the Unofficial Guide® to

Bed & Breakfasts and Country Inns in the Great Lakes

Also available from Hungry Minds

the Unofficial Guide® to

Bed & Breakfasts and Country Inns in the Great Lakes

1st Edition

Mary Mihaly

Hungry Minds™

Hungry Minds, Inc.
New York, NY • Indianapolis, IN • Cleveland, OH

Please note that prices fluctuate in the course of time, and travel information changes under the impact of many factors that influence the travel industry. We therefore suggest that you write or call ahead for confirmation when making your travel plans. Every effort has been made to ensure the accuracy of information throughout this book, and the contents of this publication are believed correct at the time of printing. Nevertheless, the publishers cannot accept responsibility for errors or omissions or for changes in details given in this guide or for the consequences of any reliance on the information provided by the same. Assessments of attractions and so forth are based upon the author's own experience, and therefore, descriptions given in this guide necessarily contain an element of subjective opinion, which may not reflect the publisher's opinion or dictate a reader's own experience on another occasion. Readers are invited to write to the publisher with ideas, comments, and suggestions for future editions

Published by Hungry Minds, Inc.
909 Third Avenue
New York, NY 10022

Copyright © 2002 by Mary Mihaly
1st edition

Produced by Menasha Ridge Press
Cover design by Michael J. Freeland
Interior design by Michele Laseau

Unofficial Guide is a registered trademark of Hungry Minds, Inc.

ISBN 0-7645-6500-1

ISSN 1536-9722

Manufactured in the United States of America

10 9 8 7 6 5 4 3 2 1

Contents

List of Maps

About the Author

Ohio native Mary Mihaly specializes in writing about "travel and lifeways." She has traveled on assignment from Uzbekistan to Ecuador for dozens of publications including *Continental, Country Living, USAirways Attaché,* and *Endless Vacation*—though her favorite trip is a 450-mile flea market she covers each August. Mihaly is a member of the Society of American Travel Writers (SATW) and the American Society of Journalists and Authors (ASJA). She collects bakelite purses, elephants, and art gourds, and is a certified feng shui practitioner.

Acknowledgments

Nearly four months were spent traveling for this book before the writing even began. Keeping one's life intact during that sort of undertaking does not happen without a great deal of help.

I'm grateful to friends and colleagues in the Society of American Travel Writers (SATW) and American Society of Journalists and Authors (ASJA) for their generous advice and support. Everyone should have such networks of smart, kind individuals in their professional lives. They all had better things to do, I'm sure.

A handful of tourism gurus worked hard to help me organize stops in their regions. I appreciate their efforts—and those of dozens of innkeepers who worried that I might need a pillow under my head, nourishment to send me down the road, and, for a few weeks, a stool to prop up my injured leg. I am privileged to have met so many good people.

My neighbors who tended my mail and my shelter during long absences, and a long list of friends and family who asked nothing of me for months on end—dudes, you're the very best and I love you madly. I am indebted to my feng shui teacher, Carol Bridges, and the "fabu girls" for their exquisite friendship. Lastly, I thank my travel buddies: my sisters Carol, always afraid she'll miss something; Margie, who always had a glass of dry red waiting for me; and my nieces—Emily, the whirlpool princess, and Audrey, who takes impeccable notes. Happy trails to all of us!

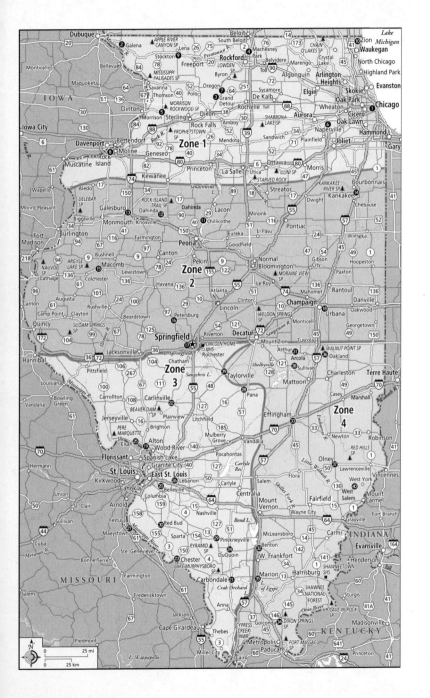

Illinois Map Legend

Zone 1 *Northern Illinois*

1) **Chicago** Windy City Bed and Breakfast Inn, 23
2) **Galena**
   Annie Wiggins Guest House, 24
   Goldmoor Inn, 25
   John Henry Guest House, 26
   Main Street Inn, 27
3) **Grand Detour** Colonial Rose Inn, 28
4) **Machesney Park** River House Bed and Breakfast, 29
5) **Morrison** Hillendale Bed and Breakfast, 30
6) **Naperville** Harrison House, 31
7) **Oregon** Patchwork Inn, 32
8) **Rock Island**
   Potter House, 32
   Top O' the Morning Bed and Breakfast Inn, 33
9) **Stockton** Hammond House Bed and Breakfast, 34
10) **Zion** Emanuelson Inn, 35

Zone 2 *Central Illinois*

11) **Chillicothe**
    Glory Hill Bed and Breakfast, 38
    Homolka House, 39
12) **Dahinda** The Barn Bed and Breakfast, 39
13) **Galesburg** Fahnestock House, 40
14) **Kankakee** River Decks Bed and Breakfast Garden Resort, 42
15) **Macomb** Pineapple Inn, 42
16) **Petersburg** The Oaks, 44
17) **Springfield** Inn at 835 Bed and Breakfast, 45
18) **Urbana** Lindley House, 46

Zone 3 *Southwest Illinois*

19) **Alton** Jackson House, 49
20) **Belleville** Victory Inn, 50

21) **Carbondale** Sassafras Ridge, 51
22) **Carlinville** Victoria Tyme Inn, 52
23) **Chester** Stone House Bed and Breakfast, 53
24) **DuQuoin** Francie's Inn On-Line, 54
25) **Elsah**
    Corner Nest Bed and Breakfast, 54
    Green Tree Inn, 55
26) **Lebanon** Landmark on Madison, 56
27) **Maeystown** Corner George Inn, 57
28) **Pana** Apothecary's Inn at Captain Kitchell's Mansion, 58
29) **Pinckneyville** Oxbow Bed and Breakfast, 59
30) **Red Bud** Magnolia Place Bed and Breakfast, 60

Zone 4 *Southeast Illinois*

31) **Arthur** Marsha's Vineyard, 62
32) **Benton** Hard Day's Nite Bed and Breakfast, 62
33) **Effingham** Garnet Hall Bed and Breakfast, 63
34) **Golconda** Mansion of Golconda, 64
35) **Marion** Olde Squat Inn, 65
36) **Oakland** Inn on the Square, 66
37) **Olney** Fessel's Cabbage Rose, 67
38) **Sullivan** Little House on the Prairie Bed and Breakfast, 68
39) **Taylorville** Market Street Inn, 69
40) **West Salem** Thelma's Bed and Breakfast, 70

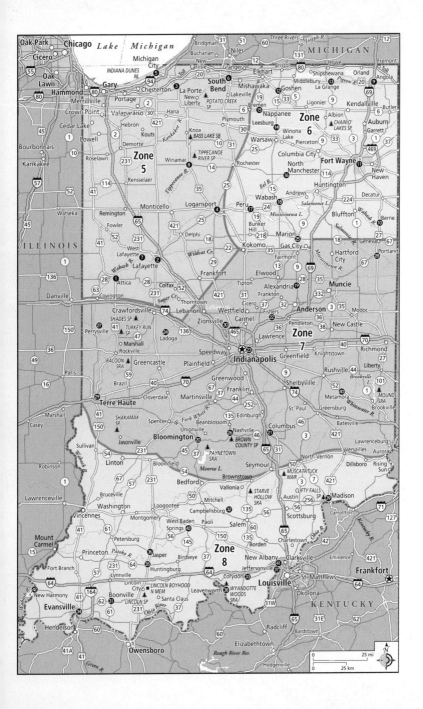

Indiana Map Legend

Zone 5 *Northwest Indiana*

1) **Attica** Apple Inn Museum Bed and Breakfast, 76
2) **Lafayette** Loeb House Inn, 84
3) **LaPorte** Arbor Hill Inn, 77
4) **Logansport** Inntiquity Inn, 83
5) **Michigan City**
   Creekwood Inn, 80
   Feallock House, 81
   Hutchinson Mansion Inn, 82
6) **South Bend**
   Book Inn, 78
   Oliver Inn, 85
7) **West Lafayette**
   Commandant's Home Bed and Breakfast, 79
8) **Winamac** Tortuga Inn, 86

Zone 6 *Northeast Indiana*

9) **Angola** Tulip Tree Inn, 89
10) **Berne** Schug House Inn, 89
11) **Fort Wayne**
   At the Herb Lady's Garden, 90
   Carole Lombard House, 91
12) **Goshen**
   Front Porch Inn, 92
   Ol' Barn Bed and Breakfast, 95
13) **LaGrange** M&N Bed and Breakfast, 96
14) **Leesburg** Prairie House Bed and Breakfast, 97
15) **Nappanee**
   Homespun Country Inn, 94
   Victorian Guest House, 94
16) **North Manchester** Fruitt Basket Inn, 98
17) **Peru** Rosewood Mansion Inn, 98
18) **Wabash** Lamp Post Inn, 99

Zone 7 *Central Indiana*

19) **Alexandria** Country Gazebo Inn
20) **Bloomington** Scholars Inn, 106
21) **Columbus** Ruddick-Nugent House, 102
22) **Fishers** Frederick-Talbot Inn at the Prairie, 107

23) **Indianapolis**
   Looking Glass Inn, 108
   Stone Soup Inn, 109
   Tranquil Cherub Bed and Breakfast, 103
24) **Ladoga** Vintage Reflections
25) **Marion** Burke Place Bed and Breakfast
26) **Nashville**
   Always Inn Bed and Breakfast, 110
   Artists Colony Inn, 109
27) **Perrysville** Hoosier Haven Inn
28) **Portland** Hilltop Farm Bed and Breakfast
29) **Terre Haute** Farrington Bed and Breakfast
30) **Zionsville** Country Gables Bed and Breakfast, 104

Zone 8 *Southern Indiana*

31) **Boonville** Godbey Guest House Bed and Breakfast, 122
32) **Campbellsburg** James Wilkins House, 122
33) **Corydon**
   Hummingbird Bed and Breakfast, 113
   Kintner House Inn, 114
34) **Evansville** Starkey Inn Bed and Breakfast, 114
35) **Huntingburg** Van Buren Street Inn, 116
36) **Jasper** Powers Inn, 123
37) **Jeffersonville** Old Bridge Inn Bed and Breakfast, 117
38) **Leavenworth** Leavenworth Inn, 118
39) **Madison** Schussler House, 118
40) **Metamora** Thorpe House, 119
41) **New Albany** Honeymoon Mansion Bed and Breakfast and Wedding Chapel, 121
42) **New Harmony** Wright Place, 124
43) **West Baden Springs** E.B. Rhodes House Bed and Breakfast, 125

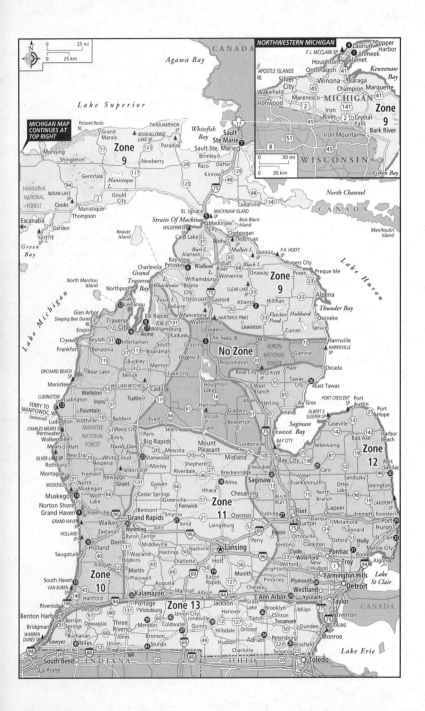

Michigan Map Legend

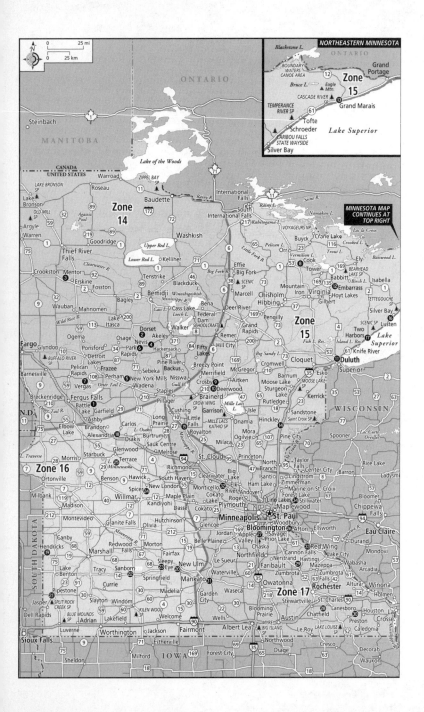

Minnesota Map Legend

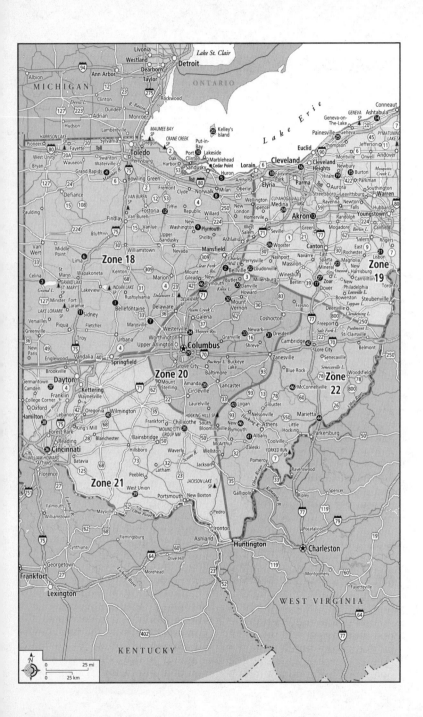

Ohio Map Legend

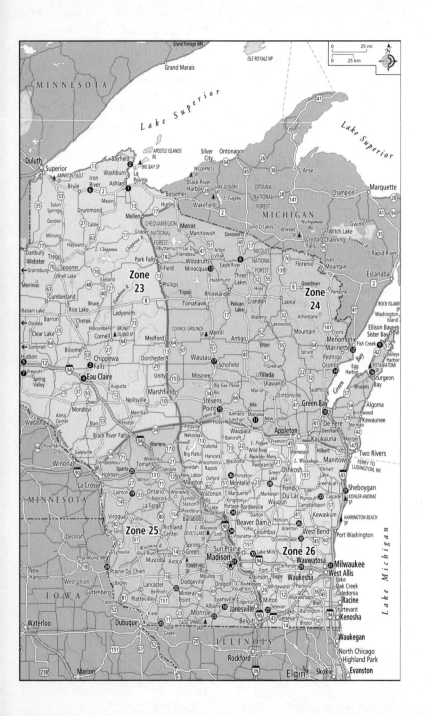

Wisconsin Map Legend

Mini Indexes

TOP (20) OVERALL

Five Stars ★★★★★

Illinois
Fahnestock House
Fessel's Cabbage Rose
Windy City Bed and Breakfast Inn

Indiana
Book Inn
Hutchinson Mansion Inn
Oliver Inn

Michigan
Chateau Chantal Winery and Bed
   and Breakfast
Fountain Hill
Grey Hare Inn
Laurium Manor Inn

Saravilla Bed and Breakfast
Schoenberger House

Minnesota
Cotton Mansion
Elephant Walk, A Bed and Breakfast

Ohio
Georgian Manor Inn

Wisconsin
Allyn Mansion Inn
Brownstone Inn
Inn at Pine Terrace
Mansion Hill Inn
Scofield House Bed and Breakfast

TOP 35 BY ROOM QUALITY

Illinois
Fahnestock House
Fessel's Cabbage Rose

Indiana
Apple Inn Museum Bed and Breakfast
Book Inn
Carole Lombard House
Country Gables Bed and Breakfast
Hutchinson Mansion Inn
Loeb House Inn
Oliver Inn
Ruddick-Nugent House

Michigan
Fountain Hill
Saravilla Bed and Breakfast
Schoenberger House

Minnesota
Cotton Mansion
Elephant Walk, A Bed and Breakfast

Ohio
Blackfork Inn
College Inn Bed and Breakfast
Elson Inn
Georgian Manor Inn
GreatStone Castle
Greenhouse Bed and Breakfast
Gunckel Heritage Bed and Breakfast
House on Harmar Hill
Inn at Cedar Falls
Inn at Willow Pond
Outback Inn
Pitzer-Cooper House
Rossville Inn
Searle House
Spitzer House
Zelkova Country Manor

Wisconsin
Allyn Mansion Inn
Brownstone Inn
Inn at Pine Terrace
Mansion Hill Inn

TOP VALUES

Illinois

Fahnestock House
Fessel's Cabbage Rose
Glory Hill Bed and Breakfast
John Henry Guest House
Sassafras Ridge
Stone House Bed and Breakfast
The Barn Bed and Breakfast

Indiana

Book Inn
Carole Lombard House
Country Gables Bed and Breakfast
E.B. Rhodes House Bed and Breakfast
Hutchinson Mansion Inn
James Wilkins House
Kintner House Inn
Oliver Inn
Rosewood Mansion Inn
Ruddick-Nugent House
Van Buren Street Inn

Michigan

Centennial Inn
Chicago Street Inn
Fountain Hill
Laurium Manor Inn
Peaches Bed and Breakfast
Saravilla Bed and Breakfast
Stuart Avenue Inn

Minnesota

Calumet Inn
Hallett House
Lottie Lee's Bed and Breakfast
Whistle Stop Inn

Ohio

Blackfork Inn
Brownstone Inn
Georgian Manor Inn
GreatStone Castle
Greenhouse Bed and Breakfast
House on Harmar Hill
Inn at Willow Pond
Outback Inn
Rossville Inn
Russell Cooper House
Searle House
Spitzer House

Wisconsin

Albany House
Artesian House
Breese Waye Bed and Breakfast
Brumder Mansion Bed and Breakfast
Inn at Pine Terrace
Lindsay House Bed and Breakfast
Mansion Hill Inn
Rosenberry Inn
Strawberry Lace Inn

BUDGET ACCOMODATIONS

Illinois

Corner George Inn
Fessel's Cabbage Rose
Francie's Inn On-Line
Hard Day's Nite Bed and Breakfast
Hillendale Bed and Breakfast
Homolka House
Inn on the Square
Landmark on Madison
Little House on the Prairie Bed
   and Breakfast
Magnolia Place Bed and Breakfast
Olde Squat Inn
Oxbow Bed and Breakfast
River Decks Bed and Breakfast
   Garden Resort
Sassafras Ridge
Stone House Bed and Breakfast
Thelma's Bed and Breakfast
Top O' the Morning Bed and
   Breakfast Inn
Victoria Tyme Inn
Victory Inn

BUDGET ACCOMODATIONS *(continued)*

Indiana

Arbor Hill Inn
Artists Colony Inn
Burke Place Bed and Breakfast
Carole Lombard House
Country Gables Bed and Breakfast
Country Gazebo Inn
E.B. Rhodes House Bed and Breakfast
Fruitt Basket Inn
Godbey Guest Huose Bed and
   Breakfast
Homespun Country Inn
Hoosier Haven Inn
James Wilkins House
Kintner House Inn
Lamp Post Inn
Leavenworth Inn
M&N Bed and Breakfast
Ol' Barn Bed and Breakfast
Olde Magnolia Inn
Powers Inn
Prairie House Bed and Breakfast
Ruddick-Nugent House
Schug House Inn
Thorpe House
Van Buren Street Inn
Victorian Guest House
Vintage Reflections

Michigan

Borchers Ausable Canoe Livery with
   Bed and Breakfast
Briley Inn
Buffalo Inn
Garden Gate Bed and Breakfast
Laurium Manor Inn
Mendon Country Inn
Raymond House Inn
Terrace Inn
Union Hill Inn
Victorian Villa Inn

Minnesota

Afton House Inn
Butler House

Calumet Inn
Dakota Lodge
Deautsche Strasse Bed and Breakfast
Heartland Trail Bed and Breakfast
Lund's Guest House
Mrs. B's
Nordic Inn Medieval Brew and Bed
Pillars Bed and Breakfast
Scanlon House Bed and Breakfast
Triple L Farm Bed and Breakfast
Whistle Stop Inn

Ohio

Bailey's Bed and Breakfast
Blackfork Inn
Cowger House Bed and Breakfast
Dum-Ford House
Fort Ball Bed and Breakfast
Frederick Fitting House
Harbor Hill's Black Squirrel Inn
Heiser haus
House on Harmar Hill
Michael Cahill Bed and Breakfast
Mirabelle Bed and Breakfast
Olde World Bed and Breakfast
Outback Inn
Russell Cooper House
Spitzer House
Whitmore House

Wisconsin

Addison House
Albany House
Breese Waye Bed and Breakfast
Brumder Mansion Bed and Breakfast
Dreams of Yesteryear Bed and
   Breakfast
Iron River Trout Haus
Lauerman Guest House Inn
McGilvray's Victorian Bed and
   Breakfast
Residenz
Rosenberry Inn
Wisconsin House Stage Coach Inn

THREE ROOMS OR FEWER

Illinois

Barn B&B
Corner Nest B&B
Fahnestock House
Fessel's Cabbage Rose
Glory Hill B&B
Homolka House
Inn on the Square
John Henry Guest House
Landmark on Madison
Marsha's Vineyard
Sassafras Ridge
Stone House B&B
Victory Inn

Indiana

At the Herb Lady's Garden
Country Gables B&B
E.B. Rhodes House B&B
Hilltop Farm B&B
James Wilkins House
Ol' Barn B&B
Old Bridge Inn B&B
Powers Inn
Schussler House
Vintage Reflections
Wright Place

Michigan

Briar Oaks Inn
Centennial Inn
Chateau Chantal Winery
Grey Hare Inn
Horse & Carriage B&B
Main Street Manor
Parsonage 1908 B&B

Minnesota

Lighthouse B&B
Lottie Lee's B&B

Miller's House
Moosebirds
Sod House on the Prairie
Triple L Farm B&B
Wildwood Lodge B&B

Ohio

Bailey's B&B
Bourbon House
Cedar Hill B&B
Claire E.
Cowger House B&B
Dum-Ford House
Fitzgerald's Irish B&B
Frederick Fitting House
Glendennis B&B
Gunckel Heritage B&B
La Grande Flora
Mill House B&B
Mirabelle B&B
Mt. Adama B&B
Outback Inn
Pitzer-Cooper House
Rossville Inn
September Farm
Whitmore House

Wisconsin

Addison House
Grapevine Inn
McGilvray's Victorian B&B
Neumann House B&B
Red Shutters B&B
Residenz
Tamarack B&B
Victorian Garden B&B

20 ROOMS OR MORE

Indiana
Artists Colony Inn

Michigan
Metivier Inn

Stafford's Bay View Inn
Terrace Inn

Minnesota
Calumet Inn

SOLO-ORIENTED

Illinois
Fahnestock House
Fessel's Cabbage Rose
Goldmoor Inn
Green Tree Inn
Hard Day's Nite B&B
Inn on the Square
Jackson House
Lindley House
Little House on the Prairie
Market Street Inn
Olde Squat Inn
Sassafras Ridge
Stone House B&B
Thelma's B&B
Top O' the Morning' B&B
Victoria Tyme Inn
Victory Inn
Windy City B&B

Indiana
Always Inn
Apple Inn Museum B&B
Arbor Hill Inn
Burke Place B&B
Creekwood Inn
Front Porch Inn
Godbey Guest House
James Wilkins House
Kintner House Inn
Looking Glass Inn
Ruddick-Nugent House
Schug House Inn
Stone Soup Inn
Tortuga Inn
Tranquil Cherub B&B

Tulip Tree Inn
Van Buren Street Inn

Michigan
Boyden House
Centennial Inn
Chicago Street Inn
Garden Gate B&B
Laurium Manor Inn
Montague Inn
Peaches B&B
Stuart Avenue Inn
Terrace Inn
Union Hill Inn
Water Street Inn

Minnesota
Calumet Inn
Deutsche Strasse B&B
Finnish Heritage Homestead
Lake Le Homme Dieu B&B
Lottie Lee's B&B
Snuggle Inn

Ohio
Blackfork Inn
Bourbon House
Brownstone Inn
Cedar Hill B&B
College Inn B&B
Edgewater Estates
Fitzgerald's Irish B&B
Gunckel Heritage B&B
Harbor Hill's Black Squirrel Inn
Heiser Haus
House on Harmar Hill
Inn at Cedar Falls

SOLO-ORIENTED (continued)

Ohio (continued)
Inn at Willow Pond
Michael Cahill B&B
Mirabelle B&B
Rossville Inn
Searle House
Spitzer House
Victorian Inn of Hyde Park
Yesterday Again B&B

Wisconsin
Addison House
Ages Past Country House
Albany House
Allyn Mansion Inn
Arbor Inn
Astor House
Brumder Mansion B&B
Ellison's Gray Lion Inn
Fargo Mansion Inn
Juniper Inn
Lauerman Guest House
Neumann House B&B
Red Shutters B&B
Residenz
Stoppenbach House
Wisconsin House

ROMANTIC (Extremely)

Illinois
Corner George Inn
Fahnestock House
Fessel's Cabbage Rose
Garnet Hall B&B
Goldmoor Inn
Hillendale B&B
Jackson House
Little House on the Prairie
Market Street Inn
The Oaks
River House B&B
Stone House B&B
Victory Inn
Windy City B&B

Indiana
Book Inn
Carole Lombard House
Honeymoon Mansion B&B
Hutchinson Mansion Inn
Loeb House Inn
Oliver Inn
Rosewood Mansion Inn
Scholars Inn

Michigan
Boyden House
Chateau Chantal Winery and B&B
Country Hermitage B&B
Davidson House
English Inn
Fountain Hill
Grey Hare Inn
Laurium Manor Inn
Martha's Vineyard
Munro House
932 Penniman, a B&B
Sand Hills Lighthouse
Saravilla B&B
Victorian Villa Inn

Minnesota
Ann Bean Mansion
Berwood Hill Inn
Candlelight Inn
Cotton Mansion
Elephant Walk B&B
Hallett House
Lake Le Homme Dieu B&B
Log House & Homestead at
    Spirit Lake
Manor on the Creek
Peacock Inn
Rand House
Rosewood Inn
Thorwood Inn
Whistle Stop Inn

ROMANTIC (Extremely) *(continued)*

Ohio

Blackfork Inn
Elson Inn
Georgian Manor Inn
House on Harmar Hill
La Grande Flora
Murphin Ridge Inn
Olde World B&B
O'Neil House
Ravenwood Castle
Stone Gables B&B
Water's Edge Retreat
Yesterday Again B&B

Wisconsin

Allyn Mansion Inn
Arbor House
Arbor Inn
Artesian House
Astor House
Baker Brewster Inn
Brownstone Inn
Brumder Mansion B&B
Fargo Mansion Inn
Grapevine Inn
Inn at Pine Terrace
Jamieson House Inn
Mansion Hill Inn
Otter Creek Inn
Phipps Inn
Scofield House B&B
Strawberry Lace Inn
White Lace Inn

FAMILY-ORIENTED

Illinois

Barn B&B
Emanuelson Inn
Fahnestock House
Harrison House
Homolka House
Lindley House
Marsha's Vineyard
Olde Squat Inn
Oxbow Inn
Thelma's B&B

Indiana

Artists Colony Inn
Commandant's House B&B
Country Gables B&B
Country Gazebo Inn
E.B. Rhodes House B&B
Farrington B&B
Frederick-Talbott Inn at the Prairie
Fruitt Basket Inn
Hilltop Farm B&B
James Wilkins House
Kintner House Inn
Leavenworth Inn

Looking Glass Inn
M & N B&B
Ol' Barn B&B
Olde Magnolia Inn
Powers Inn
Ruddick-Nugent House
Schug House Inn
Stone Soup Inn
Thorpe House
Tortuga Inn
Van Buren Street Inn
Vintage Reflections
Wright Place B&B

Michigan

Borchers Au Sable
Buffalo Inn
Cloghaun B&B
H.D. Ellis Inn
Harbor House Inn
Hess Manor
Horse & Carriage B&B
Outback Lodge
Stafford's Bay View Inn
Terrace Inn

FAMILY-ORIENTED (continued)

Michigan (continued)
Union Hill Inn
William Hopkins Manor

Minnesota
Afton House Inn
Calumet Inn
Finnish Heritage Homestead
Heartland Trail B&B
Lighthouse B&B
Lund's Guest Houses
Moosebirds
Pillars B&B
Sod House on the Prairie
Triple L Farm B&B
Whistle Stop Inn
Xanadu Island B&B

Ohio
Albany House
Castle B&B
Claire E.
Glendennis B&B

Greenhouse B&B
Gunckel Heritage B&B
Harbor Hill's Black Squirrel Inn
Heiser Haus
Inn at Brandywine Falls
Inn at Dresden
Laurel Brook Farm
Michael Cahill B&B
Pitzer-Cooper House
Ravenwood Castle
Red Maple Inn
Rossville Inn

Wisconsin
Albany House
Inn at Pinewood
Iron River Trout Haus
Lindsay House B&B
Neumann House B&B
Old Rittenhouse Inn
Residenz
Whistling Swan Inn
Wisconsin House

HISTORIC INNS

Illinois
Fahnestock House
Fessel's Cabbage Rose

Indiana
Book Inn
Commandant's Home Bed and
 Breakfast
Hutchinson Mansion Inn
James Wilkins House
Loeb House Inn

Michigan
Fountain Hill
Laurium Manor Inn
Saravilla Bed and Breakfast

Minnesota
Cotton Mansion
Elephant Walk, A Bed and Breakfast

Ohio
Georgian Manor Inn
House on Harmar Hill

Wisconsin
Allyn Mansion Inn
Brownstone Inn
Brumder Mansion Bed and Breakfast
Inn at Pine Terrace
Mansion Hill Inn
Scofield House Bed and Breakfast

NO CREDIT CARDS

Illinois
Barn B&B
Fessel's Cabbage Rose
Inn on the Square
Little House on the Prairie
Marsha's Vineyard
Olde Squat Inn
Thelma's B&B

Indiana
Country Gazebo Inn
Hoosier Haven Inn
Ol' Barn B&B

Michigan
Buffalo Inn
Centennial Inn
Chicago Street Inn
Davidson House
Emery House
Grey Hare Inn
Horse & Carriage B&B
Parsonage 1908 B&B
Pebbles of Brandywine Creek
Sand Hills Lighthouse
Union Hill Inn

Minnesota
Bally's B&B
Lund's Guest Houses
Mrs. B's
Pillars B&B
Sod House on the Prairie
Triple L Farm B&B
Wildwood Lodge B&B

Ohio
Cedar Hill B&B
Frederick Fitting House
Michael Cahill B&B
Outback Inn
Whitmore House

Wisconsin
Addison House
Artesian House
Breese Waye B&B
Brumder Mansion B&B
Ellison's Gray Lion Inn
McGilvray's Victorian B&B
Neumann House B&B
Red Shutters B&B
Residenz
Tamarack B&B

PETS PERMITTED

Illinois
Olde Squat Inn
River Decks B&B

Indiana
Country Gazebo Inn
Frederick-Talbott Inn at the Prairie
Hilltop Farm B&B
Inntiquity
Old Bridge Inn B&B
Thorpe House
Tortuga Inn
Wright Place

Michigan
H.D. Ellis Inn
Outback Lodge

Minnesota
Calumet Inn
Xanadu Island B&B

Ohio
Brownstone Inn
College Inn B&B
Edgewater Estates
Harbor Hill's Black Squirrel Inn
Heiser Haus
Laurel Brook Farm
Stone Gables B&B
Zelkova Country Manor

Wisconsin
Stoppenbach House

SMOKING PERMITTED

Illinois
Glory Hill B&B
Little House on the Prairie
Thelma's B&B

Indiana
Artists Colony Inn
Rosewood Mansion Inn
Thorpe House
Tortuga Inn

Michigan
Buffalo Inn

Minnesota
Calumet Inn
Nordic Inn

Ohio
Brownstone Inn

Wisconsin
Lauerman Guest House

FARM OR RURAL SETTINGS

Illinois
Barn B&B
Finnish Heritage Homestead
Glory Hill B&B
Goldmoor Inn
Little House on the Prairie
Olde Squat Inn
Oxbow B&B
Sassafras Ridge

Indiana
Always Inn
Country Gables B&B
Country Gazebo Inn
Creekwood Inn
Hilltop Farm B&B
Inntiquity
Leavenworth Inn
Ol' Barn B&B
Prairie House B&B
Tortuga Inn

Michigan
Buffalo Inn
Centennial Inn
Chateau Chantal Winery B&B
Country Hermitage B&B
English Inn
Grey Hare Inn
Horse & Carriage B&B
Martha's Vineyard
Outback Lodge

Pebbles of Brandywine Creek
Sand Hills Lighthouse

Minnesota
Berwood Hill Inn
Dakota Lodge
Heartland Trail B&B
Lindgren's B&B
Log House & Homestead at
   Spirit Lake
Miller's House
Sod House on the Prairie
Triple L Farm B&B
Wildwood Lodge B&B
Xanadu Island B&B

Ohio
Cedar Hill B&B
Inn at Brandywine Falls
Inn at Cedar Falls
Inn at Willow Falls
Laurel Brook Farm
Misty Meadow Farm
Murphin Ridge Inn
Olde World B&B
Pitzer-Cooper House
Ravenwood Castle
September Farm
White Oak Inn
Yesterday Again B&B
Zelkova Country Manor

FARM OR RURAL SETTINGS *(continued)*

Wisconsin
Addison House
Ages Past Country House
Artesian House
Hillwind Farm B&B
Inn at Pinewood
Iron River Trout Haus
Juniper Inn
Otter Creek Inn
Tamarack B&B

GROUPS/WEDDINGS EASILY ACCOMMODATED

Illinois
Fessel's Cabbage Rose
Francie's Inn On-Line
Inn at 835 B&B
River House B&B
Windy City B&B

Indiana
Arbor Hill Inn
At the Herb Lady's Garden
Commandant's Home B&B
Creekwood Inn
Farrington B&B
Frederick-Talbott Inn at the Prairie
Honeymoon Mansion B&B
Hutchinson Mansion Inn
Leavenworth Inn
Oliver Inn
Ruddick-Nugent House
Scholars Inn
Schug House Inn
Victorian Guest House

Michigan
Christmere House
English Inn
Harbor House Inn
Laurium Manor Inn
Munro House
Outback Lodge
Saravilla B&B
Schoenberger House
Seymour House

Stafford's Bay View Inn
Terrace Inn
Victorian Villa Inn

Minnesota
Afton House Inn
Ann Bean Mansion
Berwood Hill Inn
Inn at Maple Crossing
Manor on the Creek
Peacock Inn
Rand House
Whistle Stop Inn

Ohio
Emerald Necklace Inn
Frederick Fitting House
GreatStone Castle
Inn at Brandywine Falls
Inn at Cedar Falls
La Grande Flora
Murphin Ridge Inn
O'Neil House
Red Maple Inn
Russell Cooper House
Searle House
Whitmore House

Wisconsin
Arbor House
Inn at Pine Terrace
Lauerman Guest House
White Lace Inn

RUSTIC SETTING

Illinois
Olde Squat Inn
Oxbow Inn

Indiana
Thorpe House

Michigan
Borchers Au Sable
Mendon Country Inn
Outback Lodge

Minnesota
Finnish Heritage Homestead
Sod House on the Prairie

Lindgren's B&B
Xanadu Island B&B

Ohio
Claire E.
Cowger House B&B
Inn at Brandywine Falls
Inn at Cedar Falls
Laurel Brook Farm

Wisconsin
Addison House
Inn at Pinewood
Iron River Trout Haus
Tamarack B&B

SWIMMING POOL

Illinois
River House B&B
Oxbow B&B

Indiana
Front Porch Inn
Vintage Reflections

Ohio
Albany House
Heiser Haus
Misty Meadow Farm
Zelkova Country Manor

Wisconsin
Otter Creek Inn

ISLAND SETTING

Michigan
Cloghaun B&B
Metivier Inn

Ohio
Getaway Inn
Water's Edge Retreat

Minnesota
Xanadu Island B&B

WATERSIDE SETTING

Illinois
River Decks B&B
River House B&B
Stone House B&B

Indiana
Leavenworth Inn

Michigan
Borcher's Au Sable
Briley Inn
Davidson House
East Tawas Junction B&B
Harbor House Inn
Main Street Manor

WATERSIDE SETTING (continued)

Michigan (continued)
Montague Inn
Pebbles of Brandywine Creek
Sand Hills Lighthouse
Stafford's Bay View Inn
Water Street Inn
William Hopkins Manor

Minnesota
Green Lake Inn
Inn at Maple Crossing
Lake Le Homme Dieu B&B
Lighthouse B&B
Lindgren's B&B
Moosebirds
Park Street Inn
Wildwood Lodge B&B
Xanadu Island B&B

Ohio
Claire E.
Edgewater Estates
Inn at Willow Pond
Laurel Brook Farm
Mill House B&B
Water's Edge Retreat

Wisconsin
Inn at Pinewood
Iron River Trout Haus
Lindsay House B&B
McConnell Inn

Introduction

How Come "Unofficial"?

The book in your hands is part of a unique travel and lifestyle guidebook series begun in 1985 with *The Unofficial Guide to Walt Disney World.* That guide, a comprehensive, behind-the-scenes, hands-on prescription for getting the most out of a complex amusement park facility, spawned a series of like titles: *The Unofficial Guide to Chicago, The Unofficial Guide to New Orleans,* and so on. Today, dozens of *Unofficial Guides* help millions of savvy readers navigate some of the world's more complex destinations and situations.

The *Unofficial Guides to Bed-and-Breakfasts and Country Inns* continue the tradition of insightful, incisive, cut-to-the-chase information, presented in an accessible, easy-to-use format. Unlike in some popular books, no property can pay to be included—those reviewed are solely our choice. And we don't simply rehash the promotional language of these establishments. We visit the good, the bad, and the quirky. We finger the linens, chat with the guests, and sample the scones. We screen hundreds of lodgings, affirming or debunking the acclaimed, discovering or rejecting the new and the obscure. In the end, we present detailed profiles of the lodgings we feel represent the best of the best, select lodgings representing a broad range of prices and styles within each geographic region.

We also include introductions for each state and zone to give you an idea of the nearby general attractions. Area maps with the properties listed by city help you pinpoint your general destination. And detailed mini-indexes help you look up properties by categories and lead you to places that best fit your needs.

With *The Unofficial Guides to Bed-and-Breakfasts and Country Inns,* we strive to help you find the perfect lodging for every trip. This guide is unofficial because we answer to no one but you.

Letters, Comments, and Questions from Readers

We expect to learn from our mistakes, as well as from the input of our readers, and to improve with each book and edition. Many of those who use the

Unofficial Guides write to us to ask questions, make comments, or share their own discoveries and lessons learned. We appreciate all such input, both positive and critical, and encourage our readers to continue writing. Readers' comments and observations will contribute immeasurably to the improvement of revised editions of the *Unofficial Guides.*

How to Write the Author

Mary Mihaly
*The Unofficial Guide to Bed-and-Breakfasts
    and Country Inns in the Great Lakes*
P.O. Box 43673
Birmingham, AL 35243

Be an Unofficial Correspondent

Look out for new or special properties not profiled in this book. If you provide us with five new lodgings that we choose to visit and write about in the next edition, we'll credit you and send a copy when the edition is published. That's reason enough to get out and explore the majesty of the Great Lakes.

When you write, be sure to put your return address on your letter as well as on the envelope—they may get separated. And remember, our work takes us out of the office for long periods of research, so forgive us if our response is delayed.

What Makes It a Bed-and-Breakfast?

Comparing the stale, sterile atmosphere of most hotels and motels to the typical bed-and-breakfast experience—cozy guest room, intimate parlor, friendly hosts, fresh-baked cookies, not to mention a delicious breakfast— why stay anywhere other than a bed-and-breakfast? But this isn't a promotional piece for the bed-and-breakfast life. Bed-and-breakfasts are not hotels. Here are some of the differences:

A bed-and-breakfast or small inn, as we define it, is a small property (about 3 to 25 guest rooms, with a few exceptions) with hosts around, a distinct personality, individually decorated rooms, and breakfast included in the price (again, with a few exceptions). Many of these smaller properties have owners living right there; at others, the owners are nearby, a phone call away.

Recently, the bed-and-breakfast and small inn trade has taken off—with mixed results. This growth has taken place on both fronts: the low and high ends. As bed-and-breakfasts gain popularity, anyone with a spare bedroom can pop an ad in the Yellow Pages for "Billy's Bedroom B&B." These enterprises generally lack professionalism, don't keep regular hours or days of operation, are often unlicensed, and were avoided in this guide.

On the other end of the spectrum are luxury premises with more ameni-ties than the finest hotels. Whether historic homes or lodgings built to be bed-and-breakfasts or inns, interiors are posh, baths are private and en suite, and breakfasts are gourmet affairs. In-room whirlpool tubs and fireplaces are the norm, and extras range from in-room refrigerators (perhaps stocked with champagne) to complimentary high tea to free use of state-of-the-art recre-ational equipment to . . . the list goes on! (One longtime innkeeper, whose historic home was tidily and humbly maintained by hours of elbow grease and common sense, dubbed this new state of affairs "the amenities war.")

The result is an industry in which a simple homestay bed-and-breakfast with a shared bath and common rooms can be a budget experience, while a new, upscale bed-and-breakfast can be the luxury venue of a lifetime.

Who Stays at Bed-and-Breakfasts?

American travelers are finally catching on to what Europeans have known for a long time. Maybe it's a backlash against a cookie-cutter, strip-mall landscape, or a longing for a past that maybe never was. Maybe it's a need for simple pleasures in a world over-the-top with theme parks and high-tech wonders. Who can say for sure?

The bed-and-breakfast trade has grown so large that it includes niches catering to virtually every need: some bed-and-breakfasts and small inns are equipped to help travelers conduct business, others provide turn-down ser-vice and fresh flowers by the honeymooners' canopied bed, and still others offer amenities for reunions or conferences. Whatever your needs, there is a bed-and-breakfast or small inn tailored to your expectations. The chal-lenge, and one this guide was designed to help you meet, is sifting through the choices until you find the perfect place.

Romantics

More and more, properties are establishing at least one room or suite with fireplace, whirlpool, canopied king, and the trappings of romance. Theme rooms can also be especially fun for fantasizing. Always check out the pri-vacy factor. Sometimes a property that caters to families has a carriage house in the back or a top-floor room away from the others. If an inn allows children under 16, don't be surprised if it's noisy; look for ones that are for older children or adults only.

Families

Face it, Moms and Dads: rumpled surroundings will sometimes have to be accepted where children are welcome. You may have to give up pristine decor and breakfast tea served in bone china for the relaxed, informal mood, but on the upside, you won't have to worry as much about Anna or Sam knocking over the Wedgwood collection on the sideboard.

When an establishment says "Yes" to kids, that usually means a really kid-friendly place. Check the age restrictions. If your children are under-aged but well-behaved, let the host know; often they will make exceptions. (But be sure it's true—other guests are counting on it.) On the flip side, honeymooners or other folks who might prefer common areas free of crayons, and breakfasts without sugar-frosted confetti, may want to look elsewhere.

Many bed-and-breakfasts with cottages, cabins or accommodations that really separate guests are perfect for families with trouble-free infants and well-behaved kids. This gives parents with good intentions an alternative to "sweating-it-out" in case easy-going Raley decides to break a tooth and cries through the night.

Generally, bed-and-breakfasts are not ideal for high-action kids. But if your children enjoy games, puzzles, books, a chance for quiet pleasures, and meeting others; if they don't need TVs; and if they can be counted on to be thoughtful and follow instructions ("whisper before 9 a.m.," "don't put your feet on the table"), you and your kids can have a wonderful experience together—and so can the rest of the guests.

Business Travelers

For individual business travelers, bed-and-breakfasts and small inns are becoming much more savvy at anticipating your needs, but in differing degrees. While phone lines and data ports are fairly common, they vary from one bed-and-breakfast to another. Some say they offer data ports when in fact they have two phone jacks in every room but only one phone line servicing the entire property. This can be fine for a three-room inn in the off-season, but if you're trying to conduct business, look for properties with private lines and/or dedicated data ports. If in doubt, ask. Rooms are often available with desks, but these also vary, particularly in surface area and quality of lighting. If this is an important feature, ask for specifics and make sure you secure a room with a desk when you reserve.

Some establishments even offer couriers, secretarial support, and laundry services. And for business travelers who don't have time to take advantage of a leisurely and sumptuous breakfast, hosts often provide an early-morning alternative, sometimes continental, sometimes full.

Finally, there are intangibles to consider. After the sterile atmosphere of the trade show, meeting hall, or boardroom, a small inn with a host and a plate of cookies and a personal dinner recommendation can be nice to come home to. The atmosphere is also a plus for business meetings or seminars. The relaxed surroundings are quite conducive to easygoing give and take. During the week when guest rooms are often available, some bed-and-breakfasts and small inns are usually eager to host business groups. Discounts are often included and special services such as catering and equipment are offered if you rent the entire property. But forget weekends; these properties are still tourist oriented.

Independents

If you are on your own, small lodgings are ideal. Look for a place with single rates, and even if a special rate isn't listed, you can often negotiate a small discount. If you want some interaction, just sit in the parlor, lounge, or common rooms, and talk to people before meals. Most of the time if you're friendly and interested, you'll get an invite to join someone at a table. You could talk to the innkeepers about this even before you arrive, and they might fix you up with friendly folks. (And if you are traveling with others, invite a single to join you.) As for breakfast, communal tables are perfect for singles. Note our profiles to choose properties with that in mind.

Groups

Whether you are part of a wedding, reunion, or just a group of people who want to travel together, an inn or bed-and-breakfast is a delightful place to stay. The atmosphere is special, your needs are taken care of in a personal way, the grounds are most often spacious and lovely, and in the evening you can all retire in close proximity. It's especially fun when you take over the whole place—so you may want to choose an especially small property if that's your goal.

Those with Special Needs

Look in our profiles for mention of disabled facilities or access. Then call for details to determine just how extensive the accessibility is. Remember also that some of these houses are quite old, and owners of a small bed-and-breakfast will not have a team of accessibility experts on retainer, so be specific with your questions. If doorways must be a certain width to accommodate a wheelchair or walker, know how many inches before you call; if stairs are difficult for Great Aunt Mary Ann, don't neglect to find out how many are present outside, as well as inside. And if a property that seems otherwise special doesn't seem to have facilities, perhaps you can patch things together, such as a room on the first floor. Realistically, though, some historic properties were built with many stairs and are situated on hilltops or in rural terrain, so you will have to choose very carefully.

If you suffer from allergies or aversions, talk this over when you book. A good innkeeper will make every attempt to accommodate you. As for food, if you request a special meal and give enough notice, you can often get what you like. That's one of the joys of a small, personalized property.

You and Your Hosts

Hosts are the heart of your small inn or bed-and-breakfast experience and color all aspects of the stay. They can make or break a property, and sometimes an unassuming place will be the most memorable of all because of the care and warmth of the hosts. Typically, they are well versed in navigating the area and can be a wealth of "insider information" on restaurants, sightseeing, and the like.

While many—most, in these guides—hosts live on the premises, they often have designed or remodeled their building so that their living quarters are separate. Guests often have their own living room, den, parlor, and sitting room; you may be sharing with other guests, but not so much with your hosts. The degree of interaction between host families and guests varies greatly; we try to give a feel for the extremes in the introduction to each profile. In most cases, hosts are accessible but not intrusive; they will swing through the common areas and chat a bit, but are sensitive to guests' need for privacy. Sometimes hosts are in another building altogether; in the other extreme, you intimately share living space with your hosts. This intimate, old-style bed-and-breakfast arrangement is called a "homestay." We try to note this.

In short, most bed-and-breakfast hosts are quite gracious in accommodating travelers' needs, and many are underpinning their unique small lodging with policies and amenities from hotel-style lodgings. But bed-and-breakfasts and small inns are not the Sheraton, and being cognizant of the differences can make your experience more pleasant.

Planning Your Visit

When You Choose

If you're not sure where you want to travel, browse through our listings. Maybe something in an introduction or a description of a property will spark your interest.

If you know you are going to a certain location, note the properties in that zone, and then read the entries. You can also call for brochures or take a further look at websites, especially to see rooms or to book directly.

WEBSITES

bbchannel.com	bbinternet.com	bbonline.com
bnbcity.com	bnbinns.com	epicurious.com
getawayguides.com	innbook.com	inns.com
innsandouts.com	innsnorthamerica.com	johansens.com
relaischateaux.fr/[name of inn]	travel.com/accom/bb/usa	travelguide.com
trip.com	triple1.com	virtualcities.com

When You Book

Small properties usually require booking on your own. Some travel agents will help, but they may charge a fee, because many small properties don't give travel agents commissions. The fastest, easiest ways to book are through the Internet or a reservation service, but if you have special needs or questions, we suggest contacting properties directly to get exactly what you want.

Ask about any special needs or requirements, and make sure your requests are clear. Most of these properties are not designed for people in wheelchairs, so be sure to ask ahead of time if you need that accessibility. Specify what's important to you—privacy, king-size bed, fireplace, tub versus shower, view or first-floor access. A host won't necessarily know what you want, so make sure you decide what is important—writing it down will help you remember. Note the room you want by name, or ask for the "best" room if you're not sure. Remember to ask about parking conditions—does the property have off-street parking or will you have to find a place on the street? And if air-conditioning is a must for you, always inquire—some bed-and-breakfasts do not have it.

Verify prices, conditions, and any factors or amenities that are important to you. The best time to call is in the early afternoon, before new guests arrive for the day and when hosts have the most free time. Book as soon as possible; for weekends and holidays, preferred properties could be filled a year or more in advance.

A Word about Negotiating Rates

Negotiating a good rate can be more straightforward at a bed-and-breakfast than at a hotel. For starters, the person on the other end of the line will probably be the owner and will have the authority to offer you a discount. Second, the bed-and-breakfast owner has a smaller number of rooms and guests to keep track of than a hotel manager and won't have to do a lot of checking to know whether something is available. Also, because the number of rooms is small, each room is more important. In a bed-and-breakfast with four rooms, the rental of each room increases the occupancy rate by 25%.

To get the best rate, just ask. If the owner expects a full house, you'll probably get a direct and honest "no deal." On the other hand, if there are rooms and you are sensitive about price, chances are you'll get a break. In either event, be polite and don't make unreasonable requests. If you are overbearing or contentious on the phone, the proprietor may suddenly discover no rooms available.

Some Considerations

Like snowflakes, no two bed-and-breakfasts are alike. Some are housed in historic homes or other buildings (churches, schoolhouses, miner's hotels, and more). Some are humble and cozy, some are grand and opulent. Some are all in one building, while others are scattered amongst individual, free-standing units. Some offer a breakfast over which you'll want to linger for hours, others…well, others make a darn good muffin. Bed-and-breakfasts are less predictable than hotels and motels but can be much more interesting. A few bed-and-breakfast aficionados have discovered that "interesting" sometimes comes at a price. This guide takes the "scary" out of "interesting" and presents only places that meet a certain standard of cleanliness, predictability, and amenities. However, there are certain questions and issues common to bed-and-breakfasts and small inns that first-time visitors should consider:

Choosing Your Room

Check out your room before lugging your luggage (not having elevators is usually part of the charm). This is standard procedure at small properties and saves time and trouble should you prefer another room. When a guest room has an open door, it usually means the proud innkeeper wants you to peek. You may just find a room that you like better than the one you are assigned, and it may be available, so ask.

Bathrooms

Americans are picky about their potties. While the traditional bed-and-breakfast set-up involved several bedrooms sharing a bath, this is becoming less common. Even venerable Victorians are being remodeled to include private baths. In fact, many bed-and-breakfasts offer ultra-luxurious bath facilities, including whirlpool tubs, dual vanities, and so forth. Our advice is not to reject shared bath facilities out of hand, as these can be excellent values. Do check the bedroom-to-bath ratio, however. Two rooms sharing a bath can be excellent; three or more can be problematic with a full house.

Security

Many bed-and-breakfasts have property locks and room locks as sophisticated as hotels and motels. Others do not. For the most part, inns with three stars or more have quality locks throughout the premises. (Many with lower rankings do as well.) Very often, bed-and-breakfasts will leave the key in the room or in the door if you choose to use one. Beyond locks, most bed-and-breakfasts provide an additional measure of security in that they are small properties, generally in a residential district, and typically with live-in hosts on the premises.

Privacy

At a hotel, you can take your key and hole up in solitude for the duration of your stay. It's a little harder at a bed-and-breakfast, especially if you take part in a family-style breakfast (although many inns offer the option of an early continental breakfast if you're pressed for time or feeling antisocial, and some offer en suite breakfast service). Most bed-and-breakfast hosts we've met are very sensitive to guests' needs for privacy and seem to have a knack for being as helpful or as unobtrusive as you wish. If privacy is hard to achieve at a given property, we've noted that in the profile.

Autonomy

Most bed-and-breakfasts provide a key to the front door and/or an unlocked front door certain hours of the day. While you might be staying in a family-style atmosphere, you are seldom subject to rules such as a curfew. (A few properties request that guests be in by a specific time; these policies are noted and rare.) Some places have "quiet hours," usually from about 10 or 11 p.m. until about 7 a.m. Such policies tend to be in place when properties lack sufficient sound insulation and are noted in the profile. Generally, higher ratings tend to correspond with better sound insulation.

What the Ratings Mean

We have organized this book so that you can get a quick idea of each property by checking out the ratings, reading the information at the beginning of each entry and then, if you're interested, reading the more detailed overview of each property. Obviously ratings are subjective, and people of good faith (and good taste) can and do differ. But you'll get a good, relative idea, and the ability to quickly compare properties.

Overall Rating The overall ratings are represented by stars, which range in number from one to five and represent our opinion of the quality of the property as a whole. It corresponds something like this:

★★★★★	The Best
★★★★½	Excellent
★★★★	Very Good
★★★½	Good
★★★	Good enough
★★½	Fair
★★	Not so good
★½	Barely Acceptable
★	Unacceptable

The overall rating for the bed-and-breakfast or small inn experience takes into account all factors of the property, including guest rooms and public rooms, food, facilities, grounds, maintenance, hosts, and something we'll call "specialness," for lack of a better phrase. Many times it involves the personalities and personal touches of the hosts.

Some properties have fairly equal star levels for all of these things, but most have some qualities that are better than others. Also, large, ambitious properties that serve dinner would tend to have a slightly higher star rating for the same level of qualities than a smaller property (the difference, say, between a great novel and a great short story; the larger it is the harder it is to pull off, hence the greater the appreciation). Yet a small property can earn five stars with a huge dose of "specialness."

Overall ratings and room quality ratings do not always correspond. While guest rooms may be spectacular, the rest of the inn may be average, or vice versa. Generally, though, we've found through the years that a property is usually consistently good or bad throughout.

Room Quality Rating   The quality ratings, also given on a five-star scale, represent our opinion of the quality of the guest rooms and bathrooms only. For the room quality ratings we factored in view, size, closet space, bedding, seating, desks, lighting, soundproofing, comfort, style, privacy, decor, "taste," and other intangibles. A really great private bathroom with a claw-foot tub and antique table might bring up the rating of an otherwise average room. Conversely, poor maintenance or lack of good lighting will lower the rating of a spacious, well-decorated room. Sometimes a few rooms are really special while others are standard, and we have averaged these where possible. It's difficult to codify this, but all factors are weighed, and the ratings seem to come up easily.

Value Rating   The value ratings—also expressed using a one-to-five -star scale—are a combination of the overall and room quality ratings, divided by the cost of an average guest room. They are an indication rather than a scientific formulation—a general idea of value for money. If getting a good deal means the most to you, choose a property by looking at the value rating. Otherwise, the overall and room quality ratings are better indicators of a satisfying experience. A five-star value, A room quality, overall five-star inn or bed-and-breakfast would be ideal, but most often, you'll find a three-star value, and you are getting your money's worth. If a wonderful property is fairly priced, it may only get a three-star value rating, but you still might prefer the experience to an average property that gets a five-star value rating.

Price   Our price range is the lowest-priced room to the highest-priced room in regular season. The range does not usually include specially priced times such as holidays and low season. The room rate is based on double occupancy and assumes breakfast is included. It does not assume that other meals are included in the rate. However, be sure to check the inn's Food & Drink category. Lodgings where MAP, which stands for the hotel industry's standard Modified American Plan, is applicable offer breakfast and dinner in the room rate. Unless specifically noted, prices quoted in the profiles do not include gratuities or state and local taxes, which can be fairly steep. Gratuities are optional; use your own discretion. Prices change constantly, so check before booking.

The Profiles Clarified

The bulk of information about properties is straightforward, but much of it is in abbreviated style, so the following clarifications may help. They are arranged in the order they appear in the profile format. Many of the properties have similar names. Town names, too, can be strikingly similar. Make sure you don't confuse properties or town names when selecting an inn.

Location

First, check the map for location. Our directions are designed to give you a general idea of the property's location. For more complete directions, call the property or check its Web site.

Building

This category denotes the design and architecture of the building. Many of the properties in the *Unofficial Guides* are historically and architecturally interesting. Here are a few architectural terms you may want to brush up on, in no particular order: Colonial, Craftsman, Queen Anne, Princess Anne, Cape Cod, Hand-hewn Log, Foursquare, Art Deco, Georgian, Victorian, Arts and Crafts, Ranch, Farmhouse, Gabled, Boarding House, Miner's Hotel, Teepee, Duncan Phyfe accessories, Sandstone, Timber Sided, Bunkhouse, Carriage House, Chalet, William Morris wallpaper, Sheepherder's Wagon, Eastlake, Greek Revival, Edwardian, claw-foot tub, pedestal sink, and many more. The more you know the jargon, the better you can select the property you want.

Food & Drink

For food and drink, we offer a taste of the inn or bed-and-breakfast, so to speak. Most properties go all out to fill you up at breakfast, so that you could easily skip lunch (factor that into the value). In some areas, however, the tourist board regulates that properties can only serve a continental breakfast without a hot dish. Note whether we state "gourmet breakfast," if that experience is paramount. In most cases, a bed-and-breakfast breakfast—even a continental—tends to include more homemade items, greater selection, and greater care in presentation.

In this category, what we call "specialties" are really typical dishes, which may not always be served, but should give you a good idea of the cuisine. Very few bed-and-breakfasts and inns do not include the breakfast in the price. However, it is almost always offered as an option.

Many inns and bed-and-breakfasts offer afternoon tea, snacks, sherry, or pre-dinner wine and after-dinner desert. Note that if an inn offers meals to the public as well as guests, the atmosphere becomes less personal. Also, if MAP is noted in this category, it means the inn offers meals other than breakfast as part of the room rate.

Some inns provide alcoholic beverages to guests, some forbid consumption of alcohol—either extreme is noted in the inn's profile. The norm is that alcohol consumption is a private matter, and guests may bring and consume their own, if they do so respectfully. Glassware is generally provided. Bed-and-breakfasts are not well suited to drunkenness and partying.

A diet and a bed-and-breakfast or small inn go together about as well as a haystack and a lighted match. Come prepared to eat. Some bed-and-breakfasts will serve dinner on request, and we included that info when it was available.

Most bed-and-breakfasts are sensitive to dietary needs and preferences but need to be warned of this in advance. When you make your reservation, be sure to explain if you are diabetic, wheat- or dairy-intolerant, vegetarian/vegan, or otherwise restricted. Many proprietors pride themselves on accommodating difficult diets.

Recreation

We do not usually spell out whether the activities noted in the profile are on-site. With some exceptions, assume that golf, tennis, fishing, canoeing, skiing, and the like are not on-site (since these are small properties, not resorts). Assume that games and smaller recreational activities are on the property. But there are some exceptions, so ask.

Amenities & Services

These blend a bit. Generally, amenities include extras such as swimming pools and games, and services cover perks such as business support and air conditioning. Business travelers should note if any services are mentioned, and if there are public rooms, group discounts, and so forth to back them up. Almost all bed-and-breakfasts and inns can provide advice regarding touring, restaurants, and local activities; many keep maps, local menus and brochures on hand.

Deposit

Be pretty confident that you will be staying at a particular bed-and-breakfast when you make a reservation. The more popular the property, usually the more deposit you'll have to put down, and the further ahead. Many cancellation policies are very strict, and many innkeepers are recommending that guests purchase travelers insurance in case there is an unforeseen circumstance. When canceling after the site's noted policy, most will still refund, less a fee, if the room is re-rented. Check back on this.

Discounts

Discounts may extend to singles, long-stay guests, kids, seniors, packages, and groups. Even though discounts may not be listed in the text, it doesn't hurt to ask, as these sorts of things can be flexible in small establishments, midweek, off-season, last-minute, and when innkeepers may want to fill their rooms. This category also includes a dollar figure for additional persons sharing a room (beyond the two included in the basic rate).

Credit Cards

For those properties that do accept credit cards (we note those that do not), we've listed credit cards accepted with the following codes:

V	VISA	MC	MasterCard
AE	American Express	D	Discover
DC	Diner's Club International	CB	Carte Blanche

Check-In/Out

As small operators, most bed-and-breakfast hosts need to know approximately when you'll be arriving. Many have check-in periods (specified in the profiles) during which the hosts or staff will be available to greet you. Most can accommodate arrival beyond their stated check-in period but need to be advised so they can arrange to get a key to you. Think about it—they have to buy groceries and go to the kids' soccer games just like you. And they have to sleep sometime. Don't show up at 11:30 p.m. and expect a smiling bellhop—the same person who lets you in is probably going to be up at 5 or 6 a.m. slicing mushrooms for your omelet!

Check-in times are often flexible, but, as with any commercial lodging, check-out times can be critical, as the innkeeper must prepare your room for incoming guests. If you need to stay longer, just ask. Sometimes a host will let you leave your bags and enjoy the common areas after check-out, as long as you vacate your room. Please take cancellation policies seriously. A "no-show" is not a cancellation! If an establishment has a seven-day, or 72-hour, or whatever cancellation policy, you are expected to call and cancel your reservation prior to that time, or you could be liable for up to the full amount of your reserved stay. After all, a four-unit bed-and-breakfast has lost 25% of its revenue if you arbitrarily decide not to show up.

Smoking

We've indicated in the inn's profile if smoking is banned outright or if it is OK to smoke outside, but ask your hosts before you light up. Be mindful, too, of how you dispose of the butts—when you flick them into a nearby shrub, it's likely that your hosts, not some sanitation team, will be plucking them out next week.

Pets

We have not mentioned most of the in-house pets in the profiles, as this situation changes even more frequently than most items. Many properties have pets on the premises. Don't assume that because an establishment does not allow guests to bring pets that pets aren't present. Dogs and cats and birds (and horses, pigs, goats, llamas, etc.) are often around. If you foresee a problem with this, be sure to clarify "how around," before booking. If properties allow pets, we have noted this, but most do not. And if you can't bear to leave your own beloved Fido or Miss Kitty for long periods, and want to stay in an inn that does not allow them, good innkeepers often know of reputable boarding facilities nearby.

Open

Properties often claim they are open all year, but they can close at any time—at the last minute for personal reasons or if business is slow. Similarly, properties that close during parts of the year may open specially for groups. If you can get a bunch of family or friends together, it's a great way to stay at popular inns and bed-and-breakfasts that would be otherwise hard to book. And remember, in low-season things slow down, dinners may not be served, and even when some properties are "open," they may be half-closed.

An Important Note

Facts and situations change constantly in the small-lodging business. Innkeepers get divorced, prices go up, puppies arrive, chefs quit in the middle of a stew, and rooms get redecorated, upgraded, and incorporated. So use this format as a means to get a good overall idea of the property, and then inquire when you book about the specific details that matter most. Changes will definitely occur, so check to be sure.

Making the Most of Your Stay

Once you're settled in, it's a good idea to scope out the entire place, or you may not realize until too late that your favorite book was on the shelf, or that an old-fashioned swing would have swung you into the moonlight on a warm evening. If you are alone in the inn, it can feel like the property is yours (and that, in fact, is a good reason to go midweek or off-season). Take advantage of the charms of these lodgings: the fireplace, the piano, other guests, the gardens. What makes an inn or bed-and-breakfast experience an integral part of a trip are moments that become cherished memories.

Did you love it? You can perhaps duplicate in your daily life some of the touches that made the experience special, whether it was warm towels, an early weekend breakfast by candlelight, fancy snacks in the afternoon or a special recipe for stuffed French toast. Hosts usually enjoy sharing ideas and recipes. You can also make small "bed-and-breakfast" type changes at your own home that may make all of the difference in your world—a small rose in a vase, a new throw rug, a handmade quilt from a local craft fair—or really splurge and install a whirlpool tub with waterfall faucet!

These small lodgings are stress-busters, far away from sitcoms and the media mania of the day. They are cozy places to settle into and curl up with a book, a honey, or a dream. Or, if you must, a laptop and a cell phone.

Great Lakes Bed-and-Breakfasts

The industries that powered this country in the late nineteenth century—steel, autos, shipping, even oil—hatched and developed in the Great Lakes region. Their tycoons, executives of our first mega-corporations, built lavish mansions for their families, as did leaders of hundreds of spinoff companies and small-town success stories.

Today, a multitude of B&Bs throughout the Upper Midwest are tied to those industrial pioneers. We find some in the big cities, such as the Cotton Mansion in Duluth, built by John D. Rockefeller's attorney. Many are in tiny towns you never heard of—Elson Inn in Magnolia, Ohio, for instance, or the elegant Fessel's Cabbage Rose in Olney, Illinois.

We glimpse the grandeur of their lives when we stay in such inns, and we experience the quality that distinguishes B&Bs throughout the Great Lakes region: their heritage of entrepreneurialism. It launched the careers and built the fortunes of the individuals who built the homes, and keeps them thriving today. We're not talking about cookie-cutter mansions. While the majority of B&Bs are housed in Victorian structures (it was, after all, the fashion when the homes were built), the region's B&Bs run the gamut from Queen Annes and Prairie School architecture to barns, four-square colonials, posh lakeshore "cottages," Georgian mansions, humble farm houses and fishing lodges, and lighthouses. And even among the Queen Annes, no two are alike. A century ago and today, creativity reigns in the region's historical inns as well as its newer homes—which, in the population of Upper Midwest bed-and-breakfasts, are a small minority.

Gathering Information

While each zone has a brief introduction, and each profile lists nearby attractions, this book in no way purports to be a guidebook to the Great Lakes.

In addition to consulting one or more of the many useful Great Lakes guidebooks on the market, we suggest turning to the Internet and to your prospective bed-and-breakfast hosts as sources of information. Don't abuse your hosts, but they can (a) steer you to some good phone numbers and other resources, and (b) perhaps mail you a flyer or two about local sites and happenings with your reservation confirmation.

Some of the bed-and-breakfasts profiled in this guide have links from their websites to other websites of interest in their region.

Bed-and-Breakfasts on the Internet

The World Wide Web is full of websites for bed-and-breakfasts and small inns. It's full of booking services and tourism information sites that link you to home pages and listings for bed-and-breakfasts and small inns. Once you link up to one of the thousands of bed-and-breakfast or small inn websites, you can revel in detailed descriptions and click your way through colored photographs until your head spins (believe us, we know). If you see something you like, you can, in some cases, submit a reservation request on-line, or e-mail the hosts directly for a little cyberchat about your specific needs.

There's no denying that the Internet is a great resource for travelers in general, and for bed-and-breakfast/small inn seekers in particular. The problem comes in sorting the wheat from the chaff and in remembering that a great website does not necessarily equal a great lodging experience. (Think about it: do you want your bed-and-breakfast host spending his time whipping up omelets and cruising the local farmer's market or sitting in front of a computer until 3 a.m. in his underwear scanning photos of his backyard gazebo?)

Out-of-date information is another serious problem with Internet listings. We found many Great Lakes databases and Internet Yellow Page listings that showed us hundreds of inns, conveniently separated into geographic areas. Too good to be true, right? Calling the telephone numbers, we discovered that over half the listings were defunct. Many others were the scary type of bed-and-breakfast we're trying to avoid—the "let's-rent-Cindy's-room-while-she's-at-college" type.

A Few of My Favorite Things
about Great Lakes Bed-and-Breakfasts

Favorite Food

- Breakfast Meat   Fresh ham, Park Street Inn (Nevis, MN)

- Coffee   (Tie) Hallett House Inn (Deerwood, MN) and Fahnestock House (Galesburg, IL)

- Dessert — (3-Way Tie) Lemon Squares, Hutchinson Mansion (Michigan City, IN); Croissant Cookies with Honey, Water's Edge Retreat (Kelleys Island, OH); and Decadent Brownies, Murphin Ridge Inn (West Union, OH)

- Entree — Wild Rice Soup, Calumet Inn (Pipestone, MN)

- French Toast — Blueberry, Finnish Heritage Homestead (Embarrass, MN)

- Frittata — Zucchini, Scofield Mansion (Sturgeon Bay, WI)

- Fruit Dish — Baked Grapefruit with coconut topping, Brumder Mansion (Milwaukee, WI)

- International Cuisine — Bea's Mexican Breakfast, Inn at Willow Pond (Lisbon, OH)

- Muffins — (Tie) Strawberry, Front Porch Inn (Goshen, IN) and Banana Nut, English Inn (Eaton Rapids, MI)

- Pancakes — (Tie) Buckwheat, Van Buren Street Inn (Huntingburg, IN) and Blueberry, Olde Squat Inn (Marion, IL)

- Quiche — Wild Mushroom Quiche, House on Harmar Hill (Marietta, OH). (Honorable Mention: Wild Rice Quiche, Rosewood Mansion, Hastings, MN)

House and Garden Features

- Bath — Historic Loeb House (Lafayette, IN)

- Clever Theme Room — Lily Pad Room, Scofield Mansion (Sturgeon Bay, WI)

- Deco Echo — Carole Lombard House (Fort Wayne, IN)

- Family Manse Brought Back to Life — Brownstone Inn (Sheboygan, WI)

- Faux Painting — Awesome ceiling art, guest rooms, Brumder Mansion (Milwaukee, WI)

- Feng Shui — (4-Way Tie) Baker-Brewster Mansion (Hudson, WI), Fountain Hill (Grand Rapids, MI), Elephant Walk (Stillwater, MN), and River House Inn (Machesney, IL)

- Fireplace — (Tie) Glass tile fireplace, dining room, Brumder Mansion (Milwaukee, WI) and Penny-art hearth, Otter Creek Inn (Eau Claire, WI)

- Garden — At the Herb Lady's Garden (Fort Wayne, IN)

- Gift Shop — Inn at Cedar Falls (Logan, OH)

- Small-Town   Fessel's Cabbage Rose (Olney, IL)
  Restoration

- Southern   Commandant's Home B&B (West Lafayette, IN)
  Elegance

- Spot for   Chaise longue in the King's Suite, Lindley House (Urbana, IL)
  Watching TV

- Strategic Fine   Oliver Inn & Book Inn, flanking elegant-but-affordable
  Dining Position   Tippecanoe Restaurant in the Studebaker Mansion
                      (Fort Wayne, IN)

- Urban   Columbus Inn (Columbus, IN)
  Restoration

- Use of Family   Elson Inn (Magnolia, OH)
  Artifacts

- Wall Treatment   (Tie) Schussler House (Madison, IN) and Book Inn
                      (Fort Wayne, IN)

Innkeeping Amenities, and Quirks

- Bath Amenities   (Tie) Lip gloss, Goldmoor Inn (Galena, IL) and "Sex on the Beach"
                      soap, River House Inn (Machesney, IL)

- Best Pet Trick   The evening dog and pony show, Glory Hill B&B (Chillicothe, IL)

- Deal of the   Room & full breakfast for $25, Thelma's B&B (West Salem, IL)
  Midwest

- Entrepreneurial   Discreet antiques sales, Van Buren Street Inn (Huntingburg, IN)
  Spin-Off

- Hospitality   The only innkeeper to walk out to the car to greet us, James
                      Goldthorpe, Goldmoor Inn (Galena, IL)

- Mad Collectors   (Tie) Janet Rogers, Spitzer House (Medina, OH) and Dee Shoe-
                      maker, Greenhouse Bed and Breakfast (Chillicothe, OH)

- Mother-Daughter September Farm (Hudson, OH)
  Act

- Pottery   Albany House (Albany, WI)
  Collection

- Service Above   For taping Survivor so we could go to dinner, Bea Delpapa, Inn at
  & Beyond   Willow Pond (Lisbon, OH)

- Single-Handed   Olde Squat Inn (Marion, OH)
  Preservation Effort

Illinois

Had we been the ones to nickname Illinois, we would have called it the "Whiplash State." One night we slept in a dripping-with-velvet mansion in southeast Illinois, the next in a drafty log house just a few miles away in a town where the priciest restaurant was Pizza Hut. Then we crossed the plains to a beautiful, limestone bluff–rimmed river road no one had told us about, and over the next three days came across giant statues of **Popeye, Abraham Lincoln,** and a terra cotta warrior. On the way home we spent two half-days in traffic jams—one in the 50-mile **Spoon River Flea Market** outside **Peoria** (we finally gave up, pulled off the road, and started shopping), and the other outside **Chicago,** where traffic is worse because the only ones driving are tourists like us.

Illinois is a state of dramatic contrasts, with much of the affluence concentrated across the top quarter; the farther south one ventures, the less money one sees. There are exceptions, of course, but no one blinks at spending $250 a night to stay at a premium bed-and-breakfast in Chicago, whereas in southern Illinois, few rooms top $100, and those are likely to be suites with all the trimmings.

As a traveler, this dichotomy was an advantage. We ate better in the south (because we could afford to), found more deals in antiques shops, and made great time on the almost-deserted country roads. Driving in the south was a pleasure; in that northern slice, especially from **Rockford** to Chicago, it was intense.

That said, we also found some of the most creative innkeeping along that northern corridor and some of the best reasons to leave home and go be a tourist in Illinois. **Galena** is a tidy little shopping spectacle, and everyone needs a Chicago fix every few years. The museums, the lakefront, the restaurants, the architecture—it's a big city, with all the package implies.

We've already planned our return trip. Our problem is, now that we've seen the rest of Illinois, we need extra time to indulge. We found that a little whiplash is a good thing.

FOR MORE INFORMATION

Illinois Department of Commerce and Community Affairs
www.enjoyillinois.com/

Illinois Bed & Breakfast Association
6130 Old Highway 50
Breese, Illinois 62230
(888) 523-2406
www.bbonline.com/il/ilbba

Northern Illinois

It doesn't take a sociologist to discern the socioeconomic differences between the northern slice of Illinois and the southern regions. With tourist-clogged **Galena,** the **Quad Cities, Rockford, Chicago,** and the **Lake Michigan** lakefront, this is where visitors find a faster pace, wealthier towns, and clear winners in the race for tourism dollars.

The northwestern corner manages to keep a quaint, small-town feel while bringing in throngs of tourists. We visited Galena in late fall, when the inns weren't full and Main Street's sidewalks could be negotiated. It's a picturesque, historic town; 85% is a National Register Historic District whose residences and inns run the gamut of architectural styles—Federal, Italianate, Greek Revival, Queen Anne, Second Empire, even Galena Vernacular. Bring comfortable walking shoes; we counted more than 130 shops downtown, and about 50 bed-and-breakfasts in the town—almost all of which are historic homes.

At the southern tip of the zone you'll find the Quad Cities—four cities in two states, bisected by the **Mississippi River.** They work together as one large metro area, so it can be confusing. We found three **riverboat casinos** here and a 65-mile bike path along the river—plenty of diversions. This region has only a few bed-and-breakfasts, especially if you don't head across the bridge into Iowa; we found both of ours in the **Broadway Historic District** in **Rock Island.**

Heading west across the state, bed-and-breakfasts tend to be historic homes in small towns such as **Morrison** and **Oregon.** An exception is Rockford, the second-largest city in the state, where one finds a small mix of bed-and-breakfast styles; we stayed at River House, a contemporary jewel on the banks of the **Rock River**—the centerpiece of the Blackhawk Waterways region.

It all changes in the northeast corner of the state. Chicago commands the region; we began two hours' north of the city in Bible-grounded Zion and followed the lakefront south.

Listing Chicago's tourism highlights would be futile; they're simply too numerous—but we do have our favorites. We like to take in a **baseball game** while we're there (Cubs or White Sox? Take your pick—both ballparks are very cool.), and everyone should do an architectural tour once. Shopping on the **Magnificent Mile** is fun in any season, as are the comedy shows at **Second City** and blues bands almost anywhere. A number of bed-and-breakfasts in the city are historic townhouses; most are luxury properties.

WINDY CITY B&B INN, Chicago

OVERALL ★★★★★ | QUALITY ★★★★★ | VALUE ★★★ | PRICE RANGE $125–$225
GUEST ROOMS, $165–$325 COACH HOUSE APARTMENTS

Mary Shaw learned about luxury bed-and-breakfasts before she opened her own, by running Chicago's bed-and-breakfast reservation service. She also understands that Windy City isn't a destination inn: "People come here to do Chicago—they don't show up and say, 'what do we do now?'" She pampers them accordingly, with enough Chicago books and materials on hand to guide anyone's urban adventure. Rooms are named after Chicago authors, and much of the art adorning the inn is by renowned Chicago artists. Plantings in the ivy-covered courtyard were developed by the Chicago Botanical Gardens especially for the toddlin' town's peculiar climate.

SETTINGS & FACILITIES

Location 2 mi. north of Michigan Ave. shops in Lincoln Park neighborhood **Near** Wrigley Field, Field Museum, Art Institute of Chicago, Steppenwolf Theater, Navy Pier, Comiskey Park, Second City Comedy Club, Museum of Contemporary Art, Museum of Science and Industry, Soldiers Field, United Center, Old Town, Sears Tower, Magnificent Mile shops. **Building** 1886 brick Victorian mansion & coach house. **Grounds** Oversized, deep city lot w/ rear courtyard, landscaped gardens, wrought-iron fence. **Public Space** Entry, LR, DR, common rooms on 1st, 2nd, & 3rd floors. **Food & Drink** Hearty expanded cont'l breakfast. Coffee available any time in common-room kitchenettes & apartments. **Recreation** Pro sports, comedy clubs, museums, galleries, zoos, historic & architectural touring, world-class shopping, live theater, opera, symphony. **Amenities & Services** AC. Fresh flowers in rooms & common areas, robes in some rooms. Honor bars stocked w/ Chicago-brewed beers. Can host groups or meetings up to 20 guests.

ACCOMMODATIONS

Units 3 suites, 5 guest rooms. **All Rooms** Sitting area, alarm clock. **Some Rooms** Whirlpool tub, fireplace, fridge, TV/VCR, skylight, kitchen, desk & chair. **Bed & Bath** Kings (2), queens (5), 3/4 bed (1). Some full baths, hall bathroom, Sara Paretsky Room has Jacuzzi w/ full bath. **Favorites** Bill Zehme Suite in coach house, w/ large living room, full kitchen, dining area. **Comfort & Decor** It's a rare B&B that actually feels like someone's home instead of a contrived space to show off acquired possessions. Windy City is furnished with a superb mix of fine antiques and shabby-chic items that made us feel right at home, and we had the feeling Mary Shaw must have tested each chair and bed for comfort before she bought it. The home was gutted during renovation; the only original feature is the stained-glass window in front—but the mansion is still somehow loaded with character.

RATES, RESERVATIONS, & RESTRICTIONS

Deposit Credit card number **Discounts** Corp. rates **Credit Cards** V, MC, AE, D, DC **Check-In/Out** 3 p.m./11 a.m. **Smoking** No **Pets** No **Kids** Over age 10 welcome; can be younger if guests rent the full house or carriage house. **No-Nos** N/A **Minimum Stay** 2 nights on weekends, but can include Sat. night **Open** All year **Hosts** Mary & Andy Shaw, 607 West Deming Place, Chicago 60614 **Phone** (773) 248-7091 or toll-free (877) 897-7091 **Fax** (773) 897-7091 **Email** stay@chicago-inn.com **Web** www.chicago-inn.com

ANNIE WIGGINS GUEST HOUSE, Galena

OVERALL ★★★★½ | QUALITY ★★★★½ | VALUE ★★★ | PRICE RANGE $125–$175

The engineer who built the Annie Wiggins home so long ago had a novel idea: he constructed the upper two floors, raised them off the ground, then built the first floor while the others were suspended. Today, "Annie" appears in flowing period costume to greet guests and host the inn's many special events, including Queen Victoria's birthday weekend, a Robert Burns weekend, and Kentucky Derby weekend, which includes Southern-style meals of beignets and Southern fried chicken. Be sure to notice the pre–Civil War rope bed in Jenny's Room.

SETTING & FACILITIES

Location Several doors off US 20 in central Galena **Near** Downtown Galena, Galena River, Mississippi River, Scales Mound, Apple River, Alpine Slide **Building** 1846 Greek Revival, white exterior, w/ 1857 addition. **Grounds** City lot w/ flower gardens **Public Space** Foyer, double parlor, screened side porch, DR, 2nd-floor parlor. **Food & Drink** Early coffee available, lemonade any time, Friday afternoon tea. "Bountiful cont'l" breakfast includes signature baked cheese blintzes. **Recreation** Antiquing, historic touring, downhill & cross-country skiing, boating, canoeing, swimming, snowmobiling, horseback riding, riverboat cruising; more than 90 shops in downtown Galena. **Amenities & Services** AC. Logo soaps, special events including "Ghost Tour" of Galena. Ghost walk is complimentary to guests.

ACCOMMODATIONS

Units 7 guest rooms. **All Rooms** N/A **Some Rooms** Ceiling fan, claw-foot tub, soaking tub for 2. **Bed & Bath** Queens (7). All private baths. **Favorites** Durius Room, named after home's builder, w/ anthica leaf molding motif, piano, Eastlake settee & chair, & wedding dress display. **Comfort & Decor** Rhett Butler would feel right at home here. Every room whispers of the home's pre–Civil War past, in the wavy original window glass, original Ionic column room dividers, marble fireplaces with original coal fittings, the rooms' midcentury women's names (Molly, Nellie, India), even a summer kitchen recently converted to a guest room and connected to the main house by a screened porch. Those "bumpy" windows are even more appreciated in winter—they are positioned to capture solar warmth.

RATES, RESERVATIONS, & RESTRICTIONS

Deposit Credit card number **Discounts** Weekday off-season rates **Credit Cards** V, MC, AE **Check-In/Out** 4–7 p.m./11 a.m. **Smoking** No **Pets** No **Kids** Weekdays; only 2 guests per room **No-Nos** N/A **Minimum Stay** 2 nights weekends **Open** All year **Hosts** Wendy & Bill Heiken, 1004 Park Ave., Galena 61036 **Phone** (815) 777-0336 **Email** bheiken@galenalink.net **Web** www.anniewiggins.com

GOLDMOOR INN, Galena

OVERALL ★★★★½ | QUALITY ★★★★½ | VALUE ★★★ | PRICE RANGE ROOMS
$115–$145, SUITES $175–$265, COTTAGES $255–$295

We knew Goldmoor Inn would get our vote for best hospitality when the innkeeper greeted us at the car—the only innkeeper to do so in some 300 bed-and-breakfasts we visited. Patricia Goldthorpe's years in designing interiors are evident; we especially loved our fabric/faux wicker headboard (Veranda Room), so realistic we didn't realize it wasn't wicker until we laid down our heads. The food is great, the pampering is just as good—but get there before dark. The dirt roads leading to Goldmoor are isolated and not well marked.

SETTING & FACILITIES

Location 7 mi. west of Galena & US 20 **Near** Mississippi River, downtown Galena, Apple River, Scales Mound, Vinegar Hill Lead Mine, Galena River, Alpine Slide. **Building** Contemporary luxury inn, A-frame w/ cottages **Grounds** 12.5 acres above Mississippi River w/ flower gardens, enclosed gazebo. **Public Space** Deck, gazebo, great room, small overflow DR. **Food & Drink** Complimentary sodas, coffee any time; cookies at night. Full breakfast includes hot entree; ours was spinach soufflé quiche, sausage patties, & home-baked muffins. **Recreation** Antiquing, historic touring, downhill & cross-country skiing, snowmobiling, canoeing, horseback riding, riverboat cruising, more than 90 shops in downtown Galena. **Amenities & Services** AC. Logo bath amenities (including lip balm), hair dryer, robes, bicycles.

ACCOMMODATIONS

Units 3 cottages, 4 suites, 2 guest rooms. **All Rooms** Phone w/ voicemail, modem hookup, coffee machine, fridge stocked w/ beverages, clock radio, satellite TV, chair. **Some Rooms** Whirlpool tub, fireplace, Mississippi River view, patio/grill area (cottages), wet bar, microwave, bidet, VCR, CD/cassette player, big-screen TV, private entry, table & chairs, patio. **Bed & Bath** Kings (7), queens (2). All private baths. **Favorites** Mississippi Suite, w/ natural limestone hearth, entertainment center, oversized whirlpool, expansive Mississippi River view, table & chairs, large sitting area. **Comfort & Decor** Most furnishings in Goldmoor Inn are contemporary and lush. Because the target clientele includes honeymooners and business travelers, every convenience and amenity is provided, with plenty of work space and task lighting in the suites and cottages. Two cottages have atrium ceilings, all have private patios, and all guest rooms are carpeted.

RATES, RESERVATIONS, & RESTRICTIONS

Deposit Full payment within 4 days of reservation **Discounts** Midweek, multiple-night **Credit Cards** V, MC, D **Check-In/Out** 3–6 p.m./11:30 a.m. **Smoking** Outside **Pets** Inquire **Kids** Inquire **No-Nos** N/A **Minimum Stay** 2 nights on weekends, 3 nights some holiday weekends **Open** All year **Hosts** Patricia & James Goldthorpe, 9001 Sand Hill Rd., Galena 61036 **Phone** (815) 777-3925 or toll-free (800) 255-3925 **Fax** (815) 777-3993 **Email** goldmoor@galenalink.com **Web** www.galena-il.com

JOHN HENRY GUEST HOUSE, Galena

OVERALL ★★★★½ | QUALITY ★★★★½ | VALUE ★★★★★ | PRICE RANGE
$100–$110

Some of the elegant touches in this house tell you that a pillar of the community had to have lived here. The builder, John Henry Grimm, was editor of the *Galena Gazette,* and he obviously loved his clubby, warm-wood Arts & Crafts touches—built-in dining room cabinets with stained-glass fronts, for instance, plenty of window seats, and the original (and unusual) porch swing with foot rest. The Huotaris fell for the house when they first saw it, in spite of water-soaked walls and other evidence of 35 years of neglect; they found an Oriental rug under the dining room linoleum. Peek into the downstairs half-bath, formerly the pantry, to see Lyndi's darling collection of framed poetry. Peek out the window for a magnificent river view.

SETTING & FACILITIES
Location 3 blocks from downtown Galena **Near** Downtown shops, Mississippi River, Apple River, Galena River, Scales Mound, Alpine Slide. **Building** "1914-ish" Prairie four-square, brick exterior **Grounds** Gazebo, lawns perched on bluff overlooking Galena River **Public Space** Wraparound porch, entry, foyer, LR, DR, 2nd-floor sitting/coffee area, 2nd-floor balcony. **Food & Drink** Soda, water any time, early coffee available 7:30 a.m. Full breakfast includes egg dish, meat, cheese assortment, 2–3 home-baked breads. **Recreation** Antiquing, horseback riding, downhill & cross-country skiing, snowmobiling, horseback riding, riverboat cruises, 90 shops in downtown Galena. **Amenities & Services** AC.

ACCOMMODATIONS
Units 2 suites. **All Rooms** Sitting room w/ bay, sofa, reading lights, ceiling fan, TV, river view. **Some Rooms** N/A **Bed & Bath** Queens (2). All private baths. **Favorites** Gertrude's Suite, w/ larger bedroom. **Comfort & Decor** This B&B is one of the Midwest's best examples of disaster-to-delightful restoration. A decade ago, John Henry Guest House had a dirt cellar and no heating, plumbing, electricity, or porches; in 1995 the National Trust for Historic Preservation named it one of only 14 Great American Homes nationwide that year. Look for surprises here, including the foyer's built-in courting bench on the cold-air return, five steps built of "mystery" wood, and a signed mystery antique in the upstairs sitting room. Furnishings are mostly period antiques, compatible with the Arts & Crafts elements of the home.

RATES, RESERVATIONS, & RESTRICTIONS
Deposit Credit card number **Discounts** $20 off Sun.–Thurs., except holidays **Credit Cards** V, MC, D **Check-In/Out** 4–6 p.m./11 a.m. **Smoking** Outside **Pets** No **Kids** Over age 12; younger if whole-house rental **No-Nos** N/A **Minimum Stay** 2 nights weekends, May–Nov. **Open** Closed only Thanksgiving, Christmas Eve, Christmas Day **Hosts** Craig & Lyndi Huotari, 812 South Bench St., Galena 61036 **Phone** (815) 777-3595

MAIN STREET INN, Galena

OVERALL ★★★½ | QUALITY ★★★½ | VALUE ★★★ | PRICE RANGE $85–$125

At Main Street Inn, you find the most convenient location possible, a hot breakfast, and clean, pleasant surroundings. The lobby is carpeted; paneling is original wainscot; and the seating is comfortable wicker. Here, guests find the phone, coffee station, microwave, and ice machine. It's not a place that will inspire poetry, it's just a simple, old-fashioned inn.

SETTING & FACILITIES
Location In the heart of downtown Galena **Near** Downtown shops, Mississippi River, Galena River, Alpine Slide, Apple River, Scales Mound. **Building** 1850s brick storefront inn **Grounds** N/A **Public Space** 2nd-floor lobby **Food & Drink** Coffee, soda (50 cents) available any time. Full breakfast, includes hot entree. **Recreation** Downtown shopping,

downhill & cross-country skiing, antiquing, historic touring, canoeing, snowmobiling, horseback riding, riverboat cruises. **Amenities & Services** AC.

ACCOMMODATIONS

Units 6 guest rooms. **All Rooms** TV, clock radio, seating, reading lamps, armoire. **Some Rooms** Main Street view, sitting area, pull-out sofa. **Bed & Bath** Kings (3), 2 queens (1), queen (1), 2 doubles (1). All private baths. **Favorites** Galena Suite, w/ Victorian oak beds, sitting area, pull-out sofa. **Comfort & Decor** This second-floor inn is positioned perfectly for antiquing and shopping. Floral bedspreads and period-reproduction wall coverings create a homey haven for relaxing after a long day of touring. Most beds are antiques.

RATES, RESERVATIONS, & RESTRICTIONS

Deposit Credit card number **Discounts** N/A **Credit Cards** V, MC **Check-In/Out** 2 p.m./11 a.m. **Smoking** No **Pets** No **Kids** Over age 7 **No-Nos** N/A **Minimum Stay** None **Open** All year **Hosts** Tracey & Jeff Crowder, 404 South Main St., Galena 61036 **Phone** (815) 777-3454 **Fax** (815) 776-0057 **Email** rooms@mainstinn.com **Web** www.mainstinn.com

COLONIAL ROSE INN, *Grand Detour*

OVERALL ★★★½ | QUALITY ★★★½ | VALUE ★★★★ | PRICE RANGE $75–$85,
3-BR COTTAGE $225 (NO BREAKFAST)

This is a lovely home, enhanced by murals painted by the innkeeper. The cottage sits away from the main inn, with a full kitchen, living room, screened porch, and one king and two queen bedrooms. Ninety percent of the clients for Colonial Rose Inn are on getaways from Chicago's suburbs. We did see one down side: During our tour, the innkeepers' black lab followed us everywhere, including the restaurant, where tables had been set for dinner—not a healthy practice from allergy and hygiene standpoints.

SETTING & FACILITIES

Location Just off IL 2 between Oregon & Dixon, IL **Near** John Deere Historic Site, Chocolate Trail, Ronald Reagan Trail, Mississippi River, Rock River. **Building** 1855 Italianate w/ additions, brick exterior **Grounds** 2.4 acres of lawns, woods, perennial gardens **Public Space** Front parlor, TV room, library, inn DR, front porch, loft sitting area. Also restaurant serving dinner to the public 4 days/week. **Food & Drink** Early coffee delivered to guest rooms. Full breakfast includes hot entree, may include signature omelets. **Recreation** Antiquing, historic touring, swimming, canoeing, boating, cross-country skiing, swimming, fishing, hunting, horseback riding. **Amenities & Services** AC. Logo soaps; sells mugs of the inn. Will make bonfire for guests on request.

ACCOMMODATIONS

Units 5 guest rooms. (Also rents 3-BR cottage—breakfast not included.) **All Rooms** Ceiling fan. **Some Rooms** High-back Victorian bed. **Bed & Bath** Queens (4), double (1). All private baths. **Favorites** Queen room w/ antique iron bed; it seems brighter. **Comfort & Decor** The Italian marble fireplace in the dining room matches the one in the front parlor, and original white pine plank flooring connects most rooms on the first floor. Another marble fireplace is located in the library. Also in the parlor are desk and chair and baby grand piano; all three rooms feature 12-foot ceilings with floor-to-ceiling windows. The TV room doubles as the innkeepers' family room.

RATES, RESERVATIONS, & RESTRICTIONS

Deposit Credit card number or 50% of stay **Discounts** None **Credit Cards** V, MC **Check-In/Out** 4–10 p.m./11 a.m. **Smoking** No **Pets** No; resident dog is permitted in public areas **Kids** Over age 14; only 2 guests per room **No-Nos** N/A **Minimum Stay** None **Open** All year **Hosts** Jeffrey & Jayne Rose, 8230 South Green St., Grand Detour 61021 **Phone** (815) 652-4422 **Email** roseinn@essex1.com **Web** www.colonialroseinn.com

RIVER HOUSE BED & BREAKFAST, Machesney Park

OVERALL ★★★★½ | QUALITY ★★★★½ | VALUE ★★★★ | PRICE RANGE $135–$185; TEPEE $95 MAY–OCT.

Even if you're not a fan of Southwest decor, you'll love your surroundings at River House. We noticed an air of serenity to the place and thought perhaps it was because of the beautiful Native American art adorning the walls. The beauty of this inn, however, is hard-earned. Innkeeper Patty Rinehart learned—after she'd bought the place—that it was built on top of an old cemetery. Fearing restless nights (or worse!) for her future guests, Rinehart called in every spiritual expert she could think of, and the inn underwent blessings, clearings, feng shui, and Native American ceremonies to cleanse away any "lower energies" that might linger. It worked; we slept like babies.

SETTING & FACILITIES

Location Off Rt. 251, 5 mi. north of Rockford **Near** Rockford, Anderson Japanese Gardens, Klehm Arboretum, antiques malls, Rockford Art Museum, Tinker Swiss Cottage Museum. **Building** Contemporary, remodeled luxury ranch home **Grounds** 5.5 acres on the Rock River w/ in-ground pool, fire pit, totem pole, tepee, woods **Public Space** Common Room, DR, entry, enclosed patio, swimming pool. **Food & Drink** Sodas, bottled water any time. Full gourmet breakfast; ours included not-too-sweet apple puff pancake & "egg in a nest" (shirred egg wrapped in bacon). **Recreation** Antiquing, municipal gardens, arboretum, museums, galleries, live theater, symphony, golf courses. **Amenities & Services** AC. Gel-can fireplace system, robes, hair dryer. Can accommodate parties or luncheons to 40 persons, or arrange massage, manicure, flowers, other extras.

ACCOMMODATIONS

Units 3 guest rooms & tepee. **All Rooms** (Except tepee) Coffeepot, stocked refrigerator, alarm clock, snack pack, TV, fireplace. **Some Rooms** Hot tub, private screened porch & outside entrance, river view, table & chairs, loveseat, hide-a-bed. **Bed & Bath** King (1), queens (2). All private baths. Tepee lodge includes bedding, towels, firewood, porta-potty, wash basin, use of designated in-house bathroom. **Favorites** Garden Suite, w/ handicap/triple-head shower, & private screened porch & entrance. **Comfort & Decor**

Furnishings in guest rooms and common areas alike are sumptuous and romantic, all with an upscale Southwest flavor. The baths are oversized, the rooms are spacious, and the beds swallow you up in comfort. We loved the look of the log bed in the Timber Suite. Take time to snoop at the Native American collections decorating the common area; the drums, pipes, and art all are genuine.

RATES, RESERVATIONS, & RESTRICTIONS
Deposit 1 night's stay **Discounts** Corp., midweek, multinight **Credit Cards** V, MC, AE, D **Check-In/Out** By arrangement/noon **Smoking** Outside **Pets** Inquire (2 resident cats stay in innkeepers' quarters on request; we experienced no allergic reactions) **Kids** Inquire **No-Nos** N/A **Minimum Stay** None **Open** All year **Hosts** Patty Rinehart, 11052 Ventura Blvd., Machesney Park 61115 **Phone** (815) 636-1884 **Fax** (815) 636-1884 **Email** innkeeper@riverhouse.ws **Web** www.riverhouse.ws

HILLENDALE BED & BREAKFAST, Morrison

OVERALL ★★★★½ | QUALITY ★★★★½ | VALUE ★★★★ | PRICE RANGE $70–$175

Take a cultural journey through Hillendale's guest rooms, and visit the ancient Mayans, deep Africa, an Italian vineyard, and the Irish countryside, among other stops. The Winandys have great fun sharing their travel adventures via their inn's decor. Outside, a bagua-shaped gazebo, with bagua-shaped table in the center, set off the prairie grass garden. A Japanese tea house stands behind the bed-and-breakfast; the water garden is stocked with Japanese koi. Guarding the tea house door is a life-sized granite replica of one of the famous 7,000 terra cotta warriors of Xian. (Mike Winandy tried to convince us he'd greased palms overseas to have one stolen for himself, but reproductions are sold online.) Still, it's an imposing presence.

SETTING & FACILITIES
Location On the Lincoln Highway (US 30) in residential Morrison **Near** Morrison Rockwood State Park, Blackhawk Chocolate Trail, Lock and Dam No. 13, Heritage Canyon, Odell Agricultural Museum, Ronald Reagan Birthplace. **Building** 1891 Tudor home w/ portico & porch **Grounds** 2 acres of landscaped gardens, w/ fountains, Japanese tea house, pool **Public Space** Conservatory/breakfast room, front parlor, billiards room, fitness room, DR. **Food & Drink** Served at guests' convenience, full gourmet breakfast may feature signature marinated French toast or baked-apple pancakes. **Recreation** Antiquing, museums, swimming, historic touring, biking, canoeing, fishing, live theater, eagle-watching (Jan.-Mar.). **Amenities & Services** AC. Robes, white noise machines, chocolates in rooms, 3 different soaps.

ACCOMMODATIONS
Units 3 suites, 7 guest rooms. **All Rooms** Phone, TV/VCR. **Some Rooms** Double whirlpool tub, desk & chair, fireplace, sitting area, refrigerator. **Bed & Bath** Kings (4), queens (5), 2 twins (1). Private baths, some w/ whirlpool. **Favorites** Bonjour, w/ matching high-Victorian bedroom suite, desk, & claw-foot tub. **Comfort & Decor** We almost named Welkom as our favorite room, for its turret, marble sink, and double shower.

Rooms are named for greetings in different languages—Hau Kola, Aloha, Ciao, Sayonara, Fáilte—and the surroundings follow. It's a great scheme for the innkeepers to display artifacts from their world travels; our favorite was a painted Tibetan gold-on-cotton piece hanging in the dining room, so intricate it would take us a lifetime to complete.

RATES, RESERVATIONS, & RESTRICTIONS
Deposit Credit card number; 1 night's stay if reserving more than 1 room **Discounts** Corp., special packages **Credit Cards** V, MC, AE, D, DC **Check-In/Out** 3 p.m./11 a.m. **Smoking** No **Pets** No **Kids** Over age 12 **No-Nos** N/A **Minimum Stay** None **Open** All year **Hosts** Mike & Barb Winandy, 600 West Lincolnway, Morrison 61270 **Phone** (815) 772-3454 **Fax** (815) 772-7023 **Email** hillend@hillend.com **Web** www.hillend.com

HARRISON HOUSE, Naperville

OVERALL ★★★★ | QUALITY ★★★★ | VALUE ★★ | PRICE RANGE $118–$158

Many people come to Naperville to visit Naper Settlement, a simulated "living museum," and Harrison House is a hospitable, friendly inn for families. Those with children might choose the Blue Room, adorned with teddy bears; the Victorian Room, decorated in Battenburg lace and rich tones of rose and black, is more romantic. Harrison House isn't a particularly elegant inn, so we thought prices were a bit high, but they do offer plenty of extras.

SETTING & FACILITIES
Location In residential Naperville, blocks from downtown, 25 mi. west of Chicago **Near** Naper Settlement, downtown Naperville, Centennial Beach, Riverwalk, North Central College. **Building** 1904 Colonial, white exterior **Grounds** City lot w/ shrubs, flower beds **Public Space** Porch, foyer, LR, DR **Food & Drink** Evening snack or dessert. Guest refrigerator is stocked w/ sodas, beer, wine, sometimes cheese. Cont'l breakfast weekdays, full breakfast weekends w/ signature Texas French toast. **Recreation** Historic touring, swimming, boating, antiquing, biking, golf courses. **Amenities & Services** AC. Logo bath amenities, scratch pads & pens, fresh flowers, snacks, robes in rooms.

ACCOMMODATIONS
Units 4 guest rooms. **All Rooms** Chair, TV/VCR, clock radio. **Some Rooms** Table & chairs, whirlpool tub, desk, claw-foot tub, vintage pull-chain toilet. **Bed & Bath** Queens (4). All private baths (1 detached). **Favorites** Garden Room, w/ four-poster bed, armoire. **Comfort & Decor** Much of Harrison House's original features have been preserved, including woodwork, pocket doors, old pine plank flooring, and some light fixtures. Bed coverings are hand-stitched quilts, and guest rooms are individually furnished in white wicker, Victorian, European, or "country blue" styles, and guests in all rooms sleep on feather beds.

RATES, RESERVATIONS, & RESTRICTIONS
Deposit Credit card number **Discounts** Weekday corp. **Credit Cards** V, MC, AE **Check-In/Out** 5–7 p.m./11 a.m. **Smoking** No **Pets** No **Kids** Yes, but not babies on weekends **No-Nos** N/A **Minimum Stay** None **Open** All year **Hosts** Neal & Lynn Harrison, 26 North Eagle St., Naperville 60540 **Phone** (630) 420-1117 or toll-free (800) 842-7968

PATCHWORK INN, Oregon

OVERALL ★★★★ | QUALITY ★★★★ | VALUE ★★★★ | PRICE RANGE $75–$150

You've heard the saying "Lincoln slept here." In the case of Patchwork Inn, he really did, in the mid-1850s. At that time, much of the basement—now a common area with a TV—probably was the livery stable for the inn. They believe Abe lodged in the front room, though all rooms successfully recall the spirit and slower pace of that time. Guests from Chicago who want to meander instead of rushing to their getaway can just head west on North Avenue in the city; also Route 64, it leads to downtown Oregon.

SETTING & FACILITIES
Location Blocks from the Rock River in downtown Oregon, near IL 2 & 64 **Near** Rock River, Oregon business center, Rockford, John Deere Historic Site, 3 state parks. **Building** 1840s stagecoach inn, wood construction **Grounds** Courtyard, flower garden **Public Space** Parlor, breakfast room, lower-level common area **Food & Drink** Soda, water available any time for 50 cents; cont'l breakfast. **Recreation** Historic touring, canoeing, biking, cross-country skiing, antiquing, golf courses. **Amenities & Services** AC. 3 low-side, step-in showers.

ACCOMMODATIONS
Units 10 guest rooms. **All Rooms** TV, sitting area, phone, clock. **Some Rooms** Antique rope bed, whirlpool tub, fireplace, door to shared front porch. **Bed & Bath** "Modern/large" doubles (5), doubles (2), 2 twins (2), twin (1). Detached baths. **Favorites** Lincoln Room, because Abe slept here, w/ original brick fireplace, Jenny Lind "hired man's bed," chairs. **Comfort & Decor** Though the inn had to be gutted for restoration, it's retained original features that count, such as the pre–Civil War brick fireplace, yellow pine floors, and walnut rail. The exposed brick in the breakfast room is the original back wall. Innkeepers have added clever decorating touches to enhance the historic ambience, such as "sewing machine" breakfast tables, and shutters from one innkeeper's childhood home. Decorative stenciling is tasteful and spare.

RATES, RESERVATIONS, & RESTRICTIONS
Deposit Credit card number **Discounts** Corp., multiple-night, off-season, special packages **Credit Cards** V, MC, D **Check-In/Out** Inquire **Smoking** No **Pets** No **Kids** Over age 12 **No-Nos** N/A **Minimum Stay** None **Open** All year **Hosts** Jean & Mike McNamara, Ron Bry, 122 North 3rd St., Oregon 61061 **Phone** (815) 732-4113 **Fax** (815) 732-6557 **Email** patchworkinn@essex1.com **Web** www.essex1.com/people/patchworkinn

POTTER HOUSE, Rock Island

OVERALL ★★★½ | QUALITY ★★★★ | VALUE ★★★★ | PRICE RANGE $75–$95

Potter House hasn't changed much since it was built by Rock Island's newspaper publisher. The town's proximity to the Rock and Mississippi Rivers as well as Davenport and northern Illinois make it a major destination for both leisure and business travelers, and the inn caters to both. Period antiques throughout the house are of high quality, and three guest rooms feature old wrought-iron beds. Our favorite accent was in the Guest Room: a writing table made from an old sewing machine.

SETTING & FACILITIES
Location In residential Rock Island, several blocks from bridges to Davenport, IA **Near** Riverboat casinos, Mississippi River, "The District" arts & entertainment area, other Quad Cities. **Building** 1907 Colonial Revival, on National Register of Historic Places **Grounds** City lot; flower beds **Public Space** Foyer, LR, DR, solarium parlor **Food & Drink** Full breakfast includes hot entree. **Recreation** Boating, gambling, antiquing, live theater, museums, river cruises, canoeing, cross-country skiing. **Amenities & Services** AC. Computer modems.

ACCOMMODATIONS
Units 4 guest rooms, 1 suite. **All Rooms** TV, phone, desk, sitting area, clock radio. **Some Rooms** Fireplace, claw-foot tub. **Bed & Bath** Queens (3), 2 doubles (1), 1 double (1). All private baths (1 detached). **Favorites** Marguerite's Room, w/ queen antique brass bed, fireplace, & soft coral & aqua colors. **Comfort & Decor** Stained-glass double doors at the entry and 13 stained-glass windows are testimony to the glamour built into this home. A grand central staircase, embossed leather wall coverings in the foyer and up the stairwell, mahogany paneling in the dining room, and a "coffin" shower in the Palladian Room are just a few of the eyebrow-raisers here. Some of the public areas felt a bit gloomy, but new lighting and paint are an easy fix.

RATES, RESERVATIONS, & RESTRICTIONS
Deposit Credit card number or 1 night's stay **Discounts** Gov't. rates, Midwest Living promotions **Credit Cards** V, MC, D, AE, DC **Check-In/Out** 3–7 p.m./11 a.m. **Smoking** No **Pets** No; resident dog is permitted throughout inn **Kids** No **No-Nos** N/A **Minimum Stay** 2 nights on a few select weekends. **Open** All year. **Hosts** Frank L. Skradski, 1907 7th Ave., Rock Island 61201 **Phone** (309) 788-1906 or toll-free (800) 747-0339 **Fax** (309) 794-3947 **Email** potterhouse@qconline.com **Web** www.qconline.com/potterhouse

TOP O'THE MORNING BED & BREAKFAST INN,
Rock Island

OVERALL ★★★★ | QUALITY ★★★★ | VALUE ★★★★★ | PRICE RANGE $40–$100

Guests here have choices for lounging and privacy: they can watch TV on the sleeping porch if they rent the suite—the best room, a corner space with TV, six windows, and a jaw-dropping view of the Mississippi River—or they can choose the tiered deck that slopes down the hillside toward the river. We liked the chandeliered great room, where innkeeper Peggy Doak, a music teacher, displays her harp, organ, and grand piano. Views of the river valley are extraordinary from most public rooms.

SETTING & FACILITIES

Location In residential Rock Island, 1 mi. from Rt. 67. **Near** Riverboat casinos, Mississippi River, "The District" arts & entertainment area, other Quad Cities. **Building** 1912 Prairie home, brick **Grounds** 3 acres of lawns, forest of 200-year-old oaks, fenced by wrought iron **Public Space** Foyer, DR, LR, tiered deck, great room, screened porch, den **Food & Drink** Full breakfast includes 3 entrees; doesn't serve eggs 2 days in a row. **Recreation** Historic touring, gambling, museums, live theater, antiquing, boating, river cruises, canoeing, cross-country skiing. **Amenities & Services** AC. Champagne included if renting "sleeping porch" as sitting room w/ Ethan Allen Room.

ACCOMMODATIONS

Units 4 guest rooms, or 3 guest rooms & 1 suite. **All Rooms** Phone, alarm clock. **Some Rooms** Whirlpool tub, ceiling fan, desk & chair, table & chair. **Bed & Bath** Queen, double & twin, double, 3 twin. 2 private baths, 1 shared. **Favorites** Ethan Allen Room w/ four-poster bed, "dressing desk" & chair, built-in window bench, original tiled bath. **Comfort & Decor** The former home of the Rock Island Railroad president, we weren't surprised to find train decor in one guest room; even the phone ring is a train whistle. Details mattered when tycoons built their homes, such as the doors upstairs: the mahogany side, facing the master's quarters, features a "globe"-style crystal doorknob, while the pine side facing the maid's quarters has a plain brass knob. Mahogany is the primary wood throughout, used for trim and fireplaces.

RATES, RESERVATIONS, & RESTRICTIONS

Deposit 1 night's stay **Discounts** Gov't. rate if guest stays 5 nights **Credit Cards** V, MC **Check-In/Out** Inquire **Smoking** In designated areas **Pets** No **Kids** Yes **No-Nos** N/A **Minimum Stay** None **Open** All year **Hosts** Sam & Peggy Doak, 1505 19th Ave., Rock Island 61201 **Phone** (309) 786-3513

HAMMOND HOUSE BED AND BREAKFAST, Stockton

OVERALL ★★★½ | QUALITY ★★★½ | VALUE ★★★ | PRICE RANGE $125

Hammond House has some interesting features, such as the original yellow pine, carved-urn newels with ribbon frieze, and pocket doors. If you're looking for a romantic getaway, you'll need to tune out the gift shop downstairs; it pretty much dominates the inn's identity. Couples might want to rent the suite, with a whirlpool alcove, chaise longue, and lots of space.

SETTING & FACILITIES

Location On IL 78 in residential Stockton **Near** Apple River Canyon State Park, Stockton Memorial Park, Kidstown, Highland Community College, Galena. **Building** 1900 Colonial Revival, white exterior **Grounds** Oversized town lot w/ flower gardens **Public Space** 2nd-floor LR, DR, sunroom, deck **Food & Drink** Full breakfast includes hot entree. **Recreation** Antiquing, historic touring, biking, canoeing, golf courses, fishing, hunting. **Amenities & Services** AC. Welcome basket with bottle of wine.

ACCOMMODATIONS

Units 1 suite, 4 guest rooms. **All Rooms** Coffeemaker, TV, clock radio. **Some Rooms** Whirlpool tub, ceiling fan. **Bed & Bath** Queens (4), 2 twins (1). Small overflow room has 3/4 bed. Private baths (5). **Favorites** Charles & Nelly's Room, with contemporary furnishings, black-and-white color scheme. **Comfort & Decor** Most public spaces are on the second floor because the downstairs is largely taken by a multiple-room gift shop. The dining room features a domed skylight, and the living room has a big-screen TV, table, and chairs. The tiered deck with wisteria vine is a restful, aromatic spot for relaxing in summer.

RATES, RESERVATIONS, & RESTRICTIONS

Deposit Credit card number or $25 **Discounts** Weekday corp. rates **Credit Cards** V, MC, D **Check-In/Out** Noon/noon **Smoking** No **Pets** No **Kids** No **No-Nos** Guests staying out very late at night. "We like people in by 11 p.m." **Minimum Stay** 2 nights weekends May–Dec. **Open** All year **Hosts** LaVonneda & Spencer Haas, 323 North Main St., Stockton 61085 **Phone** (815) 947-2032 **Email** haas@blkhawk.net **Web** www.hammondhouse.com

EMANUELSON INN, Zion

OVERALL ★★★★ | QUALITY ★★★★ | VALUE ★★★★ | PRICE RANGE $105 (SHARED BATH) TO $125 (PRIVATE BATH OR COTTAGE ROOM)

How well did you pay attention in church school? You can test your Bible aptitude by driving around Zion, whose streets are named after biblical characters, and reciting their stories—Gideon, Ezra, Ezekiel, and dozens more. Emanuelson Inn was founded by a Mennonite elder; today, many of its weekend guests are visitors to the cancer treatment center across the street. The Metro Train Station, a short walk from the inn, takes visitors into Chicago.

SETTING & FACILITIES

Location Just off Lake Dr., 1.5 hrs. north of Chicago **Near** Lake Michigan, Zion Parks & Recreation Area, downtown Zion, skating rink. **Building** 1903 Victorian, red wood exterior **Grounds** Oversized city lot, flower beds **Public Space** DR, breakfast turret room, parlor, 3rd-floor turret room **Food & Drink** Complimentary snack & wine or champagne. Full breakfast includes hot entree such as signature peach-stuffed French toast. **Recreation** Boating, biking, swimming, fishing, cross-country skiing, antiquing, historic touring, ice skating. **Amenities & Services** AC. Elevator, bikes, business facilities, laundry facilities.

ACCOMMODATIONS

Units 17 guest rooms, 2-bedroom cottage, efficiency apartment. **All Rooms** TV, phone w/ voicemail, alarm clock, fridge, sitting area. **Some Rooms** Turret area, stained glass window, table & chairs, built-in dressing table. Cottage has fireplace & full kitchen. **Bed & Bath** Kings (4), queen (1), 2 twins (4), doubles (8). Apartment has 2 doubles; each cottage bedroom has 2 twins. 14 rooms w/ private baths. **Favorites** Room #1 w/ king canopy bed, coffered ceiling, bow window w/ curved glass, carved fireplace w/ Italian tile, love seat. **Comfort & Decor** One imagines that this inn appears exactly as it did in the early 1900s.

Furnishings respect original features such as the chandelier, sconces, and fireplace in the parlor and the curved-glass turret window in the breakfast room. Nor were guest rooms mucked up by thoughtless remodeling; windows, bath fixtures, and ceiling lamps were preserved wherever possible.

RATES, RESERVATIONS, & RESTRICTIONS

Deposit Credit card number **Discounts** None **Credit Cards** V, MC **Check-In/Out** 2 p.m./noon **Smoking** No **Pets** No **Kids** Over age 8 **No-Nos** Candles **Minimum Stay** None **Open** All year **Hosts** Judy Lucero, 1241 Shiloh Blvd., Zion 60099 **Phone** (847) 872-8488 ext. 119, or toll-free (877) 872-8488 ext. 119 **Email** innkeeper@emanuelson inn.com **Web** www.emanuelsoninn.com

Central Illinois

After driving the central zone, we know why Illinois is called the Plains State. It looks like Kansas, punctuated with midsized cities.

Sure, we found rural bed-and-breakfasts in microscopic villages—and visitors will be happy to discover both their quality and their prices. **Glory Hill** is a dab of class in the middle of nowhere, and **the Barn in Dahinda** is a rustic find, especially for families. But more than the other zones, central Illinois is characterized by college towns and small cities. Some are strung along the **Spoon River** to the east of **Peoria,** where—with much regret—we had to cancel appointments because the massive annual flea market had us trapped in traffic on the two-lanes. Instead, we spent the night in **Galesburg,** a popular antiques center and birthplace of **Carl Sandburg.** Several streets lined with stately mansions make up the city's National Register Historic District; our lodging there was the Fahnestock House, a mansion owned by the same team who run the local coffee roastery in Galesburg's restored commercial district.

We found the same quality of inns in **Springfield**—not surprising, as it's the state capital, but its tourism draws are the **Abraham Lincoln** sites, so you'll see much budget lodging as well. Start your tour in the cobblestone neighborhood where he and **Mary Todd Lincoln** lived for 17 years and end at his tomb in **Oak Ridge Cemetery.** (You'll know it when you see it.)

Kankakee has a different personality. It's centered mostly on the **Kankakee River** and the sports and seasonal events held there. There are 18 riverfront parks, a dozen boat launches, and a state park in the immediate area; aside from antiquing, diversions in this river valley seem to be almost exclusively river-related. The bed-and-breakfast scene follows that lead, catering to visitors who come for the canoeing, horseback riding, and other sports.

The tone switches again in Illinois's twin cities, **Urbana-Champaign.** Bed-and-breakfast guests in both cities are there largely because of the

University of Illinois—they're parents of students, visiting academics, or prospective faculty. In Champaign bed and breakfasts are located both in the historic Sesquicentennial neighborhood and farmhouses outside the city core; **Urbana's** Lindley House is found in that college town's historic district.

GLORY HILL BED & BREAKFAST, Chillicothe

OVERALL ★★★★½ | QUALITY ★★★★½ | VALUE ★★★★★ | PRICE RANGE $75–$85

We couldn't decide which was the bigger sensation at Glory Hill, the Lincoln artifacts or the impressive dog-and-pony show (literally) that happens each evening. The Lincoln items include a card with a photo of the president's funeral on the front, and a letter signed only "Abraham"—a rare signature. As for what the Russells call "the show," guests can watch each evening as Stormy, the border collie, brings in the horses from the pasture; it's great theater.

SETTING & FACILITIES
Location Off Rt. 29, between Chillicothe & Peoria **Near** Illinois River, Peoria, downtown Chillicothe. **Building** 1841 Federal home, brick **Grounds** 5 acres of woods, lawns, pasture **Public Space** Veranda, parlor, patio, screened porch, family room, DR **Food & Drink** Fresh-baked welcome snack, early coffee delivered to room. Full breakfast served at guest's convenience features any of 41 different entrees, including signature poached pears & eggs Benedict, or French strawberry soup. **Recreation** Cross-country skiing, canoeing, feeding & petting horses, fishing, museums, live theater. **Amenities & Services** AC. Robes, fax, data port.

ACCOMMODATIONS
Units 2 guest rooms. **All Rooms** Desk or table, chairs, TV/VCR, clock radio. **Some Rooms** Double whirlpool tub. **Bed & Bath** Double (1), 2 twins (1). All private baths. **Favorites** Lincoln Room, decorated in authentic Lincoln memorabilia. **Comfort & Decor** The brick pillared front veranda, the parlor with a baby grand piano, and the impressive art collection won us over before we even knew Abraham Lincoln had stayed here many times. Bricks to build the house were kilned on site. The portraits in the dining room are no reproductions; they're the innkeeper's great-great-great grandparents.

RATES, RESERVATIONS, & RESTRICTIONS
Deposit $50 **Discounts** None **Credit Cards** V, MC, D, AE **Check-In/Out** 3 p.m./11 a.m. **Smoking** Downstairs **Pets** No; 2 resident dogs are permitted in common areas **Kids** Over age 12 **No-Nos** N/A **Minimum Stay** None **Open** All year **Hosts** Bonnie Russell, 18427 North Old Galena Rd., Chillicothe 61523 **Phone** (309) 274-4228

HOMOLKA HOUSE, Chillicothe

OVERALL ★★★½ | QUALITY ★★★½ | VALUE ★★★★ | PRICE RANGE $60–$80

A casual, comfortable stop in a tiny town, Homolka House is a family-friendly stop for groups visiting Peoria who would rather stay outside the city. Vintage school chairs, a game table, couches and sitting areas in the game room, and a sunny deck give every family member a place to relax in privacy. For romantic getaways, the suite works best; it's furnished with antiques and a faux fireplace.

SETTING & FACILITIES
Location In residential Chillicothe, 15 min. north of Peoria on IL 29 **Near** Chillicothe town center, Illinois River, Peoria, Dixon Mounds, Wildlife Prairie Park, Spoon River Scenic Drive. **Building** 1901 Victorian w/ additions **Grounds** Oversized town lot w/ flower beds, shrubs **Public Space** Foyer, DR, 3-season porch, game room, deck **Food & Drink** Expanded cont'l breakfast w/ home-baked goods. **Recreation** Pool, pinball, cross-country skiing, canoeing, fishing, museums, live theater. **Amenities & Services** AC.

ACCOMMODATIONS
Units 2 guest rooms, 1 suite. **All Rooms** TV, clock radio. **Some Rooms** Library alcove, ceiling fan, VCR. **Bed & Bath** King (1), queen (1), 2 twins & crib (1). In overflow loft, daybed & crib. All private baths (1 detached), or 1 shared if loft room rented for overflow. **Favorites** Suite, on 1st floor w/ brick fireplace, stained & beveled glass, sitting room. **Comfort & Decor** Homolka House has undergone so much remodeling that visitors are challenged to see that it's a Victorian; it looks and feels like a contemporary home, with open staircases, hardwood floors, and much newer furniture in the public areas.

RATES, RESERVATIONS, & RESTRICTIONS
Deposit 50% of stay **Discounts** Extended stay **Credit Cards** V, MC, AE **Check-In/Out** 4 p.m./11 a.m. **Smoking** No **Pets** No **Kids** Yes **No-Nos** N/A **Minimum Stay** None **Open** Call ahead **Hosts** Kathy Homolka, 721 5th Ave., Chillicothe 61523 **Phone** (309) 274-5925

THE BARN BED AND BREAKFAST, Dahinda

OVERALL ★★★★½ | QUALITY ★★★★½ | VALUE ★★★★★ | PRICE RANGE $80
COUPLE; KIDS UNDER AGE 10 STAY FREE

Sixty oaks and "a few walnut trees," all from the Dunphys' farm, were sacrificed to create the Barn. The innkeepers wanted to build a barn using long-discarded techniques—it's secured with 700 hand-carved wooden pegs—and took board and batten siding from 11 different area barns to finish the job. Their guests often are families but also include ladies wanting a girls' night out, quilters, scrapbookers, and honeymooners. Be ready for delicious isolation; the Barn sits alone at the end of a dead-end road.

SETTING & FACILITIES

Location 0.5 mi. west of the Dahinda Post Office, 15 mi. east of Galesburg **Near** Dixon Mounds, Dahinda town center, Illinois River, Galesburg, Spoon River Scenic Drive, Dixon Mounds, Wildlife Prairie Park. **Building** 1992 barn, turn-of-century reproduction w/ timber frame, post & beam, mortise & tenon construction **Grounds** 215 acres of woods & farmland **Public Space** LR/great room, full kitchen **Food & Drink** Private-label coffee & raspberry wine available any time. Cont'l breakfast included in room rate; full breakfast available in main house for $7 extra. **Recreation** Antiquing, historic touring, galleries, museums, billiards, cross-country skiing. **Amenities & Services** AC. Complimentary chocolates. Pool table, washer & dryer.

ACCOMMODATIONS

Units 1 "hay loft" dorm, sleeps 10. **All Rooms** N/A **Some Rooms** N/A **Bed & Bath** Doubles (4), twins (2). Bath w/ shower & claw-foot tub indoors; also outdoor shower. **Favorites** N/A **Comfort & Decor** This is old-fashioned farm living with a modern twist: in the horse stall is a full working kitchen, and the bath is an oat bin. Art Deco chandeliers light the loft, where a variety of antique iron and carved-wood beds line the wall, dorm-style. Trunks, chairs, and benches furnish the entire space; some, like the washing machine used by innkeeper Mike Dunphy's great-grandmother, are family artifacts.

RATES, RESERVATIONS, & RESTRICTIONS

Deposit $40 **Discounts** 20% off 3 or more nights' stay **Credit Cards** Call ahead **Check-In/Out** 4–6 p.m./10 a.m. **Smoking** No **Pets** No **Kids** Yes **No-Nos** N/A **Minimum Stay** None **Open** Jan. to Thanksgiving **Hosts** Sandy & Mike Dunphy, P.O. Box 92, Dahinda 61428 **Phone** (309) 639-4408 **Fax** (309) 639-4408 **Email** dunphy@winco.net **Web** www.bbonline.com/il/thebarn

FAHNESTOCK HOUSE, Galesburg

OVERALL ★★★★★ | QUALITY ★★★★★ | VALUE ★★★★★ | PRICE RANGE $125

Class and comfort are the hallmarks of this bed-and-breakfast, an easy choice for our short list of perfect bed-and-breakfasts. The built-in features, such as the tile fireplace that tells the story of the four seasons or the three-story turret and three-story bow window alcove, set a tone of grandeur. Add the innkeepers' own creations, such as the chair-leg bathroom sink in the Victorian Suite, and the wall and ceiling treatments in the foyer—and to cinch the prize, they own a coffee roaster shop & roastery (called "Innkeeper's," natch), so guests wake to the aroma of top-quality beans grinding and brewing.

SETTING & FACILITIES

Location In Galesburg's historic district, off US 150 **Near** Seminary Street Historic commercial District, Orpheum Theater, Carl Sandburg birthplace, Bishop Hill Swedish utopian settlement, Knox College, antiques malls. **Building** 1890 Queen Anne, gray-blue palette, listed as an Anchor Structure by the National Register of Historic Places **Grounds** Large city lot w/ lawns, formal perennial garden, fountain, patio **Public Space** Front porch, foyer, double parlor, DR **Food & Drink** Stocked guest fridges include soft drinks; complimentary bottle of wine in room. Full gourmet breakfast includes home-baked breads, hot entree, served on China & silver w/ fresh flowers. **Recreation** Historic touring, antiquing, architectural touring, museums, live theater, concerts, golf course, water park, public swimming pool. **Amenities & Services** AC. Fresh flowers in room; pick-up service for guests traveling by Amtrak, bicycles.

ACCOMMODATIONS

Units 2 suites. **All Rooms** Kitchenette w/ fridge & coffeemaker, CD player, private balcony, turret parlor. **Some Rooms** TV, claw-foot tub, 14-foot bow window. **Bed & Bath** Queens (2). All private baths. **Favorites** Victorian Suite, w/ private "opera-box" balcony overlooking historic street, turret sitting room, desk & chair. **Comfort & Decor** These innkeepers added their own creativity to an already-spectacular home, designing the gorgeous stained-glass window in the foyer, designing and painting the wall treatments, stenciling the ceiling in the Victorian Suite to match the wallpaper. Their elegant collections are right at home here, including the Pickard gold china in the dining room, Mexican majolica, and Iranian rugs made from the neck-wool of lambs. In the parlor stands a rare, walnut "baby-plus" grand piano.

RATES, RESERVATIONS, & RESTRICTIONS

Deposit Credit card number **Discounts** None **Credit Cards** V, MC **Check-In/Out** Inquire **Smoking** No **Pets** No **Kids** Yes, "we don't discriminate against children." **No-Nos** Walk-in guests; reservations are required **Minimum Stay** None **Open** Open Jan.–Oct.; closed Nov. & Dec. **Hosts** Mike Bond & Johan Ewalt, 591 North Prairie St., Galesburg 61401 **Phone** (309) 344-0270 **Email** fahnestock@gallatinriver.net **Web** www.misslink.net/fahnestock

RIVER DECKS B & B GARDEN RESORT, Kankakee

OVERALL ★★★½ | QUALITY ★★★½ | VALUE ★★★ | PRICE RANGE $65–$125

River Decks offers packages year-round: winter spa retreats include fasting and deep relaxation; April brings herb tours and river park picnics; horseback riding is arranged with May packages; June begins the canoeing season; and late fall and winter offerings include leaf peeping, cross-country skiing packages, and holiday activities. With the NFL Chicago Bears' preseason training camp in Kankakee, the inn has begun a series of Bears tailgate parties beginning in August.

SETTING & FACILITIES

Location On the banks of the Kankakee River in residential Kankakee **Near** Downtown Kankakee, Kankakee River, Haigh Quarry, Old Pratt Boathouse, antiques malls, Kankakee River State Park. **Building** 1900 home, white exterior, w/ 9 decks **Grounds** Private small beach, gardens, beach houses, garden house, blue spruce, & river growth **Public Space** 2nd-floor sitting room, dining area, common area **Food & Drink** Full breakfast, may include signature breakfast pizza. **Recreation** Boating, fishing, swimming, canoeing, rock climbing, cross-country skiing, kayaking, antiquing, museums. **Amenities & Services** AC. Kayaks, paddleboats, canoes available, massage by appointment.

ACCOMMODATIONS

Units 4 guest rooms, 1 suite. **All Rooms** Balcony, river view. **Some Rooms** Whirlpool tub. **Bed & Bath** King & twin (1), kings (2), queens (2). 3 private baths, 1 shared. **Favorites** Bridal suite, w/ whirlpool tub, 25-foot private deck. **Comfort & Decor** More than 20 French doors throughout the house, coupled with the river breeze, give the inn a most open feel. Common areas are furnished with overstuffed sofas and chairs. The scheme is rather hodgepodge and in need of fresh paint when we visited, but it was not uncomfortable.

RATES, RESERVATIONS, & RESTRICTIONS

Deposit Full payment in advance; in case of cancellation, payment is transferable or guest can take a rain check **Discounts** None **Credit Cards** V, MC, AE, D **Check-In/Out** Inquire **Smoking** On balconies **Pets** Yes. **Kids** Yes. **No-Nos** N/A **Minimum Stay** None **Open** All year **Hosts** Angela Aimes & Jimmy Holmes, 494 West River St., Kankakee 60901 **Phone** (815) 933-9000 **Fax** (815) 939-4281

PINEAPPLE INN, Macomb

OVERALL ★★★★ | QUALITY ★★★★½ | VALUE ★★★★ | PRICE RANGE $79–$149

How can anyone find fault with a bed-and-breakfast whose guest rooms are named Faith, Hope, Love, and Charity? In the Love Room, appropriately, guests sleep on an iron bed adorned with Cupids. Both business and leisure travelers are welcome, and private rooms are available for lunch or dinner meetings for up to 20 people. Also on the property is a gift shop specializing in Haeger pottery and Kinkade paintings.

SETTING & FACILITIES

Location Off US 136 in residential Macomb **Near** St. Louis Rams training camp, Western Illinois Univ., Macomb Community Theater, parks. **Building** 1882 Queen Anne Victorian, red exterior **Grounds** City lot w/ flower beds, surrounded by 1882 ornamental iron fence brought from Alabama **Public Space** V-shaped porch, breakfast room, DR, parlor. Haeger/Kinkade shop in rear **Food & Drink** Welcome beverage; evening dessert. Full breakfast includes entree such as signature praline French toast w/ Canadian bacon. **Recreation** Pro sports activities, live theater, concerts, galleries, cross-country skiing. **Amenities & Services** AC. Robes, fresh flowers, bottled water in room. Copier, fax available. Can host small events.

ACCOMMODATIONS

Units 4 guest rooms, 1 suite. **All Rooms** TV/VCR, CD player, table & chairs, phone, modem, ceiling fan, hair dryer, lap desk. **Some Rooms** Private screened porch, answering machine. **Bed & Bath** King (1), queens (3), 2 twins (1). All private baths (1 detached). **Favorites** Charity Suite w/ wicker furnishings, king platform bed, window beds, 2 half-baths, treetop view. **Comfort & Decor** Pineapple Inn looks much as it did in the early 1880s, with such original features as pine plank floors, pocket doors, and light fixtures well preserved. The original pantry and built-in cabinets highlight the breakfast room; in the dining room, a painted-glass chandelier and original plaster-of-Paris faux fireplace complement berry-colored walls.

RATES, RESERVATIONS, & RESTRICTIONS

Deposit 50% of stay **Discounts** None **Credit Cards** V, MC **Check-In/Out** 4 p.m./ 10 a.m. **Smoking** On designated porches **Pets** No **Kids** Inquire **No-Nos** 2-person limit in guest rooms; extra charge for 3rd person **Minimum Stay** None **Open** All year **Hosts** Dale & Wanda Adkins, 204 West Jefferson St., Macomb 61455 **Phone** (309) 837-1914 **Fax** (309) 837-6232 **Email** pineappl@macomb.com **Web** www.macomb.com/pineapple

THE OAKS, *Petersburg*

OVERALL ★★★★½ | QUALITY ★★★★½ | VALUE ★★★★ | PRICE RANGE $75–$135

Referred to as "the Oaks" even in its post–Civil War heyday, this mansion has retained many original features, including a hat-and-cane closet in the entry, an old "intercom" system, interior shutters, a three-story walnut staircase, and seven fireplaces—five marble, two walnut. The egg-and-dart plasterwork is superb, and the craftsmanship continues throughout the house. The Oaks hosts a long menu of special packages and events each year, such as ten murder mystery weekends (with scripts written by the innkeeper) that include two dinners, appetizers, and cocktails.

SETTING & FACILITIES
Location At the edge of Petersburg, perched on a high knoll off IL 97 **Near** Lincoln's New Salem reconstructed 1830s village, Edgar Lee Masters Home, Sangamon River, downtown Petersburg, Springfield, Lincoln Home, Lincoln Tomb. **Building** 1875 brick Italianate, in Victorian neighborhood **Grounds** 5.5 acres of sloping lawns, flower gardens, oak stands **Public Space** Foyer, front parlor, library, ladies' parlor/breakfast room, DR, back patio **Food & Drink** Afternoon snack or wine & cheese. Full breakfast includes hot entree; candlelit 7-course dinner and picnic lunches also available. **Recreation** Historic touring, canoeing, kayaking, antiquing, golf courses, biking, hunting, fishing, horseback riding, live theater. **Amenities & Services** AC. Robes; Caswell-Massey bath amenities.

ACCOMMODATIONS
Units 4 guest rooms, 1 suite. (2 new rooms in progress during our visit.) **All Rooms** N/A **Some Rooms** Whirlpool tub, fireplace, TV, VCR, private porch, in-room sink. **Bed & Bath** Queens (2), 2 doubles (1), doubles (2). All private baths. **Favorites** Edward Laning Suite, w/ sitting room, best town view, & surprising mix of Italian furniture & antiques.

Comfort & Decor The elegance is striking as soon as guests step into the Oaks and notice the newel post, carved from an organ even older than the house. The Oaks gets the prize for best wall and ceiling medallions, but there are more sensations: unusual yellow Italian tile fireplace surround in the ladies' parlor, that room's ornate ceiling frieze, the front parlor's etched glass transom, and built-ins and parquet floors galore. Furnishings are a blend of fine period antiques and compatible contemporary pieces.

RATES, RESERVATIONS, & RESTRICTIONS

Deposit Credit card number; no-shows are charged 1 night's stay **Discounts** 20% off for seniors & business travelers **Credit Cards** V, MC, D **Check-In/Out** 3–6 p.m./11 a.m. **Smoking** Front & back patios **Pets** No; resident cat stays in office **Kids** Yes; please inquire first **No-Nos** N/A **Minimum Stay** None **Open** All year **Hosts** Susan & Ken Rodger, 510 West Sheridan, Petersburg 62675 **Phone** (217) 632-5444 or toll-free (888) 724-6257 **Web** www.petersburgil.com

INN AT 835 BED & BREAKFAST, Springfield

OVERALL ★★★★½ | QUALITY ★★★★½ | VALUE ★★★ | PRICE RANGE $109–$189

Miss Bell Miller was a rarity in her day—she was a florist to Springfield's turn-of-the-century elite and a successful, single businesswoman while in her 20s. Her floral business expanded to a city block–sized greenhouse complex, and before she was 40, she built Inn at 835, a luxury apartment house in the neighborhood once called Aristocracy Hill. It does give off a dignified air, with three-story verandas outside and marvelous oak detailing inside, and a working elevator. As a nod to the business that built her fortune, Bell named guest rooms after her favorite flowers, among them magnolia, lily, iris, hyacinth, and hydrangea.

SETTING & FACILITIES

Location In Springfield's Historic District, just off I-55 & I-72 **Near** State Capitol, Frank Lloyd Wright's Dana-Thomas House, Lincoln Home, Lincoln Tomb, Washington Park. **Building** 1909 Classical Revival inn, listed on National Register of Historic Places **Grounds** Oversized lot w/ flower gardens **Public Space** Entry, foyer, LR, DR **Food & Drink** Early coffee available; evening wine served. Full breakfast includes hot entree. **Recreation** Historic touring, cross-country skiing, biking, canoeing, golf courses, antiquing. **Amenities & Services** AC. Can host 100 for dinners, 150 for receptions, seat 200 outdoors, outdoor reception for 300. Special packages available.

ACCOMMODATIONS

Units 8 guest rooms, 2 suites. **All Rooms** TV/VCR, phone. **Some Rooms** Porch, fireplace, double whirlpool tub, double shower, claw-foot tub, CD stereo. **Bed & Bath** Kings (3), queens (8). All private baths. **Favorites** Orchid Suite, w/ 3 rooms (king & queen beds), private veranda, sitting room w/ fireplace. **Comfort & Decor** Common areas of the Inn at 835 have that classic Arts & Crafts look: richly colored walls and warm dark woodwork accented by ferns. Deep purples and greens set the tone for the sunny foyer and dining room, with both antique and modern furnishings alongside vintage features, such as numerous transoms, original light fixtures, and a beveled-glass entry.

RATES, RESERVATIONS, & RESTRICTIONS
Deposit 50% of stay **Discounts** None **Credit Cards** V, MC, AE, D **Check-In/Out** 3–6 p.m./noon **Smoking** On verandas **Pets** No **Kids** Over age 13 **No-Nos** N/A **Minimum Stay** 2 nights on holidays **Open** All year **Host** Court Conn, 835 South 2nd St., Springfield 62704 **Phone** (217) 523-4466 **Fax** (217) 523-4468 **Email** info@innat835.com **Web** www.innat835.com

LINDLEY HOUSE, Urbana

OVERALL ★★★★½ | QUALITY ★★★★½ | VALUE ★★★★ | PRICE RANGE $75–$150

Lindley House is a wonderful example of modernizing an old Victorian without sacrificing its historic appeal and glamour. Past the curved, pillared porch, guests step into the foyer with maple, walnut, and oak inlaid parquet floors. The beveled, leaded glass windows in the parlor, butternut pocket doors, fireplace, and other vintage elements are only enhanced by the contemporary art that graces every room—a fanciful, harmonious juxtaposition of the old and the new. The king's suite may be the most soothing room in the Midwest, and we defy anyone to leave the "magic chaise" without a quick visit to dreamland.

SETTING & FACILITIES
Location In downtown Urbana, within walking distance of the university. **Near** Univ. of Illinois, Champaign, Salt Fork of the Vermilion River. **Building** 1895 Queen Anne, remodeled, tan exterior **Grounds** City lot w/ flower beds **Public Space** Foyer, DR, LR, parlor **Food & Drink** Complimentary sodas, water. Gourmet breakfast. **Recreation** Canoeing, antiquing, museums, cross-country skiing, galleries. **Amenities & Services** AC. Robes, airport/train pickup, computer w/ Internet access in LR. Guests receive $10 discount for treatments at massage center across the street.

ACCOMMODATIONS
Units 4 guest rooms & carriage house. **All Rooms** TV/VCR, CD player, ceiling fan. **Some Rooms** Kitchenette w/ sink, fridge, coffeemaker, table & chairs. Carriage house is wheelchair accessible w/ roll-in shower. **Bed & Bath** King (1), queens (3). Carriage house, 2 twins & 1 double. In main house, 2 shared baths, 1 private. **Favorites** King's Suite w/ 20-foot attic cathedral ceiling, stained glass windows, wet bar, table & chairs, couch, chaise, private bath. **Comfort & Decor** The decor at Lindley House is sumptuous without being overdone. It was built with a whimsical design—mismatched Palladian, baroque, and lancet windows; asymmetrical gables and octagonal turret; along with touches of elegance such as starburst-pattern molding, original brass light fixtures, and ornate gingerbread stair rail. This is no stodgy Victorian; modern art adorns the walls, furnishings are plush and contemporary, and the colors fall somewhere between Martha Stewart and the Dalai Lama. Check out the deep purple and soft green palette in the king's suite.

RATES, RESERVATIONS, & RESTRICTIONS
Deposit Credit card number or 1 night's stay **Discounts** Single traveler's rate; 3-plus night discount **Credit Cards** V, MC **Check-In/Out** 4–6 p.m./11 a.m. **Smoking** No **Pets** No **Kids** Yes; families w/ children under age 8 are asked to rent the carriage house **No-Nos** N/A **Minimum Stay** None **Open** All year **Hosts** Carolyn Baxley, 312 West Green St., Urbana 61801 **Phone** (217) 384-4800 **Fax** (217) 384-8280 **Email** lindley@shout.net **Web** www.lindley.cc

Southwest Illinois

We confess: This is where the Mighty Mississippi captured our hearts. The **Great River Road** continues up—and up some more, all the way to Galena —but here in the southern zone, along the **Meeting of the Great Rivers Scenic Byway** (same road, different marketing angle), we were smitten.

Zone 3 is about the history that shaped it, so blatantly that you feel you should be wearing a calico dress and bonnet. Why? We cannot say for sure, except that spending so much time along the river inspires something; you want to read **Mark Twain** and write your own poem and appreciate what happened there. It's ol' man river, joined here by the **Missouri** and **Illinois Rivers.**

The Great River Road actually stretches for 550 miles. A good starting place is **Chester,** the little town where Popeye was created high atop the limestone bluffs. Do spend a few minutes at the **Popeye Museum** and, next door, at the **Spinach Can** collectibles. The bed-and-breakfast we profiled there is a former church with the most heavenly river view we've seen. Follow the road north to **Alton,** the starting point for eagle-watching on the river. The Visitors Center will give you a fact sheet on where, when, and how to spot American bald eagles.

After Alton, we drove 20 miles north to the walkable, New England–like historic hamlet of **Elsah,** tucked into the bluffs like a handkerchief in a pocket. The entire village is a Historic District of stone cottages and clapboard inns. Another five minutes on the river road takes you to **Grafton,** another scenic town.

A few miles inland is **Maeystown,** a 150-year-old community founded by German immigrants. The 60 limestone, wood, and brick buildings along narrow, steep streets include the Corner George Inn, a five-building bed-and-breakfast. By the time you get to **Belleville,** another 40 miles east, you'd never know you were in river country; it's a typical small town with a town square, entrepreneurial Main Street, and one of our favorite bed-and-breakfasts in the state—Victory Inn

As we explored the small towns of the region—**Pana, Taylorville, Carlinville, Lebanon**—we began to think we'd never see variety again; the bed-and-breakfasts are lovely, but they're all Italianates and Queen Ann Victorians. Then we came to **Carbondale,** almost in the **Shawnee National Forest,** and we snapped back to this century at Sassafras Ridge—a modern home in the woods, furnished with contemporary pieces with only a few antiques—just what we needed.

JACKSON HOUSE, Alton

OVERALL ★★★★½ | QUALITY ★★★★½ | VALUE ★★★★ | PRICE RANGE $95, $135 (BARN, CAVE)

When Jackson House opened the Cave in 2001, it created such a sensation that local television crews showed up to document the event. It is a marvel, with luxuriant features—skylights, double whirlpool tub, stone fireplace. In the main house, guests are treated to artifacts from the three generations of women who have loved this home—a sampler embroidered in 1838, a rosewood couch, cherished quilts. It's not easy to present so many styles in one property, but at Jackson House they manage it beautifully.

SETTINGS & FACILITIES
Location Just north of Route 140 in the Upper Alton Historic District. **Near** Great Mississippi River Road, St. Louis, wineries, Cahokia. **Building** 1870s Early Victorian w/wraparound porch, white exterior. Also barn & earth house. **Grounds** Sloping yard w/oak & maple trees; creek below in rear **Public Space** Porch, parlor, DR. **Food & Drink** Soda, juice anytime. Full breakfast includes hot entrée & dessert pie; menu might include asparagus frittata, French toast w/French bread, & breakfast pork chops. **Recreation** Riverboat cruises & gambling, cross-country skiing, antiquing, golf courses. **Amenities & Services** AC. Fresh flowers in rooms. Cave is handicap-accessible w/roll-in shower.

ACCOMMODATIONS
Units 4 (2 guest rooms, renovated barn, earth house). **All Rooms** TV/VCR, sitting area, clock radio. **Some Rooms** Fireplace, table & chairs, private patio, refrigerator, coffeemaker, whirlpool tub. **Bed & Bath** Kings (3), queen (1). All private baths. **Favorites** The Cave, w/modern furnishings, tall windows, French doors to private patio. **Comfort & Decor** Styles run the gamut at Jackson House, from post-Civil War ambience in the main house, to rustic-but-luxurious country trappings in Barth's Barn, and the modern digs—literally—in the earth house. The barn has a loft bedroom; ceiling and exterior wood is restored-original, and the ramp and stone step outside the door were used in the 1870s for the original owners' buggy.

RATES, RESERVATIONS, & RESTRICTIONS

Deposit Credit card number. **Discounts** Guests staying 2 nights or more receive a gift; discounts for those staying more than a week who don't want full breakfast. **Credit Cards** V, MC. **Check-In/Out** 3-8/11 **Smoking** No **Pets** No **Kids** Over 13. **No-Nos** No candles. **Minimum Stay** N/A **Open** All Year **Hosts** "Grace, Hope, & Janice," 1821 Seminary St., Alton 62002 **Phone** (618) 462-1426 or toll-free (800) 462-1426 **Web** www.jacksonbb.com

VICTORY INN, Belleville

OVERALL ★★★★½ | QUALITY ★★★★½ | VALUE ★★★★ | PRICE RANGE $60–$115

The previous owner of Victory Inn played piano for her guests in the parlor: "There's music in these walls," Jo Brannon says. We would agree; Jo is a part-time pastor, and guests immediately feel the warmth of this place. "People go into innkeeping for all sorts of reasons," she says. "We do it to welcome guests." You know she means it, too—and her coffee is great. Victory Inn is welcoming and a true stress-reliever.

SETTINGS & FACILITIES

Location In Belleville Historic District, just off State Rte. 159. **Near** Cahokia Mounds, Historic Lebanon, Scott Air Force Base, Mississippi River, downtown Jackson, historic Maeysville, Scenic River Road, St. Louis MO. **Building** 1877 Late Victorian brick w/prevalent Charles Eastlake influence. **Grounds** City lot, flower gardens. **Public Space** Patio, foyer, LR, DR. **Food & Drink** Sodas anytime; early coffee. Expanded continental breakfast w/home-baked goods. **Recreation** Boating, historic touring, riverboat cruises, canoeing, antiquing, winery touring. **Amenities & Services** AC. Robes, turndown service, morning newspaper, logo soaps, "keyless locks" on rooms & outside doors. Fax, copier & computer available.

ACCOMMODATIONS

Units 2 suites, 1 guest room. **All Rooms** TV, clock radio. **Some Rooms** Sitting room, double whirlpool tub, skylight, claw-foot tub. **Bed & Bath** Queens (3). All private baths. **Favorites** Eastlake Suite, w/large sitting room, daybed, double whirlpool. **Comfort & Decor** Every room at Victor Inn is designed for luxury; most major furnishings are reproductions, but the innkeepers have great taste and they work well with the Victorian décor. Eastlake touches extend to the second-floor exterior wood trim; indoors, woodwork is mahogany-stained. We noticed the unusual side-opening transoms; some light fixtures are original.

RATES, RESERVATIONS, & RESTRICTIONS

Deposit Credit card number. **Discounts** Corp., multiple-night. **Credit Cards** V, MC, AE. **Check-In/Out** 4-7/11 **Smoking** No **Pets** No; 2 adorable resident dachsunds are permitted in public areas. **Kids** No **No-Nos** N/A **Minimum Stay** No **Open** All Year **Hosts** Jo & Tom Brannan, 712 S. Jackson St., Belleville 62220 **Phone** (618) 277-1538 or toll-free (888) 277-8586 **Email** innkeeper@victoryinn.com **Web** www.victoryinn.com

SASSAFRAS RIDGE, Carbondale

OVERALL ★★★★½ | QUALITY ★★★★½ | VALUE ★★★★★ | PRICE RANGE $70–$85

Both of these innkeepers are collectors, and their handouts explain the provenance of nearly everything in the inn: the grandmother's 1903 wedding present–hall rack, the Hall teapots in the kitchen, the artists connected to every painting and sculpture in the place—and "Lindbergh Library," the small balcony office where Myers displays his collection of Lindbergh memorabilia. It's a lot to take in, but the Walkers' enthusiasm for their treasures is contagious. Don't miss the "flower bed" in the garden.

SETTINGS & FACILITIES

Location 1 mi. outside Carbondale off Rte. 51. **Near** Southern Illinois University, downtown Carbondale, Shryock performing arts center, Lusk Creek, Max Creek, wineries. **Building** 1970s-contemporary home w/atrium sun porch & window wall. **Grounds** 18 wooded acres w/ponds, walking trails. **Public Space** Common room w/dining area, sun porch, front & rear decks. **Food & Drink** Cookies, soft drinks anytime. Hearty breakfast includes choice of 6 entrees (egg scrambles, omelet, buckwheat pancakes, French toast), home-baked breads, meats, & fruits. **Recreation** Biking, cross-country skiing, live theatre, college sports, galleries, antiquing, concerts, winery touring. **Amenities & Services** AC. "Yard Sale" bookcase (guests leave cash or another book). Individual heating & cooling, computer access, small gift shop area. Limousine wine tours available.

ACCOMMODATIONS

Units 3 guest rooms. **All Rooms** Chairs, TV, clock radio, armoire. **Some Rooms** Desk & chair. **Bed & Bath** Queens (3). All private baths. **Favorites** Room 2. Bedcovering is a quilt signed by every couple who spent an anniversary or wedding night under it. **Comfort & Decor** This place is an original, starting with the sassafras theme. The inn is surrounded by sassafras trees, and rooms are marked by pottery "numbers"—i.e., sassafras leaves with one, two, or three points, crafted by a local sculptor. Another great touch is the "grapevine picture rail" in the upstairs hall; the innkeeper uses it to display her needle-point collection. Rooms are individually decorated; our favorite, No. 2, has a gorgeous bed-room suite, love seat, and Aladdin electric lamp.

RATES, RESERVATIONS, & RESTRICTIONS
Deposit Credit card number. **Discounts** No **Credit Cards** V, MC, D **Check-In/Out** 4/11 **Smoking** Outside **Pets** No; will arrange kennel. Resident cats stay outside. **Kids** Over 12. **No-Nos** No candles. **Minimum Stay** On select weekends. **Open** All Year **Hosts** Frances & Myers Walker, 382 Fawn Trail, Carbondale 62901 **Phone** (618) 529-5261 **Fax** (618) 529-1901 **Email** sassybb@bbonline.com **Web** www.sassafrasbb.com

VICTORIA TYME INN, *Carlinville*

OVERALL ★★★★½ | QUALITY ★★★★½ | VALUE ★★★★ | PRICE RANGE $69, $135 SUITE

This inn's claim to fame is birthplace of author Mary Hunter Austin, whose most famous book is, *The Land of Little Rain,* published in 1903. Austin once collaborated on a book with Ansel Adams and, over the years, was a friend of Jack London, Sinclair Lewis, Willa Cather, and others. She also was a pioneering naturalist and advocate for Native Americans; Victoria Tyme's library is decorated with Lakota Sioux artwork in her honor. In the Mary Austin Suite, family quilts, Austin's own cross-stitch and other arti-facts are displayed.

SETTINGS & FACILITIES
Location The corner of Rtes. 4 & 108 in residential Carlinville. **Near** Downtown Car-linville, Victorian town square, Blackburn College, world's largest collection of Sears mail-order homes, original Route 66, Beaver Dam State Park, Loveless Park Recreation Complex. **Building** 1857 gray & white Italianate w/1876 addition (2 homes joined), on National Register of Historic Places. **Grounds** 0.5 acres of lawns, flower beds. **Public Space** Porch, foyer, sitting room, library, DR, parlor. **Food & Drink** Refreshments at check-in. Full gourmet breakfast includes hot entrée such as "decadent" stuffed French toast. **Recreation** Antiquing, historic touring, canoeing, cross-country skiing, fishing, hunt-ing. **Amenities & Services** AC. Logo soaps; turndown service w/chocolate biscotti.

ACCOMMODATIONS
Units 1 suite, 3 guest rooms. **All Rooms** Clock radio, miniature jigsaw puzzle, chairs. **Some Rooms** Desk & chair, claw-foot tub. **Bed & Bath** Queens (4). Private baths (4). **Favorites** Bergdorf Bedchamber, w/peacock Eastlake walnut bed w/half-tester, claw-foot tub. **Comfort & Decor** Rich colors set the tone, trimmed with faux-grained burled woodwork, ornately fretted transoms, pocket doors, and walnut faux-marbled fireplaces in the library and sitting room. A highlight of the first floor is the 6-ft. lighted newel.

RATES, RESERVATIONS, & RESTRICTIONS
Deposit Credit card or 50% of stay. **Discounts** Weekday, more than 4 nights. **Credit Cards** V, MC, D **Check-In/Out** 4-6/11 **Smoking** Outside **Pets** No **Kids** Over 12

No-Nos No candles. **Minimum Stay** On select weekends. **Open** All Year. **Hosts** Jodie & Jeff Padgett, 511 E. First South St., Carlinville 62626 **Phone** (217) 854-8689 or toll-free (877) 355-6105 **Email** victyme@accunet.net **Web** www.victoriatymeinn.com

STONE HOUSE BED & BREAKFAST, Chester

OVERALL ★★★★½ | QUALITY ★★★★½ | VALUE ★★★★★ | PRICE RANGE $65–$90

Spending a lazy afternoon rocking on the front porch, watching tugboats make their way down the Mississippi River, one surmises that in the 1840s, when this stone inn was a Presbyterian church, this view would have been most conducive to finding faith. It sits atop the bluffs above the river road in the town where Popeye was born. Inside, we found some of the most imaginative decorating touches of our trip: a seemingly leather-covered wall (actually sections of brown paper bags, applied with wallpaper paste), lamps made of chairs, and a backdrop of masks, prayer robes, and other authentic Egyptiana—including a set of doors.

SETTINGS & FACILITIES

Location In residential Chester, 0.5 mi. from Rte. 150. **Near** Mississippi River, downtown Chester, Ste. Genevieve French colonial village, Shawnee National Forest, Popeye Statue, Randolph State Fish & Wildlife Area, Turkey Bluff, Delta Queen, antique malls. **Building** 1846 former church, brick. **Grounds** Expansive sloping lawns overlooking Mississippi River. **Public Space** Porches up & down, breakfast room, 2nd-floor parlor. **Food & Drink** Evening coffee; full breakfast w/hot entree. **Recreation** Antiquing, birding (American eagles), biking, hunting, fishing, swimming, historic touring, golf courses. **Amenities & Services** AC. Robes.

ACCOMMODATIONS

Units 3 guest rooms. **All Rooms** Sitting area. **Some Rooms** River view, garden view. **Bed & Bath** Queens (2), twin (1). Shared baths. **Favorites** Bedouin Room, w/river view and exotic Egyptian artifacts. **Comfort & Decor** All guest rooms are decorated with quality memorabilia from the innkeeper's travels. An intricately embroidered Bedouin dress and embellished veil are displayed in the Bedouin Room; in the River Room, walls are upholstered in fine European fabric. With their magnificent bluff view of the mighty Mississippi, though, the porches are the main attraction here.

RATES, RESERVATIONS, & RESTRICTIONS

Deposit 1 night's stay. **Discounts** Extended-stay & seasonal packages. **Credit Cards** V, MC **Check-In/Out** 2/11 **Smoking** No **Pets** No **Kids** Over 14 **No-Nos** N/A **Minimum Stay** N/A **Open** All Year **Hosts** Sandra Starr, 509 W. Harrison, Chester 62233 **Phone** (618) 604-9106 or (618) 826-5465 **Email** stonehse@egyptian.net **Web** www.thestone housebandb.com

FRANCIE'S INN ON-LINE, DuQuoin

OVERALL ★★★★ | QUALITY ★★★★ | VALUE ★★★★★ | PRICE RANGE $60–$85

Francie's is a sun-filled, cheery establishment, though the meeting & banquet side of the business appears to have equal priority with the B&B. Fluffy comforters, spacious rooms, and plenty of lighting make the rooms even more attractive and guest-friendly. Families should consider renting the Family Suite—actually the Esther and Francie Rooms with a bath between them; when rented as a suite, the rooms sleep four and are booked at a combined, reduced rate of $100.

SETTINGS & FACILITIES
Location In residential DuQuoin, 3 blocks east of Rte. 51. **Near** Downtown DuQuoin, Rend Lake, Southern Illinois University, Shawnee National Forest, DuQuoin State Fairgrounds, wineries. **Building** 1908 Prairie home, white w/red trim. **Grounds** 3 acres w/lawns, flower gardens. **Public Space** Deep front porch, foyer, DR, LR, rear tiered porch, 2nd-floor balcony, 2nd-floor common area. **Food & Drink** Early coffee available. Full breakfast includes hot entrée, home-baked pastries. **Recreation** Antiquing, fishing, canoeing, cross-country skiing, boating, historic touring, swimming, wine touring. **Amenities & Services** AC. Robes, logo soaps, morning newspaper.

ACCOMMODATIONS
Units 1 suite & 5 guest rooms, or combine for 2 suites & 3 guest rooms. **All Rooms** TV, phone hookup, sitting area, ceiling fan. **Some Rooms** Table & chairs, VCR, claw-foot tub, writing desk. **Bed & Bath** King & 2 twins (1), King or 2 twins (1), King & queen sofa (1), queen & daybed (1), queen (1). 4 private baths, 1 shared. **Favorites** Ciara Room w/white décor, claw-foot tub, 2 tables & 5 chairs. **Comfort & Decor** Guest rooms are individually decorated, but most feature a floral theme and deep, comforting colors and understated Victorian furnishings. A small gift shop area in the foyer includes handicrafts by local artisans sold on consignment. The banquet room, located in what would have been first-floor parlors, seats 30 comfortably.

RATES, RESERVATIONS, & RESTRICTIONS
Deposit Credit card number. **Discounts** Seniors 10%, corp. 15%, special packages. **Credit Cards** V, MC, AE, D. **Check-In/Out** 3/11 **Smoking** On porches. **Pets** No **Kids** Yes **No-Nos** N/A **Minimum Stay** 2 nights on select weekends. **Open** All Year **Hosts** Benny & Cathy Trowbridge, 104 S. Line St., DuQuoin 62832 **Phone** (618) 542-6686 or toll-free (877) 877-2657 **Fax** (618) 542-4834 **Email** cathy@franciesinnonline.com **Web** www.franciesinnonline.com

CORNER NEST BED & BREAKFAST, Elsah

OVERALL ★★★★ | QUALITY ★★★★ | VALUE ★★★★ | PRICE RANGE $110

The entire town of Elsah is listed on the National Register of Historic Places—a perfect setting for a peaceful little inn. Just a block from the 400-

foot limestone bluffs banking the Mississippi River, the Corner Nest sits halfway between the towns of Alton and Grafton, and just a few minutes from the 8,000-acre Pere Marquette State Park. During breakfast, guests can expect to see American bald eagles circling over the river. Come in the fall; the foliage along the bluff drive looks like a box of Trix.

SETTINGS & FACILITIES

Location In village of Elsah, 1 block from the Great River Road. **Near** Mississippi River, Sam Vadalabene Bicycle Trail, Pere Marquette State Park, limestone bluffs, Grafton, Alton, wineries. **Building** 1883 Franco-American home, on National Register of Historic Places. **Grounds** Town lot, small yard. **Public Space** Sitting room, DR, sun porch. **Food & Drink** Snacks, sodas anytime. Full breakfast includes hot entrée. **Recreation** Canoeing, biking, birding (American bald eagles), cross-country skiing, historic touring, winery touring, casino gambling, riverboat cruises. **Amenities & Services** AC. Logo soaps.

ACCOMMODATIONS

Units 3 guest rooms. **All Rooms** TV, chairs. **Some Rooms** Claw-foot tub, river view. **Bed & Bath** Doubles (3). All private baths (1 detached). **Favorites** Primitive Room, w/river view and "primitive" antique furnishings. **Comfort & Decor** A mix of early American and country would describe the style in guest rooms. Heirloom quilts cover the beds, which include a four-poster canopy and an iron bed, and public spaces likewise are furnished with quality antiques. The dining area is a window-walled sunroom.

RATES, RESERVATIONS, & RESTRICTIONS

Deposit Credit card number. **Discounts** Winter rates. **Credit Cards** V, MC, D. **Check-In/Out** 2/11. **Smoking** On porch. **Pets** No **Kids** On weekdays. **No-Nos** N/A **Minimum Stay** No **Open** All Year **Hosts** Bob & Judy Doerr, P.O. Box 220, 3 Elm St., Elsah 62028 **Phone** (618) 374-1892 **Web** www.elsahbedandbreakfast.com

GREEN TREE INN, Elsah

OVERALL ★★★★ | QUALITY ★★★★½ | VALUE ★★★★ | PRICE RANGE $95–$110

You won't even notice that Green Tree Inn is one of the newer buildings in town; innkeeper Kim Crocker does a wonderful job of re-creating a historical setting in this town that is a National Historic Place. For dinner, walk to My Just Desserts, then drive for a glass of fine local wine to the winery in Grafton, just a few miles up the road. If you must watch television, there's one in the common room—but the reception is lousy because the town is nestled in the limestone bluffs. No matter; between the river, the parks, the eagles, and the antiques shops, there's plenty to keep anyone occupied.

SETTING & FACILITIES

Location In village of Elsah, several blocks from the Great River Road **Near** Mississippi River, Sam Vadalabene Bicycle Trail, Pere Marquette State Park, limestone bluffs, Grafton, Alton, wineries. **Building** Late-1980s inn w/ green exterior, porches **Grounds** Small yard, flower beds **Public Space** Porches, breakfast/common room, gift shop. **Food & Drink** Early coffee available, 7:30 a.m. Full breakfast served 8:30 a.m. w/ hot entree; typical menu includes egg scramble, "garlic spray" toast, bacon. **Recreation** Canoeing, biking, birding (American bald eagles), cross-country skiing, historic touring, winery touring, casino gambling, riverboat cruises, antiquing. **Amenities & Services** AC. Logo soaps.

ACCOMMODATIONS

Units 6 guest rooms. **All Rooms** Private entrance, chairs, clock radio. **Some Rooms** Desk & chair. **Bed & Bath** Queens (2), 2 doubles (2), 1 double (2). All private baths. **Favorites** Birdcage Room, w/ canopy bed, desk & chair, rear porch access. **Comfort & Decor** Individually decorated rooms are furnished in period reproductions, including canopy beds and four-posters, in a pre–Civil War style. All beds have pillowtop mattresses; porches with rockers look out onto the panorama of historic stone buildings and surrounding hills.

RATES, RESERVATIONS, & RESTRICTIONS

Deposit Payment in advance **Discounts** Group rates, special packages **Credit Cards** V, MC **Check-In/Out** 2 p.m./11 a.m. **Smoking** No **Pets** Inquire **Kids** Over age 12 **No-Nos** N/A **Minimum Stay** None **Open** All year **Hosts** Kim Crocker, P.O. Box 96, 15 Mill St., Elsah 62028 **Phone** (800) 701-8003 **Email** info@greentreeinn.com **Web** www.greentreeinn.com

LANDMARK ON MADISON, Lebanon

OVERALL ★★★★ | QUALITY ★★★★ | VALUE ★★★★★ | PRICE RANGE $69–$80 WEEKNIGHTS, $85–$95 WEEKENDS

The scent of magnolia trees and honeysuckle vines brings images of the Old South to this Midwestern inn, standing on the site of a pioneer-days hotel and stagecoach stop. The front columns are recycled from the 1904 World's Fair in St. Louis, and more pillars are found at the side porch and as trim in the living room. The only television is in the upstairs library; the formal parlor has a piano. Take a stroll through downtown; more than a dozen antiques and gift shops are located along St. Louis Street.

SETTING & FACILITIES

Location Off Rt. 4 in residential Lebanon **Near** Historic downtown Lebanon, McKendree College, Carlyle Lake, St. Louis, Mississippi River. **Building** 1906 Classic Greek Revival, 2-story pillared entry, white exterior **Grounds** Double lot w/ lawns, flower beds **Public Space** Foyer, LR, front & side porches, library, enclosed back porch. **Food & Drink** Coffee, soda any time. Full breakfast includes hot entree. **Recreation** River cruises, antiquing, boating, swimming, fishing, biking, historic touring, galleries, museums, golf courses. **Amenities & Services** AC. Will order flowers, theater tickets.

ACCOMMODATIONS

Units 3 guest rooms. **All Rooms** Chairs, clock radio. **Some Rooms** Bay window, ceiling fan, robes, original bath fixtures. **Bed & Bath** King (1), queens (2). All private baths (2

detached). **Favorites** Verandah Room, w/ queen brass bed & large bay window sitting area. **Comfort & Decor** These innkeepers love florals and lace. The home is graced with original chandeliers, lots of wicker seating in various rooms, and, on the glassed-in back porch, a guest coffeemaker, fridge, and microwave. The ornate trays—copper with pearl inlay, and copper with tin accents—along with the "yogurt table" are from Turkey, where innkeeper John Carter once worked.

RATES, RESERVATIONS, & RESTRICTIONS

Deposit I night's stay or credit card number **Discounts** 10% off 3 days or longer; 10% senior discount **Credit Cards** V, MC, D, AE **Check-In/Out** 3:30 p.m./11 a.m. **Smoking** No **Pets** No **Kids** "Not suitable for children" **No-Nos** N/A **Minimum Stay** None **Open** All year **Hosts** Betty & John Carter, 118 South Madison, Lebanon 62254 **Phone** (618) 537-9532 **Web** www.bbonline.com/il/landmark

CORNER GEORGE INN, Maeystown

OVERALL ★★★★½ | QUALITY ★★★★½ | VALUE ★★★★ | PRICE RANGE $67–$87; SUMMER KITCHEN $99; CABIN, LOFT, SUITE $129–$149

Maeystown strikes us as the quintessential quiet, historic village. As one St. Louis newspaper reporter wrote, "the main attraction of Maeystown may be the fact that it doesn't have many attractions." The centerpiece of the 150-year-old German settlement is a one-lane, 1881, arched stone bridge leading into town; visitors either come here for specific festivals—such as Oktoberfest, the old-fashioned German Christmas celebration, or the spring Fruehlingsfest crafts festival—or to escape in an authentic, serene setting.

SETTING & FACILITIES

Location In central Maeystown, 8 mi. south of Rt. 156 at Valmeyer **Near** 60 historic buildings, Bluff Road Scenic Route, Fort de Chartres Historic Site, Waterloo, Fults Hill Prairie Nature Preserve, wineries. **Building** 1884 saloon, hotel, and general store of brick & stone; also summer kitchen/smoke house, 1862 rock house, 1860s log cabin **Grounds** 2 acres of historic buildings, gardens, creek **Public Space** In original inn, 2nd-floor sitting room, ballroom/common area & breakfast room, gift shop; also sweet shop. **Food & Drink** Full breakfast includes hot entree. **Recreation** Horse-drawn carriage rides, biking, antiquing, historic touring, winery touring, boating, canoeing, riverboat cruises. **Amenities & Services** AC. Logo bath amenities.

ACCOMMODATIONS

Units 7 guest rooms in 5 buildings. **All Rooms** Claw-foot tub & pedestal sink (main inn), chairs. **Some Rooms** Claw-foot whirlpool tub, kitchen, exposed stone wall, cathedral ceiling. **Bed & Bath** Queens (2), double & twin (1), doubles (4). All private baths. **Favorites** Dave and Mayme's cottage-style 4-room suite in 1862 Mae Green rock house, w/ LR, kitchen, bedroom and large bathroom w/ claw-foot whirlpool. **Comfort & Decor** Choosing favorite rooms in this historic complex isn't easy. The summer kitchen, with exposed stone and original limestone walls, has a primitive appeal, and the Roever Room, with its "champagne colors," walnut Victorian high-back bed, matching marble-top dresser and lace curtains, is just as much fun. We also loved the cannonball bed in the log cabin. The general store itself has the original store shelves, antique counters, and glass candy case.

RATES, RESERVATIONS, & RESTRICTIONS
Deposit Credit card number **Discounts** Seasonal specials **Credit Cards** V, MC **Check-In/Out** 4 p.m./11 a.m. **Smoking** No **Pets** No **Kids** "Limited appeal for children under age 12" **No-Nos** N/A **Minimum Stay** None **Open** All year **Hosts** David & Marcia Braswell, Corner of Main & Mill, Maeystown 62256 **Phone** (618) 458-6660 **Fax** (618) 458-7770 **Email** cornrgeo@htc.net **Web** www.cornergeorgeinn.com

APOTHECARY'S INN AT CAPTAIN KITCHELL'S MANSION, Pana

OVERALL ★★★★ | QUALITY ★★★★½ | VALUE ★★★★ | PRICE RANGE $80–$111

Innkeeping is one of pharmacist Paula Dunlap's two careers, and she takes time to have fun with it. The dining room, or "gold room," is the most ostentatious, with a six-foot golden ceiling medallion, ornate gold ceiling frieze, and brass floor inlay. Dunlap displays her collection of teacups and teapots and treasures the "jade bath," wedding dress, and two-tone marble fireplace in Paulina's Room. We liked the original etched glass in the front doors; it looks new.

SETTING & FACILITIES
Location In residential Pana off US 51 **Near** Lake Taylorville, Lake Shelbyville, Eagle Creek State Park, Ramsey Lake State Park. **Building** 1876 Second Empire w/ tower, pale yellow exterior **Grounds** 2.6 acres of lawns, gardens, statuary, garden path, beautiful brick drive **Public Space** Parlor, DR, 2nd-floor lounge, screened porch **Food & Drink** Welcome snack. 2-course gourmet breakfast might include crêpes & fruit salsa, or asparagus-onion-garlic fritatta. **Recreation** Boating, canoeing, historic touring, antiquing, fishing, biking, cross-country skiing. **Amenities & Services** AC. Robes.

ACCOMMODATIONS
Units 4 guest rooms. **All Rooms** Table or desk, chairs. **Some Rooms** Stained-glass windows, window seat, four-poster bed. **Bed & Bath** Kings (2), queens (2). All private baths. **Favorites** Louise's Room w/ stained-glass window, chandelier, king four-poster bed. **Comfort & Decor** It's unusual that an old home carries the same elegant features upstairs as down. Various guest rooms at Apothecary's Inn have inlaid parquet floors, a marble fireplace, ceiling medallions, and original light fixtures. The bed covering in Louise's Room is a family heirloom. Eastlake woodwork, marble fireplaces, and pocket doors are found throughout the floral-country styled home.

RATES, RESERVATIONS, & RESTRICTIONS
Deposit Credit card number **Discounts** Weekday corp.; special rates for guests not eating breakfast **Credit Cards** V, MC, AE **Check-In/Out** By arrangement/noon **Smoking**

No **Pets** No; resident cat stays outdoors **Kids** No **No-Nos** N/A **Minimum Stay** 2-night minimum holidays **Open** All year **Hosts** Paula Dunlap, 208 South Spruce St., Pana 62557 **Phone** (217) 562-3108 or (888) PANAILL (726-2455) **Email** apothecarysinn @mcleodusa.net

OXBOW BED & BREAKFAST, Pinckneyville

OVERALL ★★★★ | QUALITY ★★★★ | VALUE ★★★★★ | PRICE RANGE $50–$60, BARN APARTMENT $70

Innkeepers Al & Peg Doughty are even more interesting than their inn. Al worked as a rural veterinarian for 23 years, wrote a Civil War novel, and now hand-crafts oxbow-style, four-poster beds. Peg raised purebred Arabian horses. The barn housing the party room and swimming pool was moved from another location and rebuilt by Al. The place is a bit quirky, but it grew on us, and it's easy to find—just turn right when you see the two full-sized windmills in the front yard.

SETTING & FACILITIES
Location On US 127, 1 mi. south of Pinckneyville **Near** Downtown Pinckneyville, Pyramid State Park, Crab Orchard Wildlife refuge, Shawnee National Forest, Southern Illinois Univ. **Building** 1929 home, exact copy of first owner's house in Germany **Grounds** 11 acres of forest w/ 2 barns, indoor pool **Public Space** Screened porch, LR, music room, DR, breakfast room, screened porch, party room, lower-level fitness room. **Food & Drink** Full breakfast includes hot entree. **Recreation** Antiquing, biking, cross-country skiing, canoeing, fishing, hunting, swimming. **Amenities & Services** AC. Pool open to guests.

ACCOMMODATIONS
Units 5 guest rooms & honeymoon suite/barn apartment; also bed in party room. **All Rooms** TV, clock radio. **Some Rooms** Desk & chair. **Bed & Bath** Queens (7). All private baths. **Favorites** Pilot Knob Room, w/ oxbow-frame canopy bed, bath sided w/ aged barn siding, fainting couch, desk & chair. **Comfort & Decor** The style here is country, with splashes of Victorian, western, and, in the party room, "Early Jim Beam." Furnishings run the gamut from a hand-hewn oxbow canopy, to several beautiful Eastlake beds and marble-top pieces. The fitness room also has a hot tub, queen pullout bed, and private entrance. Rooms are named for Civil War generals and battles.

RATES, RESERVATIONS, & RESTRICTIONS
Deposit Credit card number or $25 **Discounts** Federal employees' rate, $50 **Credit Cards** V, MC **Check-In/Out** 3 p.m./11 a.m. **Smoking** No **Pets** No; resident cats stay outside **Kids** Yes, over age 6 **No-Nos** N/A **Minimum Stay** None **Open** All year **Hosts** Al & Peg Doughty, 3967 IL 13/127, Pinckneyville 62274 **Phone** (618) 357-9839 or toll-free (800) 929-6888

MAGNOLIA PLACE BED AND BREAKFAST, Red Bud

OVERALL ★★★★ | QUALITY ★★★★ | VALUE ★★★★ | PRICE RANGE $60–$75, $110–$140 SUITES

Located in Red Bud's midtown historic district, Magnolia Place is a good choice for visitors to St. Louis, 40 miles northwest of Red Bud, who don't want to stay in the city. This is a German farming community, worth a walk past other restored homes. Or just relax in the landscaped gardens under ancient, towering trees. In winter, the 1,500-square-foot Magnolia Suite is a good place to park. Of the smaller rooms, we would choose the Wisteria Room for its huge curved glass windows and grand Victorian fireplace.

SETTING & FACILITIES
Location At Rts. 3 & 154 in residential Red Bud **Near** Baldwin Lake, Illinois Caverns, Mississippi River, French Colonial District, King State Fish & Wildlife Area, downtown Red Bud. **Building** 1856 brick mansion; began as a shotgun house w/ additions **Grounds** Oversized city lot w/ patios, gazebo, statuary, flower gardens **Public Space** Parlor, DR, patios. **Food & Drink** Afternoon tea & dessert. Full breakfast includes hot entree. **Recreation** Fishing, boating, canoeing, historic touring, riverboat cruises, cross-country skiing, birding (American bald eagles), antiquing. **Amenities & Services** AC. Can host weddings, parties.

ACCOMMODATIONS
Units 2 guest rooms, 2 suites. **All Rooms** TV. **Some Rooms** Private balcony, fireplace, double whirlpool tub, double shower, VCR. **Bed & Bath** Kings (2), queen (1), double (1). 2 private baths, 1 shared. **Favorites** Magnolia Suite, entire 3rd floor w/ deep window seat, double whirlpool & sinks, 12-foot antique tin ceiling, big-screen TV, VCR. **Comfort & Decor** Original white oak woodwork, pocket doors, transoms and Eastlake-style trim create an air of stateliness. Not all furnishings are antiques; some beds and crystal chandeliers are reproductions, but they go well with the trappings—neoclassic brick pillars in the dining room, beveled mirrors, intricately carved fireplaces.

RATES, RESERVATIONS, & RESTRICTIONS
Deposit Credit card number or 1 night's stay **Discounts** Corp. **Credit Cards** V, MC **Check-In/Out** 3–9 p.m./noon **Smoking** In designated areas **Pets** No; resident dog stays in innkeeper's quarters **Kids** Inquire **No-Nos** N/A **Minimum Stay** None **Open** All year **Hosts** Dolly Krallman, 317 South Main St., Red Bud 62278 **Phone** (618) 282-4141

Southeast Illinois

Did we say we liked the river country best? We take it back.

Here's what we loved about southeast Illinois. First, there's plenty of big river here; the **Ohio River Scenic Route,** forming the southwest boundary of the state, is full of pirate caves, colonial forts, and rock formations with names like **Devil's Smokestack** and **Camel Rock** in the **Garden of the Gods Recreation Area.**

This is the state's inexpensive region, and we loved that, too. The cookies we ate on Thelma's brick front porch—that's Thelma's B&B in **West Salem,** best value in the Midwest, where $25 gets you a clean, comfortable room and hearty breakfast—would not have tasted better if she had charged five times that rate, which would have been a cheap room at the other end of the state! Nor could our room at Fessel's Cabbage Rose, the wonderfully restored mansion in little **Olney,** have been more beautiful in another setting (pricier, yes, but not better).

Sullivan didn't make an impression, but the real destination there is Little House on the Prairie. Theater buffs should travel to this spot, just to hear the innkeeper's stories of working with and entertaining the stars of yesteryear. He knew them all. We also recommend a side trip to **Oakland**—it looks like an abandoned town, except for the "Open" signs in the antiques shops.

And what would they have done with the Olde Squat Inn in **Chicago?** To be honest, we heard disparaging remarks about this no-frills complex of rescued log homes as we traveled in other regions—and as we say "no frills," we remember the blueberry pancakes with berries from their own patch, and local meats heaped high in front of us. Okay, so the log homes aren't very dressy—but we adored the folk art hanging around the place. The shower was hot, the TV worked, and we applaud the effort to save dozens of discarded log buildings and make them useful again. For those prices, a spider on the wall is in the acceptable range.

MARSHA'S VINEYARD, Arthur

OVERALL ★★★★ | QUALITY ★★★★ | VALUE ★★★★ | PRICE RANGE $93

Arthur is a tiny but busy town, and Marsha's Vineyard is located in a new development several blocks from downtown. A short walk away is a driving range. The home was built by a local Amish contractor, and many nearby activities have an Amish ring to them: Mennonite Auction, Apple Dumpling Festival, Broomcorn Festival, Cheese Festival, buggy rides. Also on the property is a treehouse with a bed and electricity—a lodging option, perhaps, for a teenager or single parent traveling with a child.

SETTING & FACILITIES
Location Off IL 133, 10 mi. west of I-57 **Near** Amish Country, Eastern Illinois Univ., Lake Shelbyville, Little Theater on the Square, Rockome Gardens Theme Park, Univ. of Illinois. **Building** New (2000) saltbox cottage, white exterior **Grounds** Almost 1 acre w/ gardens, tiny vineyard **Public Space** Kitchen **Food & Drink** Snacks (Amish cheese) & sparkling cider available any time. Full breakfast in season, served at innkeeper's quarter; off-season (Sept.–April), breakfast weekends only. **Recreation** Boating, swimming, live theater, gardens, Amish touring, golf driving range, antiquing. **Amenities & Services** AC. Bicycles, gas grill available.

ACCOMMODATIONS
Units 2 guest rooms. **All Rooms** TV/VCR, clock. **Some Rooms** Private patio, children's play area. **Bed & Bath** King & twin (1), queen & twin (1). All private baths. **Favorites** Garden Room w/ piano, sofa, patio, on first floor. **Comfort & Decor** Marsha's Vineyard is decorated in country and Amish style, with Amish quilts hand-sewn by local women as wall hangings. The loft bedroom includes a small library and sitting area with table and benches.

RATES, RESERVATIONS, & RESTRICTIONS
Deposit 1 night's stay **Discounts** None **Credit Cards** N/A **Check-In/Out** 4 p.m./10 a.m. **Smoking** No **Pets** No **Kids** Yes **No-Nos** Alcohol **Minimum Stay** None **Open** All year **Hosts** Marsha Hershberger, 212 Chaise Lane, Arthur 61911 **Phone** (217) 543-4001 **Email** mhersch@hotmail.com **Web** www.douglascotourism.com

HARD DAY'S NITE BED & BREAKFAST, Benton

OVERALL ★★★★ | QUALITY ★★★★ | VALUE ★★★★ | PRICE RANGE $65

It was eerie enough for us Beatlemaniacs visiting George Harrison's former haunt last fall, several months before he passed away. Beatles album covers, original concert posters, and other paraphernalia are everywhere in this home once owned by his sister, Louise, and where he visited her in September 1963—five months before the Beatles' pivotal (for all of us) appearance on The Ed Sullivan Show. While George stayed here, he actually played his first U.S. "concert"—a performance with a buddy at the local VFW hall.

The Ed Sullivan deal was made during that visit, and the room where he stayed is now the mini-museum. We'd love to upgrade the value rating for this bed-and-breakfast if the innkeepers would upgrade the breakfast; currently it's on par with that at a budget motel.

SETTING & FACILITIES

Location On a side street in residential Benton, 1 mi. east of I-57 exit **Near** Southern Illinois Artisans Shop & Visitors Center, wineries, Shawnee National Forest, Tele-Tracks, casinos. **Building** 1930s wood-frame house, blue-white exterior **Grounds** Small city lot, shrubs **Public Space** Porch, LR, DR, deck, mini-museum **Food & Drink** Cont'l breakfast, w/ juice, toast, bagels, toaster waffles, microwave pancakes, & cereal. **Recreation** Antiquing, biking, historic touring, Beatles research, golf courses, crafts demonstrations, museums, winery touring. **Amenities & Services** AC. Gift shop. Available for small parties & special events.

ACCOMMODATIONS

Units 4 guest rooms. **All Rooms** TV, chair, clock radio. **Some Rooms** Handicap access. **Bed & Bath** Kings (2), queens (2). All private baths. **Favorites** Ringo Room, w/ lilac decor & handicap access. **Comfort & Decor** John, Paul, George, and Ringo! Furnishings in this modest home are circa mid-1960s—in other words, it looks like the house where most of us grew up—and Beatles music softly, constantly plays over the sound system. The mini-museum is a room full of Beatles artifacts and photos, many donated by George's sister, Louise Harrison. We asked about security of these valuable collectibles during our visit; now that George is gone, we hope security has been beefed up.

RATES, RESERVATIONS, & RESTRICTIONS

Deposit Credit card number **Discounts** Corp. **Credit Cards** V, MC **Check-In/Out** Individual arrangement **Smoking** Outside **Pets** No **Kids** Inquire **No-Nos** N/A **Minimum Stay** None **Open** All year **Hosts** Jim Chady, 113 McCann St., Benton 62812 **Phone** ((618) 438-2328 **Email** jimchady@midwest.net **Web** www.harddaysnitebnb.com

GARNET HALL BED & BREAKFAST, Effingham

OVERALL ★★★★½ | QUALITY ★★★★½ | VALUE ★★★★ | PRICE RANGE $90–$120

Given its history, it's amazing that Garnet Hall survived with any original features intact. Originally a private residence, the home later became the Illinois College of Photography, with students enrolled over the years from every state in the United States, every Canadian province, and 52 foreign countries. (Because it was a photography school, those students and their times here are well documented.) During World War I, it served as a training center for disabled soldiers; later it became an office for an oil company, an apartment building, and, for a decade, a vacant building. The Martins rescued and restored it, and we couldn't decide which was our favorite spot—the cheery, window-walled turret breakfast nook, or the awesome secret garden under the eaves of the Secret Garden Room, complete with dollhouse and chirping birds.

SETTING & FACILITIES

Location In residential Effingham, 2 mi. SW of I-57, 1 block from Route 45 **Near** Lake Sara, Effingham Industrial Park, K-Square Outlet Mall, Little Wabash River. **Building** 1892 Queen Anne, red brick exterior, w/ 3-story turret & wraparound porch **Grounds** 9 city lots w/ gazebo, lawns, flower gardens **Public Space** Porch, foyer, parlor, DR, turret breakfast room, pantry, sun room, conference room **Food & Drink** Soft drinks any time. Full breakfast includes hot entree. **Recreation** Boating, swimming, antiquing, historic touring, canoeing, cross-country skiing. **Amenities & Services** AC. Hot tub in sun room.

ACCOMMODATIONS

Units 7 guest rooms. **All Rooms** TV/VCR, phone, ceiling fan. **Some Rooms** Claw-foot tub, private balcony, garden view, fold-out couch. **Bed & Bath** Queens (7). All private baths. **Favorites** Austin Room w/ 4 beveled glass windows, desk, fireplace, chairs, four-poster bed. **Comfort & Decor** Restoration of this home was carefully planned, with special care given to the rich oak paneling in the foyer, the cherry trim, the (miraculously preserved) curved-glass turret windows in the parlor, and the unusual pocket doors with glass panels. The parlor also sports a faux-marble cove ceiling and massive fireplace with Italian tile surrounding it and a beveled glass mirror. The pillared fireplace, chandelier, and ceiling frieze in the dining room are just as striking. Most furnishings throughout the house are quality antiques.

RATES, RESERVATIONS, & RESTRICTIONS

Deposit Credit card number **Discounts** Corp. weekdays **Credit Cards** V, MC **Check-In/Out** Inquire **Smoking** No **Pets** No **Kids** No **No-Nos** Alcoholic beverages **Minimum Stay** None **Open** Closed major holidays **Hosts** Donna & Newlin Martin, 1007 South 4th St., Effingham 62401 **Phone** (217) 342-5584 or toll-free (888) 376-7207 **Fax** (217) 342-5629 **Email** info@garnethall.com **Web** www.garnethall.com

MANSION OF GOLCONDA, *Golconda*

OVERALL ★★★★ | QUALITY ★★★★ | VALUE ★★★ | PRICE RANGE $85–$110

Details of life in Golconda a century ago sneak up on you. Chamber pots are under every bed, scented bundles of cinnamon sticks are used as room fresheners, and there are even built-in corner closets—a reminder of the days when a four-sided closet was taxed as a room. Even more unusual is the original Italian stained-glass window at the stair landing, bringing light not from sunshine but from another hallway on the other side. The parlors are sumptuous, but alas, they're reserved for dinner guests.

SETTING & FACILITIES

Location In the Shawnee National Forest at IL 146 on the Ohio River **Near** "Silk Stocking Row," downtown Golconda, Smithland Dam & Pool, National Cross Country Bike Trail, Ohio River Scenic Route, Golconda Marina. **Building** 1894 gabled mansion, white exterior, on National Register of Historic Places **Grounds** More than an acre of lawns, tree stands, flower beds **Public Space** Porch, foyer, breakfast room, restaurant, small lounge **Food & Drink** Full breakfast w/ entree, ordered from menu. Dinner offered in 3-parlor restaurant. Homemade evening snack. **Recreation** Horseback riding, fishing, biking, cross-country skiing, antiquing, canoeing, historic touring, boating. **Amenities & Services** AC. Logo bath amenities; TV on request

ACCOMMODATIONS

Units 4 guest rooms. **All Rooms** Chairs, decorative fireplace. **Some Rooms** Double whirlpool tub, river view, street view, exposed brick. **Bed & Bath** King (1), queen (1), 2 doubles (1), double (1). All private baths. **Favorites** Azalea Room, w/ European tile fireplace w/ topper & beveled glass mirrors; turret alcove w/ Ohio River view, Eastlake trim. **Comfort & Decor** The almost-gloomy elegance of this mansion will appeal to many bed-and-breakfast fans (we like spaces a little brighter, but that's just our taste). Parlors were transformed into the public restaurant, so guests retreat to their rooms for relaxation. The former mayor of Golconda built this home with high ceilings, pocket doors, and transoms throughout, with intricate Eastlake trim in the arches between parlors. The innkeeper's teapot collection is displayed in the breakfast room, an enclosed rear porch.

RATES, RESERVATIONS, & RESTRICTIONS

Deposit Credit card number **Discounts** Weekday, winter weekends, multiple nights **Credit Cards** V, MC, AE, D **Check-In/Out** 2 p.m./11 a.m. or by arrangement **Smoking** No **Pets** No **Kids** "We discourage children under age 10 years, but inquire" **No-Nos** N/A **Minimum Stay** None **Open** All year **Hosts** Marilyn Kunz, P.O. Box 339, Golconda 62938 **Phone** (628) 683-4400 **Fax** (618) 683-6800 (call first) **Email** mansiongol@aol.com **Web** www.members.aol.com/~mansiongol

OLDE SQUAT INN, *Marion*

OVERALL ★★★½ | QUALITY ★★★½ | VALUE ★★★★★ | PRICE RANGE $59–$65

Aptly-named innkeeper Jim Grisley hauled his first rescued log building to this old soybean farm in 1976. Each log—some weighing more than 400 pounds—was labeled and set back in place. It became a hobby; Grisley has

collected 28 log buildings of varying sizes and styles; 12 have been re-assembled (including his favorite, a rare 1861 double-crib barn) and 4 are fitted with electricity and plumbing and rented as bed-and-breakfast rooms. The driveway is an old buggy trail. Eventually, he and innkeeper Katy Lockwood, an official with the Southern Illinois Tourism Office, hope to create a living-history pioneer museum on the farm, with festivals and historical re-enactments.

SETTING & FACILITIES

Location 5 mi. east of I-57, 1 mi. past Pittsburg **Near** Shawnee National Forest, downtown Marion, Crab Orchard National Wildlife Refuge, Lake Egypt. **Building** 4 rescued, moved, & reassembled log cabins, 1820–1870 **Grounds** 300+ acres of forest, trails, meadows, picnic area, & fire pits **Public Space** Porches, breakfast room **Food & Drink** Gourmet country breakfast; ours included blueberry pancakes (using Olde Squat–grown berries), hash browns, bacon, cooked apples, homemade pear butter. **Recreation** Antiquing, biking, cross-country skiing, historic touring, swimming, canoeing, fishing, horseback riding. **Amenities & Services** AC. Grills available; cookouts & s'mores weekends.

ACCOMMODATIONS

Units 4 cabins. **All Rooms** TV, coffeepot. **Some Rooms** Kitchen, fireplace, electric heater, wood-burning stove. **Bed & Bath** Queens (2), 2 doubles & 2 twins (1), double (1). All private baths. **Favorites** Golconda cabin w/ full kitchen, living room area, porch overlooking garden. **Comfort & Decor** Historic lodging doesn't get much more authentic than these wonderfully drafty, reconstructed log cabins. We're duty-bound to give Olde Squat a relatively low quality rating because it's inelegant, but every family should sample pioneer living here—but with great coffee and a small TV to take the edge off. Antique quilts and toys decorate the rooms, and spacious porches are perfect spots to watch the sun set over the vast meadows and gardens. The floor is cold and you'll find the occasional spider into your room, but you will love being here.

RATES, RESERVATIONS, & RESTRICTIONS

Deposit 1 night's stay **Discounts** Single travelers ($40), children age 6–18 w/ parents ($10), weekday rates **Credit Cards** Call ahead **Check-In/Out** Inquire **Smoking** On porches **Pets** Yes, on leash; resident farm dogs stay outside **Kids** Yes **No-Nos** N/A **Minimum Stay** None **Open** All year **Hosts** Katy Lockwood & James Grisley, 14160 Liberty School Rd., Marion 62959 **Phone** (618) 982-2916 **Email** osquat@poweruser.com

INN ON THE SQUARE, *Oakland*

OVERALL ★★★★ | QUALITY ★★★★ | VALUE ★★★★★ | PRICE RANGE $55–$60

Inn on the Square is the centerpiece of a remote, tiny, almost silent village—so we were surprised and delighted to find three thriving antiques shops open during our visit, as well as a country gift shop. One of those antiques outlets—along with stores selling candles, women's clothing, Christmas year-round, and miscellaneous gifts—is in the inn. The tea room is open to the public and serves lunch and dinner; visitors also can buy homemade baked goods and tea mixes to go. Come to this town in a shopping mood.

SETTING & FACILITIES

Location Near Charleston, (20 miles), I 57, Exit #203 then east 14 miles **Near** Amish country, Lincoln Log Cabin State Park, Univ. of Illinois, Walnut Point, Eastern Illinois Univ. **Building** Late 1830s Colonial-style mansion, white exterior **Grounds** Oversized town lot; gardens **Public Space** Porch, library, 5 shops, tea room **Food & Drink** Early coffee available. Full country breakfast w/ eggs, ham, hash browns; 2nd day guests have French toast & bacon. **Recreation** Amish touring, historic touring, antiquing, cross-country skiing, canoeing, biking, fishing. **Amenities & Services** AC. Robes.

ACCOMMODATIONS

Units 3 guest rooms. **All Rooms** Ceiling fan, writing table, chairs. **Some Rooms** N/A **Bed & Bath** 2 doubles (3). All private baths (2 detached). **Favorites** Pine Room, w/ fireplace & Eastlake seating. **Comfort & Decor** The pine plank flooring creaks as guests walk through this lovely old inn. The hitching post in front is original, and the best spot for relaxing before dinner is in a rocking chair on the front porch, gazing out over the town square and, possibly, the sleepiest village in the Midwest. Rooms are furnished with a mix of quality antiques, and a web of small, interesting shops occupies most of the first floor. A television and coffee machine are in the library.

RATES, RESERVATIONS, & RESTRICTIONS

Deposit Credit card number **Discounts** Seasonal specials **Credit Cards** V, MC **Check-In/Out** 3 p.m./11 a.m. **Smoking** No **Pets** No **Kids** Yes **No-Nos** N/A **Minimum Stay** None **Open** All year **Hosts** Gary & Linda Miller, 3 Montgomery, Oakland 61943 **Phone** (217) 346-2289 **Fax** (217) 346-2005 **Email** innonsq@advant.net **Web** www.bedandbreakfast.com/bbc/p210688.asp

FESSEL'S CABBAGE ROSE, Olney

OVERALL ★★★★★ | QUALITY ★★★★★ | VALUE ★★★★★ | PRICE RANGE $59–$89

Fessel's Cabbage Rose has everything we look for in a bed-and-breakfast—a home with grandeur, tantalizing features, seductive lore, a dynamite breakfast, and warmhearted hospitality—plus rock-bottom prices! This inn easily wins a slot on our list of near-perfect bed-and-breakfasts. Two highlights: First, the Van Briggle tile fireplace in the sun-bathed breakfast room—1 of only 86 such fireplaces ever produced—titled, "Roses and Sailing Ship." The piece is probably priceless. Second, the bath in the Red Room Suite. One wall is totally devoted to three cabinets and matching drawers—all with locks, custom-built for the three sisters who originally lived here, so each would have a private place for her clothes and jewelry and could lock out her snoopy sisters.

SETTING & FACILITIES

Location In residential Olney, 3 blocks from US 50 **Near** Fox River, East Fork Lake, Olney Central College, downtown Olney, Red Hills State Park. **Building** 1883 limestone mansion, newly restored **Grounds** City block (1.75 acres) w/ more than 100 species of trees **Public Space** Foyer, DR, library, parlor, conservatory, breakfast room **Food & Drink** Full gourmet breakfast w/ hot entree. Water, sodas any time. **Recreation** Historic touring, antiquing, swimming, boating, fishing, canoeing, cross-country skiing. **Amenities & Services** AC. Hosts parties, meetings, weddings.

ACCOMMODATIONS

Units 3 suites. **All Rooms** TV, phone jack, clock radio, sitting area. **Some Rooms** Hand-sewn quilt bed coverings, dressing table, sun porch, extra bed. **Bed & Bath** Queens (5). All private baths. **Favorites** Red Room Suite, w/ original wallpaper, sun porch, dressing table, bath w/ original tile & fixtures. **Comfort & Decor** The Fessels did every bit of the renovation themselves, comforted by the knowledge that their work was a masterpiece to begin with. Starting at the original marble foyer, guests can progress to the dining room, with white oak floor and walnut inlay; the 16-place, 1904 Lammerts table and chairs belonged to the former owners and matches the marble-topped sideboard. On the wall hangs a 1905 Lhermitte mystery painting (what does it mean???)—and so it goes through the house, past genuine Frank Lloyd Wright windows, seven original fireplaces, and surprise features such as the Peach Suite's "disappearing" closet door.

RATES, RESERVATIONS, & RESTRICTIONS

Deposit 1 night's stay **Discounts** None **Credit Cards** Call ahead **Check-In/Out** Inquire **Smoking** No **Pets** No **Kids** Over age 12 **No-Nos** N/A **Minimum Stay** None **Open** All year **Hosts** Bruce & Karen Fessel, 409 North Boone St., Olney 62450 **Phone** (618) 392-0281 or (877) 337-7357

LITTLE HOUSE ON THE PRAIRIE BED AND BREAKFAST, Sullivan

OVERALL ★★★★½ | QUALITY ★★★★½ | VALUE ★★★★ | PRICE RANGE $60–$138

Each guest room is decorated differently in this elegant bed-and-breakfast: the parlor bedroom probably looked much as Little's grandmother kept it in her day, with the marble tabletops and cranberry glass on display. In the Star room, vintage sheet music covers the bath walls, a tribute to the many musicians who slept here; the suite is more modern. Expect to hear great yarns about celebrities Little has hosted, including Betty Grable, Alan Alda, Leonard Nimoy, and Mickey Rooney.

SETTING & FACILITIES

Location Off IL 32, 1 mi. south of Sullivan **Near** Amish country, downtown Sullivan, Lake Shelbyville, Arthur, Rockome Gardens, Little Theater on the Square. **Building** 1894 Queen Anne farmhouse, pale blue exterior w/ red accents **Grounds** 800 acres of corn & bean farm; gardens w/ outdoor pool & cabana **Public Space** Entry, LR, DR, patio, sun room. **Food & Drink** Afternoon wine & cheese. 5-course candlelight breakfast may include "heavenly bananas," eggs, Belgian waffle, bacon, home-baked muffins. Served on Florentine Wedgwood China, "the same pattern as the Queen Mum's." **Recreation** Amish touring, historic touring, antiquing, swimming, boating, canoeing, fishing, live theatre, golf courses. **Amenities & Services** AC. Guests have golf privileges at nearby country club; after they leave, innkeepers send a photo postcard of themselves as souvenir.

ACCOMMODATIONS
Units I suite, 4 guest rooms. **All Rooms** Sitting area. **Some Rooms** Skylights, whirlpool tub, TV, VCR, CD player, gas fireplace, sun room entrance. **Bed & Bath** King (1), queen (1), doubles (2), 3/4 bed (1). All private baths. **Favorites** Suite w/ whirlpool, TV, VCR, CD, 2 couches, curtained four-poster king bed. **Comfort & Decor** Guy Little loves to escort guests down the "hall of stars," where he showcases photos of celebrities he's hosted over the years. He kept the original windows and woodwork of the home built by his grandparents, adding a garden patio and other upgrades over the years. Furnishings are a mix of silky-smooth stuffed couches, fine antiques, and family artifacts such as the 1860 square grand piano in the living room.

RATES, RESERVATIONS, & RESTRICTIONS
Deposit 50% of stay **Discounts** Extended stay, weekday rates **Credit Cards** Call ahead **Check-In/Out** 4 p.m./11 a.m. **Smoking** On patios & in sun room **Pets** No; will arrange a nearby kennel stay **Kids** Over age 12 **No-Nos** N/A **Minimum Stay** None **Open** April–Dec.; closed Jan.–March **Hosts** Guy S. Little Jr. & Kirk McNamer, R.R. 2, P.O. Box 525, Sullivan 61951 **Phone** (217) 728-4727 **Fax** (217) 728-4727 **Email** gsljr@juno.com **Web** www.bbonline.com/il/littlehouse

MARKET STREET INN, Taylorville

OVERALL ★★★★½ | QUALITY ★★★★½ | VALUE ★★★★ | PRICE RANGE $85–$95 GUEST ROOMS; $135 KING ROOMS

"This house came to town in 14 boxcars," Joe Hauser says of his and Myrna's "kit home." Targeting business travelers, the Hausers operate the only bed-and-breakfast in Taylorville, designed to appeal to both men and women in furnishings and accessories. They've avoided "clutter and cute fad schemes," focusing instead on the look of an affluent century home. Third-floor guest rooms, just developed in 1998, make good use of the attic level's roof lines, gables, beveled windows, and cozy nooks.

SETTING & FACILITIES
Location At Rts. 48 & 29, 20 mi. SE of Springfield **Near** Lincoln Heritage Trail to Pana, downtown Taylorville, Sangchris Lake State Park, Nashville North-USA, Manners Park. **Building** 1892 Queen Anne kit home, bordered by original wrought-iron fence in bird of paradise pattern **Grounds** City lot, shrubs, flower beds **Public Space** Wraparound porch, foyer, DR, front parlor, 2nd-floor "smoker's porch," 3rd-floor common area, loft sitting area. **Food & Drink** Complimentary soda & water. Full breakfast at guests'

convenience w/ egg dish, meat. **Recreation** Historic touring, antiquing, fishing, canoeing, biking, cross-country skiing, swimming, tennis, golf courses. **Amenities & Services** AC. Private phone lines in rooms. Bicycles available.

ACCOMMODATIONS

Units 8 guest rooms (plus 3 overflow/long-term-stay rooms in annex). **All Rooms** TV, chairs, phone, ceiling fan, data port, fax, clock radio. **Some Rooms** Fireplace, bay, single or double whirlpool tub, desk. **Bed & Bath** Kings (2), queens (6). All private baths. **Favorites** Clocktower Room w/ king bed, double whirlpool, town view; most spacious room. **Comfort & Decor** From the front parlor's ornate fireplace and beveled glass window, to the Clocktower Room's alcoves and transoms—originally the home's outer windows—Market Street Inn is a showplace. No need to read during breakfast; guests can gaze on a large Arts & Crafts stained-glass chandelier, built-ins with original etched-glass fronts, and a Medford tile fireplace with columns and beveled-glass mirror. The third-floor common room is lit with skylights, and most rooms are furnished with a mix of antiques and contemporary pieces.

RATES, RESERVATIONS, & RESTRICTIONS

Deposit Credit card number **Discounts** Corp. **Credit Cards** V, MC, AE **Check-In/Out** By individual arrangement **Smoking** No **Pets** No **Kids** Yes **No-Nos** N/A **Minimum Stay** None **Open** All year **Hosts** Myrna & Joe Hauser, 220 East Market St., Taylorville 62568 **Phone** (217) 824-7220 or toll-free (800) 500-1466 **Fax** (217) 824-7229 **Email** jhauser@chipsnet.com **Web** www.marketstreetinn.com

---

THELMA'S BED AND BREAKFAST, West Salem

OVERALL ★★★½ | QUALITY ★★★½ | VALUE ★★★★★ | PRICE RANGE $25/PERSON; $100/WK., $300/MO.

Everywhere we went in southern Illinois, innkeeper's asked us, "How's Thelma doing?" Her legions of fans care about her, and parked on her front porch with a plateful of cookies in our laps, studying her rate card (does it really say $25?), it's easy to see why. You won't get French hand-milled soap here or half a dozen menu choices for breakfast—but you'll get a lot more than $25 worth of hospitality. Before you leave, notice the birdhouse on the backyard deck; it's a model of Thelma's family home—the one where she was raised—and is built with wood taken from that house before it was demolished.

SETTING & FACILITIES

Location Off IL 130 in residential West Salem **Near** Moravian Settlement, Indian Hill Museum, Indian Creek, Bonpas River. **Building** 1919 Prairie four-square, brick **Grounds** City lot, flower beds **Public Space** Porch, LR, den, deck **Food & Drink** Cookies in afternoon. Full breakfast includes meat, homemade breads, coffee cake. **Recreation** Historic touring, canoeing, fishing, cross-country skiing, chowders, Rendezvous at Indian Hill historic festivals. **Amenities & Services** AC. Portable TV on request; can host dinners up to 25 guests.

ACCOMMODATIONS
Units 3 guest rooms. **All Rooms** Chair, clock. **Some Rooms** TV. **Bed & Bath** Queen & 2 twins (1), queen (1), double (1). 1 shared bath. **Favorites** Room 1, w/ sleeping porch. **Comfort & Decor** It's clean, it's modest, it's your grandmother's home. The quarter-sawed red oak woodwork on the first floor was hauled from the Wabash River bottoms and milled on-site, and the bricks are from Albion. Guests can relax with the fireplace or TV in the den, on the deck, or—our choice—that great brick front porch, the kind they don't make anymore.

RATES, RESERVATIONS, & RESTRICTIONS
Deposit None **Discounts** N/A **Credit Cards** Call ahead **Check-In/Out** By individual arrangement **Smoking** Outside **Pets** No **Kids** Yes **No-Nos** N/A **Minimum Stay** None **Open** All year **Hosts** Thelma Lodwig, 201 South Broadway, West Salem 62476 **Phone** (618) 456-8401

Indiana

Of all the states in the Upper Midwest, Indiana showed us the strongest small-town state of mind—even more than Minnesota and Wisconsin, though they're more rural. Somehow, even the most isolated farm outposts in those states seemed determined to be "connected" in a progressive way, but we felt that Indiana resisted a big-city mentality, even in the big cities.

That, as Martha Stewart says, is a good thing. Every town, it seemed, had at least one antiques mall. Antiquing and fishing are two of the most popular pastimes among Hoosiers. Those are quiet hobbies, but this is a mellow state; the absence of brashness and arrogance is noticeable. We went into cities such as **South Bend** and **Lafayette**—places not so obscure that we hadn't heard of them—and came away saying things like "adorable" and "warm."

All of this made the state's offerings even more impressive because without the swagger and aggressive tourism promotion, we didn't expect to find much of interest. We couldn't have been more wrong.

From **Indiana Dunes National Lakeshore** in the northwest corner of the state (we looked around at the tall grasses and sand dunes and wondered how we ended up in South Carolina) to the cliffs over the **Ohio River,** Indiana gave us more than we'd expected. Only two cities, **Indianapolis** and **Fort Wayne,** would classify as major cities, but they're surrounded by midsized towns—South Bend and Lafayette with their great eateries and historic neighborhoods; **Bloomington,** which boasts the best health-food store (in our view) in the Midwest; **Columbus,** with its innovative architecture—and smaller places we hated to leave: spanking-clean **Amish country** in the north, artsy **Nashville** in the central zone, and **New Harmony,** tucked into the riverbank in the southwest corner.

One note of warning: Supposedly, Indiana is in the Eastern Standard Time zone, the same as New York and Atlanta. However, Indiana does not adjust for Daylight Savings Time, so if you cross the Ohio or Michigan borders in those six months, you'll have to adjust your watch there, rather than when you cross into Illinois. Confused? Wait, it gets better. When we got to southern Indiana, we learned that (sometimes) the individual counties, not the state, decide what time it is. In one day, we traveled in four different time zones; all day long we were either an hour early or an hour late for our appointments. We finally stopped looking at our watches and just enjoyed the view.

FOR MORE INFORMATION

Indiana Tourism Division
Indiana Department of Commerce
One North Capitol, Suite 700
Indianapolis, IN 46204-2288
(888) ENJOY-IN; www.enjoyindiana.com/

Indiana Bed & Breakfast Inn Travel Guide
www.ibbp.com/obb/indiana.html

Indiana Bed & Breakfast Association
1210 16th Street
Columbus, Indiana 47201
www.bbonline.com/in

Northwest Indiana

The formative triangle of cities in the first zone—**Michigan City, South Bend,** and **Lafayette**—couldn't be more dissimilar.

Just an hour's drive from Chicago, Michigan City is a lakeside resort town, perched on the edge of turbulent Lake Michigan, with its own **Mount Baldy**—a 123-foot sand dune, part of the **Indiana Dunes National Lakeshore,** just west of town. Past the beaches and dunes is **Pinhook Bog,** formed by a marooned chunk of ice when the glaciers retreated some 14,000 years ago.

Unless you know Michigan City, you might well drive past the casino and chain motels and take away the wrong impression. More than a mere tourist town, this is a historic city eager to share its lore of shipwrecks and shipping tycoons. The four bed-and-breakfasts we selected in this city are only a microcosm of the lodgings here and the kinds of travelers they serve—Creekwood Inn with space and facilities for business groups, Arbor Hill for corporate travelers and those flying solo, Feallock House for romance and pampering, and Hutchinson Mansion for sheer elegance.

In South Bend—home to the **University of Notre Dame,** the **College Football Hall of Fame,** and the **Studebaker National Museum**—tourism is a given. We found two of the classiest bed-and-breakfasts in the region here, both flanking the sumptuous Studebaker Mansion: the posh Oliver Inn and the Book Inn, the only AAA four-diamond bed-and-breakfast in the state.

You'll cross beautiful country heading south toward Lafayette, especially **Tippecanoe River State Park** and the forested **Winamac Wildlife Area.** It's not easy to choose a bed-and-breakfast in these parts; Lafayette's Centennial Historic District is full of stately mansions, but the Commandant's Home in West Lafayette and the Apple Inn in Attica are just as nice. **Purdue University** is here, so clientele of many bed-and-breakfasts tend to be academics and visiting parents.

APPLE INN MUSEUM BED & BREAKFAST, Attica

OVERALL ★★★★½ | QUALITY ★★★★½ | VALUE ★★★★ | PRICE RANGE $75–$135
DOUBLE OCCUPANCY, LESS FOR SINGLES

This home has been in innkeeper Carlson's family for three generations; it was once her grandmother's house, so she tries to "treat you like your grandmother does." About 80 percent of the furnishings and artifacts were her grandmother's or, she says, "belong to Attica." Her mother's bell collection, her grandfather's shaving mug, an 1823 burled walnut buffet, and a James Whitcomb Riley autographed collection of poems all contribute to the "museum" feel of the inn—but not uncomfortably. Ask about the French doors through which actor James Dean once walked.

SETTING & FACILITIES
Location In Attica's Brady Street Historic District, 20 mi. SE of Lafayette off I-74 **Near** Wabash River Heritage Nature Trail, Turkey Run State Park, Portland Arch Nature Preserve, 4 Historic Districts. **Building** 1903 Colonial Revival w/ columns, dormers, widow's walk; Carriage House in rear is 1999 country-rustic style. **Grounds** Flower gardens **Public Space** In main house, porch, foyer, LR, DR, library. In carriage house, common room w/ breakfast area, kitchenette area. Courtyard, deck in rear. **Food & Drink** Snacks served on arrival. Full 5-course breakfast; in main house it's served on fine china. For guests who don't want breakfast, the cost is deducted from the bill. Coffee, tea, and sodas are available any time. **Recreation** Antiquing, canoeing, off-road riding, historical touring, golf courses. **Amenities & Services** Robes in rooms, AC, outdoor hot tub.

ACCOMMODATIONS
Units 10 (5 in main house) **All Rooms** Sitting area **Some Rooms** Balcony, fireplace, desk, claw-foot tubs **Bed & Bath** All private baths in carriage house; 1 shared bath in main house. 6 queens, 2 doubles, 2 rooms w/ 2 twin beds. **Favorites** The Doll Room w/large collection of dolls & Steiff bears, an 1800s Victorian baby bed and high iron bed for guests. **Comfort & Decor** Collections rule this carefully renovated home: Toby mugs, Bing & Grondahl Christmas plates and figurines, antique postcards and Brier horses, and art by

Emma Hudson Culvert, among others. Hand-painted china is displayed in the dining room; much artwork and murals were done by a local artist. Original stained glass and pocket doors appear throughout the house.

RATES, RESERVATIONS, & RESTRICTIONS
Deposit Credit card number or pay 1 night in advance. **Discounts** No **Credit Cards** V, MC **Check-In/Out** 3 p.m./11 a.m. **Smoking** In courtyard only; guests caught smoking inside are charged $200 **Pets** No **Kids** By prior arrangement. **No-Nos** Eating in rooms. **Minimum Stay** 2 nights on select weekends; prices remain the same. **Open** All year **Hosts** Carolyn Carlson, P.O. Box 145, 604 S. Brady St., Attica 47918 **Phone** (317) 762-6574 **Email** appleinn@tctc.com **Web** www.appleinninc.com

ARBOR HILL INN, LaPorte

OVERALL ★★★½ | QUALITY ★★★★ | VALUE ★★★ | PRICE RANGE $64–$229

Built by Chicago businessman W. A. Jones, this home once housed his renowned firearms collection of nearly 1,000 guns—which, we were relieved to find, have been moved to a museum. Interesting beveled glass windows grace the first floor, but the second-story terrace was our favorite spot. The best view is from the Regal Manor guest room, from which much of the county can be seen.

SETTING & FACILITIES
Location 0.25 mi. west of Rt. 35, minutes from I-80/90 **Near** LaPorte Lakes, antiques shops, Blue Chip Casino, Lake Michigan **Building** 1910 Greek Revival w/ pillared porches up & down **Grounds** Lawn, flower beds **Public Space** Foyer, common room w/ fireplace, DR **Food & Drink** Evening snack, full breakfast. Dinner served w/ 48 hours' notice. **Recreation** Boating, fishing, antiquing, gambling, historical touring, golf courses. **Amenities & Services** AC, business services available (overhead projectors, flip charts), breakfast delivered to room, private parties.

ACCOMMODATIONS
Units 7 (includes 4 suites) **All Rooms** Dataport phone, cable TV, VCR, sitting area. **Some Rooms** Suites have small fridge, table, sitting room; some rooms have see-through fireplace, microwave, skylight, handicap access, fieldstone fireplace. **Bed & Bath** All private baths. 2 king beds, 5 queens. **Favorites** W. A. Jones Retreat w/ wet bar, oversized whirlpool & original vaulted wainscot ceiling. **Comfort & Decor** French country, a bit on the romantic side, is a good description of this home's furnishings. The trim throughout the house is oak, and the innkeeper displays her small collection of cranberry glass. Guest rooms and suits all have distinct personalities, with beds of white or black iron, cherry wood, brass, or walnut panel.

RATES, RESERVATIONS, & RESTRICTIONS
Deposit 50% of stay, refundable 10 days before scheduled visit. **Discounts** Corp. rate **Credit Cards** V, MC, AE, D **Check-In/Out** 4 p.m./11 a.m. **Smoking** Outside in designated areas. **Pets** No **Kids** Well-behaved children welcome. **No-Nos** N/A **Minimum Stay** 2 nights on holiday & Notre Dame game weekends **Open** All year **Hosts** Kris

Demoret, Lora Kobat, and Mark Wedow, 263 W. Johnson Rd., LaPorte 46350 **Phone** (219) 362-9200 **Fax** (219) 326-1778 **Email** arborh@netnitco.net **Web** www.arborhillinn.com

BOOK INN, South Bend

OVERALL ★★★★★ | QUALITY ★★★★★ | VALUE ★★★★★ | PRICE RANGE
$100–$160

Book Inn's distinction as the only four-diamond bed-and-breakfast in Indiana and Illinois is well deserved. The rooms, most named after authors, are decorated in soft, rich colors and top-quality furnishings. On the first floor, pocket doors, wood transoms, and stained glass lend more class, crowned by the stunning window at the stair landing. On the lower level, more than 9,000 used books make great browsing. Ask to see the hand-painted tile backsplashes in the kitchen.

SETTING & FACILITIES
Location Walking distance from intersection of US 31/33 and Rt. 20 **Near** Studebaker Mansion (next door), Copshaholm "living museum," Convention Center, College Football Hall of Fame, Coveleski Baseball Stadium, St. Joseph River **Building** 1872 Second Empire, brick **Grounds** Small yard, city lot **Public Space** Large front porch, so-big-it-echoes foyer, LR, DR, library **Food & Drink** Complimentary wine, beer, soda any time. Gourmet breakfast served on antique Haviland china by candlelight. **Recreation** Historic touring, Minor League baseball, boating, antiquing. **Amenities & Services** Fresh flowers in rooms, AC, used bookstore in basement, robes in rooms, logo soaps & note paper.

ACCOMMODATIONS
Units 2 suites, 3 guest rooms **All Rooms** Phones w/ dataports, cable TV, sitting area, desk **Some Rooms** N/A **Bed & Bath** Kings (4), queen (1), all private baths. **Favorites** Cush-

ing Suite, the largest space, with bay alcove and hand-painted walls replicating vintage wall-paper. **Comfort & Decor** Now this is elegance, from the 12-foot ceilings and ornate carved entry doors, to the stained glass and butternut woodwork throughout the house. Check out the gilded muslin walls in the Jessie Willcox Smith suite, decorated with framed prints of the famous illustrator's work.

RATES, RESERVATIONS, & RESTRICTIONS
Deposit I night's stay, refunded if room is rented after cancellation. **Discounts** AARP, AAA, other groups **Credit Cards** V, MC, AE **Check-In/Out** 5–7 p.m./11 p.m. **Smoking** No **Pets** No **Kids** Welcome if in second room; only 2 persons per room. **No-Nos** N/A **Minimum Stay** None **Open** All year **Hosts** John & Peggy Livingston, 508 West Washington, South Bend 46601 **Phone** (219) 288-1990 **Fax** (219) 234-2338 **Email** info@book-inn.com **Web** www.book-inn.com

COMMANDANT'S HOME BED & BREAKFAST,
West Lafayette

OVERALL ★★★★½ | QUALITY ★★★★ | VALUE ★★★★★ | PRICE RANGE $95

It's the majestic grand staircase (think Gone with the Wind) that sets the tone, makes you gasp, and draws you in. Then you notice other reminders of the era: original pine and walnut plank flooring, original transoms, and light fixtures—not to mention the life-sized "soldiers" guarding the front door. Commandants of the veterans' home complex—a plum position bestowed on leaders who had distinguished themselves in the military—once lived in this grand home on the hill, now a National Historic Place.

SETTING & FACILITIES
Location On the grounds of the Indiana Veterans' Home on SR 43 **Near** Wabash River, Purdue Univ., Tippecanoe Battlefield, city of Lafayette **Building** Approx. 1900 Federal style w/ massive 2-story Ionic columns **Grounds** Surrounded by 130-acre grounds of the Veterans' Home **Public Space** Front porch, back porch, 2nd-story porch, house-size foyer, parlor/TV room, LR, DR, 2nd-floor foyer **Food & Drink** Complimentary soda, coffee, tea, sweet snacks. 4-course candlelight breakfast includes 2 entrees. **Recreation** Canoeing, fishing, exploring 10-acre veterans' cemetery. **Amenities & Services** Fax/modem access, AC, logo bath amenities.

ACCOMMODATIONS
Units 7 guest rooms **All Rooms** Ceiling fans, sitting area **Some Rooms** River view, expansive view of grounds & carriage house, original bath fixtures. **Bed & Bath** All private baths. 2 kings, 4 queens. **Favorites** Commandant Seybert's Room, for its oak bed, Mission rocker, and 2-window view of the carriage trail & library. **Comfort & Decor** Furnishings and decor of the Commandant's Home are as dignified as the home itself. A majestic frieze of the Battle of Tippecanoe presides over the living room, complemented by a marble pillared fireplace and grand piano. The crystal chandelier defines the dining room, set off by 10-foot ceilings.

RATES, RESERVATIONS, & RESTRICTIONS
Deposit Credit card number **Discounts** None **Credit Cards** V, MC, D, AE **Check-In/Out** 3 p.m./11 a.m. **Smoking** On porches **Pets** No **Kids** Yes **No-Nos** N/A **Minimum Stay** No **Open** All year **Hosts** Gene & Carolyn Brown, 3848 St. Rd. 43 N, West Lafayette 47906 **Phone** (765) 463-5980 **Fax** (765) 463-5982 **Email** rooms @commhomeb-b.com **Web** www.commhomeb-b.com

CREEKWOOD INN, Michigan City

OVERALL ★★★★ | QUALITY ★★★★ | VALUE ★★ | PRICE RANGE $135–$170

More an inn for business travelers than a bed-and-breakfast, Creekwood Inn creates a decidedly corporate ambience. (Promotional literature, in fact, touts the inn as "the perfect mix of business and pleasure.") Rooms are furnished comfortably and attractively but impersonally. It's an ideal setting for a corporate retreat; guests will feel they've been to a country inn but not to a bed-and-breakfast. Their restaurant is called The Ferns.

SETTING & FACILITIES
Location On Rts. 20/35 at I-94 **Near** Lake Michigan, Blue Chip Casino, Indiana Dunes State Park, Warren Dunes State Park, Michigan City harbor & public beach, wetlands **Building** 1930s country manor, stone & wood construction **Grounds** 33 wooded acres w/ jogging & ski trails, small lake **Public Space** Conservatory (great room), entry, DR, sun porch, terrace deck, game-table loft **Food & Drink** Cont'l breakfast of homemade breads & fruit; honor bar in conservatory. Full breakfast & dinner available weekends at an additional charge. **Recreation** Fishing, tennis, boating, horseback riding, golf courses, skiing, swimming, gambling. **Amenities & Services** Robes, hair dryers in rooms; logo bath amenities, bicycles & lawn croquet available, AC. Fax, copier, AV equipment available.

ACCOMMODATIONS
Units 12 guest rooms, 1 suite. **All Rooms** Fridge w/ icemaker & soft drinks, overstuffed chairs, desk, reading lamp. **Some Rooms** Fireplaces, private terraces. Suite has meeting room for 10 people, sun porch, fireplace, & beverage bar. **Bed & Bath** All private baths. King bed in suite; guest rooms have kings (4), 2 queens (4), or 2 twins (4). **Favorites** The Hinkleberry Room, spacious w/ fireplace and view of gardens. **Comfort & Decor** The inn is decorated in a rustic/contemporary style; rooms are spacious with an English country feel. Most furnishings are reproduction antiques.

RATES, RESERVATIONS, & RESTRICTIONS
Deposit Credit card number **Discounts** AAA, group rates, weekend & seasonal packages. **Credit Cards** V, MC **Check-In/Out** 4 p.m./noon **Smoking** Outdoors only **Pets** No **Kids** Inquire **No-Nos** N/A **Minimum Stay** None **Open** All year **Hosts** Mary Lou Linnen, Route 20-35 at I-94, Michigan City 46360 **Phone** (219) 872-8357 **Fax** (219) 872-8357 **Email** creekwd@adsnet.com **Web** www.creekwoodinn.com

FEALLOCK HOUSE, Michigan City

OVERALL ★★★½ | QUALITY ★★★½ | VALUE ★★★★ | PRICE RANGE $75–$109

Where service is concerned, no one works harder at pampering guests than these innkeepers. Harold brought our car from the locked compound when we needed it, coffee was delivered on cue, and they will even arrange to pick up guests at O'Hare Airport—more than an hour's drive away. The house looks small, but it actually boasts 52 windows and 49 doors, all restored by the Smiths.

SETTING & FACILITIES

Location Central Michigan City **Near** Lake Michigan, Indiana Dunes State Park, Warren Dunes State Park, Blue Chip Casino, Michigan City harbor & beaches **Building** 1866 gable-front Italianate of 3-brick wall construction **Grounds** City lot with enclosed parking compound **Public Space** Library, parlor, DR **Food & Drink** Soda, coffee, tea, snacks any time. Coffee brought to 2nd-floor kitchen area before breakfast. Full breakfast includes home-baked pastry, custom-cooked omelet, smoothie. **Recreation** Boating, swimming, charter boat fishing, antiquing, historic touring **Amenities & Services** Robes in rooms, turn-down service, fresh fruit in room, candy & bottled water & ice water in room at night, logo bath amenities

ACCOMMODATIONS

Units 4 guest rooms **All Rooms** Ceiling fans **Some Rooms** Sleigh bed, desk, recliner **Bed & Bath** Queens (3), double (1). Private bath (1), shared (2). **Favorites** Lewis Room w/ sitting alcove, writing desk, four-poster bed, original light fixtures **Comfort & Decor** Every room is designed for comfort, with easy chairs and strong reading lights. Some will find the Pullman Room and in-progress Lighthouse Room a tad cornball, but not overly so. The innkeepers are keen on local history and have scattered artifacts of Michigan City's heritage throughout the property.

RATES, RESERVATIONS, & RESTRICTIONS

Deposit Credit card number **Discounts** Senior discount 10%, business rates, repeat-guest discount of 15% or previous year's rate, whichever is less. Special packages available, including train to Chicago ($6). **Credit Cards** V, MC **Check-In/Out** 3 p.m./11 a.m. (flexible) **Smoking** No **Pets** No **Kids** Occasionally, by prior arrangement **No-Nos** N/A **Minimum Stay** None **Open** All year **Hosts** Jan & Harold Smith, 402 East 8th St., Michigan City 46360 **Phone** (219) 878-9543 **Fax** (219) 878-9623 **Email** feallock@netnitco.net

HUTCHINSON MANSION INN, *Michigan City*

OVERALL ★★★★★ | QUALITY ★★★★★ | VALUE ★★★★★ | PRICE RANGE
$85–$140 (CARRIAGE HOUSE SUITES)

If homes were women, the Hutchinson Mansion would be Cleopatra. The very floors are a work of art. More than a century after the parquet floors were laid—and after years of research by the innkeepers—the intricate designs were identified by a guest who recognized them as quilting patterns! A bronze newel lady, an unsigned Tiffany window in the Tower Suite, a hallway light fixture of "Vaseline glass," and 12-foot ceilings all contribute to the grandeur. The Carrera marble angel in the garden was a gift from Hutchinson family descendents. In the carriage house, don't miss the awesome clouds in Suite 2. Did we mention that half the rooms are priced at $100 or less—with $10 more deducted for singles?

SETTING & FACILITIES

Location Michigan City's Historic District, several blocks from Rts. 20/35 **Near** Lake Michigan, Indiana Dunes State Park, Michigan City harbor & beaches **Building** 1875 red-brick mansion with Queen Anne, Classic Revival, & Italianate elements **Grounds** Just under an acre w/ richly landscaped gardens, patios, bittersweet vine. Side lawn is perfectly sized for a croquet field. **Public Space** Parlor, "book nook," DR, library, sun porch, 2nd-floor game room **Food & Drink** Juice, water, coffee, tea, sodas available any time, plus popcorn, brownies, and the world's most excellent lemon squares. Breakfast is full, including entrees such as puffy rarebit. ("I've never served a scrambled egg," says innkeeper Mary DuVal.) **Recreation** Swimming, charter boat fishing, hiking, tennis, golf courses, cross-country skiing, horseback riding, canoeing, birding, croquet. **Amenities & Services** AC, fresh flowers in rooms, plush robes

ACCOMMODATIONS
Units 5 suites, 5 guest rooms (4 of the suites in carriage house) **All Rooms** Individual climate control, writing table or desk, sitting area, phone, modem **Some Rooms** Double whirlpool, private terrace, private porch w/ swing, marble fireplace **Bed & Bath** King (1), queens (9), all private baths. Original bath in the Servants' Quarters might have been the first in the city. **Favorites** Patterson Room w/ 1820 Southern plantation-style tester bed, once a rope bed (the Rockefeller Foundation wanted to buy it for the Smithsonian, but the DuVals think people should still sleep in it), and marble fireplace. **Comfort & Decor** Paneling and wood trim doesn't darken this home a bit; it's cheery yet dignified. Eleven stained-glass windows, secret panels, fine antiques, and a "shaker porch" for shaking and airing linens are a few highlights.

RATES, RESERVATIONS, & RESTRICTIONS
Deposit 1 night's stay or credit card number, refundable with more than 7 days' notice **Discounts** Single occupancy, long-term stays, or business rates **Credit Cards** V, MC, **Check-In/Out** 4 p.m./11 a.m. **Smoking** Outside only **Pets** No **Kids** Over age 12 **No-Nos** N/A **Minimum Stay** None **Open** All year **Hosts** Mary & Ben DuVal, 220 W. 10th St., Michigan City 46360 **Phone** (219) 879-1700 **Fax** (219) 872-8357 **Email** N/A

INNTIQUITY INN, *Logansport*

OVERALL ★★★ | QUALITY ★★★½ | VALUE ★★★ | PRICE RANGE $75–$110

Converting a barn into a bed-and-breakfast might be one of those ideas that sounds better than the actual result. Creating a polished space takes a small fortune, and these innkeepers cut many corners: vintage fireplaces could be a nice shabby chic touch, but the recycled slate flooring, paneling fashioned from Holiday Inn headboards, and many other "found" elements add up to a hodgepodge that's a bit rough around the edges. A slight cigarette smell from the bar, just off the common room, pervades the public spaces. Still, the antiques, including a Tiffany window, are first-rate.

SETTING & FACILITIES
Location On SR 25, 1.5 mi. north of Logansport **Near** Eel River, Wabash River, 35 mi. from Purdue **Building** Converted 1849 barn w/ pale blue exterior **Grounds** 23 acres of meadows, gardens, canal **Public Space** Common room, 2nd-floor sitting room, bar/restaurant, breakfast room, library, meeting room **Food & Drink** Coffee, tea, soft drinks available anytime. Full breakfast of fruit, nut breads, rolls, entree. **Recreation** Golf courses, canoeing, tennis, biking **Amenities & Services** AC, business facilities, robes & fresh flowers in room, hair dryers, laundry service for long-term guests, hot tub in silo. Candlelight champagne dinners available for $50.

ACCOMMODATIONS
Units 10 guest rooms **All Rooms** Deck, cable TV, sitting area **Some Rooms** Whirlpool or double whirlpool tub, fireplace, double shower **Bed & Bath** Queens (8), doubles (2)

Favorites Handicapped room, with roll-in shower, terrace & view of canal, gardens, & meadows. **Comfort & Decor** The innkeepers, former antiques dealers, furnished the inn with a mix of fine antiques, including an Eastlake bed and a canopied Lincoln bed, and recycled finds, such as marble trim from an airport that closed.

RATES, RESERVATIONS, & RESTRICTIONS
Deposit 1 night's stay or credit card number, refundable with 1-week notice. **Discounts** Government employee, corporate, whole-house (at least 6 rooms), and extended-stay discounts **Credit Cards** V, MC, D **Check-In/Out** 3 p.m./11 a.m. **Smoking** On decks or in bar **Pets** By arrangement, depending on the pet. Resident cat lives outdoors. **Kids** Occasionally; use of a roll-away bed is $25. If the child breaks an antique, the parents have to pay for it. **No-Nos** No eating in room except snacks **Minimum Stay** None **Open** All year **Hosts** George & Lee Naftzger, 1075 SR 25 N, Logansport 46947 **Phone** (219) 722-2398 or toll-free (877) 230-7870 **Email** inntiquity@cqc.com **Web** www.inntiquity.com

LOEB HOUSE INN, *Lafayette*

OVERALL ★★★★½ | QUALITY ★★★★½ | VALUE ★★★★ | PRICE RANGE $85–$175

This home, listed on the National Register of Historic Places, has all the elements you look for in a grand historic inn—fireplaces, pillars, stained glass, brass door pulls, down to the original cypress planking and parquet floors. Nagel operates the bed-and-breakfast with his mother, and it's hard to say who pampers guests the most. They're a smart, interesting pair who don't mind joining guests for an aperitif in the parlor. We were delighted that no "instruction cards" appeared in our room—these folks assume their guests are grown-ups.

SETTING & FACILITIES
Location Lafayette's Centennial Historic District **Near** Columbian Park, Fort Ouiatenon, Tippecanoe Battlefield, Purdue Univ., Wabash River **Building** 1882 Grand Ital-

ianate brick w/ rare double-bay windows in front **Grounds** Flower beds, growing urn collection **Public Space** Foyer, formal double parlor, sitting parlor, DR, front & back porches. **Food & Drink** Soda, water available any time. Full candlelight breakfast, served on china & crystal, includes entree. **Recreation** Swimming, canoeing, petting zoo, historical touring, museums. **Amenities & Services** Port & sherry served in the evening, turn-down service w/ chocolates, copy & fax available.

ACCOMMODATIONS

Units 5 guest rooms **All Rooms** Cable TV, phone, ceiling fan **Some Rooms** Claw-foot tub, whirlpool tub, closeted toilet **Bed & Bath** Queens (1), 2 doubles (1), double (3). All private baths. **Favorites** Carrie's Retreat, w/ hand-painted tiles floor tiles, muraled Jacuzzi "pavilion" & basket-weave Eastlake bedroom suite. **Comfort & Decor** Everyone stops at the lamp newel post—"the reason I bought the house," says innkeeper Dick Nagel—with shades rescued from a local church. First-floor trim is black walnut, topped by 12-foot ceilings, restored plaster medallions, and crown moldings. Furnishings are luxurious (we counted 11 pillows on our bed) and top quality.

RATES, RESERVATIONS, & RESTRICTIONS

Deposit 1 night's stay or credit card. **Discounts** None **Credit Cards** V, MC, AE **Check-In/Out** 4 p.m./11 a.m. **Smoking** On porches only **Pets** No (resident cat lives outdoors) **Kids** Well-behaved, over age 12 **No-Nos** N/A **Minimum Stay** None **Open** All year **Hosts** Dick Nagel, 708 Cincinnati St., Lafayette 47901 **Phone** (765) 420-7737 **Email** N/A **Web** www.loebhouseinn.com

OLIVER INN, *South Bend*

OVERALL ★★★★★ | QUALITY ★★★★★ | VALUE ★★★★★ | PRICE RANGE $145

Oliver Inn forms an elegant sandwich with the Book Inn, two doors away, and the lavish Studebaker Mansion between. No detail has been overlooked in this home, built as a wedding present, and original touches—such as the servants' call boxes, the old "silver vault" and curved leaded glass windows—have been preserved. Rooms were interconnected, as in many

Victorian mansions, so the family would not be seen in their bed clothes by servants. Front rooms, with original maple flooring, are the largest—that's where Steve Thomas from public television's This Old House stays.

SETTING & FACILITIES
Location Walking distance from intersection of Rts. 31/33 and Rt. 20 **Near** Studebaker Mansion, Univ. of Notre Dame, St. Joseph River, East Race Waterway **Building** 1886 Queen Anne Victorian, peach & deep green exterior **Grounds** 1 acre—gazebo w/ glider, inviting seating areas, fountains, gardens, and 1910 play house **Public Space** Library, front parlor/gift shop, DR, entries, 2 gingerbread porches, 2nd-floor sitting area **Food & Drink** Beverages, snacks available any time in "Butler's Pantry." Full candlelight breakfast by the fire w/ "live" music from player piano **Recreation** Boating, canoeing, kayaking, carriage rides, historic touring **Amenities & Services** AC, private phone lines, fax, computer hook-up, meeting rooms

ACCOMMODATIONS
Units 9 guest rooms **All Rooms** Cable TV, phone **Some Rooms** Fireplace, private balcony, double Jacuzzi, claw-foot tub, panoramic views **Bed & Bath** Kings (5, or 4 and 2 twins that make a king), queens (4). Private baths except 1 shared, for 3rd-floor overflow guest rooms. **Favorites** Knute Rockne Room, w/ private balcony, Art Deco furnishings, original bath w/ marble sink & claw-foot tub, original chrome plumbing, & "shimmy" machine **Comfort & Decor** The restoration of this soaring, distinguished mansion was superb, from the sculpted plaster dining room ceiling to the black-cherry carved newel lamp, original cut-glass sconces, and "green man" wood sculpture high on the exterior trim. No flea-market finds here; Oliver Inn is pure elegance.

RATES, RESERVATIONS, & RESTRICTIONS
Deposit Credit card number or arrange deposit when reservations are placed **Discounts** AAA, corporate, senior, extended stay **Credit Cards** V, MC, AE, D, **Check-In/Out** 4–6 p.m./11 a.m. **Smoking** On porches only **Pets** Occasionally by arrangement **Kids** With well-behaved parents **No-Nos** N/A **Minimum Stay** None **Open** All year **Hosts** Richard & Venera Monahan, 630 West Washington St., South Bend 46601 **Phone** (219) 232-4545 or toll-free (888) 697-4466 **Fax** (219) 288-9788 **Email** oliver@michiana.org **Web** www.oliverinn.com

TORTUGA INN, *Winamac*

OVERALL ★★★★ | QUALITY ★★★★½ | VALUE ★★★★★ | PRICE RANGE $75–$125

Perched atop a slope leading down to the Tippecanoe River, Tortuga Inn's setting is one of the prettiest in northern Indiana. It's a popular stopover for bird-watchers, who have spotted about ten varieties of woodpeckers alone. The innkeepers, both working artists, keep the grounds and inside adorned with their fabric, metal, and wood sculptures, as well as their paintings. Though smoking is permitted, we detected no odor in those areas—and

Tortuga holds the distinction of the only horse-friendly bed-and-breakfast in this book. For those looking for a laid-back, artsy place in a wooded setting, this inn is ideal.

SETTING & FACILITIES

Location Just off Rt. 14 north of Winamac, on the Tippecanoe River **Near** Tippecanoe River State Park, horse stables, Fort Wayne, Amish country **Building** 1994 lodge-style inn, multilevel **Grounds** 275 acres on the Tippecanoe River w/ 2 miles of walking trails, stables, facilities for riding lessons **Public Space** Parlor, DR, patios, deck **Food & Drink** Evening snack & sherry. Full breakfast includes home-baked breads, egg dish, entree such as crêpes or pancakes, breakfast meat. **Recreation** Canoeing, horseback riding, cross-country skiing, birding, Amish & historic touring. **Amenities & Services** AC. Champagne included w/ rental of bridal suite. Much of the art on display is for sale.

ACCOMMODATIONS

Units 5 guest rooms. **All Rooms** TV, VCR, sitting area. **Some Rooms** Skylight, whirlpool tub, double sinks, desk & chair. **Bed & Bath** Queens (4), double (1), plus full-size sofa bed or daybed. All private baths. **Favorites** Master Suite, adjacent to walk-out patio. **Comfort & Decor** This is not your grandma's B&B! Both owners are artists, and the decor—mostly their own art—is funky, eclectic, and beautiful. We loved Lee's collection of masks, and Gordon's room screens are irresistible. Two rooms are handicap-accessible.

RATES, RESERVATIONS, & RESTRICTIONS

Deposit Credit card number or $25. **Discounts** AARP, weekly rental. **Credit Cards** V, MC, D, AE. **Check-In/Out** 1 p.m./11 a.m. or by prior arrangement. **Smoking** In designated areas. **Pets** Yes; guests traveling w/ horses can board them here. Pets permitted in 2 guest rooms. **Kids** Yes **No-Nos** N/A **Minimum Stay** None **Open** All year **Hosts** Lee & Gordon Ligocki, 2142 N. 125 East., Winamac 46996 **Phone** (219) 946-6969 **Fax** (219) 946-6969 **Email** N/A

Northeast Indiana

Get used to hearing people go on and on about antiques here. Between the **Shipshewana Flea Market** and antiques malls lining virtually every town's Main Street, it seems likely that if you're a diligent shopper, you will see every item ever produced by humankind in this corner of the state.

Our first Indiana appointment was in **Berne**, a tiny hamlet just south of **Fort Wayne.** We saw no shoppers and no one walking the streets but we did notice two antiques malls to explore (with great prices, we hasten to add). Fort Wayne is a bigger city, so of course it offers more typical city attractions—a zoo, an art museum, a performing arts center—but it also prides itself on its proximity to antiques centers and the third-largest Amish community in the country.

Once we drove north to make our way across the top of the state, we felt that we needed to submit and start antiquing. Shipshewana boasts not only 90 shops in its town center but also the largest outdoor flea market in the Midwest every Tuesday and Wednesday, May through October, as more than 1,000 vendors set up shop in the auction grounds.

We encountered the same love of antiques in **Goshen, Nappanee,** and other towns sprinkled across northern Indiana. Nappanee also holds the distinction of the "home of home and garden," with more than 35 home shops strung along U.S. 6, including some that specialize in hand-crafted Amish furniture.

Most bed-and-breakfasts throughout this area are Victorians, located in their towns' residential or historic districts. One nostalgic exception is the Carole Lombard House in Fort Wayne, furnished in quality Art Deco pieces—more sexy than romantic, we thought, in a Clark Gable–Carole Lombard way. In Nappanee, about half the town is included in a "historic architecture walk," a mix of Prairie School, Queen Anne, Foursquare, and other styles, plus at least one wildly ornate Queen Anne.

TULIP TREE INN, Angola

OVERALL ★★★★ | QUALITY ★★★★ | VALUE ★★★★ | PRICE RANGE $90–$125

The well-tended flower beds and inviting wicker on the front porch can make a guest forget that he or she is on a major thoroughfare. The craftsmanship of the carved woodwork and windows is impressive. This is a special place where locals can indulge in an in-town getaway and enjoy their own discount.

SETTING & FACILITIES
Location Less than 0.25 mi. north of intersection of US 20 & IN 127 **Near** Tri-State Univ., Pokagon State Park, Shipshewana Auction, Amish country **Building** 1886 Queen Anne Victorian **Grounds** Flower beds **Public Space** Foyer, LR, DR, porch **Food & Drink** Coffee, tea, soda any time. Full candlelight breakfast includes gourmet coffee, muffin, & entree; signature dishes are eggs Benedict & Spanish tortilla **Recreation** Boating, fishing, golf courses, tennis, ice fishing, winter sports, antiquing **Amenities & Services** Music at breakfast, business meetings, fax & computer available, massages & afternoon tea available, laundry facilities. AC, robes in rooms.

ACCOMMODATIONS
Units 3 rooms, 1 suite **All Rooms** TV, VCR, sitting area **Some Rooms** Kitchen, wraparound sun deck **Bed & Bath** King (1), queen (2), 2 doubles (1). 2 private baths, 1 shared. **Favorites** Rose Room, largest room w/ spacious sitting area, king bed. **Comfort & Decor** The original oak woodwork in the Tulip Tree may be its most striking feature, yet the spacious public rooms, soft colors, and many windows give the first floor a breezy, open feel. Pocket doors, beveled leaded windows, and Oriental rugs lend a luxurious note.

RATES, RESERVATIONS, & RESTRICTIONS
Deposit Credit card, refundable w/ 7 days' notice and cancellation fee of $15/room. **Discounts** Single occupancy, corp., local, extended-stay rates. **Credit Cards** V, MC **Check-In/Out** Noon/2 p.m., both flexible **Smoking** Porch & deck only **Pets** No **Kids** Occasionally, by arrangement **No-Nos** N/A **Minimum Stay** None **Open** All year **Hosts** Kathy & Mac Friedlander, 411 N. Wayne St., Angola 46703 **Phone** Toll-free (888) 401-0002 **Fax** Toll-free (888) 356-0002 **Email** tuliptree@tuliptree.com **Web** www.tuliptree.com

SCHUG HOUSE INN, Berne

OVERALL ★★★★ | QUALITY ★★★★ | VALUE ★★★★★ | PRICE RANGE $38

The restored woodwork in Schug House is of heart virgin pine, floors in the public rooms are inlaid oak parquet, and the antiques—such as the Eastlake washstand of tiger maple, the sleigh bed in the third-floor turret bedroom, or the high-back oak bed in the Sun Room guest room—are well chosen. Why, then, can guests stay here for a mere $38? "We can't manufacture an ocean or mountains or a university," Jane says. The spacious carriage house, with flooring from an 1860s log cabin and a 1910 porcelain stove as the TV stand, is just $2 more. Welcome to the best bed-and-breakfast deal in the Midwest.

SETTING & FACILITIES

Location I block west of Berne's only traffic light **Near** Amish community, antiques malls **Building** 1907 twin-towered Queen Anne Victorian **Grounds** Flower beds **Public Space** Foyer, parlor, DR, 2nd-floor screened sleeping porch **Food & Drink** Soft drinks available any time. Breakfast is deluxe cont'l, w/ croissants, coffee cake, sweet rolls, fruit, juices, cold cereal, and cheeses served on antique china & glassware **Recreation** Antiquing, historic touring, Amish interests **Amenities & Services** Catered dinners arranged; AC

ACCOMMODATIONS

Units 3 guest rooms plus carriage house **All Rooms** Cable TV in antique armoire, phone, sitting area, desk **Some Rooms** Claw-foot tub, ceiling fan, canopy bed **Bed & Bath** Queens (3), double (1), 2 twins (1). All private baths. **Favorites** Wenner Room w/ large bath, private door to porch, claw-foot tub. **Comfort & Decor** This Queen Anne stands out because its walls are nearly unadorned. "We prefer to let the beauty of the house show," says innkeeper Jane Minch. One iron bed had to be restored by an auto body shop, and several rooms feature small "hired man's beds."

RATES, RESERVATIONS, & RESTRICTIONS

Deposit Credit card or I night's stay **Discounts** None **Credit Cards** V, MC **Check-In/Out** "Any time"/noon **Smoking** On front porch only **Pets** "Never!" **Kids** Yes **No-Nos** N/A **Minimum Stay** None **Open** All year **Hosts** Jane & John Minch, 706 W. Main St., Berne 46711 **Phone** (219) 589-2303 or owners' residence, (219) 589-2448 **Email** N/A

AT THE HERB LADY'S GARDEN, Fort Wayne

OVERALL ★★★★ | QUALITY ★★★★ | VALUE ★★★★★ | PRICE RANGE $75

Gardeners, prepare to be wowed. The Herb Lady's garden is the focal point of this bed-and-breakfast—and as wonderful as it looks, the fragrance is even better. Take a few steps in any direction and the aromas change. Roger Swain of public television's The Victory Garden stayed here and, we hear, learned a thing or two about growing herbs. The garden is divided by function: herbs for baking and confections, soups and sauces, cosmetics and fragrances; herbs to be dried; herbs for teas; medicinal herbs; those for fabrics and dyes; and herbs for salves and dressings. Somewhere in there are more than a dozen varieties of thyme alone.

SETTING & FACILITIES

Location East of Fort Wayne near I-469 **Near** Amish country, antiques malls, coliseum sports arena **Building** Post–Civil War brick **Grounds** Magnificent gardens, including a raised 22' x 35' herb garden **Public Space** Parlor, great room, DR, screened porch **Food & Drink** Choice of full or cont'l breakfast, served on grandmother's oak table or screened porch. Coffee available before breakfast. **Recreation** Antiquing, Amish interests, enjoying the herbal scents & gardens **Amenities & Services** Herb library, AC, special events. Classes offered in herb gardening, herbal jelly & vinegar making, preserving herbs, and crafting with herbs, depending on the season.

ACCOMMODATIONS

Units 2 guest rooms **All Rooms** TV, sitting area, books, ceiling fan **Some Rooms** Canopy bed, mantel **Bed & Bath** Queens (2), all private baths. **Favorites** Indiana Artists Room, overlooking the herb garden, with original art by Indiana painters. **Comfort & Decor** Ms. Rennecker, the "herb lady," uses some antiques that have been in her family for generations. You'll do a double-take at the massive, hand-carved English oak huntboard in the parlor; up the (steep, curving) stairs the floors are original butternut planking. Our favorite feature: good bedside reading lights.

RATES, RESERVATIONS, & RESTRICTIONS

Deposit 1 night's stay or credit card **Discounts** Single & senior rates **Credit Cards** V, MC, D **Check-In/Out** 4–6 p.m./10 a.m. for room stay, 11:30 a.m. for "An Herbal Experience" (classes) stay **Smoking** On back porch **Pets** No **Kids** No **No-Nos** Candles in rooms. Also, no eating in rooms: "If you have a snack, please enjoy it in the public rooms." **Minimum Stay** None **Open** All year **Hosts** Louise & Ralph Rennecker, 8214 Maysville Rd., Fort Wayne 46815 **Phone** (219) 493-8814 **Email** N/A

CAROLE LOMBARD HOUSE, Fort Wayne

OVERALL ★★★★½ | QUALITY ★★★★½ | VALUE ★★★★★ | PRICE RANGE $65–$85

Built by film star Carole Lombard's grandfather, this home is filled with Gable-and-Lombard memorabilia, all displayed most tastefully. One almost expects to see Lombard swooping into her room wearing that 1930s chenille robe; the Clark Gable room is for swooning at the many photos of that

handsome mug. In the morning, have coffee in the window-walled breakfast porch overlooking the Carole Lombard Memorial Bridge or watch a Lombard screwball comedy classic on the VCR.

SETTING & FACILITIES

Location In the historic West Central Neighborhood on the Heritage Trail **Near** Children's Zoo, River Greenway, Performing Arts Center, Lincoln Museum **Building** 1902 brick home with spruce green, berry, & taupe exterior trim **Grounds** Flower beds **Public Space** Foyer, indoor porch/TV room, LR, DR, breakfast porch **Food & Drink** Soft drinks available any time. Full breakfast includes fresh fruits, gourmet coffee or tea, entree such as buckwheat/corn pancakes, & Canadian bacon **Recreation** Bicycling on the Greenway, theater, antiquing **Amenities & Services** AC, fresh flowers in room, will occasionally pick up guests at airport.

ACCOMMODATIONS

Units 5 guest rooms **All Rooms** Cable TV, phone, chenille spreads **Some Rooms** Ceiling fans, claw-foot tub **Bed & Bath** King (1), queen (1), double (2), 2 twins (1). All private bathrooms. **Favorites** Carole Lombard, with photos of the star, chenille bedcover & sofa, chenille robe hanging, & "oil crayon" stenciling—the room where she was born. **Comfort & Decor** The scheme here, in Lombard's honor, is Art Deco—and it works beautifully. Deco furnishings and lamps fill nearly every room, accented perfectly by the sunburst-pattern oak wood trim.

RATES, RESERVATIONS, & RESTRICTIONS

Deposit 1 night's stay or credit card **Discounts** Travel agent commission **Credit Cards** V, MC, D **Check-In/Out** 4–5:30 p.m./noonish **Smoking** No **Kids** By arrangement **No-Nos** N/A **Minimum Stay** None **Open** All year **Hosts** Bev & Dave Fiandt, 704 Rockhill St., Fort Wayne 46802 **Phone** Toll-free (888) 426-9896 or (219) 426-9896 **Fax** (219) 426-9896 **Email** N/A

FRONT PORCH INN, Goshen

OVERALL ★★★★ | QUALITY ★★★★ | VALUE ★★★★★ | PRICE RANGE $79

This inn has everything going for it—lots of character, comfortable rooms, pillars, porch, patio, and one of the tastiest dishes we've tried—Meyer's baked oatmeal pudding. The stained glass in the transoms came from an old train. We also enjoyed Meyer's dollhouse and the antique Valentines displayed in the upstairs hall. The home is located on Goshen's Greenway bike and walking trail.

SETTING & FACILITIES
Location A few yards from US 33 in downtown Goshen **Near** Shipshewana Flea Market, Mennonite Relief Sale, Amish Acres, Goshen College **Building** 1887 Italianate Victorian, on National Register of Historic Places **Grounds** Small front yard; backyard offers pool, perennial garden, ivy-laden private patio **Public Space** Parlor, LR, DR, foyer, large front porch, rear patio **Food & Drink** Soft drinks any time. Gourmet breakfast includes such dishes as strawberry muffins, egg bake, oatmeal pudding. **Recreation** Antiquing, theater, canoeing, kayaking, fishing, golf courses, tennis, white-water rafting. **Amenities & Services** AC. Small parties and meetings can be hosted.

ACCOMMODATIONS
Units 4 guest rooms **All Rooms** Ceiling fans, sitting area or desk **Some Rooms** Bay window, fireplace, walk-in shower, stained-glass window **Bed & Bath** Queens (4), all private baths. **Favorites** Fireside Room w/ trundle & working fireplace **Comfort & Decor** Relax on this front porch and you may not want to leave. Ditto for the backyard patio, a small sanctuary that should appear in some home-design magazine. Inside, choose a spot near the living room's 8-foot windows.

RATES, RESERVATIONS, & RESTRICTIONS
Deposit 50% of total **Discounts** Corp. rate **Credit Cards** V, MC **Check-In/Out** 3 p.m./10:30 a.m. **Smoking** No **Pets** No (innkeeper has a quiet, friendly dog) **Kids** No **No-Nos** N/A **Minimum Stay** None **Open** All year **Hosts** Marsha Meyer, 320 S. Fifth St., Goshen 46528 **Phone** (219) 533-4258 **Email** marsh@npcc.net **Web** www.bedandbreakfast.com/bbc/p600253.asp

HOMESPUN COUNTRY INN, Nappanee

OVERALL ★★★★ | QUALITY ★★★★ | VALUE ★★★★★ | PRICE RANGE $59–$79

Naming guest rooms for their original occupants a century ago creates the sort of connection many guests look for in a bed-and-breakfast; that link is personalized with photos of those long-ago occupants in each of their rooms. Guests can even view the wedding china of the original owners, Frank and Alma Brown, and Alma's hand fan. A more contemporary artifact is the Art Deco cedar chest in the parlor, once owned by innkeeper Dianne Debelak's mother. Keepsakes of the inn are sold in the front parlor.

SETTING & FACILITIES
Location Central Nappanee, near the intersection of Rts. 19 and 6 **Near** Dutch Village, Amish Acres, Shipshewana Flea Market, Lake Wawasee **Building** 1902 Queen Anne w/ beveled glass windows **Grounds** Lawn, shrubs—city lot **Public Space** Foyer, TV room, LR, DR, porch **Food & Drink** Coffee, soft drinks, hot chocolate and "candy all over the house" any time. Full breakfast includes fruit plate, baked goods, & entree. **Recreation** Antiquing, flea marketing, Amish interests, historic touring, water sports. **Amenities & Services** AC, special-occasion packages. Two cordless phones are available for guest use.

ACCOMMODATIONS
Units 5 guest rooms **All Rooms** Sitting area, ceiling fan, cable TV/VCR, clock radio **Some Rooms** Pullout sofa, robes in room **Bed & Bath** Queens (3), double (1), 2 twins (1). All private baths. **Favorites** Miss Allman's Room w/ large bath, named for an elementary school teacher who rented the room a century ago, decorated w/ antique school memorabilia. **Comfort & Decor** Homespun has the classic Queen Anne elements—quarter-sawn oak trim, pocket doors, mantels, original oak floors, and some original light fixtures—all lovingly restored. The paneling in the foyer is hand-carved.

RATES, RESERVATIONS, & RESTRICTIONS
Deposit Credit card **Discounts** Special midweek rate, Mon.–Thurs. **Credit Cards** V, MC, D **Check-In/Out** 4–6 p.m./10 a.m. **Smoking** Only on porch **Pets** No **Kids** By arrangement and if supervised **No-Nos** N/A **Minimum Stay** None **Open** All year **Hosts** Dennis & Dianne Debelak, 302 N. Main, Nappanee 46550 **Phone** Toll-free (800) 311-2996 or (219) 773-2034 **Email** home@hoosierlink.net **Web** www.homespuninn.com

VICTORIAN GUEST HOUSE, Nappanee

OVERALL ★★★★ | QUALITY ★★★★ | VALUE ★★★★ | PRICE RANGE $69–$149

The lush woods in this inn make sense: Frank Coppes, the original owner, was a renowned cabinetmaker. Furnishings are well chosen—Eastlake seating, ornamental iron bed, soft pinks and purples in several rooms—and custom touches, such as the original stained-glass sconce and swinging door, survived changes to the home. Racks of clothes for sale in the living room, however, detract from the features we should be noticing. (The innkeeper paints designs on clothing items, then offers them for sale.) They cheapen the room—removing them would greatly improve the ambience.

SETTING & FACILITIES

Location 2 blocks from Nappanee's town square **Near** Amish Acres, Dutch Village, Shipshewana Flea Market, Lake Wawasee **Building** 1887 Victorian w/ pink exterior, on National Register of Historic Places **Grounds** Lawn, flower beds—city lot **Public Space** Foyer, great room/DR, porch **Food & Drink** Cider, hot beverages, snack in evening. Full breakfast includes dishes such as crab quiche and poppyseed bread **Recreation** Antiquing, flea marketing, Amish interests, historic touring, water sports. **Amenities & Services** AC. Sells dolls & painted clothes in great room. Weddings, showers, business meetings, private parties can be arranged.

ACCOMMODATIONS

Units 1 suite, 5 guest rooms **All Rooms** TV, ceiling fan, sitting area, phones **Some Rooms** Pullout sofa, claw-foot tub, pull-chain toilet, stained-glass window, private balcony **Bed & Bath** Queens (6), single (1 in suite), day bed **Favorites** Coppes Suite with large bath, four-poster bed, stained glass window, 110-year-old tub **Comfort & Decor** A wall was knocked out between two parlors, giving the first floor much more openness. The mantel and trim throughout the first floor are quarter-sawed oak, and we loved the huge dining room table, original to the house.

RATES, RESERVATIONS, & RESTRICTIONS

Deposit Credit card **Discounts** None **Credit Cards** V, MC, D **Check-In/Out** 4 p.m./10 a.m. **Smoking** No **Pets** No **Kids** Occasionally by arrangement; an extra $25 is charged if the child is a 3rd person. **No-Nos** No **Minimum Stay** On select holiday weekends **Open** All year **Hosts** Bruce & Vickie Hunsberger, 302 E. Market St., Nappanee 46550 **Phone** (219) 773-4383 **Email** vghouse@npcc.net **Web** victorianb-b.com

OL' BARN BED & BREAKFAST, Goshen

OVERALL ★★★★ | QUALITY ★★★★ | VALUE ★★★★★ | PRICE RANGE $69–$75

The Ol' Barn—actually dismantled and moved to its present location with much help from family, friends, and Amish barn builders—is located in the heart of Indiana's Amish country. Both innkeepers had Amish grandparents, so their ties to the community are strong. If you're lucky, you'll arrive just in time to see Lynette's freshly baked donuts cooling on the rack.

SETTING & FACILITIES

Location On CR 33, just east of Goshen **Near** Goshen city center, Shipshewana Flea Market, the Old Bag factory, Amish country **Building** Approx. 1880 barn, rebuilt & moved in 1990 **Grounds** 9 acres, including 2 wooded acres w/ walking trails, 7 acres of soybeans, corn, & meadow **Public Space** Entry, DR, guest kitchenette, cupola **Food & Drink** Early coffee;

sodas, coffee available any time. Full breakfast includes egg dish, baked oatmeal. **Recreation** Antiquing, historic & Amish touring, opera. **Amenities & Services** Logo soaps

ACCOMMODATIONS
Units 2 guest rooms **All Rooms** AC. Whirlpool tub, TV, ceiling fan, sitting area. **Some Rooms** VCR. **Bed & Bath** Queens (2), both private baths. **Favorites** The Loft, because it's larger. **Comfort & Decor** The style in the barn is "tasteful country." Bed coverings are hand-sewn quilts. A shared kitchenette contains table and chairs, microwave, guest fridge, and a small window looking onto the host family's private quarters. Don't leave without taking your turn on the rope swing; it hangs from the highest open point in the building, actually located in the innkeepers' area, but guests are invited to give it a whirl.

RATES, RESERVATIONS, & RESTRICTIONS
Deposit 1 night's stay **Discounts** Weekly **Credit Cards** Call ahead **Check-In/Out** 4–6 p.m./noon, or by prior arrangement **Smoking** Outside **Pets** No **Kids** Yes **No-Nos** N/A **Minimum Stay** None **Open** All year **Hosts** Conrad & Lynette Showalter, 63469 CR 33, Goshen 46528 **Phone** (219) 642-3222 **Email** clshowal@bnin.net **Web** www. amishcountry.org

M & N BED & BREAKFAST, LaGrange

OVERALL ★★★★ | QUALITY ★★★★ | VALUE ★★★★★ | PRICE RANGE $59

Sentiment rules in this home, whose flowers once grew in the garden of the innkeeper's grandmother, and Victorian teas are hosted regularly. With fitness center privileges, a full breakfast for up to three people, and home-baked cookies in the afternoon, we don't know how the Carneys can afford to operate; it's a lovely home and a perfect base for Shipshewana flea marketers. Don't miss Sam's pencil sharpener collection.

SETTING & FACILITIES
Location Just off IN 20, halfway between South Bend & Fort Wayne **Near** Shipshewana Flea Market, horse auction, historic & Amish touring **Building** 1869 Victorian, brick exterior, white exterior, w/ 1871 addition **Grounds** Old-fashioned garden, gazebo, goldfish pond, patio **Public Space** Porch, DR, LR, foyer **Food & Drink** Early coffee delivered upstairs, evening coffee & tea served, welcome snack. Full breakfast includes assortment of home-baked breads, hot entree, dessert. **Recreation** Antiquing, Amish & historic touring, golf courses. **Amenities & Services** AC. Robes in rooms; stocked guest fridge. Guests have complimentary use of the nearby fitness center.

ACCOMMODATIONS
Units 3 guest rooms, 1 guest cottage. **All Rooms** Cable TV, ceiling fans, sitting area. **Some Rooms** Claw-foot tub, desk, & chair. **Bed & Bath** Queen & single (3), all private baths (1 detached). **Favorites** Wicker Room, for sentimental reasons—the innkeeper's grandmother made the quilt bed covering before the innkeeper was born. **Comfort & Decor** Victorian and country mix easily in this home, adorned with ornate Eastlake-style oak and hickory woodwork, a faux marble fireplace in the living room, recliners, and delicate wicker

furniture on the porch. In the foyer, the trim is faux burled walnut, and more warm wood greets guests in the Third Room—an antique birds-eye maple sleigh bed and dresser.

RATES, RESERVATIONS, & RESTRICTIONS

Deposit Credit card number. **Discounts** None **Credit Cards** V, MC, D, AE **Check-In/Out** 2 p.m./2 p.m. or by individual arrangement **Smoking** On porch only **Pets** No **Kids** Yes **No-Nos** N/A **Minimum Stay** None **Open** All year **Hosts** Sam & Estella Carney, 215 North Detroit, LaGrange 46761 **Phone** (219) 463-2961 or (219) 463-2699 **Email** N/A

PRAIRIE HOUSE BED & BREAKFAST, Leesburg

OVERALL ★★★★ | QUALITY ★★★★ | VALUE ★★★★★ | PRICE RANGE $45–$65

The spaciousness of the public areas of Prairie House is striking; guests can easily find a spot for a private talk without retreating to their room. Most like to congregate in the lower-level common room, equipped with TV/VCR, a guest kitchen, table tennis, and an exercise bike. They're also invited to read or use the piano in the music room. The dining room table is an old hickory piece that seats 18; it's always topped with fresh flowers.

SETTING & FACILITIES

Location 1 mi. off IN 15 **Near** Shipshewana Flea Market, biblical Gardens, Winona Lake Historical Area, Amish country **Building** 1974 ranch home, remodeled 1995 **Grounds** 7,000-acre farm, raising tomatoes, corns, beans; flower beds, gazebo **Public Space** Entry room, DR, LR, music room, patio, lower-level common room **Food & Drink** Coffee & soda any time, evening snack. Full breakfast includes hot entree & breakfast meat. **Recreation** Amish & historic touring, birding, canoeing, fishing, swimming, horseback riding. **Amenities & Services** AC. Logo soaps, hair dryers, fresh flowers in rooms. Farm tours & small-meeting facilities available to 10 people.

ACCOMMODATIONS

Units 4 guest rooms. **All Rooms** Clock radio, sitting area. **Some Rooms** Robes, desk & chair, private entry, skylights. **Bed & Bath** Queens (2), double (1), twin (1). All private baths. **Favorites** Room 1, for its spaciousness, desk, private access. **Comfort & Decor** It's refreshing to be in a modest but lovely home that doesn't try to be something it isn't. Everett and Marie Tom choose instead to add personal, pleasurable touches to their ranch house: an Eastlake family heirloom organ in the entry, a piano in the music room, a stone fireplace in the common room. Notice Marie's framed Sears & Roebuck "Cinderella dress" on display.

RATES, RESERVATIONS, & RESTRICTIONS

Deposit 1st night's stay. **Discounts** Multiple nights. **Credit Cards** V, MC. **Check-In/Out** 4–6 p.m./11 a.m. **Smoking** No **Pets** No; resident cat is permitted in guest areas **Kids** Inquire **No-Nos** No alcoholic beverages permitted in the home **Minimum Stay** None **Open** All year **Hosts** Everett & Marie Tom, 495 East 900 North, Leesburg 46538 **Phone** (219) 658-9211 **Fax** (219) 453-4787 **Email** marietom3@yahoo.com **Web** www.prairiehouse.net

FRUITT BASKET INN, North Manchester

OVERALL ★★★½ | QUALITY ★★★★ | VALUE ★★★★ | PRICE RANGE $65–$75

Interesting features give Fruitt Basket Inn its unique look, including elaborate original fretwork on the first floor and the tiered, Greek-pattern mantel of the dining room fireplace. A guest telephone and fridge are located in the second-floor lounge. In the History Room, the innkeepers showed ingenuity by creating an Eastlake-style shelf, actually a headboard from an old twin bed, turned upside-down and mounted on the wall. The Fruitts also own a home-based interior decorating business.

SETTING & FACILITIES
Location Residential North Manchester, just off Rt. 114 **Near** Wabash River, Amish country **Building** 1904 Arts & Crafts/Victorian mix, white exterior **Grounds** City lot; flower beds, shrubs **Public Space** Parlor, LR, DR, turret "tea room," 2nd-floor lounge **Food & Drink** Soft drinks any time. Full breakfast includes hot breads, egg dish, breakfast meat. **Recreation** Canoeing, swimming, Amish touring, antiquing. **Amenities & Services** AC.

ACCOMMODATIONS
Units 4 guest rooms. **All Rooms** Ceiling fan, clock, sitting area. **Some Rooms** Bay window, window seat. **Bed & Bath** Kings (2), queen (1), double (1). All private baths. **Favorites** History Room because of its antiques, including an old Victrola and a 150-year-old cradle. **Comfort & Decor** The Fruitts are collectors, and that passion is on display here. The most interesting are the glass pieces in the dining room and Randy's collection of fruit plates. The home's original features, including pocket doors, column partition between the foyer and parlor, and egg-and-dart trim throughout, make a comfortable backdrop.

RATES, RESERVATIONS, & RESTRICTIONS
Deposit Credit card number **Discounts** None **Credit Cards** V, MC **Check-In/Out** Flexible; arrange at time of reservation **Smoking** On porch **Pets** No **Kids** Yes **No-Nos** N/A **Minimum Stay** None **Open** All year **Hosts** Randy & Sharon Fruitt, 116 West Main St., North Manchester 46962 **Phone** (219) 982-2443 **Fax** (219) 982-2443 **Email** fbinn@hoosierlink.net

ROSEWOOD MANSION INN, Peru

OVERALL ★★★★½ | QUALITY ★★★★½ | VALUE ★★★★★ | PRICE RANGE $75–$90

This is one of those homes where guests are transported back to a time of grandeur and grace. From the antique velvet furnishings and wood-burning fireplace in the library, to the bowed walls of the "tower" rooms, we felt the pull of romance and history in this home. Guest rooms are designed to attract both leisure and business travelers with data ports and ample desk space.

SETTING & FACILITIES
Location Residential Peru near downtown, off Rt. 24. **Near** Cole Porter Birthplace and Burial Site, Mississinewa Reservoir, International Circus Hall of Fame **Building** 1880 brick Jacobean mansion w/ Eastlake exterior trim **Grounds** Shares a city block with another mansion; lawns, flower beds **Public Space** DR, LR, parlor, library, guest butler pantry **Food & Drink** Soda, coffee, snacks available any time in pantry. Breakfast is deluxe cont'l, with home-baked breads & fruits. **Recreation** Historic touring, museums, fishing, water-skiing, swimming, biking, antiquing, golf. **Amenities & Services** AC. Fax, copy services; can accommodate business meetings.

ACCOMMODATIONS
Units 10 guest rooms & carriage house. **All Rooms** Phone, TV, sitting area, clock radio. **Some Rooms** Fireplace (some of Italian marble), daybed, desk & chair, couch, closet w/ built-in drawers & cupboards. **Bed & Bath** King (1), queens (7), doubles (2), twin (1). All private baths. **Favorites** Victoria's Suite, sunny corner room w/ window seats flanking the queen-size iron bed, desk & chair. **Comfort & Decor** This mansion was designed for glamour. Quarter-sawed tiger oak trim and paneling greet guests in the foyer; their eyes are immediately drawn to the spectacular three-story staircase with a stained-glass panel at the landing rumored to be a Tiffany. The dining room is round and anchored by a massive chandelier—a sumptuous touch. Our elegance rating would be much higher with updating; replacing the torn, worn carpet will make a world of difference.

RATES, RESERVATIONS, & RESTRICTIONS
Deposit Credit card number **Discounts** $20 discount for single travelers **Credit Cards** V, MC, D, AE **Check-In/Out** 2 p.m./11 a.m. **Smoking** In library **Pets** No **Kids** Yes **No-Nos** N/A **Minimum Stay** None **Open** All year **Hosts** David & Lynn Hausner, 54 North Hood St., Peru 46970 **Phone** (765) 472-7151 **Fax** (765) 472-5575 **Email** rosewood@ cqc.com **Web** www.rosewoodmansion.com

LAMP POST INN, Wabash

OVERALL ★★★★ | QUALITY ★★★★ | VALUE ★★★★★ | PRICE RANGE $50–$65

The mere chance to stare at Lamp Post Inn's exterior for a couple of days makes it worth visiting this place. The Wedgwood-style sandstone turret windows are a spectacle in themselves, with curved glass and wrought-iron toppers. Flanking the windows and stone porch, one slowly becomes aware of ornamental architectural elements: angels, urns, seahorses, guys with beards. The windows are no less impressive when viewed indoors, in the living room and Pink Room. An original globe fixture lights the foyer, where ceilings reach 12 feet, set off by original oak trim and paneling.

SETTING & FACILITIES
Location 6 blocks west of Rts. 15 & 13 in central Wabash **Near** Honeywell Center, library, historical museum **Building** 1895 Romanesque home of Indiana sandstone, w/

Bluestone porch **Grounds** Shady city lot w/ shrubs, flagstone terrace, brick patio **Public Space** Foyer, LR, DR, entry **Food & Drink** Sodas available any time. Full breakfast includes entree such as Belgian waffles. **Recreation** Historical touring, swimming, golf. **Amenities & Services** AC. White noise machine, CD player in rooms.

ACCOMMODATIONS
Units 4 guest rooms. **All Rooms** Clock, phone, ceiling fan, sitting area. **Some Rooms** Fireplace, claw-foot tub. **Bed & Bath** Queens (2; 1 w/ pillowtop mattress), double (1), double plus twin (1). All private baths. **Favorites** Pink Room, because of the turret window; also features a lounging area & true grandfather four-poster bed. **Comfort & Decor** A home couldn't make a better first impression. First, the turret windows make the visitor gasp (they're really quite extraordinary!). The eight-foot oval, beveled-glass window in the giant front door seals the impact. Most furnishings are fine antiques—pedestal or marble lavatory, wrought-iron bed, antique chandelier in the dining room—of a quality that's appropriate to their setting.

RATES, RESERVATIONS, & RESTRICTIONS
Deposit 1 night's stay **Discounts** Corp. **Credit Cards** V, MC **Check-In/Out** Noon/noon **Smoking** Outside **Pets** At innkeeper's discretion **Kids** At innkeeper's discretion **No-Nos** N/A **Minimum Stay** None **Open** All year. **Host** Janet Conner, 261 West Hill St., Wabash 46992 **Phone** (219) 563-3094 **Email** lamppostbb@comteck.com

Central Indiana

This is Indiana's zone of cities—**Terre Haute, Indianapolis, Blooming-ton, Columbus, Muncie**—and barely there hamlets, such as **Perrysville** and **Ladoga.** This is mostly flat land of farms and forest, and even the city-side bed-and-breakfasts have a family-gathering feel.

Tourism is big business in Indianapolis—the zoo and children's museum are a draw, and of course the Indy 500—but because we already knew about those attractions, we explored the suburbs and beyond.

Bloomington, about 50 miles southeast of Indianapolis, is home to **Indi-ana University,** but it's known as more than just a college town. Several miles outside the city lie **three major lakes—Lemon, Griffy, and Mon-roe**—that are renowned destinations for fishing, camping, and wildlife. Lake Monroe is especially famous for its annual crappie tournaments. The city's museums, too, bring visitors, particularly the internationally recog-nized **Lilly Library,** featuring a pre-1456 Gutenberg Bible on continuing exhibit; the **Hoagy Carmichael Museum** on campus; and **Indiana Uni-versity's Art Museum,** designed by I. M. Pei and housing works by Pablo Picasso and Claude Monet.

Leaving Bloomingtom, the antiquing heats up again as one gets near **Nashville.** The terrain is hilly in **Brown County,** a bit more rugged than the farm country, and the centerpiece is Nashville. Settled as an art colony early in the twentieth century, Nashville today is a shopper's mecca, with more than 300 shops, galleries, and studios lining the narrow streets. We visited in early November, when the shops still were open all day but most of the tourists had gone home.

In Nashville, most bed-and-breakfasts are private homes, though several establishments are larger, such as the **Artists Colony Inn.** Any location there is as good as the next; the entire town is only ten blocks long.

Half an hour west is Columbus, possibly the most visually interesting city we visited. In 1942, a local church received national attention for its modern design. Over the years, the Cummins Foundation offered to pay the architect fees for other public buildings, bringing in the biggest names—Eero Saarinen, I. M. Pei, Richard Meier—and famous artists such as Dale Chihuly and Henry Moore to create public art. All of this effort was to create a small city that is deliberately "different by design."

The bed-and-breakfasts in Columbus—a refurbished downtown Art Deco hotel and a sumptuous Greek Revival—are beautifully juxtaposed in style. Two worthwhile historic destinations, Metamora and the Conner Prairie Pioneer Settlement are both informative, "living history" communities. Metamora's Thorpe House was more rustic than the Frederick-Talbott Inn across from Conner Prairie, but it's also a much older inn.

RUDDICK-NUGENT HOUSE, Columbus

OVERALL ★★★★½ | QUALITY ★★★★½ | VALUE ★★★★★ | PRICE RANGE **$69–$99**

The Orwins are well traveled, so mementoes of their journeys are displayed throughout the house—and they blend well, even the African display from Dennis's long-ago years in the Peace Corps. The dining room has a Far Eastern flavor and a Federal-style fireplace—but the home has survived far greater identity crises, particularly when Lizzie Ruddick converted the home's exterior to Colonial Revival, using massive columns salvaged from the 1904 St. Louis Exposition. It's eclectic and it all works.

SETTING & FACILITIES

Location Off US 31 in residential Columbus **Near** Columbus, a renowned modern-architecture showplace; city parks, golf courses. **Building** 1884 Victorian w/ facade rebuilt to look neoclassical/Colonial Revival **Grounds** Entire city block of gardens (including a "literary rose garden," growing only varieties named after authors & fictional characters), statuary, fountains, lawns. **Public Space** Porches, foyer, DR, LR **Food & Drink** Complimentary soda, snacks in room; full candlelight breakfast (served family-style) includes gourmet coffee, several juices, several breads, entrees such as bananas Foster eggs or honey-mustard eggs. **Recreation** Antiquing, historical & architectural touring. **Amenities & Services** Hair dryers, smoke masks in rooms, AC.

ACCOMMODATIONS

Units 3 guest rooms, 1 suite **All Rooms** Phone, TV/VCR, sitting area **Some Rooms** Jet bath, fireplace, sitting room, claw-foot tub, balcony overlooking the rose garden **Bed & Bath** King or 2 twins (1), queens (3) **Favorites** Martha's room with large jetted tub, marbleized cast-iron fireplace & headboard made from the original front doors of the home. **Comfort & Decor** Two "eternal flames" light the way through this beautiful home—lighted newel posts with oak and brass lamps, always casting a flickering glow over the leaded glass, bull's-eye moldings, and original crown molding in the first floor. A green slate Eastlake fireplace graces the dining room.

RATES, RESERVATIONS, & RESTRICTIONS

Deposit Credit card number **Discounts** Long-term, repeat guests, corp. & gov't per diem rates. Special off-season & holiday packages. **Credit Cards** V, MC, D, AE **Check-In/Out** 3–6 p.m./11 a.m. **Smoking** No **Pets** No (resident cat stays in innkeepers' quarters) **Kids** Yes **No-Nos** N/A **Minimum Stay** None **Open** All year **Hosts** Dennis & Joyce Orwin, 1210 16th St., Columbus 47201 **Phone** (812) 379-1354 or toll-free (800) 814-7478 **Fax** (812) 379-1357 **Email** innkeepers@ruddick-nugent-house.com **Web** www.ruddick-nugent-house.com

TRANQUIL CHERUB BED & BREAKFAST, Indianapolis

OVERALL ★★★★ | QUALITY ★★★★ | VALUE ★★★★ | PRICE RANGE $85–$140

Reuse of interesting antiques is a rare skill that these innkeepers have mastered. A hand-operated clothes washer now serves as an end table, a twin cradle becomes a coffee table, a TV stand was once a cream separator, and the desk in the foyer is an 1870 Victorian Eastlake organ. Another fun feature are the U.S. and world maps hanging in the upstairs common room; guests are invited to stick pins in their hometowns.

SETTING & FACILITIES

Location Near I-65 & US 31 in residential Indianapolis **Near** Indianapolis Zoo, downtown, Convention Center, Children's Museum, Indianapolis Motor Speedway, NCAA Hall of Champions, Butler Univ., White River State Park **Building** 1890 Classical Revival **Grounds** Flower beds, small pond **Public Space** Front porch, foyer, parlor, DR, 2nd-floor common room w/ TV **Food & Drink** Juices, soft drinks, snacks available any time. Full breakfast includes muffins, entree such as stuffed French toast, potato, & breakfast meat. **Recreation** Museums, spectator car racing & other sports, birding **Amenities & Services** Robes in rooms, logo bath amenities, hair dryers, AC

ACCOMMODATIONS

Units 1 suite, 3 guest rooms **All Rooms** Dataports, sitting area **Some Rooms** TV, phone **Bed & Bath** King (2), queen (2). All private baths. **Favorites** Gatsby Room w/ four-poster cannonball bed, 1930 square soaking tub, and Art Deco dresser & vanity **Comfort & Decor** The theme is cherubs—not angels, but cherubs. This house is blessed with dozens (if not hundreds) but they don't overpower—they just hang in the background, looking pudgy. The angelic wall covering in the dining room is adorable. Contrast it with the stairwell photos of a generations-ago medical school "gross anatomy" class—ick.

RATES, RESERVATIONS, & RESTRICTIONS

Deposit Credit card or 1 night's stay **Discounts** Corp. & gov't. per diem rates **Credit Cards** V, MC, D, AE **Check-In/Out** 4–6 p.m./noon **Smoking** On porch only **Pets** No (resident dog, cat, & canary live on premises) **Kids** Occasionally, by prior arrangement **No-Nos** No **Minimum Stay** On special occasions. 3-day min. required during Indy 500 weekend. **Open** All year **Hosts** Barb & Thom Feit, 2164 North Capitol Ave., Indianapolis 46202 **Phone** (317) 923-9036 **Fax** (317) 923-8676 **Email** host@tranquilcherub.com **Web** www.tranquilcherub.com

COUNTRY GABLES BED & BREAKFAST, *Zionsville*

OVERALL ★★★★½ | QUALITY ★★★★½ | VALUE ★★★★★ | PRICE RANGE
$68–$115 OFF-SEASON, $88–$135 IN SEASON

This inn promotes a "warm, family-oriented environment" and, according to their literature, "will accommodate unmarried couples in separate sleeping rooms." Aside from that values-based overtone, however, we found

Country Gables to be a delightful spot. It feels secluded, though downtown Indy is just 20 minutes away, and historic Zionsville, known for its antiquing, is one mile away. The setting and style of the home reminded us of a country getaway in Sonoma or rural Pennsylvania—so much greenery!

SETTING & FACILITIES
Location Rt. 334 between I-65 & US 421 **Near** White River Park, Indianapolis Children's Museum, Museum of Art, Indianapolis Motor Speedway **Building** Restored late-1800s Victorian farmhouse **Grounds** 3 acres of sprawling lawns, flower beds, vegetable garden, deck, fountain, gazebo **Public Space** Entry, porches, breakfast room, deck, parlor, reading room, LR **Food & Drink** Welcome basket of fruit, homemade cookies, snacks; evening dessert; soft drinks available any time. Full breakfast includes home-baked bread or scones, eggs or quiche, waffles or pancakes, sausage, fruits, served on antique china w/ fresh flowers & soft music. **Recreation** Historic interests, antiquing, museums, spectator professional & amateur sports, birding, cross-country skiing. **Amenities & Services** AC. Hair dryers, bath amenities. Fax service available.

ACCOMMODATIONS
Units 3 suites **All Rooms** sitting rooms, cable TV, VCR, videos, phones, modem jack, chair & table or desk **Some Rooms** Office layout, DVD, CD player, microwave, refrigerator, kitchen w/ dishwasher, disposer, coffeemaker, cooking & eating utensils, piano. **Bed & Bath** Queen & full-sized sofa bed (1), queen (1), double (1), all private baths. **Favorites** Helen Mabel Suite, w/ 3 rooms (750 sq. ft.), private entrance from wraparound porch, modern kitchen & dining area **Comfort & Decor** Innkeeper Garland Elmore built much of the furniture in the suites, including desks and cabinetry. The decor is tasteful country, with a blend of quilt or cutwork bed coverings, antiques, and more contemporary-style furnishings.

RATES, RESERVATIONS, & RESTRICTIONS
Deposit 1 night's stay **Discounts** 3-night stays are discounted 10%; also single & extended-stay rates. **Credit Cards** V, MC **Check-In/Out** 4 p.m./noon **Smoking** Outside **Pets** No (resident dog is quiet) **Kids** Yes **No-Nos** N/A **Minimum Stay** None **Open** All

year **Hosts** Jean & Garland Elmore, 9302 St. Rt. 334, Zionsville 46077 **Phone** (317) 873-5382 **Email** Innkeeper@countrygables.com **Web** www.countrygables.com

SCHOLARS INN, Bloomington

OVERALL ★★★★ | QUALITY ★★★★½ | VALUE ★★★★ | PRICE RANGE $79–$125

Perched on a hill overlooking the busy one-way street, Scholars Inn looks like a distinguished professor's home—elderly and aloof yet engaging. Next door, a 150-year-old mansion serves as the Scholars Inn Gourmet Cafe and Wine Bar and is the sort of noisy, crowded eatery one expects to find on the East Coast; in tweed-jacket Bloomington it's a pleasant surprise. Wine tastings, a summer jazz concert series, and an expansive dessert menu eliminate any hints of stuffiness. The setting is elegant, but come for fun.

SETTING & FACILITIES
Location 5 blocks from downtown Bloomington, near Indiana Univ. **Near** Museums, college sports events **Building** 1900 brick mansion **Grounds** Patios, back lawn, flower gardens **Public Space** Foyer, LR/DR w/ fireplace, terraces **Food & Drink** Cookies, coffee, soda all day. Full breakfast includes fresh pastry from owners' bakery & hot entree. On Sundays, scones & coffee available 8 a.m., then guests can use $20 vouchers for brunch or lunch at owners' restaurant next door. **Recreation** Sports events, fine arts, historic touring **Amenities & Services** AC, robes in rooms, hair dryers. Breakfast delivered to guest rooms, fax & private phone available. Indiana Univ. theater or basketball tickets sometimes included with night's stay; formal teas served twice monthly.

ACCOMMODATIONS
Units 6 guest rooms **All Rooms** Cable TV, VCR, ceiling fans, desk or sitting area **Some Rooms** Jacuzzi, fireplace, private terrace entrance **Bed & Bath** Kings (5), queen (1), all with pillowtop mattresses; all private baths. **Favorites** Garden Room, with ceramic tile floor, stone wall fountain, private stone patio and sitting area in bath. **Comfort & Decor** The style here in casual elegance, attracting an upscale clientele of visiting academics, business travelers, and parents of students. Oriental rugs and warm woods dominate the decor; one guest room features the schoolmaster's armoire from the movie Hoosiers.

RATES, RESERVATIONS, & RESTRICTIONS
Deposit Credit card number or 50% of stay. **Discounts** Corp. rates, midweek multiple-day rates. **Credit Cards** V, MC, D **Check-In/Out** After 3 p.m. or by arrangement/11 a.m. **Smoking** No **Pets** No (resident dog) **Kids** Over age 12, younger by special arrangement **No-Nos** N/A **Minimum Stay** 2 nights on special weekends **Open** All year **Hosts** Lyle & Kerry Feigenbaum, 801 North College, Bloomington 47404 **Phone** (812) 332-1892 or toll-free (800) 765-3466 **Fax** (812) 335-1490 **Email** scholarsinn@earthlink.com **Web** www.scholarsinn.com

FREDERICK-TALBOTT INN AT THE PRAIRIE, Fishers

OVERALL ★★★★ | QUALITY ★★★★ | VALUE ★★★★ | PRICE RANGE $99–$199

Restoring the Frederick-Talbott as a bed-and-breakfast was a five-year effort for Muller and Irvine, who were next-door neighbors as children. They oversaw every detail of the renovation, even ensuring that the stairs were wide enough to accommodate a person toting suitcases. A 1906 cottage on the grounds houses the kitchen, breakfast room, and honeymoon suite. They specialize in hosting group weekends; two of their favorites are quilters and scrapbookers, who "sit there long into the night, snipping and pasting," Muller says. "You've never seen a happier bunch of women."

SETTING & FACILITIES

Location 20 mi. north of Indianapolis, 6 mi. north of I-465 Exit 35 **Near** Conner Prairie Museum (living history museum), Benjamin Harrison House **Building** 1875 farmhouse, teal clapboard **Grounds** Courtyard, flower beds **Public Space** Upstairs sitting room, deck, sun porch/breakfast room, conference room, business DR **Food & Drink** Coffee station w/ soda, hot drinks, homemade cookies all day. Buffet breakfast typically includes an egg dish, French toast, potatoes, homemade muffins, breakfast meats. **Recreation** Historic touring, art museums, pro sports (Indianapolis Motor Speedway, Indiana Pacers, Indianapolis Colts, Indianapolis Fever basketball), children's museum, zoo, Indianapolis symphony, opera & live theater. **Amenities & Services** Hair dryers in rooms, logo bath amenities, meeting facilities for up to 24.

ACCOMMODATIONS

Units 10 guest rooms **All Rooms** AC, cable TV, phone **Some Rooms** Writing desk, fireplace **Bed & Bath** Kings (4), queens (5), 2 queens (1), all private baths. **Favorites** Honeymoon Suite, w/ Jacuzzi, daybed, oversized shower; the Hamilton Room, with an entry ceiling border of vintage hats. **Comfort & Decor** The theme is country, though rooms are individually decorated with nostalgic "finds" from Indianapolis-area tea rooms and other businesses that folded.

RATES, RESERVATIONS, & RESTRICTIONS

Deposit Credit card number. **Discounts** Corporate rates available **Credit Cards** V, MC, D, AE **Check-In/Out** 3 p.m./11 a.m. **Smoking** Designated areas only. **Pets** Yes—please inquire. **Kids** Yes—please inquire. **No-Nos** N/A **Minimum Stay** On select weekends, such as Indy race weekends. Inquire. **Open** All year **Hosts** Susan Muller & Ann Irvine, 13805 Allisonville Rd., Fishers 46038 **Phone** (317) 578-3600 or toll-free (800) 566-beds (2337) **Fax** (317) 578-3600 **Email** fredtal@indy.net **Web** www.fredericktalbottinn.com

LOOKING GLASS INN, Indianapolis

OVERALL ★★★½ | QUALITY ★★★★ | VALUE ★★★★ | PRICE RANGE $105–$135

After naming her first bed-and-breakfast (see the next listing) for her favorite childhood story ("Stone Soup"), innkeeper Jeneane Life decided to continue the theme with Looking Glass Inn, just a few doors from Stone Soup. This inn is designed to take any visitors, from singles to families. Set in a historic area perfect for strolling, both properties have been favorably reviewed in national publications, including Country Inns magazine and the New York Times Travel section. In restoring Looking Glass, Life was able to save the home's best features, including original fireplaces, stained glass, moldings, and pocket doors. Special accommodations are made for guests needing an allergen-free environment.

SETTING & FACILITIES

Location Indianapolis, historic Old Northside neighborhood **Near** Zoo, children's museum, Indianapolis Motor Speedway, Convention Center, downtown Indianapolis **Building** 1905 Free Classic–style mansion w/ wine-red exterior **Grounds** City lot w/ flower beds, brick patio w/ fish pond **Public Space** Foyer, DR, sunroom, butler's pantry, LR, porch **Food & Drink** Snacks & nonalcoholic beverages in butler's pantry. Full breakfast includes hot entree. **Recreation** Museums, pro sports, antiquing. **Amenities & Services** Dry cleaning available, on-call massage therapists, phone w/ voicemail in rooms, fax & copy machines available. Wine gift baskets & flowers available on request; innkeepers speak German & Japanese.

ACCOMMODATIONS

Units 5 guest rooms, 1 suite. **All Rooms** Cable TV, VCR, bath amenities. **Some Rooms** Jacuzzi or double Jacuzzi, claw-foot tub; Hideaway Suite has fully equipped kitchen & LR. **Bed & Bath** Kings (1), king & 2 twins (or 4 twins, 1), queens (3), double (1). All private baths. **Favorites** Willow Room, w/ Empire-style antiques and queen sleigh bed. **Comfort & Decor** Victorian themes appear throughout this B&B, though not overwhelmingly so; just enough lace accents the rooms that, for the most part, allow the wood and architectural features—such as a tile fireplace in the Rose Room—proper spotlight.

RATES, RESERVATIONS, & RESTRICTIONS

Deposit 50% of stay **Discounts** Long-term stay **Credit Cards** V, MC, D, AE **Check-In/Out** By arrangement/11 a.m. **Smoking** Outside only **Pets** No **Kids** Yes **No-Nos** N/A **Minimum Stay** On special weekends **Open** All year **Hosts** Jeneane Life, 1319 North New Jersey St., Indianapolis 46202 **Phone** (317) 639-9550 **Fax** (317) 684-9536 **Email** stonesoupinn@iquest.net or through Web site **Web** www.stonesoupinn.com

STONE SOUP INN, Indianapolis

OVERALL ★★★★ | QUALITY ★★★½ | VALUE ★★★★★ | PRICE RANGE $85–$135

Innkeeper Life runs a seamless operation with two bed-and-breakfasts on the same block. We loved the Mission-style decor in Stone Soup's public spaces, with original quarter-sawed oak paneling, Mission oak chairs, and stained-glass windows. We were especially drawn to the Mission-furnished sitting area on the second floor. The floor lamp in the dining room is a special piece. We felt we had to lower ratings on this one for the shared baths and continental breakfasts, but it's a beautiful home nonetheless.

SETTING & FACILITIES
Location Historic Old Northside neighborhood **Near** Zoo, children's museum, Indianapolis Motor Speedway, Convention Center, downtown Indianapolis **Building** Modified Tudor, turn-of-century **Grounds** 0.75 acre, flower beds, pond **Public Space** Library, LR, DR, foyer, sunroom, 2nd-floor sitting area **Food & Drink** Soda, snacks any time. Weekdays, cont'l breakfast; full breakfast weekends w/ hot entree. **Recreation** Museums, pro sports, antiquing. **Amenities & Services** AC, on-call massage therapist, wine gift baskets & flowers available, fax & copy machines available. Phone w/ voicemail in rooms. Innkeepers speak German & Japanese.

ACCOMMODATIONS
Units 7 guest rooms **All Rooms** Cable TV/VCR **Some Rooms** Garden view, fireplace, Jacuzzi or double Jacuzzi **Bed & Bath** King (1), queens (5), double (1). 5 private baths, 1 shared. **Favorites** Lily Room, with bay window seat overlooking lily pond, wicker bedroom suite **Comfort & Decor** Guest rooms are individually decorated, mostly in Victorian or Craftsman antiques. Each offers some feature worth choosing it for; the Blue Room—the most spacious—features an ornate 6-foot-high headboard, and 2 others have window seats.

RATES, RESERVATIONS, & RESTRICTIONS
Deposit 50% of stay **Discounts** Long-term stay **Credit Cards** V, MC, D, AE **Check-In/Out** By arrangement/11 a.m. **Smoking** Outside only **Pets** No **Kids** Yes **No-Nos** N/A **Minimum Stay** On select weekends **Open** All year **Hosts** Jeneane Life, 1304 North Central Ave., Indianapolis 46202 **Phone** (317) 639-9550 **Fax** (317) 684-9536 **Email** stonesoupinn@iquest.net or through Web site **Web** www.stonesoupinn.com

ARTISTS COLONY INN, Nashville

OVERALL ★★★★ | QUALITY ★★★★½ | VALUE ★★ | PRICE RANGE $70–$170 GUEST ROOMS, $110–$250 SUITES

Artists Colony definitely is not without style and appeal. Nashville has been an art colony since the early 1900s, and pieces from the innkeepers' collection of those artists' work adorn the walls. Much care went into furnishing the inn using skills of local artisans. However, it's not a true bed-and-breakfast. Breakfast is not included during peak touring months—an inducement to get guests into the inn's on-site restaurant, serving three meals daily to the public—and there is no common room for relaxing. Nashville today is a crowded retail center with more shops selling commercial doodads, it seemed, than original art or handicrafts. We found the packed sidewalks and long lines oppressive.

SETTING & FACILITIES

Location In the heart of downtown Nashville **Near** Shops, museums, flea markets, winery **Building** 1992 wood-frame inn **Grounds** Flower beds **Public Space** Entry hall, restaurant, gift shop, roof hot tub deck **Food & Drink** Cont'l breakfast only included during off-season; no complimentary food or drink in summer. **Recreation** Galleries, flea marketing, antiquing, historical touring. **Amenities & Services** Individually controlled AC, rooftop hot tub, logo bath amenities. Conference facilities, handicapped-accessible rooms available.

ACCOMMODATIONS

Units 20 guest rooms, 3 suites **All Rooms** Phone, cable TV, Windsor table & chairs. **Some Rooms** Conference room, VCR, sitting area, sofa, private balcony. **Bed & Bath** All queens, all private baths. Suites include kitchenette w/ microwave, fridge, coffeemaker; 1 includes 2 queen beds. **Favorites** Ada Walter Shulz room with table for 4 & large private balcony looking down on downtown Nashville. **Comfort & Decor** Owner Ellen Carter, daughter of Indiana artist Frederick Rigley, named rooms after Hoosier artists and decorated the inn with their paintings. The style is 19th-century Shaker, with nearly 500 beds, cupboards, tables, and chairs custom-built by an Indiana woodworker; a Nashville weaver wove the rugs; and a local seamstress made the curtains and bed coverings.

RATES, RESERVATIONS, & RESTRICTIONS

Deposit 1 night's stay, due when reservation is made. **Discounts** Group rates & seasonal specials available. **Credit Cards** V, MC, AE **Check-In/Out** 4 p.m./noon **Smoking** In designated rooms **Pets** No **Kids** Yes **No-Nos** N/A **Minimum Stay** 2 nights most weekends **Open** All year **Hosts** Jay & Ellen Carter, P.O. Box 1099, Franklin & Van Buren, Nashville 47448 **Phone** (812) 988-0600 or toll-free (800) 737-0255 **Fax** (812) 988-9023 **Email** info@artistscolonyinn.com **Web** www.artistscolonyinn.com

ALWAYS INN BED & BREAKFAST, Nashville

OVERALL ★★★★ | QUALITY ★★★½ | VALUE ★★★ | PRICE RANGE $75–$200

We liked many things about Always Inn: the innkeeper, a transplant from the East Coast, loved conversation. Sitting on the deck, sipping wine from the winery a mile up the road and watching for deer (who never appeared) was great relaxing fun. Our room was quite cramped, however, and the toilet leaked; our impression was that the owner, who resides in California, needs to invest in an update. Most distressing was the innkeeper's boast that "no food is ever wasted here," and that he often recycles leftovers—even those left on guests' plates.

SETTING & FACILITIES
Location On IN 46 between Columbus and Nashville **Near** Nashville, Gnaw Bone, winery **Building** 1970s lodge with decks, patios **Grounds** 4 acres w/ paths, flower gardens, deer-watching spots, hot tub gazebo **Public Space** Terraces, LR/DR, gazebo **Food & Drink** Complimentary soda any time. Full country breakfast includes egg dish, pastry, breakfast meat, fruit, home fries, sometimes popovers. **Recreation** Flea marketing, birding, deer-watching, antiquing. **Amenities & Services** Logo bath amenities, AC. Dinner prepared & delivered to room for special occasions. Computer, copy & fax machines available.

ACCOMMODATIONS
Units 5 guest rooms **All Rooms** Entry to deck or patio, cable TV, love seat or chairs. **Some Rooms** Jacuzzi, fireplace, sofa bed **Bed & Bath** King bed & queen sofa bed (1), queens (3), double (1). All private baths. **Favorites** White Pine Room w/ king bed, private entry to front balcony, VCR, queen-sized sofa bed, marble fireplace. **Comfort & Decor** All rooms are smaller than expected, but the only ones uncomfortably small (meaning, too small for space along both sides of the bed) were the rear first-floor rooms. Still, they opened onto a small patio and were a good vantage point for an evening deer-watch. All guest rooms are decorated in soft, muted colors with no specific theme but a strong Southwest influence.

RATES, RESERVATIONS, & RESTRICTIONS
Deposit 50% of stay **Discounts** AAA, senior, midweek, corp., off-season **Credit Cards** V, MC, AE, D. **Check-In/Out** 4–6 p.m. or by prior arrangement/11 a.m. **Smoking** Outside only **Pets** No **Kids** Age 12 and older, well-behaved **No-Nos** N/A **Minimum Stay** None **Open** All year **Hosts** Doug Clickenger, 8072 East IN 46, Nashville 47448 **Phone** (812) 988-2233 or toll-free (888) 457-2233 **Fax** (812) 988-9688 **Email** innkeeper@alwaysinn.com **Web** www.alwaysinn.com

Southern Indiana

You don't have to be a river buff to appreciate the towns along this slice of Indiana. The zone is bounded on three sides by the **Wabash and Ohio Rivers,** and the towns evoke images of riverboat gambling and **Huck Finn.** When we visited inland towns in Zone 4 , we were lucky enough to find some frankly spectacular historic properties in the middle of nowhere. In **Campbellsburg,** we wondered how such a rococo home as the **James Wilkins House** came to be built in a tiny crossroads where we saw not one other person during our stay. Huntingburg's Van Buren Street Inn presented a fine antiques sale and even finer buckwheat pancakes. In **West Baden,** a.k.a. Wellville, we thought we were on a movie set, the cityscape is that bizarre.

Along the river, **New Harmony** was a placid discovery—not surprisingly, as it was settled originally by a German communal group, the Harmonie Society, and later home to Utopians. It's not your predictable, run-of-the-mill historic tourist town; among its attractions are a meditation labyrinth.

Following the Ohio River east, we reach **Evansville**—a city of economic challenges but with a striking riverfront historic district, where the Tara-like Starkey Inn is located. By **Leavenworth,** the bluffs overlooking the river are high, making wonderful panoramas for front-porch gazing.

We found two additional towns memorable for different reasons. One is a few miles inland: **Corydon,** a National Historic District, is the site of the **Squire Boone Caverns,** where Daniel Boone's little brother narrowly escaped capture—a thrilling place of rushing underground streams, waterfalls, and formations. The other standout for us was **Madison,** a river town that has developed its waterfront intelligently, and it is accessible to everyone. It's a fun town to explore, with a winery, crafts shops, several antiques malls, and a variety of restaurants within a few blocks of the town center.

HUMMINGBIRD BED & BREAKFAST, Corydon

OVERALL ★★★★ | QUALITY ★★★★ | VALUE ★★★★ | PRICE RANGE $81–$95

All guest rooms but one are located on the third floor. The home is furnished in warm woods, mostly family artifacts, and the parlors are inviting places to pause before dinner. The Reading Parlor features a gas fireplace and Wurlitzer organ, and the more casual TV parlor has a VCR and large video library. Our favorite spot was the porch, fronting on Corydon's main street.

SETTING & FACILITIES

Location 3 blocks from Corydon town square **Near** Antiques shops, caves, winery, riverboat casino **Building** 1885 Victorian, gutted & restored, with pale yellow exterior **Grounds** City lot; flower gardens **Public Space** Foyer, DR, TV parlor, reading parlor, wraparound porch **Food & Drink** Full hot breakfast **Recreation** Antiquing, caving, gambling, birding, canoeing, historic touring **Amenities & Services** AC, morning newspaper, phone available.

ACCOMMODATIONS

Units 4 guest rooms **All Rooms** Clock radios, writing desk, sitting area **Some Rooms** Bay window **Bed & Bath** Doubles (3), 2 twins (1). All private baths. **Favorite** Seascape Room, for its open, airy ambience. **Comfort & Decor** Though the house was gutted, the wood trim, including bull's-eye molding, looks decades old. Hummingbird is furnished with many Eastlake antiques; the rails, with oak and walnut spindles, are original.

RATES, RESERVATIONS, & RESTRICTIONS

Deposit Full amount for 1 night's stay; 50% for 2 or more nights. **Discounts** None **Credit Cards** V, MC **Check-In/Out** 4–6 p.m./10:30 a.m.; early or late arrivals can be accommodated with notice. **Smoking** Outdoors in designated areas **Pets** No (resident cat is permitted throughout house) **Kids** Over age 12 **No-Nos** N/A **Minimum Stay**

None **Open** All year **Hosts** Jerry & Barbara Hess, 400 East Chestnut St., Corydon 47112 **Phone** (812) 738-0625 or toll-free (877) 422-0625 **Email** Through Web page **Web** www.corydon.iswired.com or www.tourindiana.com

KINTNER HOUSE INN, Corydon

OVERALL ★★★★½ | QUALITY ★★★★½ | VALUE ★★★★★ | PRICE RANGE
$49–$79 WEEKDAYS, $59–$99 WEEKENDS; CHILDREN UNDER AGE 12 STAY FREE

Guests "live" in post–Civil War Indiana at Kintner House. We easily imagined sharing the parlor with visiting statesmen doing business just across the road in the state's first Capitol building. Rooms are furnished with antiques of the highest quality, but we loved the spacious, inexpensive third-floor rooms, some renting for just $49 and featuring hand-sewn quilt coverlets. One favorite was the Lincoln Suite with its elaborate, double-shelf columned fireplace. It wasn't easy to leave those wonderful rooms to tackle downtown Corydon's antiques malls, but we forced ourselves.

SETTING & FACILITIES
Location In the center of historic downtown Corydon **Near** Museums, antiques malls, live theater, fairgrounds, glass factory, nature reserve **Building** 1873 brick inn, on National Register of Historic Places **Grounds** Small city lot; flower beds **Public Space** Porch, DR, TV parlor, entry, registration parlor **Food & Drink** Coffee, tea, cookies available any time. Full breakfast includes hot entree. **Recreation** Historic touring, caving, fishing, boating, picnicking, canoeing, antiquing. **Amenities & Services** AC, free gifts for honeymooners.

ACCOMMODATIONS
Units 15 guest rooms (some called "suites" but are 1 room) **All Rooms** Phones, cable TV **Some Rooms** Fireplace, VCR, Victorian tub, wet bar. **Bed & Bath** Kings (3), queens (2), 2 doubles (1), double plus twin (2), double (7). All private baths. **Favorites** Presidential Suite—corner room w/ 4 windows, claw-foot tub, brick-front fireplace w/ carved wood columns, poplar floors w/ square-head nails. **Comfort & Decor** Every item in this historic inn seemed to belong here, along with the 12-foot ceilings, original walnut and chestnut floors, transoms, and vintage plumbing. Rooms on the first 2 floors are furnished in Victoriana, while 3rd-floor rooms are done in a tasteful country style.

RATES, RESERVATIONS, & RESTRICTIONS
Deposit Credit card number or 1 night's deposit **Discounts** Corp. rates **Credit Cards** V, MC, D, AE **Check-In/Out** 1 p.m./11 a.m. **Smoking** No **Pets** No **Kids** Yes **No-Nos** N/A **Minimum Stay** None **Open** All year **Hosts** Dee Windell, 101 South Capitol Ave., Corydon 47112 **Phone** (812) 738-2020 **Email** reservations@kintnerhouse.com **Web** www.kintnerhouse.com

STARKEY INN BED & BREAKFAST, Evansville

OVERALL ★★★★ | QUALITY ★★★★ | VALUE ★★★★ | PRICE RANGE $95–$185

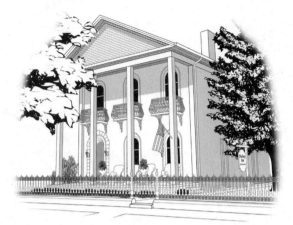

This home, built by local attorney Thomas Garvin to ease his wife's home-sickness, is deliberately reminiscent of a mansion in the Deep South. Two of their children's names are etched in an upstairs bedroom window. In these elegant rooms, people with names like Rhett and Scarlett flirted behind white gloves and satin drapes. Furnishings, including a grand piano in the parlor, dining room furniture designed by the current innkeeper, and fabric wall coverings reflect that high-mannered time.

SETTING & FACILITIES

Location Downtown Evansville, a block from the Ohio River **Near** Downtown shops, Reitz Home Museum, zoo, Angel Mounds, Wesselman Park Nature Reserve, casino **Building** 1850 Neoclassical, w/ pillars & white exterior **Grounds** Slate sidewalks, flower beds (city lot) **Public Space** Foyer, parlor, LR, DR, porch, 2nd-floor sitting area w/ large-screen TV **Food & Drink** Soda, coffee, water available any time. Full gourmet breakfast with homemade muffins or coffee cake, and egg strata or "loaded" omelets. **Recreation** Historic touring, antiquing, gambling, boating. **Amenities & Services** AC, bath amenities, hair dryers, breakfast in room on request.

ACCOMMODATIONS

Units 4 guest rooms **All Rooms** 2 comfortable chairs, ceiling fans **Some Rooms** Mantel, canopy bed, sleigh bed **Bed & Bath** King (1), queens (2), double (1). All private baths. **Favorites** Grande Room, with king four-poster bed, much natural light, and antique wardrobe. **Comfort & Decor** This is a grand residence, emphasized by a white decorating scheme, 12-foot ceilings, and rescue of early features such as Italianate cast-iron enframement windows, balconies, original carved oak rail and newel post, and original beveled glass in the front door.

RATES, RESERVATIONS, & RESTRICTIONS

Deposit 1 night's stay or credit card number **Discounts** Corp. (10%) and gov't rates **Credit Cards** V, MC, AE **Check-In/Out** 3–6 p.m. or by arrangement/11 a.m. **Smoking**

On porches only **Pets** No **Kids** Over age 12 **No-Nos** N/A **Minimum Stay** Occasional special-event weekends **Open** All year **Hosts** Veda & Walt Taylor, 214 SE First St., Evansville 47713 **Phone** (812) 425-7264 or toll-free (800) 580-0305 **Fax** (812) 425-7233 **Email** contact@starkeyinn.com **Web** www.starkeyinn.com

VAN BUREN STREET INN, Huntingburg

OVERALL ★★★★½ | QUALITY ★★★★½ | VALUE ★★★★★ | PRICE RANGE $65–$95

There may be more elegant bed-and-breakfasts in the Midwest, but none are more fun to visit. Jim Ward is a genial host, avid reader, Civil War buff, and art lover; if you're in a chatty mood, he'll probably invite you for a beer on the patio. The literature table in the entry includes a price sheet for many of the inn's furnishings; offerings when we visited included a three-piece East-lake settee for $575 and a ten-foot oak church pew for just $375. Visit a year later, and the rooms will have morphed into an entirely different look. The built-in cupboards in guest rooms seem incongruous but are a feature of the inn's history, installed by the Sisters of St. Benedictine who once lived there. Breakfast is a feast—ask for Jim's signature buckwheat pancakes.

SETTING & FACILITIES
Location Downtown Huntingburg, just off Rt. 64 **Near** Downtown antiques district, Patoka Lake, Marengo Caves **Building** 1900 former nunnery, red brick exterior **Grounds** Small yard, enclosed patio, flower beds **Public Space** Entry, guest lounge, DR, upstairs reading area, porch, patio. Also front parlor if not rented as part of Robert E. Lee suite. **Food & Drink** Full custom-prepared breakfast from menu; beverages any time. Guests can help themselves to anything in the refrigerator, including wine & beer. **Recreation** Antiquing, caving, boating, golf courses, Minor League baseball (played in stadium featured in the movie A League of Their Own). **Amenities & Services** AC. Phone, toys, & big-screen TV in guest lounge, outdoor hot tub, robes & slippers in rooms; babysitting services available.

ACCOMMODATIONS
Units 4 guest rooms (one available as suite w/ large parlor for extra fee) **All Rooms** Sitting area **Some Rooms** N/A **Bed & Bath** Queens (2), doubles (2). All private baths, 1 detached. **Favorites** Robert E. Lee Room is the largest; with parlor (including original tiled fireplace) it's nearly half of the first floor. Double Eastlake bedroom suite; wall hangings include tintype of a relative who served in the Civil War. **Comfort & Decor** This innkeeper appreciates and displays books and art of all genres. His personal collection ranges from contemporary John Wesley pieces in the upstairs hall to an 1861 watercolor of a Union soldier boy. Original beveled and stained glass is found throughout. If you like the furnishings—mostly quality antiques—you can take many of them home: the owner sells antiques on the side.

RATES, RESERVATIONS, & RESTRICTIONS
Deposit Credit card **Discounts** Single traveler, weekly, corp. **Credit Cards** V, MC, DC **Check-In/Out** Flexible **Smoking** Outside **Pets** No **Kids** Yes **No-Nos** N/A **Minimum**

Stay None **Open** Most of the year; owner takes a Caribbean respite for several weeks in January. **Host** Jim Decker-Ward, 401 North Van Buren Street, P.O. Box 259, Huntingburg 47542 **Phone** (812) 683-2471 **Email** deckward@vanburenstreetinn.com **Web** www.vanburenstreetinn.com

OLD BRIDGE INN BED & BREAKFAST, Jeffersonville

OVERALL ★★★½ | QUALITY ★★★½ | VALUE ★★★ | PRICE RANGE $75–$115

This home is architecturally distinguished. The creaking plank floors tell you that you're in a very old place with much history—though no one can say exactly how much, because documentation was lost when the town's courthouse burned, years ago—dating from "at least 1840," according to innkeeper Williams. Many of the furnishings are family artifacts, but we would suggest refurbishing. Some of the Art Deco pieces were badly nicked, carpet upstairs was worn, and rooms were cramped with too much furniture. With a few design touches and updates, Old Bridge Inn could be a showplace.

SETTING & FACILITIES
Location In Jeffersonville's historic district, 1 minute from I-65 and Louisville, KY **Near** Antiques shops, Ohio River Falls of the Ohio fossil beds, Louisville Slugger Museum, downtown Louisville & museums, Univ. of Louisville, Churchill Downs **Building** 1840 Georgian colonial, on National Register of Historic Places **Grounds** Ample lawn, landscaped gardens **Public Space** DR, parlor w/ big-screen TV & fireplace, sun porch **Food & Drink** Complimentary sodas, water any time. Full breakfast includes entree, breakfast meats. **Recreation** Antiquing, fine arts museums, canoeing, fine arts, steamboat rides, historic touring, horse races. **Amenities & Services** AC, cordless phones available, fax available.

ACCOMMODATIONS
Units 2 guest rooms, 1 suite **All Rooms** TV, radio, sitting area **Some Rooms** Double whirlpool tub, robes in room w/ detached bath. **Bed & Bath** Queens (3). All private baths (1 detached). **Favorites** Dr. Hancock Room, with largest bath, fireplace w/ electric insert, robe, and prettiest antiques, including Eastlake bed. **Comfort & Decor** Rooms are furnished individually: the Garden Room is decorated with reproduction Victorian garden prints and the bed has an ornate iron headboard. Furniture in the Nautical Suite is "Art Deco waterfall;" the suite is designed to resemble a seaside cottage and features a ship-clock collection.

RATES, RESERVATIONS, & RESTRICTIONS
Deposit Credit card or 1 night's stay **Discounts** Extended stay; corp., special packages **Credit Cards** V, MC, D **Check-In/Out** 3 p.m./11 a.m. **Smoking** Outdoors **Pets** Inquire; will be permitted if they're housebroken and stay in carrier or on leash, and must be confined. Two resident dogs stay in innkeeper's quarters. **Kids** Yes; well-behaved children welcome. "They have to respect the antiques." **No-Nos** N/A **Minimum Stay** None **Open** All year **Host** Linda Williams, 131 West Chestnut St., Jeffersonville 47130 **Phone** (812) 284-3580 **Fax** (812) 284-3561 **Email** innbridge@aol.com **Web** www.oldbridgeinn.com

LEAVENWORTH INN, *Leavenworth*

OVERALL ★★★★½ | QUALITY ★★★★½ | VALUE ★★★★ | PRICE RANGE $69–$119

We could have stayed in the front porch rockers, gazing down at the lazy Ohio River, for a very long time. The view from the porch—and many rooms—is expansive, and most conducive to dozing, daydreaming, and writing poetry. More disciplined types will spend time on the Stairmaster in the well-equipped fitness room. A game of croquet or horseshoes is as rigorous as most would get in this dreamy place.

SETTING & FACILITIES

Location On SR 62, 3 mi. south of I-64 **Near** Downtown Leavenworth, Blue River, Harrison-Crawford State Forest, Wyandot & Marengo Caves **Building** 2 renovated turn-of-the-century farm homes **Grounds** 6 acres w/ large gazebo, flower gardens, tennis court, walking/biking paths, Ohio River overlook across road **Public Space** In main inn, DR, porch, front room, Great Room. In cottage, DR, LR, sun room, porch, computer room, fitness room. **Food & Drink** Cookies, hot beverages, juice available all day. Full breakfast served at the Overlook Restaurant across the road, owned by innkeepers. **Recreation** Biking, fishing, canoeing, tennis, caving, antiquing, swimming. **Amenities & Services** AC. Bicycles & helmets available to guests. Hair dryer, logo bath amenities, in room. Fax, copier, computer, conference rooms available. Fitness room.

ACCOMMODATIONS

Units 11 guest rooms **All Rooms** Phone, cable TV/VCR, modem port **Some Rooms** Desk, sitting area (some both), fireplace, futon or pullout couch **Bed & Bath** Main inn: King (1), king or 2 twins (1), queens (4). Cottage: Kings (2), queens (3). Cots available. All private baths. **Favorites** Holly Room—sunny corner windows w/ porch & river view, sleigh bed, handicap access. **Comfort & Decor** Rooms are furnished in a modernized country style, with no clutter—plenty of room to move around. Chenille bed coverings in main inn guest rooms add a sentimental touch. Rooms in the cottage are smaller but very bright and upbeat, painted in tropical yellows and creams. The Great Room, with two window walls, is especially inviting.

RATES, RESERVATIONS, & RESTRICTIONS

Deposit 50% of stay **Discounts** AAA, AARP **Credit Cards** V, MC, D, AE, **Check-In/Out** 4 p.m./noon **Smoking** No **Pets** No **Kids** Yes; kids under age 12 stay free. Crib is available. **No-Nos** N/A **Minimum Stay** None **Open** All year **Hosts** Bert Collins, 930 West St., Rt. 62, Leavenworth 47137 **Phone** (812) 739-2120 or toll-free (888) 739-2120 **Fax** (812) 739-2012 **Email** leavenworthinn@aol.com **Web** www.leavenworthinn.com

SCHUSSLER HOUSE, *Madison*

OVERALL ★★★★½ | QUALITY ★★★★½ | VALUE ★★★★ | PRICE RANGE $120

There wasn't a room we didn't like at this gracious inn. Guest rooms are individually decorated, with interesting twists on wall treatments: in the

Rose Room, walls were papered only from the ceiling down to the tops of the ten-foot windows, so the walls weren't as "busy" as many are with flowered paper and don't compete with the lace canopy. Ceilings upstairs and down are 12 feet high. Linger in this town; with two wineries, three antiques malls, and many other shops—all perched on the banks of the Ohio River—filling a weekend is no problem.

SETTING & FACILITIES

Location On US 421 in central Madison **Near** Downtown Madison, antiques malls, Clifty Falls State Park, Ohio River, Hanover College **Building** 1849 Federal/Greek Revival, on National Register of Historic Places **Grounds** Double lot; flower beds, statuary **Public Space** Foyer, DR, parlor **Food & Drink** Soft drinks, juice available any time; coffee delivered upstairs 7:30 a.m. Full, hot candlelight breakfast served on china and silver with classical music playing; signature dish is raspberry-peach coffee cake. **Recreation** Antiquing, historic architecture touring (Madison boasts 133 city blocks listed on the National Register of Historic Places). **Amenities & Services** Morning newspaper delivered to room, evening turn-down service, AC, fresh flowers in room.

ACCOMMODATIONS

Units 3 guest rooms **All Rooms** Fireplace, sitting area, reading lights **Some Rooms** Canopy bed, brass bed **Bed & Bath** Queens (3). All private baths. **Favorites** Rose Room, with tall windows, street view, and most comfortable seating. **Comfort & Decor** Taste reigns at this historic inn, almost to the point of formality. Many original features survived the inn's 150-plus years, including surface-nailed thin oak board flooring, cast-iron mantels with faux-marble paint, inlaid floors, and cherry stair rails. Throughout the house hang limited-edition prints by P. Buckley Moss, a personal friend of the innkeeper.

RATES, RESERVATIONS, & RESTRICTIONS

Deposit Credit card **Discounts** Gov't, travel agent, single traveler **Credit Cards** V, MC, D **Check-In/Out** 3 p.m./11 a.m. **Smoking** No **Pets** No **Kids** Over age 12 **No-Nos** N/A **Minimum Stay** None **Open** All year **Hosts** Bill & Judy Gilbert, 514 Jefferson St., Madison 47250 **Phone** (812) 273-2068 or toll-free (800) 392-1931 **Email** schussler@voyager.net **Web** www.schusslerhouse.com

THORPE HOUSE, Metamora

OVERALL ★★★½ | QUALITY ★★★½ | VALUE ★★★★ | PRICE RANGE $70–$125

Thorpe House's guest rooms are named after the innkeepers' paternal ancestors who settled Indiana. "Country casual" describes more than the decor; it's also the inn's personality, with family-style breakfasts and drinks served in Mason jars. You'll find no phones, TV, radio, or alarm clocks in the rooms, though phones and TV are available on request. You won't need your car to explore Metamora; but be prepared for commercialism—more shops sell mass-produced goods than antiques or handicrafts. Tip: Many shops are closed on Mondays—come later in the week.

SETTING & FACILITIES

Location In Metamora, a historic village on the National Register of Historic Places **Near** Walking distance of more than 100 art galleries, museums and shops in town; also Whitewater Canal State Historic Site, including grist mill, canal boat, locks. Near Whitewater State Park, Quakertown & Mounds State Recreation Areas, Mary Gray Bird Sanctuary. **Building** Mid-1840s inn w/ 1860s additions **Grounds** Flower beds **Public Space** 2nd-floor deck, restaurant, gift shop, deck behind restaurant, small front porch, sitting room of suite if not booked. **Food & Drink** Coffee available before breakfast. Full breakfast in restaurant: menu selections weekdays, buffet weekends. **Recreation** Historic touring, museums, antiquing, canoeing, golf courses, biking trails. **Amenities & Services** Will arrange boating for guests.

ACCOMMODATIONS

Units 4 guest rooms, 1 suite **All Rooms** Sitting area **Some Rooms** Hide-a-bed, table **Bed & Bath** King or 2 twins (1), doubles (4). All private baths. **Favorites** Shedric Owens & William Rose Room, suite w/ table, 2 trundles, sitting room. **Comfort & Decor** The decorating theme here is "country casual," with handmade quilts covering beds. Floors are original pine and poplar planks. Once you reach the second floor you might want to stay there—the stairs are so steep, you'll know they're original. Transoms, pine trim, and bull's-eye moldings enhance the sense of history.

RATES, RESERVATIONS, & RESTRICTIONS

Deposit 1 night's stay **Discounts** Travel agents, special packages **Credit Cards** V, MC, AE, D **Check-In/Out** 3 p.m./11 a.m. **Smoking** Courteous, cautious smoking allowed in designated areas. **Pets** Yes, with well-trained owners. **Kids** Yes, with well-trained parents. **NoNos** N/A **Minimum Stay** None **Open** Open April–Dec; closed Jan–March **Hosts** Mike & Jean Owens, 19049 Clayborne St., P.O. Box 36, Metamora 47030 **Phone** (765) 647-5425 or toll-free (888) 427-7932 **Email** thorpehouse@cnz.com **Web** www.metamora.com/thorphouse

HONEYMOON MANSION BED & BREAKFAST AND WEDDING CHAPEL, New Albany

OVERALL ★★★★½ | QUALITY ★★★★½ | VALUE ★★★ | PRICE RANGE $80–$170

More than 300 couples are wed each year at this mecca of marital senti-mentality. Rooms are named for famous people living in the 1800s, includ-ing the Florence Nightingale Suite (the former owner was Florence's great-niece) and the 944-square-foot Ralph Waldo Emerson Suite; Emer-son often visited New Albany on lecture tours and stayed in a nearby man-sion. Two ordained ministers are on staff and are paid separately for both rehearsals and wedding services, with the amount ($30–$60) depending on the length of the service. Use of the chapel is according to number of guests ($75–$250), and with extra fees for candles and reception space.

SETTING & FACILITIES
Location In New Albany's Historic District, once called Mansion Row **Near** Ohio River, downtown Louisville KY, Churchill Downs, Kentucky Derby Museum, Kentucky Center for the Arts **Building** 1850 Victorian mansion, ornate white exterior, on National Regis-ter of Historic Places **Grounds** City lot, flower beds **Public Space** Foyer, chapel, DR, parlor, breakfast room. **Food & Drink** All-you-can-eat country breakfast includes sweet bread, biscuits, breakfast meats, potatoes, and specialty, twice-baked peaches. **Recreation** Canoeing, horse races, theater, boating **Amenities & Services** Victorian weddings, for-mal & informal services (religious or civil) available for up to 70 guests. AC.

ACCOMMODATIONS
Units 6 guest rooms, 1 suite. **All Rooms** Cable TV/VCR, sitting area **Some Rooms** Pri-vate entrance, marble Jacuzzi, double Jacuzzi, fireplace, mirrored walls, stained-glass win-dows, canopy beds, private balcony, private entrance. **Bed & Bath** Queens (6), double (1). All private baths. **Favorites** Stephen Foster room—spacious with marble columns, dou-ble Jacuzzi, private entrance, hand-carved cherry bed. **Comfort & Decor** Entering this inn is like walking into a wedding cake, all white, lacy, and gold-trimmed—either ornate or gaudy, depending on one's taste. Stained-glass doors, parquet floors, and an original pewter and brass chandelier greet guests, along with inlaid grape molding in the parlor and huge, original medallion.

RATES, RESERVATIONS, & RESTRICTIONS
Deposit 1 night's stay **Discounts** 10% Mon.–Thurs. on suite **Credit Cards** V, MC, AE, D **Check-In/Out** 3 p.m./11 a.m. **Smoking** Outside **Pets** No **Kids** Over age 12, with responsible adults **No-Nos** N/A **Minimum Stay** None **Open** All year **Hosts** Bill & Donna Stepp, 1014 East Main St., New Albany 47150 **Phone** (812) 945-0312 or toll-free (800) 759-7270 **Fax** (812) 945-6615 **Email** wdshoneymoon@earthlink.net **Web** www.bbonline.com/in/honeymoon

GODBEY GUEST HOUSE BED & BREAKFAST, Boonville

OVERALL ★★★½ | QUALITY ★★★½ | VALUE ★★★★ | PRICE RANGE $60–$75

Built by one of Boonville's founding families, Godbey Guest House was the town's first bed-and-breakfast. It's a comfortable stop on the way to the bluffs of the Ohio River; Cora loves to cook for guests and relax with them on the porches. The shady lot is a habitat for birds and rabbits.

SETTING & FACILITIES

Location Off Rt. 62, about 15 mi. NE of Evansville **Near** Little Pigeon River, Ohio River **Building** 1856–65 "remuddled" Victorian, originally Queen Anne **Grounds** Half acre of lawns, flower beds **Public Space** Tea room/porch, patio, LR, breakfast room, DR, loft sitting area, back porch. **Food & Drink** Soda, water, teas any time; home-baked afternoon snack. Full breakfast includes hot entree. **Recreation** Canoeing, birding, biking, historic touring. **Amenities & Services** AC. If guests are visiting their family in town, those family members are invited to breakfast at no charge. Sunday dinners served once a month, open to the public.

ACCOMMODATIONS

Units 4 guest rooms. **All Rooms** TV, ceiling fan, clock, sitting area. **Some Rooms** Table & chairs, tin fireplace. **Bed & Bath** Queen (1), doubles (2), 2 twins (1). 4 private baths, 1 shared. **Favorites** Bay room w/ table & chairs in alcove. **Comfort & Decor** The style is a combination of Victorian and French country, on the busy side. The living room is adorned with the innkeeper's collection of musical instruments, including both a piano and an organ. The theme extends to the wall covering in the first-floor guest bath: instead of wallpaper, the walls are covered in old sheet music.

RATES, RESERVATIONS, & RESTRICTIONS

Deposit Credit card number **Discounts** None **Credit Cards** V, MC, AE, D **Check-In/Out** "When you get here and when you leave." **Smoking** On back porch **Pets** No; resident dog is permitted in guest areas **Kids** Inquire **No-Nos** N/A **Minimum Stay** None **Open** All year **Hosts** Don & Cora Alyce Seaman, 401 South 4th St., Boonville 47601 **Phone** (812) 897-3902 **Email** N/A

JAMES WILKINS HOUSE, Campbellsburg

OVERALL ★★★★½ | QUALITY ★★★★½ | VALUE ★★★★★ | PRICE RANGE $55–$65

Many owners of Victorians claim that their homes are "painted ladies," but Diane Callahan didn't fudge: with 13 colors, James Wilkins House is a true lady. The home is near-perfection without formality; Callahan will join guests in the library to watch Survivor or on a front-porch rocker for a glass of wine. She had fun decorating the inn; notice the wallpaper trick in the nursery and the look of the wicker settee and chairs in front of the Magnolia Room's "horseshoe" window.

SETTING & FACILITIES

Location Off Rt. 60, 9 mi. NW of Salem **Near** John Hay Lake, Spring Mill State Park, Paoli Peaks, Delaney Park, Salem Genealogy Library **Building** 1894 Painted Lady Victorian **Grounds** 0.25-acre lot w/ gazebo, flower beds **Public Space** Foyer, parlor, library, DR **Food & Drink** Sodas any time; early coffee available. Full breakfast includes home-baked muffins, hot entree. **Recreation** Historic touring, skiing, antiquing, horseback riding, cave exploring, fishing, swimming. **Amenities & Services** AC. Logo bath amenities; fax available, can accommodate meetings or luncheons to 14 people.

ACCOMMODATIONS

Units 3 guest rooms. **All Rooms** Ceiling fans, clock radio, sitting area. **Some Rooms** Table & chairs, bay window, four-poster bed, handmade quilt bed covering. **Bed & Bath** Queen (1), double (1), 2 twins (1). 1 private bath, 1 shared. **Favorites** Paisley Room, w/ queen bed, table & chairs, pill-box toilet, slipper tub, private bath. **Comfort & Decor** Diane Callahan took nearly 3 years to renovate her home. The dining room is the pearl, with original wainscot paneling and an original Italian tile/carved wood fireplace with topper. Ceiling medallions are original, as are the imported English fretwork and pine plank floors. The Eastlake parlor furniture suits the room perfectly.

RATES, RESERVATIONS, & RESTRICTIONS

Deposit Credit card number or 1 night's stay **Discounts** 10% for 3 nights or longer **Credit Cards** V, MC **Check-In/Out** 4 p.m./11 a.m. **Smoking** Outside **Pets** No **Kids** Yes, if well behaved **No-Nos** Candles **Minimum Stay** None **Open** All year **Hosts** Diane Callahan, 225 West Oak St., Campbellsburg 47108 **Phone** (812) 755-4274 **Fax** (812) 755-5239 **Email** jwhbnb@blueriver.net **Web** www.jameswilkinshousebnb.com

POWERS INN, Jasper

OVERALL ★★★★ | QUALITY ★★★★ | VALUE ★★★★★ | PRICE RANGE $60

A log-cabin inn once stood on this site, built and operated by settler Lewis Powers. Then, as now, a warm bed welcomed travelers to the county seat. The inn is sparsely but tastefully furnished, adding to the historic-"colonial" ambience. Floors are original wood. Notice the sink in the detached bath upstairs; it's a converted dresser.

SETTING & FACILITIES

Location On US 231, 2 blocks west of the courthouse **Near** Downtown Jasper, Abraham Lincoln's Boyhood Home, Paoli Peaks, Patoka Lake & Tillery Hill Recreation Area **Building** 1880s Second Empire, gray exterior **Grounds** City lot w/ shrubs, flower beds **Public Space** Porch, DR, parlor **Food & Drink** Sodas available any time. Full breakfast includes home-baked breads or muffins & hot entree. **Recreation** Skiing, canoeing, swimming, biking, birding, historic touring. **Amenities & Services** AC. Bottled water in room.

ACCOMMODATIONS

Units 3 guest rooms. **All Rooms** Ceiling fan, sitting area, clock radio. **Some Rooms** Claw-foot tub, table & chair. **Bed & Bath** Double & twin (1), doubles (2). All private baths

(1 detached). **Favorites** Room w/ detached bath—the largest bath, with sitting area. **Comfort & Decor** A mix of Shaker-style and other antiques furnish this inn. Old wood walls in the entry give the place a cottage feel; inlaid wood floors, bull's-eye molding, transoms, and pocket doors make a warm setting for the Eastlake furniture in public areas. A TV is in the parlor; phones are available on request.

RATES, RESERVATIONS, & RESTRICTIONS
Deposit Credit card number or 1 night's stay **Discounts** Extended stay **Credit Cards** V, MC **Check-In/Out** 3 p.m./11 a.m. or by prior arrangement **Smoking** On porch **Pets** No **Kids** Yes **No-Nos** N/A **Minimum Stay** None **Open** All year **Hosts** Larry & Alice Garland, 325 West 6th St., Jasper 47546 **Phone** (812) 482-3018 **Email** N/A

WRIGHT PLACE, New Harmony

OVERALL ★★★★ | QUALITY ★★★★ | VALUE ★★★ | PRICE RANGE $95–$150

New Harmony will be quite a discovery for first-time visitors. Settled in 1814 by the Harmonie Society, a German communal group, the town was sold a decade later. By the 1850s it was home to scientists and educators hoping to create a utopian society. Much of their dream remains in the historic shops, meditation labyrinth, and galleries. Wright Place sits at the town's edge—a good starting point for walking tours.

SETTING & FACILITIES
Location In historic village on the IN–IL line **Near** Museums, shops, art galleries, labyrinth, Harmonie State Park, theater **Building** 1982 replica of an 1840s saltbox home **Grounds** 5 acres, mostly undeveloped, w/ lawns, gardens, patio, goldfish pond **Public Space** Entry, library, music room, DR **Food & Drink** Cookies, sodas, bottled water all day. Full gourmet breakfast includes hot entree; meat. **Recreation** Historic touring, antiquing, canoeing, live theater **Amenities & Services** AC. Can accommodate small group dinners, parties.

ACCOMMODATIONS
Units 1 guest room, 1 suite. **All Rooms** TV/VCR, fridge, clock radio, sitting area. **Some Rooms** Reading room. **Bed & Bath** Queens (2). Both private baths. **Favorites** Suite w/ "new Eastlake" bedroom set, daybed in TV room. **Comfort & Decor** The cherry-trimmed library nods to local history with bookcases milled from a former owner's farm and built by a local cabinetmaker. A fireplace and baby grand piano warm the music room. Best spot in the house: a couch in the music room, where a large picture window gives lovely, relaxing views of the rose and perennial gardens.

RATES, RESERVATIONS, & RESTRICTIONS
Deposit Credit card number **Discounts** None **Credit Cards** V, MC **Check-In/Out** 3 p.m./11 a.m. or by arrangement **Smoking** No **Pets** Yes, if housebroken, and kept in a travel crate when guests are out **Kids** Yes. **No-Nos** N/A **Minimum Stay** None **Open** All year **Hosts** Duane & Laurie Wright, 515 South Arthur St., New Harmony 47631 **Phone** (812) 682-3453 **Web** www.newharmony.evansville.net

E. B. RHODES HOUSE BED & BREAKFAST,
West Baden Springs

OVERALL ★★★★½ | QUALITY ★★★★½ | VALUE ★★★★★ | PRICE RANGE $50–$75

Think The Road to Wellville, and you have the precise image of West Baden Springs Domed Hotel, a spectacle of a health resort, built by E. B. Rhodes and two partners. The resort stands empty, but his house remains a viable legacy. The third floor, once a gymnasium, is now the innkeepers' quarters; in Rhodes's day it was rumored to have been used for gambling. Rhodes spared no expense in building and adorning his grand home; in addition to ornate Eastlake trim, he installed twin pillared Italian tile fireplaces in the common room and dining room. Perched as it is on a bluff overlooking the park, town, and resort, one can easily imagine the prominence this home—and its occupants—once commanded in West Baden.

SETTING & FACILITIES
Location On a hill overlooking the town, off Rt. 37. **Near** West Baden Springs Domed Hotel, French Lick, Patoka Lake, Paoli Peaks **Building** 1899 Late Victorian w/ white exterior, stone porch **Grounds** Garden, fish pond, canary aviary **Public Space** Porch, foyer, common room, DR **Food & Drink** Fruit basket & snack in room. Full breakfast includes hot entree. **Recreation** Antiquing, historic touring, biking, spelunking, tennis, skiing, swimming, boating, snowboarding, golf. **Amenities & Services** AC. Will arrange wine, flowers, or other special touches on request.

ACCOMMODATIONS
Units 2 guest rooms and carriage house. **All Rooms** Sitting area. **Some Rooms** Park view, double shower, whirlpool tub, fireplace, table, desk. Carriage house has 2-sided gas fireplace, daybed, claw-foot tub, coffee station, table w/ benches. **Bed & Bath** Queens (2), double (1). All private baths. **Favorites** Lavender Room, w/ table & chairs, desk & chair, and "altar chair." **Comfort & Decor** The detail and workmanship in this home is extraordinary. The cut-beveled glass in the front door is extremely ornate, and the Eastlake ornamentation continues in the foyer. Most of the wood is mahogany, mixed with some red oak, and each of the egg-and-dart panels is a separate piece. The stained-glass windows and painted light fixtures are original—lots to stare at in this house.

RATES, RESERVATIONS, & RESTRICTIONS
Deposit Credit card number **Discounts** For repeat guests **Credit Cards** V, MC, D, AE **Check-In/Out** 3–6 p.m./11 a.m. **Smoking** Outside **Pets** No **Kids** Yes **No-Nos** N/A **Minimum Stay** None **Open** All year **Hosts** Marlene & Frank Sipes, 726 Rhodes Ave., P.O. Box 7, West Baden Springs 47469 **Phone** (812) 936-7378 or toll-free (800) 786-5176 **Fax** (812) 936-3597 **Email** ebrhodes@bluemarble.net **Web** www.bluemarble.net\~ebrhodes

Michigan

Michigan should be advertised as one giant water park. How else would you characterize a land of two peninsulas, 3,000 miles of shoreline, and more than **100 lighthouses?**

The most oddly shaped of any state, we also found that it's one of the most fun. In one 12-day sweep across the state, we stayed at bed-and-breakfasts masquerading as a canoe livery, a stately English mansion, a winery, and a Victorian with elephant-hide wallpaper. We ate pasties (rhymes with "nasties") in the Upper Peninsula and contributed to the economy in **Antique Alley** across the bottom of the state. There's so much of Michigan, in fact, that it borders four of the five Great Lakes (only Lake Ontario is left out).

Zone 9 consists of the **Upper Peninsula**—or, as Michiganers refer to it, the U.P.—and the northern portion of the **Lower Peninsula** (L.P.). It's a diverse region, with national forestlands, sandy beaches, and limestone bluffs outlining the U.P. lakeshores and **Bay View** (Michigan's Chautauqua) and beautiful **Mackinac** (pronounced Mackinaw) **Island** distinguishing the northern L.P. The two land masses are connected by the five-mile suspension (and suspenseful) bridge spanning the **Straits of Mackinac.** Michigan's state parks just embarked on a five-year, $100 million upgrade, and many of those overhauls will be to the beaches and timberlands of the U.P.

Visitors who can afford the time would be well advised to attend a class or two in Bay View, Michigan's Chautauqua. The community is one of a network of such towns across the United States that began in the 1880s as Methodist "tent cities" for prayer meetings, and evolved into citywide "summer universities." Eventually, Victorian homes replaced the tents and a year-round population grew, but the mission of intellectual enlightenment and cultural growth endures.

We were glad to be touring Zone 10, the western sliver bordering **Lake Michigan** from **South Haven** north to **Charlevoix,** in the fall. The beaches fill with laughing, splashing tourists in summer; in the fall, shore villages are golden, with plenty of space for browsing in the galleries.

Michigan's interior is the land of midsized cities—**Grand Rapids, Lansing, Kalamazoo**—and, in the north, lake and river towns. The forestlands here make for great snowmobiling: the **Cadillac area** alone has more than 600 miles of trails.

Most of the eastern coast, nicknamed the Sunrise Side, borders **Lake Huron** and the "thumb" and its "crook" make up the quieter coast of Zone 12. Here you'll find the mouth of the **Au Sable River,** site of some of the best canoeing and kayaking in the Midwest; the historic shore towns bordering the thumb; and, anchoring the mitten in the south, **Detroit.** Across the bottom of the state, nothing defines Zone 13 as vividly as **Antique Alley**—dozens of antiques emporiums, strung along an 80-mile route. Rounding out the zone are the restored Victorian towns of **Coldwater, Sturgis,** and **Three Rivers.**

FOR MORE INFORMATION

Travel Michigan
(888) 78-GREAT
travel.michigan.org

Michigan Lake to Lake Bed & Breakfast Association
444 Oak Street
Holland, MI 49424
(616) 738-0135
innfo@laketolake.com

Upper Peninsula and Northern Michigan

If the **Upper Peninsula** were as expensive as it is beautiful, no one could afford to visit. For nearly 400 miles, the peninsula stretches out from northern Wisconsin to **Sault Sainte Marie,** with scenic lakeshores and remote wilderness in between—though even the most isolated spot is at most only 30 miles from travel services.

It's easy to plot one's own lake tour; scenic roads nearly encircle the peninsula—as much a water park as the **Lower Peninsula,** with 150 major waterfalls, 4,300 inland lakes, and 12,000 miles of trout streams. Yet the bed-and-breakfasts we toured were all luxury properties, particularly the Laurium Manor Inn on the **Keweenaw Peninsula,** atop the U.P. These inns offer deluxe treatment after a long day of fishing, hiking, snowmobiling, rafting, skiing, hunting, or kayaking.

We crossed to the U.P. over the famous **Mackinac Bridge,** where staff members offer assistance to drivers too frightened to drive the five-mile span alone. A Bridge Authority staffer will rescue you on the ramp and drive your car across—a handy service for those with phobias; according to our driver (yes, we confess, we made the call), they take about ten drivers across the bridge each day.

One of the best stories of northern Michigan is **Bay View,** the Chautauqua of the north. It's a resort community that attracts tens of thousands of visitors each year for its cultural and educational programs. People come from across the country to attend summer classes in skills ranging from chair caning and yoga to sailing. Its bed-and-breakfasts most often are larger, historic inns rather than private homes; that's also the case with **Mackinac Island,** the standout on the **Lake Huron** side. The town sits just outside **Petoskey,** a romantic town known for its historic Gaslight District shopping area.

One more northern Michigan spot deserves highlighting: **Grayling,** where the Au Sable and Manistee Rivers welcome thousands of visitors each spring for fishing, canoeing, morel mushrooming, and birders hoping to catch a glimpse of the endangered Kirtland's warbler.

SAND HILLS LIGHTHOUSE INN, Ahmeek

OVERALL ★★★★ | QUALITY ★★★★ | VALUE ★★★ | PRICE RANGE $125–$185

Location, location, location is the mantra that brings guests to this otherwise institutional-looking lighthouse. Built in 1917 to house three lightkeepers and their families, it later served as a training site for 200 soldiers during World War II. Because it perches lakeside near the Upper Peninsula's northernmost point, guests can watch both sunrise and sunset here—not to mention the Northern Lights. Best spot: 101 feet up, in the lighthouse tower.

SETTING & FACILITIES

Location On the north shore of the Keweenaw Peninsula, 25 mi. NE of Houghton **Near** Ahmeek Village, Lake Superior, Copper Harbor, Brockway Mountain Drive. **Building** 1912 blonde-brick lighthouse w/ signal tower **Grounds** 35 acres of lawns & forest, including walking paths & 3,000 ft. of lakefront **Public Space** Common room, dining area, upper-level sitting room, tower, recreation room **Food & Drink** Evening dessert, full breakfast. (Breakfast not served until 9:30 a.m.; guests who can't wait are offered juice, coffee, pastries.) **Recreation** Antiquing, historic & copper mine touring, museums, cross-country skiing. **Amenities & Services** AC. Innkeeper plays piano evenings.

ACCOMMODATIONS

Units 1 suite, 7 guest rooms. **All Rooms** Ceiling fan, 2 chairs, music box, hair dryer. **Some Rooms** Private balcony overlooking Lake Superior, whirlpool tub, table, fireplace. **Bed & Bath** King (1), queens (7). All private baths. **Favorites** Sir Laurence Olivier, w/ marble-inlaid fireplace & custom-designed canopy. **Comfort & Decor** Seven years prior to our visit, Sand Hills was a pile of rubble. Rooms were all refurbished, and fireplaces and other Victorian-style design features, such as 70-pound ceiling medallions and bronze lighted newel posts, were installed. In the rec room, guests find a vintage pool table and game tables. Photograph and most paintings adorning walls are by innkeeper Bill Frabotta.

RATES, RESERVATIONS, & RESTRICTIONS

Deposit Full payment in advance **Discounts** None **Credit Cards** No. Cash, check, or traveler's checks only **Check-In/Out** 4 p.m./noon **Smoking** No **Pets** No **Kids** No; "it's an adult environment" **No-Nos** "We discourage coolers—this isn't a campground" **Minimum Stay** 2 nights May-Oct. **Open** All year **Hosts** Bill & Mary Frabotta, Five Mile Point Rd., P.O. Box 414, Ahmeek 49901 **Phone** (906) 337-1744 **Web** www.sandhillslighthouseinn.com

BRILEY INN, Atlanta

OVERALL ★★★★ | QUALITY ★★★★ | VALUE ★★★★★ | PRICE RANGE $65–$75

Tucked away in the forest at the end of a long dirt road, Briley Inn provides a restful stop for travelers heading toward the north shores. We had fun browsing Carla's collections of rare antique dolls (her avocation is teaching doll-making), antique glass Aladdin's lamps, and especially her antique silver cruet sets from England and Germany. Take a walk in the woods—this is northern Michigan's elk country; you might also spot bears, bobcats, deer, wild turkey, and—our biggest thrill—bald eagles.

SETTING & FACILITIES
Location Just off MI 32 on Atlanta's west edge **Near** Thunder Bay River, wilderness area. **Building** 35-year-old lodge home **Grounds** 6 acres on Thunder Bay River. **Public Spaces** Great room w/ TV, atrium; DR w/ sitting room; 2nd-floor sitting area, deck **Food & Drink** Snacks, hot beverages in afternoon. Breakfast is full—"hearty country." **Recreation** Cross-country skiing, mushroom picking, fishing, snowmobiling, hunting, canoeing, golf. **Amenities & Services** AC. Full use of inn's canoes, rowboats, paddleboat; gift & doll shop.

ACCOMMODATIONS
Units 5 guest rooms. **All Rooms** Chandelier, sitting area, river view. **Some Rooms** Whirlpool tub. **Bed & Bath** Doubles w/ pillowtop mattresses (5). All private baths (1 detached). **Favorites** McKenzie Room—the most spacious, off the great room, w/ rose color scheme. **Comfort & Decor** The look throughout is country, with Victorian touches. Bed coverings are rare "one-hander" quilts from Pennsylvania, and all beds are oak with high, carved headboards. One room is handicap-accessible.

RATES, RESERVATIONS, & RESTRICTIONS
Deposit 1 night's stay **Discounts** None; golf packages offered **Credit Cards** V, MC, AE **Check-In/Out** 3 p.m./11 a.m. **Smoking** No **Pets** No (2 resident schnauzers stay in innkeepers' quarters) **Kids** Over age 14; only 2 guests per room **No-Nos** Alcohol on premises **Minimum Stay** 2 nights on July 4 **Open** All year, except Nov., "because we don't want deer hunters" **Hosts** William & Carla Gardner, 11021 McArthur Rd., Atlanta 49709 **Phone** (989) 785-4784 **Email** briley@northland.lib.mi.us **Web** www.laketolake.com/briley

STAFFORD'S BAY VIEW INN, Bay View/Petoskey

OVERALL ★★★★½ | QUALITY ★★★★½ | VALUE ★★★ | PRICE RANGE IN SEASON, 5 LEVELS OF ROOMS—$145, $180, $208, $250, $280

On the edge of what used to be a Methodist tent city, Stafford's Bay View is part of a resort community that developed to host a Chautauqua series of cultural and intellectual summer programs. Today, the programs continue in many of the 400 Victorian cottages that replaced the early tents. Bay View Inn, itself a National Historic Place, is the largest of several inns in the cottage colony. Come on the weekend; Sunday brunch here was named Michigan's best by *Michigan Living* magazine.

SETTING & FACILITIES

Location On Lake Michigan's Little Traverse Bay, 1 mi. north of Petoskey **Near** Petoskey shopping area, Bay View Woods, Lake Michigan, Nub's Nob, Boyne Mountain & Boyne Highlands ski slopes, Winter Sports Park, Petoskey Concerts in the Park, Chautauqua sites. **Building** 1886 Grand Dame Victorian **Grounds** 2 city blocks of bayside lawns, flower & herb gardens **Public Space** Lobby w/ fireplace, sun room, 2 DRs, library, gift shop, 3rd-floor parlor **Food & Drink** Complimentary soft drinks, hot beverages. Full breakfast. Sat. night guests get Sun. brunch. **Recreation** Sleigh rides, cross-country or downhill skiing, galleries, Chautauqua programs (performing arts, lectures, educational programs), tennis, swimming, boating, canoeing. **Amenities & Services** Bath amenities, bicycles, croquet. Can accommodate parties & banquets to 250 guests, depending on the room & event.

ACCOMMODATIONS

Units 31. **All Rooms** Sitting area, clock radio. **Some Rooms** Writing desk, bay view, balcony, whirlpool tub, fireplace, robes, sitting room. **Bed & Bath** Mostly queen beds. All private baths. **Favorites** "Trillium" Rooms—5 guest rooms w/ bay views. **Comfort & Decor** Rooms are individually decorated, most with a Victorian flair. Stafford's really is a full-service inn, so convenience is a priority; a coffee station, phones, the elevator, and cozy conversation areas are easily found. This is a classic lakeside resort inn, set in a Historic Landmark District.

RATES, RESERVATIONS, & RESTRICTIONS

Deposit Credit card number or 1st night's stay **Discounts** None **Credit Cards** V, MC, AE, D **Check-In/Out** 3 p.m./11 a.m. **Smoking** No **Pets** No **Kids** Yes **No-Nos** Nonguest diners can't bring alcohol into DR **Minimum Stay** None **Open** All year **Host** Dean Smith, 2011 Woodland Ave., P.O. Box 3, Petoskey 49770 **Phone** (231) 347-2771 or toll-free (800) 258-1886 **Fax** (231) 347-3413 **Email** bayview@staffords.com **Web** www.staffords.com

TERRACE INN, Bay View/Petoskey

OVERALL ★★★★½ | QUALITY ★★★★ | VALUE ★★★★ | PRICE RANGE $77–$107 IN SEASON; $49–$74 NOV. 1–MAY 31. JACUZZI SUITE, $159 IN SEASON, $99 NOV.–MAY

The Chautauqua movement is an intriguing slice of American history, made more special by virtue of continuing success of such "summer university" communities. Bay View's cottages, like those in other Chautauquas, are heavily adorned with gingerbread; inside, Terrace Inn's nod to the past includes original oak furniture used in guest rooms, porches, lobby, and dining room since the inn's opening. We were impressed by the spirit of the

Somewhere in Time Room, reminiscent of the Christopher Reeve movie: 5% of proceeds from that room are donated to Reeve's foundation for spinal cord injuries.

SETTING & FACILITIES

Location In residential Bay View, 2 blocks off US 31 **Near** Boyne Highlands, Boyne Mountain & Nub's Nob ski areas, Petoskey Gaslight Shopping District, casino, Bay Harbor Marina District, Crooked Tree Arts Council, Kilwin's Chocolate Factory, Petoskey Concerts in the Park, Chautauqua programs. **Building** 1911 late-Victorian neo-Gothic inn, on National Register of Historic Places **Grounds** Hillside city lot w/ shrubs, flower beds **Public Space** Lobby, DR, lower-level TV room, front & rear porches **Food & Drink** Cont'l breakfast. **Recreation** Downhill & cross country skiing, historic touring, birding, mushroom hunting, biking, canoeing, fishing, gambling, museums, concerts, boat rides, sleigh rides, snowshoeing, golf. **Amenities & Services** AC. Boat tours, ferry service, complimentary use of bicycles & snowshoes, dogsled rides, golf privileges at Petoskey–Bay View Country Club; specialty packages include jazz, women-only "Pamper Yourself" weekends, quilters' getaways, Victorian weekends.

ACCOMMODATIONS

Units 43 guest rooms. **All Rooms** Sitting area. **Some Rooms** Whirlpool tub. **Bed & Bath** Queen & double-bed sofa (1), queens (30), 2 twins (8), doubles (4). All private baths. **Favorites** Hemingway Room, in cottage decor, highlighting Hemingway's childhood & northern Michigan experience. **Comfort & Decor** It's rare to find an Arts & Crafts–style interior intact, in a building of this size. The rich, solid northern Michigan hemlock paneling that graces the lobby and dining room, along with the wide hallways and huge windows looking onto the veranda, give the space a "yesteryear summer holiday" feel. You just know Mark Twain played cards in this lobby.

RATES, RESERVATIONS, & RESTRICTIONS

Deposit Credit card number **Discounts** 10% for 5 days or more **Credit Cards** V, MC, AE **Check-In/Out** 11 a.m./4 p.m. **Smoking** No **Pets** No **Kids** Yes **No-Nos** N/A **Minimum Stay** 2 nights on select weekends **Open** All year **Hosts** Tom & Denise Erhart, 1549 Glendale, P.O. Box 266, Petoskey (Bay View) 49770 **Phone** (231) 347-2410 or toll-free (800) 530-9898 **Fax** (231) 347-2407 **Email** info@theterraceinn.com **Web** www.theterraceinn.com

BORCHERS AUSABLE CANOE LIVERY WITH BED & BREAKFAST, *Grayling*

OVERALL ★★★½ | QUALITY ★★★½ | VALUE ★★★★ | PRICE RANGE $69–$89

Introducing guests to the beauty of the 130-mile AuSable River is the Hunters' mission—either from a canoe or, if they prefer, from a rocking chair on the balcony. The river has a gentle current, so both active and armchair canoers have an easy experience; staff members can arrange river trips from two hours to more than a week long. For those who don't know what to bring on a canoe trip, supply and safety information is provided by Borchers.

SETTING & FACILITIES
Location 1 mi. north of I-75 Exit 256, on the AuSable River **Near** Hartwick Pines State Park, Hansen Hills Recreation Area, Huron National Forest. **Building** 1930s livery inn, red stain exterior & wraparound balcony **Grounds** 1-acre riverside lot w/ forest, bushes, flower beds **Public Space** Foyer, kitchen/dining area, LR **Food & Drink** Cold beverages any time. Full breakfast includes hot entree. **Recreation** Canoeing, hunting, fish hatchery, downhill & cross-country skiing, mountain biking, historic touring, swimming, golf. **Amenities & Services** AC. Baskets made by innkeeper Cheri Hunter are for sale in foyer, along with other gift items. Canoes, kayaks for rent.

ACCOMMODATIONS
Units 6 guest rooms. **All Rooms** Ceiling fan, TV, clock, sitting area. **Some Rooms** Private door to balcony, loveseat, desk, chaise. **Bed & Bath** 2 queens (2), 1 queen (1), double (2), 2 twins (1). 3 private baths, 1 shared. **Favorites** AuSable Room, w/ 2 queen beds, desk & chair, balcony access. **Comfort & Decor** "Casual country with taste" is the style at Borchers. Pine paneling and stuffed furniture set the tone in the public spaces. The balcony, hovering over the quiet river, was the ideal spot for coffee at sunrise. This bed-and-breakfast is a relaxing break from the formality of most bed-and-breakfasts—think jeans and plaid flannel shirts.

RATES, RESERVATIONS, & RESTRICTIONS
Deposit 1 night's stay **Discounts** AARP, weekday **Credit Cards** V, MC, D **Check-In/Out** 1 p.m./noon **Smoking** No **Pets** No **Kids** Yes **No-Nos** N/A **Minimum Stay** 2 nights preferred most weekends **Open** All year **Hosts** Cheri & Mark Hunter, 101 Maple St., Grayling 49738 **Phone** (517) 348-4921 or toll-free (800) 762-8756 **Email** chunter@borchers.com **Web** www.canoeborchers.com

LAURIUM MANOR INN, Laurium

OVERALL ★★★★★ | QUALITY ★★★★½ | VALUE ★★★★★ | PRICE RANGE $69–$109

This 45-room mansion is the largest in the western Upper Peninsula and no doubt the most sumptuous. One could spend a weekend here just wandering, taking it all in; the Art Nouveau–styled foyer hallway alone, with vaulted, canvas-covered ceiling, is 10 feet wide and 50 feet long. Every room is packed with rare details. Note the original thermostats (each room had one, even in 1908), with four settings: freezing, temperate, summer heat, and blood heat. The vaulted dome ceiling in the parlor is hand-painted canvas, covered with silver leaf. In the dining room, gold-backed mirrors and a possible Tiffany custom-designed glass fireplace set off the elephant-hide walls (innkeepers estimate two and a half elephants were sacrificed).

SETTING & FACILITIES

Location In residential Laurium, just off US 41 on the Keweenaw Peninsula **Near** Copper Harbor Lighthouse, Delaware Copper Mine, Eagle Harbor Light Station Museum, Brockway Mountain Drive, Mt. Bohemia, Ft. Wilkins State Park. **Building** 2 Victorian mansions—Laurium Manor (1908, white exterior w/ Corinthian columns, on National Register of Historic Places) and Victorian Hall (1906, brick & sandstone mansion) **Grounds** Oversized city lots, flower beds **Public Space** Laurium Manor: Wraparound porch, foyer, parlor, den, DR, library. Victorian Hall: Wraparound porch, kitchen, parlor, library, foyer, DR **Food & Drink** Early coffee available. Full breakfast buffet includes hot egg dish, breakfast meat. **Recreation** Historic touring, fishing, museums, lighthouse touring, biking, canoeing, kayaking, downhill & cross-country skiing, snowmobiling. **Amenities & Services** AC. Can accommodate dinners & parties for 100 guests.

ACCOMMODATIONS

Units 18 in 2 homes. **All Rooms** Sitting area, clock. **Some Rooms** Fireplace, dressing table & chair, desk & chair. **Bed & Bath** Queens (4), 2 doubles (1), double & twin (2), double (11). 13 private baths, 2 shared. **Favorites** Room #3, originally the nursery, w/ fireplace, antique iron bed, canvas-covered walls, & hand-painted frieze of rabbits, birds, & other small animals. **Comfort & Decor** These mansions must have been the showplaces of the U.P. when they were built by copper barons. We loved the painted ceiling plaster crown work in the library of Victorian Hall, designed to match the flowers in the nearby stained-glass window. In the parlor, curly birch trim was stained to resemble mahogany; wood trim upstairs and down is from the Black Forest in Germany. In Laurium Manor, opulence defines every space—especially in the dining room, where wall coverings (don't touch!) are embossed and gilded elephant hide.

RATES, RESERVATIONS, & RESTRICTIONS

Deposit Credit card number **Discounts** Corp., gov't. rates **Credit Cards** MC, V, D **Check-In/Out** 4–11 p.m./11 a.m. **Smoking** No **Pets** No (resident cat on premises Nov.–May) **Kids** Yes **No-Nos** N/A **Minimum Stay** N/A **Open** All year **Hosts** Julie &

Dave Sprenger, 320 Tamarack St., Laurium 49913 **Phone** (906) 337-2549 **Fax** (815) 328-3692 **Email** innkeeper@lauriummanorinn.com **Web** www.lauriummanorinn.com

CLOGHAUN BED & BREAKFAST, *Mackinac Island*

OVERALL ★★★★ | QUALITY ★★★½ | VALUE ★★★ | PRICE RANGE $100–$165

For more than a century, Cloghaun (pronounced, "clo-haun") has been a family affair, built by the owner's great-grandparents. Marti Carey adorns the hallways with displays of Victorian and vintage artifacts she's collected—combs, jewelry, other small pieces—but the plate collection lining the walls of the back parlor are a mystery to her: "They've always been here," she says. Even more mysterious are the bizarre mannequins in the upstairs hallway; one end is guarded by a figure in a white wedding dress, flanked by an Eastlake pump organ and an antique square piano, while at the other end stands the "lady in black"—unsettling late at night.

SETTING & FACILITIES

Location In downtown Mackinac Island, just off the coast of northern Michigan **Near** Downtown shops, Grand Hotel, marina, historic fort, Mackinac Bridge, Upper Peninsula. **Building** 1884 Renaissance Revival, white exterior w/ deep porch & twin balconies **Grounds** Small yard w /landscaped flower gardens **Public Space** DR, front parlor w/ TV, back parlor, entry **Food & Drink** Afternoon tea. Cont'l breakfast, served on china & silver. **Recreation** Boating, historic touring, biking, horseback riding, tennis, golf, horse & buggy rides. **Amenities & Services** Fresh flowers at breakfast. Fax, phone, & copier on site.

ACCOMMODATIONS

Units 11 guest rooms. **All Rooms** Sink, if not private bath. **Some Rooms** Private front balconies w/ town & lake view; private entrance. **Bed & Bath** 2 doubles (9), double (2). 9 private baths, 1 shared. **Favorites** Front balcony rooms—largest rooms, w/ quality antique furnishings & deep balconies. **Comfort & Decor** Country and French country are the decorating styles throughout Cloghaun. The feel is that of a lakeside inn, especially sitting on the room-sized porches and watching tourists pass by. Our room had a built-in closet with glass-front door, lined with lace curtains—an unusual feature, we thought—and Eastlake bed and dresser.

RATES, RESERVATIONS, & RESTRICTIONS

Deposit 1 night's stay **Discounts** Midweek, off-season **Credit Cards** V, MC **Check-In/Out** 3 p.m./10 a.m. **Smoking** On porch **Pets** No **Kids** Over age 2 **No-Nos** Watching TV late at night; the TV parlor is adjacent to a guest room **Minimum Stay** 2 nights weekends in season **Open** All year **Hosts** Marti & Paul Carey, Market St., P.O. Box 1540, Mackinac Island 49757 **Phone** (906) 847-3885 or toll-free (888) 442-5929 **Email** cloghaun@aol.com **Web** www.cloghaun.com

METIVIER INN, Mackinac Island

OVERALL ★★★★ | QUALITY ★★★½ | VALUE ★★★ | PRICE RANGE $125–$205 LOW SEASON, $190–$285 HIGH SEASON

Metivier Inn isn't as renowned as some other lodgings on Mackinac Island, but it's one of the lovelier properties in town. Because it sits on an oversized lot, the side yards encourage migrating birds—much to the entertainment of guests. The breakfast area feels a bit cramped, but the spacious rooms and porches more than compensate. Tourists crowd the streets in summer, but Metivier's flower gardens help create an escape from the multitudes on the other side of the gate.

SETTING & FACILITIES
Location In downtown Mackinac Island, just off the coast of northern Michigan **Near** Downtown shops, Grand Hotel, Mackinac Bridge, marina, historic fort, Upper Peninsula. **Building** 1877 Victorian home w/ additions **Grounds** About 0.5 acre of landscaped gardens, lawns **Public Space** Front & side porches, common room/breakfast area, coffee area, small 2nd-floor sitting area w/ writing desk **Food & Drink** Cont'l breakfast. **Recreation** Boating, historic touring, biking, horseback rides, tennis, golf, horse & buggy rides. **Amenities & Services** Logo soaps; phone & modem access.

ACCOMMODATIONS
Units 1 suite, 20 guest rooms. **All Rooms** Sitting area, clock. **Some Rooms** Garden view, TV, roll-away bed, settee, whirlpool tub, private patio, access to quiet side porch. **Bed & Bath** King (1), 2 queens (1), queens (19). All private baths. **Favorites** John Jacob Astor room w/ turret area, canopy bed, garden view. **Comfort & Decor** The style throughout Metivier Inn is country. We liked the ambience of the front rooms; although you get more street noise than in other rooms, we also found it soothing to hear the clip-clop of horses' hooves passing by on their buggy tours. The suite (#12) offers the most amenities, including sink, coffeemaker, TV, table, chairs, and microwave.

RATES, RESERVATIONS, & RESTRICTIONS
Deposit 1 night's stay **Discounts** Mid-week, off-season **Credit Cards** V, MC, AE, D **Check-In/Out** 3 p.m./11 a.m. **Smoking** On porches **Pets** No **Kids** Yes **No-Nos** N/A **Minimum Stay** 2 nights Sat. and special weekends **Open** May–Oct. **Hosts** Angie Leonard, Box 285, Mackinac Island 49757 **Phone** (906) 847-6234 **Email** metinn@lighthouse.net **Web** www.metivierinn.com

WATER STREET INN, Sault Sainte Marie

OVERALL ★★★★ | QUALITY ★★★★ | VALUE ★★★★ | PRICE RANGE $75–$105

Another great location Water Street Inn sits high above the St. Mary River, providing guests with an unobstructed view of Canada. Sault Sainte Marie is the country's third-oldest city, so there's plenty of history to explore here, through Native American, French, British, and American eras, to the current status as the busiest lock system in the world. That means hours of porch-front gazing at freighters gliding by. Inside, two collections caught our eye: the owner's porcelain doll collection and her teacup collection in the dining room.

SETTING & FACILITIES
Location Just outside downtown, a block from the Sault Locks, across the St. Mary's River from Canada **Near** Downtown shopping, Sault Locks, Seney Wildlife Refuge, Agawa Canyon Tour Train, Les Cheneaux Island Area, Great Lakes Shipwreck Historical Museum. **Building** 1904 yellow brick Princess Anne Victorian **Grounds** Double lot sloping to the river, w/ gazebo & flower gardens **Public Space** Wraparound porch, foyer w/built-in benches, DR, parlor **Food & Drink** Hot chocolate, spiced cider, hot beverages, cookies any time. Early coffee delivered to rooms. Full breakfast includes egg dish, pancakes, meat. **Recreation** Historic touring, museums, birding, downhill & cross-country skiing, antiquing, biking, fishing, golf. **Amenities & Services** AC. Logo soaps, robes.

ACCOMMODATIONS
Units 4 guest rooms. **All Rooms** Sitting area, ceiling fans, settee. **Some Rooms** Bay window, fireplace, river view, dressing table, desk. **Bed & Bath** Queen (1), double plus twin (1), doubles (2). All private baths (1 detached). **Favorites** Flagship Room, largest guest room w/ beveled-glass mirror, desk & chair, curved-glass window. **Comfort & Decor** We're always impressed by vintage curved glass in windows. Water Street Inn also features ornately carved fireplace with beveled glass, and a possible Tiffany window at the staircase landing—one of many stained-glass windows. Trim throughout the house is hard wood (oak, cherry, maple); we especially liked the elaborate built-in serving butler in the dining room, designed after a room in the White House.

RATES, RESERVATIONS, & RESTRICTIONS
Deposit Credit card number **Discounts** None **Credit Cards** V, MC **Check-In/Out** 3 p.m./11 a.m. **Smoking** No **Pets** No; resident dog stays in innkeepers' quarters **Kids** Over age 16 **No-Nos** N/A **Minimum Stay** None **Open** All year **Hosts** Anna & Duane Henion, 140 East Water St., Sault Sainte Marie 49783 **Phone** (906) 632-1900 or toll-free (800) 236-1904

Western Michigan

Put **Traverse City** on your to-do list—and we mean the entire region from **Elk Rapids** at the north of Zone 10, past the **Old Mission and Leelanau Peninsulas,** down past **Sleeping Bear Dunes National Lakeshore**—or, as they say all over the Midwest, "the Dunes." Give yourself the whole summer if you can, because that's how long you can spend here without seeing and experiencing everything.

Traverse City itself is a hopping-busy resort town at the foot of **Grand Traverse Bay,** which is actually twin bays, divided by the Old Mission Peninsula. Follow Route 37 for about eight miles up the peninsula and you're treated to a panoramic view of both bays; the road takes you past award-winning wineries, **cherry orchards,** and lakeside cottages you wish you lived in.

Spend the next day exploring the more hilly Leelanau Peninsula, a few miles west of town. Artsy villages, galleries, and more wineries (including the one Madonna recently purchased for her father) await—and do stop at some of the wineries for tastings. Vintners in this region are known for their quality dry wines and semi-sweets.

Along the coast, we found one lakeside resort town after another—and they are not cookie-cutter communities by any means. **Saugatuck** began as an artists' colony and still is filled with galleries and boutiques; many former artists' cottages now serve as inns. **Ludington State Park,** six miles north of Ludington, might be the least crowded beach on the west coast—it's worth the drive. In **Grand Haven,** the old stone pier attracts fishermen and sight-seers alike, and everyone should see the windmills and tulip gardens of **Holland.**

Aside from **Lake Michigan's** attractions, the one similarity between most of the towns is their bed-and-breakfast style. Most are Victorians, and because their primary industry is tourism, many serve a no-frills continental breakfast of bagels, cold cereals, and juice. If you look forward to a hearty morning meal at bed-and-breakfasts, be sure to ask the innkeeper about breakfast when you make your reservation.

CANDLELIGHT INN, *Elk Rapids*

OVERALL ★★★½ | QUALITY ★★★½ | VALUE ★★★★★ | PRICE RANGE $75

For those visiting northwest Michigan, who want to avoid more tourist-crowded resort towns, Elk Rapids is a slower-paced alternative. It's a coastal village on the bay, 15 miles north of Traverse City, whose entire waterfront is open to the public. Candlelight Inn, just three blocks inland, is an unassuming little spot for resting weary bones. Some original features of the house have been preserved, including ash stair rails and woodwork, the oak front door, and a stained-glass window.

SETTING & FACILITIES
Location In residential Elk Rapids, several blocks west of US 31 **Near** Grand Traverse Bay, downtown Elk Rapids, Sleeping Bear National Park, Elk Rapids Harbor. **Building** 1890 Gothic cottage, white exterior **Grounds** 0.5 acre w/ lawns, flower gardens **Public Space** Common area, DR, side porch **Food & Drink** Hot beverages available any time. Cont'l-plus breakfast. **Recreation** Fishing, boating, biking, swimming, golf, historic touring.

ACCOMMODATIONS
Units 3 guest rooms, plus 1 overflow room. **All Rooms** Ceiling fan, sitting area. **Some Rooms** N/A. **Bed & Bath** Queens (3), double (1). All private half-baths. **Favorites** Amish Room, most spacious, w/ Amish-made furniture. **Comfort & Decor** This is a modest home, but the innkeepers have taken care to ensure guests' comfort with double-pillowtop mattresses, hand-sewn quilted bed coverings, and bedside reading lights. Bed styles vary—Eastlake, antique iron, or Amish—and we liked the Americana Room, decorated in patriotic colors.

RATES, RESERVATIONS, & RESTRICTIONS
Deposit 1 night's stay **Discounts** None **Credit Cards** V, MC **Check-In/Out** 11 a.m./3 p.m. **Smoking** No **Pets** No (resident dog was elderly at time of our visit; stays in innkeepers' quarters) **Kids** Yes, but rooms have only 1 bed; air mattress available for $10/night **No-Nos** Food or drinks in guest rooms **Minimum Stay** 2 nights weekends in July & Aug. **Open** All year **Hosts** Jean & Dick Lamphier, 310 Spruce St., P.O. Box 476, Elk Rapids 49629 **Phone** (231) 264-5630

BOYDEN HOUSE BED & BREAKFAST, *Grand Haven*

OVERALL ★★★★½ | QUALITY ★★★★½ | VALUE ★★★★ | PRICE RANGE $110–$150

Of the 300 bed-and-breakfasts we visited, Boyden House most successfully proves our theory: If you love your stuff and choose it carefully, it works. The Kowalskis blend their artist daughter's contemporary pieces with Midwest pottery, Caribbean pizzazz, occasional American antiques, and whatever beads, ribbons, or scarves complete the vision for that room. Imagine such frivolity in a home with inlaid parquet floors and rich cherry paneling—a quality experience all around.

SETTING & FACILITIES

Location Residential Grand Haven, 0.5 mi. off US 31 **Near** Lake Michigan, museums, marina, beaches, downtown Grand Haven. **Building** 1874 gray-shingled Queen Anne Victorian **Grounds** Flower gardens, fish pond, tiered deck, fountain **Public Space** Porch, DR w/ alcove, second DR w/ fireplace, massage room, guest kitchen **Food & Drink** Coffee/tea any time. Candlelight gourmet breakfast w/ fresh flowers; specialty is breakfast pizza w/ mushrooms, bacon, bleu cheese, sun-dried tomatoes, egg, cheese. **Recreation** Swimming, boating, museums, historic touring, biking. **Amenities & Services** AC. Hair dryer, curling iron, fax available; massage therapist available by appointment. TGIF social hour when inn is full.

ACCOMMODATIONS

Units 7 guest rooms & carriage house. **All Rooms** Clock, phone, TV/VCR, CD player. **Some Rooms** Double whirlpool tub, fireplace, private porch, private entrance, sofas, chaise. **Bed & Bath** Kings (3), queens (5). All private baths. **Favorites** Carriage House— not the most elegant space, but the privacy, king bed, sofas, & kitchenette make it special. **Comfort & Decor** Unlike most Victorian bed-and-breakfasts, Boyden House is not filled with lace and heavy antiques and foo-foo accessories—thank heavens! With ornately carved woodworking, massive pocket doors, arched doorways, and elaborate fretwork as the backdrop, the Kowalskis furnished the inn with contemporary paintings, sculptures and funky items they've picked up over the years. The effect is hip and bold, yet romantic.

RATES, RESERVATIONS, & RESTRICTIONS

Deposit Credit card number or 50% of stay **Discounts** Off-season rates **Credit Cards** V, MC, AE **Check-In/Out** 1 p.m./11 a.m. **Smoking** Outside **Pets** No **Kids** Inquire **No-Nos** N/A **Minimum Stay** 2 nights weekends May 1–Nov. 1; 3 nights holidays **Open** All year **Hosts** Tony & Gail Kowalski, 301 South 5th St., Grand Haven 49417 **Phone** (616) 846-3538 **Email** gkowalski@triton.net **Web** www.bbonline.com/mi/boyden

HARBOR HOUSE INN, *Grand Haven*

OVERALL ★★★★ | QUALITY ★★★★ | VALUE ★★★ | PRICE RANGE $140–$190 IN SEASON; $130–$180 SHOULDER SEASON WEEKENDS

Reminiscent of a modernized farmhouse, Harbor House is a typical seaside resort inn, with enough porch space for every guest. Originally intended as condos, the rooms are spacious and individually decorated, most with a harbor view. Just across the road is Grand Haven's boardwalk, giving guests an easy stroll to white sandy beaches, shops, and galleries, or they can grab a bench and enjoy the Lake Michigan dune vistas.

SETTING & FACILITIES

Location Facing Grand Haven harbor on the Grand River, Lake Michigan **Near** Downtown Grand Haven, Lake Michigan, dunes, Grand Haven Lighthouse, museums, marina, beaches. **Building** 1987 Victorian-style inn w/ screened & open porches **Grounds** Corner lot across the road from the riverfront **Public Space** Porch, screened porch, foyer/reception area, LR, library, coffee station **Food & Drink** Hot beverages, cookies available any time. Cont'l-plus buffet breakfast includes fresh-baked cinnamon bread, cereals, cheeses, other baked goods. **Recreation** Swimming, biking, boating, cross-country skiing, fishing, antiquing, golf. **Amenities & Services** AC. Catering, meeting facilities, gift baskets, icemaker & ice buckets available.

ACCOMMODATIONS

Units 17 guest rooms. **All Rooms** TV/VCR, phone, clock radio, modem, sitting area. **Some Rooms** Gas log fireplace, river view, garden view, whirlpool tub, galley kitchen. **Bed & Bath** Kings: (10), queen & sofa bed (1), queens (6). All private baths. **Favorites** Cottage Garden View Suite, w/ queen bed & queen sofa bed, galley kitchen, fireplace, & whirlpool tub. **Comfort & Decor** This almost-Victorian inn strikes a rare balance of being both romantic and family-friendly. The Federal-style living room offers a wood-burning stove, much appreciated in cool October evenings on Lake Michigan, whereas the library is more clubby—wood-paneled with TV and newspapers—giving guests two comfortable options for relaxing, depending on their mood.

RATES, RESERVATIONS, & RESTRICTIONS

Deposit Credit card number **Discounts** Corp. & off-season weekday rates **Credit Cards** V, MC, AE **Check-In/Out** 2 p.m./11 a.m. **Smoking** On porches **Pets** No **Kids** Yes; $25 charge for 3rd person requiring roll-away or trundle bed **No-Nos** N/A **Minimum Stay** 2 nights on summer weekends **Open** All year; closed only on Thanksgiving Day, Christmas Eve, & Christmas **Hosts** Linda Dybevik, 114 South Harbor Dr., Grand Haven 49417 **Phone** (616) 846-0610 or toll-free (800) 841-0610 **Web** www.harborhousegh.com

PARSONAGE 1908 BED & BREAKFAST, Holland

OVERALL ★★★★ | QUALITY ★★★★ | VALUE ★★★★ | PRICE RANGE $100–$130

The Parsonage could be nicknamed House of Creativity. Witness the doll house on the front porch—an exact replica of the Parsonage. Inside, walls are adorned with paintings by the innkeeper's grandfather, a self-taught artist who died young; we thought his work was quite good. Even the back yard holds creative touches: as you walk to the patio, look down at the stepping-stones; they're old iron wall registers.

SETTING & FACILITIES

Location Just off US 31 in residential Holland **Near** Lake Michigan, antiques malls, Hope College, Saugatuck Resort. **Building** 1908 former Christian Reformed Church parsonage **Grounds** Very private hedge-walled city lot w/ flower gardens, brick patio, seating **Public Space** Glassed-in porch, foyer, 2 front sitting rooms, DR **Food & Drink** Lemonade, cookies any time. Full breakfast includes entree such as puff pancakes or baked egg dish, breakfast meats. **Recreation** Boating, swimming, tennis, biking, antiquing, live theater, cross-country skiing, golf. **Amenities & Services** AC. Fresh flowers from innkeeper's garden in guest rooms, logo soaps, robes.

ACCOMMODATIONS

Units 3 guest rooms. **All Rooms** Ceiling fans, reading lights, sitting area. **Some Rooms** Claw-foot tub. **Bed & Bath** Doubles (2), 2 twins (1). 2 private baths; 2 shared if inn is full. **Favorites** Parson's Room w/ 8-foot-high Eastlake headboard, French desk & chair, & marble-topped English washstand w/ slop jar. **Comfort & Decor** "My kids think I have too much stuff in some of these rooms," innkeeper Bonnie laments. Perhaps, but we love the ambience of cozy, tongue-in-cheek parson's residence. A Gothic stained-glass window in the foyer reminds guests of the home's heritage, and original features, including pillared room dividers and beveled-glass windows, class it up. A rare hired man's bed sits in a front parlor.

RATES, RESERVATIONS, & RESTRICTIONS

Deposit Payment in advance **Discounts** Extended-stay **Credit Cards** No **Check-In/Out** 4 p.m. or by prior arrangement/noon **Smoking** No **Pets** No **Kids** "The B&B is adult-oriented" **No-Nos** Guests who bring wine are encouraged to drink it on the patio or porch, rather than in guest rooms **Minimum Stay** 2 nights on weekends **Open** All year **Hosts** Bonnie McVoy-Verwys, 6 East 24th St., Holland 49423 **Phone** (616) 396-1316 **Web** www.bbonline.com/mi/parsonage

BETWEEN THE LAKES BED & BREAKFAST, Interlochen

OVERALL ★★★½ | QUALITY ★★★½ | VALUE ★★★ | PRICE RANGE $95–$110

Guest rooms are individually decorated; themes include Michigan harbors, Scandinavian art, and African art. Upon returning from dinner at about 8:30 p.m., however, we were surprised to find all common areas dark, sending the clear message that guests were not welcome to relax there after dinner.

SETTING & FACILITIES

Location On isthmus between Duck Lake & Green Lake, off MI 137 **Near** Traverse City, Sleeping Bear Dunes National Park, Interlochen State Park, Interlochen Center for the Arts, Crystal Mountain. **Building** 1980s ranch home w/ green exterior **Grounds** Residential lot; bushes, trees **Public Space** Common room, DR, heated lap pool **Food & Drink** Cont'l breakfast. Afternoon tea 4–6 p.m. **Recreation** Boating, downhill & cross-country skiing, swimming, performing arts, birding. **Amenities & Services** AC.

ACCOMMODATIONS

Units 5 guest rooms. **All Rooms** Sitting area, clock. **Some Rooms** Desk & chair, window seat, fireplace, private entrance. **Bed & Bath** King (1), Queen & double (1), queens (2), 2 doubles (1). All private baths. **Favorites** Inuit room, w/ Native American art from Hudson Bay area, desk & chair. **Comfort & Decor** Common areas are furnished w/ contemporary seating. In the living room, Asian art and a gas log fireplace set the tone; African sculpture and masks decorate the dining room, all gathered during the innkeeper's career in the U.S. Foreign Service.

RATES, RESERVATIONS, & RESTRICTIONS

Deposit 1 night's stay **Discounts** Senior; off-season rates; children under 24 months stay free **Credit Cards** V, MC, AE **Check-In/Out** 3–7 p.m./11 a.m. **Smoking** No **Pets** No (during our stay, resident German shepherd knocked down baby gate intended to keep him away from guest rooms and repeatedly growled at us) **Kids** Yes **No-Nos** Eating in room, candles **Minimum Stay** 2 nights June, July, Aug., holiday weekends **Open** All year; closed several days a week **Hosts** Barbara & Gordon Evans, 4570 Case Blvd., P.O. Box 280, Interlochen 49643 **Phone** (231) 276-7751 **Fax** (231) 276-6242 **Email** info@between lakes.com **Web** www.betweenlakes.com

CENTENNIAL INN, *Lake Leelanau*

OVERALL ★★★★½ | QUALITY ★★★★½ | VALUE ★★★★★ | PRICE RANGE $85

The setting, across the road from a cherry orchard, is perfect for the image: a historic inn where over the generations notables and common folk alike have found respite and a warm welcome. We were dazzled by the innkeepers' collections—candle molds, pewter, German miniature sheep, Bennington pottery, Beaumont pottery, and a collection of fine quilts that has taken more than half a century to build. We loved being here and will use it as our base when we return to explore northwest Michigan's wineries.

SETTING & FACILITIES

Location 3.6 mi. north of Leland, off CR 641 **Near** Sugar Loaf Resort, Leelanau State Park, Sleeping Bear National Lakeshore, Suttons Bay, Leland. **Building** 1865 country farm house w/ German flavor **Grounds** 5 acres of meadows, woods; historic barns, granary, & carriage house **Public Space** LR, DR, patio, deck, coffee area off kitchen **Food & Drink** Snacks, beverages available during day; occasional dessert served. Full country breakfast includes egg dish (usually omelets), meat. **Recreation** Biking, fishing, boating, downhill & cross-country skiing, winery tours. **Amenities & Services** AC. TV in living room cabinet.

ACCOMMODATIONS

Units 3 guest rooms. **All Rooms** Sitting area. **Some Rooms** N/A. **Bed & Bath** Doubles (3). 1 private bath, 1 shared. **Favorites** Apple Room, for the private bath. **Comfort & Decor** These hosts pride themselves on the authenticity of their furnishings and collections, and we were duly impressed. Common areas feature one-of-a-kind early-century pine furniture; we found the small plank table and window seat in the coffee area especially endearing. Glass doors leading to the dining room are more than 150 years old.

RATES, RESERVATIONS, & RESTRICTIONS
Deposit 50% of stay **Discounts** None **Credit Cards** No **Check-In/Out** 3 p.m./11 a.m. **Smoking** No **Pets** No **Kids** No **Minimum Stay** None **Open** All year **Hosts** Karl & JoAnne Smith, 7251 East Alpers Rd., Lake Leelanau 49653 **Phone** (231) 271-6460

SCHOENBERGER HOUSE, Ludington

OVERALL ★★★★★ | QUALITY ★★★★½ | VALUE ★★★★ | PRICE RANGE $145–$245

Innkeeper Marlene Schoenberger's family has lived here for more than 50 years; she remembers, as a little girl, roller-skating across the third-floor gymnasium (rumor has it that the gym once held trapezes). Every corner holds a family yarn; one of the best concerns the area rugs in the living and music rooms. Decades ago, a former owner asked Schoenberger's mother if he could use the house for a party, as his new home was too small. She consented and he gave her the valuable rugs, which had been original to the house, as a thank-you gift. Our favorite feature, though, is the dining room radiator—with a built-in bun warmer! That was a first for us.

SETTING & FACILITIES
Location On Ludington's main artery, 0.5 mi. west of US 31 **Near** Lake Michigan, city marina, car ferry, Ludington State Park. **Building** 1903-4 Neoclassical home of yellow brick w/ pillared double porch **Grounds** City lot; flower beds **Public Space** Front porches up & down, side porch, foyer, LR, DR, music room, library **Food & Drink** Full breakfast. **Recreation** Swimming, boating, cross-country skiing, snowmobiling, performing arts. **Amenities & Services** AC. Sat. musical events, Sun. brunch w/ music, both on select weekends. Can accommodate meetings & retreats.

ACCOMMODATIONS
Units 4 guest rooms, 1 suite. **All Rooms** Sitting area. **Some Rooms** Private balcony, claw-foot tub, fireplace. **Bed & Bath** King (1), queens (4). All private baths. **Favorites**

Master suite, w/ antique bath fixtures (including old foot tub), fireplace flanked by built-in benches, private balcony. **Comfort & Decor** Every room displays sophistication and opulence, with four different patterns of inlaid parquet floors, rich cherry trim in the living room, mahogany woodwork in the music room, and black walnut in the library, set off by dramatic wall stenciling original to the house—all background for custom-tile fireplaces, pocket doors, and other Craftsman features. Furnishings are formal, appropriate to the grandeur of the home.

RATES, RESERVATIONS, & RESTRICTIONS
Deposit Credit card number **Discounts** None **Credit Cards** V, MC, AE **Check-In/Out** By arrangement **Smoking** No **Pets** No **Kids** Over age 14 **No-Nos** N/A **Minimum Stay** 2 nights on music weekends **Open** All year **Hosts** Marlene Schoenberger, 409 East Ludington Ave., Ludington 49431 **Phone** (231) 843-4435 **Fax** (231) 843-4435 **Web** www.bbonline.com/mi/schoenberger

EMERY HOUSE, Muskegon

OVERALL ★★★★ | QUALITY ★★★★ | VALUE ★★★★ | PRICE RANGE $80

Once a home for runaways (and, more recently, a complex of crafts boutiques), Emery House still retains features of its first life as a bank president's home. Tile flooring and leaded glass mark the entry; throughout the first floor one finds bays and Federal-style wood trim. In guest rooms, fine antiques—including a primitive "rope" bed—furnish the rooms; baths have original marble sinks, claw-foot tubs, and medicine cabinets.

SETTING & FACILITIES
Location On US B 31, several blocks from Muskegon Lake **Near** Hackley Park, Muskegon Museum of Art, Muskegon County Museum, Frauenthal Center of Performing Arts **Building** 1903–6 brick Georgian Colonial, in Heritage Village (National Historic District) **Grounds** City lot, English garden & courtyard **Public Space** Porch, foyer, DR, parlor/game room, 2nd-floor guest kitchenette **Food & Drink** "Super cont'l" breakfast of muffins, breads, cereals, hard-boiled eggs, hot applesauce. **Recreation** Live theater, swimming, boating, historic touring, antiquing, museums. **Amenities & Services** AC.

ACCOMMODATIONS
Units 4 guest rooms & carriage house room. **All Rooms** Ceiling fans, sitting areas. **Some Rooms** Hand-sewn quilted bed covering, fireplace, built-in closet, dressing table & chair, bay window. **Bed & Bath** Doubles (5). All private baths. **Favorites** Carriage house, for the privacy. **Comfort & Decor** The Georgian influence is most visible in the mahogany staircase in the center hall. The home went through much "remuddling" over the years, but some features survived: the Jacobean oak wainscoting in the parlor is in great shape, and the original French sconces and matching etched-glass dining room chandelier are unique. The dining room table also is original to the house.

RATES, RESERVATIONS, & RESTRICTIONS
Deposit $25 **Discounts** Extended stay (more than 3 nights) **Credit Cards** No **Check-In/Out** 3–5 p.m./11 a.m. **Smoking** No **Pets** No **Kids** Over age 4 **No-Nos** Alco-

hol on the premises, coolers **Minimum Stay** 2 nights summer weekends **Open** May 1–Oct. 31 **Hosts** Bill & Barbara Frame, 446 West Webster (B 31 South), Muskegon 49440 **Phone** (231) 722-6978 **Web** www.bbonline.com/mi/emery

HACKLEY-HOLT HOUSE BED & BREAKFAST, Muskegon

OVERALL ★★★½ | QUALITY ★★★½ | VALUE ★★★ | PRICE RANGE $89 SUMMER, $75 WINTER

Built by a lumber baron, the Hackley-Holt House is an impressive sight from the street. Inside, the grapevine chandelier in the foyer caught our eye immediately. In the parlor, an organ occupies a cozy alcove set off by fretwork trim. Some updating will be beneficial but isn't an urgent need; this home is comfortable and decorated with taste and restraint.

SETTING & FACILITIES

Location Behind the Hackley & Hume historic sites in Heritage Village, a National Historic District **Near** Frauenthal Theater, Muskegon Lake, Cherry County Playhouse, L. C. Walker Arena, Muskegon County Museum, Muskegon Museum of Art. **Building** 1857 brick Italianate w/ wraparound porch **Grounds** Oversized city lot; lawns, flower beds **Public Space** Porch, foyer, parlor, DR, library **Food & Drink** Sodas, snacks available any time. Full breakfast includes hot entree. **Recreation** Live theater, historic touring, art museum, boating, swimming, fishing, cross-country skiing, ice skating. **Amenities & Services** AC. Robes, bicycles available.

ACCOMMODATIONS

Units 4 guest rooms. **All Rooms** TV, clock radio, sitting area. **Some Rooms** Phones, claw-foot tub. **Bed & Bath** King/2 twins (1), queens (3). All private baths (1 detached). **Favorites** Rose Room, for the sitting alcove. **Comfort & Decor** Furnishings in most rooms are Victorian, following the home's design features—original ceiling medallions, bull's-eye moldings, the original stained-glass window in the parlor alcove, and an ornate fireplace in the parlor with mirror, Eastlake topper and deep blue tile surround. Restoration is ongoing.

RATES, RESERVATIONS, & RESTRICTIONS

Deposit Credit card number or 1 night's stay **Discounts** None **Credit Cards** V, MC, AE, D **Check-In/Out** 4–7 p.m./11 a.m. **Smoking** Outside **Pets** No; resident cat and dog are confined to innkeepers' quarters **Kids** Inquire **No-Nos** N/A **Minimum Stay** N/A **Open** All year **Hosts** Bill & Nancy Stone, 523 West Clay Ave., Muskegon 49440 **Phone** (231) 725-7303 or toll-free (888) 271-5609 **Email** hhhbb@gte.net **Web** www.bbonline.com/mi/hhhbb

MARTHA'S VINEYARD BED & BREAKFAST, South Haven

OVERALL ★★★★½ | QUALITY ★★★★½ | VALUE ★★★★ | PRICE RANGE $120–$165

The marble walkway leading to the front porch is your first clue that Martha's Vineyard is about opulence and being pampered. From there, the soft classical music (indoors and out), the marble fireplace and baby grand piano in the living room, and gold-plated fixtures in the guest room all affirm your high expectations. The Donnans set out to create a true escape from the pressures of daily living, and they achieved their goal, down to Paul's expert gardening; his flowers practically pour over the picket fence.

SETTING & FACILITIES
Location On the Blue Star Highway, 2 mi. north of South Haven **Near** Lake Michigan, South Haven shopping. **Building** 1852 Federal farm house, remodeled, white exterior **Grounds** 4 acres enclosed by white picket fence, pond w/ geese, private beach on Lake Michigan, flower gardens **Public Space** Porch, entry, LR, DR **Food & Drink** Early coffee available at 7:30 a.m., brownies & sodas available all day. "Lavish workhorse" 4-course breakfast w/ "careful presentation" includes caramel apple pancakes; served on linens & heirloom china. **Recreation** Swimming, boating, charter fishing, biking, snowmobiling, antiquing, dinner cruises, golf. **Amenities & Services** Robes, hors d'oeuvres tray in guest rooms. Massage therapist, catered dinners on veranda, picnic baskets available.

ACCOMMODATIONS
Units 5 guest rooms. **All Rooms** Private veranda, gas fireplace, sitting area, ceiling fan. **Some Rooms** Whirlpool tub, oversized shower. **Bed & Bath** Queens (5), all custom-made w/ pillowtop mattresses. All private baths. **Favorites** The Arbor, w/ iron bed, French doors opening to veranda, 2-person shower. **Comfort & Decor** Martha's Vineyard is aptly named; the ambience is luxury cottage. We thought the rooms were on the small side, but no matter—they're elegantly appointed and romantic as any we've seen. The verandas give a calming, beautiful view from every room; if you take work on your getaway, choose the Manchester Suite with a built-in window desk.

RATES, RESERVATIONS, & RESTRICTIONS
Deposit 50% of stay **Discounts** Seasonal specials **Credit Cards** V, MC, D **Check-In/Out** 3–8 p.m./11 a.m. **Smoking** No **Pets** No **Kids** Yes, but only 2 guests per room **No-Nos** N/A **Minimum Stay** 2 nights weekends in season **Open** All year **Hosts** Paul & Pamela Donnan, 473 Blue Star Highway, South Haven 49090 **Phone** (616) 637-9373 **Fax** (616) 639-8214 **Email** Donnans@marthasvy.com **Web** www.marthasvy.com

SEYMOUR HOUSE, South Haven

OVERALL ★★★★ | QUALITY ★★★★ | VALUE ★★★ | PRICE RANGE $110–$140 IN SEASON; $100–$135 Nov.-April

With the attention she gives to details, it's not surprising that innkeeper Friedl Scimo is a former hotelier. Subtleties are evident even in the themed guest rooms: deck chairs are the seating for the Michigan Room's nautical look; a willow loveseat sits in the Colorado Room; and where else would you find skylights but in the Austrian Room? The peach farmer who built this stately home would be pleased.

SETTING & FACILITIES
Location On Blue Star Highway, 8 mi. north of South Haven **Near** South Haven shopping, Saugatuck, Kal-Haven Trail, Lake Michigan. **Building** 1862 Italianate, brick **Grounds** 11 acres w/ 1-acre pond, paddleboat, canoe, groomed walking trails **Public Space** Vestibule, parlor, DR, library, pantry, 3-season porch **Food & Drink** Early coffee available; cookies & sodas all day. Full breakfast includes hot entree. **Recreation** Biking, cross-country skiing, canoeing, birding, boating, swimming, antiquing. **Amenities & Services** Small gift shop area in vestibule. Massage therapist, picnic baskets available. Can accommodate parties & weddings to 50 guests. Theme packages, horse-drawn wagon rides, progressive dinners (Dec.).

ACCOMMODATIONS
Units 5 guest rooms; also secluded 2-BR log cabin available (no meals or maid service in cabin). **All Rooms** Sitting area. **Some Rooms** TV/VCR, ceiling fan, whirlpool tub, claw-foot tub, CD player, skylights, pond view. **Bed & Bath** King (1), queens (4). All private bath. **Favorites** Austrian Room, decorated w/ pictures & pottery from Salzburg & Vienna, lit by 2 skylights. **Comfort & Decor** Fretwork, original window glass and light fixtures, and unusual Eastlake spoon-carved woodwork in the dining room have been enhanced by newer features, such as the trompe-l'oeil dining room painting that matches the wallpaper and the murals in the Colorado guest room. Painted wainscoting in the dining room is original, but the best spot for morning coffee is the sunny three-season porch.

RATES, RESERVATIONS, & RESTRICTIONS
Deposit Credit card number **Discounts** Weekday **Credit Cards** V, MC, D **Check-In/Out** 4–7 p.m./11 a.m. **Smoking** No **Pets** No (resident cat stays outdoors) **Kids** In cabins only **No-Nos** N/A **Minimum Stay** 2 nights weekends (in cabins, 2 nights always) **Open** All year **Hosts** Friedl Scimo, 1248 Blue Star Highway, South Haven 49090 **Phone** (616) 227-3918 **Fax** (616) 227-3010 **Email** seymour@cybersol.com **Web** www.seymourhouse.com

CHATEAU CHANTAL WINERY AND BED & BREAKFAST, Traverse City (Old Mission Peninsula)

OVERALL ★★★★★ | QUALITY ★★★★½ | VALUE ★★★★ | PRICE RANGE $125–$150

In the evening, when the fire's roaring in the great room and you've poured yourself a glass of the best dry red in the state, Chateau Chantal feels like your personal villa. Perched atop a knoll miles from the tourist clamor of Traverse City, this winery and bed-and-breakfast is a haven with stunning, layered, panoramic views of West Bay and East Bay. They produce a dozen wines, from Cabernet Franc to a pricey ($50/half bottle) but exquisite ice wine. Book your room a year in advance; the inn, as they say, is full.

SETTING & FACILITIES
Location On MI 37, Old Mission Peninsula, 12 mi. north of Traverse City **Near** Wineries, Traverse City, Shanty Creek Resort, Bowers Harbor, Mapleton. **Building** Chateau-style

winery building, 1983 **Grounds** 65 acres, mostly vineyards. **Public Space** Tasting room, winery, great room, breakfast nook **Food & Drink** Full breakfast includes egg dishes, home-baked breads. **Recreation** Winery tours, antiquing, boating, historic touring, swimming, golf. **Amenities & Services** AC. Wine seminars offered. Guests can help themselves to open wine bottles after tasting room closes each evening.

ACCOMMODATIONS

Units 2 suites, 1 guest room. **All Rooms** TV. **Some Rooms** N/A **Bed & Bath** Queens (3). All private baths. **Favorites** Either suite, for the extra space—but any room in this hilltop winery is cozy and luxurious. **Comfort & Decor** The inn just opened in 1993—a decade after CEO Bob Begin started farming the surrounded vineyards—so every space feels new. The winery and common areas reminded us of places we'd seen in France, with a deliberate Old World texture. Guest rooms are furnished with fine contemporary pieces.

RATES, RESERVATIONS, & RESTRICTIONS

Deposit Credit card number or $25 **Discounts** None **Credit Cards** V, MC **Check-In/Out** 3–7 p.m./noon **Smoking** No **Pets** No **Kids** Yes. **No-Nos** N/A **Minimum Stay** 2 nights weekends **Open** All year **Host** Bob Begin, 15900 Rue du Vin, Old Mission Peninsula, Traverse City 49686 **Phone** (231) 223-4110 or toll-free (800) 969-4009 **Email** wine@chateauchantal.com **Web** www.chateauchantal.com

GREY HARE INN, *Traverse City*

OVERALL ★★★★★ | QUALITY ★★★★½ | VALUE ★★★★ | PRICE RANGE $115–$185

The Ruzaks must have had great fun planning their inn. In the Grange du Bois ("barn wood") suite, Cindy designed the wrought-iron grape trellis bed, adding a hickory floor and a mantel made of a close friend's ancestral barn. The design of the breakfast bistro mimics the winery's exterior; even the breakfast is made of Michigan food with French style. The innkeepers were awaiting their first harvest during our visit; if the wine is of the same quality as the winery, it will be a very good year.

SETTING & FACILITIES

Location On MI 37 on the Old Mission Peninsula, 7 mi. north of Traverse City **Near** Wineries, Mapleton, Traverse City, Bowers Harbor, Shanty Creek Resort. **Building** 1998 winery/inn designed to resemble an old stone farm house **Grounds** 27 acres of vineyards, forest, cherry orchard **Public Space** Common room, breakfast "bistro," front & rear patios **Food & Drink** Snack in evening. 2-course breakfast served at guests' convenience before 9:30 a.m.; typical dishes are cherry pecan sausage and egg crêpe w/ 7-grain wild rice & mushrooms. **Recreation** Winery tours, boating, swimming, historic touring, antiquing, golf. **Amenities & Services** AC. Logo bath amenities. Winter special events include a "macaroni & cheese cookoff."

ACCOMMODATIONS

Units 3 guest rooms. **All Rooms** Ceiling fan, bay view, armoire, sitting area, TV. **Some Rooms** Claw-foot tub, gas fireplace, sitting room, whirlpool tub. **Bed & Bath** Queens (3). All private baths. **Favorites** Vineyard Suite, w/ four-poster mahogany canopy bed, private patio, vineyard view, whirlpool tub. **Comfort & Decor** This stylish inn was carefully planned down to the last detail. The common room floor, for instance, is a custom pattern using five sizes of Italian stone tiles, setting off the soft grapevine pattern of the fabric covering the sofa and chairs. The trompe l'oeil in the common room, done by a local artist, is one of the best we've seen, and the rabbit-and-grapevine frieze on the hearth is adorable.

RATES, RESERVATIONS, & RESTRICTIONS

Deposit 50% of stay **Discounts** Repeat referral, travel agent **Credit Cards** No; cash, check, or money order only **Check-In/Out** 4–6 p.m./noon **Smoking** No **Pets** Occasionally by arrangement (resident cats stay in innkeepers' quarters) **Kids** Yes; only 2 guests per room. **No-Nos** "We ask that guests refrain from using perfume during their stay" **Minimum Stay** 2 nights July & Aug.; 2 nights weekends **Open** All year **Hosts** Cindy & Jay Ruzak, P.O. Box 1535, Old Mission Peninsula, Traverse City 49685 **Phone** (231) 947-2214 or tollfree (800) 873-0652 **Email** greyhare@pentel.net **Web** www.pentel.net/greyhare

COUNTRY HERMITAGE BED & BREAKFAST, Williamsburg

OVERALL ★★★★½ | QUALITY ★★★★½ | VALUE ★★★★ | PRICE RANGE $110–$165

Country Hermitage had no plumbing or electricity when the Veliquettes purchased it, so the inn is more modernized than most historic homes. They were able to save the original striped maple and black walnut wainscoting in the dining room, however, along with built-in china cabinets, restored wood trim throughout the house, and other Craftsman touches. If it's warm outside, guests can eat breakfast on the wraparound deck. Keep your eyes peeled for a photo op up the road—a sign indicating the halfway point between the North Pole and the Equator.

SETTING & FACILITIES

Location On US 31 5 mi. NE of Traverse City **Near** Traverse City, VASA Trail, Music House Museum, East Grand Traverse Bay, wineries, Turtle Creek Casino. **Building** 1883 Victorian farmhouse, yellow exterior, on National Register of Historic Places **Grounds** 350 acres of cherry trees & hiking trails **Public Space** Deck, DR, sun room, parlor, library, "gallery" LR, small kitchen gift shop **Food & Drink** Complimentary sodas all day; complimentary wine, beer in evening. Full farm-style breakfast. **Recreation** Historic touring, casino, charter fishing, boating, sailing, swimming, antiquing, cross-country skiing, winery touring, golf. **Amenities & Services** AC. Logo soaps & bath grains; offers golf packages, access to spa & workout facilities, modem hookup, fax. Will arrange flowers, special baskets.

ACCOMMODATIONS

Units 5 guest rooms. **All Rooms** TV, ceiling fan, sitting area, bay view. **Some Rooms** Panoramic orchard view, fireplace, whirlpool tub. **Bed & Bath** King (1), queens (4). All private baths. **Favorites** Amon Room—the smallest guest room, but sunny, private corner room with orchard views in 2 directions. **Comfort & Decor** This farmhouse had been abandoned for 30 years before the Veliquettes purchased it, so nearly every surface and feature is new. That accounts for its surprisingly sunny, airy quality—rare in Victorians—but certain aspects, such as the Eastlake-style fireplace in the gallery living room, give a tasteful nod to the past. It's a pleasing juxtaposition to the contemporary local art displayed on the walls, all for sale.

RATES, RESERVATIONS, & RESTRICTIONS

Deposit Credit card number or 50% of stay **Discounts** Corp. **Credit Cards** V, MC, AE, D **Check-In/Out** 4–7 p.m./11 a.m. **Smoking** No **Pets** No **Kids** Yes, but "this is a romantic getaway" **No-Nos** N/A **Minimum Stay** 2 nights weekends in season, 3 nights holidays **Open** All year **Hosts** Nels & Michelle Veliquette, 7710 US 31 North, Williamsburg 49690 **Phone** (231) 938-5930 **Fax** (231) 938-5931 **Email** michelle@countryhermitage.com **Web** www.countryhermitage.com

Central Michigan

Some of the most amazing spots we've never heard of—and a few that we have—were located in Michigan's central zone.

We had never visited any of this zone's midsized cities—**Lansing, Kalamazoo,** and **Grand Rapids**—and each held surprises. Kalamazoo's two historic districts, with oak-lined streets and ornate Victorians set far back across expansive lawns and gardens, made a terrific afternoon stroll.

In Lansing, the **Michigan Historical Museum** was a real eye-opener: five floors of state history, from prehistoric times into the twentieth century. The **Olds Museum and Science Center** are impressive as well; the English Inn, our destination for the night, was elegant and tasteful.

Perhaps the biggest surprise was Grand Rapids. We would not have expected to find a dazzler such as the **Frederik Meijer Gardens and Sculpture Park** in a smaller Midwestern city. Its permanent collection includes more than 100 major works by such internationally renowned artists as Alexander Calder and one of only two 24-foot-tall bronze Leonardo da Vinci's horse sculptures in the world. The **Van Andel Museum Center, Children's Museum,** and **John Ball Zoo**—along with the hundreds of restored mansions in the **Heritage Hill Historic District** (two of which we profiled as bed-and-breakfasts)—convinced us to plan a return visit.

But the smaller towns in the region drew us in as well. In **Alma,** the attraction was Saravilla Bed-and-Breakfast itself—a palatial estate, built as a father's gift to his daughter, with the ballroom alone measuring 1,200 square feet. **Ionia** is another town without pretense, and just outside **Stanwood,** the Outback Lodge is one of the few bed-and-breakfasts we found that actually encourages children. We were touched by the innkeeper's devotion to Native American heritage and all things natural, both in the programs she presents for school groups and in her own gift shop.

SARAVILLA BED & BREAKFAST, Alma

OVERALL ★★★★★ | QUALITY ★★★★½ | VALUE ★★★★★ | PRICE RANGE $85–$140

Saravilla's ballroom alone, at 1,200 square feet, is bigger than most houses. It's a doozy, with built-in bench seating, a musicians' nook, fireplace with more benches, leaded glass, and elaborate wood trim. Even the porch is grandiose, supported by 19 modified Ionic pillars. This is one of those homes with secrets everywhere: floor tile in the Highland Room's bath actually is wall tile; when it was removed during renovation, workers found an old fireplace and exposed brick—creating the rare bathroom with an original fireplace. Breakfast is served in the turret dining room.

SETTING & FACILITIES

Location 1 mi. south of US 27/MI 46 exit, in geographic center of Michigan's Lower Peninsula **Near** Alma College, Heritage Center for Performing Arts, Midland Center for Performing Arts, Central Michigan Univ. **Building** 1894 Dutch Colonial w/ 1902 added wing, 11,000 sq. ft. total **Grounds** 1.25 acres of lawns & English walking garden **Public Space** Wraparound porch, foyer, billiards room, sun room, DR, library, parlor, ballroom, 2nd-floor sitting area, deck **Food & Drink** Iced tea, water, snacks available all day. Formal full breakfast is served on antique crystal & china, includes hot entree. **Recreation** Cross-country skiing, birding, antiquing, historic touring, spectator college sports, symphony, regional theater. **Amenities & Services** AC in 6 of 7 guest rooms. Logo soaps, robes.

ACCOMMODATIONS

Units 1 suite, 6 guest rooms. **All Rooms** TV, ceiling fan, sitting area. **Some Rooms** Desk & chair, whirlpool tub, dressing table, fireplace, original bath fixtures, claw-foot tub, sitting room. **Bed & Bath** Kings (3), queen & twin (4). All private baths (3 detached). **Favorites** Ammi Wright Suite, w/ large windows on 3 sides of the room, sitting room & fireplace. **Comfort & Decor** This house is massive and posh, but dark-wood nooks and conversation corners give it coziness. The foyer sets the tone, with English quarter-sawed oak woodwork and a mural custom-painted on gold leaf on canvas in Paris and brought here. The library is the most Craftsman-like room, with built-in benches and ornate carved fireplace. The TV parlor is the most casual room; our favorite was the sunroom with skylights and a hot tub.

RATES, RESERVATIONS, & RESTRICTIONS
Deposit Credit card number or 50% of stay **Discounts** Corp. & Sun.–Thurs. rates **Credit Cards** V, MC, D **Check-In/Out** 4 p.m./11 a.m. or by arrangement **Smoking** Outside **Pets** No **Kids** Yes; up to 4 guests allowed in room **No-Nos** N/A **Minimum Stay** None **Open** All year **Hosts** Linda & Jon Darrow, 633 North State St., Alma 48801 **Phone** (517) 463-4078 **Fax** (517) 463-8624 **Email** ljdarrow@saravilla.com **Web** www.saravilla.com

ENGLISH INN, Eaton Rapids

OVERALL ★★★★½ | QUALITY ★★★★½ | VALUE ★★★ | PRICE RANGE $105–$175

Originally the private residence of Olds Motor Car Company president Irving Jacob Reuter, English Inn is a fitting estate for a late-1920s auto tycoon. In that era, names on the guest list included Fords and Firestones—the industry's upper crust. The home exudes quiet elegance in its furnishings, architectural details, food, and service; even the wine list, featuring more than 20 wines by the glass and selected by *Wine Spectator* magazine for an Award of Excellence for the last four consecutive years, distinguishes the inn.

SETTING & FACILITIES
Location On MI 99, 10 mi. south of Lansing **Near** Michigan State Univ., Wharton Center, Potter Park Zoo, R. E. Olds Museum, Impression V Science Center. **Building** 1928 brick Tudor Revival home **Grounds** 15 acres of gardens, lawns sloping down toward the Grand River; gazebo, swimming pool, croquet court, fishpond **Public Space** Foyer, DR, restaurant, library, lower-level pub **Food & Drink** Early coffee delivered to room, cont'l breakfast weekdays, full breakfast weekends. Restaurant is open to the public for lunch & dinner. **Recreation** Historic touring, golf courses, tennis, croquet, swimming, Class A baseball (Lansing Lugnuts), live theater, concerts. **Amenities & Services** AC. Soda, full ice bucket given guests at check-in. Logo bath amenities. Can accommodate meetings to 40 people.

ACCOMMODATIONS
Units 6 guest rooms, 2 cottages (1- and 2-BR). **All Rooms** Several seating options, TV, clock radio. **Some Rooms** Table/chairs/chandelier in bath; sitting alcove, river view, marble fireplace. **Bed & Bath** Queens (9). All private baths in main inn; shared bath in Honeysuckle Cottage. **Favorites** Somerset Room, for the immense lavender tile bath, four-poster bed original to the home, and the inn's best sunset view. **Comfort & Decor** English formality dictates the style in this gracious home. Fine antiques furnish every guest room—which, if the inn isn't full, guests can glimpse according to the open-door policy. The restaurant is paneled in rich Honduran mahogany; diners can admire the ornamental Della Robbia carvings bordering the mantel and ceiling while they eat.

RATES, RESERVATIONS, & RESTRICTIONS

Deposit I night's stay **Discounts** N/A **Credit Cards** V, MC **Check-In/Out** 3 p.m./11 a.m. **Smoking** Outside **Pets** No **Kids** Yes **No-Nos** N/A **Minimum Stay** None **Open** All year, except Christmas Eve & Day **Hosts** Gary & Donna Nelson, 677 South Michigan Rd., Eaton Rapids 48827 **Phone** (517) 663-2500 or toll-free (800) 858-0958 **Fax** (517) 663-2643 **Email** englishinn@arq.net **Web** www.englishinn.com

UNION HILL INN, Ionia

OVERALL ★★★½ | QUALITY ★★★½ | VALUE ★★★★★ | PRICE RANGE $50–$65; $115 FOR LOWER-LEVEL APARTMENT

Union Hill's slogan is, "Where love and peace abide," and we believe it. This mature couple are deeply in love and treat visitors like their own kids. In the foyer, guests walk past an extensive Christmas village collection of 50 lighted buildings, peopled by Mary Kay's teddy bear collection. Our favorite piece indoors is the marble-top Eastlake hutch in the dining room. The downstairs apartment is the best choice for business travelers, with a roll-top desk, treadmill, exercise bike, stepping machine, and private porch and entrance.

SETTING & FACILITIES

Location Several blocks from MI 21 in residential Ionia **Near** Ionia State Recreation Area, Grand River, Ionia Theater, Ionia County Bertha Brock Park, downtown Ionia. **Building** 1868 red brick Italianate w/ wraparound porch **Grounds** City lot w/ flower beds, sloping lawns **Public Space** Porch, foyer, LR, DR, upstairs sitting room **Food & Drink** Sodas, hot beverages available any time. Full country breakfast includes homemade breads & jams. **Recreation** Swimming, biking, antiquing, live theater, tennis, golf, horse races, cross-country skiing, sailing, fishing. **Amenities & Services** AC.

ACCOMMODATIONS

Units 5 guest rooms & apartment. **All Rooms** TV, ceiling fan, clock radio, sitting area, desk & chair. **Some Rooms** VCR, claw-foot tub, fireplace, private entrance & porch. **Bed & Bath** Queen & twin (1), queens (3), doubles (2). 2 shared baths; apt. has private bath. **Favorites** Kate's Room, sunny corner room w/ desk & chair. **Comfort & Decor** Much of this home looks as it did when it was built, just after the Civil War. Original stained-glass windows mark the entry and living room where unusual "black drape" moldings set the stage for the "apartment grand" piano. Nearby stands a spinning wheel that belonged to the original owner. The decorating style is a mix of country and Antebellum, with antiques in all rooms.

RATES, RESERVATIONS, & RESTRICTIONS

Deposit 50% of stay or credit card number **Discounts** Couples who stay at Union Hill on their honeymoon can return for their 1st anniversary free of charge **Credit Cards** N/A **Check-In/Out** 2 p.m./11 a.m. **Smoking** No **Pets** Inquire; resident dog is quiet **Kids** "Kids under control are welcome" **No-Nos** N/A **Minimum Stay** None **Open** All year **Hosts** Tom & Mary Kay Moular, 306 Union St., Ionia 48846 **Phone** (616) 527-0955

STUART AVENUE INN, Kalamazoo

OVERALL ★★★★½ | QUALITY ★★★★½ | VALUE ★★★★★ | PRICE RANGE $95; SUITES $140–$175

Tom and Mary Lou Baker did a statewide search to find the perfect inn for themselves. The main building, the Bartlett-Upjohn House, was once owned by Dr. James T. Upjohn, youngest of the four brothers who founded the Upjohn (Pharmaceuticals) Company. Next door in the Chappell House are the inn's VIP suites, highlighting Mission and Art Nouveau details, with a twist: the original owner stood 6'5", so ceilings are 12 feet high and doorways and kitchen cupboards stretch far above guests' heads. The complex, including both homes, McDuffee Gardens (formerly a Shakespearean garden), and original carriage house, are surrounded by a white picket fence. During your stay, ask to see Tom's lightning rod collection; if you haven't seen vintage rods up close, you'll be surprised at how delicate and pretty they are.

SETTING & FACILITIES

Location Off I-94 & US 131 in Kalamazoo's Stuart Ave. Historic District **Near** Western Michigan Univ., Vine Historic District, South Street Historic District, Kalamazoo College, Kalamazoo Air Zoo, Kalamazoo Nature Center, Ballet Arts, Arts Council Gallery. **Building** 1886 Eastlake Queen Anne & 1902 Arts & Crafts homes **Grounds** More than an acre of award-winning gardens, patios, gazebo, fountain, lily pond **Public Space** Bartlett-Upjohn House has foyer, 2 parlors, DR; both homes have porches (Chappell House also has 2nd-floor screened porch) **Food & Drink** Cont'l-plus buffet breakfast 6 days/week, 7–9 a.m.; hot entree Sat. **Recreation** Performing arts, galleries, museums, zoo, historic touring, antiquing, biking. **Amenities & Services** AC.

ACCOMMODATIONS

Units 3 suites, 16 guest rooms. **All Rooms** TV, clock radio, fridge, phone. **Some Rooms** VCR, stereo, fireplace, double whirlpool tub, wet bar, complimentary champagne. **Bed & Bath** King/2 twins (4), queens (15). All private baths. **Favorites** Honeymoon suite, for the extra space, double whirlpool, champagne, sound system. **Comfort & Decor** Both homes have been restored with hand-printed art wallpapers, Belgian lace curtains, and furnished with quality period antiques. Conveniences for business travelers (the inns' target clientele) include good lighting and plenty of desk and tables space in guest rooms. The Bartlett-Upjohn House makes the most dramatic impression indoors and out, with fretwork, quarter-sawed and hand-carved oak doors, multiple gables and bays, and original light fixtures throughout. The entire property is stunning.

RATES, RESERVATIONS, & RESTRICTIONS

Deposit 1 night's stay or credit card number **Discounts** None **Credit Cards** V, MC, AE, D, DC **Check-In/Out** 4 p.m./noon **Smoking** No **Pets** No **Kids** Yes **No-Nos** N/A **Minimum Stay** N/A **Open** All year **Hosts** Tom & Mary Lou Baker, 229 Stuart Ave., Kalamazoo 49007 **Phone** (616) 342-0230 or toll-free (800) 461-0621 **Fax** (616) 385-3442 **Email** tom@stuartaveinn.com **Web** www.stuartaveinn.com

FOUNTAIN HILL, Grand Rapids

OVERALL ★★★★★ | QUALITY ★★★★★ | VALUE ★★★★★ | PRICE RANGE
$85–$105 WEEKNIGHTS, $110–$125 WEEKENDS

Of the 300 bed-and-breakfasts profiled for this book, we found 5 that we'd rate near-perfect, and this is one of them. So many innkeepers complain that guests "want something for nothing," but Fountain Hill manages to bestow an extraordinary, lavish experience for under $100. Carol Dubridge's response when asked about providing so many thoughtful amenities: "I know what I need when I travel, so that's what I offer our guests." Kudos to congenial innkeepers with standards. During your visit, take a driving or walking tour of the neighborhood: some 1,300 historic homes in more than 60 architectural styles, dating from 1848, make up the Heritage Hill Historic District, including homes built by Albert Stickley, Frank Lloyd Wright, and James Gallup.

SETTING & FACILITIES
Location 5 blocks from both I-196 & US 131, a short walk from downtown Grand Rapids **Near** Business district, Frederik Meijer Gardens & Sculpture Park, Grand Lady Riverboat, John Ball Zoo, Cannonsburg Ski Area, Blandford Nature Center. **Building** 1874 Italianate, painted brick **Grounds** City lot; small gardens in rear **Public Space** Foyer, sitting room, parlor, DR, sunset porch **Food & Drink** Complimentary sodas, wine, snacks. Full gourmet breakfast served at guests' convenience on silver & china w/ fresh flowers, newspaper. **Recreation** Downhill & cross-country skiing, historic & architectural touring, museums, galleries, performing arts. **Amenities & Services** AC. Fresh flowers in room, robes, hair dryer, bottled water, wake-up tray delivered to room, free passes to YMCA. Fax, photocopier, laundry facilities, catering services available.

ACCOMMODATIONS
Units 4. **All Rooms** TV/VCR, sitting area, phone w/private line & message recorder. **Some Rooms** Private sun porch, double-sunken whirlpool tub, seating in bathroom, desk & chair. **Bed & Bath** Queens (4). All private baths. **Favorites** Jamie Room, w/ the biggest bath, sunken whirlpool, expansive room, massive carved plantation four-poster bed. **Comfort & Decor** Class and luxury define this elegant, yet not-too-formal bed-and-breakfast. From the foyer's curved staircase to the parlor's huge bakelite four-seashell ceiling light cover (you have to see it to believe it), to the curved walls, ubiquitous leaded glass, 12-foot ceilings, and oversized guest rooms and baths—all furnished in a classy mix of upscale contemporary furnishings and period antiques—this inn is a destination in itself.

RATES, RESERVATIONS, & RESTRICTIONS
Deposit Credit card number **Discounts** Corp., weekday **Credit Cards** V, M, AE **Check-In/Out** 2 p.m./noon **Smoking** No **Pets** No **Kids** Yes **No-Nos** N/A **Minimum Stay** None **Open** All year **Hosts** Carol & Tom Dubridge, 222 Fountain NE, Grand Rapids

49503 **Phone** (616) 458-6621 or toll-free (800) 261-6621 **Fax** (616) 235-7536 **Web** www.fountainhillbandb.com

PEACHES BED AND BREAKFAST, Grand Rapids

OVERALL ★★★★½ | QUALITY ★★★★½ | VALUE ★★★★★ | PRICE RANGE $88— "ANY ROOM, ANY DAY"

Business travelers often are too rushed to appreciate their surroundings, but every Peaches guest should see the basement game room, originally a ballroom. Depression-era murals depicting the four seasons of sports in Michigan decorate the walls, painted there as payment for a long-ago debt. In the workout room are a weight machine, stepper, stationery bike, and free weights; some guests actually use them.

SETTING & FACILITIES
Location Several blocks from US 131 and I-196, a short walk from downtown Grand Rapids **Near** Davenport College, VanAndel Arena, Grand Rapids Community College, Frederik Meijer Gardens & Sculpture Park, John Ball Zoo, Grand Lady Riverboat, Blandford Nature Center. **Building** 1916 Georgian, red brick **Grounds** City lot, flower gardens, w/ flower-lined brick drive lit by brick columns **Public Space** Porch, foyer, LR, library, DR, sun room, lower-level workout room, lower-level game room **Food & Drink** Sodas, water any time, early coffee available. Full breakfast includes hot entree. **Recreation** Historic & architectural touring, performing arts, galleries, downhill & cross-country skiing, antiquing. **Amenities & Services** AC. TV/VCR available; hair dryer, coffeemaker, instant hot water in rooms; dry cleaning available.

ACCOMMODATIONS
Units 5 guest rooms. **All Rooms** Phone, data port, desk, alarm clock, fax service, sitting area. **Some Rooms** Fireplace. **Bed & Bath** Queens (2), doubles (3). 3 private baths, 1 shared. **Favorites** 2-fireplace room (rooms not named) w/ private, vintage bath. **Comfort & Decor** Art Nouveau best characterizes the style, with conveniences, such as special lighting in guest rooms aimed at the business traveler. Wood in most rooms was designed to be painted, but the library's built-in walnut bookcases were left natural. Original moldings and fireplaces, French doors leading to the dining room, and a skylit foyer lend a straightforward elegance.

RATES, RESERVATIONS, & RESTRICTIONS
Deposit Credit card number **Discounts** After 10 nights, 11th night free **Credit Cards** V, MC, D **Check-In/Out** 4 p.m./10 a.m. **Smoking** No **Pets** No; resident dog stays in innkeeper's quarters **Kids** Yes, "but the house isn't kid-friendly" **No-Nos** "We encourage women guests to take off their spike heels indoors; they cause permanent gouges in the wood floors" **Minimum Stay** None **Open** All year **Hosts** Jane E. Lovett, 29 Gay Ave. SE, Grand Rapids 49503 **Phone** (616) 454-8000 or toll-free (888) 210-6910 **Fax** (616) 459-3692 **Email** JL@peaches-inn.com **Web** www.peaches-inn.com

OUTBACK LODGE BED & BREAKFAST, *Stanwood*

OVERALL ★★★★ | QUALITY ★★★★ | VALUE ★★★★ | PRICE RANGE $79–$119

At Outback Lodge, it's about horses and nature. A former teacher, innkeeper Sue Parker teaches school groups about Michigan trees and the effects of lumbering in the woods surrounding her inn. Up to 30 horses live in these stables, and guests nine years and older of any experience level can go for rides. Western riding students can be younger, and pony rides also are offered. If you're up in time to ride into dawn's rising mist, you might glimpse fox, wild geese, partridge, and turkey greeting the day; at dusk you're likely to see whitetail deer at the pond.

SETTING & FACILITIES

Location Several miles east of US 131 **Near** Big Rapids, Mecosta, Blanchard's Loafers Glory, Soaring Eagle Casino, state forest land. **Building** Rustic-style inn, 2 years old **Grounds** 20 acres of woods and trails, adjacent to 2,500 acres of state-protected forest w/ wooded trails **Public Space** Upstairs & downstairs common areas, 2-story wrap-around deck, patio, campfire area & pavilion, stables, gift shop **Food & Drink** Snacks & cold beverages any time. Hearty breakfast is different every day, includes custom-cooked eggs, home-baked breads, ranch-fried potatoes. No tofu or sprouts. **Recreation** Horseback riding, swimming, fishing, biking, canoeing, hunting, rodeo, antiquing, boating, golf, wagon & sleigh rides, nature lessons, riding lessons, cross-country skiing, snowmobiling. **Amenities & Services** AC. Robes in rooms; TV, microwave, guest fridge in common area. Horseback riding & other programs open to public; can accommodate groups, meetings, weddings. All items in gift shop are nature-related; "no plastic & silk-type things."

ACCOMMODATIONS

Units 6 guest rooms. **All Rooms** Sitting area. **Some Rooms** Double whirlpool tub. **Bed & Bath** King & twin (1), Queen & twin (2), queen (1), 2 doubles & twin (1), double (1). 4 private baths, 1 shared. **Favorites** Queen room, w/ double whirlpool & log canopy bed. **Comfort & Decor** The Western decor works well at this lodge, which had been a riding stable for several years before becoming a bed-and-breakfast. An imposing stone fireplace dominates the upstairs common area, and the deck gives panoramic views of the surrounding countryside. But the attraction at this new-but-historic-looking inn is the outdoors; nature programs and horses are why families, photographers, and sportsmen come here.

RATES, RESERVATIONS, & RESTRICTIONS

Deposit 50% of stay **Discounts** Midweek rates **Credit Cards** V, MC **Check-In/Out** 3 p.m./noon **Smoking** Outside, but not near the stables. "We prefer smoking on the porches or at the fire pit." **Pets** Horses only. Resident greyhound is permitted in common areas; resident cats stay outdoors **Kids** Yes **No-Nos** N/A **Minimum Stay** None **Open** All year; stables are closed during deer hunting season **Hosts** Sue Parker, 12600 Buchanan, Stanwood 49346 **Phone** (231) 972-7255 **Email** outbacklodge@centurytel.net **Web** www.laketolake.com/outback_lodge

Eastern Michigan

It's a quieter, gentler vacation land here on the **Lake Huron** coast, where the **Saginaw Bay** indents the coastline to form the famous "thumb." Choices run the spectrum from tiny **East Tawas Junction** to midsized **Saginaw** and **Ann Arbor,** to **Detroit,** the major metropolis of the state.

State parks and public beaches line much of the coast, where an exhilarating waterfront drive keeps the lake in view along almost the entire eastern edge of the zone. Coastal towns where we stopped, including **Port Huron, Port Sanilac,** and **East Tawas,** to tour bed-and-breakfasts were not only much more reserved than their counterparts along **Lake Michigan** on the western coast but also not quite as upscale. Shopping districts had a less polished look, and we saw fewer designer boutiques and artists' galleries.

This wasn't a bad thing, in our view. The **Sunshine Side** along **Lake Huron** appeared to be a more affordable family destination while still offering the character and beaches—and without the traffic-clogged roads we found along Lake Michigan. We loved driving along the lake through nineteenth-century villages, admiring the restored century homes as well as works in progress. Bed-and-breakfasts tended to be Victorians with a water view that welcomed children and offered some rooms for less than $100.

Inland, the thumb is a farming region—less forested than inland northern Michigan, with one popular tourist town we should mention: **Frankenmuth,** known as Little Bavaria, where visitors come from all over the Midwest to shop for Christmas collectibles.

But there's much more to Zone 12 than the "thumb towns." In the crook and at the southern tip are the zone's two midsized cities, **Saginaw** and **Ann Arbor.** The latter is a culture-filled college town where we toured the Midwest's best-named bed-and-breakfast, The Artful Lodger—an upscale property supplying guests with robes, slippers, and a hearty gourmet breakfast at affordable prices. Ditto for Saginaw, where Montague Inn sits on two acres with manicured flower and herb gardens; the city itself is a lesser destination than most Midwestern cities, and it lacked a restaurant scene, but the inn won us over and has economical rooms—especially appropriate for business travelers.

Detroit anchors that corner of the state. Although we had to venture into the suburbs to find bed-and-breakfasts we wanted to profile, the Motor City can't be overlooked as a vacation and business travel spot. Hitsville U.S.A. houses the original studios of **Motown Records,** and we've visited the **Henry Ford Museum & Greenfield Village** in **Dearborn**—the largest and most-visited indoor-outdoor museum in North America—many times. Exhibits there include Thomas Edison's laboratory (really!), the Wright Brothers' bicycle shop (moved to this site), and vintage cars. Two new favorites in Detroit: the new **Museum of African American History** and the stirring **Underground Railroad Museum.**

ARTFUL LODGER, Ann Arbor

OVERALL ★★★★½ | QUALITY ★★★★ | VALUE ★★★★ | PRICE RANGE $79–$119

Since it was built nearly 150 years ago, Artful Lodger has always been a professor's home—and it easily wins the prize for the best bed-and-breakfast name. Current owner Fred Bookstein is a professor of morphometrics, a field he invented, which relates to quantifying the changes of shapes of biological data. Edith is a professional costume designer; her talents created our favorite spot in the house: the faux "peeling wallpaper" of the many-windowed cupola aerie, designed to incorporate the room's actual peeling walls.

SETTING & FACILITIES

Location In the heart of the Univ. of Michigan campus **Near** Art museum, Mendelssohn Theater, U-M stadium, Yost Arena, Power Center. **Building** 1858 Italianate, "an earnest attempt at Upper Midwest Tuscan," on National Register of Historic Places **Grounds** 1 acre, trees, lawns **Public Space** Porch, foyer, LR, screened porch, winter dining area, patio, side deck **Food & Drink** Hot beverages available any time. Gourmet breakfast options include heart-healthy & vegetarian. **Recreation** Galleries, live theater, orchestra, college sports, cross-country skiing. **Amenities & Services** AC. VCR in music room. Robes, slippers, iron & board, bath amenities in rooms. String & keyboard instruments available for informal chamber music.

ACCOMMODATIONS

Units 4 guest rooms & 1 overflow room w/ kitchenette. **All Rooms** TV, phones, coffeemaker. **Some Rooms** Small balcony, desk, deck access, claw-foot tub. **Bed & Bath** King (1), queens (3), double (1). All private baths (2 detached). **Favorites** First 2nd-floor queen room w/ balcony. **Comfort & Decor** This sturdy mansion, with butternut wood trim and fieldstone walls 18 inches thick, is softened by the innkeepers' display of delicate Chinese and Japanese artifacts, including happy coats designed by innkeeper Edith Bookstein, a costume designer. Furnishings juxtapose the new against the old—Wassily chairs and contemporary sofas in the living room, for example, with old transoms and window chamfering in the background.

RATES, RESERVATIONS, & RESTRICTIONS

Deposit 1 night's stay **Discounts** None **Credit Cards** V, MC, AE **Check-In/Out** 4:30–7:30 p.m./11:30 a.m. **Smoking** No **Pets** No **Kids** Inquire; 3rd person in room is $35 extra; families discouraged on football weekends **No-Nos** Cooking in rooms **Minimum Stay** 2 nights **Open** All year **Hosts** Fred & Edith Leavis Bookstein, 1547 Washtenaw, Ann Arbor 48104 **Phone** (734) 769-0653 **Fax** (734) 769-0833 **Email** Inn keeper@artlodger.com **Web** www.artlodger.com

GARDEN GATE BED & BREAKFAST, Caro

OVERALL ★★★★ | QUALITY ★★★★ | VALUE ★★★★★ | PRICE RANGE $65–$95

Evelyn White prides herself on the service she gives her guests: when asked about amenities, she replied, "They get whatever they want." Garden Gate is deliberately reminiscent of a cottage on Cape Cod, and furnishings are mostly quality antiques. White's most unusual collection is a display of christening dresses, hanging on a bedroom wall; among other family heirlooms, White also displays a doll whose dress is a fragment of her great-grandmother's wedding dress.

SETTING & FACILITIES

Location In residential Caro, in the thumb of Michigan's Lower Peninsula **Near** Cass River, Saginaw Bay. **Building** 1985 Cape Cod cottage, built to be a B&B **Grounds** City lot, fenced w/ a vintage "garden gate," flower gardens **Public Space** Garden room, DR, LR, entry, patio **Food & Drink** Snack basket, bottled water in rooms; early coffee delivered to door. Full breakfast might include oatmeal, croissants w/ ham & eggs, Belgian waffles. **Recreation** Canoeing, cross-country skiing, boating, swimming. **Amenities & Services** AC. Fresh flowers in rooms. Logo bath amenities, paper.

ACCOMMODATIONS

Units 4 guest rooms. **All Rooms** Sitting area, desk, TV, phone. **Some Rooms** Robes. **Bed & Bath** Queen (1), 2 twins (1), doubles (2). All private baths. **Favorites** First-floor room, spacious, sunny, furnished with quality antiques. **Comfort & Decor** This small but attractive cottage is a restful place. The garden room, actually the skylighted sun room where breakfast is served, opens onto the back gardens, a scene right off of an Impressionist's canvas. Indoors, there's good browsing with innkeeper White's collection of P. Buckley Moss prints and Hummel plates and figurines.

RATES, RESERVATIONS, & RESTRICTIONS

Deposit Credit card number **Discounts** None **Credit Cards** V, MC **Check-In/Out** "Flexible—I work with people" **Smoking** No **Pets** No (resident dog is permitted in public areas) **Kids** Inquire **No-Nos** N/A **Minimum Stay** None **Open** All year **Hosts** Evelyn White, 315 Pearl St., Caro 48723 **Phone** (517) 673-2696 **Fax** (517) 672-1451

EAST TAWAS JUNCTION B&B, *East Tawas*

OVERALL ★★★½ | QUALITY ★★★½ | VALUE ★★★ | PRICE RANGE $119–$149

Sitting in a fantasy location—across the two-lane from a beach and Lake Huron—East Tawas Junction also has a train chugging across its front yard once a day, but innkeeper Leigh Mott says guests love the mini-spectacle. This is a farmhouse-style inn, with typical features of the era—pocket doors, bull's-eye molding, some leaded glass—that Mott has updated with French doors to the deck and other newer additions. She's created mini-environments in her guest rooms: in addition to the stockade-fence headboard, Il Jardino is decorated with photos of garden windows. The Rose Room resembles a tropical getaway, with breezy front view, canopy bed, and cedar closet.

SETTING & FACILITIES

Location On US 23, facing Lake Huron's Tawas Bay **Near** Lake Huron, city parks, beaches, harbor, marinas. **Building** Early-1900s Country Victorian, white exterior, w/ glassed front porch **Grounds** 1.5 acres of lawns, flower beds. House sits far back from road w/ train tracks across front yard **Public Space** Glassed porch, deck, parlor, LR, 2 DRs, 2nd-floor sitting area **Food & Drink** Full breakfast, served at guests' convenience, might include berry crêpes w/ cream cheese, quiche w/ homemade crust, bacon. **Recreation** Boating, swimming, biking, birding, canoeing, cross-country skiing. **Amenities & Services** Robes in rooms, coffee center.

ACCOMMODATIONS

Units 5 guest rooms. **All Rooms** Sitting area, TV, clock, ceiling fan. **Some Rooms** Canopy bed, private entrance. **Bed & Bath** King (1), queens (2), doubles (2). All private baths (1 detached). **Favorites** Il Jardino, w/ king bed, private entrance to deck, clever headboard made of stockade fence. **Comfort & Decor** Vacationers are the clientele in this lakeside resort town, and East Tawas Junction offers them respite away from the predictable family motels. Public rooms are small but cozy; guests usually gather in the living room, where they find a big-screen TV and butterfly grand piano—a rare piece (only 400 were produced). Two dining areas, the porch and deck, give guests choices for morning socializing or dining alone, depending on their moods.

RATES, RESERVATIONS, & RESTRICTIONS

Deposit 50% of stay or credit card number **Discounts** $30 discount off season **Credit Cards** V, MC, D, but prefer payment by cash or check **Check-In/Out** 3 p.m./noon or by arrangement **Smoking** No **Pets** Not usually, but inquire **Kids** Inquire **No-Nos** Candles in rooms **Minimum Stay** 2 nights in summer, sometimes in Sept. & Oct. **Open** All year **Hosts** Donald & Leigh Mott, 514 West Bay St., East Tawas 48730 **Phone** (989) 362-8006 **Email** info@east-tawas.com **Web** www.east-tawas.com

MAIN STREET MANOR, Flushing

OVERALL ★★★★ | QUALITY ★★★★ | VALUE ★★★★ | PRICE RANGE $95–$110

Done in florals and lace (but not overdone), Main Street Manor is a picture-pretty inn. Built by a Civil War veteran, the manor features Victorian medallions and other interesting design elements; one room has a white-on-white stenciled ceiling, creating a textured effect. In the Garden Suite, a rocking love seat in the reading alcove is an intimate spot with a garden view. Items in the gift shop are from the innkeeper's antiques store, a welcome change from the usual inventory of mugs and T-shirts.

SETTING & FACILITIES

Location Off I-75, 4 mi. west of Flint **Near** Riverview Park, Frankenmuth, Crossroads Village, Flint College & Cultural Center, outlet malls, antiques malls; less than 1 hr. NW of Detroit. **Building** 1888 Queen Anne/Stick style, gray exterior **Grounds** Double city lot w/ river walk behind house **Public Space** Porch, gift shop, parlor, deck, DR **Food & Drink** Homemade cookies & coffee on arrival, beverages all day. Full candlelight breakfast served on antique china & silver includes hot entrees, meat, signature 9-fruit medley, custom blend of coffee. **Recreation** Antiquing, museums, historic touring, performing arts, canoeing, birding, cross-country skiing, biking, galleries. **Amenities & Services** AC. Robes, logo bath amenities, white noise machines in guest rooms, & fresh roses from innkeeper's rose bushes. Dinner chocolates, take-home cookies.

ACCOMMODATIONS

Units 2 guest rooms. **All Rooms** Ceiling fan w/ remote control. **Some Rooms** Double whirlpool tub, desk, garden view. **Bed & Bath** Queens (2) w/ pillowtop mattresses. Private baths. **Favorites** Sewing Room, w/ pine plank floor, double whirlpool, canopy bed, old sewing machine-turned-dressing table. **Comfort & Decor** Innkeeper Tim Sodeman is an antiques dealer in nearby Frankenmuth, so the home is full of his finds. The dining room's tin ceiling is from a demolished firehouse in the Upper Peninsula. Architectural elements decorating some rooms, as well as much of the home's furniture, arrived via Tim's antiques business.

RATES, RESERVATIONS, & RESTRICTIONS

Deposit 50% of stay **Discount** "Frequent sleeper program," also credits for referrals **Credit Cards** V, MC, AE, D, DC **Check-In/Out** 3 p.m./11 a.m. or by prior arrangement **Smoking** No **Pets** No **Kids** No—with steep steps and high beds, innkeepers don't think guest rooms are safe for small children **No-Nos** N/A **Minimum Stay** None **Open** All year **Hosts** Tim & Sue Sodeman, 516 East Main St., Flushing 48433 **Phone** (810) 487-1888 or toll-free (877) 487-1888 **Email** mainstreetmanor@worldnet.att.net **Web** www.bbon-line.com/mi/mainstreet

932 PENNIMAN, A BED & BREAKFAST, Plymouth

OVERALL ★★★★ | QUALITY ★★★★ | VALUE ★★★ | PRICE RANGE $109–$175

If part of your ideal bed-and-breakfast experience is a gourmet breakfast, put 932 Penniman on your list—both innkeepers are culinary arts instructors. They also know how to design a comfortable getaway space. Their new carriage house suites—Tower Suite and Up North—have comfortable furniture around a blazing hearth, private entrances, and double whirlpools. We liked the contrast of Up North with the more romantic rooms—Mission furniture, stone fireplace, and log bed. It's a good place to rest after the short walk to dinner downtown.

SETTING & FACILITIES

Location 0.5 mi. from MI 14 in residential Plymouth **Near** Kellogg Park, downtown Plymouth, Detroit, Ann Arbor. **Building** 1903 Queen Anne Victorian w/ Arts & Crafts interior **Grounds** City lot; elaborate flower gardens, small courtyard **Public Space** Reception hall, parlor, 3-season front porch, library, patio **Food & Drink** Sodas, hot beverages, cookies available all day. Full breakfast w/ hot entrees. **Recreation** Antiquing, cross-country skiing, galleries, museums, historic touring, live theater, pro sports (in Detroit). **Amenities & Services** AC. Ceiling fans, robes, hair dryers, logo bath amenities.

ACCOMMODATIONS

Units 3 guest rooms, 2 suites. **All Rooms** Desk, TV, alarm clock, phone, sitting area, wardrobe. **Some Rooms** Claw-foot tub, chaise, gas fireplace, balcony, double whirlpool, private entrance. **Bed & Bath** Queens (5). All private baths. **Favorites** Rose Haven, w/ bay window, fainting couch, street view. **Comfort & Decor** When the Garys furnished this inn, they found pieces in perfect sync and scale with the house itself. The most formal room is the library with Empire furniture, contrasted to the more clubby reception hall with its oak and tile fireplace, original bric-a-brac on the balustrade, and turret area. The home has seven bays and plenty of interesting light fixtures and original woodwork to occupy wandering eyes. If some of the doors seem extra-wide, it's because they're called coffin doors, built to accommodate caskets when residents passed away.

RATES, RESERVATIONS, & RESTRICTIONS
Deposit Credit card number **Discounts** None **Credit Cards** V, MC, D, AE **Check-In/Out** 4–6 p.m./10 a.m. weekdays, 11 a.m. weekends **Smoking** No **Pets** No (resident dog is considered hypo-allergenic, doesn't shed) **Kids** Inquire; only 2 guests per room **No-Nos** N/A **Minimum Stay** None **Open** All year **Hosts** Carey & Jon Gary, 932 Penniman Ave., Plymouth 48170 **Phone** (734) 414-7444 or toll-free (888) 548-4887 **Fax** (734) 414-7445 **Web** www.bbonline.com/mi/penniman

DAVIDSON HOUSE, Port Huron

OVERALL ★★★★½ | QUALITY ★★★★½ | VALUE ★★★★ | PRICE RANGE $90–$150

The Military Street district of historic homes was a perfect spot for Wilbur Davidson to built his residence, alongside other lakeside homes of the town's elite. A friend to Thomas Edison (who grew up in Port Huron), Davidson later helped found one of the parent companies of Detroit Edison. In a later historic phase, Davidson House was where Fr. Flanagan founded the first Boys' Town; miraculously, the fine woodwork—butternut, cherry, black oak—along with vintage windows, tile fireplace surrounds, and (in the dining room) the original light shades survived all of that rambunctious energy.

SETTING & FACILITIES
Location On MI 25, facing the St. Clair River **Near** Lake Huron, St. Clair River, Black River, Blue Water Bridge to Canada, marinas, beaches, antiques malls, Fort Gratiot Lighthouse, 3 river walks. **Building** 1890 Queen Anne w/ cedar shingles & beveled white pine siding, on National Register of Historic Places **Grounds** City lot w/ patio, flower beds **Public Space** Entry, foyer, front parlor, LR, DR **Food & Drink** Juices, soft drinks available any time. Full breakfast served in Victorian setting w/ salt cellars, knife rests, and other period accessories. **Recreation** Boating, fishing, canoeing, swimming, river walking, antiquing, historic touring. **Amenities & Services** AC. Wake-up service, logo soaps, robed for detached bath. Hosts teas for little girls' birthday parties.

ACCOMMODATIONS
Units 4 guest rooms. **All Rooms** Fireplace, sitting area. **Some Rooms** Whirlpool tub, claw-foot tub, TV. **Bed & Bath** Queens (3), double (1). All private baths (1 detached). **Favorites** Balcony Room. It's the smallest, but we liked the balcony. **Comfort & Decor** Indoors and out, Davidson House is a place crammed with detail. The entry alone is a work of art, with beveled stained glass, an unusual griffin frieze, and colorful tile floor. A wreath and garland frieze adorns the foyer, set off by black oak trim. Stained-glass windows and bays are found throughout the house, and its dramatic open oak staircase makes it a great spot for weddings. Ask Odette to point out the carriage waiting nook.

RATES, RESERVATIONS, & RESTRICTIONS
Deposit 50% of stay **Discounts** 3rd night half-price **Credit Cards** No; cash or check only **Check-In/Out** 4–7 p.m./11 a.m. **Smoking** On porch or balcony **Pets** No **Kids** Yes,

over age 10 **No-Nos** N/A **Minimum Stay** None **Open** All year **Hosts** Mark & Odette LaPrairie, 1707 Military St., Port Huron 48060 **Phone** (810) 987-3922 **Web** www.davidsonhouse.com

RAYMOND HOUSE INN, *Port Sanilac*

OVERALL ★★★★ | QUALITY ★★★★ | VALUE ★★★★ | PRICE RANGE $65–$85 OFF SEASON, $85–$105 PEAK SEASON

This home was occupied by the Raymond family for 112 years before innkeepers Gary and Cristy Bobofchak bought and restored it. Port Sanilac is a tourist town, busy in summer with sailboat races, art and antiques fairs, fishing tournaments, and other lake-resort events. Off-season, the town empties and the Bobofchaks get busy producing their handicrafts and professional photography, which they sell in the gift shop. In 1992, Raymond House was placed on the Michigan Register of Historical Sites.

SETTING & FACILITIES
Location On MI 25, 90 mi. north of Detroit on Lake Huron **Near** Lake Huron, Huron City, petroglyphs, Sanilac Lighthouse, marina, Loop-Harrison Museum, antique centers, Barn Theater, beaches. **Building** 1872 Italianate w/ gingerbread portico **Grounds** More than an acre of lawns, flower beds **Public Space** Parlor, DR, gift shop, rear deck, 2nd- & 3rd-floor loft seating area **Food & Drink** Early coffee; "staggered" full breakfast served 8:30–10 a.m. on china & crystal, includes hot entree & meat. **Recreation** Boating, canoeing, historic touring, scuba diving, antiquing, live theater, golf, swimming. **Amenities & Services** AC. Robes.

ACCOMMODATIONS
Units 7 guest rooms. **All Rooms** TV/VCR, phones, sitting area. **Some Rooms** Hide-a-bed, canopy or wraparound iron bed. **Bed & Bath** King/2 twins (2), queens (4), double (1). 5 private baths, 1 shared. **Favorites** Red Room, for the painted Art Deco bed and the bed covering from innkeeper's great-great grandmother. **Comfort & Decor** The style of Raymound House is Victorian, but the feel is almost Colonial. Original painted floor planking and some original light fixtures remain on the first floor, which is decorated with historic family photos, lace curtains, and quality antiques. The stair rail is mahogany.

RATES, RESERVATIONS, & RESTRICTIONS
Deposit Credit card number **Discounts** AAA, weekdays, senior, military, extended stay, whole-house Apr.-Nov. **Credit Cards** V, MC, D, AE **Check-In/Out** 3 p.m./11 a.m. **Smoking** On porch & deck **Pets** No (2 small resident dogs don't shed) **Kids** Over age 12 **No-Nos** N/A **Minimum Stay** None **Open** All year **Hosts** Gary & Cristy Bobofchak, P.O. Box 439 (M-25), Port Sanilac 48469 **Phone** (810) 622-8800 or toll-free (800) 622-7229 **Fax** (810) 622-8485 **Email** rayhouse@greatlakes.net **Web** www.bbonline.com/mi/raymond

MONTAGUE INN, Saginaw

OVERALL ★★★★½ | QUALITY ★★★½ | VALUE ★★★★ | PRICE RANGE $75–$125

GUEST ROOMS; $160–$175 SUITES

Montague Inn is one of Saginaw's most prestigious properties. Surrounded by expansive lawns and city parks, it's popular for parties and weddings. Scott Kelly, chef and innkeeper, is responsible for the lush gardens and takes special pride in the herb garden; he uses his own produce for vinegars and salad dressings served in the restaurant (and sold by the bottle). The wine list is impressive; Kelly's dual goal is to raise culinary awareness in Saginaw and to earn recognition from *Wine Spectator* magazine for Montague Inn's extensive wine list.

SETTING & FACILITIES
Location On MI 13, on Lake Linton in Saginaw's cultural district **Near** Frankenmuth, Birch Run outlets, Japanese tea house, Saginaw Children's Zoo, sculpture gallery, museums, antiques malls. **Building** 1930 Georgian mansion, brick **Grounds** 2 acres of lawns, flower gardens, herb gardens on Lake Linton **Public Space** Lobby, dining rooms, library, patios **Food & Drink** Cookies in room; coffee, sodas available any time, cont'l breakfast. Lunch & dinner (open to public) Tues.–Sat. **Recreation** Zoo, antiquing, galleries, swimming, tennis, historic touring, golf. **Amenities & Services** AC. Early coffee, logo scratch pads & pencils, off-site dry cleaning, fax, photocopy available. Complimentary YMCA passes.

ACCOMMODATIONS
Units 16 guest rooms, 2 suites. **All Rooms** TV, phone, sitting area, clock. **Some Rooms** Lake or garden view, sun room, whirlpool tub, fireplace, sitting room. **Bed & Bath** Kings (4), queens (7), doubles (7). Roll-aways & cribs available free of charge. Private bath (16), Jacuzzi (1). **Favorites** Montague Suite, w/ gas-log fireplace, 3 window seats, sun room w/ sofa bed. **Comfort & Decor** The entire inn is furnished with period antiques. The most comfortable spot for socializing or reading is the library, with a long bay window seat and private corners; try to find the secret compartment in the bookcases. The dining room overlooks the lawns and Lake Linton. Some of the guest rooms are more elegant than others; splurging for an upgrade here is worth it.

RATES, RESERVATIONS, & RESTRICTIONS
Deposit 50% of stay or credit card number **Discounts** AAA, corp., senior **Credit Cards** V, MC, AE, D **Check-In/Out** 3 p.m./noon **Smoking** No **Pets** No **Kids** Yes **No-Nos** N/A **Minimum Stay** None **Open** All year **Hosts** Scott Kelly, 1581 South Washington Ave., Saginaw 48601 **Phone** (517) 752-3939 **Fax** (517) 752-3159 **Email** montagueinn@aol.com **Web** www.montagueinn.com

HESS MANOR, Romeo

OVERALL ★★★½ | QUALITY ★★★½ | VALUE ★★★★ | PRICE RANGE $79–$85

Hess Manor is a straightforward, not overly adorned house in an unusual place: the Village of Romeo is a Historic Place (established 1838), full of early and mid-nineteenth-century homes and shops. Sidewalks downtown are brick, and antiques stores abound. The innkeepers also own a Victorian bed-and-breakfast and wedding chapel across the street, Brabb House, built about 20 years after Hess Manor.

SETTING & FACILITIES
Location On Romeo's Main St. at 32-Mile Rd., 30 mi. north of Detroit **Near** Historic village shops, pre–Civil War sites, orchards, parks, small lakes. **Building** 1854 Gothic home, white exterior **Grounds** Small yard on city lot, flower beds **Public Space** Deck, DR/kitchen area, LR, hot tub **Food & Drink** Full breakfast includes hot entree, meat, & sweet ending. **Recreation** Historic touring, swimming, boating, canoeing, antiquing, golf. **Amenities & Services** AC. Copy machine, fax, modem available.

ACCOMMODATIONS
Units 4 guest rooms. **All Rooms** TV/VCR, clock radio, sitting area. **Some Rooms** N/A **Bed & Bath** Queens (4) w/ pillowtop mattresses. 2 private baths, 1 shared. **Favorites** Wine Room, for the Gothic bed. **Comfort & Decor** One would never guess this home is nearly a century and a half old; it's been completely refurbished and looks like a relatively new construction. Furnishings are a mix of antiques and contemporary pieces. In the living room, guests find a big-screen TV and fireplace; a handy magazine rack stands along the 2nd-floor hallway.

RATES, RESERVATIONS, & RESTRICTIONS
Deposit 25% **Discounts** 10% off for AAA members or single travelers **Credit Cards** V, MC **Check-In/Out** 4 p.m./11 a.m. **Smoking** On deck **Pets** No **Kids** Yes **No-Nos** Guests are welcome to use the microwave in the kitchen for snacks, but are asked not to cook food. **Minimum Stay** None **Open** All year **Hosts** Thom & Kelly Stephens, 186 South Main St., Romeo 48065 **Phone** (810) 752-4726

WILLIAM HOPKINS MANOR, St. Clair

OVERALL ★★★★ | QUALITY ★★★★ | VALUE ★★★★ | PRICE RANGE $80–$100

This is a mansion to ramble in. The snooping is great—when was the last time you saw a collection of Grace Livingston Hill books? Innkeeper Sharon Llewellyn's other collection is even more interesting—antique cardboard-framed photos of little girls in Communion dresses. Several are displayed in each guest room, somehow bringing serenity to their assigned spaces. Llewellyn and her business partner, Terry Mazzarese, excel at making guests feel at home. We hope they can persevere in improving the property; both keep full-time jobs (Llewellyn is a math professor, Mazzarese works for the National Guard) and they're challenged to keep up.

SETTING & FACILITIES

Location On MI 25 overlooking the St. Clair River, 45 mi. NE of Detroit **Near** Lake Huron, downtown St. Clair, Blue Water Bridge to Canada, antiques centers, beaches, marinas. **Building** 1876 Second Empire Victorian, brick **Grounds** Nearly a city block of lawns & shrubs w/ original wrought-iron fence **Public Space** Grand hallway, porch, Sun. parlor, casual parlor, sun room, DR, pool room, massage studio **Food & Drink** Sodas available any time. Full gourmet breakfast includes hot entree, meat; signature dish is stuffed French toast w/ homemade apple syrup. **Recreation** Boating, swimming, antiquing, historic touring, canoeing, golf, billiards. **Amenities & Services** AC. Certified massage therapist on site.

ACCOMMODATIONS

Units 5 guest rooms. **All Rooms** N/A. **Some Rooms** Table & chairs, sitting area, fireplace. **Bed & Bath** Queens (5). Private full bath (1), half bath (2), shared bath (2). **Favorites** Riverside Room, corner room w/ 3 tall windows, oversized closet w/ built-in dresser, cove ceiling. **Comfort & Decor** With 12.5-foot ceilings, one always expects elegance—but, walking into the Sunday parlor, we didn't expect to gasp. Hand-painted flowers around the recently restored cove ceilings, a turret alcove, an eight-pillar arched room divider, round window, bay seats, a square grand piano . . . you, too, will need to catch your breath when you see this magnificent space. Add in original acid-etched windows, a mahogany stair rail with carved newel post, and a 17-foot dining room table. We only wish we could have seen the Christmas tree they put up in that immense parlor.

RATES, RESERVATIONS, & RESTRICTIONS

Deposit 50% of stay **Discounts** N/A **Credit Cards** V, MC, AE **Check-In/Out** Inquire **Smoking** No **Pets** No **Kids** Yes **No-Nos** N/A **Minimum Stay** None **Open** All year **Hosts** Sharon Llewellyn & Terry A. Mazzarese, 613 North Riverside Ave., St. Clair 48079 **Phone** (810) 329-0188 **Fax** (810) 329-6239 **Email** whmanor@aol.com **Web** www.laketolake.com/whmanor

Southern Michigan

Sometimes, the best getaway is the simplest. If your idea of a perfect weekend is a few hours of canoeing, some antiques shops, and a simple country breakfast, and you don't want to fight tourist traffic or worry about restaurant reservations, then head for southwest Michigan's **River Country.**

Like the other zones, this southernmost region is diversified, but without crowds or pretense. Michigan's lesser-known **wine region** is centered here in the area between **Niles** and **Paw Paw**. Just east of Niles is the Victorian town of **Three Rivers,** whose circa-1870 Main Street is a National Register Historic District and the starting point of a 100-mile self-guided leaf-peeping tour that winds through **Amish country,** ending in **Coldwater,** the western edge of **Antique Alley.**

You can shop your way through a dozen towns clustered along US 12 in more than 40 antiques malls and emporiums, crossing half a state until you reach the **Detroit** suburbs. The landscape is mostly agricultural—corn, beans, tomatoes—and shopkeepers sell jars of home-grown peppers and jams throughout the season. When you reach the eastern edge of the state, you're on the Great Lakes once again—**Lake Erie** this time, where you find arguably the finest walleye fishing in the region. Walleye season is relatively short; from mid-May through mid-July, fishing is the number-one activity in **Monroe** and **Luna Pier.**

We would characterize the bed-and-breakfasts in Zone 13 as more lovely than elegant—though, as always, there are exceptions. Munro House in **Jonesville** not only fits our image of deliciously decadent, it's also historically important as a former stop on the **Underground Railroad.** Victorian Villa Inn in **Union City** is posh, and the Chicago Street Inn in **Brooklyn** is smaller but stately.

The others we visited reached high standards but were more modest homes. The eyebrow-raiser of the bunch was Pebbles of Brandywine Creek in **Niles;** the innkeeper is a British lady who offers a traditional English tea in the afternoon—and hosts readings in Akashic records, a method for tracing the path of one's soul in past and present lives. We don't want to play favorites, but between the antiques, the wineries, and the soul-tracking, we know where we'll spend our next "girlfriends' getaway."

BRIAR OAKS INN BED & BREAKFAST, Adrian

OVERALL ★★★★ | QUALITY ★★★★ | VALUE ★★★ | PRICE RANGE $100–$120 WEEKDAYS, $150–$170 WEEKENDS

The spacious rooms in this inn are named after the home's builder and previous owners. Though children are welcome, Briar Oaks really aims for romance and corporate guests. At the time of our visit, a new wing was being added, though the inn will keep the well-preserved oak floors, which were rescued in the 1930s from a mansion being torn down in Ann Arbor to make way for University of Michigan expansion. For the benefit of overseas corporate clients, Karin Whitcher speaks fluent German. (We did think a $50 price hike on weekends was excessive; we'd schedule our stay on a weekday.)

SETTING & FACILITIES
Location On MI 52 just north of Adrian **Near** Michigan International Speedway, Michigan State Univ., Hidden Lake Gardens, antiques malls, Irish Hills, Adrian Historical Museum, Adrian Croswell Opera House. **Building** Renovated 1930s home, white exterior **Grounds** 4 acres of oak forest, back slope to Beaver Creek, patio **Public Space** LR/dining room, deck, patio **Food & Drink** Complimentary bottle of champagne. Full breakfast includes hot entree & meat. **Recreation** Historic touring, antiquing, gardens, opera, train rides, car racing, fishing, golf. **Amenities & Services** AC. Pillowtop mattresses.

ACCOMMODATIONS
Units 3 guest rooms. **All Rooms** Fireplace, TV/VCR, stereo, seating, clock radio, minifridge, whirlpool tub, CD player, iron & board. **Some Rooms** Desk & chair, private balcony. **Bed & Bath** Kings (2), queen (1). All private baths. **Favorites** Tuttle Suite, w/ French doors to patio, double whirlpool, mahogany king bed. **Comfort & Decor** Lots of floral fabrics and wallpaper borders decorate Briar Oaks. The Russell Suite features a hand-carved mahogany bedroom suite from Indonesia and a private balcony overlooking Beaver Creek. Bed coverings were hand-sewn by the innkeeper, Karin Whitcher.

RATES, RESERVATIONS, & RESTRICTIONS
Deposit Credit card number **Discounts** Corp., multiple-night **Credit Cards** V, MC **Check-In/Out** 3 p.m./noon **Smoking** No **Pets** Inquire **Kids** Yes **No-Nos** N/A **Minimum Stay** 2 nights on race weekends **Open** All year **Hosts** Gene & Karin Whitcher, 2980 North Adrian Hwy. (M-52), Adrian 49221 **Phone** (517) 263-7501 or toll-free (888) 606-2568 **Fax** (517) 266-8802 **Email** info@briaroaksinn.com **Web** www.briaroaksinn.com

H. D. ELLIS INN, Blissfield

OVERALL ★★★★ | QUALITY ★★★★ | VALUE ★★★★ | PRICE RANGE $80–$100

A cornerstone attests to Ellis Inn's original resident, Hiram D., who was one of the town's pillars—banker, grocery and hardware store owner, postmaster, and township supervisor. Today, this neighborhood is being restored, building by building. With five antiques malls nearby, Ellis Inn is handy for flea-marketing weekends. Only 20 minutes from Toledo, it's also popular with business travelers who don't want to stay in the city.

SETTING & FACILITIES
Location On US 223, 45 min. south of Ann Arbor **Near** Croswell Opera House, Lenawee Historical Museum, Michigan International Speedway, Toledo Museum of Art, Center of Science & Industry, antiques malls. **Building** 1883 Italianate, red brick exterior **Grounds** City lot; shrubs, flower beds **Public Space** Porch, common room/parlor, DR, 2nd-floor sitting room **Food & Drink** Coffee, bottled water available all day; full breakfast buffet (8:30–10 a.m.) includes hot entree & foods made from inn's own apple & peach trees. **Recreation** Historic touring, antiquing, dinner & murder mystery trains, car racing, museums. **Amenities & Services** AC. Bath amenities, robes for detached bath. Spa services available.

ACCOMMODATIONS
Units 4 guest rooms. **All Rooms** TV, sitting area, clock radio, phone. **Some Rooms** Desk & chair, private fridge. **Bed & Bath** Queens (2), doubles (2). All private baths (1 detached). **Favorites** Hiram Ellis Room—largest room w/ queen high-headboard Eastlake bed, fridge. **Comfort & Decor** Antiques, lace curtains, and dark woods create the ambience for this quiet bed-and-breakfast. Doors still feature the original beveled-glass window panes, and guests in the Hervey Bliss room can enjoy their own private entrance. A microwave is found in the 2nd-floor sitting room.

RATES, RESERVATIONS, & RESTRICTIONS
Deposit Credit card number or full payment **Discounts** Corp., extended stay, AAA, seniors **Credit Cards** V, C, AE **Check-In/Out** 4 p.m./noon **Smoking** Front porch. **Pets** If small and in its own cage; when guests leave they must take the pet with them (resident dog is permitted in common areas) **Kids** Yes; cribs are available **No-Nos** N/A **Minimum Stay** None **Open** All year **Hosts** Christine Webster & Frank Seely, 415 West Adrian St., Blissfield 49228 **Phone** (517) 486-3155 **Fax** (517) 486-5002 **Email** ellisinn@cass.net **Web** www.cass.net/~ellisinn

BUFFALO INN, Brooklyn

OVERALL ★★★★ | QUALITY ★★★★ | VALUE ★★★★★ | PRICE RANGE $50–$90

Carol Zarr named her inn for her late younger brother, nicknamed Buffalo, who loved everything Southwestern. Theme decorating isn't easy, but she's pulled it off nicely; her blankets, animal skins, artwork, and other decorating touches are of good quality and easy to be around. The deck overlooks wetlands behind the inn. Route 12 is a busy two-lane with lots of character and, we can say firsthand, some wonderful antiques malls down the road.

SETTING & FACILITIES
Location On US 12, halfway between Brooklyn & Onsted **Near** Michigan Speedway, Hidden Lake Garden, Antique Alley, Hayes State Park, Michigan Space Museum, Walker Tavern Historic Complex. **Building** 1876 farmhouse, white exterior, w/ additions **Grounds** 6 acres of pond, meadows, wetlands **Public Space** Game room, Buffalo Room/LR/dining area, deck **Food & Drink** Coffee, sodas, beer, water any time. Full breakfast buffet includes hot entrees. **Recreation** Antiquing, swimming, boating, hunting, fishing, NASCAR races, historic touring, golf. **Amenities & Services** AC. Robes for shared baths; specialize in family reunions.

ACCOMMODATIONS
Units 5 guest rooms. **All Rooms** Ceiling fans, sitting area. **Some Rooms** Fireplace. **Bed & Bath** Kings (2), queen (1), 2 twins (1), double (1). 1 private bath, 2 shared. **Favorites** Saloon Room w/ round king bed, red velvet bed covering, red chandelier. **Comfort & Decor** With its Western decor, this inn is made for families. Kids can stay busy at the pinball machine in the game room while parents relax in front of the stone fireplace. A piano, stereo, work or game table, and TV provide other options, but our favorite pastime here was snooping at the buffalo collection (which begins in the front yard). Notice the hatbox dresser in the Country Room.

RATES, RESERVATIONS, & RESTRICTIONS
Deposit 50% of stay; full payment on select dates **Discounts** Weekly, whole-house **Credit Cards** N/A **Check-In/Out** 3 p.m./noon. **Smoking** On smoking porch **Pets** No **Kids** Yes **No-Nos** Prefer that guests eat & drink in the game room only **Minimum Stay** 3 nights race weekend & select weekends **Open** All year **Hosts** Carol A. Zarr, 10845 US 12, Brooklyn 49230 **Phone** (517) 467-6521 **Web** www.bbonline.com/mi/buffaloinn

CHICAGO STREET INN, *Brooklyn*

OVERALL ★★★★½ | QUALITY ★★★★½ | VALUE ★★★★★ | PRICE RANGE
$80–$85, JACUZZI SUITES $150–$165

Once they see both buildings, guests will surely be torn between the Victorian house, glowing with its original oak and cherry woodwork, original light fixtures, and lit newel post, and the more contemporary 1920s bungalow—the more private option. The bungalow was moved to this site from across town; we liked the more secluded Ivy Arbor suite.

SETTING & FACILITIES

Location In central Brooklyn, off US 12 & 127 **Near** Downtown Brooklyn, Antique Alley, Hidden Lake Gardens, Hayes State Park, Michigan Space Museum, Walker Tavern Historic Complex. **Building** 1886 Queen Anne Victorian, gray-blue exterior, and 1920s bungalow in rear **Grounds** Oversized town lot, flower gardens **Public Space** Porch, DR, common room, parlor **Food & Drink** Juice & water any time. Full breakfast includes hot entree & homemade baked goods. **Recreation** Antiquing, bowling, biking, historic touring, swimming, boating, canoeing, golf, cross-country skiing. **Amenities & Services** AC. Robes & coffee pots in Jacuzzi suites.

ACCOMMODATIONS

Units 3 guest rooms, 3 suites. **All Rooms** TV, fridge. **Some Rooms** VCR, fireplace, double whirlpool tub, bidet, private enclosed porch, private entrance, private patio. **Bed & Bath** Queens (5), double (1). **Favorites** Emily's Suite, entire attic w/ 2-sided gas fireplace, table & chairs, large sitting room area. **Comfort & Decor** Victorian-country style is the decor for the main building, though we found it elegant and not too lacy or overdone. The main home has been carefully restored; the dining room features a bull's-eye coffered ceiling and alcove built to showcase the stained-glass window, and the focus in the common room is the ornate cherry Eastlake fireplace with original Romeo and Juliet tile.

RATES, RESERVATIONS, & RESTRICTIONS

Deposit 1 night's stay **Discounts** Sun.–Thurs. $15 discount in bungalow; corp. rates **Credit Cards** N/A **Check-In/Out** 4–8 p.m./11 a.m. **Smoking** No **Pets** No **Kids** Yes **No-Nos** N/A **Minimum Stay** None **Open** All year **Hosts** Carl & Mary Frances Moore, 219 Chicago St., Brooklyn 49230 **Phone** (517) 592-3888 **Email** chiinn@aol.com **Web** www.chiinn.com

BENEDICT DOLL BED & BREAKFAST, Coldwater

OVERALL ★★★★ | QUALITY ★★★★ | VALUE ★★★★ | PRICE RANGE $90–$100

Brewmaster Benedict Doll, who built this home a century ago for his family of 11 children, undoubtedly would have approved of the renovations here. As a nod to the inn's history, innkeepers Christina Towell and Richard Christensen display a collection of bottles from the Benedict Doll Brewery, which operated next door. Christina also collects fabric angels, resting on the window seat across the back of the house and looking down on the meadows guarding the Sauk River. One of the best times to visit is during the famous Magic Festival in nearby Colon, where some of the best magicians in the world gather to learn from each other and show off. Reserve your room early.

SETTING & FACILITIES

Location On MI 12 & US 64 **Near** Antique Alley, Amish country, Shipshewana Flea Market, beaches, boat launch, Michigan International Speedway, Hayes State Park. **Building** 1900 Queen Anne Victorian, green exterior palette, on National Register of Historic Places **Grounds** 9 acres w/ groomed hiking & biking trail **Public Space** Deck, porch, kitchen/breakfast area, DR, sitting room, front parlor, loft sitting area **Food & Drink** Soft drinks any time, wine in evening. Afternoon tea on request. Full breakfast includes home-baked breads, hot entree; signature dish is Eggs Benedict Doll. **Recreation** Antiquing, downhill & cross-country skiing, sledding, horseback riding, biking, swimming, boating, historic touring. **Amenities & Services** AC. TV, VCR, & stereo located in sitting room. Sells locally hand-made soaps.

ACCOMMODATIONS

Units 4 guest rooms. **All Rooms** Sitting area, alarm clock. **Some Rooms** Fridge, ceiling fan. **Bed & Bath** Queen & twin (1), queen (1), doubles (2). 2 private baths, 1 shared. **Favorites** Storyville Room, w/ bold red furnishings & claw-foot tub. **Comfort & Decor** What's interesting about this house is a range of moods in different rooms: The rear dining area, with a window wall overlooking the river valley behind and undeveloped meadows, has a farm house feel, while the front rooms are more formal and elegant. Original pine flooring and floor-to-ceiling pine cupboards are right at home in the kitchen. In the parlor, the unusual Victorian parlor seating, stained glass, and the ornate carved fireplace with frieze and tile clearly were meant for Sunday company.

RATES, RESERVATIONS, & RESTRICTIONS

Deposit 1 night's stay **Discounts** Corp., extended stay **Credit Cards** V, MC, D **Check-In/Out** 4–7 p.m./11 a.m. **Smoking** Outside **Pets** No; resident small dog is permitted in common areas **Kids** Inquire **No-Nos** N/A **Minimum Stay** None **Open** All year **Hosts** Christina Towell & Richard Christensen., 665 West Chicago St., Coldwater 49036 **Phone** (517) 279-2821 or toll-free (866) 279-2821 **Email** benedictdoll@cbpu.com **Web** www.benedictdoll.com

HORSE & CARRIAGE BED & BREAKFAST, Jonesville

OVERALL ★★★★ | QUALITY ★★★★ | VALUE ★★★★ | PRICE RANGE $85–$100

If you want to give your kids a glimpse of farm life, Horse & Carriage is a good choice. It's remote—get directions from the innkeepers—and historic. In fact, it's a designated Centennial Farm, meaning it's been farmed continuously by one family for more than a century. The Rainbow Room has an adjacent cubbyhole playroom, stocked with toys, dolls, and vintage clothes so kids can play dress-up. At one time, the home also served as a small schoolhouse; the fireplace now stands where the schoolmarm had her desk and chalk board

SETTING & FACILITIES
Location 7 mi. east of Jonesville, 2 mi. off US 12 **Near** Jonesville, Moscow, Buck Lake, Antique Alley, Michigan International Speedway, Amish Country, Shipshewana Flea Market. **Building** Country farm house, white wood exterior, homesteaded 1835 **Grounds** Working sheep farm w/ lake, gazebo **Public Space** Dining area, sun porch, LR, small porch, kids' playroom **Food & Drink** Hearty breakfast w/ eggs from farm's own chickens (signature dish is coddled eggs on home-baked breads), fruit popovers w/ sour cream. **Recreation** Antiquing, Amish & historic touring, horse & buggy rides, cross-country skiing, NASCAR races, sleigh rides. **Amenities & Services** AC. Carriage rides, $25.

ACCOMMODATIONS
Units 3 guest rooms. **All Rooms** Phones. **Some Rooms** N/A. **Bed & Bath** King (1), queen (1), 2 twins (1). 1 private bath, 1 shared. **Favorites** Starry Night, most spacious room, decorated w/ tramp art. **Comfort & Decor** This renovated farmhouse is decorated in the style that works best—that is, everything the innkeepers love. Hand-hewn twig furniture and Mission chairs furnish the common rooms, contrasting with the light walls and sunny windows. Don't expect dark and clubby, just inviting.

RATES, RESERVATIONS, & RESTRICTIONS
Deposit $40 per room, per night **Discount** Extended stay **Credit Cards** No; cash or check only **Check-In/Out** 4–6 p.m./11 a.m. Mon.–Sat., 9:30 a.m. Sunday **Smoking** No **Pets** No **Kids** Yes, "we love children" **No-Nos** Alcohol on premises **Minimum Stay** On a few select weekends **Open** All year **Hosts** Keith L. Brown & Family, 7020 Brown Rd., Jonesville 49250 **Phone** (517) 849-2732 **Fax** (517) 849-2732 **Email** horsecarriagebb@yahoo.com **Web** www.hcbnb.com

MUNRO HOUSE, Jonesville

OVERALL ★★★★½ | QUALITY ★★★★½ | VALUE ★★★★ | PRICE RANGE $99–$179

If these walls could talk! Native Americans once slept on the floor of the library, where a big-screen TV now stands. In the breakfast room, the hearth is formed with bricks from the county jail, the doors are from a nearby brothel, and the ceiling beams and floor planks are from a church. Could Munro House's history be any more eclectic and interesting? Sure—add in two secret rooms and a tunnel from its days as a stop on the Underground Railroad. An old pull-bell at the front door, 12-foot ceilings, and eighteenth-century mirrors in the parlor enhance the intrigue.

SETTING & FACILITIES

Location Residential Jonesville, 2 blocks south of US 12 **Near** Downtown Jonesville, Amish country, Antique Alley, Michigan International Speedway, Shipshewana Flea Market. **Building** 1840 Greek Revival, white exterior **Grounds** Oversized city lot, lawns, flower beds **Public Space** Foyer, parlor, DR, library, breakfast room **Food & Drink** Soft drinks, cookies any time. Full country breakfast; specialty is omelets w/ fresh eggs from nearby Amish farms. **Recreation** Antiquing, NASCAR races, historic & Amish touring, cross-country skiing. **Amenities & Services** AC. Robes in whirlpool rooms. Can host parties to 100, sit-down dinners up to 65 guests.

ACCOMMODATIONS

Units 7 guest rooms. **All Rooms** TV/VCR, sitting area, phone, modem jack. **Some Rooms** Desk & chair, double whirlpool tub, gas stove or fireplace. **Bed & Bath** Queens (7). All private baths. **Favorites** Clara's Room, w/ expertly hand-painted trees & flowers on walls, picket-fence headboard, & coordinating fabrics. **Comfort & Decor** The charm of this inn's decor is couched in its heritage. It's one of several we found where the windows are recessed with shutters folding into a wall casing, a feature invented by Thomas Jefferson. Original iron hardware on doors, the original Louis XVI–style chandelier in the foyer, ten fireplaces, and floors of poplar, maple, and cherry perfectly fit Munro House's history as a stop on the Underground Railroad, where 400 slaves hid on their path to freedom.

RATES, RESERVATIONS, & RESTRICTIONS

Deposit Credit card number; on full-house rentals, advance cash payment is required **Discounts** Whole-house; corp. Sun–Thurs. ($69) **Credit Cards** V, MC, AE, D, DC **Check-In/Out** 3 p.m./11 a.m. **Smoking** Outside **Pets** No (2 quiet resident dogs stay in innkeepers' quarters) **Kids** No **No-Nos** Candles; guests will be charged clean-up fees **Minimum Stay** Only on select weekends **Open** All year **Hosts** Mike & Lori Venturini, 202 Maumee St., Jonesville 49250 **Phone** (517) 849-9292 or toll-free (800) 320-3792 **Fax** (517) 849-7685 **Email** info@munrohouse.com **Web** www.munrohouse.com

MENDON COUNTRY INN, Mendon

OVERALL ★★★★ | QUALITY ★★★★ | VALUE ★★★★ | PRICE RANGE $69–$129, $139 COTTAGE ROOMS, $159 LODGE ROOMS

Originally, Mendon Country Inn was a stagecoach tavern & inn, but in later incarnations it became a cow shed, a church, and even a bakery. Innkeepers Geff and Cheryl Clarke, who lived in England and South Africa, bring new perspectives and traditions, partly in the cuisine, partly in their decorating touches. Cheryl's collection of dolls from around the world is displayed in the foyer. Canoe trips can be arranged by the inn; every sixth canoe is free. Mendon Inn also hosts bicycle groups and children's book retreats.

SETTING & FACILITIES

Location On MI 60, halfway between Kalamazoo and Sturgis **Near** Centreville Antiques Market, Shipshewana Flea Market, Amish country, Colon/Magic Capital, Swiss Valley Ski Resort, St. Joseph River, Diamond D Ranch. **Building** 1843 stagecoach inn, brick construction w/ gallery porch across the front **Grounds** Many-acre complex of forest, outbuildings, creek, putting green **Public Space** Gift shop, DR/social room. Lodge has common room **Food & Drink** Full gourmet breakfast buffet; specialty is French soufflé omelets. **Recreation** Antiquing, historic & Amish touring, magic shows, downhill & cross-country skiing, canoeing, horseback riding. **Amenities & Services** AC. Ceiling fans, clock radios, on-site massage therapist, theme weekends.

ACCOMMODATIONS

Units 17, including cottage (2 rooms) & lodge (4 rooms). **All Rooms** Antique bed coverings, chair, reading lamps. **Some Rooms** Double whirlpool tub, coffeemaker, desk, microwave, robes, fridge, private entrance, fireplace, creek view, TV (in cottage). **Bed & Bath** Queens (9), 2 doubles (4), double & twin (4). All private baths. **Favorites** Old Wakeman Room, w/ high Eastlake queen bed, double whirlpool, ornate painted woodwork, fireplace. **Comfort & Decor** Mendon Inn still looks like a stagecoach stop, with the original walnut staircase, 18-foot ceilings—probably the highest we saw in 300 inns!—and huge, tall transoms. Throughout the inn, host Cheryl Clarke displays her museum-quality collection of antique quilts. Rooms are individually decorated with themes such as Amish, barn, and "country cousin." The log lodge is furnished in American Southwest style.

RATES, RESERVATIONS, & RESTRICTIONS

Deposit Payment in advance **Discounts** Weekday, repeat guest, travel agent, AARP 10% **Credit Cards** V, MC, D, AE **Check-In/Out** 3 p.m./11 a.m. **Smoking** Outside **Pets** No **Kids** Over age 12 **No-Nos** N/A **Minimum Stay** 2 nights weekends in season & on select weekends off-season **Open** All year **Hosts** Geff & Cheryl Clarke, 440 West Main St., Mendon 49072 **Phone** (616) 496-8132 or toll-free (800) 304-3366 **Fax** (616) 496-8403 **Email** vasame@aol.com **Web** www.rivercountry.com/mci

---

PEBBLES OF BRANDYWINE CREEK, Niles

OVERALL ★★★★½ | QUALITY ★★★★ | VALUE ★★★ | PRICE RANGE $85–$95; $95–$125 NOTRE DAME FOOTBALL WEEKENDS

Innkeeper Madeline Day characterizes her guests' experience as rustic elegance, provided with an English flair. Recently retired from Notre Dame's Center for Ethics, Ms. Day pampers her guests with authentic teas and genuine tranquility. "Let nature lift your soul," her brochure gently persuades us. If your soul can use a nudge in achieving its goals, she also hosts readings in Akashic Records, a technique for tracing the path of one's soul in the past and present, thereby giving it more informed guidance in the future. Whether your aim is inner reflection or simple escape from football madness, Pebbles of Brandywine Creek provides one of the loveliest settings in the state.

SETTING & FACILITIES

Location In Niles, 0.25 mi. north of US 12 **Near** Notre Dame Univ., Potato Creek State Park, College Football Hall of Fame, Brandywine Creek, South Bend (IN), wineries. **Building** 1920s cottage w/ additions **Grounds** 5.5 acres of forest, paths, gardens, & trout-filled creek **Public Spaces** DR, deck, LR, sun porch **Food & Drink** Traditional English tea (simple, cream, or full afternoon tea) on request. Full breakfast served on silver & antique china, often British mixed grill w/ muffins & fruit. **Recreation** Canoeing, biking, cross-country skiing, antiquing, historic & winery touring, museums, college football, minor league baseball (South Bend Silver Hawks). **Amenities & Services** AC.

ACCOMMODATIONS

Units 3 guest rooms, plus lower-level guest room & dorm for overflow. **All Rooms** Sitting area. **Some Rooms** N/A. **Bed & Bath** Queens (2), 2 twins (1). Overflow rooms, 2 twins & 4 twins. 1 private bath, 1 shared upstairs; lower-level bath for overflow guests during football weekends. **Favorites** Bedroom 1, w/ private bath & queen bed. **Comfort & Decor** With a setting like this, the interior is bound to be secondary regardless of style choices. We stood at the large picture window in the living room, staring down two deer who accepted our presence—an everyday occurrence at Pebbles. A tiered deck behind the inn slopes down a ravine to Brandywine Creek, a meandering waterway sheltered by old-growth beech, sycamore, and maple trees. This is a peaceful, wooded sanctuary you won't want to leave.

RATES, RESERVATIONS, & RESTRICTIONS

Deposit 50% of stay **Discounts** None **Credit Cards** No **Check-In/Out** 4–6 p.m./11 a.m. **Smoking** No **Pets** No **Kids** Inquire **No-Nos** Eating or alcohol in guest rooms **Minimum Stay** 2 nights during football weekends **Open** All year **Hosts** Madeline Day, 1564 South 3rd St., Niles 49120 **Phone** (616) 687-8924 **Fax** (616) 687-8935 **Email** Mday@PebblesofBWC.com **Web** www.PebblesofBWC.com

CHRISTMERE HOUSE, Sturgis

OVERALL ★★★★½ | QUALITY ★★★★½ | VALUE ★★★★ | PRICE RANGE $80–$145

Built by a Civil War physician as a hospital, Christmere House served for more than 30 years as both community clinic and home to Dr. Nelson Packard and his family. Innkeeper Janette Parr Johns expresses her various interests in the rooms: One is done in French Country style with French Provincial furniture hand-painted by a local artist; three others pay tribute to U.S. presidents Roosevelt, Lincoln, and Washington.

SETTING & FACILITIES

Location Several blocks south of US 12 in residential Sturgis **Near** Shipshewana Flea Market, Amish country, Centreville Antiques Market, Antique Alley, Michigan International

Speedway, downtown Sturgis. **Building** 1869 Queen Anne Victorian, brick construction **Grounds** City lot; flower gardens **Public Space** Enclosed porch, foyer, 2 DRs, 2nd-floor sitting area **Food & Drink** Full breakfast includes a hot entree, usually a meat & egg baked dish, & signature cinnamon rolls. **Recreation** Antiquing, historic & Amish touring, cross-country skiing, golf. **Amenities & Services** AC. Full-service restaurant in inn, dinner by order. Can accommodate parties up to 100 guests.

ACCOMMODATIONS
Units 7 guest rooms. **All Rooms** TV, phone, sitting area. **Some Rooms** Whirlpool tub, claw-foot tub, four-poster fireplace, microwave, fridge, desk & chair. **Bed & Bath** Queen + 2 twins (1), queens (5), double + 2 singles (1). All private baths. **Favorites** Queen's Tower Room, 3rd-floor room w/ canopy bed, desk & chair, kitchenette area w/ microwave & fridge. **Comfort & Decor** Glowing fruitwood is the backdrop for such features as carved fireplaces, stained-glass windows, and pocket doors in Christmere House. Much of the ornamentation focuses on the public dining rooms, open for dinner five days a week. Period antiques furnish the individually themed guest rooms: an Austrian stove and antique musical instruments in Austrian Melody, local art and memorabilia in Indiana's Pride, a cozy spot to nestle under the eaves in Emily Dickinson and Friends.

RATES, RESERVATIONS, & RESTRICTIONS
Deposit 1 night's stay or credit card number **Discounts** Corp., weekly **Credit Cards** V, MC, AE, D **Check-In/Out** 3 p.m./11 a.m. or by prior arrangement **Smoking** No **Kids** Yes **Pets** No **No-Nos** N/A **Minimum Stay** None **Open** All year **Hosts** Janette Parr Johns, 110 Pleasant St., Sturgis 49091 **Phone** (616) 651-8303 or toll-free (888) 651-8303 **Web** www.rivercountry.com/christmere

VICTORIAN VILLA INN, Union City

OVERALL ★★★★½ | QUALITY ★★★★½ | VALUE ★★★★ | PRICE RANGE $70–$120 WEEKDAYS, $110–$160 WEEKENDS

We didn't visit Victorian Villa in winter, but it's easy to visualize the Victorian Christmas hosted here each year, complete with Dickens Dinners. Happiness is relaxing in one of the home's many alcoves with a cordial or glass of bubbly from the extensive wine list, which has received *Wine Spectator's* "Best of Award of Excellence" each year since 1993. On weekends, guests can participate in a complimentary wine tasting. The cuisine, too, has earned national recognition from *Victoria* and *Midwest Living* magazines.

SETTING & FACILITIES
Location In residential Union City, 8 mi. west of I-69 near MI 60 **Near** Antique Alley, Colon/Magic Capital, Binder Park Zoo, Amish country, Chain-of-Lakes. **Building** 1876 brick Victorian, on National Register of Historic Places **Grounds** 2 acres w/ gazebo, landscaped flower gardens **Public Space** Foyer, parlor, DR, breakfast room **Food & Drink** Coffee available 7:30 a.m. Tea at 3 p.m., cont'l breakfast weekdays, gourmet breakfast

buffet weekends. Dinners served to the public. **Recreation** Antiquing, magic shows & magic museum, zoo, historic & Amish touring, canoeing, fishing, cross-country skiing, golf. **Amenities & Services** AC. Robes, logo bath amenities, breakfast delivered to room, pillow mints, in-room snack basket w/ bottled water. Can accommodate Victorian dinners, weddings, & other events.

ACCOMMODATIONS

Units 2 suites (including 1 2-BR), 8 guest rooms. **All Rooms** Ceiling fan, sitting area. **Some Rooms** TV, claw-foot tub, marble bath fixtures, seating alcove, fireplace, exposed brick, hot tub. **Bed & Bath** Queens (3), doubles (8). All private baths. **Favorites** Art Nouveau Suite, secluded carriage house room w/ ornate iron bed. **Comfort & Decor** Every space is elegantly appointed in this inn. Guest rooms are furnished with intricately carved high-headboard Eastlake, four-poster, sleigh, or other specialty antique beds with quality accessories. Original light fixtures, carved moldings, fretwork, and medallions accentuate the 12-foot ceilings on the first floor, and third-floor rooms feature exposed brick. Quality reproduction wall coverings are used throughout the home.

RATES, RESERVATIONS, & RESTRICTIONS

Deposit 1 night's lodging or half of stay, whichever is greater **Discounts** N/A **Credit Cards** V, MC, D **Check-In/Out** 3–9 p.m./11 a.m. **Smoking** No **Pets** No **Kids** Inquire **No-Nos** Because the inn has a liquor license, guests cannot consume their own liquor in public spaces. **Minimum Stay** Only on Victorian Christmas weekends **Open** All year **Hosts** Rob Gibson & Cindy Shattuck, 601 North Broadway St., Union City 49094 **Phone** (517) 741-7383 or toll-free (800) 34-villa **Fax** (517) 741-4002 **Email** innkeeper@avictorianvilla.com **Web** www.avictorianvilla.com

Minnesota

It isn't exactly a foreign country, but Minnesota definitely is different.

Take winter, please. In most Midwestern states, people cope with the cold and snow. They tolerate it, grit their teeth as they shovel and trudge through it, and celebrate each spring when the white stuff is finally gone. But in Minnesota, the most frigid state of all, they love the stuff. It's true: Look at their scrapbooks, you'll see photos of grown men and women sledding, building igloos, creating snow people—and smiling the entire time.

Then there's the current governor, a former professional wrestler. Can you name another state where the most popular T-shirt reads, "My governor can beat up your governor"?

Their state bird is the loon. We didn't see a coffee shop in **Starbuck, Two Harbors** only had one harbor, **Sleepy Eye** was wide awake, and **Embarrass** probably feels that way because the town has no downtown. We found Minnesotans to be progressive and fiercely independent—and they live in a very funky state.

The touring possibilities cover the extremes, from the wilderness lakes of **Voyageurs National Park** in the northwest to the megametropolis of Minneapolis–St. Paul in the opposite corner. In between is the **Land of 10,000 Lakes**—an accurate tag; once you leave the congested **Twin Cities,** Minnesota seems to be one long causeway. We add a note of caution, in fact: Do take curves slowly on the back roads. There's water waiting around every bend.

To capitalize on its variegated landscape, Minnesota has designated more than 2,000 miles of roads as scenic byways, taking visitors through wetlands, prairies, forests, bluffs, and river country, and they make a handy way to explore the state. Booklets with maps are available from the Minnesota Office of Tourism, call (800) 657-3700. We hate to play favorites, but the North Shore drive, stretching along **Lake Superior** from **Duluth** to Canada, probably offers the most dramatic scenery. It passes within a few miles of the **Boundary Waters Canoe Area,** a national treasure.

FOR MORE INFORMATION

Minnesota Office of Tourism

100 Metro Square, 121 7th Place E.

St. Paul, MN 55101

(800) 657-3700

www.exploreminnesota.com

Minnesota Bed & Breakfast Guild

305 E. Roselawn Avenue

St. Paul, Minnesota 55117

(651) 778-2400; (651) 778-2424

info@hospitalitymn.com

www.bbonline.com/mn/mbbg

Zone 14

Northwest Minnesota

In this northernmost corner of Minnesota you will find the most undeveloped land in the state and remote lakes best explored with a guide. If we were to bisect the zone diagonally, in fact, the northwest half would be almost totally devoid of bed-and-breakfasts; lodging is more likely to come in the form of campgrounds, motels, and fishing cabins. This is a land frequented by hunters and fishermen.

We found one upscale inn in the northern reaches: the Inn at Maple Crossing. Rescued by its current owners from woeful deterioration, it's a departure from the more rugged accommodations of the region, with gourmet dining and an extensive gift shop.

Most bed-and-breakfasts in the zone are clustered in the southeast corner. Our northernmost stops were in **Nevis** and its baby sister, Dorset.

If you're in central Minnesota, you've got to make it to Dorset. This make-believe town plunked in the middle of nowhere and surrounded by nothing, consists of about a dozen businesses—gift shops, antique shops, book stores, restaurants, and the Heartland Trail bed-and-breakfast—and, as far as we could tell, nothing else. Its four-page *Daily Bugle*—"published once a year . . . whether there's news or not,"—proclaims that the U.S. Census Bureau undercounted the town's population by 3.2 million. In another article, a former mayor sued Dorset because his key to the city didn't work.

Heartland Trail bed-and-breakfast is a former grade school on the rails-to-trails path of the same name. A few minutes' down Route 34 is **Park Rapids** and Wildwood Lodge; from there, most of the bed-and-breakfasts tend to be Victorians and other historic homes in larger towns, such as **Vergas** and **New York Mills. Xanadu Island,** and Spirit Lake's Log House and Homestead, are both waterside inns. The Whistle Stop Inn is a favorite with options—elegance in the Victorian, or the same high-end treatments in the three railroad cars. They're all beautiful; it's not an easy decision, but we like the Pullmans for the novelty.

XANADU ISLAND BED & BREAKFAST, Battle Lake

OVERALL ★★★★ | QUALITY ★★★★ | VALUE ★★★ | PRICE RANGE $95–$155;
COTTAGES $550–$660/WEEK (W/O BREAKFAST)

Built by an in-law of the J. P. Morgan family, Xanadu was once a summer gathering place for socialites. Legend has it that one of those visitors lost her walnut-sized diamond ring on the beach, and it was never recovered—"You can't imagine how many hours I spent on my hands and knees looking for that stone," she said later. The current innkeeper is a former college administrator who had to haul away some 150 car tires before opening the bed-and-breakfast. It's a dreamy spot right at lakeside; Battle Lake is stocked with walleye, crappie, bass, and perch.

SETTING & FACILITIES
Location Just north of MN 210 & CR 83 **Near** Battle Lake (town & lake), Glendalough State Park, Clitherall Lake, Otter Tail Lake, Scenic Lake Route. **Building** 1922 lake lodge w/ red shingle siding, & 3 cottages **Grounds** 5 acre forested island at end of causeway, surrounded on 3 sides by Battle Lake w/ sandy beach **Public Space** Great room, enclosed porch, 2nd-floor sun room, dock **Food & Drink** Full breakfast includes hot entree, "Xanadu Frost" smoothie. **Recreation** Antiquing, turtle races, art gallery, horseback riding, cross-country skiing, boating, canoeing, fishing, paddle boating. **Amenities & Services** AC. Paddle boat, canoe, fishing boats available.

ACCOMMODATIONS
Units 5 guest rooms, 3 cottages. **All Rooms** Alarm clock, chairs. **Some Rooms** Double shower, double whirlpool tub, heart-shaped whirlpool tub, fireplace, lake view. **Bed & Bath** Guest Rooms, queens (4), double (1). Cottages sleep 7, 6, & 3 in double & single beds. Private baths (3), half-baths (2), Jacuzzi (1). **Favorites** Lake Side Room w/ window wall overlooking lake, queen white iron bed, heart-shaped whirlpool. **Comfort & Decor** It's a rare innkeeper who achieves shabby chic style without making it look too foo-foo, contrived, or junky. At Xanadu, it's do just right. The inviting Adirondack chairs sprinkled around the property were built by the innkeeper, as was one of the four-poster beds. A massive stone fireplace dominates the great room; most furnishings are antiques—some original to the house—including cozy, leather-covered Mission chairs in the great room and select Victorian pieces.

RATES, RESERVATIONS, & RESTRICTIONS
Deposit 1 night's stay **Discounts** None **Credit Cards** V, MC, D **Check-In/Out** 3 p.m./11 a.m. **Smoking** No **Pets** In cottages only, leashed **Kids** All ages in cottages; over age 12 in house **No-Nos** N/A **Minimum Stay** None **Open** All year **Hosts** Bryan & Janet Lonski, R.R. 2, Box 51, Battle Lake 56515 **Phone** Toll-free (800) 396-9043 **Email** xanadu@prtel.com **Web** www.xanadu.cc

HEARTLAND TRAIL BED & BREAKFAST, Dorset

OVERALL ★★★★ | QUALITY ★★★★ | VALUE ★★★★★ | PRICE RANGE $65–$85

The grade-school ambience here is adorable; both kids and adults will have fun staying here. Guest rooms are named by grade number (Grade 1, Grade 2, and so on) and, being former classrooms, are unusually spacious with characteristic 12-foot ceilings. Dorset is worth a stop; you'll find a fine little bookstore and four restaurants, in the village with only 26 residents.

SETTING & FACILITIES

Location 1 block from downtown Dorset, off the Heartland Trail **Near** Heartland bike trail, Dorset shopping hamlet, Paul Bunyan State forest, Itasca State Park. **Building** 1920 schoolhouse, white exterior **Grounds** 3 acres of lawn, forest, flower gardens **Public Space** Great Room w/ dining area, 2 2nd-floor landing sitting areas, deck **Food & Drink** Full breakfast, includes entree & breakfast meat. **Recreation** Biking, in-line skating, birding, cross-country skiing, antiquing, snowmobiling. **Amenities & Services** AC. Bicycle & in-line skate rental; helmets provided. Robes in rooms w/ detached baths.

ACCOMMODATIONS

Units 5 guest rooms, 1 suite. **All Rooms** Ceiling fans, clocks. **Some Rooms** Sitting room. **Bed & Bath** Queens (4), queen plus twin (1), double plus twin (1). All private baths (3 detached). **Favorites** Grade 6 suite, w/ alcove room. **Comfort & Decor** School-day memories come flooding back the minute you step onto the shallow steps, which were built for small children. The Great Room is a comfortable space and has the inn's only TV. In the spacious guest rooms, school blackboards mix well with the country theme.

RATES, RESERVATIONS, & RESTRICTIONS

Deposit 1 night's stay **Discounts** Stay a week, 7th night is free **Credit Cards** MC, V **Check-In/Out** 3 p.m./noon **Smoking** Outside on deck **Pets** Inquire; "we make sure they're under constant supervision" **Kids** Yes **No-Nos** N/A **Minimum Stay** None, except during the busiest season, at owner's discretion **Open** During winter to groups only **Hosts** John & Pat Corbid, 20220 Friar Rd., Dorset 56470 **Phone** (218) 732-3252 **Email** corbidpj@aol.com **Web** www.heartlandbb.com

INN AT MAPLE CROSSING, *Mentor*

OVERALL ★★★★ | QUALITY ★★★★ | VALUE ★★★★★ | PRICE RANGE $79–$125

This inn might be subtitled "an inn for every taste." The food is better than good (Jim Thomasson is a foodie and cookbook author), the gift shop offers handmade pieces by more than 100 artists, and every room has a different theme. We were touched by Dora's Room and Clariece's Room, nods to the sisters who once ran the inn, decorated in colors they loved and artifacts reflecting their time here. Also housed at Maple Crossing is a study center whose scholars-in-residence work to "extend understanding through the integration of the disciplines."

SETTING & FACILITIES
Location Off US 2 at Maple Lake **Near** Mentor, Maple Lake **Building** 1860 log house, covered w/ 1890 additions **Grounds** 7.2 lakeside acres, w/ 2-mi. & 4-mi. walks around lake **Public Space** Lobby, parlor, DR, breakfast room, large gift shop, "summer porch," 2nd-floor library **Food & Drink** 2-course breakfast: baked fruit course & entree, w/ home-baked breads. **Recreation** Swimming, boating, kayaking, canoeing, ice skating, cross-country skiing, birding. **Amenities & Services** AC. Logo bath amenities, special events on lawn (such as Shakespeare productions, free & open to the public).

ACCOMMODATIONS
Units 16 guest rooms. **All Rooms** Sitting area. **Some Rooms** Cathedral ceiling, desk, balcony, patio, lake view, handicap access. **Bed & Bath** King (1), king/2 twins (1), queens (11), double (3), extra twin (2), double sleeper sofas (2). **Favorites** Innkeeper's Choice, lakeside grand dormer room w/ cathedral ceiling, walnut beams, rare empire chest, double burled walnut wardrobe. **Comfort & Decor** The theme throughout is best described as "classy Williamsburg." Every detail in this inn was planned, down to the keychains matching the room themes. No mirror hangs in the Amish room, furnished with a Shaker bed and Amish quilt. In Innkeeper's Choice, the bed is positioned so that lovers can see the moon through the upper window and its reflection on the lake through the window below—one of the most romantic notions in guest room planning we've come across.

RATES, RESERVATIONS, & RESTRICTIONS
Deposit 1 night's stay **Discounts** Winter specials **Credit Cards** V, MC **Check-In/Out** 3–7 p.m./11 a.m. **Smoking** Outside **Pets** No **Kids** Children of well-behaved parents are welcome **No-Nos** N/A **Minimum Stay** None **Open** All year **Hosts** Nancy & Jim Thomasson, R.R. 1, Box 129, Maple Lake, Mentor 56736 **Phone** (218) 637-6600 **Email** maplexing@gvtel.com

PARK STREET INN, Nevis

OVERALL ★★★½ | QUALITY ★★★½ | VALUE ★★★★ | PRICE RANGE $75–$125

It's not easy to read Irene or her taste. We admired her home's oak lamp posts and columns with carved roses, and her hobnail glass collection and other antiques—and then she showed us the Grotto. It's a bizarre, deliberately cave-like lower-level guest room with a cascading stone fountain, stone-painted walls, a clean-air machine, and double whirlpool. All doubts disappeared at breakfast, however. Irene's fresh mushroom soufflé and off-the-farm ham made up one of the best breakfasts we ate in Minnesota.

SETTING & FACILITIES

Location Just off MN 34, 10 min. from Dorset **Near** Lac de Belle Taine, Nevis city park, Heartland Trail, Itasca State Park, Village of the Smokey Hills, Leech Lake. **Building** 1912 Bungalow, white exterior **Grounds** Small front yard **Public Space** Foyer, LR, DR, 2nd-floor loft area w/ TV, 2nd-floor deck **Food & Drink** Beverages in evening, early coffee. Full breakfast includes home-baked breads, egg dish, & breakfast meat. **Recreation** Swimming, boating, antiquing, golf courses, birding, biking, snowmobiling, cross-country skiing, fishing

ACCOMMODATIONS

Units 3 guest rooms, 1 suite. **All Rooms** Sitting area. **Some Rooms** Deck access, whirlpool tub, thermal massage tub, claw-foot tub, private sun porch. **Bed & Bath** King (1), Queen & double (1), 2 doubles (1), double (1). All private baths. **Favorites** The Suite, w/ thermal massage tub framed by oak columns, private sun porch, deck access. **Comfort & Decor** This modest home has interesting features, including a Mission-style gas fireplace with cabinet topper and stained-glass cabinet doors. Corinthian columns separate the foyer and living room. In the dining room, the home's original plate rail has egg-and-dart trim to match the woodwork. The dining suite is Eastlake, and the pillared sideboard came from a local church.

RATES, RESERVATIONS, & RESTRICTIONS

Deposit 1 night's stay **Discounts** Extended stay (7 nights for the price of 6), winter specials **Credit Cards** V, MC **Check-In/Out** 3 p.m./noon **Smoking** On porch or balcony **Pets** By arrangement **Kids** Inquire; usually age 10 & older **No-Nos** N/A **Minimum Stay** 2 nights holidays; 2 nights if staying Saturday in July & Aug. **Open** All year **Hosts** Irene & Len Hall, 106 Park St., Nevis 56467 **Phone** (218) 652-4500 or toll-free (800) 797-1778 **Email** psi@eot.com **Web** www.parkstreetinn.com

WHISTLE STOP INN, New York Mills

OVERALL ★★★★½ | QUALITY ★★★★½ | VALUE ★★★★★ | PRICE RANGE
$65–$109 SUN.–THURS., $65–$135 WEEKENDS

Any railroad buff would be impressed at the quality workmanship and careful restoration in Whistle Stop Inn's 80-foot-long railroad cars. Such a glamorous outcome doesn't happen overnight; each of the three cars took more than a year to restore. When the Lees acquired the cars, they were full of "birds' nests, bees' nests, and things living there that left awful smells." You'd never know it to see the beautiful spaces today. The main house, a dramatic Victorian trimmed with carved oak, is furnished with period antiques, including a pre–Civil War four-poster canopy bed in the suite.

SETTING & FACILITIES
Location On US 10, 3 mi. SE of Detroit Lakes **Near** Finn Creek Open Air Museum, Itasca State Park, Detroit lakes, New York Mills Regional Cultural Center, downtown New York Mills. **Building** 1903 Victorian w/ turret & white exterior, & 3 refurbished railroad cars **Grounds** 1 acre of lawns, 150-year-old oak & pine trees **Public Space** Foyer, parlor, DR **Food & Drink** Coffee/tea service in rooms. Full breakfast includes hot entree. **Recreation** Museums, antiquing, historic touring, canoeing, cross-country skiing, biking, snowmobiling. **Amenities & Services** AC. Tandem & single bikes available; can accommodate parties.

ACCOMMODATIONS
Units 1 guest room, 1 suite, 3 railroad cars. **All Rooms** TV, sitting area, alarm clock. **Some Rooms** Refrigerator, microwave, VCR, fireplace, single or double whirlpool tub, ceiling fan, claw-foot tub. **Bed & Bath** Queens (5). All private baths. **Favorites** Imperior Car, most elegant railroad car, w/ brass bed, stained-glass windows, fridge, microwave, fireplace. **Comfort & Decor** Our "quality rating" doesn't apply to all spaces; the Palace and Imperial Cars are a bit more opulent. One was a 1909 dining car, the other a day coach on the Yellowstone Park Line, built in 1895; both are furnished for a sumptuous "ride" to pampering and luxury. We even loved the 1893 Caboose, the least opulent of the three cars, with a whirlpool in the former crew quarters, and the original john—for display only—in the rear.

RATES, RESERVATIONS, & RESTRICTIONS
Deposit $25 **Discounts** Seasonal specials **Credit Cards** V, MC, D, AE **Check-In/Out** 4–6 p.m./11 a.m. **Smoking** Outside **Pets** No **Kids** Age 10 and older **No-Nos** N/A **Minimum Stay** None **Open** All year **Hosts** Jann & Roger Lee, Route 1, Box 85, New York Mills 56567 **Phone** (218) 385-2223 or toll-free (800) 328-6315 **Fax** (501) 421-5005 **Email** whistlestop@wcta.net **Web** bbonline.com/mn/whistlestop

WILDWOOD LODGE BED & BREAKFAST, Park Rapids

OVERALL ★★★★½ | QUALITY ★★★★ | VALUE ★★★ | PRICE RANGE $125–$160

WildWood Lodge is a true lakeside retreat, set far back into the woods and positioned for watching sunsets. And it's a bed-and-breakfast with a heart: If "no highway travel advised" bulletins are issued for your departure day, either in Park Rapids or at your destination, you may stay free of charge until it's safe to travel. WildWood has received a *Better Homes & Gardens* Award.

SETTING & FACILITIES
Location On Fish Hook Lake, off MN 71 & 34 **Near** Lake, Heartland Trail, Itaska State Park. **Building** Remodeled 1950 log home **Grounds** 2 lakeside acres w/ lawns, forest **Public Space** Great Room, deck **Food & Drink** Full breakfast includes hot entree. **Recreation** Cross-country ski trails, swimming, antiquing, biking, golf courses, tennis, snowmobiling, birding, canoeing, snowshoeing. **Amenities & Services** AC. Robes in rooms, logo bath amenities, massage therapist available, complimentary snowshoes & canoe, complimentary lake tour in 1954 Chris Craft, small meeting facilities.

ACCOMMODATIONS
Units 3 guest rooms **All Rooms** TV. **Some Rooms** Deck access, private deck, single or double whirlpool, large sitting area. **Bed & Bath** King/2 twins (2), queen (1). All private baths. **Favorites** Eagle's Nest, hideaway above carriage house w/ expansive lake view, private deck, double whirlpool, large sitting area. **Comfort & Decor** Remodeled to update the rustic look of the cabin, this inn is furnished with period reproductions and luxury linens. We especially liked the handmade trout design comforter in the Cove. In the Great Room, floor-to-ceiling windows provide a sweeping lake view; a massive stone fireplace focuses the living area.

RATES, RESERVATIONS, & RESTRICTIONS
Deposit None **Discounts** Extended stay (10%), $10 off Sun.–Thurs. **Credit Cards** Call ahead **Check-In/Out** 3–6 p.m./11 a.m. **Smoking** No **Pets** No **Kids** No **No-Nos** N/A **Minimum Stay** Weekends in peak season and some holidays, 2-night minimum **Open** All year **Hosts** Phil & Liz Smith, HC06, Box 45A; 15301 Forget Me Not Drive, Park Rapids 56470 **Phone** (218) 732-1176 or toll-free (888) wwlodge **Web** www.wildwoodbb.com

LOG HOUSE & HOMESTEAD ON SPIRIT LAKE, Vergas

OVERALL ★★★★½ | QUALITY ★★★★½ | VALUE ★★★ | PRICE RANGE $110–$195

Two sisters operate this bed-and-breakfast: Patrice is the on-site innkeeper, and Suzanne handles the books, ordering, and other desk work from her home in St. Louis. "I have my wish list," Patrice says, "and she orders according to our budget." The log house, built on land homesteaded by the sisters' ancestors, was moved 80 miles, coming to rest on a knoll overlooking Spirit Lake, where it still wears its original whitewash. Newspapers found in the walls during restoration are framed and hang on the walls.

SETTING & FACILITIES
Location 5 mi. west of Vergas off CR 4 **Near** Detroit Lakes, downtown Vergas, Detroit Mountain Ski Area. **Building** 1902 lakeside home, white exterior w/ balconies; 19th-century log house **Grounds** 115 acres of fields, hills, maple woods, trails, Spirit Lake **Public Space** Common room, screened porch at the log house **Food & Drink** Greeting tray in

room; early coffee & snack. Gourmet breakfast served in guest rooms or common area. Recreation; Biking, swimming, cross-country skiing, snowshoeing, antiquing, golf courses. **Amenities & Services** AC. Robes, morning newspaper, snowshoes, canoes, rowboats, carriage & sleigh rides. Candlelight dinner, picnics available with advance notice.

ACCOMMODATIONS

Units 4 guest rooms, 1 suite. **All Rooms** Balcony or porch, sitting area. **Some Rooms** Skylights, fireplace, double whirlpool tub, fridge, wet bar, slipper tub. **Bed & Bath** King (1), queens (4). All private baths. **Favorites** Anna's Room in log house, w/ screened porch, deck, sunrise view over the lake. **Comfort & Decor** Family artifacts, including the innkeepers' great-great-grandfather's immigrant trunk, are mixed with other period antiques in both houses. The three-story log house is furnished in a slightly rustic country style; the decor in the homestead is more French Country, though both are elegant.

RATES, RESERVATIONS, & RESTRICTIONS

Deposit Credit card number or $45 **Discounts** Seasonal specials, midweek winter rates **Credit Cards** V, MC, D **Check-In/Out** 4–7:30 p.m./noon **Smoking** On open porches **Pets** No **Kids** Cannot accommodate young children; inquire. **No-Nos** N/A **Minimum Stay** None **Open** All year **Hosts** Suzanne Tweten & Patrice Allen., P.O. Box 130, Vergas 56587 **Phone** (218) 342-2318 or toll-free (800) 342-2318 **Email** loghouse@tekstar.com **Web** www.loghousebb.com

Northeast Minnesota

Here as in the opposite corner, bed-and-breakfasts tend to cluster—in this instance along the **Lake Superior** shoreline—but we also found good touring and great bed-and-breakfasts inland.

In the north-central part of the zone, we'd send everyone to **Embarrass** if we could tell them what to look for. There's no town center, no official buildings, no Welcome to Embarrass signs. Charles Kuralt once did a story on the town that isn't there—how embarrassing! (Sorry; we had to say it once.)

Settled by Finns, Embarrass sits almost directly on the **Laurentian Divide;** two rivers within three miles of town flow in opposite directions The Finnish Heritage Homestead is a century-old farm and former boarding house for loggers, owned today by innkeepers who came to escape big-city traffic; Buzz isn't Finnish, but he spins a good yarn with an accent.

Toward the center of the state, the memorable bed-and-breakfasts distinguish themselves by their individuality. Lottie Lee's in **Little Falls,** near **Charles Lindbergh's boyhood home,** is full of Arts and Crafts touches and surrounded by the innkeeper's carefully tended flower gardens, regularly featured in the town's garden tours. The Hallett House in **Deerwood** is an exquisite example of Art Deco architecture and styling, and the innkeepers make some of the best coffee in the state. The Nordic Inn in **Crosby** is—we'll say it—downright bizarre, with a pauper's tower, Viking ship loft, and Thor guarding the door, all housed in a former church.

We were especially taken by the shoreline drive along Lake Superior on the eastern edge of the zone. We started in **Duluth,** a city we'd never visited and fell in love with. Its historic district of mansions built by shipping tycoons, some of which now are opulent bed-and-breakfasts, is worth touring, and the harbor views are magnificent. Moving up the coast, towns, and bed-and-breakfasts take on a simpler tone, catering to those who visit for the canoeing, skiing, fishing, and hiking.

MOOSEBIRDS ON LAKE VERMILION, Cook

OVERALL ★★★½ | QUALITY ★★★½ | VALUE ★★★★ | PRICE RANGE $79–$109

The name comes from the gray Canadian jay, a northern bird (also called "camp robber") so friendly it will eat out of your hand. This bed-and-breakfast is ultra-casual, but higher quality than you'd guess as you wind past the bait and fishing supplies. Whole-house rentals are popular here, and Lake Vermilion is a beautiful spot with 1,200 miles of shoreline and excellent walleye fishing.

SETTING & FACILITIES

Location On US 24, 9 mi. outside Cook **Near** Lake Vermilion, Voyageurs National Park. **Building** General store, bait & tackle shop, bayside B&B in rear **Grounds** 5 acres of forest **Public Space** Great Room, deck, DR, full kitchen **Food & Drink** Full skillet breakfast includes entree & signature "fresh salsa." **Recreation** Boating, canoeing, fishing, birding, wildlife viewing, golf courses. **Amenities & Services** Pontoon rental, fishing licenses available, souvenir sales.

ACCOMMODATIONS

Units 3 guest rooms. **All Rooms** Sitting area. **Some Rooms** Bay view, skylight. **Bed & Bath** King (1), king w/ daybed (1), 2 twins (1). 1 private bath, 1 shared. **Favorites** Lake View room, for private bath & view of Spring Bay. **Comfort & Decor** This comfortable B&B is almost a secret space, tucked behind the general store and bait shop. The sunken living room has a large fireplace and opens onto the bayside deck. Furnishings are contemporary and comfortable.

RATES, RESERVATIONS, & RESTRICTIONS

Deposit N/A **Discounts** None **Credit Cards** V, MC **Check-In/Out** Inquire **Smoking** Outside **Pets** No **Kids** Yes **No-Nos** N/A **Minimum Stay** None, but $10 extra for staying just 1 night **Open** All year, must book in advance Sept.–Apr. **Hosts** Ron & Sue Martin, 3068 Vermilion Dr., Cook 55723 **Phone** (218) 666-2627 **Web** www.lakevermilion. com/moosebirds

NORDIC INN MEDIEVAL BREW AND BED, Crosby

OVERALL ★★★★ | QUALITY ★★★★ | VALUE ★★★★ | PRICE RANGE $55–$125

If there's a prize for the most out-there bed-and-breakfast, Nordic Inn takes first place. As the brochure says, "We're the only building with a Viking out front." His name is Thor—although, according to innkeeper Steinarr, "He fell the other day. If I fell, I'd be Thor, too" (arrgh). No inhibitions are permitted at this inn, where every Saturday is dinner theater night, including "The Spells of Odin," when guests must cast the right magic spells to end Ragnarok, the Viking apocalypse. This place is great fun; Steinarr even takes guests in Viking costume to storm the football stadium for Minnesota's home games. Bring kids for a weekday getaway; weekend shows offer adult humor. Mead is served on tap.

SETTING & FACILITIES

Location Central Crosby, in Brainerd Lakes region **Near** Antiques shops, Paul Bunyan Trail, Cuyuna Mine Pit Lakes, Brainerd Arboretum, Croft Mine Historical Park, Brainerd International Raceway. **Building** Converted 1909 church **Grounds** City lot **Public Space** Great Room ("Valhalla") w/ bar, DR (dungeon), adjacent hot tub room for 10, game room ("Asgard") **Food & Drink** "Huge" Viking breakfast includes meat pie, Viking potatoes, parsley toast (an authentic Viking bread). Viking Feast served w/ Sat, dinner theater; bar offers wide selection of spirits; $5 carry-in tax per each person bringing own beverages. **Recreation** Everything Viking happens here, including education on Viking history & lore in Asgard library; weekend interactive dinner theater on-site; antiquing, snowmobiling, kayaking, canoeing, biking, fishing, golf courses, scuba diving, snorkeling, fishing. **Amenities & Services** AC. Soap cutting, lessons in Viking culture & influence, dinner theater.

ACCOMMODATIONS

Units 5 guest rooms **All Rooms** Cable TV, VCR, phone, sitting area. **Some Rooms** Single or double whirlpool tub, bidet, double shower. **Bed & Bath** Kings (2), queen (1), 2 doubles (1), double (1). All private baths (1 detached). **Favorites** Odin's Loft, where guests relax in a Viking ship's prow hovering above the Great Room, king bed, double whirlpool. **Comfort & Decor** Choose your poison, no extra charge for bad jokes: Odin's Loft comes "fully stocked" (featuring a prisoner's stockade), or guests can be locked in the pauper's tower overnight. Valhalla is furnished with couches made of 2,400-year-old pine and a sunken whirlpool in the church's former altar. Stained-glass windows were custom-made. A clever twist on the bizarre theme is the Locker Room, dedicated to the Minnesota Vikings; carpet is Astroturf, clothes are stored in lockers, headboards are goal posts—you get the picture.

RATES, RESERVATIONS, & RESTRICTIONS

Deposit Credit card number; whole-house weekend rentals require a nonrefundable $500 deposit **Discounts** Senior weekday discount 10% **Credit Cards** V, MC, D, AE **Check-In/Out** 4–8 p.m./noon **Smoking** In Valhalla only **Pets** No; will arrange a kennel; inquire **Kids** Yes **No-Nos** N/A **Minimum Stay** 2 nights on select weekends **Open** All year **Hosts** Steinarr the Crazy Viking, 210 First Ave. NW, Crosby 56441 **Phone** (218) 546-8299 **Email** nordic@vikinginn.com **Web** www.vikinginn.com

HALLETT HOUSE, Deerwood

OVERALL ★★★★½ | QUALITY ★★★★½ | VALUE ★★★★★ | PRICE RANGE $75–$115 WEEKDAYS, $10 MORE WEEKENDS

Graceful curves and rounded bays shape this home. From the original wool carpet downstairs to original French parchment wallpaper throughout, we felt warmly welcomed here. Various rooms cater to the mood: The dining room is sunny and semiformal, whereas the sunken library, with contemporary leather furniture, wood-burning fireplace and TV, is more casual. We especially enjoyed the new gazebo, a second home for the arched screens that once sheltered the home's original porch.

SETTING & FACILITIES
Location On MN 6 just outside Deerwood **Near** Crosby antique district, Paul Bunyan Trail, Cuyuna Mine Pit Lakes, Croft Mine Historical Park, Brainerd Arboretum, Brainerd International Raceway. **Building** 1920 Art Deco home, white exterior, w/ 1936 additions **Grounds** 13 acres, includes woods, flower gardens, gazebo, fountains, 4-hole golf course **Public Space** Porch, foyer, DR, LR, library **Food & Drink** Coffee available at 7 a.m., full breakfast (7:30–10 a.m.) served on vintage Fiestaware, includes hot entree & meat. Complimentary wine served afternoons. **Recreation** Antiquing, birding, golf, biking, snowmobilers, cross-country skiing, fishing, scuba diving, snorkeling. **Amenities & Services** AC. Fresh flowers in rooms, TV/VCR in LR, free shuttle service to Brainerd-Crow Wing Airport.

ACCOMMODATIONS
Units 2 suites, 3 guest rooms. **All Rooms** Ceiling fans, sitting area. **Some Rooms** TV, VCR, private entrance, fireplace, whirlpool, private balcony. **Bed & Bath** Queens (2), doubles (3). All private baths (1 detached). **Favorites** Agathie Christie Suite, w/ 1936 mirrored dressing room, glass curtain rod, writing desk, room-sized alcove, original chandelier, & 1940 drapes. **Comfort & Decor** Named after the innkeepers' favorite authors (e.g., Grey, Hitchcock, Steinbeck, Hemingway), guest rooms exhibit each character's personality. The John Steinbeck is furnished much like the author's boyhood home in Calinas, with hardwood flooring and period furniture; the Zane Grey has Deco lighting and authentic Native American artifacts. A lift chair totes guests up the stairs. Fireplaces warm the library and living room, all accented by an impressive collection of genuine Art Deco lamps.

RATES, RESERVATIONS, & RESTRICTIONS

Deposit Credit card number **Discounts** Midweek or multiple-night, $10 off **Credit Cards** V, MC, D, AE **Check-In/Out** 4–7:30 p.m./11 a.m. **Smoking** Balcony, porch, gazebo **Pets** No (resident cat is permitted in common areas) **Kids** Over age 12 **No-Nos** N/A **Minimum Stay** None **Open** All year **Hosts** Bob Novak & Scott Berg, 22418 MN 6, Deerwood 56444 **Phone** (218) 546-5433 or toll-free (877) 546-5433 **Web** www.halletthouse.com

COTTON MANSION, Duluth

OVERALL ★★★★★ | QUALITY ★★★★★ | VALUE ★★★★ | PRICE RANGE $175–$245

Cotton Mansion was a fitting residence for Joseph Bell Cotton, corporate attorney for John D. Rockefeller. Every room is sumptuous, from the entry with its hand-carved wooden angels and stunning stained-glass barrel ceiling to the elevated built-in chess nooks in the parlor—an ideal spot for a late-night cognac. Even the wooden ceiling under the portico is coffered. Brass sconces are original, and the antique desk in the parlor—originally the library—was Cotton's personal desk. Be sure to notice the original, vintage appliqués on the dining room chairs; the innkeeper was advised to remove them, but she wisely resisted.

SETTING & FACILITIES

Location In Duluth's historic East End district **Near** Downtown Duluth, Lake Superior, museums, harbor. **Building** 16,000-sq.-ft. Italian Renaissance Revival mansion of yellow brick **Grounds** Almost an acre of lawn, flower garden **Public Space** Entry, foyer, parlor, great room, DR **Food & Drink** Evening snack, wine & cheese, shrimp appetizer, desserts. Full candlelight breakfast served on fine china, crystal, & silver; signature dishes are eggs Benedict (Saturdays only), stuffed French toast w/ Italian sausage. **Recreation** Antiquing, boating, museum touring, historic interests. **Amenities & Services** AC. Breakfast served in bed in Terrace Suite; massage therapy available w/ other spa services, including herbal wrap & hydrotherapy.

ACCOMMODATIONS

Units 1 suite, 5 guest rooms. **All Rooms** CD player, sitting area. **Some Rooms** Duluth harbor view, fireplace, slipper tub, private terrace. **Bed & Bath** Queens (5). All private baths. **Favorites** Bella Flora Suite, 3 rooms atop the carriage house, w/ wet bar, coffeemaker, fridge, whirlpool. **Comfort & Decor** The grandeur of this home is difficult to believe, from the rare, carved woods—white oak in the foyer, Russian walnut in the Great Room, mahogany in the dining room, and Flemish oak in the parlor—to the ornate carved plaster ceilings. The six-foot alabaster mantel in the great room is one of a kind, along with the limestone fireplace in the ceramic tile-floored sun room, and the six-foot marble fireplace in the parlor. Wall coverings are silk tapestry fabric.

RATES, RESERVATIONS, & RESTRICTIONS

Deposit Credit card **Discounts** None **Credit Cards** MC, V, D, AE **Check-In/Out** 4–6 p.m./11 a.m. **Smoking** No **Pets** No **Kids** No **No-Nos** N/A **Minimum Stay** 2 nights, June 1–Oct. 31 **Open** All year **Hosts** Ken & Kimberly Aparicio, 2309 East First St., Duluth 55812 **Phone** (218) 724-6405 or toll-free (800) 228-1997 **Email** cottonmansion@msn.com **Web** www.cottonmansion.com

MANOR ON THE CREEK INN, Duluth

OVERALL ★★★★½ | QUALITY ★★★★½ | VALUE ★★★★ | PRICE RANGE
$119–$189; CARRIAGE HOUSE $199–$219

The rich, deep woods—African mahogany and tiger grain oak, among others—is no surprise; the manor was built by a lumber baron. The innkeepers aren't sure who installed the "bullet glass" doors to the billiards room, but this mansion, once church-owned, retains most of its original features, including arched Gothic ceilings and lighted newel post. In the living room stands another glass tile fireplace and baby grand piano. The window wall to the billiards room is a new addition, but it works; that space was formerly a bishop's chapel.

SETTING & FACILITIES

Location In Duluth's historic East End District **Near** Downtown Duluth, Lake Superior, Oregon Creek. **Building** 1907 Arts & Crafts mansion, yellow brick **Grounds** 2 acres w/ ravine & path running along Oregan Creek **Public Space** Porch, DR, foyer, LR, sun porch, music room, billiards room, 3rd-floor sitting room **Food & Drink** Afternoon snack & beverages. Full breakfast includes hot entree w/ breakfast meat. **Recreation** Antiquing, boating, museum touring, historic interests. **Amenities & Services** AC. Fresh flowers, candy in rooms. Available for small parties, weddings, meetings; bicycle available.

ACCOMMODATIONS

Units 5 suites, 2 guest rooms, plus 2-BR carriage house w/ sunken LR & full kitchen. **All Rooms** Ceiling fan, telephone. **Some Rooms** Desk & chair, claw-foot tub, single or double whirlpool tub, fireplace, cast iron stove, private deck, private screened porch. **Bed & Bath** Kings (5), queens (2); in carriage house, queen (1), double (1). All private baths. **Favorites** Carriage house, for maximum privacy, sunken LR, full kitchen, TV, 2 balconies, gas fireplace. **Comfort & Decor** Arts & Crafts touches are found throughout the house, in leaded glass windows, sconces, and the museum-quality glass tile mantel in the dining room—the best room of all, with a ten-foot window for viewing the gardens and ravine, built-in cabinets with curved-glass mirrors, burled mahogany trim, and a unique, ornate oval ceiling recess.

RATES, RESERVATIONS, & RESTRICTIONS

Deposit 1 night's stay **Discounts** Midweek, multiple-night, winter **Credit Cards** V, MC, D **Check-In/Out** 3–6 p.m./11 a.m. **Smoking** Outside **Pets** No **Kids** Over age 12 **No-Nos** Guests aren't permitted in kitchen **Minimum Stay** 2 nights with Saturday stay; 3 nights during Grandma's Marathon **Open** All year **Hosts** Chris & Tom Kell, 2215 East 2nd St., Duluth 55812 **Phone** (218) 728-3189 or toll-free (800) 428-3189 **Email** manor@cpinternet.com **Web** www.manoronthecreek.com

FINNISH HERITAGE HOMESTEAD, Embarrass

OVERALL ★★★★ | QUALITY ★★★½ | VALUE ★★★★★ | PRICE RANGE $78–$105

Bring your sweater to the land of Northern Lights; in these parts, snow in July and August isn't uncommon and down comforters stay on the beds year-round. Don't be alarmed by the howling at night—it's a lone wolf, possibly one of those who contributed to Buzz's decision to stop raising poultry. Instead, explore the farm on cross-country skis, or, in spring, pick a pail of berries or a bunch of wildflowers for the breakfast table. Finnish Heritage Homestead is the real deal, in spite of the innkeepers' non-Finnish background (they're fast-track escapees from Arizona). And although "beautiful downtown Embarrass" doesn't exist, the town does sit atop the Laurentian Divide, and its two rivers flow in opposite directions.

SETTING & FACILITIES

Location Off MN 21 in Embarrass (Note: Embarrass has no "downtown" and the B&B posts no signs at the road. Get directions before you go) **Near** Boundary Waters Canoe Area, Giants Ridge. **Building** 1901 log farmhouse **Grounds** 16 acres of working farm (oats, hay) w/ raspberry patch, vegetable gardens, log outbuildings, large gazebo **Public Space** LR, DR, small gift shop **Food & Drink** Full gourmet breakfast includes homemade breads, entree such as farm-style soufflé, berry or wild rice pancakes, cheesy wild rice. **Recreation** Cross-country skiing, canoeing, moose-watching, snowmobiling, igloo-building, fishing, golf courses, historic touring. **Amenities & Services** Robes in room, guest fridge, nonskid socks in room for cold weather, Finnish wood-fired sauna (restrictions in winter).

ACCOMMODATIONS

Units 5 guest rooms, **All Rooms** Sitting area. **Some Rooms** Half-bath. **Bed & Bath** Queens & twin (1), queens (3), 2 twins (1). 1 private, 1 half-bath, 1 shared bath (for 3 rooms). **Favorites** Elmina, with queen & twin beds and private bath. **Comfort & Decor** The shared bath situation here gets tricky, and brings down the quality rating—but everything else about Finnish Heritage is about comfort. The style is early farmhouse and very appropriately so, with original logs exposed and creaky wood floors. Quilts and family artifacts are the accessories, including innkeeper Elaine's expertly handmade bark creations and her teacup collection. The fireplace is inviting, but the real hot spot for socializing is the gazebo, in all seasons.

RATES, RESERVATIONS, & RESTRICTIONS

Deposit 1 night's stay **Discounts** None **Credit Cards** V, MC **Check-In/Out** 4 p.m./11 a.m. **Smoking** In gazebo only **Pets** No (resident barn cats stay outdoors) **Kids** Yes **No-Nos** N/A **Minimum Stay** None **Open** All year **Hosts** Buzz & Elaine Brayinton, 4776 Waisanen Rd., Embarrass 55732 **Phone** (218) 984-3318 or toll-free (800) 863-6545

BALLY'S B&B, *Grand Marais*

OVERALL ★★★½ | QUALITY ★★★½ | VALUE ★★★★★ | PRICE RANGE $75

Everyone's grandmother could have lived in this house. Many furnishings are original to the house and it's still operated by the family who built it. The ambience is intimate but casual. Our favorite piece was the unusual wicker library table in the parlor

SETTING & FACILITIES

Location In central Grand Marais, at gateway to Boundary Waters Canoe Area **Near** Lake Superior, Superior Hiking Trail, Boundary Waters, downtown Grand Marais. **Building** 1915 frame home, originally built as a boarding house **Grounds** City lot; flower gardens **Public Space** Sun porch, small foyer, LR, parlor, DR **Food & Drink** Full breakfast w/ entree, including egg dish, breakfast meat, & drop biscuits. **Recreation** Kayaking, canoeing, snowshoeing, fishing, sailing, skiing, dog sledding **Amenities & Services** Fresh flowers in rooms.

ACCOMMODATIONS

Units 4 guest rooms. **All Rooms** Old radio. **Some Rooms** Sitting area. **Bed & Bath** Doubles (3), 2 twins (1). All private baths. **Favorites** Twin-bed room; it gets the most sun, feels cheery. **Comfort & Decor** Pocket doors and leaded glass are original to this house, which has a farmhouse-lakeside cottage feel. Glass-front cabinets dress up the dining room. The wood trim throughout is probably cedar.

RATES, RESERVATIONS, & RESTRICTIONS

Deposit None **Discounts** Single travelers, $5 off **Credit Cards** No **Check-In/Out** By individual arrangement **Smoking** No **Pets** No **Kids** No **No-Nos** Coolers in rooms **Minimum Stay** None **Open** All year **Hosts** Karen Holte Bally, 121 East 3rd St., P.O. Box 524, Grand Marais 55604 **Phone** (218) 387-1817 or toll-free (888) 383-1817 **Email** schoenr@hutchtel.com **Web** www.bbonline.com/mn/ballys/index.html

SNUGGLE INN, Grand Marais

OVERALL ★★★★ | QUALITY ★★★★ | VALUE ★★★★ | PRICE RANGE $90–$95

Service, value, and great cooking are the hallmarks of this cozy bed-and-breakfast. Guests staying multiple nights can have clean linens and room cleaning every morning on request. The lakeside drive to Grand Marais alone is worth the trip, a handy stop-off on the Great Lakes Circle Tour or en route to the Boundary Waters. Consider a class at the North House Folk School; take home a pair of Cree mukluks or learn to mushroom.

SETTING & FACILITIES

Location In central Grand Marais, at gateway to Boundary Waters Canoe Area **Near** Lake Superior, Superior Hiking Trail, Boundary Waters, downtown Grand Marais. **Building** 1903 bungalow, white exterior **Grounds** City lot; perennial gardens **Public Space** Common room w/ cable TV/VCR, DR, deck **Food & Drink** Coffee, sodas available any time. Full breakfast includes specialties such as banana–macadamia nut French toast, wild rice waffles w/ fresh blueberry sauce, & pumpkin-apple streusel muffins. **Recreation** Canoeing, kayaking, fishing, sailing, showshoeing, skiing, dog sledding. **Amenities & Services** AC. Fresh flowers in rooms.

ACCOMMODATIONS

Units 4 guest rooms. **All Rooms** N/A **Some Rooms** Sitting area, lake view. **Bed & Bath** Queens (2), doubles (2). **Favorites** Harbor Room, for the best view of Lake Superior. **Comfort & Decor** This small home with rather small rooms compensates with grand hospitality. Rooms feature prints, books and original art by local artists, maple hardwood floors, and handmade quilts; decorating themes reflect the surroundings—Flycaster, Nor'Shore, B.W.C.A. (Boundary Waters Canoe Area).

RATES, RESERVATIONS, & RESTRICTIONS

Deposit 50% of total stay **Discounts** AAA & AARP weekdays; also discounts for students of North House Folk School & Art Colony **Credit Cards** V, MC, D, AE **Check-In/Out** 2–4 p.m. or by prior arrangement/11 a.m. **Smoking** Outside **Pets** No; resident cat stays in innkeepers' quarters **Kids** Only w/ whole-house rental **No-Nos** Coolers in guest rooms **Minimum Stay** 2 nights, select summer weekends **Open** All year **Hosts** Tim Nauta & Greg Spanton, 8 Seventh Ave., P.O. Box 915, Grand Marais 55604 **Phone** (218) 387-2847 or toll-free (800) 823-3174 **Email** info@snuggleinnbb.com **Web** www.snuggleinnbb.com

DAKOTA LODGE, Hinckley

OVERALL ★★★½ | QUALITY ★★★½ | VALUE ★★★ | PRICE RANGE $58–$110; $135 CABIN (DOUBLE OCCUPANCY)

A former nightclub called Chrissy's Place, Dakota Lodge is a casual place to spend a country weekend. The owner raises ducks and exotic chickens, which kids enjoy. Some of the antique furnishings, such as the 1920s armoire in one of the guest rooms, were striking, and we liked the bed-and-breakfast's "lending library" program: Check out any book that you may have started reading during your stay, including antique editions, and return it by mail within 10 days. Cabin guests should note, though it sleeps six, the $135 price is for two guests; additional guests are $20 each per night—and breakfast is not included in cabin rental.

SETTING & FACILITIES

Location On MN 48, 10 mi. east of Hinckley **Near** St. Croix State Park, Willard Munger State Trail, Bohn's Ark Zoo, Hinckley Fire Museum, Hinckley Flea Market. **Building** 1974 log lodge plus cabin **Grounds** Over 6 acres of fields & forest **Public Space** DR, LR, small TV room, porch **Food & Drink** Complimentary beverages 3–8 p.m. Full country breakfast w/ hot entree. **Recreation** Cross-country skiing, fishing, canoeing, antiquing, canoeing. **Amenities & Services** AC. Will arrange flowers, wine for special occasions.

ACCOMMODATIONS

Units 5 guest rooms, 1 cabin. **All Rooms** Ceiling fans. **Some Rooms** Double whirlpool tub, sitting area (4 of 5 rooms), canopy bed, table & chairs, desk, wood-burning fireplace (4 of 5 rooms). **Bed & Bath** King (1), queens (4) in lodge; queens (2) and queen sleeper sofas (2) in cabin. All private baths in lodge (1 detached), 1 bath in cabin. **Favorites** Cabin, for the privacy, 3-season sleeping porch, full kitchen & TV/VCR. **Comfort & Decor** Furnishings at Dakota Lodge are a bit of a hodgepodge but comfortable. The plethora of fireplaces makes most rooms a good choice in cold months. The lodge isn't particularly elegant, but there are quality features, such as the old pump organ in dining room, and the piano and wall of books—some dating back to 1857—in the living room. We did detect a cigarette smell in the lodge.

RATES, RESERVATIONS, & RESTRICTIONS

Deposit 1 night's stay **Discounts** Single traveler **Credit Cards** V, MC, D **Check-In/Out** 3–9 p.m./11 a.m. **Smoking** Outside **Pets** No (resident cat comes into the lodge) **Kids** Yes, in cabin **No-Nos** N/A **Minimum Stay** None **Open** All year **Hosts** Michael Schmitz, R.R. 3, Box 178, Hinckley 44307 **Phone** (320) 384-6052 **Web** www.dakotalodge.com

LOTTIE LEE'S B&B, Little Falls

OVERALL ★★★★½ | QUALITY ★★★★½ | VALUE ★★★★★ | PRICE RANGE
$75–$85 SUN.–THURS., $85–$95 WEEKENDS, ROSE SUITE $120–$135

This home is a marvel of juxtaposition. Alongside such interesting original features as the "wavy" oak woodwork and stained glass–fronted servers in the dining room, one finds whimsy in Earl's metal creations and the yellow sun room. Originally, the home featured an intricate doorbell system with different sounds for each door. Lottie Lee's gardens are featured in the town's annual garden tours, and include Diane's ten-bloom Easter lily,

Monet sunflowers, her mother's perennials and raspberries, and, of course, Earl's metal sculptures.

SETTING & FACILITIES

Location In Little Falls, 4 blocks from Mississippi River **Near** Charles A. Lindbergh State Historic Site (boyhood home) & State Park, Minnesota Fishing Museum, Pine Grove Park & Zoo, Minnesota Military Museum. **Building** 1907 Arts & Crafts w/ Victorian & Tudor elements **Grounds** Double lot w/ lush sculpted gardens **Public Space** Screened porch, foyer, "turret room," LR, DR, sun room **Food & Drink** Full breakfast w/entree, breakfast meat. **Recreation** Historic touring, cross-country skiing, canoeing, antiquing, birding. **Amenities & Services** AC. Fresh flowers in rooms.

ACCOMMODATIONS

Units 2 guest rooms (or 1 guest room & 1 suite if nursery is included). **All Rooms** Antique iron beds, sitting area. **Some Rooms** Claw-foot tub, dressing room, vintage intercom, table, window seat, garden view. **Bed & Bath** All private baths (or, if renting nursery w/ Rose Room, 1 shared). Queen beds (3). **Favorites** Rose Room, with a spacious, sunny seating area, table, and dressing room. **Comfort & Decor** Original light fixtures, Arts & Crafts wood trim, and a beautiful Tiffany-inspired stained-glass window at the landing help make this home a warm haven. Some of the sculptures throughout the house were done by innkeeper Earl Pilloud, a retired industrial arts teacher. Pocket doors and Tudor arches add to the charm; our favorite detail was the "iris garden" in the Rose Room's bath, hand-painted in 1908.

RATES, RESERVATIONS, & RESTRICTIONS

Deposit Advance payment for entire stay **Discounts** None **Credit Cards** V, MC **Check-In/Out** 4–7 p.m./11 a.m. **Smoking** No **Pets** No **Kids** Yes **No-Nos** N/A **Minimum Stay** None **Open** May–Sept. **Hosts** Earl & Diana Pilloud, 206 SE Third St., Little Falls 56345 **Phone** (320) 632-8641 **Email** epilloud@upstel.net **Web** www.upstel.net/~lotlee

LINDGREN'S BED & BREAKFAST, Lutsen

OVERALL ★★★★ | QUALITY ★★★½ | VALUE ★★★ | PRICE RANGE $105–$150

There's plenty to do in this remote lodge, even if you never leave the property. A fire pit, volleyball court, horseshoe pit, hammock, and swing keep guests relaxed. Summers are cooler here—expect a 20° drop if you're driving north from the Twin Cities—but winters often are warmer than the rest of the state. Set your alarm early; sunrise on Lake Superior is worth getting up for.

SETTING & FACILITIES
Location 0.5 mi. off MN 61 on Lake Superior **Near** Lake Superior, Boundary Waters Canoe Area, Lutsen Mountain, North Shore Corridor Snowmobiling Trail, Superior National Forest. **Building** 1926 hunting lodge **Grounds** 450-ft. rocky lakefront w/ wild-flower garden, horseshoe pit, fire pit **Public Space** Common Room w/ breakfast area, small patio, Finnish sauna hut **Food & Drink** Cont'l-plus breakfast w/ homemade jams, wild raspberry muffins & breads; cereals, fruit. Sodas and "box wine" served afternoons. **Recreation** Downhill & cross-country skiing, golf courses, canoeing, fishing, kayaking, mountain biking, snowmobiling, antiquing, snowshoeing. **Amenities & Services** Robes & fresh flowers in rooms, bedside candies.

ACCOMMODATIONS
Units 3 guest rooms, plus lower-level dorm. **All Rooms** TV, coffeemaker, sitting area. **Some Rooms** Double whirlpool. **Bed & Bath** Kings (2), queen, all private bath. Dorm has king, double, 8 twin beds, shared bath. **Favorites** Bobby's Room, with the double whirlpool. **Comfort & Decor** This rustic, north-woods lodge is perched on the edge of Lake Superior in Superior National Forest. Lakeside windows give panoramic water views. A massive stone fireplace and baby grand piano in the common room add to the woodsy ambience, though we admit cringing at the large collection of moose, bear, birds, and timberwolf heads—hunting trophies—looking down on us.

RATES, RESERVATIONS, & RESTRICTIONS
Deposit N/A **Discounts** None **Credit Cards** V, MC **Check-In/Out** 4 p.m./11 a.m. **Smoking** Outside **Pets** No **Kids** No **No-Nos** N/A **Minimum Stay** 2 nights weekends, 3 nights holidays **Open** All year **Hosts** Shirley Lindgren, P.O. Box 56, CR 35, Lutsen 55612 **Phone** (218) 663-7450 **Email** stay@lindgrenbb.com **Web** www.lindgrenbb.com

LIGHTHOUSE BED & BREAKFAST, Two Harbors

OVERALL ★★★★ | QUALITY ★★★★ | VALUE ★★★★ | PRICE RANGE $115

You won't find glamour here, but you will find thrills as an assistant light-house keeper. In that role, you become a registered "keeper of the light" during your stay, and the cost of staying overnight is actually a donation to maintaining the historic lighthouse. You'll also have a magnificent view of Lake Superior's North Shore, a close-up view of giant freighters on the lake and in the adjacent harbor, and a front-row seat for some of the prettiest sunsets in the Midwest. If a storm comes up, not to worry—the light tower is three bricks thick.

SETTING & FACILITIES

Location On Lake Superior's North Shore on the water-edge of Two Harbors **Near** Downtown Two Harbors, Sonju Trail, Superior Hiking Trail, Agate Bay Harbor, Cloquet Valley State Forest, Duluth (25 mi.). **Building** 1892 working lighthouse, red brick **Grounds** Lakeside yard sloping to Lake Superior, outbuildings, pier **Public Space** Kitchen, LR, DR, light tower **Food & Drink** "Simple, homey" full breakfast. **Recreation** Lighthouse maintenance, biking, birding, canoeing, downhill & cross-country skiing, kayaking, snowshoeing, snowmobiling. **Amenities & Services** Caters small private luncheons, meetings.

ACCOMMODATIONS

Units 3 guest rooms. **All Rooms** Lake view, alarm clock, chairs. **Some Rooms** N/A **Bed & Bath** Double & twin (1), doubles (2). Shared bath. **Favorites** Forest Room, the largest space. **Comfort & Decor** Guest rooms and common areas alike are simply and sparsely furnished, with antique iron or wood beds, quilted bed coverings, simple rugs covering the floors, and almost no wall art. The focus is the lake and the historical aspects of the lighthouse, with little emphasis on pampering.

RATES, RESERVATIONS, & RESTRICTIONS

Deposit Payment in advance **Discounts** None **Credit Cards** V, MC **Check-In/Out** 3 p.m./10 a.m. **Smoking** No **Pets** No **Kids** Yes **No-Nos** N/A **Minimum Stay** None **Open** All year **Hosts** Lake County Historical Society, 1 Lighthouse Point, P.O. Box 128, Two Harbors 55616 **Phone** (218) 834-4814 or toll-free (888) 532-5606 **Email** lakehist @lakenet.com **Web** www.lighthousebb.org

Zone 16

Southwest Minnesota

In this region we visited some of Minnesota's most affordable bed-and-breakfasts. There were exceptions, such as the new Lake Le Homme Dieu bed-and-breakfast, and the fully outfitted Miller's House in **Terrace.** This area caters largely to families, serving up hearty breakfasts in simple settings.

One of the most homespun is the Triple L Farm in **Hendricks,** a 20-minute walk from the South Dakota border, perfect for family farm getaways. The innkeeper happily demonstrates the sack swing, and those who really want to rough it can sleep in the bunkhouse for $35. Just down the road stands a spectacle: a "wind farm," more than 125 gigantic propellers towering over the rolling landscape, as far as the eye can see. Each blade is 82 feet long, and turbines stretch 165 feet into the sky. Pick the right side road and you'll be surrounded by massive propellers for at least five miles; it looks like a scene out of the Tele-Tubbies.

Almost directly south of Hendricks is Pipestone, where we stayed at the historic Calumet Inn, built of Sioux quartzite, which was quarried just a mile down the road. Much of Main Street is a National Register Historic District, many displaying sandstone relief sculptures on their facades—gargoyles, Eve with apples, the serpent in Eden, baby Moses in the bulrushes, and other architectural details.

Two other stops are important to tourism in the southwest zone: **New Ulm,** a German settlement complete with performing glockenspiel in the town center, is known for its heritage, parks, and **August Schell Brewery,** the second-oldest family brewery. Probably the biggest tourism draw in the region is the **Laura Ingalls Wilder Historic Highway,** including the **Ingalls Home** and other sites made famous in the *Little House on the Prairie* series. We visited the Sod House on the Prairie, built with sod from a nearby virgin prairie. The innkeepers are in the process of restoring the prairie grasses on their land.

CEDAR ROSE INN, *Alexandria*

OVERALL ★★★★ | QUALITY ★★★★ | VALUE ★★★ | PRICE RANGE $75–$130

Throughout the first floor of Cedar Rose, a sculpted plaster frieze trickles across the ceiling, from one room to the next in an acorn and leaf motif, trailing vines and leaves—a traditional symbol of hospitality in these parts. That's not the only evidence of hospitality at this inn, however. It was once known as the "Hostess House" because so many special events were held here, and the former owner baked more than 200 dozen caramel and cinnamon rolls each week for catering and entertaining. Today, a trail of blooming roses greets guests along the circular path leading to the house, and the aroma of fresh-baked cinnamon rolls still wakes guests in the morning.

SETTING & FACILITIES
Location 2 mi. from I-94 in residential Alexandria **Near** Lake Winona, Carlos State Park, Carlos Creek Winery, Fort Alexandria, Runestone Viking Museum, Inspiration Peak, Theatre Le Homme Dieu. **Building** 1900 Tudor Revival w/ wraparound porch, on National Register of Historic Places **Grounds** City lot w/ pond garden, rose gardens **Public Space** Porch, entry, parlor, library, LR, BR, infrared sauna **Food & Drink** Early coffee. Full country breakfast may include pancakes, omelets, French toast, sausage, scones, muffins. **Recreation** Swimming, boating, canoeing, kayaking, biking, winery touring, historic touring, antiquing, live theater. **Amenities & Services** AC.

ACCOMMODATIONS
Units 4 guest rooms. **All Rooms** chairs, clock. **Some Rooms** Thermo-massage bath, double whirlpool tub, claw-foot tub, stereo system, fireplace, bay window seat. **Bed & Bath** King (1), queens (3). All private baths. **Favorites** Alma Anderson Room, w/ window seat, thermo-massage bath in Balneo claw-foot tub, fireplace. **Comfort & Decor** This is a romantic setting without going overboard on floral designs or lace. Original maplewood floors, oak woodwork, and several stained-glass windows blend with diamond-pane windows, oversized gables, Tiffany-style chandeliers, and a vast open staircase. Common areas are furnished with quality antiques.

RATES, RESERVATIONS, & RESTRICTIONS
Deposit 1 night's stay **Discounts** None **Credit Cards** V, MC **Check-In/Out** 4–6 p.m./11 a.m. **Smoking** No **Pets** No **Kids** Age 12 and over **No-Nos** N/A **Minimum Stay** None **Open** All year **Hosts** Florian & Aggie Ledermann, 422 7th Ave. West, Alexandria 56308 **Phone** (320) 762-8430 or toll-free (888) 203-5333 **Email** cedarose @gctel.com **Web** www.echopress.com/cedarose

LAKE LE HOMME DIEU BED & BREAKFAST, *Alexandria*

OVERALL ★★★★½ | QUALITY ★★★★½ | VALUE ★★★ | PRICE RANGE $165–$195

Although this contemporary home will appeal to business travelers and younger bed-and-breakfast guests, its features cater to traditional bed-and-breakfast fans as well, including a lift down the hillside, leading to the pier below. Most guests opt to have breakfast on the porch rather than the dining room because the porch's window walls overlook Lake Le Homme Dieu—a sunny, expansive view, a fine start to one's day.

SETTING & FACILITIES
Location 2 mi. from Alexandria along Lake Le Homme Dieu **Near** Downtown Alexandria, Fort Alexandria, Runestone Viking Museum, Carlos Creek Winery, Inspiration Peak, Lake Carlos State Park, Theatre Le Homme Dieu. **Building** 1999 contemporary country home, brick w/ stained cedar siding **Grounds** 2 acres of lakeside lawns, trees **Public Space** LR, 4-season porch, deck w/ hot tub, DR **Food & Drink** Soft drinks any time; full breakfast includes hot entree. **Recreation** Cross-country skiing, boating, antiquing, swimming, historical touring, snowmobiling, snowshoeing, winery touring, golf courses. **Amenities & Services** AC. Robes, fresh flowers, chocolates in rooms, candles in baths.

ACCOMMODATIONS
Units 4 guest rooms. **All Rooms** TV/VCR, chairs, clock radio. **Some Rooms** Single or double whirlpool tub, CD player. **Bed & Bath** Queens (4). All private baths. **Favorites** Ash Room, w/ Mission-style furniture. **Comfort & Decor** It occurred to us as we toured this new home, built as a B&B, that Lake Le Homme Dieu would appeal to a younger clientele than many inns, with its clean lines, un-frilly decor, contemporary furnishings, and open quality to the space. Each guest room features a different wood bed, including a cherry Amana bed, a maple sleigh bed, the ash Mission bed, and an old iron bed in the one room furnished in family antiques.

RATES, RESERVATIONS, & RESTRICTIONS
Deposit $100 **Discounts** None **Credit Cards** V, MC **Check-In/Out** 3–6 p.m./11 a.m. **Smoking** No **Pets** No **Kids** Over age 12 **No-Nos** N/A **Minimum Stay** None **Open** All year except Feb. **Hosts** Judy Radjenovich, 441 South Le Homme Dieu Dr. NE, Alexandria 56308 **Phone** (320) 846-5875 or (800) 943-5875

PILLARS BED AND BREAKFAST, *Alexandria*

OVERALL ★★★★ | QUALITY ★★★★ | VALUE ★★★★ | PRICE RANGE $65–$105

The entry to this stately home is impressive, with Corinthian pillars framing the front door. The dining and sitting rooms are both pleasant spots for lingering with coffee. Each guest room has a focal point; in the Fireside Room it's the ornately carved mantel over the copper fireplace, whereas the Rose Room features a canopy brought from Norway. During the holidays, each room has its own full-size Christmas tree.

SETTING & FACILITIES

Location Just off I-94, in residential Alexandria **Near** Runestone Viking Museum, Fort Alexandria, Carlos Creek Winery, Inspiration Peak, Theatre Le Homme Dieu, Lake Carlos State Park. **Building** 1903 Neoclassical, white exterior **Grounds** City lot; shrubs, flower beds **Public Space** Foyer, front & rear porches, sitting room, DR **Food & Drink** Early coffee available. Full breakfast includes hot entree; may feature signature "designer pancakes." **Recreation** Downhill & cross-country skiing, antiquing, historical touring, swimming, snowmobiling, snowshoeing, winery touring, golf courses. **Amenities & Services** AC.

ACCOMMODATIONS

Units 5 guest rooms. **All Rooms** Clock, chairs. **Some Rooms** TV, fireplace, sitting area, fresh roses in season. **Bed & Bath** Queens (3), double (1), 3/4 bed (1). Private full bath (1), private half bath (1), shared bath (3). **Favorites** Fireside Room, w/ private bath, fireplace, sitting area, queen bed. **Comfort & Decor** The innkeepers used imagination in decorating guest rooms: The Anne of Green Gables is done in Victorian style with memorabilia, and Eleanor's Room is a sensitive space, named for the innkeeper's late sister and decorated with Eleanor's wedding dress, shoe collection, and other possessions. Common areas are trimmed in original oak woodwork, notably the sunny dining room with a built-in oak buffet.

RATES, RESERVATIONS, & RESTRICTIONS

Deposit 1 night's stay **Discounts** None **Credit Cards** V, MC **Check-In/Out** 4 p.m./11 a.m. **Smoking** No **Pets** No **Kids** By prior arrangement **No-Nos** N/A **Minimum Stay** None **Open** All year **Hosts** Jim & Anita Tollefson, 1004 Elm St., Alexandria 56308 **Phone** (320) 762-2700 **Email** pillarbb@rea-alp.com **Web** www.pillarsbandb.itgo.com

TRIPLE L FARM BED & BREAKFAST, Hendricks

OVERALL ★★★½ | QUALITY ★★★½ | VALUE ★★★★★ | PRICE RANGE $55–$75; $100 SUITE (ALL 3 UPSTAIRS BEDROOMS). BUNKHOUSE $35 FOR 2 GUESTS, KIDS FREE; BREAKFAST $5 EXTRA PER BUNKHOUSE GUEST

With this backdrop, Triple L Farm will easily imagine the settlers' prairie experience: winds blowing across miles of fields, kittens at play, wildflowers blooming, country roads that lead nowhere but to more country roads. For many miles south and west of Triple L, there's a real rural bonus: hundreds of gigantic propellers scattered across the prairie, the world's second-largest "wind farm," an image so surreal you expect the Tele-Tubbies to appear, skipping along through the grasses. The bunkhouse is a favorite with hunters, but be ready for rustic. That means washing in water you carry in a pail and visiting an outhouse.

SETTING & FACILITIES

Location On MN 19, 1 mi. from SD border **Near** Pipestone National Monument, Laura Ingalls Wilder Trail, "Harness the Wind" turbine project. **Building** 1890s farmhouse on prairie **Grounds** 283 acres of working farm & prairie; take a turn on the "sack swing" **Public Space** Common room w/ dining area **Food & Drink** Welcome snack. Full breakfast served on pottery crafted by innmaker's cousin, includes hot entree. **Recreation**

Antiquing, fishing, boating, swimming, cross-country skiing, biking, birding, hunting, golf courses, tennis courts. **Amenities & Services** AC. Robes, hair dryers provided.

ACCOMMODATIONS

Units 1 suite (3 bedrooms), 1 guest room. **All Rooms** Sitting area. **Some Rooms** TV/VCR, ceiling fan, phone, writing desk, sofa bed. **Bed & Bath** Queens (2), doubles (2). 1 private bath, 1 shared. **Favorites** Grandparents' Room, features spoon-carved bed by a local artist and wall weavings by former guests. **Comfort & Decor** This home is country all the way, with quilted bed coverings and comfortable stuffed furniture. Two Gary Smith prints adorn the living room. The farmhouse is almost always shaded.

RATES, RESERVATIONS, & RESTRICTIONS

Deposit 80% of total stay **Discounts** 10% off 3 nights or more **Credit Cards** No **Check-In/Out** 2 p.m./11 a.m. or by prior arrangement **Smoking** No **Pets** Only in kennels, occasionally in bunkhouse **Kids** Yes **No-Nos** N/A **Minimum Stay** None **Open** All year **Hosts** Lanford & Joan Larson, R.R. 1, Box 141, Hendricks 56136 **Phone** (507) 275-3740 **Email** lll@itctel.com

DEUTSCHE STRASSE BED & BREAKFAST, New Ulm

OVERALL ★★★½ | QUALITY ★★★½ | VALUE ★★★★ | PRICE RANGE $69–$89

New Ulm is an oom-pah-pah town; its giant glockenspiel puts on a show three times a day, and the Heritagefest is one of the top 100 festivals in the country. The Dakota uprising happened here in 1862. A good place to ponder the battle is the August Schell Brewery, after five generations the second-oldest family brewery in the United States.

SETTING & FACILITIES

Location In New Ulm's historic district, off MN 15 **Near** Flandrau State Park, downtown New Ulm, Martin Luther College, Minnesota River, Swan Lake, Scenic Lake Route. **Building** 1893 Victorian w/ all-season sun porch, side porch **Grounds** City lot; flower beds **Public Space** Porches, foyer, parlor, formal DR **Food & Drink** Early coffee. Full breakfast may include signature Deutsche Strasse Potato Hash, German apple pancakes, or made-to-order omelets. **Recreation** Canoeing, cross-country skiing, historical touring, boating, fishing, antiquing, Oktoberfest, Heritagefest. **Amenities & Services** AC. Can host parties, meetings, luncheons to 24 guests. Flowers & fruit baskets available w/ 2-day advance notice.

ACCOMMODATIONS

Units 5 guest rooms. **All Rooms** Clock, chair. **Some Rooms** N/A **Bed & Bath** Queens (2), doubles (3). Private full bath (1), private half bath (2), shared bath (2). **Favorites** 4-poster room w/private bath. **Comfort & Decor** This is a modest home overlooking the Minnesota River Valley; it is furnished with antiques and trimmed with original woodwork. The dining room features the original chandelier and sconces. All rooms are clean and comfortable—a cozy, welcoming place to stay when touring the German shops or festivals.

RATES, RESERVATIONS, & RESTRICTIONS
Deposit Credit card number **Discounts** Single rates **Credit Cards** V, MC **Check-In/Out** 4:30–6:30 p.m./11 a.m. **Smoking** No **Pets** No **Kids** By arrangement **No-Nos** N/A **Minimum Stay** None **Open** All year **Hosts** Gary & Ramona Sonnenberg, 404 South German St., New Ulm 56073 **Phone** (507) 354-2005 or toll-free (866) 226-9856 **Email** glsonnen@newulmtel.net **Web** www.newulmtel.net/~glsonnen/deutsche.html

CALUMET INN, Pipestone

OVERALL ★★★★½ | QUALITY ★★★★½ | VALUE ★★★★★ | PRICE RANGE $67–$82, WHIRLPOOL ROOMS $100–$130

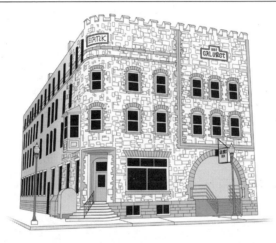

Every room at the Calumet is furnished in quality antiques—all different, all elegant. The inn underwent a $3 million restoration and renovation in 1979, with the aim of retaining its original appearance but with modern conveniences. We kept expecting Miss Kitty to descend the grand staircase from our favorite spot—the lobby gift shop of antiques, particularly the affordable Midwest pottery. The dining room serves the most exquisite wild rice soup in Minnesota. Had breakfast been more than bagels and cold cereal, the quality rating would have been several points higher.

SETTING & FACILITIES
Location Downtown Pipestone, among 20 Main St. buildings on National Historic Register **Near** Pipestone National Monument, Pipestone Health & Recreation Center, Pipestone County Museum, Fort Pipestone. **Building** 1887 stone inn of Sioux quartzite, w/ Pipestone trim, on National Register of Historic Places **Grounds** N/A **Public Space** Lobby, gift shop

area, meeting room, DR, pub & lounge **Food & Drink** Cont'l breakfast. **Recreation** Antiquing, historic touring. **Amenities & Services** AC. Fresh flowers in rooms.

ACCOMMODATIONS

Units 41 guest rooms. **All Rooms** Tables & sitting area, cable TV, phone. **Some Rooms** Claw-foot tub, single or double whirlpool tub, desk, turret sitting alcove. **Bed & Bath** Mix of doubles & queen beds (precise number fluctuates w/ renovations & "model" rooms); several rooms w/ 2 doubles or 2 queens. One "family suite" has 4 doubles. All private baths. **Favorites** Honeymoon Room w/ queen four-poster, double whirlpool nestled along a Sioux quartzite wall. **Comfort & Decor** Guests to the Calumet will feel as if they're on a movie set or in an elegant stagecoach tavern inn. All rooms are spacious, many with high-backed Victorian or Eastlake beds. Wall art is well selected, with many historic Pipestone photos throughout the inn; Native American artifacts of the region are displayed in the lobby, and an elevator makes the inn handicapped-friendly.

RATES, RESERVATIONS, & RESTRICTIONS

Deposit Credit card number **Discounts** None **Credit Cards** MC, V, AE **Check-In/Out** 2 p.m./11 a.m. **Smoking** Only in the 10 smoking-permitted guest rooms, "and that number keeps going down" **Pets** Only if they're small & kenneled; guests with pets are assigned smoking rooms **Kids** Yes **No-Nos** N/A **Minimum Stay** None **Open** All year **Hosts** Colleen & Steve Klinkhammer, 104 West Main St., Pipestone 56164 **Phone** (507) 825-5871 or toll-free (800) 535-7610 **Fax** (507) 825-4578 **Email** calumet@calumetinn.com **Web** www.calumetinn.com

---

SOD HOUSE ON THE PRAIRIE, Sanborn

OVERALL ★★★½ | QUALITY ★★★½ | VALUE ★★★★★ | PRICE RANGE $100 FOR 1 COUPLE; $130 FAMILY OF 3; $140 FAMILY OF ★★★★; KIDS UNDER AGE 6 STAY FREE

When Laura Ingalls Wilder's family arrived on this prairie, the "tall grass"— big bluestem and Indian grass—was so tall that they had to stand on their horses to see ahead. Stan McCone built the sod replicas as a tribute to those homesteaders who settled the prairie, and he is working to restore the eight-foot-tall "sea of grass" surrounding the house. The sod home was featured in a 2001 History Channel special on frontier homes. Spend an evening sitting in the spindle chair by the crackling wood stove, trying to read by the oil lamp. Stroll the wildflower paths by day, try to find the outhouse at night. It's a glimpse at pioneer living—though, chances are, no one delivered hot biscuits and fresh coffee to the Ingalls' door in the morning.

SETTING & FACILITIES

Location On the Laura Ingalls Historic Highway, 0.25 mi. south of MN 71 & 14 junction **Near** Walnut Grove (Wilder Museum & Ingalls Homestead), Jeffers Petroglyphs. **Building** Authentic replica of 1880s sod house, built 1987 **Grounds** 25 acres of prairie in process of restoring grasses, wildflowers **Public Space** 1-room sod house, also enclosed gazebo w/ seating, coffeepot **Food & Drink** Coffee any time. Full breakfast delivered to sod house includes home-baked pastry, muffins, hot entree w/ breakfast meats. **Recreation** Be a pioneer family for a day, in authentic dress. Also historic touring, waterslide & swimming pool, golf course. **Amenities & Services** AC.

ACCOMMODATIONS

Units 1-room house. **All Rooms** Wood-burning stove, outhouse, furs & traps displayed, table & chairs. **Some Rooms** N/A **Bed & Bath** Doubles (2), fainting couch. Outhouse; wash pitcher & bowl. **Favorites** N/A **Comfort & Decor** This is a true pioneer experience, so be sure your kids are ready to use an outhouse and wash pitcher. About the size of one of the homes Laura Ingalls Wilder lived in, the Sod House walls are of sod squares (two feet thick) brought from virgin prairie on a nearby farm—an authentic prairie soddy. Light is from oil lamps, heat is from a wood-burning stove, and 1880-style dresses, bonnets, and other clothing are available. Handmade quilt bedcovers and a horsehide robe will keep you warm.

RATES, RESERVATIONS, & RESTRICTIONS

Deposit $50 per couple, $100 for family or adult group **Discounts** None **Credit Cards** No **Check-In/Out** 4–5 p.m./noon **Smoking** Yes **Pets** No **Kids** Yes **No-Nos** Alcoholic parties **Minimum Stay** None **Open** Inquire during winter months **Hosts** Stan & Virginia McCone, 12598 Magnolia Ave., Sanborn 56083 **Phone** (507) 723-5138

W. W. SMITH INN, Sleepy Eye

OVERALL ★★★★½ | QUALITY ★★★★½ | VALUE ★★★★ | PRICE RANGE $75–$125

This historic home makes a beautiful setting for the antiques placed here; some, including volumes in the library and its carved oak chairs, were acquired from the estate of W. W. Smith, the banker who built the house. We loved the dressing table and fainting couch in the Garden Room, but our favorite touches were the "corset shades" in the parlors—Victorian lamp shades (now refurbished but retaining the original wires), over which women used to fit their corsets when they removed them at night.

SETTING & FACILITIES

Location Off MN 14, 10 min. from New Ulm **Near** Laura Ingalls Wilder childhood home, Martin Luther College, Milford State Monument, Flandrau State Park, Cottonwood River, Minnesota River. **Building** Early 1900s Queen Anne, on National Register of Historic Places **Grounds** Oversized city lot; Victorian garden, carriage house **Public Space** Deep porch w/ turret, foyer, 2 front parlors, DR, library **Food & Drink** Early coffee. Full breakfast includes hot entree. **Recreation** Antiquing, historical touring, canoeing, kayaking, swimming, cross-country skiing, golf courses. **Amenities & Services** AC. First floor available for special events.

ACCOMMODATIONS

Units 3 guest rooms, 2 suites. **All Rooms** Sitting area, clock. **Some Rooms** Robes, claw-foot tub, 2-person hot tub, breakfast delivered to room, fireplace, stained-glass window, TV. **Bed & Bath** King (1), king/2 twins (1), doubles (3). Private/shared baths.

Favorites Queen's Suite, w/ high-backed cherry bedroom set, sunrise view, parlor w/ fireplace. **Comfort & Decor** The glamour of this home begins just inside the heavy oak front door, at the Tiffany newel light. Beautiful surprises are found in every room, from stained-glass windows in closets to the original plank walls in the carriage house, the guest room built into the horse's "box stall," and the home's elaborate light fixtures, including the library's original brass chandelier with Steuben shades. Period antiques furnish all rooms.

RATES, RESERVATIONS, & RESTRICTIONS

Deposit I night's stay **Discounts** Single traveler rates **Credit Cards** Call ahead **Check-In/Out** Inquire **Smoking** No **Pets** No **Kids** Yes **No-Nos** N/A **Minimum Stay** None **Open** All year **Hosts** Dennis & Mary Hoffrogge, 101 Linden St. SW, Sleepy Eye 56085 **Phone** (507) 794-5661 or toll-free (800) 799-5661 **Web** www.bbonline.com/mn/smithinn/index.html

GREEN LAKE INN, Spicer

OVERALL ★★★½ | QUALITY ★★★★ | VALUE ★★★ | PRICE RANGE $99–$109 OFF SEASON; IN SEASON $119–$129

Unlike several bed-and-breakfasts, Green Lake Inn isn't a destination in itself; guests come to Spicer because of the lake, and the inn happens to be there. It's not an elegant inn; we thought some updating of the furnishings and a coat of paint would add appeal. Still, it's clean; we'd be happier with the prices if the inn underwent a historic restoration.

SETTING & FACILITIES

Location In resort town of Spicer, across road from Green Lake **Near** Glacial Ridge bike trail, Saulsbury public beach & fishing pier, Green Lake. **Building** 1913 inn alongside storefronts **Grounds** N/A **Public Space** Porch, 2nd-floor sitting area, great room, DR for meetings, kitchen area w/ microwave & fridge **Food & Drink** Voucher for breakfast at O'Neil's Restaurant next door. **Recreation** Beach, swimming, fishing, boating, biking. **Amenities & Services** AC. Bath amenities, laundry facilities, can accommodate small meetings & parties up to 50.

ACCOMMODATIONS

Units 4 guest rooms. **All Rooms** TV, sitting area, table & chairs. **Some Rooms** Lake view, claw-foot tub, high four-poster bed. **Bed & Bath** Queens (4). All private baths. **Favorites** Windsor, w/ ceiling border of porcelain roses, claw-foot tub, & high four-poster. **Comfort & Decor** Stained glass, leaded glass, and bull's-eye molding throughout the inn are original. The upstairs sitting room features an organ and skylight, and the great room's picture windows and couches make an inviting spot for evening cocktails and lake viewing.

RATES, RESERVATIONS, & RESTRICTIONS

Deposit Credit card number; cash deposit required for select event weekends **Discounts** Extended-stay, whole-house, & group rates **Credit Cards** V, MC, AE, D

Check-In/Out 2:30 p.m./11 a.m. **Smoking** No **Pets** No **Kids** Yes, "but please let us know in advance" **No-Nos** No food from O'Neil's allowed in guest rooms **Minimum Stay** None **Open** All year **Hosts** Tasha Fostervold, 152 Lake Ave. North, Spicer 56288 **Phone** (320) 796-6523 **Web** www.bbonline.com/mn/greenlake

MILLER'S HOUSE, Terrace

OVERALL ★★★★½ | QUALITY ★★★★½ | VALUE ★★★ | PRICE RANGE $200

If isolation is the goal, you'll love Terrace, a tiny settlement of 23 year-round residents, 13 miles from the nearest traffic light. (The Italian restaurant in town, the Terrace Store, seats more than twice the population.) Two former New York schoolteachers own both the restaurant and cottage. Terrace's main attraction is the old flour mill, now a museum operated by a foundation, which hosts orchestra concerts and classes. Don't miss the tiny 1860 log home that once housed a family of nine.

SETTING & FACILITIES
Location Terrace Historic District **Near** Terrace Mill, Terrace Store restaurant, Keystone Bridge, Lake Johanna, Glacial Lakes State Park, Ordway Prairie, Mill Pond. **Building** 1930 stone cottage, 1.5 stories **Grounds** Small plot in 3-acre open village setting **Public Space** N/A **Food & Drink** Full gourmet breakfast; sodas, water, coffee, & tea service any time. **Recreation** Historic touring, antiquing, nature study, canoeing, fishing, rosemale, other crafts classes, cross-country skiing, ice skating. **Amenities & Services** AC. Dinner available in Terrace Store, special events (Fiddlers' Contest, Heritage Festival).

ACCOMMODATIONS
Units 1 whole-house rental, 2 bedrooms sleep 5. **All Rooms** Sitting area, clock, TV. **Some Rooms** Daybed. **Bed & Bath** 1 full bath. **Favorites** Daybed room w/ extra space. **Comfort & Decor** Innkeepers have furnished this cottage with grandma's-house antiques characteristic of rural Minnesota. Iron and wood beds, quilts, benches, and regional handicrafts (baskets, hand-woven rugs, woodcrafts) are displayed; exposed rafter ends and timbering, and other original features have been preserved. The kitchen is fully refurbished with modern appliances.

RATES, RESERVATIONS, & RESTRICTIONS
Deposit 1 night's stay **Discounts** None **Credit Cards** V, MC **Check-In/Out** 3 p.m./11 a.m. **Smoking** Outside **Pets** No **Kids** Yes **No-Nos** N/A **Minimum Stay** None **Open** June 1–Sept. 16, 4 nights/week (Wed., Thurs., Fri., Sat.) **Hosts** Bob Greenfield & Dick Grella, Box 15, Old Mill Pond Rd., Terrace 56380 **Phone** (320) 278-2233

Southeast Minnesota

It's back to the city in Zone 17—and back to big-city prices, even in smaller towns.

Most of the tourism—and, consequently, most of the bed-and-breakfasts—collects in bluff country in the southeast corner of the state, along the **Mississippi River** and **St. Croix River Valley** and on the outskirts of **Minneapolis.** We found glamorous old mansions of every architectural style, built by industrial titans after the Civil War, throughout the zone.

Along the **Root River** in bluff country, bed-and-breakfasts were filled with canoe and biking enthusiasts on week-long adventures among the limestone cliffs. Several wineries are found in the region, producing both fruit and grape wines. There also is a significant **Amish community** in southeast Minnesota; we stopped several times to check out breads, jams, and small quilts offered at roadside stands.

We spent time in **Red Wing** as well, home to the highly collectible Red Wing pottery. The town is a center for pottery and antiques shoppers, and the bed-and-breakfasts we visited here were all fairly affluent establishments.

They get pricier as you make your way north along the river to **Hastings** and **Stillwater.** They're also quite elegant, most with whirlpools, wine and cheese in the afternoons, and all the trappings. **Hastings** is another worthwhile shopping town with more than 60 National Register historic structures, including a copper-roofed **Frank Lloyd Wright** building. We wanted to linger at Elephant Walk in Stillwater, too; the place had such a calming effect, in spite of the bustling antiques mecca several blocks down the hill. **Afton** is an idyllic little burg that looks as if it belongs in a Mark Twain novel. A good strategy for seeing this region is via the **Great River Road.** It starts on Route 26 in the southeast corner of the state and follows the Mississippi River for 562 miles. It winds through the St. Croix River Valley, into the **Twin Cities,** and north through **Monticello** (where we visited the stately

Rand House) and continues north into loon country, ending at the mighty river's source in a lake at **Itasca State Park,** just past **Bemidji.**

AFTON HOUSE INN, Afton

OVERALL ★★★★ | QUALITY ★★★★ | VALUE ★★★★ | PRICE RANGE $60–$155

Its name was inspired by Robert Burns's poem "Flow Gently, Sweet Afton," and this historic town lives up to the expectation of tranquility and a place for respite. New England settlers plotted the village in 1855 and built a town of simple, straightforward architecture, near springs that still give clear drinking water. Afton House Inn is one of many nineteenth-century homes where businesses operate today; among its most interesting features is a one-of-a-kind spiral staircase carved by local woodcarver Elmo Ericksen.

SETTING & FACILITIES

Location On the St. Croix Trail/CR 21, off I-94 **Building** 1867 inn, saloon, & restaurant **Grounds** Terrace **Public Space** Small lobby w/ TV, 2nd-floor lounge area w/ coffee center, restaurant (Catfish Saloon) **Food & Drink** Early coffee available. Full buffet breakfast includes entree, breakfast meats. **Recreation** Historic touring, river cruises, antiquing, mountain biking, skiing, snowboarding, sailing, fishing, golf. **Amenities & Services** AC. Hair dryer in room. Meeting facilities available.

ACCOMMODATIONS

Units 16 guest rooms. **All Rooms** TV, phone. **Some Rooms** Single or double whirlpool tub, fireplace, handicap features (grab bars, tub benches, high toilets), skylight, private balcony, desk & chair, terrace access, river view. **Bed & Bath** Kings (2), queens (14). All private baths. **Favorites** Room 46, w/ whirlpool, direct exit to terrace. **Comfort & Decor** In keeping with its historic-town setting, Afton Inn's decor is a mix of country and early American, with fine antiques in many of the rooms. Favorites include an unusual antique dressing table with pull-out arms (room 25), a heart-shaped table (room 31) and a spoon-carved commode (room 27).

RATES, RESERVATIONS, & RESTRICTIONS

Deposit Full payment in advance **Discounts** None **Credit Cards** V, MC, AE, D **Check-In/Out** 2 p.m./11 p.m. **Smoking** In designated rooms **Pets** No **Kids** Yes **No-Nos** N/A **Minimum Stay** None **Open** All year **Hosts** Gordon & Kathy Jarvis, P.O. Box 326, Afton 55001 **Phone** (651) 436-8883 or toll-free (877) 436-8883 **Fax** (651) 436-6859 **Email** info@aftonhouseinn.com **Web** www.aftonhouseinn.com

PEACOCK INN, Chaska

OVERALL ★★★★½ | QUALITY ★★★★½ | VALUE ★★★★ | PRICE RANGE $119–$199

One easily imagines lounging with an evening cocktail on the wide, made-for-entertaining wraparound veranda, admiring the 1910 English garden while a chamber quartet performs in the town gazebo across the road. The careful restoration and refurnishing of Peacock Inn is capable of time travel, indoors and out. Meals are memorable occasions, staged with the dining room's sumptuous backdrop of original hand-painted murals and gliding-swan stained-glass windows. The use of deep peacock blue carpet and accents is a surprise, but it works.

SETTING & FACILITIES

Location In Chaska off US 41, across from City Square Park **Near** Mall of America, downtown Minneapolis, Minnesota River, Minnesota Landscape Arboretum, Old Log Theater **Building** 1910 Neoclassic Georgian, on National Register of Historic Places **Grounds** Oversized city lot w/ English gardens **Public Space** Original tile-floor wraparound porch, foyer, LR, small second-floor common room, DR, back porch **Food & Drink** Complimentary sodas, coffee; evening dessert tray w/ wine, champagne. Full candlelight breakfast includes fruit plate, entree such as frittata, breakfast meats. **Recreation** Live theater, antiquing, horse racing, biking, cross country skiing, golf courses. **Amenities & Services** Guest refrigerator. AC. Monogrammed robes, hair dryer, bath amenities; will put phone or TV in room on request. Can host weddings, teas, parties.

ACCOMMODATIONS

Units 5 **All Rooms** Fireplace, music system, sitting area. **Some Rooms** Ceiling fans, original tile floor, double whirlpool tub, claw-foot tub, park view, desk & chair, cushioned window seat. **Bed & Bath** Queens (5), all private baths. **Favorites** Peterson Room, with large sitting area, shared sitting room, remote-control blinds, Eastlake bed. **Comfort & Decor** A long list of elegant features welcome guests—original mahogany rail in the grand foyer, ten-foot coffered ceilings whose egg-and-dart trim matches the ornamentation in the light fixture, two-sided pocket doors, velvety parlor sofas, and beveled-glass fireplaces—but it is the Witte Brothers stained-glass window at the landing, depicting a woman feeding a peacock, that takes your breath away. Take in the serenity; the piece is, literally, priceless.

RATES, RESERVATIONS, & RESTRICTIONS

Deposit Credit card number; in season, card is put through at time of reservation **Discounts** Corp. **Credit Cards** V, MC **Check-In/Out** 4–7 p.m./11 a.m. **Smoking** On porch or fire escape **Pets** No (resident parrot lives in basement) **Kids** Over age 12 **No-Nos** "We ask guests to be mindful of our custom-made bedding." **Minimum Stay** None **Open** All year **Hosts** Jens & Joyce Bohn, 314 Walnut St., Chaska 55318 **Phone** (952) 368-4343 or toll-free (800) 484-5810 (code 0465) **Email** joyce314@aol.com **Web** www.peacock-inn.com

LUND'S GUEST HOUSES, Chatfield

OVERALL ★★★ | QUALITY ★★★ | VALUE ★★★★★ | PRICE RANGE $70 ($65 IF GUESTS DON'T WANT BREAKFAST; SINGLE ROOM-ONLY $35)

If you're looking for affordable lodging with the freedom of a home setting—and if elegance isn't a factor—then Lund's Guest Houses can be the right choice. It works especially well for families and adventure travelers who might feel inhibited in a Victorian full of pricey antiques. The 1900 house is more comfortable than the cottage, though both offer equipped kitchens. Breakfast is served in Oakenwald Terrace, the assisted living facility; ambience there is a bit gloomy, but go early for a good look at Ms. Lund's many collections and antiques.

SETTING & FACILITIES
Location In central Chatfield, just off MN 52 **Near** Historic Bluff country, Amish country, state parks. **Building** Two modest homes, built 1900 and 1920 **Grounds** Small yards, flower beds **Public Space** Each house has screened porch, LR, DR, kitchen **Food & Drink** Expanded cont'l breakfast. **Recreation** Antiquing, Amish touring, historic touring, canoeing, biking, cross-country skiing, birding. **Amenities & Services** AC. 1 home has phone & TV.

ACCOMMODATIONS
Units 8. An extra room in innkeeper's mansion, now serving as assisted-living quarters, is sometimes used for overflow guests. **All Rooms** Chair or sitting area. **Some Rooms** Screened porch w/ daybed, writing desk, clock. **Bed & Bath** Doubles (7), 2 twins (1). Overflow room, 2 twins. All private baths in 1920 house; 2 private 1 shared bath in 1900 house. **Favorites** Deco Suite in older home; Art Deco furnishings include chair & dressers. **Comfort & Decor** These guest houses are no-frills lodging, though the 1900 house has much dark wood and trim, a "solid" feel, and features such as pocket doors, brick fireplace, leaded glass–front built-in cabinets in the dining room, and an authentic 1950s kitchen, down to the linoleum floor and yellow cabinets.

RATES, RESERVATIONS, & RESTRICTIONS
Deposit 1 night's stay **Discounts** None **Credit Cards** No **Check-In/Out** By individual arrangement. **Smoking** No **Pets** Inquire **Kids** Over age 12 **No-Nos** N/A **Minimum Stay** None **Open** All year **Hosts** Marian Lund, 218 Winona St. SE, Chatfield 55923 **Phone** (507) 867-4003

ROSEWOOD INN, Hastings

OVERALL ★★★★½ | QUALITY ★★★★½ | VALUE ★★★ | PRICE RANGE $97–$277

As massive a home as Rosewood is, we were delighted to find so many spots throughout the home where we could find privacy—on the screened porch where coffee service is set up, in the various bays and alcoves, on the porch.

Even at dinner, tables are arranged in the alcoves and "tented" in the dining room to create privacy. We stayed in Mississippi Under the Stars, where an heirloom collection of elephants lines the shelves, and luxuriated in the teak double whirlpool. The baths throughout the house are grand, but not all have showers; if you're a "shower person," ask before you choose a room.

SETTING & FACILITIES

Location In residential Hastings, in the St. Croix Valley off US 61 **Near** Mississippi River, Stillwater, downtown Hastings, Twin Cities, Vermillion River, St. Croix River. **Building** 1880 brick Queen Anne Victorian, on National Register of Historic Places **Grounds** City lot w/ landscaped rose gardens **Public Space** Porch, DR, parlor, foyer, screened back porch, library **Food & Drink** Coffee service, hot chocolate, sodas any time; evening snack. 3-course gourmet breakfast may include signature wild rice quiche. **Recreation** Boating, canoeing, antiquing, historic touring, kayaking, snowshoeing, cross-country skiing. **Amenities & Services** AC. Breakfast served w/ linens & roses in season; delivered to guest room on request. Dinner available. Hosts parties, business meetings.

ACCOMMODATIONS

Units 8 guest rooms. **All Rooms** Sitting area. **Some Rooms** Fireplace (7 of 8 rooms), double whirlpool tub, bay window, antique copper soaking tub, Swedish Duxianna bed. **Bed & Bath** Queens (8). All private baths. **Favorites** Mississippi Under the Stars, attic room w/ Duxianna bed, teak double whirlpool, round shower, many numerous alcoves. **Comfort & Decor** Indulgence is the key word at Rosewood Inn. Public rooms are trimmed in restored cherry woodwork, furnished in period antiques, and highlighted with many alcoves and bays so spacious, one writer wrote, you could "fit a Volkswagen in them." The parlors and library have fireplaces, as do most guest rooms. If you haven't slept on a Swedish Duxianna bed, give it a try; Rosewood's are covered with Nikken "therm quilts," activated by body temperature—not a bad idea in frigid Minnesota.

RATES, RESERVATIONS, & RESTRICTIONS

Deposit Payment in advance up to 2 nights; 1 night's payment for longer stays **Discounts** Seasonal packages **Credit Cards** V, M, D, AE **Check-In/Out** 4 p.m./"noonish" **Smoking** No **Pets** Inquire **Kids** Inquire **No-Nos** N/A **Minimum Stay** None **Open** All year **Hosts** Pam & Dick Thorsen, 620 Ramsey St., Hastings 55033 **Phone** (651) 437-3297 or toll-free (888) 846-7966 **Fax** (651) 437-4129 **Email** mrthorwood@aol.com **Web** www.thorwoodinn.com

THORWOOD INN, *Hastings*

OVERALL ★★★★½ | QUALITY ★★★★½ | VALUE ★★★ | PRICE RANGE $137–$247

It's surprising that two brick mansions, built in the same year and owned by the same innkeepers, can be so different in tone—and speaking of tones, at least one musical group has recorded an album in Thorwood's dining room, originally designed as a music room. Apparently, the maple floors are ideal for resonance; today an 1890 square grand piano rests in the room's unusual, square-shaped bay. Hastings is bursting with creativity—Gumby was invented here, and Frank Lloyd Wright supervised one of his student's building designs in town—and we couldn't recall when we'd seen so many antiques shops in one small town. Be sure to set aside an afternoon for exploring vintage stores.

SETTING & FACILITIES

Location In a wooded residential neighborhood near downtown, off US 61 **Near** Mississippi River, St. Croix River, Vermillion River, Stillwater, Twin Cities, downtown Hastings. **Building** 1880 French Second Empire mansion, dark brick, on National Register of Historic Places **Grounds** City lot w/ trees, flower gardens **Public Space** Porch, foyer, 2 parlors, DR **Food & Drink** Coffee, sodas any time; evening snack. Gourmet breakfast may include Swiss biscuit eggs w/ fresh dill. **Recreation** Antiquing, boating, canoeing, crosscountry skiing, historic touring, galleries, museums, fishing. **Amenities & Services** AC. Breakfast served in guest room on request; dinners available. Can accommodate family reunions, parties, business retreats.

ACCOMMODATIONS

Units 4 guest rooms, 2 suites. **All Rooms** Sitting area, clock. **Some Rooms** Double whirlpool, 1 or 2 fireplaces, skylight, loveseat. **Bed & Bath** Queens (6). All private baths. **Favorites** Oh Promise Me! - 3-level suite w/15-foot ceilings, skylight above bed in loft bedroom, marble shower, corner fireplace. **Comfort & Decor** Thorwood's sister inn, Rosewood, is decorated in roses and dark greens, but Thorwood is done in muted teals and purples—a more opulent Victorian palette (though some rooms have a more contemporary romantic feel). It's not easy to choose between Beautiful Dreamer, with its round whirlpool set into the 27-foot circular steeple, or Shenandoah—a smaller, sunny room with five showerheads in the shower. Most furnishings are period antiques.

RATES, RESERVATIONS, & RESTRICTIONS

Deposit Payment in advance for up to 2-night reservations; 1 night's prepayment for longer stays **Discounts** Seasonal packages **Credit Cards** V, MC, D, AE **Check-In/Out** 4 p.m./noon **Smoking** No **Pets** Inquire **Kids** Inquire **No-Nos** N/A **Minimum Stay** None **Open** All year **Hosts** Pam & Dick Thorsen, 315 Pine St., Hastings 55033 **Phone** (651) 437-3297 or (888) 846-7966 **Fax** (651) 437-4129 **Email** mrthorwood@aol.com **Web** www.thorwoodinn.com

MRS. B'S, Lanesboro

OVERALL ★★★★ | QUALITY ★★★★ | VALUE ★★★★ | PRICE RANGE $90–$100 WEEKENDS, $70–$80 WEEKDAYS

Tiny Lanesboro (pop. 900) is called the "hidden town," surrounded by limestone bluffs, with more than a dozen inns and bed-and-breakfasts. Most of its visitors come for the Root River and environs—canoeing, biking, hiking, leaf-peeping. A regional livestock auction also swells the population every few weeks. Take the self-guided walking tour of historic homes and have a picnic at the 1869 dam and waterfall. Mrs. B's is one of the most comfortable inns in town, but be alerted to its restaurant policy: Guests staying 2 nights are required to eat a dinner at the inn.

SETTING & FACILITIES

Location In central Lanesboro, 3 blocks off US 16 **Near** Winery, antiques shops, cheese & sausage makers, Root River, limestone bluffs, Sylvan Park. **Building** 1870 limestone inn w/ classic facade **Public Space** Lobby, lower-level restaurant/breakfast DR **Food & Drink** Lemonade available all day. Full breakfast includes oatmeal & buttermilk pancakes, "cottage bacon," seasonal frittata, signature orange ricotta bread. Restaurant serves lunch & dinner to public Wed.–Sun. evenings, one seating (7 p.m.), $27.95 prix fixe, and wine & beer are available. **Recreation** Biking, canoeing, Amish & historic touring, fishing, tennis, hunting, downhill & cross-country skiing, golf **Amenities & Service** AC. Logo soaps.

ACCOMMODATIONS

Units 9, plus 1 overflow room. **All Rooms** Sitting area, writing desk. **Some Rooms** Gas fireplace, access to deck. **Bed & Bath** Queens (8), 2 twins (1), all private baths. **Favorites** Blue & White Room, sunny corner room w/ chaise longue, canopy bed; spacious enough to bring in cot for 3rd guest. **Comfort & Decor** The style at Mrs. B's is country. Handmade quilts cover beds in most rooms (one spread is chenille), all chosen for their natural fibers. In the lobby is a brick fireplace, game table and baby grand piano; notice the library "card catalog" near the front door.

RATES, RESERVATIONS, & RESTRICTIONS

Deposit $40 check **Discounts** None **Credit Cards** No **Check-In/Out** 3–6 p.m. or by arrangement/noon **Smoking** No **Pets** No **Kids** Inquire **No-Nos** Restaurant has a beer & wine license, so guests who bring their own liquor can't drink it in public areas **Minimum Stay** None **Open** All year, except closed for 2 days at Christmas **Hosts** Bill Sermeus & Mimi Abell, 101 Parkway, P.O. Box 411, Lanesboro 55949 **Phone** (507) 467-2154 **Web** www.lanesboro.com (click on "lodging")

SCANLAN HOUSE BED & BREAKFAST, Lanesboro

OVERALL ★★★★ | QUALITY ★★★★ | VALUE ★★★★ | PRICE RANGE $70–$110 WEEKDAYS, $80–$135 WEEKENDS

In this tourist town, bed-and-breakfasts are booked far in advance by bikers and river enthusiasts. Lanesboro sits in the dramatic Root River blufflands, with abundant wildlife and half a dozen historic towns perched above the river. Built by rags-to-riches entrepreneur and state legislator Michael Scanlon, Scanlon House is a convenient and pleasant stopping point for travelers exploring the 42-mile valley.

SETTING & FACILITIES

Location In Lanesboro, on the Root River State Trail **Near** Root River, wineries, Sylvan Park, Eagle Bluff Environmental & Learning Center, Cornucopia Art Center. **Building**

1889 Queen Anne Victorian, pink-palette exterior **Grounds** City lot w/ flower gardens **Public Space** 2 front parlors, DR, patio **Food & Drink** Complimentary split of champagne in room; beer/wine/beverage honor bar. 5-course breakfast includes hot entree, breakfast meats, dessert. **Recreation** Biking, in-line skating, cross-country skiing, canoeing, swimming, horse-drawn carriage tours, winery & historic touring, tennis, fishing, golf, Amish touring. **Amenities & Services** AC, hair dryer in room. Innkeepers also operate bicycle, canoe, & ski rental business w/ discounted rates for B&B guests.

ACCOMMODATIONS

Units 5 guest rooms. **All Rooms** TV, clock radio, sitting area. **Some Rooms** Fireplace, private turret balcony, stained-glass window, double whirlpool tub, four-poster bed. **Bed & Bath** Queens (5). All private baths. **Favorites** Sunrise Suite, largest room w/ fireplace, couch & chairs, double whirlpool, coffeemaker. **Comfort & Decor** The front parlor features a turret sitting area, stained-glass windows, and the innkeeper's doll collection, and the library parlor has a fireplace and mahogany trim. The prettiest room is the dining room, with leather wall covering, stained-glass window, and an Eastlake built-in server. Furnishings are comfortable, though parlor decor is excessively busy.

RATES, RESERVATIONS, & RESTRICTIONS

Deposit Credit card number or total advance payment **Discounts** None **Credit Cards** V, MC, AE, D **Check-In/Out** 3 p.m./noon **Smoking** No **Pets** No **Kids** Over age 8 (only 2 guests per room) **No-Nos** N/A **Minimum Stay** None **Open** All year **Hosts** Kirsten Mensing, Manager, 708 Parkway Ave. South, Lanesboro 55949 **Phone** (507) 467-2158 or toll-free (800) 944-2158 **Fax** (520) 244-3360 **Email** ScanlanBB@aol.com **Web** www.scanlanhouse.com

BERWOOD HILL INN, Lanesboro

OVERALL ★★★★½ | QUALITY ★★★★½ | VALUE ★★★ | PRICE RANGE $155–$195

The serenity on this remote hilltop, enhanced by one of the best valley views in the Midwest, put us immediately at ease here. This bed-and-breakfast is a destination in itself; come here for romance, reading, business, or meditation. Berwood Hill seems ready for any moods or dreams. The cottage is most private and even has its own porch, but it lacks plumbing—and no robes are provided for getting across the yard to the bath (in the house). Come prepared for cold-weather trips to the loo.

SETTING & FACILITIES

Location 4 mi. SW of Lanesboro, just off US 16 **Near** Root River Valley, Bluff Country, Lanesboro town center. **Building** 1878 Victorian farmhouse, white w/ much gingerbread trim **Grounds** 200 acres, most leased to farmers. B&B site sits atop a high knoll, with gazebo, fountains, sculptured flower gardens, and stunning view of surrounding valley **Public Space** DR, LR, 2nd-floor sitting area, sitting porch/library, wraparound porch **Food & Drink** Gourmet breakfast includes egg dish, meat (sometimes salmon or river trout), potato, and pancakes or waffle. Afternoon desserts. **Recreation** Canoeing, downhill or cross-country skiing, snowshoeing, horseback riding, antiquing, Amish touring, croquet. **Amenities & Services** AC. Picnic lunch or candlelight dinner available. Can accommodate weddings, business meetings.

ACCOMMODATIONS
Units 4; includes 3rd-floor suite & Garden Cottage. **All Rooms** Sitting area, access to 2nd-floor wraparound porch. **Some Rooms** Claw-foot tub, whirlpool tub, ceiling fans, window seats, writing desk. **Bed & Bath** Queen (1), doubles (3). All private baths; 1 detached, bath for Garden Cottage is in main house. **Favorites** 3rd-floor suite, w/ 2 window seats, writing desk, daybed. **Comfort & Decor** Visualize Grandma's farmhouse furnished with all of your favorite pieces and fine antiques. With original wainscoting throughout and upscale furnishings, Berwood Hill is more like a small country manor than farmhouse, though the knotty pine and fir flooring set a more casual tone.

RATES, RESERVATIONS, & RESTRICTIONS
Deposit $50 nonrefundable **Discounts** Off-season and Sun.–Thursy. **Credit Cards** MC,V **Check-In/Out** 3 p.m./11 a.m. **Smoking** Outside **Pets** No **Kids** Over age 12 **No-Nos** N/A **Minimum Stay** None **Open** All year **Hosts** Wayne Skjelstad, R.R. 2, Box 22, Lanesboro 55949 **Phone** Toll-free (800) 803-6748 **Fax** (507) 765-5291 **Email** indulge@berwood.com **Web** www.berwood.com

BUTLER HOUSE, Mankato

OVERALL ★★★★½ | QUALITY ★★★★½ | VALUE ★★★★ | PRICE RANGE $69–$119

Built by a former mayor of Mankato, Butler House is the picture of turn-of-the-twentieth-century elegance. The parlor carpet is an antique Persian sarouk rug, but the most impressive space is the 28-foot entry hall that sets the tone for the entire house. Everything is oversized here, from the 15-foot window seat in the parlor, to the antique dining table that seats 20. The effect is one of grandeur, though it might be too much "heaviness" for some tastes—a bit dark and intimidating; one instinctively wants to whisper—but opulent nonetheless.

SETTING & FACILITIES
Location Off US 14 in residential Mankato **Near** Midwest Wireless Civic Center, Gustavus Adolphus College, Mount Kato Ski Area, Sakatah Singing Hills State Trail, Red Jacket Trail, Minnesota State Univ./Mankato. **Building** 1905 English-style brick mansion **Grounds** City lot; shrubs, flower beds **Public Space** Porch, entry, parlor, DR, sitting room **Food & Drink** Early coffee. Gourmet breakfast includes hot entrees. **Recreation** Downhill & cross-country skiing, biking, ice skating, snowshoeing, antiquing, historic touring, galleries. **Amenities & Services** AC. Fax machine, conference room available.

ACCOMMODATIONS
Units 5 guest rooms. **All Rooms** TV, writing table, clock, chairs. **Some Rooms** Whirlpool tub, fireplace. **Bed & Bath** King/2 twin (1), queens (3), double (1). All private baths. **Favorites** King room w/fireplace, whirlpool, larger space. **Comfort & Decor**

Cross the expansive, wicker-filled front porch into the home trimmed with lush fumed oak and cypress woodwork, and a dining room decorated with hand-painted frescoes and leaded glass–front built-ins. A Steinway grand piano sits in the entry hall; numerous pocket doors, cozy window seats, and fine antiques are found throughout the home.

RATES, RESERVATIONS, & RESTRICTIONS
Deposit $50 **Discounts** Weekday, long-term, relocation rates **Credit Cards** V, MC, AE **Check-In/Out** 4–6 p.m./11 a.m. **Smoking** No **Pets** No **Kids** Over age 12 **No-Nos** N/A **Minimum Stay** None **Open** All year **Hosts** Sharry & Ron Tschida, 704 South Broad St., Mankato 56001 **Phone** (507) 387-5055 **Fax** (507) 388-5462 **Email** butler-house@ic.mankato.mn.us **Web** www.butlerhouse.com

RAND HOUSE, Monticello

OVERALL ★★★★½ | QUALITY ★★★★½ | VALUE ★★★★ | PRICE RANGE $105–$165

Perched on a knoll above the busy town, Rand House was built by Rufus Rand Sr., owner of the Minneapolis Gas Light Company, as a wedding gift for his bride, Susan. Current owners have restored the entire estate, earning the 1995 Award for Outstanding Historic Preservation from the Preservation Alliance of Minnesota. The grounds are as impressive as the home, ringed by New England–style stone fences filled with flowers. From the dining room chandelier to the three imported fireplaces, Rand House, once used as a rest home, is a model for rejuvenating historic mansions.

SETTING & FACILITIES
Location Just outside central Monticello, midway between St. Cloud & Minneapolis **Near** Little Mountain Settlement museum, Mississippi River, Lake Maria State Park. **Building** 1884 Queen Anne Victorian, on National Register of Historic Places **Grounds** 4 acres of landscaped flower gardens, pond, walking paths, fountain **Public Space** Foyer, screened porch, solarium, drawing room, DR **Food & Drink** Complimentary wine & sodas; early coffee delivered to room. Full breakfast includes entree w/ breakfast meat. **Recreation** Antiquing, historic touring, boating, cross-country skiing, birding, tennis, biking. **Amenities & Services** AC. Newspaper delivered to room w/ morning coffee, logo soaps, robes, can host weddings & parties up to 20 guests.

ACCOMMODATIONS
Units 4 guest rooms. **All Rooms** Sitting area. **Some Rooms** Table & chairs, desk, claw-foot tub, private porch, turret sitting area, fireplace. **Bed & Bath** King (1), queens (3). All private baths. **Favorites** Garden Room, actually a suite w/ screened porch & 4-season sun room. **Comfort & Decor** Elegance is the standard in this grand home, with wood inlay floors, original Eastlake-style oak woodwork, original light fixtures, and plenty of alcoves and fireplaces for relaxing with a good mystery novel. A baby grand piano graces the foyer, though our favorite spot was the sun room—an 1890s, shingle-style addition—with stone fireplace. All rooms are furnished with fine antiques, not a bit overdone.

RATES, RESERVATIONS, & RESTRICTIONS

Deposit 1 night's lodging, due 5 days after making reservation **Discounts** None **Credit Cards** V, MC, AE **Check-In/Out** 4–6 p.m./11 a.m. **Smoking** No—not even on porches **Pets** No **Kids** Discouraged; by arrangement for whole-house rental **No-Nos** N/A **Minimum Stay** None **Open** All year **Hosts** Duffy & Merrill Busch, One Old Territorial Rd., Monticello 55362 **Phone** (763) 295-6037 or toll-free (888) 295-0881 **Email** info@randhouse.com **Web** www.randhouse.com

CANDLELIGHT INN, Red Wing

OVERALL ★★★★½ | QUALITY ★★★★½ | VALUE ★★★★ | PRICE RANGE $129–$169

When you feel you've seen every piece of Red Wing pottery in the Midwest, Candlelight Inn will be a wonderful oasis from shopping stress. The innkeepers took great care in restoring this home, built by a leading stoneware pioneer. They kept such impressive details as the original Quesal lighting fixtures and the feather-painted marble fireplace in the parlor. We also enjoyed the Gudraises' more whimsical additions, such as the expertly folk-painted table and chairs in the Heritage Room. Live piano music accompanies breakfast; Zig twinkles the ivories from the next room.

SETTING & FACILITIES

Location Several blocks from downtown Red Wing **Near** Stoneware & pottery foundries, antiques malls, Mississippi River. **Building** 1877 Modified Italianate, on Minnesota Historical Register **Grounds** City lot, flower beds **Public Space** Open foyer, library, front parlor, DR, screened wraparound porch **Food & Drink** Coffee delivered to room 8:15 a.m., appetizers & wine at check-in, evening snack. Breakfast begins w/ dessert, then fresh baked breads, entree. **Recreation** Historic touring, live theater, biking, cross-country skiing, Mississippi River activities. **Amenities & Services** AC. Logo soaps, guest fridge, small gift shop.

ACCOMMODATIONS

Units 5. **All Rooms** Gas fireplace, table & chairs. **Some Rooms** European soaker-whirlpool, bay window, original fireplace, settee. **Bed & Bath** Queens (5). All private baths. **Favorites** Butternut Suite, w/ crotch mahogany Victorian topper bed, built-in butternut cupboards, heart-shaped double whirlpool, antique settee & chandelier. **Comfort & Decor** Tall doors with antique beveled glass take guests across the threshold from the screened wraparound porch into the open foyer, with its "bullet's-eye" chandelier—an original gas fixture—with beveled and beaded glass. Stained-glass windows reflect the butternut captain's wheel motif in the stair rail. Throughout the home, a blend of cherry, butternut, oak, and walnut set off inlaid parquet floors, seven fireplaces, and other lavish touches.

RATES, RESERVATIONS, & RESTRICTIONS

Deposit Credit card number **Discounts** 10% AAA discount; $30 midweek discount Nov. 1–May 31 **Credit Cards** MC, V, D, AE **Check-In/Out** 4 p.m./11 a.m. **Smoking** Front porch **Pets** No **Kids** Over age 12 **No-Nos** N/A **Minimum Stay** 2 nights weekends **Open** All year **Hosts** Lynette & Zig Gudrais, 818 West 3rd St., Red Wing 55066 **Phone** (651) 388-8034 or toll-free (800) 254-9194 **Email** info@candlelightinn-redwing.com **Web** www.candlelightinn-redwing.com

GOLDEN LANTERN INN, Red Wing

OVERALL ★★★★½ | QUALITY ★★★★½ | VALUE ★★★ | PRICE RANGE $95–$149 WEEKDAYS, $139–$205 WEEKENDS

Tucked behind a high wooden fence—and with no children yelling in the hallways—Golden Lantern is a good choice for an intimate getaway. It's a large home (6,000 square feet), built by the president of the Red Wing Shoe Company, and it's an easy walk to the downtown antiquing and shopping district. The marble and mahogany fireplace in the living room is an especially good spot for friends to chat over cocktails, and every guest room is nicely appointed for both business and romantic trips. The only drawback we saw was the discrepancy between weekday and weekend prices, in one instance a $60 jump for the same breakfast and services.

SETTING & FACILITIES

Location In Red Wing's historic district, 3 blocks from downtown **Near** Mississippi River, pottery factories, Twin Cities, Mall of America, Sheldon Theater. **Building** 1932 Tudor Revival, stone & stucco exterior **Grounds** Double lot w/ flower beds, 2 patios **Public Space** Foyer, LR, library, DR, screened sun porch, 6-person hot tub **Food & Drink** Soda & water in guest fridge, early coffee delivered to room. Full candlelight breakfast includes hot entree w/ breakfast meat. **Recreation** Antiquing, canoeing, boating, historic touring, theater, skiing, eagle-watching, biking. **Amenities & Services** AC. Breakfast in guest room on request, robes in rooms.

ACCOMMODATIONS

Units 3 suites, 2 guest rooms. **All Rooms** Table & chairs. **Some Rooms** Cable TV/VCR, double whirlpool tub, double shower, pull-out sofa, gas fireplace, double sinks, canopy bed, bluff views, balcony. **Bed & Bath** Kings (2), queens (3). All private baths. **Favorites** Helen's Suite; sitting room is summer sleeping porch, also has private balcony, fireplace, queen canopy, TV/VCR. **Comfort & Decor** Even though many furnishings are quality antiques, Golden Lantern feels a bit newer than early 1930s. Walnut, birch, oak, and maple are used for trim throughout the house, and numerous common areas—inside and out—make it easy to find seclusion or a good spot for a quiet talk. We loved the oak-paneled library, furnished in Mission-style furniture, but all spaces are cozy.

RATES, RESERVATIONS, & RESTRICTIONS

Deposit For large groups **Discounts** Midweek discount; check Web for specials **Credit Cards** V, MC, D **Check-In/Out** 4–5 p.m./11 a.m. **Smoking** Outside, on the patio **Pets** No **Kids** Occasionally weekdays by prior arrangement—inquire **No-Nos** N/A **Minimum Stay** None **Open** All year **Hosts** Tim & Rhonda McKim, 721 East Ave., Red Wing

55066 **Phone** (651) 388-3315 or toll-free (888) 288-3315 **Email** info@goldenlantern.com **Web** www.goldenlantern.com

LAWTHER OCTAGON HOUSE BED & BREAKFAST, Red Wing

OVERALL ★★★★ | QUALITY ★★★★ | VALUE ★★★ | PRICE RANGE $159–$225

James Lawther, a 25-year-old Irish pioneer who began building his fortune in Red Wing when it was just a small river settlement, might have dabbled in the metaphysical. He was one of the town's first mayors as well as a land speculator and philanthropist who built his home with eight sides because, he felt, such a shape "fostered the health and harmony of its inhabitants." Indeed, the octagon is the shape of the bagua in feng shui, whose followers believe eight-sided homes to be the most beneficial to their health, prosperity, and happiness.

SETTING & FACILITIES
Location Residential Red Wing, 0.5 mi. from town center **Near** Antiques malls, Mississippi River, stoneware & pottery foundries. **Building** 1857 brick octagon home, on the National Register of Historic Places **Grounds** City lot; flower beds **Public Space** Foyer, parlor, LR, DR, screened porch, cupola **Food & Drink** Afternoon snack. Full breakfast includes egg dish & home-baked muffins. **Recreation** Historic touring, antiquing, biking, cross-country skiing, Mississippi River activities. **Amenities & Services** AC. Robes in rooms.

ACCOMMODATIONS
Units 4 guest rooms, 1 suite. **All Rooms** Sitting area. **Some Rooms** Whirlpool tub, river & bluff view, claw-foot tub, small foot-washing tub, dressing table. **Bed & Bath** King (1), queens (4). All private baths. **Favorites** Sisters' Suite, w/ private staircase entrance, king bed, sitting room, and original feather-painted slate fireplace. **Comfort & Decor** Furnishings throughout the home are Victorian, including many ornate Eastlake pieces. Much of the woodwork in public areas is painted white, against a backdrop of dark fabric wall coverings—a wise choice because, except for the (unpainted) walnut stair rail, the wood is very soft fir. The effect, though, is a bit heavy with the Victorian furniture. Still, we loved the cove ceilings with tin trim, faux marbleized fireplaces, and tin mantels.

RATES, RESERVATIONS, & RESTRICTIONS
Deposit 50% of stay **Discounts** Midweek **Credit Cards** V, MC **Check-In/Out** 4 p.m./11 a.m. **Smoking** Outside **Pets** No (2 small resident dogs are permitted in common rooms) **Kids** No, unless they're older and guests rent the entire house **No-Nos** N/A **Minimum Stay** None **Open** All year **Hosts** Penny Stapleton, 927 West 3rd St., Red Wing 55066 **Phone** (651) 388-1778 or toll-free (800) 388-0434 **Email** ps@octagon-house.com **Web** www.octagon-house.com

ELEPHANT WALK, A BED AND BREAKFAST, Stillwater

OVERALL ★★★★★ | QUALITY ★★★★½ | VALUE ★★★★ | PRICE RANGE
$129–$179 WEEKDAYS, $169–$269 TOP WEEKEND/SEASONAL RATES

The best innkeepers are those who are well traveled, and we love almost everything about Elephant Walk. The ambience is a soothing, progressive product of soft music, Far Eastern artifacts, careful planning, and attention to detail. It manifests in small comforts, such as the numerous conversation areas in the parlors—smallish rooms but still affording maximum privacy. Floors are heated, privacy shades in guest rooms open from the top, and the Japanese gardens are almost a destination in themselves. And where else have you slept in a Chaing Mai Room? The tariff is high but, for this experience, reasonable—but once more, we wish the weekday/weekend discrepancy, for the same services, weren't so dramatic.

SETTING & FACILITIES

Location Side street in historic Stillwater in the St. Croix Valley **Near** Twin Cities, Mall of America, St. Croix River, downtown Stillwater. **Building** 1883 stick-style Victorian **Grounds** Oversized city lot w/ landscaped water & flower gardens, ponds, sculptures, sitting areas **Public Space** Porches, foyer, parlor, sitting room, DR **Food & Drink** Waters & sodas any time; wine, cheese & homemade crackers served evenings. Full breakfast includes entree, scones, meat (such as smoked chorizo sausage), dessert such as crème brûlée. **Recreation** Antiquing, hot-air ballooning, downhill & cross-country skiing, dinner train. **Amenities & Services** AC. Takes guests' photos, put on Web so guests can send them to friends as email attachments. Robes, irons in rooms.

ACCOMMODATIONS

Units 1 suite, 3 guest rooms. **All Rooms** Fridges, gas fireplaces, double whirlpool tubs, CD sound systems, ceiling fans. **Some Rooms** Hand-forged copper sink w/ waterfall spout, stone mantel, bamboo bed, claw-foot tub, bath-side aquarium, private rooftop terrace, water garden. **Bed & Bath** Queens (4). **Favorites** Cadiz Suite, w/ private deck garden, large corner sitting room, garden room w/ double whirlpool, 2-sided fireplace. **Comfort & Decor** Innkeepers Rita and Jon Graybill designed the guest rooms after their world travels, so the Rangoon Room features a 19th-century teak four-poster carved by Burmese craftsmen, for instance, and the Raffles Room—named for the Singapore hotel where the Singapore sling cocktail was invented—has a bamboo canopy bed and rattan seating; tropical fish guard the stone grotto whirlpool. In every space, guests are surrounded by artifacts and antiques from faraway lands.

RATES, RESERVATIONS, & RESTRICTIONS

Deposit Credit card number or advance payment **Discounts** Sun.–Thurs. **Credit Cards** V, MC, D, DC **Check-In/Out** 4–6:30 p.m./11 a.m. **Smoking** No **Pets** No **Kids** No **No-Nos** N/A **Minimum Stay** None **Open** All year **Hosts** Rita & Jon Graybill, 801 West Pine St., Stillwater 55082 **Phone** (651) 430-0359 or toll-free (888) 430-0359 **Email** info@elephantwalkbb.com **Web** www.elephantwalkbb.com

ANN BEAN MANSION, *Stillwater*

OVERALL ★★★★½ | QUALITY ★★★★½ | VALUE ★★★★ | PRICE RANGE
SUN.–THURS. $109–$139, FRI. $149–$179, SAT. $169–$199

We could have spent a day just admiring the detail in the Ann Bean Mansion—especially in the dining room with its inlaid walnut and oak flooring, built-in servers with beveled glass designed to match the fireplace, and the ceiling hand-painted to match the wallpaper. Some guests linger at the 112-year-old grand piano in the front parlor, but we were content on the magnificent front porch. Here again, though, weekend prices jump $60 for the same amenities. Our advice: Come between November and April, when every room is a cool $99 (excluding holidays).

SETTING & FACILITIES

Location Side street in historic Stillwater in the St. Croix River Valley **Near** Twin Cities, Mall of America, St. Croix River, downtown Stillwater. **Building** 1880 Victorian, brown exterior **Grounds** Oversized city lot, flower beds **Public Space** Wraparound porch, foyer, double parlor, DR **Food & Drink** 4-course breakfast served w/ linen & china, includes egg dish, homemade caramel rolls, dessert, often signature poached pears. **Recreation** Antiquing, hot-air ballooning, downhill & cross-country skiing, dinner train. **Amenities & Services** AC. Cont'l breakfast served in room on request, small weddings & parties, flowers & special baskets available.

ACCOMMODATIONS

Units 5 guest rooms. **All Rooms** Gas or wood-burning fireplace, single or double whirlpool tub, sitting area. **Some Rooms** Window seat, river & town views, bay window, marble shower. **Bed & Bath** Queens (4), double (1). All private baths. **Favorites** Guest Room, w/ hand-carved oak mantel over wood-burning fireplace, ornate trim surrounding bay window, original wainscot paneling in bath, sleigh bed, double whirlpool. **Comfort & Decor** With so much sumptuous wood trim, it's no surprise that Ann Bean Mansion was built by a lumber baron. Pocket doors, Eastlake oak trim, and wooden shutters that fold into 18-inch-thick casings draw the eye upward to ornate cove ceilings. The hand-carved marble mantel in the double parlor is a spectacle of beautiful craftsmanship; we also paused in the foyer to admire the "birdhouse" newel post and fireplace, with tiles signed by the artist in 1899.

RATES, RESERVATIONS, & RESTRICTIONS
Deposit Credit card number or advance payment in full **Discounts** Weekdays, winter **Credit Cards** V, MC, AE, D **Check-In/Out** 4:30–6 p.m./11 a.m. **Smoking** On porch **Pets** No **Kids** Inquire; discouraged on weekends **No-Nos** N/A **Minimum Stay** 2 nights weekends **Open** All year **Hosts** Kari Stimac & John Wubbels, 319 West Pine St., Stillwater 55082 **Phone** (651) 430-0355 or toll-free (877) 837-4400 **Email** info@annbeanmansion.com **Web** www.annbeanmansion.com

Ohio

It may be the most compact state in the Upper Midwest, but Ohio is as diverse as any larger state. Tucked below Lake Erie, the pocket-shaped Buckeye State offers flatlands and ski slopes, caves and cliffs, farms and major cities, balmy island breezes and lake-effect snow.

Nor can the five touring zones be pigeonholed easily. Zone 18, the windswept Northwest, stretches horizontally between horizons like a taut trampoline, yet it holds incongruities. The most brash are the **Lake Erie Islands,** full of resort towns, wineries, souvenir shops, and brightly colored cottages—a taste of the Caribbean, just a ferry ride away. **Toledo** is the jumping-off point for the state, the beginning of the chaotic Interstate 75 corridor to **Detroit.**

Cleveland dominates Zone 19, with its dramatic lakeshore, ethnic neighborhoods, and music for every taste, from the **Rock and Roll Hall of Fame** to the renowned **Cleveland Orchestra,** tagged by Time magazine the "finest band in the land." East of the city is the snow belt and wine trail that reaches almost to the Pennsylvania border, while southern roads lead to the **Cuyahoga Valley National Recreation Area,** Ohio's only national park, and **Akron,** the Rubber Capital turned polymer center.

In the center of the state is Zone 20, and in its center is busy **Columbus,** the state capital. **Ohio State University** is the city's other major industry, obscuring great attractions such as the **German Village** historic neighborhood, the gallery-filled **Short North arts district,** and world-class shopping at the new **Polaris Fashion Place.**

Zones 21 and 22 bring us to Ohio's hills—the beginning of Appalachia—and the **Ohio River. Cincinnati,** itself built on seven giant hills, anchors Zone 21 and, like Cleveland, hosts pro football and baseball teams. Its municipal park, high on a bluff overlooking the river, is one of the state's best-kept secrets.

Instead of major cities, Zone 22 has **Marietta**, boasting more area of National Register properties than any city in the Midwest. Perched above the **Ohio and Muskingum Rivers, Marietta** is a picturesque (but not sleepy) river town almost surrounded by the **Wayne National Forest.**

FOR MORE INFORMATION

Ohio Department of Development, Division of Travel and Tourism

www.ohiotourism.com

800-BUCKEYE

Ohio Bed & Breakfast Association

5310 East Main Street

Suite 104

Columbus, Ohio 43213

(614) 868-5567

www.ohiobba.com

Northwest Ohio

Vast and sparse, Zone 18 takes forever to drive across. Tomato farms cover much of the landscape in the rural areas, but one also finds some unexpected sights.

The first such surprise is Ohio's vacation hot spot, the **Lake Erie Islands.** These tiny glacial droppings have their own personalities. **Kelleys Island,** where we profiled beautiful Water's Edge Retreat (one of the most upscale bed-and-breakfasts in this book), is a serene, secluded islet, whereas Put-in-Bay on **Middle Bass Island** is noisier with shops, tourists and crowded bars on weekends. Bed-and-breakfasts on both islands generally take the form of private homes and tourist cottages, but Kelleys is priciest because it's a more exclusive destination.

Back on terra firma, the **Toledo/Bowling Green** area offers fewer inns than one would expect for such a populous region. Some of the isolated, tiny towns farther south—**Celina, Bellefontaine, Sidney**—likewise offer only a few choices in bed-and-breakfast lodging. When we get nearer to the eastern portion of the zone we find a density of bed-and-breakfasts. From **Mount Gilead** to **Bucyrus** and north to **Bellevue, Tiffin, Norwalk,** and **Sandusky,** innkeeping becomes a popular career choice for owners of the grand old homes that once belonged to shipping tycoons, mill builders, and other early captains of industry. These towns, closer to both **Lake Erie** and Ohio's rivers and canal system, were key to the state's post–Civil War growth and now have historic districts ideal for strolling and opening bed-and-breakfasts.

These towns also offer variety in activities for leisure travelers, from lake and river sports to antiquing and city attractions—galleries, shops, and more restaurant choices than in the more isolated villages. Visitors to the western end of the zone often are connected to **Bowling Green State University.** If you're headed for Toledo, set aside half a day to tour its remarkable **Museum of Art;** originally endowed by the Libby family (of Libby Glass, headquartered in Toledo), its extensive glass collection is one of the best in the country, displaying pieces from ancient Chinese and Egyptian bottles to brilliant contemporary pieces by artist Dale Chihuly.

WHITMORE HOUSE, Bellefontaine

OVERALL ★★★½ | QUALITY ★★★½ | VALUE ★★★★★ | PRICE RANGE $40–$60

At the time of our visit, guests employed by the FBI and CIA had just left; they were working at a nearby testing facility to develop new barriers around the White House. Innkeeper Musser often hosts top-secret government workers at her bed-and-breakfast. Her brochure discusses her restaurant and special-event services—the bigger business of Whitmore House.

SETTING & FACILITIES
Location On OH 47 W, 4 mi. west of town. **Near** Ohio Caverns, Mad River Mountain Ski Area, Zane Caverns, Indian Lake. **Building** 1870–73 "Country Victorian." **Grounds** Almost 4 acres of lawns, English garden, deck, large herb garden. **Public Space** LR, DR/restaurant, porch. **Food & Drink** Evening snack; full breakfast includes hot entree. **Recreation** Skiing, boating, canoeing, touring caverns, antiquing, swimming, fishing. **Amenities & Services** AC; hand-crafted soaps; full-service restaurant for dinner; catering of private parties & events up to 400 guests; and a full wedding consultant.

ACCOMMODATIONS
Units 2 guest rooms. **All Rooms** Clock radio, phone, sitting area, table or desk. **Some Rooms** Settee. **Bed & Bath** Queen (1), double (1). Shared bath. **Favorites** Settee Room, furnishings seem more inviting. **Comfort & Decor** This is a real country home; front windows look out onto cornfields and a two-lane road, and the living room overlooks the garden. It's a simple, largely unadorned interior, even in the restaurant. The only TV is in the living room; guests generally like to relax on the porch swing.

RATES, RESERVATIONS, & RESTRICTIONS
Deposit $25. **Discounts** 10% off 5-day stay. **Credit Cards** N/A; cash or check only **Check-In/Out** 4 p.m./10 a.m. **Smoking** No. **Pets** No. **Children** Yes, if well behaved **No-Nos** No alcohol; on-site restaurant has a liquor license. **Minimum Stay** None **Open** All year **Host** Sandra L. Musser, 3985 OH 47, Bellefontaine 43311 **Phone** (937) 592-4290 **Fax** (937) 592-6963 **Email** whitmore@2access.net

FREDERICK FITTING HOUSE, Bellville

OVERALL ★★★★ | QUALITY ★★★★ | VALUE ★★★★★ | PRICE RANGE $59–$83

Fans of this long-established bed-and-breakfast were nervous when it changed hands in 1997, but they needn't have worried. The stained glass and transoms remain, and Ms. Lomax has devised wonderfully creative window treatments. Her quality antiques include a century-old radio, an ornate hall tree in the foyer, and, in the Colonial Room, a "body water pitcher." Artifacts adorn the yard; true to the innkeeper's description as an Italianate country village bed-and-breakfast, this inn puts on no airs. Breakfast is a feast, and Ms. Lomax is a superb cook.

SETTING & FACILITIES

Location 3 mi. east of I-71, halfway between Columbus and Cleveland. **Near** Village center shops, Malabar Farms historical home, Mohican State Park. **Building** Restored 1863 Italianate Victorian w/ original oak plank flooring and walnut, maple & butternut staircase. **Grounds** Large residential lot w/ garden gazebo, flower beds, swing, picnic tables **Public Space** Front porch, foyer, parlor, DR, library, small loft sitting area **Food & Drink** Full breakfast with home-baked pastry, meat entree, and freshly ground coffee; evening snacks; soft drinks available any time **Recreation** Antiquing, canoeing on Mohican River, cross-country skiing, downhill skiing, hiking, spectator car racing at Mid-Ohio Raceway, golf, horseback riding. **Amenities & Services** Shampoos and lotions in rooms, breakfast served in garden gazebo on request, AC.

ACCOMMODATIONS

Units 3 guest rooms. **All Rooms** Private bath, shower. **Some Rooms** Claw-foot tub, adjacent bath. **Bed & Bath** Queen (3)—canopy, Shaker, and sleigh. **Favorites** Shaker Room, in wonderfully relaxing shades of blue, green, & burgundy, and finely stenciled bathroom walls. **Comfort & Decor** A mix of antiques with reproductions and a touch of shabby chic. Gazebo features a ceiling fan for hot evenings.

RATES, RESERVATIONS, & RESTRICTIONS

Deposit 50% of amount of stay, refunded with 10-day cancellation notice. **Discounts** N/A **Credit Cards** No; cash, check, or traveler's checks only. **Check-In/Out** 3 p.m. or by arrangement/noon **Smoking** Outside only. **Pets** N/A **Kids** By prior arrangement **No-Nos** N/A **Minimum Stay** N/A **Open** All year except Thanksgiving Day, Christmas Eve, Christmas, and New Year's Day. **Host** Barbara Lomax, 72 Fitting Ave., Bellville 44813 **Phone** (419) 886-2863 **Web** www.bedandbreakfast.com/bbc/p208262.asp

HEISER HAUS, Celina

OVERALL ★★★½ | QUALITY ★★★½ | VALUE ★★★★ | PRICE RANGE $65–$85

If you miss the 1970s, you'll love Heiser Haus. This one-of-a-kind home is an eclectic mix of flower power and quirky finds, the most bizarre of which is a pair of jail cells in the living room. Laid into the foundation before the house was built, the cells once held John Dillinger—a bit of lore perpetuated by the innkeepers, who incorporated two mannequins (a gray-suited man and a "lady in red") into their decor. Guest rooms are at the four corners of the upstairs balcony; we encountered a minor privacy issue watching TV in the upstairs loft TV area while the innkeepers' family watched a different channel in their family room below. But Heiser Haus just opened in December 2000; it's a work in progress and worth the stop.

SETTING & FACILITIES
Location 25 mi. from Lima, 50 mi. north of Dayton. **Near** Grand Lake St. Mary's, State Parks. **Building** 1972, style a cross between Frank Lloyd Wright and 1970s retro **Grounds** Large back yard; lawn, bushes, and flower beds; abandoned log cabin play house. **Public Space** Upstairs balcony sitting room w/ TV, breakfast room w/ full kitchen, outdoor patio, and heated indoor pool. Guests are sometimes invited to use innkeepers' LR **Food & Drink** Nonalcoholic beverages available any time, and each room features a bowl of fresh fruit. Breakfast is full, including meat entree. **Recreation** Antiquing, beach, swimming, canoeing, fishing, golf, hunting, sailing, tennis. **Amenities & Services** Shampoos and other bath amenities, robes, AC.

ACCOMMODATIONS
Units 4 guest rooms. **All Rooms** Private bath. **Some Rooms** Shower, bidet, sitting area. **Bed & Bath** King (1), queen (3), sofa bed (1). All private baths. **Favorites** Doc's Room, with rosewood paneling and small sitting room. **Comfort & Decor** The original red short shag carpeting is in perfect condition. The three huge bronze chandeliers came from a theater in Columbus, and the stone-encrusted walls are original. The balcony railing once surrounded a Mercer County cemetery.

RATES, RESERVATIONS, & RESTRICTIONS
Deposit 50%, with full refund if cancellation is a month prior to visit and 50% refund with 2 weeks' notice. **Discounts** N/A **Credit Cards** MC, V, D **Check-In/Out** 3 p.m./11 a.m. or by special arrangement. **Smoking** Outside. **Pets** By prior arrangement. Owners have 2 outdoor dogs and a cat that has the run of the house, and dander level is moderately high. **Kids** Welcomed **No-Nos** N/A **Minimum Stay** N/A **Open** All year, except Christmas Day. **Hosts** Sherry & Dave Heiser, 117 N. Brandon Ave., Celina 45822 **Phone** (419) 586-9179 or toll-free (800) 417-4397 **Fax** (419) 584-0460 **Email** tiggerow@bright.net **Web** www.bedandbreakfast.com/bbc/p621212.asp

MILL HOUSE BED & BREAKFAST, Grand Rapids

OVERALL ★★★★ | QUALITY ★★★★ | VALUE ★★★★ | PRICE RANGE $80–$120

Visit Mill House in spring and summer, when guests can relax on the canal-side patios. The building's industrial history is evident on the inside, softened by innkeeper Karen Herzberg's expert stenciling. Outdoors you step down a stone path into a garden haven, just feet from the Miami & Erie Canal and Maumee River. When was the last time you saw a mule-drawn canal boat? Grand Rapids is a historic "walking town" with a good day's browsing of shops and canal attractions.

SETTING & FACILITIES

Location On Rt. 578 on the Maumee River, 15 mi. SW of Toledo. **Near** Wabash Cannonball Trail, Oak Openings Preserve, Fort Meigs, Toledo Zoo, COSI Science Museum, Bowling Green State Univ., Univ. of Toledo. **Building** 1898 brick, converted steam-powered flour mill. **Grounds** Paths, decks, pond, sculptured gardens; canal & city park w/ island behind house. **Public Space** Entry, TV room, DR. **Food & Drink** Complimentary sodas, sherry, evening dessert. Full breakfast includes hot entree. **Recreation** Antiquing, historic touring, minor league baseball, museums, galleries, biking, cross-country skiing, fishing, golf, boating. **Amenities & Services** AC, bath amenities.

ACCOMMODATIONS

Units 3 guest rooms. **All Rooms** Sitting area. **Some Rooms** Table & chairs, cable TV, modem, whirlpool tub, canal view, private entrance. **Bed & Bath** Queen, twin, & roll-away (1), queen & twin (1), queen (1). All private baths. **Favorites** Garden Room, w/ corner view of the pond & patio, windows on 3 walls, table & chairs, and picket-fence headboard. **Comfort & Decor** We're torn between the Garden Room and the Edward Howard Room, named after the first white settlers in the area—the largest room, with exposed brick and original beams from its former life as a mill. If the floor has a familiar look, it's because it's made from lanes of a local bowling alley. Hand-sewn quilted wall hangings throughout the inn add personality and are enhanced by hand-painted wall treatments.

RATES, RESERVATIONS, & RESTRICTIONS

Deposit Credit card number or $50/night. **Discounts** Corp., multiple-night, whole-house rates. **Credit Cards** V, MC, D, AE. **Check-In/Out** 4–9 p.m./11 a.m.; "Try to let us know check-in time within an hour." **Smoking** No. **Pets** No; resident dog & cat stay in innkeepers' quarters. **Kids** Yes, "but we're right on the water—we emphasize safety" **No-Nos** N/A **Minimum Stay** None **Open** All year **Hosts** Karen & Jim Herzberg, 24070 Front St., P.O. Box 102, Grand Rapids 43522 **Phone** (419) 832-6455 **Email** innkeeper@themill house.com **Web** www.themillhouse.com

CAPTAIN MONTAGUE'S, Huron

OVERALL ★★★★ | QUALITY ★★★★ | VALUE ★★★ | PRICE RANGE $85–$155

Huron is largely a lakeside tourist town in summer, so Captain Montague's has become a welcome alternative to motels and other commercial lodging. Privacy is elusive in such towns, and with the large gazebo (once a carriage house), patios, and two parlors, guests can find plenty of spots for intimate chats. The beach and Huron's mile-long pier—wonderfully romantic at sunset—are a short walk from the inn.

SETTING & FACILITIES
Location Off US 6 in residential Huron. **Near** Huron Lighthouse, Huron Playhouse, Huron College, Lakefront Park, Lake Erie, Cedar Point Amusement Park, boats to Lake Erie Islands, caves. **Building** 1876 Southern Colonial, white exterior w/ 2-story pillared porch. **Grounds** Full city block w/ gazebo, gardens, in-ground pool, Amish swing **Public Space** Porch, foyer, DR, parlor, Newton's Room/2nd parlor, library, galley kitchen. **Food & Drink** Custom-blended cinnamon coffee at dawn. Expanded cont'l candlelight breakfast (when indoors) served in gazebo or poolside in summer; signature dish is Irish Cottage scones. **Recreation** Boating, swimming, antiquing, historic touring, canoeing, kayaking, theater, cross-country skiing, galleries, wineries, golf. **Amenities & Services** AC.

ACCOMMODATIONS
Units 5 guest rooms. **All Rooms** Sitting area. **Some Rooms** Ceiling fans, robes, canopy bed, fireplace, table & chairs. **Bed & Bath** King/2 twin (1), queens (4). All private baths. **Favorites** Jenny's Room, the most romantic space, with fireplace, canopy bed, robes, settee, & chair. **Comfort & Decor** More mellow than luxurious, Captain Montague's nonetheless is a stately home with much to offer. The white-on-white dining room, with its cozy alcove, is just elegant enough for a candlelight breakfast. The hand-carved fireplaces in both dining room and parlor, as well as front staircase, are of rich black walnut, a nice complement to the parlor's 1880 black walnut pump organ. Guest room furnishings are Victorian—lots of lace and florals.

RATES, RESERVATIONS, & RESTRICTIONS
Deposit 1 night or 50% of total **Discounts** None **Credit Cards** V, MC, D **Check-In/Out** 3 p.m./11 a.m. **Smoking** No **Pets** No **Kids** No **No-Nos** N/A **Minimum Stay** 2 nights weekends in season, but Sun. can be one of the nights **Open** All year **Hosts** Judy & Mike Tann, 229 Center St., Huron 44839 **Phone** (419) 433-4756 or toll-free (800) 276-4756 **Email** judytann@aol.com **Web** www.captainmontagues.com

BAILEY'S BED & BREAKFAST, Lima

OVERALL ★★★½ | QUALITY ★★★½ | VALUE ★★★★ | PRICE RANGE $55–$65

Bailey's is a Christian bed-and-breakfast, so discussions in the common room are likely to center around religious topics. If guests wish advice on being saved, the innkeeper is happy to talk with them. That said, however, religion is not forced on guests, and Diane Bailey takes a liberal view on such matters as bringing in wine; guests are welcome to have alcohol in their rooms. This is a friendly, comfortable home without remarkable furnishings or architectural features, catering mostly to business travelers. Guests are encouraged to relax and indulge in reflection and serenity; the front porch swing is ideal for a mini-escape.

SETTING & FACILITIES

Location Lima's west side, residential neighborhood. **Near** Ohio State Univ. Lima campus, Faurot Park, MacDonell House, downtown shopping. **Building** 1919 Federal/Colonial, brick with large front porch. **Grounds** City lot, flower beds. **Public Space** Common room w/ fireplace, radio, CD player, board games; DR, porch. **Food & Drink** Soft drinks & juice available all day. Coffee, tea, or juice delivered to guest rooms before full breakfast, including hot entree. **Recreation** Antiquing, golf nearby. **Amenities & Services** Robes in guest rooms, AC, fax, copy service.

ACCOMMODATIONS

Units 3 guest rooms. **All Rooms** TV, cable, phone, sitting area, ceiling fans. **Some Rooms** Queen, 2 twins. **Bed & Bath** All private baths w/ showers. **Favorites** Room #2, spacious with soft colors, period furnishings and large walk-in closet. **Comfort & Decor** This home is decorated in simple country style, yet the tone is one of "comfortable formality," with cream-colored carpeting and overstuffed furniture. The owners show appropriate restraint, keeping the lace and potpourri to a minimum.

RATES, RESERVATIONS, & RESTRICTIONS

Deposit Credit card or 1 night's stay; total refund less $10 with 48 hrs. notice. **Discounts** AAA. **Credit Cards** V, MC, AE. **Check-In/Out** 3–9 p.m. or by arrangement/11 a.m. **Smoking** On front porch. **Pets** No. **Kids** Over age 12. **No-Nos** N/A **Minimum Stay** N/A **Open** All year. **Host** Diane Bailey, 1128 State St., Lima 45805 **Phone** (419) 228-8172 **Fax** (419) 228-8172

BRODRICK HOUSE BED & BREAKFAST, *Marysville*

OVERALL ★★★★ | QUALITY ★★★★ | VALUE ★★★★ | PRICE RANGE $89–$99

Innkeeper Bill Garritt is a hobbyist inventor, and he's happy to explain his creations to visitors. Brodrick House isn't without its own curiosities, including the unusual spring-loaded Eastlake-style chandelier over the dining room table. This is a warm, welcoming place with a straightforward feel typical of Arts & Crafts homes; the front porch—built of stones made on-site—invites visitors to sit a spell.

SETTING & FACILITIES

Location Off US 33, near downtown Marysville. **Near** Marysville business district, Mad River Mountain Ski Resort, Indian Lake, Alum Creek Reservoir, Ohio & Zane Caverns.

Building 1905 home of poured stone. **Grounds** City lot; gardens w/ path. **Public Space** Porch, foyer, parlor, DR, media room, open kitchen. **Food & Drink** Snacks, sodas any time. Cont'l-plus breakfast w/ home-baked goods is served by candlelight. **Recreation** Antiquing, swimming, fishing, boating, downhill & cross-country skiing, cavern exploring, historic touring. **Amenities & Services** AC, logo soaps, robes for detached bath, nightly turn-down service.

ACCOMMODATIONS

Units 4 guest rooms. **All Rooms** TV, clock radio. **Some Rooms** Claw-foot tub. **Bed & Bath** Queens (2), doubles (2). All private baths (1 detached). **Favorites** Country Room, the largest, w/ queen high-top bed. **Comfort & Decor** The atmosphere here is relaxed. Guests are encouraged to keep their rooms as a haven for rest, rather than working there, and are provided a media room as a workplace—a converted sun room off the kitchen with a computer, fax, phone, and color copier. Style throughout the house is Arts & Crafts, with walnut trim, pocket doors, and quarter-sawed oak fireplace in the parlor.

RATES, RESERVATIONS, & RESTRICTIONS

Deposit Credit card number. **Discounts** 3rd night 50%; corp., AAA rates; guests celebrating anniversary get $1 discount for each year they were married & welcome platter in their room. **Credit Cards** V, MC, AE. **Check-In/Out** 3–8 p.m. or by arrangement/11 a.m. **Smoking** Outside. **Pets** No. **Kids** No. **No-Nos** N/A **Minimum Stay** None. **Open** All year. **Hosts** Bill & Dianne Garritt, 275 West 5th St., Marysville 43040 **Phone** (937) 644-9797 or toll-free (877) 644-9797 **Email** brodrick@midohio.net **Web** www.brodrickhouse.com

THE CASTLE BED & BREAKFAST, Marysville

OVERALL ★★★★ | QUALITY ★★★★ | VALUE ★★★★ | PRICE RANGE $85–$95

We thought the Cordells were clever to name guest rooms after the jewel colors in the stained-glass window downstairs: emerald, garnet, sapphire, and amethyst. This bed-and-breakfast is an antiques shop, and nearly everything is for sale; quality antiques are set up in both public areas and guest rooms as furnishings. They're a nice complement to permanent features of the house, including original brass light fixtures, and numerous alcoves and bays. We'd like to see a more discreet price list, though, instead of price tags garishly hanging everywhere.

SETTING & FACILITIES

Location Off US 33, at downtown Marysville's edge. **Near** Marysville business district, Mad River Mountain Ski Resort, Indian Lake, Alum Creek Reservoir, Ohio & Zane Caverns. **Building** 1884 brick Italianate Victorian, on National Register of Historic Places. **Grounds** City lot, flower beds. **Public Space** Entry, deep front porch, DR, LR, library/museum room. **Food & Drink** Cont'l-plus breakfast w/ homemade muffins & waffles, served at guests' convenience. **Recreation** Antiquing, cross-country & downhill skiing, swimming, boating, fishing, caverns. **Amenities & Services** AC, logo bath amenities.

ACCOMMODATIONS

Units 4 guest rooms. **All Rooms** TV, phone, data port, clock, sitting area. **Some Rooms** Canopy or high Victorian bed, fireplace. **Bed & Bath** Queens (2), doubles (2). All private baths. **Favorites** Emerald Room w/ antique queen bed, reading alcove, original spoon-carved fireplace w/ beveled mirror. **Comfort & Decor** Original butternut, walnut, and oak trim survives throughout this home. Period touches add character, including transoms (even over doors leading to baths and closets), the traditional bridal staircase, and, displayed in the library, artifacts from an early 1900s time capsule discovered during renovation. The stained-glass transom in the entry is original.

RATES, RESERVATIONS, & RESTRICTIONS

Deposit Credit card number. **Discounts** Corp. & extended-stay rates. **Credit Cards** V, MC. **Check-In/Out** 4–7 p.m./11 a.m. **Smoking** No. **Pets** Inquire. **Kids** Yes. **No-Nos** N/A **Minimum Stay** None. **Open** All year. **Hosts** Barry & Susan Cordell, 318 East 5th St., Marysville 43040 **Phone** (937) 644-2273 or toll-free (877) 644-4722 **Fax** (937) 644-1220 **Email** mail@thecastleb-b.com **Web** www.thecastleb-b.com

GEORGIAN MANOR INN, Norwalk

OVERALL ★★★★★ | QUALITY ★★★★½ | VALUE ★★★★★ | PRICE RANGE $95–$180

This inn is Ohio's only bed-and-breakfast with a four-diamond AAA rating, so expect a special experience here. Every interior surface, the entire exterior and extensive landscaping were redone in the restoration, but this stately home is also cozy and inviting. "We wanted it to look the period, but be comfortable—we didn't want it to look like a museum," Gene Denney says. It worked; one wants to curl up with a good mystery among the marble-top tables and lovely lamps in the living room. The antique Winthrop secretary in the library is perfect for parking with a laptop. Women business travelers will appreciate details missing in many bed-and-breakfasts, such as good reading lights, hair dryers, and mirrors. Take a walk while you're here; the street is lined with magnificent mansions.

SETTING & FACILITIES

Location Norwalk's historic, mansion-lined West Main Street. **Near** Amish country, Cedar Point Amusement Park, Thomas Edison's birthplace, Lake Erie, Kingswood Center Gardens, Pres. Rutherford B. Hayes Presidential Center, Norwalk Raceway. **Building** 1906 Georgian mansion, pale yellow exterior, underwent renovation in 1995. **Grounds** 1.4 acres with pond, stream, and waterfall; stone paths wind through the property and carefully landscaped gardens ("outdoor rooms"). **Public Space** Large foyer, parlor, DR, 600-book library, sun porch, 2 patios. **Food & Drink** Coffee, tea, soft drinks, and breakfast bars available all day. Full breakfast with entree, such as quiche w/ hash browns and bacon, or strawberry French toast w/ sausage. Some packages include cheese plate or picnic basket. **Recreation** Antiquing, Lake Erie water sports, winery touring, hiking, tennis, biking, birding, drag racing, historic home walking tours. **Amenities & Services** Robes; computer, fax, copier, CD player on site, conference rooms, barbecue grill available, AC.

ACCOMMODATIONS

Units 4 guest rooms. **All Rooms** Cable TV, VCR, phone, modem port, walk-in closets, radio, ceiling fan. **Some Rooms** Sitting area, canopy bed, Jacuzzi (1), fireplace. **Bed & Bath** Queen (3), double (1). All private baths. **Favorites** Lady Katherine Room, w/ antique bed of burled walnut; and Lady Anne Room with 2 walk-in closets and private balcony overlooking pond. **Comfort & Decor** No detail was overlooked in restoring this home, from the crystal chandeliers and large cove moldings to the two-sided pocket doors between the parlor and dining room—one side mahogany, the other side oak, to match the wood in the rooms facing the doors. Window treatments are sumptuous; paintings are by such noted artists as Alan Maley and John Stobart.

RATES, RESERVATIONS, & RESTRICTIONS

Deposit Credit card number, or check for 50% of stay. **Discounts** AAA, midweek; special packages include Valentine's Day, Golf, and Romantic Getaways. **Credit Cards** AE, MC, V, D. **Check-In/Out** 3 p.m./11:30 a.m. **Smoking** No. **Pets** No. **Kids** No. **No-Nos** N/A **Minimum Stay** 2 nights on holiday weekends. **Open** All year, except Christmas Day. **Hosts** Gene & Judy Denney, 123 West Main St., Norwalk 44857 **Phone** (419) 663-8132 or toll-free (800) 668-1644 **Fax** (419) 668-3542 **Email** GeorgianManor@neo.rr.com **Web** or www.bbonline.com/oh/georgian

SEARLE HOUSE, *Plymouth*

OVERALL ★★★★½ | QUALITY ★★★★½ | VALUE ★★★★★ | PRICE RANGE $75–$140

It took three men two years to paint this exquisite home. A former guest house for railroad passengers and crew, it was about to be condemned before the recent restoration. The warm, rich room colors are authentic to the period, and careful attention was given to details such as the wainscoting in the formal dining room. Furnishings were passed down from the former owner, a woman with diverse interests who married a Vanderbilt and once starred in a John Wayne movie. The innkeepers were both trained at the Culinary Institute of America, so breakfast is a fine-dining experience. They offer a dinner menu and will prepare individualized meals, but they need several days' notice to shop for the right ingredients—Plymouth is a very small town. They also enjoy hosting small special-interest groups, such as book clubs, for getaways.

SETTING & FACILITIES

Location Centrally located to Toledo, Columbus, & Cleveland. **Near** Amish country, Plymouth town center shops, Norwalk Raceway. **Building** Listed in the National Register of Historic Places. 1870 Victorian Second Empire painted lady (5 colors), with original hand-carved gingerbread and ornate interior millwork. **Grounds** Large landscaped lawn, flower gardens, fish pond w/ fountains & lilies. **Public Space** Parlor w/ TV, DR, garden room, foyer. **Food & Drink** Coffee, tea, & soft drinks available all day; afternoon tea served by the pond in warm weather. Inn has a liquor license, and drinks are available. Full breakfast includes home-baked muffins or rolls, fresh fruit, and made-from-scratch entree such as quiche or waffles. **Recreation** Ski resort, golf courses, auto racetrack, shopping at renowned vintage clothing store Stitches in Time. **Amenities & Services** Dinners & special events, extensive wine list, AC.

ACCOMMODATIONS

Units 9 guest rooms, some adjoining & can convert to suites. **All Rooms** Phone, TV, cable, sitting area, specialized air filters. **Some Rooms** Data port, window boxes, handicap accessible (1). **Bed & Bath** Queen beds (8), 2 singles (1). All private baths. **Favorites** Historical Medical Room, w/ medical artifacts. **Comfort & Decor** Light fixtures, wood trim, and shutters are all original. Rooms are named for categories of distinguished Ohioans; e.g., the Authors' Room features a plaque listing notable Ohio authors; the Genius Room's plaque lists Ohio inventors and industrialists, including Thomas Edison and John D. Rockefeller.

RATES, RESERVATIONS, & RESTRICTIONS

Deposit 1 night's stay; refund w/ 48 hrs. cancellation notice. **Discounts** Corp. **Credit Cards** AE, MC, V. **Check-In/Out** 2–6 p.m./11 a.m. or by prior arrangement. **Smoking** No. **Pets** No. **Kids** Yes, but innkeepers say, "We'd like them supervised." **No-Nos** Kitchen is off-limits. **Minimum Stay** N/A **Open** All year; closed Christmas, Easter, & Thanksgiving. **Hosts** Kenneth & Victoria DiBiagio, 49 Railroad St., Plymouth 44865 **Phone** (419) 687-2222 **Fax** (419) 687-2223 **Web** www.searlehouse.com

GETAWAY INN, Put-in-Bay on South Bass Island

OVERALL ★★★★ | QUALITY ★★★★ | VALUE ★★★ | PRICE RANGE $75–$165

Set back on a wooded lot several blocks behind Put-in-Bay's town center, the Getaway Inn is a quiet alternative to the boisterous lakeside inns on this resort island. The 1838 cabin was the first dwelling on South Bass Island,

and the 1940 addition mimics the log structure with weathered wood siding taken from trees in the backyard that were cleared for the expansion. Put-in-Bay is a popular family and college student destination; unregistered "stowaway" guests are charged $50 here.

SETTING & FACILITIES
Location A wooded area outside Put-in-Bay in the Lake Erie Islands. **Near** Put-in-Bay downtown shops, Lake Erie, Cedar Point amusement park, wineries. **Building** 1940 & 1998 additions to 1838 log cabin, modernized rustic style. **Grounds** Stone patio, landscaped yard. **Public Space** Foyer, sunroom, gathering room w/ sofas. **Food & Drink** Soda, bottled water available any time. "Deluxe cont'l" breakfast, can include entree such as egg casserole; specialty is beignets on weekends. **Recreation** Boating, water sports, picnicking. **Amenities & Services** AC, shampoo & bath amenities; fine china & silver are used at breakfast.

ACCOMMODATIONS
Units 1 suite, 3 guest rooms. **All Rooms** Cable TV. **Some Rooms** N/A **Bed & Bath** All private baths, all queen beds. **Favorites** Train Room; spacious, train motif w/ Amish sled bed. **Comfort & Decor** The decorating style is Western/rustic. White ash and black walnut are the primary woods used in the bed-and-breakfast, though some log beams from the original 1838 structure can be seen in the cellar, walls, and attic.

RATES, RESERVATIONS, & RESTRICTIONS
Deposit Credit card or 1 night's rate, refundable until 2 weeks prior to stay minus a $15 cancellation fee. **Discounts** 4th weekday free. **Credit Cards** MC, V, D, AE. **Check-In/Out** 3 p.m./11 a.m., but can leave bags at the inn while finishing the day on the island. **Smoking** No. **Pets** No. **Kids** Weekdays only. **No-Nos** People other than registered guests. **Minimum Stay** 2 nights on weekends. **Open** All year, "if you can get here. Lake Erie freezes from late November to mid-March and ferries don't run." **Host** Bill Cunningham, 210 Concord Ave., P.O. Box 296, Put-in-Bay 43456 **Phone** (419) 285-9012 or toll-free (877) 228-1114 **Fax** (419) 285-9008 **Web** www.getawayinn.com

GREATSTONE CASTLE, *Sidney*

OVERALL ★★★★½ | QUALITY ★★★★½ | VALUE ★★★★★ | PRICE RANGE $95–$135

Driveways like this one only appear in the movies. GreatStone, castlelike because of three huge turrets, lives up to the anticipation in every room. The first focus is the reception hall, finished in deep red African mahogany with red wainscot. The parlor is trimmed in cherry, the ballroom in carved white mahogany and the grand staircase is carved red African mahogany. On display in the library are ledgers, diaries, and other personal artifacts belonging to the first owner, businessman William H. C. Goode. The dining room is used to host Victorian dinners with musicale for the local historical society and other formal gatherings.

SETTING & FACILITIES
Location Hilltop overlooking Sidney's historic downtown. **Near** I-75, 30 mi. from Dayton and Springfield, USAF Aviation Museum. **Building** On National Register of Historic Places, a Victorian mansion of 18-in.-thick Bedford Indiana limestone. **Grounds** 2 acres of lawn, gardens, & 100-year-old oaks lining a circular drive. **Public Space** Reception hall, parlor, ballroom, DR; library; breakfast room/conservatory, wraparound porch. **Food & Drink** Dessert & nonalcoholic beverages available in evening; breakfast is cont'l-plus w/ fresh fruits & pastries. **Recreation** Fishing, golf, skiing, birding, biking, antiquing. **Amenities & Services** AC, robes, bicycles provided; full-service spa on premises, including hydrotherapy & beauty treatments. Computer, fax machine, copier, CD player, VCR, and piano are available. Weddings, corp. meetings, and other events are easily accommodated.

ACCOMMODATIONS
Units 6 guest rooms. **All Rooms** AC, cable TV, sitting area. **Some Rooms** Fireplace, bay windows. **Bed & Bath** Queen (2), double (4), private bath in 4 rooms. **Favorites** Victorian Room, with a magnificent Victorian bed & dresser. **Comfort & Decor** Exotic woods from around the world are found throughout this mansion, and the owners have selected fine antiques to match. The dining room features white oak walls and ceiling, and table and chairs willed to future occupants by the original owner; they match the columns and leaf carvings found throughout the first floor. The wallpaper in the Reception Hall is actually painted canvas.

RATES, RESERVATIONS, & RESTRICTIONS
Deposit Credit card or 1 night's lodging, refundable up to 7 days prior to visit. **Discounts** AAA, gov't. rate, long-term stay. **Credit Cards** MC, V, AE. **Check-In/Out** 3 p.m./noon. **Smoking** On porches. **Pets** No. **Kids** "We do not prohibit them, but we discourage them on Saturday nights." **No-Nos** N/A **Minimum Stay** None. **Open** All year, except closed Thanksgiving & Christmas. **Hosts** Frederick & Victoria Keller, 429 N. Ohio Ave., Sidney 45365 **Phone** (937) 498-4728 **Fax** (937) 498-9950 **Email** greatstone@west net.com **Web** www.greatstonecastle.com

FORT BALL BED & BREAKFAST, Tiffin

OVERALL ★★★★½ | QUALITY ★★★★ | VALUE ★★★★★ | PRICE RANGE $65–$110, $10 EXTRA PERSON

Named for the stockades erected nearby during the War of 1812, this inn has undergone extensive renovation; even the original plank flooring was once painted and had to be stripped. Visitors step through the cheery side entrance onto original tile floors. Vintage stained and beveled glass is found throughout the first floor, enhancing elaborately carved mantels and built-ins. The Arts & Crafts–style dining room was a 20th-century addition. This is popular lodging for families of Tiffin and Heidelberg students, so it gets busy during orientation week and other school events.

SETTING & FACILITIES

Location 40 mi. SW of Sandusky, 40 mi. SE of Toledo. **Near** Tiffin Univ., Tiffin's downtown business district, Heidelberg College, Rutherford B. Hayes Presidential Center. **Building** 1894 Queen Anne Revival, brick, restored. **Grounds** Lawn, flower beds. **Public Space** DR, parlor, TV room, wraparound porch. **Food & Drink** Water, soft drinks, & cookies available any time in upstairs fridge. Full breakfast includes hot entree. **Recreation** Riverside walking path 2 doors away; Cedar Point Amusement Park, Toledo Zoo, golf, antiquing. **Amenities & Services** AC, hair dryer, irons & ironing boards, bath amenities, fax available.

ACCOMMODATIONS

Units 4 (Room 4 only rented "if in agreement with Room 2; they would share a bath.") **All Rooms** Ceiling fans, cable TV, VCR, mantel, sitting area, phone. **Some Rooms** Tower bay, fireplace, sleeper sofa, whirlpool (single & double). **Bed & Bath** King (2), queen (1), double (1), 3 private baths if 4th room is vacant. **Favorites** Room 1 w/ fireplace and whirlpool. **Comfort & Decor** Restored before opening as a bed-and-breakfast in 1894, Fort Ball's unusual features include sliding glass cupboard doors in the pantry and ornate built-in cupboards in the parlor.

RATES, RESERVATIONS, & RESTRICTIONS

Deposit Credit Card or 50% of stay, refundable with 24 hrs. notice if room is rebooked. **Discounts** Business, long-term. **Credit Cards** V, MC, D. **Check-In/Out** 4–7 p.m./noon, or by prior arrangement. **Smoking** Outside only. **Pets** No. **Kids** Yes, "but the house isn't child-proofed." **No-Nos** N/A **Minimum Stay** N/A **Open** All year. **Hosts** Charles & Lenora Livingston, 25 Adams St., Tiffin 44883 **Phone** (419) 447-0776 or toll-free (888) 447-0776 **Fax** (419) 448-8415 **Email** ftballbanb@friendlynet.com **Web** www.fortball.com

ZELKOVA COUNTRY MANOR, Tiffin

OVERALL ★★★★½ | QUALITY ★★★★½ | VALUE ★★★★ | PRICE RANGE $75–$150

Though it's tucked just off a major byway, Zelkova Country Manor is so isolated and quiet it seems far from civilization. Gourmet dinner on the property enables guests to relax and enjoy their stay, rather than leave in search of a restaurant. From premium wines to soft jazz, carefully chosen details contribute to a quality experience, enhanced by the faintest scents from the herb garden. There's nothing like a whiff of lemon thyme at dusk to both soothe and invigorate. Repeat guests receive a special gift: a framed, individually colored photo of the inn.

SETTING & FACILITIES

Location Just off OH 224 several miles south of Tiffin. **Near** Tiffin Univ., Heidelberg College, Rutherford B. Hayes Presidential Center, downtown Tiffin. **Building** Georgian Revival, tan brick, built 1952. **Grounds** 27 acres of sprawling lawns, vegetable and flower gardens, herb garden, woodland, wetlands, outdoor pool. **Public Spaces** Foyer, LR, 2 DRs ("You don't have to eat with others if you don't want to"), library. **Food & Drink** Afternoon tea served at 4 p.m., reception daily at 6 p.m. with complimentary beer, wine, cocktails, and hors d'oeuvres. A full English breakfast includes Irish oatmeal, scones, entree, and coffee blended and shipped from Colorado. Dinner is available for an additional cost. **Recreation** Antiquing, swimming, picnicking, golf, canoeing, biking. **Amenities & Services** Logo bath amenities & note paper, AC, fresh fruit in rooms, meeting room.

ACCOMMODATIONS

Units 8 guest rooms. **All Rooms** Cable TV, CD player, data port, sitting area. **Some Rooms** Private sun room porch, woodland view, garden view, private garden, wheelchair access. **Bed & Bath** Queens (6), king (1), double (1). All private baths. **Favorites** Flynn Room, w/ queen bed and private herb garden. **Comfort & Decor** Unadorned elegance is the decorating style of this inn with a somewhat masculine tone. A grand piano anchors the living room. Antiques were less important to this innkeeper than comfort; contemporary furnishings and clean lines dominate.

RATES, RESERVATIONS, & RESTRICTIONS

Deposit First night's lodging, refundable with 2 weeks' notice. **Discounts** Full-manor rental. **Credit Cards** V, MC. **Check-In/Out** 3 p.m./noon. **Smoking** Outside. **Pets** "If they don't mind there's a chance my dog might eat it." **Kids** Yes; "We can certainly tolerate their children if they can." **No-Nos** N/A **Minimum Stay** None. **Open** All year. **Host** Michael Pinkston, 2348 South CR 19, Tiffin 44883 **Phone** (419) 447-4043 **Fax** (419) 447-6473 **Email** zelkova@bpsom.com **Web** www.zelkovacountrymanor.com

Northeast Ohio

All roads lead to **Cleveland,** the easiest city in the world to learn: everything runs either along the lake, or away from it. Downtown attractions include, of course, the **Rock and Roll Hall of Fame and Museum,** the **Great Lakes Science Center**—a hands-on science museum with a twist, the science focuses on, um, the Great Lakes—and new stadiums for the **Cleveland Browns and Indians** pro football and baseball teams. Five miles east is **University Circle,** home to the famed **Museum of Art, the Museum of Natural History, Case Western Reserve University,** and the **Orchestra's Severance Hall.**

Like any big city, Cleveland's suburban and ex-urban fingers extend a good 40 miles, stopping short of **Akron** to the south—another turnaround city with its own industrial heritage and, consequently, home of former titans that became bed-and-breakfasts. Cleveland seems to have more than its share of classy bed-and-breakfasts, nearly all in century homes, ranging from sprawling mansions, such as Edgewater Estates—just across the road from **Edgewater Park and Lake Erie**—to little **Glendennis,** a single-unit brick cottage in the Ohio City neighborhood.

East of Cleveland are the lake communities, with bed-and-breakfasts focused on visitors who come to fish, swim, and tour the wineries. In communities like **Burton** and **Hiram,** barely connected to Cleveland, we find bed-and-breakfasts converted from large, restored farm houses.

In the southern portion of Zone 19, the terrain is hilly. College towns, railroad stops, and pottery centers all have created interest in bed-and-breakfasts: in **Loudonville** and **Belleville,** guests often combine a bed-and-breakfast stay with trips to **Malabar Farm** and **Mohican State Parks.** **Sugarcreek,** a Swiss village, is worth a stop (though we confess leaving quickly to escape the polka music blasting from loudspeakers). This is Amish country; watch for slow-moving carriages on secondary roads.

O'NEIL HOUSE, Akron

OVERALL ★★★★½ | QUALITY ★★★★½ | VALUE ★★★★ | PRICE RANGE $100–$175

There are no bad spots in the O'Neil House; Grace's Room is small but beautiful, and the others are unusually spacious. The sunny breakfast room looks out onto a stone terrace and gardens, leaded windows grace nearly every room, and in the library, a secret Prohibition bar hides behind a bookcase—all reminiscent of affluent life in the roaring 1920s. (The original owner founded General Tire Co.; Akron is the Rubber Capital of the World.) The energetic innkeeper makes her own drapes, bedspreads, and slipcovers and runs a popular restaurant, the Amber Pub, on the side.

SETTING & FACILITIES

Location Akron's near-west side, 5 min. west of downtown. **Near** Metroparks, Stan Hywet Hall, Univ. of Akron, Cuyahoga Valley National Recreation Area. **Building** 1923 Tudor mansion. **Grounds** 4 acres w/ gardens, pond, terraces, benches, & paths for meandering. **Public Space** Grand foyer, LR, garden room, library, breakfast room. **Food & Drink** Full gourmet breakfast. Specialty is the "Gatsby" with filet mignon "Benedict," wine, cheese, & homemade pastry. **Recreation** Cross-country skiing, tennis, antiquing, Akron Aeros minor league baseball, Akron Museum of Contemporary Art. **Amenities & Services** Robes provided; will deliver private dinners to rooms for extra fee. Weddings, meetings, & small banquets can be arranged.

ACCOMMODATIONS

Units 1 guest room, 3 suites. **All Rooms** Cable TV, sitting area. **Some Rooms** Fireplace, kitchen, sitting room, sunroom, bidet. **Bed & Bath** King (1), queen (4) ; all private baths, Servants' Suite has 1.5 baths. **Favorites** Master Suite with spacious dressing room & Art Deco bath. **Comfort & Decor** Even the foyer is sumptuous, with hand-carved linen-fold oak panels—each square is carved in a different design! The Oriental rugs in the living room are antiques, and the light fixtures are original. In the expansive living room, a grand piano and one of the home's six working fireplaces add to the warmth.

RATES, RESERVATIONS, & RESTRICTIONS
Deposit Credit card number. **Discounts** N/A **Credit Cards** V, MC, D. **Check-In/Out** 2 p.m./11 a.m. **Smoking** No. **Pets** No; owner's dog and cats live indoors. **Kids** Yes. **No-Nos** Burning candles in rooms. **Minimum Stay** N/A **Open** All year. **Host** Gayle Johnson, 1290 West Exchange St., Akron 44313 **Phone** (330) 867-2650 **Fax** (330) 867-8211 **Web** www.bedandbreakfast.com/bbc/p208194.asp

MICHAEL CAHILL BED & BREAKFAST, Ashtabula

OVERALL ★★★½ | QUALITY ★★★½ | VALUE ★★★★★ | PRICE RANGE $55–$80

These are simple and modest but comfortable lodgings, visited most often by fishermen, on a street called Captains' Row for the number of ship captains who once lived there. The owners, who live two doors away, took four years to restore the home once covered with Insul-brick. A 1930s Sears & Roebuck stove is used in the kitchen, and the refrigerator is an old Crosley Shelvador. Guests relax on authentic Morris chairs in the second-floor sitting room; one downstairs sitting room features Art Deco chairs from the 1920s.

SETTING & FACILITIES
Location Above Walnut Beach in downtown Ashtabula, halfway between Conneaut and Geneva-on-the-Lake. **Near** Marine Museum, historic Bridge Street shops, Lake Erie, Ashtabula County wineries, numerous covered bridges. **Building** 1887 Stick Style home, on National Register of Historic Places, painted in period greens w/ brown trim. **Grounds** City lot, flower beds, shrubs. **Public Space** Sitting rooms (1 up, 2 down), 2 w/ TV, DR, kitchen, small kitchenette upstairs, wraparound porch. **Food & Drink** Full breakfast w/ muffin, entree. **Recreation** Charter boat fishing, swimming, boating, antiquing, historic interests. **Amenities & Services** N/A.

ACCOMMODATIONS
Units 4 guest rooms. **All Rooms** AC. **Some Rooms** N/A. **Bed & Bath** Queen (1), doubles (2), two 3/4-beds (1); all private baths. **Favorites** Room 1 with queen bed. **Comfort & Decor** Interior highlights include cherry woodwork downstairs, original electric chandeliers, bull's-eye moldings, and antique furnishings. On a bluff just feet from Lake Erie, the front porch cools weary travelers on hot summer nights.

RATES, RESERVATIONS, & RESTRICTIONS
Deposit 1st night, refunded with 1 week's notice. **Discounts** Multiple nights or whole-house rental. **Credit Cards** No; cash or check only **Check-In/Out** 3 p.m./noon. **Smoking** On porch. **Pets** No. **Kids** Welcome. **No-Nos** N/A **Minimum Stay** None. **Open** All year. **Hosts** Pat & Paul Goode, 1106 Walnut Blvd., P.O. Box 3024, Ashtabula 44005 **Phone** (440) 964-8449 **Email** cahillbb@apk.net

RED MAPLE INN, Burton

OVERALL ★★★★ | QUALITY ★★★★ | VALUE ★★★ | PRICE RANGE $119–$225

Red Maple Inn sits in the heart of the country's fourth-largest Amish community and Ohio's biggest maple syrup–producing town. Partly because of its size and business clientele and partly because it's not a home, the ambience here is more like that of a hotel than a bed-and-breakfast. Still, rooms are individually decorated and lovely—just don't look for a traditional bed-and-breakfast experience.

SETTING & FACILITIES

Location Burton Village, next door to "living history museum" Century Village. **Near** Historic museums, Punderson State Park, Nelson Ledges, Holden Arboretum, Ashtabula County wineries. **Building** Western Reserve-style inn, white exterior. **Grounds** Lawns in wooded setting, overlooking rolling hillside dotted with Amish farms. **Public Space** Burton Room (LR) w/ fireplace, DR, library, fitness center, conference room, patio. **Food & Drink** Weekends, cont'l or hot buffet breakfast; weekdays cont'l or cooked-to-order. Light hors d'oeuvres served at 5 p.m. In the evening, complimentary coffee, tea, soft drinks, cookies, popcorn are available. **Recreation** Boating, fishing, canoeing, golf, horseback riding, downhill & cross-country skiing, Sea World, Six Flags of Ohio Amusement Park, cheese & maple syrup production. **Amenities & Services** AC, complimentary horse-drawn carriage rides, bath amenities, robes, feather pillows available, meetings and special events for up to 100 people, fax & AV equipment available.

ACCOMMODATIONS

Units 17 guest rooms, 1 suite. **All Rooms** Phone, cable TV, Jacuzzi, desk, coffee pot, irons, ironing boards. **Some Rooms** Private balcony, fireplace, sitting area, valley view, Century Village view. **Bed & Bath** Queens (2), doubles (16), sleeper sofas (11); all private baths. **Favorites** Suite with large balcony, kitchenette, & fireplace. **Comfort & Decor** All rooms are furnished in hand-crafted Amish-built furniture. Rooms are spacious if a bit commercial in tone, decorated in Early American style.

RATES, RESERVATIONS, & RESTRICTIONS

Deposit 1 night's stay; phone reservations must use credit card. **Discounts** AAA on suite, also corner & valley view rooms. **Credit Cards** MC, V, AE, D. **Check-In/Out** 3 p.m./11 a.m. **Smoking** Balconies, patio. **Pets** No. **Kids** Welcome; children under age 5 stay free **No-Nos** N/A **Minimum Stay** None. **Open** All year. **Host** Gina M. Holk, manager, 14707 South Cheshire St., Burton 44021 **Phone** (440) 834-8334 or toll-free (888) 646-2753 **Fax** (440) 834-8356 **Email** info@redmapleinn.com **Web** www.redmapleinn.com

BROWNSTONE INN, Cleveland

OVERALL ★★★★½ | QUALITY ★★★★½ | VALUE ★★★★★ | PRICE RANGE $95–$150

A renovator by trade, Robin Yates says he "could add private baths in about ten minutes," but he'd rather people meet in the hallway and talk to each other. Yates is a sociable guy and spirited Cleveland booster: "I love single travelers," he says, "I take them around town, usually go have dinner or drinks with them in the evening." He serves "big, big breakfasts with protein," and leaves leftovers in the fridge for guests to snack on. Brownstone Inn has been his home since 1974 (he lives in the basement), just opened as an inn in 1997. The brownstone is authentic; stone to build it was brought from New York—but if you're not a good climber, ask for a lower floor; the "nosebleed room" is four flights up.

SETTING & FACILITIES
Location Main artery just east of core downtown. **Near** Museums, pro sports stadiums, Edgewater State Park, Lake Erie. **Building** 1874 Victorian brownstone, on National Register of Historic Places. **Grounds** Fenced courtyard in rear. **Public Space** DR, parlor, courtyard. **Food & Drink** Full breakfast, fruit & snacks any time in kitchenette, evening sherry or port. **Recreation** Customized tours of Cleveland; swimming, boating, water sports. **Amenities & Services** Daily newspapers, fireplace, weddings, special events, personal tours, whole-house air purifier.

ACCOMMODATIONS
Units 1 suite, 4 guest rooms. **All Rooms** Radio, ionizer. **Some Rooms** TV/VCR (3), fireplaces (2) **Bed & Bath** Queens (2), Full beds (3), Futon (1) for extra person. Shared bath e/ shower, antique fixtures on each floor. **Favorites** 2nd-floor front room w/ street view, sitting area, sumptuous colors & furnishings. **Comfort & Decor** Enter through massive, peacock-blue double front doors at top of stone steps. Elegant patented French wallpaper marks the Grand Foyer and stairway; pocket doors, marble fireplace in DR, tall arched doors set off the 14-foot ceilings on first floor, player piano in parlor. Central AC. Home was completely renovated before opening.

RATES, RESERVATIONS, & RESTRICTIONS
Deposit 25%. **Discounts** Senior, group, AAA, long-term stay, single traveler. **Credit Cards** V, MC, AE, D. **Check-In/Out** By arrangement. **Smoking** In designated areas. **Pets** By arrangement; limited accommodation. **Kids** Welcome by arrangement. **No-Nos** N/A **Minimum Stay** None. **Open** All year. **Host** Robin Yates, 3649 Prospect Ave., Cleveland 44115 **Phone** (216) 426-1753 **Fax** (216) 431-0648 **Email** ryates@iopener.net **Web** www.brownstoneinndowntown.com

BOURBON HOUSE, Cleveland

OVERALL ★★★★½ | QUALITY ★★★★ | VALUE ★★★★★ | PRICE RANGE $75–$150

This host loves his home, and it shows. The refurbishing has been carefully planned, down to the historically accurate exterior colors and the wooden screen doors. He extends himself to give everyone a comfortable, quality experience; he even rented a room last Christmas; the guest joined in the family celebration. He tastes every breakfast before it's served, offers a lengthy menu in French and English, and gladly shows off his collection of antique silver, "tarnish and all." Lonzer, who named the inn after his ancestors, is an avid student of royal family history and loves to entertain with stories behind family artifacts that fill the rooms.

SETTING & FACILITIES

Location Franklin Historic District 5 min. west of downtown. **Near** Museums, Edgewater State Park, Lake Erie, pro sports stadiums. **Building** 1901 Victorian **Grounds** Small front yard on residential blvd. **Public Space** Parlor, receiving room, DR, library, third-floor music room. **Food & Drink** Full breakfast menu, including specialty coffee drinks and 6 egg entrees; snacks, soft drinks any time. **Recreation** Antiquing; boating, swimming, picnicking, water sports in state park. **Amenities & Services** Turn-down service w/ chocolates, books, games, data port, piano, copier.

ACCOMMODATIONS

Units 1 suite, 2 guest rooms. **All Rooms** AC, cable TV, radio, fireplace, hair dryer. **Some Rooms** Private bath, sitting room. **Bed & Bath** King (1), queen (1), double (1); private bath in suite; 2 rooms share bath. **Favorites** Burgundy Suite with pink-tiled fireplace and original white-tiled bath. **Comfort & Decor** Interior style is Arts & Crafts. The home's most striking feature is a giant, finely crafted (unsigned) stained-glass window at the staircase landing. Wood throughout is original; even radiators still have their original gilding. Three pieces of Eastlake furniture are in receiving room; an old pump organ graces the parlor.

RATES, RESERVATIONS, & RESTRICTIONS

Deposit 1st night; reservations guaranteed by credit card or advance payment; 48 hrs. cancellation. **Discounts** Corp. (20%), senior citizen/AARP (15%), gov't (15%). **Credit Cards** V, MC, AE. **Check-In/Out** 4:30 p.m./11 a.m. **Smoking** On porch. **Pets** No. **Kids** No. **Minimum Stay** None. **Open** All year. **Host** Robert J. Lonzer, 6116 Franklin Blvd., Cleveland 44102 **Phone** (216) 939-0535 **Email** robert_bourbon_house@msn.com **Web** www.bbhost.com/bourbon_house

EDGEWATER ESTATES, Cleveland

OVERALL ★★★★½ | QUALITY ★★★★½ | VALUE ★★★★ | PRICE RANGE $95–$150

On a tree-lined street in Cleveland's most affluent neighborhood, Edwater Estates is a four-minute drive from the heart of downtown and a four-minute jog to the beach. The flip-side construction of the inn, with two living and dining rooms, is a handy way to keep allergic guests from the animals and affords more privacy for all guests. We wanted to stay in the sun room and watch neighbors taking their afternoon constitutionals. Ask to see the Moroccan "altar."

SETTING & FACILITIES

Location On the West Shoreway, across the road from Edgewater Park & Lake Erie. **Near** Downtown Cleveland, Rock and Roll Hall of Fame, pro football & baseball parks, Great Lakes Science Museum. **Building** 1920s English Tudor, twin public areas. **Grounds** Double lot; stone patio, flower gardens. **Public Space** 2 LRs, 2 DRs, sun room, back porch, guest kitchen. **Food & Drink** Complimentary afternoon snack & wine. Full breakfast includes entree and homemade blueberry bread or orange croissant. **Recreation** Museums, galleries, spectator sports, swimming, boating, canoeing, historic touring. **Amenities & Services** AC. robes in rooms; partnership throughout city include "rock & roll" packages and complimentary drinks or desserts at restaurants.

ACCOMMODATIONS

Units 1 suite, 3 guest rooms. **All Rooms** TV, sitting area, ceiling fan, desk & chair, clock radio. **Some Rooms** Fireplace. **Bed & Bath** King (1), queen & double (1), queens (2). **Favorites** King Room, for the space. **Comfort & Decor** Arts & Crafts touches embellish the interior of this home, occupied by the Sisters of St. Augustine in the early 1950s. Fortunately, the most striking features remained, such as the "round" main dining room, original tile fireplaces in both living rooms, and cherry beveled-glass built-ins in the dining hall. Furnishings are a mix of fine antiques and plush seating.

RATES, RESERVATIONS, & RESTRICTIONS

Deposit Credit card number. **Discounts** AAA, corp. weekday rates, 10% off for repeat guests. **Credit Cards** V, MC, D, AE. **Check-In/Out** 3 p.m./12:30 p.m. or by prior arrangement. **Smoking** In designated areas. **Pets** Yes, for extra charge (resident 2 cats & dog are permitted in half the public areas; one LR & DR are kept animal-free). **Kids** Inquire. **No-Nos** N/A **Minimum Stay** None. **Open** All year. **Host** Gayle Lopez, 9803-5 Lake Ave., Cleveland 44102 **Phone** (216) 961-1764 **Fax** (216) 961-7043 **Email** lopezgayle@hotmail.com **Web** www.edgewaterestatesbedandbreakfast.com

STONE GABLES BED & BREAKFAST, Cleveland

OVERALL ★★★★½ | QUALITY ★★★★½ | VALUE ★★★★ | PRICE RANGE $100–$125

Inside and out, Stone Gables is one of the more intriguing structures we've visited. Don't be put off by the blackened sandstone; it can't be cleaned without damaging the stone. Innkeeper Turnbull likes to describe his approach as "historic elegance meets modern comfort." Details were important during renovation of this castlelike urban bed-and-breakfast, including preservation of the tile floor in the entry.

SETTING & FACILITIES

Location In Franklin Blvd. Historic District in Ohio City neighborhood, just west of downtown. **Near** Rock and Roll Hall of Fame, Lake Erie, Edgewater State Park, Browns & Indians pro football & baseball parks, West Side Market, Public Square. **Building** 1883

Berea Sandstone duplex, eclectic Stick style. **Grounds** City lot; perennial gardens. **Public Space** Parlor, foyer, DR, 2nd-floor library. **Food & Drink** Sodas, water, juice available any time; early coffee, afternoon snack. Full breakfast includes hot entree such as egg dish or signature dark chocolate Belgian waffle w/ Frangelico cream. **Recreation** Historic touring, swimming, boating, canoeing, kayaking, birding, spectator sports, museums, galleries. **Amenities & Services** Flowers in rooms, fitness equipment & sauna available, massage therapist available, logo bath amenities. Conference room in progress at time of our visit, fax & copier available.

ACCOMMODATIONS

Units 2 suites & 3 guest rooms. **All Rooms** TV, clock radio, phone, sitting area. **Some Rooms** Single or double whirlpool, fireplace, pillowtop mattress, writing desk, pullout queen-sized sofa bed. **Bed & Bath** Kings (4), queen (1). All private baths. **Favorites** Blue Room, for its unusual decor, including the "four-poster without posters." **Comfort & Decor** Stone Gables had opened barely three months prior to our visit, so some touches, such as restoration of cove moldings, was still in progress. No matter—innkeepers went to extraordinary lengths to achieve elegance, and it shows—a hall mirror and dining room furniture imported from Paris, gray slate faux-marbled Eastlake fireplaces, and custom-made carpet, among other details.

RATES, RESERVATIONS, & RESTRICTIONS

Deposit Credit card number. **Discounts** 10% off for Web customers and readers of this *Unofficial Guide*. **Credit Cards** V, MC, AE **Check-In/Out** 3 p.m./11 a.m. or by prior arrangement. **Smoking** No. **Pets** Small dogs okay; no cats. **Kids** Yes. **No-Nos** N/A **Minimum Stay** None. **Open** All year. **Hosts** Richard Turnbull & James Hauer, 3806 Franklin Blvd., Cleveland 44113 **Phone** (216) 961-4654 or toll-free (877) 215-4326 **Email** richard@stonegables.net **Web** www.stonegables.net

INN AT BRANDYWINE FALLS, Cleveland

OVERALL ★★★½ | QUALITY ★★★★ | VALUE ★★★★ | PRICE RANGE $120–$275

Because the inn sits in a national park, the Hoys cannot own it outright, but have leased the buildings since 1988—including the inn and former grist mill, saw mill, distillery and 3 acres—for the next 50 years. Heavy restoration was necessary; the Hoys were able to save such features as the American chestnut floor in the kitchen and original fireplace with its own bread oven. The specialty of the house is pear oatmeal soup with yogurt. Guest rooms have no TVs because, George says, "we specialize in removing the trappings of society that make people anxious." The setting is true to that vision—woods, farmland, and tranquility, complete with waterfall.

SETTING & FACILITIES

Location In Cuyahoga Valley National Park, 20 mi. south of Cleveland. **Near** Hale Farm & Village, Stan Hywet Home & Gardens, Blossom Music Center, Cuyahoga Valley Train, ski sites. **Building** 1848 Greek Revival farmhouse, on National Register of Historic Places.

Grounds 33,000 acres of National Park w/ hills, forests, historic sites. **Public Space** LR, DR, kitchen, library. **Food & Drink** Full breakfast; coffee & tea any time. **Recreation** Hiking, skiing, sledding, golf, cross-country skiing, biking, historic "living museum" tours, hay rides, carriage rides. **Amenities & Services** Books, games, self-guided tour of house; available for luncheons, weddings, parties to 50 guests or afternoon tea for 20.

ACCOMMODATIONS

Units 3 suites, 3 guest rooms. **All Rooms** Phone (hidden in an antique). **Some Rooms** Jacuzzi (2); TV, microwave, fridge, fireplace in suites. **Bed & Bath** King, double sleigh beds (2); 2 double beds (1); all private baths. **Favorites** James Wallace Parlour, with sleigh bed, private entrance to the porch, scenes on window shades painted by owner, and 1844 coverlet on bed. Barrier-free. **Comfort & Decor** Rustic but classy, the inn mimics mid-19th-century life in the Heartland, with cannonball beds, four-poster beds, antique quilts, and plank flooring. Furniture is authentic to the Greek Revival period, including the tole-painted DR table, painted by a local artist. Also true to the period, closets (which would have been taxed as rooms) are shallow and armoires are provided. Wood-burning Franklin stoves help heat the carriage barn suites.

RATES, RESERVATIONS, & RESTRICTIONS

Deposit 65% with reservation. **Discounts** 10% for 3-day nonholiday stay. **Credit Cards** V, MC, D. **Check-In/Out** 4 p.m./11 a.m. **Smoking** Outside only. **Pets** If they can stay in stables with owner's pets. **Kids** Over age 6 years in guest rooms; any age in suites. **No-Nos** "Nobody absent their common sense." **Minimum Stay** 2 nights for Sat. reservations. **Open** All year. **Hosts** George & Katie Hoy, 8230 Brandywine Rd., Sagamore Hills 44067 **Phone** (330) 650-4965 or toll-free (888) 306-3381 **Fax** (330) 467-2162 **Email** brandywinefallsinn@prodigy.net **Web** www.innatbrandywinefalls.com

GLENDENNIS BED & BREAKFAST, Cleveland

OVERALL ★★★★ | QUALITY ★★★★ | VALUE ★★★★ | PRICE RANGE $110

This is the perfect inn for guests who like the idea of a bed-and-breakfast, but don't want to socialize with other guests. Unless one of the innkeepers is sitting on the deck when you're there, privacy at Glendennis is total. Its location is ideal for walking to some of Cleveland's finest restaurants, historic West Point Market, and the quickly revitalizing West 25th Street corridor.

SETTING & FACILITIES

Location In the heart of Cleveland's historic Ohio City neighborhood, just west of downtown. **Near** Business district, West Side Market, pro football & baseball stadiums, Rock & Roll Hall of Fame, Lake Erie, Great Lakes Science Museum. **Building** 1862 "Greek Revival without the columns," distressed brick. **Grounds** Small yard, shade gardens, brick & stone patio. **Public Space** Front parlor **Food & Drink** Organic cont'l-plus breakfast includes 3 juices, homemade bread, eggs, yogurt. **Recreation** Swimming, boating, museums, galleries, spectator sports, antiquing, historic touring. **Amenities & Services** AC. Breakfast served on back patio or delivered to suite. Complimentary treat for couples celebrating honeymoon or anniversary; laundry services available.

ACCOMMODATIONS

Units I suite. **All Rooms** 3rd-floor dining & sitting area, LR, bedroom, deck. **Some Rooms** N/A **Bed & Bath** Double bed & double-sized futon. Private bath. **Favorites** N/A **Comfort & Decor** A mix of antiques and contemporary pieces furnish the suite. An antique family quilt covers the bed; a desk, futon sofa, TV, and phone are in the suite's sitting room. Refrigerator, microwave, and coffee station are in the dining nook. Both innkeepers and guests use the second-floor deck, overlooking the gardens.

RATES, RESERVATIONS, & RESTRICTIONS

Deposit $25. **Discounts** Corp. rate, weekly rate (rent for 5 days, weekend is free). **Credit Cards** V, MC. **Check-In/Out** 4 p.m. or by arrangement/noon. **Smoking** Outside. **Pets** Inquire. Resident cat can be secluded for guests w/ allergies. **Kids** Yes; cribs available. **No-Nos** N/A **Minimum Stay** None. **Open** All year. **Hosts** David & Emily Dennis, 2808 Bridge Ave., Cleveland 44113 **Phone** (216) 589-0663 **Email** glendennis@rmrc.net **Web** www.glendennis.com

OLDE WORLD BED & BREAKFAST, Dover

OVERALL ★★★★ | QUALITY ★★★★ | VALUE ★★★★★ | PRICE RANGE $68–$110

Saving this landmark farmhouse was Jonna Sigrist's dream. A solid home with hardwood beams and sandstone foundation, it had been condemned in the 1970s. Sigrist was able to retain the walnut staircase, pine four-panel doors, sliding pocket doors, servants' staircase, and wood floor planks. Breakfast is served on antique china; quilts on beds were hand-sewn by Sigrist's grandmother. She grows her own herbs and vegetables, letting her garden and the seasons inspire her menus. Romantic packages and other specials, including extras such as sleigh rides and massages, are available in season.

SETTING & FACILITIES
Location Less than a mile from I-77 between Sugarcreek and Dover. **Near** Amish country, antiques malls, Schoenbrunn & Trumpet in the Land outdoor drama, Tappan Lake, 14 cheese factories. **Building** 1881 Victorian Italianate brick farm house. **Grounds** 1 acre w /pond, large wraparound deck, flower beds. **Public Space** Parlor/tea room, DR. **Food & Drink** Soda, hot beverages available 24 hours. Full breakfast w/ entree, sometimes featuring specialty butter pecan muffins, eggs Benedict casserole, or breakfast lasagna. Cookies in evening. Hosts "Queen's Tea" Tues. & Wed. **Recreation** Antiquing, downhill & cross-country skiing, water sports, theater, historic towns. **Amenities** AC; will arrange visits to a day spa, journeys into Amish country, or crafts classes. Logo soaps, shampoo.

ACCOMMODATIONS
Units 4 guest rooms, 1 suite. **All Rooms** Sitting area. **Some Rooms** Claw-foot tub, electric fireplace, TV. **Bed & Bath** King (1), queen (4); all private baths. **Favorites** Victorian Room with bay-window sitting area. **Comfort & Decor** The kitchen features exposed brick; a separate 1800s log cabin holds a two-person hot tub. The bath in the Alpine room is an old copper tub, with a surround made of three kinds of wood. The suite features Mediterranean decor; remaining rooms are the Oriental—the "Executive Room" with phone, desk, and TV—and Parisian Room.

RATES, RESERVATIONS, & RESTRICTIONS
Deposit Credit card or 50% of stay; refund if cancellation is 5 days before visit. **Discounts** AAA & senior citizen on weekdays. **Credit Cards** MC, V, D. **Check-In/Out** 3–7 p.m./11 a.m. **Smoking** No. **Pets** No. **Kids** No. **No-Nos** N/A **Minimum Stay** None. **Open** All year. **Host** Jonna Sigrist, 2982 OH 516 NW, Dover 44622 **Phone** (330) 343-1333 or toll-free (800) 447-1273 **Fax** (330) 364-8022 **Email** owbb@tusco.net **Web** www.oldeworldbb.com

EMERALD NECKLACE INN, *Fairview Park*

OVERALL ★★★★ | QUALITY ★★★½ | VALUE ★★★ | PRICE RANGE $95—$159

This storefront inn was once the town's first general store; following that merchant's tradition, any bride spending her wedding night at the inn receives a washboard. Emerald Necklace's best feature is its convenience, especially for business travelers—easy access to the international airport, NASA, and Metroparks; free morning newspaper; and airport pick-up ($10).

SETTING & FACILITIES
Location 15 mi. west of Cleveland, just north of I-480. **Near** Cleveland Metroparks, Cleveland Hopkins Airport, NASA Lewis Research Center. **Building** 1863 modernized brick storefront. **Grounds** Small patio. **Public Space** Parlor/tea room, tea shop/breakfast room, beauty salon, 2nd-floor common area. **Food & Drink** Evening snack. Full country breakfast includes hot entree. **Recreation** Horseback riding, biking, fishing, tennis, cross-country skiing, museums, golf. **Amenities & Services** AC. Robes, welcome snack basket, bottled water, fresh flowers in rooms. Hosts wedding showers, teas, other small events up to 16 guests. Beauty salon offers some spa services.

ACCOMMODATIONS

Units 4 guest rooms. **All Rooms** Ceiling fan. **Some Rooms** Table & chairs, whirlpool tub, sitting area, balcony, fireplace, canopy bed. **Bed & Bath** King (1), queens (3). All private baths. **Favorites** Emerald View room—most spacious, w/ gas fireplace, balcony, clawfoot tub. **Comfort & Decor** The decorating style isn't quite Victorian, but it's very lacy. There's a cramped feeling to this bed-and-breakfast, probably because it's several businesses—tea shop, tea party place, beauty salon, bed-and-breakfast—crammed into a space that isn't large to begin with. The look is romantic, not too overdone.

RATES, RESERVATIONS, & RESTRICTIONS

Deposit Full payment in advance. **Discounts** Multiple-night. **Credit Cards** V, MC. **Check-In/Out** 2 p.m./noon; $50 fee for late check-out unless previously arranged. **Smoking** Outside. **Pets** No. **Kids** Over age 12. **No-Nos** N/A **Minimum Stay** None. **Open** All year. **Host** Gloria Cipri Kemer, 18840 Lorain Rd., Fairview Park 44126 **Phone** (440) 333-9100 **Fax** (440) 333-9103 **Email** info@emeraldnecklaceinn.com **Web** www.emeraldnecklaceinn.com

SEPTEMBER FARM, Hiram

OVERALL ★★★★ | QUALITY ★★★★ | VALUE ★★★★ | PRICE RANGE $80–$120

This mother-and-daughter team (Flo's the mom) run a class farmhouse. Kathy spent years developing meals for Lean Cuisine, so she knows her way around a kitchen—and her Macadamia French toast, waffles, and omelets prove it. ("I'm a great chopper," Flo says of her own culinary skills.) Breakfast is served on china, crystal, and silver. Special touches of the house include antique family photos and a phone booth in the dining room. The duo hosts occasional small groups for whole-house rentals.

SETTING & FACILITIES

Location Off Rt. 82 at Hiram. **Near** Hiram College, Amish country, Six Flags over Ohio, Sea World. **Building** 1840s Greek Revival farm house, white exterior. **Grounds** 5 acres w/ gardens, parklike paths, pergola, resident free-range chickens. **Public Space** Parlor, DR, screened porch. **Food & Drink** Full breakfast, often including family's traditional cinnamon coffee cake, "killer lemonade," muffins or scones, entree w/ homemade maple sausage or homemade pepper bacon, & farm-fresh eggs from innkeepers' own chickens. Popcorn, soft drinks any time. **Recreation** Canoeing, biking, shopping from local crafters (quilters, woodworkers, basket weavers), antiquing, golf, amusement parks. **Amenities & Services** Robes provided. Parlor hearth warmed on crisp days; AC.

ACCOMMODATIONS

Units 2 guest rooms, 1 suite. **All Rooms** Hand-sewn quilts on beds. **Some Rooms** Private entrance, TV, stereo. **Bed & Bath** Queen (1), double (2), private bath with suite, guest rooms share bath. **Favorites** Katie's Room, a suite with 1820 four-poster canape bed & sitting room. **Comfort & Decor** Random-planked hardwood floors line the hallways leading to the old-fashioned kitchen, giving the home a real farmhouse feel. Guests in Marie's Room sleep on an 1800 cannonball poster bed, high enough to need a step-stool.

RATES, RESERVATIONS, & RESTRICTIONS

Deposit 1 night's stay with credit card, refundable with 1 week's cancellation notice. **Discounts** Conover workshop students. **Credit Cards** V, MC. **Check-In/Out** 2 p.m./11 a.m., or by prior arrangement. **Smoking** On porch. **Pets** No; innkeepers have outdoor dogs. **Kids** "Not little ones." **No-Nos** N/A **Minimum Stay** None. **Open** All year. **Hosts** Flo & Kathy Klingensmith, 12056 OH 700, Hiram 44234 **Phone** (330) 569-7601 **Fax** (330) 569-7603 **Email** septfarm@apk.net **Web** www.septemberfarm.com

WATER'S EDGE RETREAT, *Kelleys Island*

OVERALL ★★★★½ | QUALITY ★★★★½ | VALUE ★★ | PRICE RANGE $169–$299

Be ready for tranquility when you visit this bed-and-breakfast, because Kelleys Island is a true retreat. A small handful of shops and pubs make up the town of just over 100 permanent residents; people come here to escape and unwind. Leave your car on the mainland and take the ferry or Island Rocket. Water's Edge is a great place to be lazy, far from the madding crowd at Cedar Point, the amusement park barely visible across the bay. Elizabeth and Tim Hermes are warm, unpretentious hosts who love to share hearty food and quality wine, and their tiny dog never barks. A pricey but memorable getaway, with a range of romantic packages available.

SETTING & FACILITIES

Location Kelleys Island in the Lake Erie Islands, a 30-min. ferry or "Island Rocket" ride from Sandusky. **Near** Lake Erie, rocky beach, winery, Glacial Grooves State Memorial. **Building** New (1994) Victorian, painted in Caribbean colors. **Grounds** Flower gardens, gazebo, shoreline deck. **Public Space** Parlor w/ fireplace, DR, wraparound porch, veranda. **Food & Drink** Coffee and iced tea always available, wine and cheese every afternoon, home-baked cookies at check-in. Breakfast is gourmet buffet; ours included homemade croissants, huevos rancheros, and Starbuck's coffee. **Recreation** Lakeside walking, electric cart touring, boat-ing. **Amenities & Services** Massage therapist available; guests can arrange to borrow own-ers' golf carts to go into town for dinner, AC.

ACCOMMODATIONS
Units 3 suites, 3 guest rooms. **All Rooms** Lake Erie view, ceiling fans. **Some Rooms** TV, VCR, Jacuzzi, 2-person Jacuzzi, daybed. **Bed & Bath** All private baths. **Favorites** Jacuzzi Suite, with skylight in bath and bay-view sitting area. **Comfort & Decor** Guests are sur-prised to learn that this Victorian is a new building. Vintage wood treatments give rooms an antique feel. An outdoor whirlpool spa, veranda rockers, and period furniture mix well with modern conveniences.

RATES, RESERVATIONS, & RESTRICTIONS
Deposit Credit card number or 1 night's deposit. **Discounts** N/A **Credit Cards** V, MC. **Check-In/Out** 3–6 p.m./11 a.m. **Smoking** No. **Pets** No. **Kids** Over age 12. **No-Nos** N/A **Minimum Stay** 2 nights on weekends, 3 nights holiday weekends. **Open** All year. **Hosts** Elizabeth & Tim Hermes, 827 East Lakeshore Dr., P.O. Box 839, Kelleys Island 43438 **Phone** (419) 746-2455 **Fax** (419) 746-2411 **Email** Watersedg1@aol.com **Web** www.Waters EdgeRetreat.com

INN AT WILLOW POND, Lisbon

OVERALL ★★★★½ | QUALITY ★★★★½ | VALUE ★★★★★ | PRICE RANGE $95–$105

Once they taste her food, no guest is surprised that Bea Delpapa once ran a cooking school in Cleveland. Chuck is an artist and home furnishings designer, and their great taste shows in their many collections displayed throughout the house. You'll eat breakfast at a replica Irish Wake gate-leg table; outside, birds will dine at one of Bea's many feeders—and if you don't recognize a species, ask Bea, an avid birder who keeps meticulous records. Ask about the inn's weekend artists' and writers' workshops.

SETTING & FACILITIES
Location Off US 30, halfway between Cleveland and Pittsburgh. **Near** Fiesta Ware fac-tory, Beaver Creek State Park, historic Lisbon & Columbiana town centers. **Building** 1865 redwood New England farmhouse. **Grounds** 11 hilly acres w/ large pond, paths, meadow. **Public Space** Common room, DR, LR, TV room, foyer. **Food & Drink** Hibis-cus tea on arrival, wine & cheese in evening. Guests have choice of Mexican or full coun-try breakfast. Ingredients are from "as close to home as possible;" eggs are from free-range chickens down the road, berries & fruits are from local farmers, & salsa is made of tomatoes, tomatillos, & chiles from innkeeper's garden. **Recreation** Antiquing, pottery shopping, exploring historic canals, horseback riding, birding, golf, cross-country skiing. **Amenities & Services** Turn-down service, nighttime chocolates & candlelight, individu-ally controlled AC, fresh flowers in rooms, fax available. (In the above-and-beyond depart-ment: Distressed that we would miss an episode of Survivor if we went to dinner, the innkeeper taped it so we could watch it when we returned.)

ACCOMMODATIONS

Units 3 guest rooms. **All Rooms** Phones, writing tables, arm chairs, logo bath amenities. **Some Rooms** Jacuzzi. **Bed & Bath** King (1), queen (1), 2 twins (1); all private baths. **Favorites** Oaxaca Room with collection of masks over tub. **Comfort & Decor** All rooms are adorned with the innkeepers' Mexican folk art collections, including elaborate dioramas, dolls, many Last Suppers, funerals, baptisms, crêches—all museum-quality. Occasionally, you'll spot a non-Mexican item, such as the signed Peter Max print in the foyer.

RATES, RESERVATIONS, & RESTRICTIONS

Deposit I night's lodging, with full refund if canceling within 7 days of arrival or if room is booked. **Discounts** Midweek, special singles' rates. **Credit Cards** V, MC, D. **Check-In/Out** After 3 p.m. or by arrangement/11a.m. **Smoking** Outside only. **Pets** No; resident cats wander indoors. **Kids** By special arrangement .**Minimum Stay** None. **Open** All year. **Hosts** Chuck & Bea Delpapa, 41932 OH 517, Lisbon 44432 **Phone** (330) 424-4660 **Fax** (330) 424-4661 **Email** wilopond@raex.com **Web** virtualcities.com/oh/willowpond.htm

BLACKFORK INN, Loudonville

OVERALL ★★★★½ | QUALITY ★★★★½ | VALUE ★★★★★ | PRICE RANGE $65–$125

Both the innkeeper and her husband are writers, so the books you see everywhere are an obvious decoration. Blackfork Inn is a house of many personal connections: In one guest room, a photo of Sue's grandmother hangs near a bed; on it lies the coverlet on which the grandmother was born. In the "saloon house" across the road, her Christmas tree stands year-round, decorated not with ornaments but with drying herbs from her garden. ("I tell people to go out and dance in the garden," she says.) The builder was a railroad fan and set his home as close to the tracks as possible; the effect is either loud or charming, depending on your outlook.

SETTING & FACILITIES

Location Southern Ashland County, east of Mansfield and I-71. **Near** Malabar Farm State Park, Mohican State Park, Amish country, Schoenbrunn Village, Loudonville's "Victorian Street." **Building** 1865 French Second Empire, brick w/ ornate wood trim, on National Register of Historic Places, and 1847 former railroad saloon, then Pentecostal church. **Grounds** Two city lots, herb gardens, flower beds. **Public Space** Foyer, parlor, DR, library in Victorian; common room in saloon house. **Food & Drink** Soft drinks available any time; full European-style breakfast includes local fruits in season & local Amish meats & cheeses. Let innkeeper know if you prefer a hot breakfast; specialty is apple pancakes. **Recreation** Antiquing, canoeing, horseback riding, water sports, Amish & historic touring. **Amenities & Services** Robes in rooms, complimentary tickets to movies at Loudonville's restored opera house; massage therapist available; library of classical CDs.

ACCOMMODATIONS

Units 6 guest rooms, 2 suites. **All Rooms** CD player. **Some Rooms** Work desk, sitting area, tubs. **Bed & Bath** Kings (2), queens (2), doubles (4). All private baths. In Victorian house, old-fashioned water closets. **Favorites** Victoria, the largest room. **Comfort &**

Decor Keystone moldings, Moroccan-style arches, and exposed brick add architectural interest. Wall coverings in the parlor are silk, a lavish backdrop for the size-appropriate antiques and floor-to-ceiling windows. Hundreds of books, including an Ohioana library, warm the decor of every room.

RATES, RESERVATIONS, & RESTRICTIONS

Deposit Credit card. **Discounts** Extended stay, corp. rates, special seasonal packages. **Credit Cards** V, MC, D. **Smoking** Outside. **Pets** No. **Kids** Will consider individual requests. **No-Nos** N/A **Minimum Stay** None. **Open** All year. **Host** Sue Gorisek, 303 North Water St., Loudonville 44842 **Phone** (419) 994-3252 **Email** bfinn@ bright.net **Web** www.ohiobba.com/blackforkinn.htm

ELSON INN, Magnolia

OVERALL ★★★★½ | QUALITY ★★★★½ | VALUE ★★★★ | PRICE RANGE $100–$120

There's a story behind every piece in this home; rooms are named after the children who first lived here and decorated with artifacts of their lives. Carved wood cornices, shutters, and chandeliers in the parlor and living room are original, down to the fragile globes. Interior trim is walnut and cherry. If you're not sleeping in Debbie's Room, peek into her 1950s bathroom. Guests eat breakfast in the sunny yellow dining room, seated at great-grandmother's original family table and chairs, and eating with her fine silver.

SETTING & FACILITIES

Location In SE Stark County, between Canton and Carrollton. **Near** Amish country, Zoar Village, Atwood Lake, National Football Hall of Fame. **Building** 1879 Victorian Italianate, white painted brick (3-brick-thick walls), on National Register of Historic Places. **Grounds** Original ornate iron fence, never painted. Residential lot with flower gardens, pond w/ ducks. **Public Space** Parlor, foyer, sitting room, loft library, outdoor garden room, wraparound porch, DR. **Food & Drink** Snacks, soft drinks available any time. Full breakfast includes 2 juices, 2 home-baked muffins, & meat entree. **Recreation** Water sports, historic touring, antiquing. **Amenities & Services** Individually controlled AC & heat, shampoos & bath amenities provided; bicycles & fishing poles available.

ACCOMMODATIONS
Units 4 guest rooms. **All Rooms** Feather bedcovers. **Some Rooms** Fireplace. **Bed & Bath** King (1), queen (2), 2 doubles (1); all private baths. **Favorites** Emma's Room, with king bed, Emma's original Victorian bedroom suit, marble mantel, and Emma's Daughters of the American Revolution membership certificate on display. **Comfort & Decor** Enter through a magnificent ten-foot iron-gate and stained-glass double doors, into the foyer with curved wall. The home was built by the innkeeper's great-grandfather; the family has always lived here, and almost all furnishings are original to the house.

RATES, RESERVATIONS, & RESTRICTIONS
Deposit 1 night's stay with charge card, refundable with 14-day written notice, minus $14 service charge. **Discounts** None. **Credit Cards** V, MC, D. **Check-In/Out** 4–6 p.m./11 a.m. **Smoking** Outside. **Pets** No; "Our ducks would be scared away." **Kids** "Older children are fine." **No-Nos** N/A **Minimum Stay** N/A **Open** All year. **Hosts** Jo Lane & Gus Elson, 225 North Main St., Magnolia 44643 **Phone** (330) 866-9242 or (330) 866-9013 **Fax** (330) 866-1911 **Email** jelson@neo.rr.com **Web** www.elsoninn.com

SPITZER HOUSE, Medina

OVERALL ★★★★ | QUALITY ★★★★½ | VALUE ★★★★★ | PRICE RANGE $65–$125

Janet Rogers collects everything, it seems, and packs it all into her home— jadeite, McCoy cookie jars, vintage doll clothes and linens, even a pinball machine in the upstairs hall. A Longaberger basket collection hangs from beams in the entryway, and "turkey red" embroidered pillow shams are found throughout the house. The inn is presided over by four ghosts, but only three are former residents. The fourth is a mischievous, piano-playing little girl.

SETTING & FACILITIES
Location On Rt. 18, 4 blocks west of Medina center. **Near** Town square, Victorian tea rooms, Montrose shopping area. **Building** 1890 Queen Anne w/ Stick-style design, pastel-painted exterior; on National Register of Historic Places. **Grounds** Victorian garden w/ 1,800 roses; pond. **Public Space** Foyer, parlor, DR. **Food & Drink** Snacks, soft drinks all day. Full breakfast includes entree; specialties include "Little Brown Jug" and banana-walnut pancakes. **Recreation** Antiquing, historic tours. **Amenities & Services** Down comforters, feather beds. Innkeeper sells homemade candles.

ACCOMMODATIONS
Units 4 guest rooms. **All Rooms** AC, sitting area, phone, cable TV, vintage chenille bedspreads. **Some Rooms** Jacuzzi for 2, mood lights, coffee pot, garden view. **Bed & Bath** King (1), queen (3); all private baths. **Favorites** Evalyn's Room with antique Murphy bed & baby-pink double Jacuzzi & waterfall spout. **Comfort & Decor** Santa greets guests year-

round, dressed for the season. This innkeeper's dozens of collections are displayed in antique cupboards and on the home's original cherry mantels. Front doors are cherry with beveled glass.

RATES, RESERVATIONS, & RESTRICTIONS

Deposit 50% or credit card guarantee, refundable with 1 week's advance notice. **Discounts** Long-term (5+ days). **Credit Cards** MC, V, D. **Check-In/Out** 4–6 p.m./11 a.m. **Smoking** No. **Pets** No. **Kids** Over age 12. **No-Nos** N/A **Minimum Stay** None. **Open** All year. **Hosts** Dale & Janet Rogers, 504 West Liberty St., Medina 44256 **Phone** (330) 725-7289 or toll-free (888) 777-1379 **Fax** (330) 725-7289 **Email** spitzer@apk.net **Web** www.victorianinns.com/spitzerhouse

FITZGERALD'S IRISH BED & BREAKFAST, Painesville

OVERALL ★★★★ | QUALITY ★★★★ | VALUE ★★★★★ | PRICE RANGE $80–$90

Everything is Irish in this new (one year old at time of our visit) bed-and-breakfast, from the cuisine, prepared by Tom, to the furnishings. This inn is so near to Lake Erie that migrating birds often pause in the large yard and put on a show for guests watching from the sun porch. The innkeepers, both joggers, purchased the home from its original owners.

SETTING & FACILITIES

Location Painesville's Historic District. **Near** Lake Erie College, Painesville town center, Holden Arboretum, James A. Garfield National Historic Site, wineries, Lake Erie. **Building** 1937 French Tudor w/ turret. **Grounds** Yard w/ flower beds, picnic area. **Public Space** LR, TV room, DR, sun porch. **Food & Drink** Weekend Irish breakfast of 2 eggs, imported rashers/bacon & sausage, cereals, brown bread, potato scones, fresh Danish. Tea & cookies on arrival. Weekdays, breakfast is cont'l deluxe. **Recreation** New, 9-mi. rails to trails path one-eight mile down the street. Wineries, water sports, beaches, fishing, summer concerts in nearby park. **Amenities & Services** AC, logo bath amenities & note pads, note cards w/ photo of inn.

ACCOMMODATIONS

Units 3 guest rooms. **All Rooms** Cable TV, radio. **Some Rooms** Robes provided. **Bed & Bath** Queen (2), double (1). Mayo Room has extra bed. All private baths, 1 detached. **Favorites** Dublin Room, decorated with photos of "Dublin Doors." **Comfort & Decor** Craftsmanship in this 16-room home is evident in the ornate staircase, hardwood floors and 11-foot fireplace. Nearly all furniture is imported from Scotland & Ireland.

RATES, RESERVATIONS, & RESTRICTIONS

Deposit 1 night's stay or 50%, refundable with 2 weeks' cancellation notice. **Discounts** 10% off 5-night stay. **Credit Cards** MC, V, D, AE. **Check-In/Out** 4–8 p.m./11 a.m. **Smoking** On porch. **Pets** No. **Kids** Over age 13. **No-Nos** N/A **Minimum Stay** None. **Open** All year. **Hosts** Tom & Debra Fitzgerald, 47 Mentor Ave., Painesville 44077 **Phone** (440) 639-0845 **Email** fitz@ncweb.com **Web** www.fitzgeraldsbnb.com

HARBOR HILL'S BLACK SQUIRREL INN, *Wooster*

OVERALL ★★★½ | QUALITY ★★★½ | VALUE ★★★★ | PRICE RANGE $65–$75

The innkeepers, both retired professors, own an antiques shop in downtown Wooster, so they've placed interesting pieces in the home. Some of the nicest are a four-poster "pineapple" bed in the McIlvaine Room, a Civil War desk on the first floor, and vintage prints in various rooms. Rather than a lawn, a Victorian cottage garden greets guests in the front yard.

SETTING & FACILITIES
Location Central Wooster. **Near** College of Wooster, Freedlander Theater, Secrest Arboretum, Ohio Agricultural Research Center, Amish country. **Building** 1880 Victorian w/ Gothic side porch. **Grounds** Flower gardens, paths, turtle pond & fountain in backyard—three-quarter acre lot. **Public Space** Parlor, DR, sitting room. **Food & Drink** "We don't serve a healthy breakfast." Eggs, bacon, fresh yogurt muffins, waffles; specialty is "baked eggs in a basket." Soft drinks any time. **Recreation** Ohio Light Opera, antiquing, Amish & historic touring. **Amenities & Services** Zoned AC, bath amenities.

ACCOMMODATIONS
Units 4 guest rooms. **All Rooms** Cable TV, VCR, writing desk, chair(s). **Some Rooms** Double Jacuzzi. **Bed & Bath** King (1), queen (3); all private baths. **Favorites** Brothers Schwartz room w/ Jenny Lind bed & small chaise. **Comfort & Decor** This is not an elegant home, but it's comfortable and well maintained with ten-foot ceilings on the first floor, double parlor with pocket doors, and fireplaces in the sitting and dining rooms.

RATES, RESERVATIONS, & RESTRICTIONS
Deposit Credit card number. **Discounts** 3rd night. **Credit Cards** AE, V, M. **Check-In/Out** "We pride ourselves in not having a check-in and check-out time. You let us know." **Smoking** No. **Pets** Dogs allowed. **Kids** Welcome. **No-Nos** None. **Minimum Stay** N/A **Open** All year. **Hosts** Dan Rider & Ed Schrader, 636 College Ave., Wooster 44691 **Phone** (330) 345-9596 or toll-free (800) 760-1710 **Web** www.bbonline.com/oh/blacksquirrel

MIRABELLE BED & BREAKFAST, *Wooster*

OVERALL ★★★½ | QUALITY ★★★½ | VALUE ★★★★★ | PRICE RANGE $67–$88

The tone at Mirabelle is old world; innkeepers can greet guests in English, German, or Hungarian. They have few family artifacts, but one of the most engaging is the framed collection of counted cross-stitch bouquets, expertly embroidered by Kathy's mother and hanging in the stairwell. The bed-and-breakfast is a project by midlife newlyweds Kathy and Tom, who met in Europe as young adults and reconnected there 25 years later—a storybook romance. Mirabelle is handy, affordable, and incredibly clean lodging for families of Wooster College students.

SETTING & FACILITIES

Location City of Wooster. **Near** Wooster College, Freedlander Theater, Amish country, arboretum. **Building** 1913 Colonial. **Grounds** City lot; flower beds, shrubs. **Public Space** LR/DR, deck, porch, coffee room. **Food & Drink** Coffee, soft drinks all day. Breakfast is "European style"—homemade breads, local meats & cheeses, pastries. **Recreation** Canoeing, skiing, horseback riding, touring cheese & chocolate factories, antiquing. **Amenities & Services** AC; bath gels & shampoos. Coffee delivered to upstairs hallway early morning; breakfast served w/ linens & candlelight, fresh flowers in rooms.

ACCOMMODATIONS

Units 2 guest rooms, 1 suite. **All Rooms** Cable TV/VCR. **Some Rooms** Writing desk, fireplace, sitting area. **Bed & Bath** King (1), queen (1), daybed w/ trundle (1). All private baths. **Favorites** Salzburg Suite w/ bay window & claw-foot tub. **Comfort & Decor** Walls in the public rooms are painted the palest lemon yellow, setting off bookcases and beveled glass. Stuffed chairs in living room make a comfortable space for evening conversation.

RATES, RESERVATIONS, & RESTRICTIONS

Deposit 50%. **Discounts** Off-season & extended-stay rates. **Credit Cards** V, MC, AE, D, DC.. **Check-In/Out** Flexible/noon **Smoking** No. **Pets** No. **Kids** By prior arrangement. **No-Nos** N/A **Minimum Stay** 2 nights during graduation & parents' weekends at Wooster College. **Open** All year. **Hosts** Tom & Kathy Fordos, 1626 Beall Ave., Wooster 44691 **Phone** (330) 264-6006 or toll-free (888) 294-7857 **Email** tkfordos@aol.com **Web** www.bbonline.com/oh/mirabelle

COWGER HOUSE BED & BREAKFAST, Zoar

OVERALL ★★★★ | QUALITY ★★★★ | VALUE ★★★★ | PRICE RANGE $70–$80

The ambience of living in a log cabin is enhanced by the surrounding homes and businesses of historic Zoar Village and by guides in period dress. A cider mill, farm market, dairy, tin shop, and blacksmith shop are among the buildings run by the Historical Society; others are privately operated. Guests at Cowger House (originally the village brewmaster's cabin) eat at 1850 tavern tables in front of a 19th-century fireplace. Try to get an upstairs room; they're much older than the first-floor addition.

SETTING & FACILITIES

Location 3 mi. east of I-77 at Exit 93. **Near** Located at edge of Zoar Village, a "living museum" settled in 1817, now operated by the Ohio Historic Society. **Building** 1817 log cabin. **Grounds** Tiny yard, flower beds. **Public Space** DR. **Food & Drink** Lavish country breakfast w/ eggs, sausage, ham, biscuits. Candlelight dinners also available. **Recreation** Antiquing, historic touring of Zoar Village, canoeing, Amish country touring **Amenities & Services** N/A.

ACCOMMODATIONS

Units 3 guest rooms. **All Rooms** Commode, sink, hand-sewn Amish quilts. **Some Rooms** N/A. **Bed & Bath** King (1), double (2). Full bath (1) shared by all 3 rooms. **Favorites**

Upstairs rooms, circa 1817 (1st-floor room was early 20th-century addition) **Comfort & Decor** The rooms are spacious and, though not particularly luxurious, get four stars for their historic importance. This cabin is true to log-cabin life two centuries ago.

RATES, RESERVATIONS, & RESTRICTIONS

Deposit Total cost of stay; 6% cancellation fee. **Discounts** N/A **Credit Cards** V, M, AE. **Check-In/Out** 5–7 p.m./11 a.m. **Smoking** No. **Pets** No. **Kids** By prior arrangement, for additional cost. **No-Nos** Guests not permitted in kitchen. **Minimum Stay** None. **Open** All year. **Hosts** Ed & Mary Cowger, 197 Fourth St., P.O. Box 527, Zoar 44697 **Phone** (330) 874-3542 or toll-free (800) 874-3542 **Fax** (330) 874-4172 **Web** www.zoarvillage.com

Central Ohio

Driving along Interstate 71, the cornfields seem never-ending—then, suddenly, you're facing a skyline of interesting shapes. Modern architecture found its way to the center of this farmland, where bed-and-breakfasts range from small brick cottages in **German Village** to large Victorians in other historic neighborhoods. Home to **Ohio State University, Columbus** is known for the kind of massive, old homes that fill college towns; most were sacrificed to student housing, but a few were rescued and restored as bed-and-breakfasts.

There is variety in the small towns surrounding Columbus, and in their bed-and-breakfast landscape. **Westerville,** just north of the city, is notable as an upscale yet dry (as in no liquor) town; affluent baby boomers live there, raising their children away from what they see as damaging effects of alcohol.

In the western outskirts of the zone, **Springfield** is a small city whose main attractions are three of the largest antiques malls in the state. To the east, **Newark** and **Dresden** are farm communities, and Newark's bed-and-breakfasts are likely to be restored homes in secluded rural areas, or in historic neighborhoods near **Denison University.** Dresden is famous for the basket-shaped headquarters of the highly collectible Longaberger baskets; its largest bed-and-breakfast, the Inn at Dresden is the former home of founder Dave Longaberger. **Longaberger's Home Office,** we should mention, has been responsible for more than one fender bender along OH 16 because it's such a spectacle: a seven-story replica of a wooden Longaberger basket, complete with handles. Down the road is another landmark, Longaberger Homestead, a seven-building shopping and entertainment center.

Bordering Zone 20 on the east is the city of **Zanesville,** the center of Midwest pottery making. Some of the most collectible pottery was produced in this clay-rich region through the 1950s; today it's the mecca for pottery outlets and festivals, including the annual **McCoy Lovers' Reunion** for collectors of the once ubiquitous and elegant McCoy pieces.

DUM-FORD HOUSE, Amanda

OVERALL ★★★★ | QUALITY ★★★★ | VALUE ★★★★★ | PRICE RANGE $60–$75

The innkeepers value family history; rooms are named after their grand-mothers, and one of the beds is the one the hostess slept in as a child. On the stairway landing, notice the carpet remnant displayed on the wall: it was a piece of carpet from the old Ohio Senate chambers, with the state outlined on it. The gardens are impressive; they are Ms. Ford's passion and designed to attract butterflies, hummingbirds, and other friendly visitors.

SETTING & FACILITIES

Location Rt. 22, just west of Lancaster. **Near** Hocking Hills, Lancaster Historic District, Circleville. **Building** 1845 Federal-style home, brick. **Grounds** Large lot w/ sculpted flower beds, gardens w/ miniature waterfall. **Public Space** Parlor, DR, patio, courtyard. **Food & Drink** Soda, fresh-baked cookies in afternoon. Full breakfast, including entree. **Recreation** Antiquing, Circleville Pumpkin Festival, canoeing, picnicking, golf, fishing **Amenities & Services** AC, logo bath amenities. Fresh flowers in room; massage or special-occasion gifts can be arranged.

ACCOMMODATIONS

Units 1 guest room, 1 suite. **All Rooms** Sitting area. **Some Rooms** Garden view. **Bed & Bath** Queen (1), double (1), both private baths. **Favorites** Lucianna, the suite with sitting room, brass bed. **Comfort & Decor** Slatted wood transoms on first floor match spindles on stairway. Some rooms have original poplar and American cherry plank floors; others feature exposed brick and wainscoting.

RATES, RESERVATIONS, & RESTRICTIONS

Deposit 50%, refundable with 10-day cancellation notice. **Discounts** 10% for extended stays. **Credit Cards** V, MC. **Check-In/Out** 3–6 p.m./11 a.m. **Smoking** Outside. **Pets** No (owner has a dog). **Kids** By arrangement. **No-Nos** N/A **Minimum Stay** 2 nights on holidays. **Open** All year. **Host** Anna Ford, 123 West Main St., P.O. Box 496, Amanda 43102 **Phone** (740) 969-3010 **Email** dum-fordbb@buckeyenet.net **Web** www.dum-fordbb.com

HARRISON HOUSE BED & BREAKFAST, Columbus

OVERALL ★★★★ | QUALITY ★★★★ | VALUE ★★★★ | PRICE RANGE $109 ($169 IF TAKING OVERFLOW ROOM ALSO)

Although Innkeeper Davis adds touches of elegance, such as candlelight breakfast and crisply ironed sheets, she notes that her guests—mostly business travelers and parents of OSU students—don't care about such extras as logo soaps. Her bed-and-breakfast isn't the destination; Columbus is—though she's delighted when guests notice such details as the Waterford crystal chandelier in the dining room.

SETTING & FACILITIES

Location In Victorian Village, a National Historic District, off I-71 in the city. **Near** Ohio State Univ., Olentangy River, downtown Columbus, German Village, Columbus Zoo, Center of Science & Industry. **Building** 1890 Queen Anne Victorian, on National Register of Historic Places. **Grounds** City lot, flower beds. **Public Space** Parlor, DR, porch. **Food & Drink** Full breakfast w/ hot entree & meat. **Recreation** Galleries, museums, canoeing, kayaking, historic touring, zoo. **Amenities & Services** AC.

ACCOMMODATIONS

Units 4 guest rooms & overflow room for extra guest. **All Rooms** TV, clock radio, private phone line, desk & chair. **Some Rooms** N/A **Bed & Bath** Queens (5). 4 private baths; overflow room shares a bath. **Favorites** Christmas Room, w/ loveseat alcove and extensive Santa collection. **Comfort & Decor** In this bed-and-breakfast, quality antiques mix well with stuffed contemporary chairs and couches. It's designed for business travelers, though some special features do stand out: multiple-pane transoms, oak woodwork in an Eastlake leaf pattern, beveled-glass windows—especially the front door window.

RATES, RESERVATIONS, & RESTRICTIONS

Deposit Credit card number. **Discounts** None. **Credit Cards** V, MC, D, AE. **Check-In/Out** 1 p.m. or by arrangement/11 a.m. **Smoking** On porch. **Pets** No. **Kids** No, "we can only put two people in a room." **No-Nos** Candles. **Minimum Stay** 2 nights during OSU home football games, 6 weekends/yr. **Open** All year. **Host** Sandy Davis, 313 West 5th Ave., Columbus 43201 **Phone** (614) 421-2202 or toll-free (800) 827-4203 **Web** www.columbus-bed-breakfast.com

LA GRANDE FLORA, Columbus

OVERALL ★★★★ | QUALITY ★★★★ | VALUE ★★★★★ | PRICE RANGE $80–$90

This home is so white-and-gold Victorian that one almost needs a parasol to complete the romantic image. The lighted newel post is a bronze Cupid and Psyche, and the 8-foot-wide entry hall ends (28 feet later) at a gold-trimmed fireplace. In the dining room, the ceiling is artfully papered, set off by an art glass chandelier. The guest rooms are more restful. The decor may be a bit much for some tastes, but we liked the effect—and we're glad someone is preserving high Victorian traditions. Be sure to see the library, with Davis's ruby glass collection and artifacts from her world travels.

SETTING & FACILITIES

Location In Bryden Road Historic District, off I-71 in the city. **Near** Ohio State Univ., Olentangy River, downtown Columbus, German Village, Columbus Zoo, Center of Science and Industry. **Building** 1903 brick Colonial Revival. **Grounds** City lot w/ English gardens & statuary. **Public Space** Pillared front & side porches, foyer, library, parlor, DR, "garden room" loft sitting area. **Food & Drink** Afternoon snacks. Formal, high Victorian breakfast using china & silver includes a cold buffet, hot entree, & 2 hot meats. **Recreation** Galleries, museums, canoeing, kayaking, historic touring, zoo. **Amenities & Services** AC.

Hair dryers in rooms; can accommodate showers, weddings, & parties to 75 guests, meetings to 15 participants, and high Victorian teas.

ACCOMMODATIONS

Units 3 guest rooms. **All Rooms** Phone w/ separate phone line, fridge, microwave, coffeemaker, TV/VCR, fireplace, table & chairs, clock radio. **Some Rooms** Canopy bed, claw-foot tub, tin cove ceilings. **Bed & Bath** Queens (2), double (1). All private baths. **Favorites** Master Suite, w/ bed alcove, sitting room, large wood fireplace. **Comfort & Decor** There's so much to see in this most Victorian bed-and-breakfast, it can be a bit overwhelming. Some things, such as the arch dividers in the foyer, the Empire-style fireplace in the parlor, and the beveled-glass windows and carved oak fireplace in the dining room, are original. The foyer chandelier, though, is innkeeper Nancy Davis's design, as is the garden loft with lattice, fountain, and other veranda touches.

RATES, RESERVATIONS, & RESTRICTIONS

Deposit Credit card number or 50% of stay. **Discounts** None. **Credit Cards** V, MC, AE. **Check-In/Out** By individual arrangement. **Smoking** No. **Pets** Inquire (2 resident cats, dog). **Kids** Inquire. **No-Nos** N/A **Minimum Stay** None. **Open** All year. **Hosts** Nancy E. Davis & Ronald L. Demming, 820 Bryden Rd., Columbus 43205 **Phone** (614) 251-0262 or toll-free (800) 251-2588 **Fax** (614) 252-7693 **Web** www.bbonline.com/oh/flora

WHITE OAK INN, Danville

OVERALL ★★★★ | QUALITY ★★★★ | VALUE ★★★★ | PRICE RANGE $80–$130

Tranquility sets the tone at White Oak Inn. Whether you curl up with a mystery in front of the common room hearth or settle into an oak rocker on the front porch, you're likely to see no one all day but other guests. Warm, Amish-built wood furnishings throughout the inn are beautifully crafted, but need a few antiques shop "finds" or family artifacts to accent them and lend a more homey touch.

SETTING & FACILITIES

Location Off Rt. 62, near Mount Vernon. **Near** Kokosing Gap Trail, Amish country, Roscoe Village, Siberian Tiger Foundation, Longaberger Basket Company. **Building** 1915 country inn, white exterior. **Grounds** 15 acres of rolling hills & woodland, populated by deer & wild turkey. Across the road is a 1-mile walking path alongside a small river. A screened shelter house is available for special events. **Public Space** Common room, DR, porch. **Food & Drink** Soft drinks any time. Full breakfast includes egg entree & fresh-baked muffins. **Recreation** Historic touring of Roscoe Village (restored 1830s Erie Canal town w/ reenactments), Amish country touring, Longaberger touring & shopping, bicycling, canoeing, fishing, golf. **Amenities & Services** AC, logo bath amenities, hair dryer.

ACCOMMODATIONS

Units 10 guest rooms. **All Rooms** Ceiling fan, clock radio, ironing board. **Some Rooms** Bay windows, Victorian furniture, fireplace, double Jacuzzi. **Bed & Bath** Queens (7), queen & twin (1), doubles (2); all private baths. **Favorites** White Oak Room, spacious, w/ forest view, antique glass-shade lamps, double Jacuzzi, working fireplace. **Comfort & Decor** Each room is named for the wood it's furnished in. Flooring is the original white oak, and decor in most inn rooms is modernized early American.

RATES, RESERVATIONS, & RESTRICTIONS

Deposit Full amount, refundable up to 14 days before date of visit, 30 days for groups reserving 3 or more rooms, minus $10 cancellation fee. **Discounts** N/A **Credit Cards** V, MC, D, AE. **Check-In/Out** 3–9 p.m./11 a.m. **Smoking** Outside & on porches. **Pets** No; innkeepers have large dog. **Kids** Over age 12, by prior arrangement. **No-Nos** N/A **Minimum Stay** 2 nights most weekends & holidays. **Open** All year. **Hosts** Ian & Yvonne Martin, 29683 Walhonding Rd. (OH 715), Danville 43014 **Phone** (740) 599-6107 **Email** yvonne@ecr.net **Web** www.whiteoakinn.com

INN AT DRESDEN, Dresden

OVERALL ★★★★ | QUALITY ★★★★ | VALUE ★★★★ | PRICE RANGE $85–$165

You won't believe the hill you have to climb to reach this inn, perched high above the town of Dresden. If your car makes it (tour buses usually don't), have a glass of wine on the deck and enjoy the view; it's terrific from any angle. Chances are your inn-mates will be Longaberger collectors—for them, staying in Dave's former home is worshiping at the altar. This is an ideal getaway spot for pottery and basket shoppers.

SETTING & FACILITIES

Location Off OH 60 between Coshocton & Zanesville. **Near** Dresden, Longaberger Basket Company, Roscoe Village, pottery outlets, Amish country, wineries. **Building** 1980 Tudor, former home of Dave Longaberger (creator of Longaberger baskets). **Grounds** Hilltop lot, lawns. **Public Space** DR, veranda, social room, 2-level deck **Food & Drink** Nonalcoholic beverage on arrival, wine & cheese social hour in evening, full buffet breakfast. **Recreation** Touring Longaberger factory, pottery shopping, touring Roscoe Village (restored Erie Canal village), golf, touring Amish country. **Amenities & Services** Bath amenities, meeting room for 14 people; fax machine & copier available during business hours.

ACCOMMODATIONS

Units 4 suites, 6 guest rooms. **All Rooms** Cable TV, VCR, phone, modem hook-up, workstation, alarm clock, CD player. **Some Rooms** Wet bar, private deck, kitchenette, fridge, fireplace. **Bed & Bath** King beds (4), 2 queens (1), queen (4), 2 twins (1). All private baths, Jacuzzi (2), double Jacuzzi (5), claw-foot tub (1). **Favorites** Dresden suite, w/ gas-log fireplace, king Victorian bed, deck. **Comfort & Decor** Each room is decorated differently. The looks vary from the very contemporary City Lights suite to the Dresden, which was Dave Longaberger's room and features his half-round desk.

RATES, RESERVATIONS, & RESTRICTIONS

Deposit 50% of stay. **Discounts** 10% for AAA and AARP members; "we work with tour groups." **Credit Cards** V, MC, D, AE. **Check-In/Out** 3 p.m./11 a.m. **Smoking** On balconies. **Pets** No. **Kids** Yes. **No-Nos** N/A **Minimum Stay** N/A **Open** All year. **Hosts** Patricia Lyall & Karen Knisley, 209 Ames Ave., Dresden 43821 **Phone** (749) 754-1122 or toll-free (800) dresden **Fax** (740) 754-9856 (call first) **Email** info@theinnatdresden.com **Web** www.theinnatdresden.com

RUSSELL COOPER HOUSE, Mount Vernon

OVERALL ★★★★½ | QUALITY ★★★★½ | VALUE ★★★★★ | PRICE RANGE WEEKDAYS $65, WEEKENDS $85–$100

Respecting this home is a family affair: innkeeper Mary Dvorak's ancestors have owned it since 1856. She works to keep such features as the dining room's marble-top servers, plank flooring, tin ceiling, and Bradbury and Bradbury wall coverings in pristine condition. Cherry fretwork on the first floor is original, as are the chandelier, fireplace with frieze, and beveled-glass windows in the library—"the most authentic of the rooms," Dvorak says. The family also owns cherry orchards in Michigan, and she sells their jams and other cherry products, along with Amish baskets and other items in her small gift shop area.

SETTING & FACILITIES

Location Off Rt. 13/Main St. in residential Mount Vernon. **Near** Amish country, Mohican State Park, Malabar Farm, Roscoe Village, Mid-Ohio Raceway. **Building** 1829 low Victorian mansion, on National Register of Historic Places. **Grounds** Oversized city lot w /lawns, flower gardens, hot tub. **Public Space** Foyer, sun room, library, DR, "party room." **Food & Drink** Complimentary evening cordials. Full candlelight gourmet breakfast may include signature havarti dill baked eggs. Lunch & dinner served to the public. **Recreation** Antiquing, historic & Amish touring, canoeing, biking, birding, swimming, spectator car racing. **Amenities & Services** AC. Logo bath amenities; hosts parties to 44 guests. Fax, copies, & express mail can be arranged.

ACCOMMODATIONS

Units 6 guest rooms. **All Rooms** Ceiling fan, sitting area. **Some Rooms** TV, fireplace, desk & chair. **Bed & Bath** Queens (2), double & twin (1), doubles (3). All private baths. **Favorites** Colonel's Room, w/ sunny front exposure, decorated w/ family artifacts. **Comfort & Decor** History holds a place of honor here, and much is on display. We loved the Civil War campaign chair in the foyer, near the extensive collection of historical Russell Cooper and Civil War memorabilia, including antique medical devices and rare books. Elegance is added with classic etched and stained-glass windows, rich cherry trim, ornate Eastlake front doors, and marble fireplaces.

RATES, RESERVATIONS, & RESTRICTIONS

Deposit Credit card number. **Discounts** Single, corp., off-season. **Credit Cards** V, MC, AE. **Check-In/Out** 3 p.m./10 a.m. **Smoking** No. **Pets** No. **Kids** Over age 12. **No-Nos** N/A **Minimum Stay** 2 nights during Oct. & select weekends. **Open** All year. **Host** Mary Dvorak, 115 East Gambier St., Mount Vernon 43050 **Phone** (740) 397-8638 **Email** maryd@russell-cooper.com **Web** www.russell-cooper.com

PITZER-COOPER HOUSE, Newark

OVERALL ★★★★½ | QUALITY ★★★★½ | VALUE ★★★★ | PRICE RANGE $85–$125

In such a quiet, rural setting, it's easy to imagine yourself in a simpler time, when women really did make their own candles (as Teresa Cooper does) and colonial homes were decorated with elegant simplicity. Only the second owners, the Coopers saved the house, which had not been painted for 50 years (ask to see the before photos). Period light fixtures were custom-made for several rooms; among original features are the colored glass at the front door and the old clanger doorbell.

SETTING & FACILITIES

Location 5 mi. north of I-70, 30 min. east of Columbus. **Near** Dawes Arboretum, historic Granville, Hopewell Indian Mounds, National Heisey Glass Museum. **Building** 1858 Greek Revival farm house w/ Italianate elements, on National Register of Historic Places. **Grounds** 10 acres w/ large vegetable, herb, & perennial gardens. **Public Space** Entryway, parlor, DR, TV/VCR room. **Food & Drink** Juices, soda any time; full breakfast including home-baked breads. **Recreation** Historic touring, museums, biking, canoeing, birding, antiquing. **Amenities & Services** AC. Logo bath amenities; innkeeper makes her own soaps, scented w/ herbs from her garden. Robes, hair dryers in rooms; fax machine available.

ACCOMMODATIONS

Units 1 suite, 1 guest room. **All Rooms** Irons. **Some Rooms** Sitting room. **Bed & Bath** Queen beds (2), all private baths. **Favorites** Melissa Suite—sunny, spacious, sleeps 4 with pull-out sofa. **Comfort & Decor** Original oak flooring downstairs, plus original windows and cherry staircase, creak to let you know you're in a very old home, impeccably restored. Antique glass was used to replace any broken panes during the restoration, and woodwork was painted to be historically accurate.

RATES, RESERVATIONS, & RESTRICTIONS

Deposit I night's stay or credit card, refundable w/ 7 days' cancellation notice minus 10% cancellation fee. **Discounts** Free night after 10 nights; any referrals you make are credited toward that total. **Credit Cards** MC, V, D, AE. **Check-In/Out** 4:30 p.m./11 a.m. **Smoking** Outside.. **Pets** No **Kids** Yes. **No-Nos** Alcohol. **Minimum Stay** 2 nights if staying Fri. **Open** All year. **Hosts** Joe & Teresa Cooper, 6019 White Chapel Rd. SE, Newark 43056 **Phone** (740) 323-2680 or toll-free (800) 833-9536 **Fax** (740) 323-3157 **Email** mail@pitzercooper.com **Web** www.pitzercooper.com

COLLEGE INN BED & BREAKFAST, Westerville

OVERALL ★★★★½ | QUALITY ★★★★½ | VALUE ★★★★ | PRICE RANGE $95–$115

Everything about College Inn—from the sisal rugs and bamboo palm trees to the West Indies artwork and soft, cotton lap robes—beckons guests to pause and relax. Rohrer loves pampering guests—"I don't think people pamper themselves enough," she says, "especially travelers." She'll give you a back scratcher, a down comforter, and, if your eyes are tired, an ice pack—and that's after she picks you up at the airport, so you don't have to bother with a taxi. Westerville is a dry town (in the mid-1800s, the Anti-Saloon League was headquartered here), so she encourages guests to bring a bottle if they like wine before dinner.

SETTING & FACILITIES

Location Near Westerville town center, off I-270 (Columbus bypass). **Near** Westerville shopping, Otterbein College, Columbus Convention Center, German village, Columbus Zoo, Ohio State Univ., Ohio State fairgrounds, Anti-Saloon League Museum. **Building** 1878 brick Victorian. **Grounds** City lot—flower gardens, patio. **Public Space** 2nd-floor TV lounge w/ VCR, cable, movies; LR, DR, library. **Food & Drink** Full breakfast, including fresh-baked breads. Soft drinks any time; evening snacks—popcorn, fresh-baked cookies, or chips & salsa. **Recreation** Antiquing, biking, shopping. **Amenities & Services** AC, feather or hypo-allergenic pillows, dry cleaning, massage therapist or psychic on request, use of bicycles, ironing & unpacking services on request.

ACCOMMODATIONS

Units 4 guest rooms. **All Rooms** Phone, modem hookup, seating area. **Some Rooms** N/A **Bed & Bath** Queens (4), all private baths, extra-firm double-pillowtop mattresses. **Favorites** Front room w/ large, sunny, 2-window bath & armchairs, decorated w/ a shabby chic touch. **Comfort & Decor** Innkeeper Rohrer is a fan of homeopathic health, and the rooms reflect her calm, peaceful approach to business and life. Sheets are line-dried, ironed crisp, and stored with a lavender sachet. Dining room decor takes on a Caribbean tone; somehow it fits well with the home's original mantel, floor-to-ceiling windows, and majestic archway pocket doors.

RATES, RESERVATIONS, & RESTRICTIONS

Deposit Credit card number. **Discounts** Corp., senior, long-term stay. **Credit Cards** MC, V, D **Check-In/Out** 3 p.m./noon, both flexible. **Smoking** Outside. **Pets** With notice, if well behaved, but must be small & stay in cages. **Kids** With notice, must be well behaved. **No-Nos** N/A **Minimum Stay** Only on special weekends, such as Otterbein's graduation. **Open** All year. **Host** Becky Rohrer, 63 West College Ave., Westerville 43081 **Phone** (614) 794-3090 or toll-free (888) 794-3090 **Fax** (614) 895-9337 **Email** ClBnB@aol.com **Web** www.bbonline.com/oh/collegeinn

Southwest Ohio

There's no single way to characterize **Cincinnati.** Its historic mansions, some of which became bed-and-breakfasts, are among the most elegant we visited across the Midwest. Its **Museum of Art** gained notoriety as the naughty bastion of freedom of expression more than a decade ago, when the Supreme Court refused to shut down a suggestive photography exhibit, yet this seemingly progressive city experienced racial unrest as recently as 2000.

Built on seven hills, Cincinnati is another city of distinct neighborhoods—our favorite might be **Mount Adams,** where the streets are so narrow they're barely negotiable and nearly every building is a shotgun-skinny townhouse. It's a trendy area of edgy art galleries and nouveau cuisine eateries. In contrast, the **Hyde Park** neighborhood, where most of the city's bed-and-breakfasts reside, is elegant in a more traditional, Victorian way. As for touring, the most productive stop is the **Museum Center,** where the **History Museum, Museum of Natural History and Science, Children's Museum,** and **Omnimax Theater** share the same complex. For lunch or dinner, try the **Rookwood Pottery Restaurant,** overlooking the **Cincinnati Art Museum** and **Krohn Conservatory,** where you'll be seated in the old kilns once used for firing the now-rare vases and bowls.

Most of the other bed-and-breakfasts in Zone 21 are farm houses—that is, if you can call the stylized barn at Murphin Ridge a farmhouse. True, it sits on rural acreage, but there the resemblance ends; its cottages and barn are new and opulent, and its art festivals draw city slickers from all over the state.

Northwest of Cincinnati, **Wilmington** offers a variety of bed-and-breakfasts, from farms to renovated carriages houses. At Yesterday Again Bed & Breakfast, your lodging is also a shopping opportunity if you come on a warm-weather holiday, when the innkeepers stage a community flea market. In **Chillicothe,** the biggest attraction was the inn we profiled, Greenhouse Bed and Breakfast, with more collections—covering walls, stuffed into cabinets, inching away from the walls like ground cover—than any-place we'd ever seen.

GREENHOUSE BED & BREAKFAST, Chillicothe

OVERALL ★★★★½ | QUALITY ★★★★½ | VALUE ★★★★★ | PRICE RANGE $80–$90

As fine as Dee's breakfast is (and it is a feast), sitting down to breakfast interrupts one's snooping. These innkeepers collect everything, it seems, from spatter ware to antique match holders, children's cast-iron stoves, and old photographs. Kids' kitchen items hold a special place in Dee's heart, and they're stacked on shelves and cupboards in nearly every room. Ask for a tour of the kitchen and butler's pantry, where hundreds of miniature graniteware pieces are displayed.

SETTING & FACILITIES

Location Off Rt. 23, central Chillicothe. **Near** Epic outdoor drama Tecumseh, Hopewell Culture National Historic Park, Pump House Art Gallery, theaters, Ross County Museum. **Building** 1894 Queen Anne, green exterior, surrounded by original iron gate. **Grounds** Residential lot w/ flower gardens, elaborate playhouse "for the grandbabies." **Public Space** Library, DR, parlor, foyer, porch. **Food & Drink** Soft drinks any time. Full breakfast w/ fruit topped by sour cream & sugar, entree, breakfast meats. **Recreation** Historic touring, canoeing, fishing, golf, theater. **Amenities & Services** AC, logo bath amenities. All rooms are unusually spacious.

ACCOMMODATIONS

Units 4 guest rooms. **All Rooms** Cable TV, clock radio. **Some Rooms** Original bath fixtures, marble sinks. **Bed & Bath** King (1), queens (3). All private baths. **Favorites** Master bedroom, w/ largest bath, graniteware collection along chair rail, child's serving set in miniature oak hutch. **Comfort & Decor** This home is sumptuous, from the Italian sandstone mantel and quarter-sawed oak in the parlor to the cherry alcove off the kitchen, the cherry paneling in the dining room and awesome stained glass in the library—all set off by beautiful inlaid wood floors.

RATES, RESERVATIONS, & RESTRICTIONS

Deposit N/A **Discounts** Long-term stay, by prior arrangement. **Credit Cards** MC, V. **Check-In/Out** 3 p.m./11 a.m. **Smoking** On porch. **Pets** No (owner's cat stays outside at all times). **Kids** Yes. **Minimum Stay** N/A **No-Nos** N/A **Open** All year. **Hosts** Tom & Dee Shoemaker, 47 East 5th St., Chillicothe 45601 **Phone** (614) 775-5313 or toll-free (877) 398-0600 **Web** www.chillicotheohio.com/thegreenhouse

VICTORIA INN OF HYDE PARK, Cincinnati

OVERALL ★★★★½ | QUALITY ★★★★½ | VALUE ★★★ | PRICE RANGE $99–$189

Catering to business travelers comes naturally to Tom Possert, a long-distance runner who travels worldwide to compete in marathons and Iron Man contests. A former engineer, Possert wanted to be his own boss and fell in love with this home and its leaded glass, original brass hardware, pocket doors, and the lighted Mercury topping the newel post. Guests are invited to join him for a scenic running tour of the affluent Hyde Park neighborhood. More independent types are treated to a complimentary workout at the Cincinnati Sports Club.

SETTING & FACILITIES

Location Hyde Park neighborhood, central Cincinnati. **Near** Hyde Park Square, Ault Park gardens, riverfront, Mt. Adams, Cincinnati Art Museum. **Building** 1909 brick, Tudor features. **Grounds** Flower gardens, deck, pool. **Public Space** Foyer, parlor, DR, sitting room. **Food & Drink** Coffee early; complimentary soft drinks, yogurt, fruit any time. Full breakfast including fresh-baked bread, scones. **Recreation** Shopping, pro football & baseball, jogging, galleries. **Amenities & Services** AC, robes in room, hair dryers, fax machine & copier available.

ACCOMMODATIONS

Units 3 guest rooms, 1 suite. **All Rooms** Phone, cable TV, desk, sitting area. **Some Rooms** Fireplace, whirlpool, sitting room. **Bed & Bath** Queens (3), double (1), all feather beds. All private baths. **Favorites** Country Manor Room w/ 1840s bed and private, screened sleeping porch overlooking pool. **Comfort & Decor** When Possert restored his home in the early 1990s, the work was recognized by *Better Homes & Gardens*. The Victorian Suite showcases an 1880s Victorian Eastlake bed; on the way, notice the huge stained-glass window at the landing.

RATES, RESERVATIONS, & RESTRICTIONS

Deposit Credit card number; refundable w/ 2 weeks' notice for weekend stays, 48 hrs. notice weekdays. **Discounts** AAA, corp. **Credit Cards** V, MC, AE. **Check-In/Out** Flexible. **Smoking** No. **Pets** No. **Kids** No. **No-Nos** N/A **Minimum Stay** 2 nights on weekends. **Open** All yea.r **Host** Tom Possert, 3567 Shaw Ave., Cincinnati 45208 **Phone** (513) 321-3567 or toll-free (888) 422-4629 **Fax** (513) 533-2944

MT. ADAMS BED & BREAKFAST, Cincinnati

OVERALL ★★★½ | QUALITY ★★★½ | VALUE ★★ | PRICE RANGE $155–$165

"This is a neighborhood for grown-ups," Dellecave says, explaining his policy of discouraging guests with kids. He's right; lined with art galleries, pubs, specialty shops, and upscale restaurants, historic Mt. Adams is a great area for adult strolling. Just five minutes from downtown Cincinnati, Mt. Adams perches high above the city. At the time of our visit, this bed-and-breakfast had been open less than a year.

SETTING & FACILITIES
Location Mt. Adams neighborhood, Cincinnati. **Near** Cincinnati Art Museum, Eden Park, Krohn Conservatory, Playhouse in the Park, Mirror Lake. **Building** 1883 Shotgun row house **Grounds** Small lot; fenced garden & patio in rear. **Public Space** Living room w/ big-screen TV, VCR; sitting room. **Food & Drink** Breakfast served at restaurant next door—full breakfast weekends, cont'l weekdays, or Sun. brunch. Coffee bar in sitting room. **Recreation** Historic touring, fine arts, bicycling, remarkable overlook in Eden Park. **Amenities & Services** AC, oversized hot tub outside, gas log fire pit, central air cleaner.

ACCOMMODATIONS
Units 2 suites. **All Rooms** Cable TV, VCR, movie library, compact fridge, CD/tape player, private phone line w/ cordless phone, voicemail, fax/copier. **Some Rooms** Private deck, gas log see-through fireplace, gas log stove, spiral staircase, Jacuzzi, cathedral ceiling **Bed & Bath** King (1), queen (1); all private baths. **Favorites** Hemingway Suite, with oversized (13' x 10') bathroom & loft study. **Comfort & Decor** Every convenience is provided for guests, from auxiliary AC to humidifier and security lighting. It's not glamorous, but it works, especially for business travelers.

RATES, RESERVATIONS, & RESTRICTIONS
Deposit 1 night's stay, refundable w/ 5 days' notice. **Discounts** N/A **Credit Cards** V, MC, D, AE. **Check-In/Out** 3–8 p.m./11 a.m. **Smoking** No. **Pets** No. **Kids** No. **No-Nos** N/A **Minimum Stay** None. **Open** All year. **Host** Mike Dellecave, 1107 Belvedere St., Cincinnati 45202 **Phone** (513) 651-4449 or toll-free (888) 233-8770 **Email** dellecave@ fuse.net **Web** http://www.travelguides.com/inns/full/OH/7062.html

GUNCKEL HERITAGE BED & BREAKFAST, Germantown

OVERALL ★★★★½ | QUALITY ★★★★½ | VALUE ★★★★ | PRICE RANGE $80–$125

It's all in the family at this bed-and-breakfast—at long last. Built by innkeeper Bonnie's fourth great-grandfather Philip Gunckel for his daughter, Elizabeth, more than 175 years ago, the home changed hands several times before Bonnie and her husband bought it in 1996. Guests receive discount dinner coupons to the nearby Florentine Hotel (Ohio's second oldest hotel) and the Peerless Mill Inn. This is a romantic inn but not at all overdone, and kids get a warm welcome: the smaller dining room is filled with games and toys.

SETTING & FACILITIES

Location In Germantown's center, 9 mi. west of I-75. **Near** Dayton Art Institute, Air Force Museum, Kings Island Amusement Park, Cox Arboretum Metropark, 3 flea markets. **Building** 1826 brick Victorian Italianate, listed on National Register of Historic Places. **Grounds** Landscaped yard, 2 patios, hammock. **Public Space** Front-to-back foyer, DR, second DR, game room, parlor. **Food & Drink** Complimentary soda, wine, salty snacks, ice cream sundae bar. Full, gourmet candlelight breakfast. **Recreation** Antiquing, dinner theater, biking, swimming, golf, historic touring. **Amenities & Services** Room service on request, logo bath amenities, AC, newspaper, hair dryers, irons/ironing boards, special-occasion baskets on request.

ACCOMMODATIONS

Units 3 guest rooms. **All Rooms** Coffee pot, cable TV/VCR, video library, fridge, sitting area, table. **Some Rooms** Fireplace, sofa bed, claw-foot tub, private covered balcony. **Bed & Bath** Queen feather bed (2), double w/ pillowtop mattress (1); all private baths. **Favorites** Koogle Room with antique Queen Ann bed & fireplace. **Comfort & Decor** Restored to remarkably good condition, this home is warmed by six working fireplaces and features original plank floors, original shutters and such rare antiques as the Bible bench in the living room.

RATES, RESERVATIONS, & RESTRICTIONS

Deposit $50 or credit card. **Discounts** 10% for 3 days' stay or longer. **Credit Cards** V, MC, D. **Check-In/Out** 3–5 p.m. (flexible)/11 a.m. **Smoking** On porches and balcony only. **Pets** No. **Kids** Yes. **No-Nos** N/A **Minimum Stay** None. **Open** All year. **Hosts** Lynn & Bonnie (Gunckel) Koogle, 33 West Market St., Germantown 45327 **Phone** (937) 855-3508 or toll-free (877) 855-3508 **Email** gunckelheritage@aol.com **Web** www.gunckelheritage.com

ROSSVILLE INN, Hamilton

OVERALL ★★★★½ | QUALITY ★★★★½ | VALUE ★★★★★ | PRICE RANGE $90–$100

This bed-and-breakfast's history is as interesting as it gets. It began innocently enough as an affluent businessman's home. In the 1920s it was a juvenile detention center for boys, and during World War II it was a day-care center for "Rosie the Riveter"—women factory workers. Then, until the 1960s, it was a brothel—none of which is in evidence today. In the parlor, notice the unusual "winged" mantel.

SETTING & FACILITIES

Location Hamilton's Rossville Historic District, 30 min. from Cincinnati. **Near** Miami Univ., Hueston Woods State Park, Pyramid Hill Sculpture Park & Arboretum, Fitton Center. **Building** 1859 Greek Revival brick, white exterior. **Grounds** Pergola, brick patio, porch, elaborate flower gardens & plantings, including more than 100 varieties of hosta in backyard. **Public Space** DR, billiards room, parlor. **Food & Drink** Welcome cheese & crackers on arrival, chocolates & home-baked cookie in room, complimentary soda, beer, & wine. Full breakfast includes homemade rolls or pastry and entree w/ meat. **Recreation** Canoeing, biking, fine arts, historical home touring. **Amenities & Services** Reading lights over beds, robes provided.

ACCOMMODATIONS
Units 3 guest rooms. **All Rooms** Cable TV, phone, writing desk, computer/fax hookup, 2 phone lines. **Some Rooms** Jacuzzi, fold-out bed, sitting area. **Bed & Bath** King (1), queen (1), 2 twins (1; can be converted to king). All private baths. **Favorites** Manor Room, w/ king four-poster rice bed, crewel-covered armchairs, & Jacuzzi **Comfort & Decor** Much was retained in restoring this Greek Revival with 11.5' ceilings. Upstairs, original pine flooring survived (the first floor was destroyed in a 1913 flood); Federal-style transoms, and decorative woodwork survived downstairs.

RATES, RESERVATIONS, & RESTRICTIONS
Deposit 1 night's stay. **Discounts** Whole-house, business, & extended-stay rates. **Credit Cards** V, MC, D, AE. **Check-In/Out** 4–6 p.m./11 a.m. **Smoking** Outside. **Pets** No; owners have a large, friendly dog. "If people need a pet fix, they can take Marla for a walk," says innkeeper Bill Groth. **Kids** Yes. **No-Nos** N/A **Minimum Stay** 2 nights on major Miami Univ. weekends, such as graduation. **Open** All year. **Hosts** Bill & Jackie Groth, 117 South B St., Hamilton 45013 **Phone** (513) 868-1984 or toll-free (888) 892-0871 **Fax** (513) 863-5502 **Email** RossvilleInn@NRCI.com **Web** www.ohiobba.com/rossvilleinn.htm

MURPHIN RIDGE INN, West Union

OVERALL ★★★★ | QUALITY ★★★★★ | VALUE ★★★★ | PRICE RANGE $90–$200

The innkeepers' sense of style is apparent in the modernistic design of the guest room building; not surprisingly, one of the gift shops is an art gallery showcasing local artists' work. Their property also includes a corn crib, fire pit, smoke house, and, inside the barn, a standing 1808 log cabin that eventually will be restored as a small conference center. The McKenneys know people work on the road; all rooms but one contain a writing desk and all offer a selection of books. If you're lucky, Chef Renee will make her to-die-for brownies when you visit.

SETTING & FACILITIES

Location Off Rt. 41 between Columbus & Cincinnati. **Near** Amish country, Appalachian Highlands, Serpent Mound. **Building** Main structure is 1820s brick farm house. Guest rooms are in a new "stylized barn"–style inn; 3 cabins also available. **Grounds** 142 isolated acres of woodland, meadows, herb & vegetable gardens, a new "bird blind" and 8.5 mi. of walking trails. A working farm growing corn, winter wheat, & soybeans. **Public Space** Foyer, DR, Chicken Wing DR (so called for its chicken decor), 2 gift shops, common room (w/ the only TV on the property). **Food & Drink** Snack, soft drinks available evenings. For breakfast, "nothing is frozen food or from mixes;" includes homemade granola, entrees such as multigrain pancakes w/ homemade applesauce, or the specialty, "Farmer's scramble." Innkeepers make their own jellies, jams, and possibly the finest butter pickles on the planet. **Recreation** Swimming, tennis, shuffleboard, basketball, horseshoes, croquet, birding, Amish & historic interests. **Amenities & Services** Dinners available Wed.–Sat. nights. Pool, tennis courts, massage available, Amish baking classes, Appalachian weekends. Special events include Sept. Arts Fair, Chef's Table weekends, and chocolate weekends (Nov.–May, last week of each month). Gift baskets available

ACCOMMODATIONS

Units 10 guest rooms, 3 new cabins. **All Rooms** Phone, data port, clock radio. **Some Rooms** Robes, coffeemaker, love seat, ceiling fan, porch, fireplace, skylight. Cabins feature kitchenette, CD player, recessed reading lights, double Jacuzzi, sitting area w/ recliners. **Bed & Bath** Queens (11), 2 queens (2). **Favorites** Any cabin; the quietude is wonderfully soothing. **Comfort & Decor** Rooms are tastefully austere: "We want people to use the outdoors," says innkeeper Darryl McKenney. Furnishings were handcrafted by a local master builder. In the Chicken Wing dining room, innkeepers display their collection of Bennington & Rockingham pottery.

RATES, RESERVATIONS, & RESTRICTIONS

Deposit $50 or credit card. **Discounts** Winter specials. **Credit Cards** V, MC. **Check-In/Out** 3 p.m./11 a.m. **Smoking** In designated areas; guest rooms & cabins are nonsmoking. **Pets** No. **Kids** Yes. **No-Nos** N/A **Minimum Stay** 2 nights weekends. **Open** All year, except closed first 2 weeks of January. **Hosts** Sherry & Darryl McKenney, 750 Murphin Ridge Rd., West Union 45693 **Phone** (937) 544-2263 or toll-free (877) 687-7446 **Fax** (937) 544-8151 **Email** Murphinn@bright.net **Web** www.murphinridgeinn.com

---

CEDAR HILL BED & BREAKFAST, Wilmington

OVERALL ★★★½ | QUALITY ★★★★ | VALUE ★★★★ | PRICE RANGE $85–$95

Once you step inside your room, you would never know you were standing in a generations-old carriage house. The walls, floors, and furnishings mimic a ten-year-old building. Set back at least a quarter-mile from the road, Cedar Hill can be a true forest getaway; guests are encouraged to bring groceries and cook in their rooms if they like, rather than driving into town for meals. If you hear what seems like dozens of little creatures thundering across the roof and skylight, don't be alarmed—it's the hickory trees shedding their nuts.

SETTING & FACILITIES

Location OH 73 outside Wilmington, 3 mi. from I-71. **Near** Fort Ancient State Park, Little Miami Bike Trail, Wilmington, Little Miami River. **Building** Converted carriage house **Grounds** 10 acres of woodland, walking paths. **Public Space** Gathering room. **Food & Drink** Soft drinks, coffee, home-baked cookies always available. Breakfast includes fresh fruit & entree such as puff pancakes. **Recreation** Antiquing, canoeing, biking, horseback riding, golf. **Amenities & Services** Fresh flowers, chocolates, coffeemaker in room, hammock. Gathering room can be rented for meetings.

ACCOMMODATIONS

Units 2 guest rooms, 1 suite. **All Rooms** Cable TV/VCR, kitchenette, writing table & chairs, sitting area, stovetop. **Some Rooms** Extra sleeping area, private porch. **Bed & Bath** Queen (2), 2 queens (1); all private baths. **Favorites** Cedar Room—spacious, larger seating area, 2 beds. **Comfort & Decor** Modernized Shaker is the style, rustic but with all the conveniences.

RATES, RESERVATIONS, & RESTRICTIONS

Deposit 1 night's stay, refundable with 7 days' cancellation notice. **Discounts** Corp. & group rates. **Credit Cards** V, MC, D. **Check-In/Out** 4–6 p.m. or by arrangement/11 a.m. **Smoking** Outside, "if you're careful." **Pets** No. **Kids** Usually over age 12. "We're more lenient if they book all three rooms." **No-Nos** N/A **Minimum Stay** None. **Open** All year. **Hosts** Rick & Joan McCarren, 4003 OH 73, Wilmington 45177 **Phone** (937) 383-2525 or toll-free (877) 722-2525 **Fax** (937) 383-2525 **Email** cedarhillbb@hotmail.com **Web** www.ohiobba.com/cedarhill.htm

YESTERDAY AGAIN BED & BREAKFAST, Wilmington

OVERALL ★★★★ | QUALITY ★★★★ | VALUE ★★★★ | PRICE RANGE $125–$225 (FOR LOWER LEVEL SUITE, IN PROGRESS)

These innkeepers have thought of everything: if you feel like shopping for antiques but don't want to drive far, you can visit the gift shop in their 1836 barn. On Memorial Day, July 4, and Labor Day they hold a community yard sale on the farm—good dates for flea marketers to visit. This bed-and-breakfast feels like home, due in large part to the warm hospitality extended by the Davises; guests leave feeling more like friends than customers. Judy is a nurse—a nurturer both by trade and by personality.

SETTING & FACILITIES

Location On US 68, 2 miles from I-71. **Near** Wilmington, Wright-Patterson Air Force Base, outlet malls. **Building** 1823 farmhouse, white exterior. **Grounds** 22 acres w/ walking paths, original farm buildings. **Public Space** Foyer, LR, DR, back sun room, porch, deck. **Food & Drink** Hot/cold beverages, snacks all day; full breakfast (from menu) includes entrees and meat. **Recreation** Antiquing, golf courses, horseshoes, sand volley-ball, croquet. **Amenities & Service** Coffee served upstairs before breakfast. AC, hot tub, swimming pool. Robes provided; logo bath amenities. Fridge & microwave in upstairs hall.

ACCOMMODATIONS

Units 3 guest rooms. **All Rooms** AC, cable TV, VCR, clock radio, hair dryer. **Some Rooms** Pasture view. New suite will offer whirlpool tub & fireplace. **Bed & Bath** K (2), queen (1). All private baths. **Favorites** Country Pleasures, w/ king brass bed & 1950s linoleum. **Comfort & Decor** Inviting, sprawling front porch leads to rooms with original painted plank flooring and rooms furnished with chairs and artifacts from innkeepers' grandparents. New suite will feature private entrance, exposed stone and brick, joists made of trees, and barn siding that dates from 1836.

RATES, RESERVATIONS, & RESTRICTIONS

Deposit Card or 1 night's stay, refunded w/ 72 hrs. notice. **Discounts** Active military, corp., whole-house rates available.. **Credit Cards** V, MC, AE, D **Smoking** Outside only, but it's discouraged: "There's not one building on the farm that could be replaced," says innkeeper Judy Kirchner-Davis. **Pets** No. **Kids** By prior arrangement. **No-Nos** Bottles in pool area. **Minimum Stay** 2 nights on weekends & holidays. **Open** All year. **Hosts** Skip Davis & Judy Kirchner-Davis, 3556 US 68 North, Wilmington 45177 **Phone** (937) 382-0472 or toll-free (800) 382-0472 **Fax** (937) 382-7867 **Email** info@yesterdayagain.com **Web** www.yesterdayagain.com

Southeast Ohio

Calling **Marietta** a just historic river town is like referring to Frank Sinatra as just a singer. Settled in the 1780s by George Washington's pals—their payment, in this country's cash-poor infancy, for military services—it quickly became the Ohio River's primary trade center and a major gateway to the new frontier.

As a result of having been settled by the country's elite, Marietta boasts more square miles of historic homes than any city in the country, and, smack in the middle of a residential neighborhood, the cemetery with the most Revolutionary War soldiers' graves in the United States. Not surprisingly, the bed-and-breakfasts here are largely historic properties.

While in Marietta, history buffs will find no shortage of museums, including railroad museums, the **Ohio River Museum,** and the public library's Genealogy Department, used by visitors from across the land to trace their family histories. You might also catch a musical on the showboat *Becky Thatcher.* We would consider a special trip just to shop again at **Rossi Pasta,** the local pasta factory and maker of gourmet mustards, oils, and sauces.

Away from the river you'll find **Athens,** home of **Ohio University,** and the area known as **Hocking Hills.** This is Ohio's hilly region, and it's full of caves and cabins. Much of the zone is taken up by **Wayne National Forest;** people come to these parts for canoeing, horseback riding, and, in the fall, leaf peeping.

Much of the lodging in Zone 22 is located in secluded cabins and hunting and fishing lodges. There are notable exceptions: Laurel Brook Farm offers both creaky farm house rooms and new whirlpool suites. The Inn at Cedar Falls is both rustic and elegant, offering gourmet candlelight dinners and romantic cottages. Ravenwood Castle, on an isolated hilltop outside **New Plymouth,** is a true original, with creative medieval-themed suites equipped with fireplaces and whirlpools.

ALBANY HOUSE, Albany

OVERALL ★★★½ | QUALITY ★★★½ | VALUE ★★★ | PRICE RANGE $75–$150

The most inviting room in the house is the heated pool area with working fireplace, showers, and lots of wicker furniture poolside. Features of the house include original red oak floors, mahogany banister, transoms, and exposed brick. Resident cat is permitted indoors; innkeepers will "work with" guests' allergies to make their stay comfortable. About 65% of guests are Ohio University professors and students' parents.

SETTING & FACILITIES
Location West of Rt. 50, 10 min. from Athens. **Near** Ohio Univ., Lake Snowden, Hocking College, Hocking Valley Scenic Railroad. **Building** 1850s Greek Revival, white exterior. **Grounds** City lot, flower beds. **Public Space** Parlor, LR w/ TV & VCR, DR, indoor pool, changing room, small patio, porch. **Food & Drink** Bottled water any time, evening snacks; cont'l breakfast (eggs & breakfast meat served weekends). **Recreation** Swimming, fishing, hiking, scenic train rides, antiquing, hunting. **Amenities & Services** Robes in rooms, AC.

ACCOMMODATIONS
Units 4 guest rooms, 2 suites. **All Rooms** Ceiling fans. **Some Rooms** TV. **Bed & Bath** Queens (4), doubles (2), extra twin (1); 4 private baths, 1 shared. **Favorites** "Apartment" for extended stays, w/ TV, balcony, fridge, breakfast bar, couch. **Comfort & Decor** Rooms are decorated with quilts and other family heirlooms. The home has a "rough" feel and could use some updating and polishing.

RATES, RESERVATIONS, & RESTRICTIONS
Deposit Half the cost of visit, refundable 7 days before visit if canceling **Discounts** None **Credit Cards** No; cash or check only. **Check-In/Out** 4–9 p.m./11 a.m. **Smoking** Outside. **Pets** No; resident cat allowed indoors. **Kids** Over age 8. **No-Nos** N/A **Minimum Stay** 2 nights on special Ohio Univ. weekends, such as graduation & parents' weekends. **Open** All yea.r **Hosts** Ted & Sally Hutchins, 9 Clinton St., Albany 45710 **Phone** (740) 598-6311 or toll-free (888) 212-8163

MISTY MEADOW FARM BED & BREAKFAST, Cambridge

OVERALL ★★★★ | QUALITY ★★★½ | VALUE ★★ | PRICE RANGE $130–$190

You can't go wrong with 150 acres of blossoming apple trees, dense forest, and hilltop meadows just made for watching beautiful sunsets. Every guest should walk to see the beautiful artesian spring-fed pond, and the "Sound of Music hill" up the drive. The owners build a bonfire every night, and romantic picnic dinners, including champagne, can be arranged.

SETTING & FACILITIES
Location Off OH 22, first road east of I-77. **Near** Salt Fork, Roscoe Village, Longaberger Basket Company, "Wilds" International Animal Preserve, Living Word Outdoor Drama.

Building Circa-1930 ranch house. **Grounds** 150 acres includes stocked pond, fruit orchard, ravines, woods, trails. Cottage on property is 120 years old. **Public Space** DR, Octagon Room, large deck, patio, above-ground pool, outdoor spa. **Food & Drink** Fresh-baked chocolate chip cookies. Full 4-course breakfast includes trademark "Misty" fruit drink, home-baked coffee cake, entree. **Recreation** Antiquing, fishing, swimming, rigorous hiking trails on property, historic touring. **Amenities & Services** Robes & fresh flowers in rooms, AC, hay rides available; also fax service, dinners.

ACCOMMODATIONS

Units 3 guest rooms, 1 cottage. **All Rooms** Desk or table. **Some Rooms** N/A. **Bed & Bath** Queens (3); all private baths. Cottage has 1 queen, 2 doubles, bath & fully equipped kitchen. **Favorites** Theatrical Room, decorated w/ photos & artifacts of innkeeper Vicki's mother, who was an entertainer. **Comfort & Decor** Rooms are individually decorated, and each has a desk or table with chairs. In the cottage is a TV, wood-burning fireplace, and privacy deck with a hot tub.

RATES, RESERVATIONS, & RESTRICTIONS

Deposit $50 for each night of stay. **Discounts** None. **Credit Cards** V, MC, D. **Check-In/Out** 3–8 p.m./11 a.m. **Smoking** Outside. **Pets** No; resident dog & 3 cats are permitted indoors. **Kids** Over age 14. **No-Nos** Riding resident horses. **Minimum Stay** 2 nights in the cottage, none in guest rooms. **Open** All year, except Christmas Eve & Christmas. **Hosts** Jim & Vicki Goudy, 64878 Slaughter Hill Rd., Cambridge 43725 **Phone** (740) 439-5135 **Fax** (740) 439-5408 **Email** misty@cambridgeoh.com **Web** www.mistymeadow.com

INN AT CEDAR FALLS, Logan

OVERALL ★★★★½ | QUALITY ★★★★½ | VALUE ★★★★ | PRICE RANGE $75–$120; CABINS $125–$265

Ellen Grinsfelder is continuing the dream she started with her mother: an inn that brings nature to people, but with elegance. There are no phones, TVs, or radios in rooms, but the furnishings are fine antiques—a balance is achieved. Classes and special weekend events include guest chef weekends, star-gazing sessions with an expert during meteor showers, and classes in infused oils, where the students' first task is to pick their own herbs. No inn is perfect—it seems petty to charge guests for a bottle of water—but it's still a beguiling place, and the multilevel cabins are awesome getaway spots.

SETTING & FACILITIES

Location Off OH 664 between Rts. 33 & 56. **Near** Hocking Hills State Parks, Ash Cave, Cedar Falls, Cantwell Cliffs, Hocking River, Buckeye Trail. **Building** 1840s double log house (w/ later additions); renovated 19th-century cabins; new barnlike inn. **Grounds** 60 acres of woodlands, trails, meadows, organic vegetable garden, flower gardens, herb garden. **Public Space** Common room in barn, DR, patio dining, 2 common rooms in log building, porches. **Food & Drink** Stocked fridge in barn (coffee & tea complimentary, charge for bottled water & soda). Cookie in room; can order gourmet box lunch or dinner or have dinner in DR. Full breakfast includes homemade granola & entree. **Recreation** Birding, canoeing, caving, biking, cross-country skiing, fishing, golf, horseback riding. **Amenities & Services** Logo bath amenities, large gift shop. Hosts business meetings, nature hikes, cooking classes, massages.

ACCOMMODATIONS

Units 9 guest rooms, 5 cabins. **All Rooms** Books in rooms, writing desks, chairs. **Some Rooms** Cabins have decks w/ porch swings, cooking facilities, gas log stoves, double whirlpool. Some are handicap accessible. **Bed & Bath** Queen (13), 2 twins (1). **Favorites** Tree House Cabin in the woods, with double whirlpool tub, double shower, 2 decks, large living room, couches. **Comfort & Decor** Rooms mix a rustic/practical style with touches of shabby chic. The antique quilt hanging in the barn's common room is extraordinary.

RATES, RESERVATIONS, & RESTRICTIONS

Deposit Credit card. **Discounts** Midweek except in Oct., winter, AARP (10%), midweek AAA (10%). **Credit Cards** V, MC. **Check-In/Out** After 3 p.m./11 a.m. **Smoking** 2 smoking rooms; cabins & DR smoke-free. **Pets** No. **Kids** Welcome in cabins. **No-Nos** No phones or TVs in rooms. Inn has a liquor license, so guests can't bring liquor to meals. **Minimum Stay** 2 nights weekends. **Open** All year, but no food served Christmas Eve night or Christmas Day. **Hosts** Ellen Grinsfelder, 21190 OH 374, Logan 43138 **Phone** (740) 385-7489 or toll-free (800) 65-falls **Fax** (740) 385-0820 **Email** innatcedarfalls@hocking hills.com **Web** www.innatcedarfalls.com

LAUREL BROOK FARM, Logan

OVERALL ★★★½ | QUALITY ★★★½ | VALUE ★★★ | PRICE RANGE $90

An atmosphere of hearty, healthy country living is the aim of these innkeepers, who use all-natural materials—no plastics—as much as possible. Ten campers at a time can pitch their tents at Laurel Brook's farm for

$25 a tent; firewood is supplied and breakfast at the bed-and-breakfast is optional. The new carriage house units will offer skylights, Jacuzzis, oak floors, and private decks. Resident dogs and cats are permitted indoors.

SETTING & FACILITIES

Location 5 mi. outside Logan. **Near** Hocking Hills State Parks. **Building** Late 1880s farmhouse, nestled under a wooded hillside. **Grounds** 56 acres are a working farm w/ cattle, tree plantation, hay crops, stocked fishing pond, river walk, & 10-acre wildlife sanctuary. **Public Space** TV room, DR, patio, small foyer, 2nd-floor library/common room. **Food & Drink** Unusually good coffee, tea, raspberry iced tea made from the farm's spring-fed well water. Full breakfast includes organically grown brown eggs, low-processed meats from a local butcher, & seasonal entrees such as asparagus quiches in spring. **Recreation** Fishing, boating, camping, biking, canoeing, cross-country skiing, birding, hunting. **Amenities & Services** Refrigerator, microwave in common room, AC, hair dryers. Jan.–March, soup supper included in price of room for guests booking 2 nights or longer.

ACCOMMODATIONS

Units 2 guest rooms, 2 carriage house suites in progress. Also sleeping loft for overflow w/ kids; king mattress. **All Rooms** TV, VCR, Direct TV, CD/stereo. **Some Rooms** Extra twin bed. **Bed & Bath** King (2), both private baths. **Favorites** Hattie's Room w/ 2 beds, spacious bath. **Comfort & Decor** This is a farmhouse that creaks, feels, and looks like your grandma's farmhouse, complete with quilts thrown over couches and cattle grazing in the pasture. Original plank flooring and bull's-eye molding mark the inelegant but comfortable interior.

RATES, RESERVATIONS, & RESTRICTIONS

Deposit Credit card. **Discounts** None **Credit Cards** V, MC. **Check-In/Out** 3 p.m. (flexible)/flexible check-out. **Smoking** Only on porch. **Pets** "If they don't tear things up or bark all night"; one-time $15 fee/each pet. **Kids** Yes, including infants. **No-Nos** Keg parties. **Minimum Stay** None, but charge extra if only reserving for 1 night on weekend. **Open** All year. **Hosts** Robert & Cynthia Burris, 31345 Ansel Rd., Logan 43138 **Phone** (740) 569-4229 or toll-free (800) 578-4279 **Email** cynthia@laurelbrookfarm.com **Web** www.laurel-brookfarm.com

CLAIRE E, Marietta

OVERALL ★★½ | QUALITY ★★½ | VALUE ★★★ | PRICE RANGE $80

Think Huck Finn. The adventure begins as you step from the riverbank onto a floating wooden platform, then pull a rope hand over hand to position the platform next to the boat and climb aboard without falling into the drink. One needs to keep an open mind in places such as the *Claire E.*—it is, after all, the only bed-and-breakfast anywhere located on a diesel-powered sternwheeler (we think), and it's listed on the National Register of Historic Maritime Vessels. So ignore the diesel fumes, which are powerful, until the boat is aired out. You're safe—the boat doesn't move when occupied.

SETTING & FACILITIES
Location On the Ohio River—literally. **Near** Marietta, Fenton Art Glass Factory, Marietta College, Becky Thatcher Theater, Historic Harmar Village. **Building** 1926 diesel-powered sternwheeler boat. **Grounds** N/A **Public Space** Small DR, sitting room. **Food & Drink** Full breakfast includes entree & breakfast meat. **Recreation** Antiquing, visiting Marietta historic attractions. **Amenities & Services** N/A.

ACCOMMODATIONS
Units 1 guest room, 1 suite. **All Rooms** AC. **Some Rooms** N/A. **Bed & Bath** Doubles (2), 2 bunks (1). **Favorites** Upper deck "suite" w/ 2 rooms, better view of river. **Comfort & Decor** Walls display rare old photos of Marietta history. Furniture once belonged to "people from old Marietta."

RATES, RESERVATIONS, & RESTRICTIONS
Deposit Credit card. **Discounts** None. **Credit Cards** V, MC. **Check-In/Out** After 3 p.m./10 a.m. **Smoking** No. **Pets** Discouraged. **Kids** Yes. **No-Nos** N/A **Minimum Stay** N/A **Open** All year, except when owner is cruising on *Claire E.* for his vacation. **Host** Harley Noland, c/o Levee House Cafe, 127 Ohio St., Marietta 45750 **Phone** (740) 374-2233

HOUSE ON HARMAR HILL, *Marietta*

OVERALL ★★★★½ | QUALITY ★★★★½ | VALUE ★★★★★ | PRICE RANGE $68–$82

This gorgeous mansion gets the prize for the best porch view in Ohio. In spring, a large magnolia tree shades the veranda. Indoors, the best spot is the unique turret sitting room; one can easily imagine the whispers and stolen kisses that happened here. The innkeepers run such a polished inn that we were there for hours before we learned they had just opened for business a few months earlier. Even the shared bath is a relatively painless experience; the room is bigger than most living rooms. Don't leave without seeing Doug's collection of antique razors.

SETTING & FACILITIES

Location High atop Harmar Hill, overlooking the Ohio River and city of Marietta. **Near** Fenton Art Glass Factory, historic Harmar Village, Marietta College, Lee Middleton Doll Factory, Becky Thatcher Theater. **Building** 1901 Queen Anne Victorian, pale yellow exterior (w/ porch painted sun-dried tomato red). **Grounds** City lot, flower beds, shrubs **Public Space** Foyer, parlor, DR, sitting room, turret room w/ sitting area, set off by Corinthian columns, porch. **Food & Drink** Fruit, snacks, soda, coffee, & tea available all day; wine & cheese Sat. 5–7 p.m. Full breakfast includes fresh-baked breads, entree such as mushroom quiche. **Recreation** Historic touring, theater, museums, golf, antiquing. **Amenities & Services** Fresh flowers in room, modem port, fax service available, robes, coffee in upstairs hall before breakfast, logo bath amenities.

ACCOMMODATIONS

Units 4 guest rooms. **All Rooms** Pocket doors, AC, robes. **Some Rooms** Telescope, beveled-glass window, built-in glass fronted cabinets. **Bed & Bath** King (1), queens (2), double (1). 2 private baths, 1 shared. One features original Indiana marble sink, 2 have claw-foot tubs. **Favorites** The Custer Room (named for the home's second owners, descendants of Gen. George Custer) in turret w/ telescope and view of the city. **Comfort & Decor** The magnificent wood mantels, dentil molding, tower archway, and acorn finials on the grand staircase, were carved by two brothers who built caskets. The front parlor is Victorian formal, with a curved-glass cabinet and velvet settee and chairs, whereas the back sitting room is more casual with contemporary furniture.

RATES, RESERVATIONS, & RESTRICTIONS

Deposit Credit card number; $10 fee for cancellation within 24 hrs. of visit. **Discounts** None. **Credit Cards** V, MC, AE. **Check-In/Out** 4–8 p.m./11 a.m. **Smoking** On porch. **Pets** No; resident cats come indoors but dander level is negligible. **Kids** By prior arrangement. **No-Nos** N/A **Minimum Stay** N/A **Open** All year. **Hosts** Judy & Doug Grize, 300 Bellevue St., Marietta 45750 **Phone** (740) 374-5451 or toll-free (877) 914-5451 **Fax** (740) 374-5078

OUTBACK INN, McConnelsville

OVERALL ★★★★½ | QUALITY ★★★★½ | VALUE ★★★★★ | PRICE RANGE $65–$70

Your talented and ebullient hosts are authors, radio entertainers, and community activists, so they always have good stories to make guests feel at home. The original oak woodwork and marvelous collections throughout the house add to the appeal; there's great browsing to be done here. Start with Bob's collection of parrot art in the Roadside Room, and work up to the collections of Art Deco compacts, and the complete set of silent star tins in the living room. As we went to print, the Belfances had just announced an essay contest in which the grand prize was their inn. Guests may find new innkeepers when they next visit Outback Inn—or, if they write the best essay, they could be the new owners! The entry fee is $100 for each 500-word essay, and the Belfances encourage multiple entries. For details, visit the web site or phone (800) 542-7171.

SETTING & FACILITIES

Location Central McConnelsville, off Rt. 60. **Near** The Wilds game preserve, 1890 Opera House. **Building** 1870 Federalist home. **Grounds** Fenced back yard. **Public Space** Porch, patio, LR, foyer, DR. **Food & Drink** Soft drinks all day. Full breakfast includes fresh-baked mini-muffins and entree; specialties are Carol's apple puff-pancakes & Bob's ham & cheese morning strata. **Recreation** Hunting, fishing, historic touring, antiquing. **Amenities & Services** AC. TV in living room.

ACCOMMODATIONS

Units 3 guest rooms. **All Rooms** Radio, antique lamps. **Some Rooms** Desk, private entrance. **Bed & Bath** Queen (1), double (1), 2 twins (1). **Favorites** Hooray for Hollywood, w/ an 8-piece Art Deco bedroom suite of ebony, walnut, & chrome, and a collection of early movie art & photography. **Comfort & Decor** Art Deco rules in this house, where graceful Deco lamps and furnishings are found in nearly every room. Stained glass is nearly as ubiquitous. An early 1900s gas fireplace warms the living room.

RATES, RESERVATIONS, & RESTRICTIONS

Deposit 50% of stay, refundable up to 7 days before visit. **Discounts** Sun.–Thurs. and single occupancy. **Credit Cards** No; cash and check only. **Check-In/Out** 4–6 p.m./11 a.m. **Smoking** No. **Pets** No.. **Kids** Teens by arrangement **No-Nos** N/A **Minimum Stay** None. **Open** All year. **Hosts** Carol & Bob Belfance , 171 East Union Ave., McConnelsville 43756 **Phone** (740) 962-2158 or toll-free (800) 542-7171 **Fax** (740) 962-4824 **Email** carolbob@dragonbbs.com **Web** www.theoutbackinnbandb.com

RAVENWOOD CASTLE, New Plymouth

OVERALL ★★★★½ | QUALITY ★★★★½ | VALUE ★★ | PRICE RANGE $105–$195 IN CASTLE; $159–$275 FOR COTTAGES

I didn't want to like this place, but it's so well done, and so much fun, I couldn't help myself. The medieval decor is done just right, and the individually decorated cottages, designed to mimic the sort of small village that once surrounded castles, are creatively planned, including a merchant's, woodcutter's, and silversmith's cottage. The extra-high window in Rapunzel's Tower is a clever touch.

SETTING & FACILITIES

Location Off OH 56, 20 mi. from Athens. **Near** Hocking Hills State Park. **Building** 1995 replica 12th-century castle. **Grounds** 115 acres, half undeveloped, with 2.5 mi. of hiking trails and gardens. **Public Space** Great Hall/DR, game room/pub, library (w/ castle's only TV & VCR), gift shops. Tea room is open for lunch 4 days/wk. **Food & Drink** Full breakfast includes entree. Lunch & theme dinners available. **Recreation** Birding, antiquing, fishing, canoeing, biking. **Amenities & Services** AC, logo bath amenities. Inn has beer/wine license.

ACCOMMODATIONS

Units 8 guest rooms, 5 cottages. (Ravenwood also offers a Gypsy Cottage deep in the woods, and 5 vintage summer camp cottages with Celtic legends–themed decor, not part of the B&B.) **All Rooms** Fireplace w/ gas insert, stained-glass windows, ceiling fans. **Some Rooms** Whirlpool tub, deck, porch; cottages have kitchenette w/ microwave, fridge, & coffeemaker, TV/VCR, porch or deck. **Bed & Bath** Kings (2), queens (4), doubles (2); all private baths. Cottages have king (3) & queen (2) beds. **Favorites** Sherwood Forest Room, w/ Robin Hood aiming his bow & arrow from behind a lit tree—clever effect; a great room for families. **Comfort & Decor** The spirit of Ivanhoe lives on in this hilltop castle. Guests enter through Gothic arches. The stained glass windows in the Great Hall are from a church in Nelsonville, and windows are protected with shutters—as they would have been in the 12th century.

RATES, RESERVATIONS, & RESTRICTIONS

Deposit 1 night's payment, refundable with more than 1 week's notice. **Discounts** Week-night specials, kids free in June, other specials. **Credit Cards** V, MC, D. **Check-In/Out** 4 p.m. (flexible)/11 a.m. or so. **Smoking** No. **Pets** No (owners have dogs and outdoor cats). **Kids** Yes, over age 10. **No-Nos** "No drinking guest's own liquor in public areas." **Minimum Stay** 2 nights on weekends or by arrangement. **Open** All year. **Hosts** Jim & Sue Maxwell, 65666 Bethel Rd., New Plymouth 45654 **Phone** (740) 596-2606 or toll-free (800) 477-1541 **Fax** (740) 596-5818 **Web** www.ravenwoodcastle.com

Wisconsin

You don't have to be a cheese-head to appreciate the uniqueness of Wisconsin. From the **St. Croix River,** across the vast Northwoods forests along the **Great Divide Scenic Highway** to the **Lake Michigan Circle Tour** on the opposite shore, Wisconsin's tourism motto beckons: "Stay just a little bit longer."

The wilderness here is habitat for black bear, timberwolves, and whitetail deer. The lakes, swamps, and bogs—all accessible by the state's scenic highways—teem with beaver, loons, and bald eagles. You can drive the entire state, from the **Apostle Islands National Lakeshore** on Wisconsin's northern tip to **Milwaukee's breweries** in the south, following the same two-lane road almost the entire trip.

Oh, yes, about driving in Wisconsin. Prepare for confusion and exasperation as you try to find your destination. Apparently, the people who named Wisconsin's roads didn't know enough words and numbers, so you will find, in addition to those conventionally numbered and named, roads called "A," "B," C," and so forth. It gets better: when they ran out of letters, they doubled up: "AA," "BB," and "CC." And wait, there's even more. The letter-numbering format is for county roads—so when you cross the line into the next county, it starts all over again—and Route CC in the new county is not related to Route CC in the county you just left.

If you can get past the chaotic road names, you will find one of the greenest, most pristine states in the country. Zone 23 starts along the **Mississippi and St. Croix Rivers,** lined with historic river towns, and ends at the magnificent Apostle Islands of Lake Superior. Wisconsin is a fairly flat state, and especially in the interior, sports such as biking, snowshoeing, cross-country skiing, and snowmobiling are popular everywhere.

Zone 24 takes us through thick forests to the opposite shore and the famous **Door County** peninsula, full of tourists, orchards, and fishing towns, and offering some of Wisconsin's grandest Victorian bed-and-breakfasts. Down in Zone 3, the state's hilliest region, we're back on the Mississippi, anchored by **Prairie du Chien** on the western edge and state capital/college town Madison on the east. Finally, we make our way east through the lakeland resort towns across Zone 4, dominated by Milwaukee. At that point, we're in the Chicago–Milwaukee traffic corridor. Happy driving!

FOR MORE INFORMATION

Wisconsin Department of Tourism

P.O. Box 7976,

Madison, WI 53707-7976

(608) 266-7621

www.travelwisconsin.com

Wisconsin Bed and Breakfast Association

108 S. Cleveland Street

Merrill, WI 54452

(715) 539-WBBA

www.wbba.org

Northwest Wisconsin

"Over the river and through the woods," that describes northern Wisconsin. Well, most of it anyway. In this densely wooded region, you find such events as the American Birkebeiner cross-country ski race between **Hayward** and **Cable** and the nation's largest off-road bicycle race at the **Chequamegon Fat Tire Festival.** Fishing, hunting, birding, and scouting for arrowheads are popular pastimes.

Through the rugged interior of this zone, bed-and-breakfasts tend to be fishing lodges and rustic lakeside cabins. Even the comparatively luxurious Otter Creek Inn, sitting on a highway in **Eau Claire,** has a woody, Northwoods tone. One of Wisconsin's most prosperous lumber towns in the 1800s, Eau Claire is a good place for cyclists to explore riverside biking trails.

But Zone 23 isn't entirely timberlands. The western ridge of the zone follows the **Mississippi and St. Croix Rivers** through affluent, progressive towns that almost mirror their counterparts across the river in Minnesota. Hudson especially calls us back, with its fine mansions-turned–bed-and-breakfasts and a lively Caribbean restaurant we hope is still there when we return. **Prescott,** where the rivers meet, is worth a stop, both for a stay at Arbor Inn and for the downtown overlook, where the line delineating the blue waters of the St. Croix and the muddy waters of **Big Muddy** is clearly visible.

At the northern tip of the state, the forests end at the banks of **Lake Superior.** Ferries carry visitors to the **Apostle Islands,** a group of 22 tiny islands dotted with lighthouses, sea caves, hiking trails, and blue-water sailing. The main towns in this area are **Ashland,** a historic fishing town, and Bayfield, more touristy but pleasant nonetheless. Bed-and-breakfasts here are a small microcosm of bed-and-breakfasts everywhere: the homey, Victorian Residenz in Ashland; the gorgeous, ultra-contemporary Artesian House in **Bayfield;** and its larger neighbor in town, the Old Rittenhouse Inn.

RESIDENZ, Ashland

OVERALL ★★★★ | QUALITY ★★★★ | VALUE ★★★★★ | PRICE RANGE $70–$75

The Popes are continually surprised at the number of cross-country cyclists who stop at Residenz—but compared to many other states, Wisconsin is crazy about its bike trails, and guests can stow their bikes in the carriage house. The inn doesn't have (and doesn't need) air conditioning: "Lake Superior is our air conditioner," Pat says. Original features of the home include some light fixtures, original golden oak trim and paneling, and ornate newel posts. In season, guests are invited outside to pick their own raspberries; stow them in the guest refrigerator upstairs.

SETTING & FACILITIES
Location Near US 2, several blocks from Lake Superior **Near** Apostle Islands & National Lakeshore, Copper Falls State Park, Chequamegon National Forest. **Buildings** 1889 Queen Anne Victorian, rose exterior color scheme **Grounds** Double town lot, lavish flower beds **Public Space** L[GOTHIC]-shaped porch, foyer, parlor, DR, LR, side porch, 2nd-floor sitting room **Food & Drink** Evening snack, beverages any time. Full breakfast includes fresh-baked muffins, egg entree; signature dish is cream cheese French toast. **Recreation** Birding, boating, sailing, fishing, swimming, kayaking, downhill & cross-country skiing, snowmobiling, lighthouse touring, museums, golf. **Amenities & Services** Coffee delivered to rooms as early as you like. Communal TV is in upstairs sitting room.

ACCOMMODATIONS
Units 3 guest rooms. **All Rooms** Ceiling fan, sitting area. **Some Rooms** TV. **Bed & Bath** Doubles (2), king/2 twins (1). All private baths (1 detached). Roll-away bed & cots available. **Favorites** Sleigh Room, with sleigh bed, attached bath. **Comfort & Decor** In the parlor, guests relax on Eastlake furniture, surrounded by reproduction Grand Baroque wallpaper. An 1889 pump organ sits in the turret alcove, under stunning stained-glass lilies. The living room fireplace features beveled glass, tile important from Holland and carved wood shelves; the dining room focus is on the built-in, Federal-style serving hutch.

Deposits: 50% **Discounts** Winter corp. rates, extended stay **Credit Cards** None; cash or checks only **Check-In/Out** 3 p.m./11 a.m. **Smoking** On porch **Pets** No; resident sheltie stays in innkeepers' quarters **Kids** Yes **No-Nos** N/A **Minimum Stay** Prefer 2 nights summer weekends **Open** All year **Hosts** Reg & Pat Pope, 723 Chapple Ave., Ashland 54806 **Phone** (715) 682-2425 **Fax** (715) 685-9953 **Email** therez@ncis.net **Web** www.residenzbb.com

ARTESIAN HOUSE, Bayfield

OVERALL ★★★★½ | QUALITY ★★★★½ | VALUE ★★★★★ | PRICE RANGE
$80–$100 OFF SEASON, $100–$120 IN SEASON

Al Chechik and his wife, Margaret Rdzak, shared the dream of building Artesian House, but she passed away soon after the bed-and-breakfast opened in 1996. Her serenity still sets the tone in this place where style, tranquility, and great food rule—untainted even by cigarette smells on guests' clothing: Smokers are turned away. Chechik is a personable innkeeper who usually joins them for coffee at the breakfast table to make them feel more at home.

SETTING & FACILITIES
Location Off Hwy. 13, 2 miles south of Bayfield **Near** Lake Superior, Apostle Islands. **Building** Contemporary lodge, built 1996 **Grounds** 24 acres of forest & wetlands w/ walking trail, mountain & lake views **Public Space** Great room/DR, wraparound deck **Food & Drink** Beverages any time. Full breakfast includes 3 granolas, "at least 6 enhancements," and entree. **Recreation** Boating, kayaking, birding, downhill & cross-country skiing, golf. **Amenities & Services** Logo bath amenities, "special favors" on request, wheelchair access, phone & fax access, corkscrews & wineglasses in rooms, guest fridge.

ACCOMMODATIONS
Units 4 guest rooms. **All Rooms** Private entrance to deck, ceiling fans, clock, data ports, couch. **Some Rooms** Whirlpool (1), pocket door. **Bed & Bath** Queens (3), double (1) w/ pullout sofa. **Favorites** Mauve Room, for the Art Deco bedroom suite. **Comfort & Decor** This house is a real looker, starting with the soaring, window-walled atrium and drop-dead views across the top of the forest: "I'm trying to bring the outside in," explains innkeeper Al Chechik. The custom-built sheet-metal fireplace was finished to look like copper—a striking piece—and in the dining area, the one-of-a-kind wood-inlay table and matching chairs add more warmth.

RATES, RESERVATIONS, & RESTRICTIONS
Deposit 1st night's stay or, for 1-night guests, 50% **Discounts** Gov't rate for state employees; travel agents inquire **Credit Cards** None **Check-In/Out** 3 p.m./11 a.m.

Smoking No **Pets** No **Kids** Over age 12, or inquire **No-Nos** N/A **Minimum Stay** 2 nights on summer weekends **Open** All year **Hosts** Al Chechik, R.R. 1, Box 218K, Bayfield 54814 **Phone** (715) 779-3338 **Fax** (715) 779-535-5350 **Email** artesian@ranger.ncis.net **Web** www.artesianhouse.com

OLD RITTENHOUSE INN, *Bayfield*

OVERALL ★★★½ | QUALITY ★★★½ | VALUE ★★ | PRICE RANGE $99–$249

There's good news and bad news about the renowned Old Rittenhouse. Aside from the tiny bath (with sink outside, in the bedroom), we were surprised to be presented at checkout with a bill for our breakfast. (Some bed-and-breakfasts do charge extra for full breakfasts, but we hadn't been informed of the policy.) The podium for the restaurant hostess is also where guests check in; the restaurant takes up the entire first floor sending a clear message that the restaurant is the priority. The dining rooms are beautifully appointed, however, with numerous stained-glass windows (including a surprise feng shui bagua, complete with trigrams, on the inn's back wall) and our $10 wild mushroom omelet was, we admit, exceptionally good.

SETTING & FACILITIES
Location In the heart of Bayfield, 4 blocks from Lake Superior **Near** Shopping, marina, ravine park, National Lakeshore Visitor Center, Apostle Islands. **Building** 1890 Queen Anne, red exterior **Grounds** Small yard, hilltop city lot overlooking the town **Public Space** Wraparound porch, DR, 2nd-floor lounge **Food & Drink** Cookie plate in upstairs hall. Cont'l or full breakfast, for fee. **Recreation** Boating, birding, kayaking, golf, downhill & cross-country skiing. **Amenities & Services** Logo soaps; corkscrew & wineglasses in room. Phone in 2nd-floor lounge.

ACCOMMODATIONS
Units 10 guest rooms. **All Rooms** Sitting area. **Some Rooms** Fireplace (9), whirlpool (5), lake view (5). **Bed & Bath** Kings (6), queen (1) doubles (3), queen sleeper sofa (1). All private baths. **Favorites** Room 3, for the panoramic lake & town view. **Comfort & Decor** The porch is furnished with comfortable wicker furniture, but in cold weather, there is no place to relax but the small upstairs lounge. All three parlors are dining rooms for the inn's restaurant, which is open to the public. We loved the view from our room, but the chairs were too low to sit in comfortably, and the bathroom was so small we literally had to step outside to hike up our britches.

RATES, RESERVATIONS, & RESTRICTIONS
Deposit 1 night's lodging, nonrefundable **Discounts** Special packages; inquire **Credit Cards** V, MC **Check-In/Out** 3:30 p.m./noon **Smoking** On porch **Pets** No **Kids** Yes **No-Nos** N/A **Minimum Stay** None **Open** All year **Hosts** Larry Cicero, Managing Innkeeper, Box 584, 301 Rittenhouse Blvd., Bayfield 54814 **Phone** (715) 779-5111 or toll-free (800) 779-2129 **Web** www.rittenhouseinn.com

MCGILVRAY'S VICTORIAN BED & BREAKFAST,
Chippewa Falls

OVERALL ★★★½ | QUALITY ★★★½ | VALUE ★★★★ | PRICE RANGE $69–$99

Melanie Berg enjoys her artsy projects, and we thought they were fun—
especially the painted brick fireplace with unusual stone architectural elements. The hilltop location in a historic neighborhood lends elegance to
the home, especially with its imposing portico. Breakfast is served on collectible Depression glassware—a fitting sendoff after a night's rest on an
antique featherbed.

SETTING & FACILITIES
Location Just off Hwy. 29, near the Chippewa River **Near** Lake Wissota State Park,
museums, brewery, Chippewa Cultural Center. **Building**1893 Neoclassic & Georgian
Revival w/ 2-story columns **Grounds** Flower & herb gardens **Public Space** 4 porches
(including screened side porch), DR, great room, large "faux tower room," 2nd-floor loft
sitting area **Food & Drink** Beverages any time. Full breakfast includes local sausages &
homemade muffins or scones. **Recreation** Boating, fishing, swimming, biking, museums,
antiquing, golf. **Amenities & Services** AC, fresh flowers in rooms, robes in room w/
detached bath, hot tub, guest coffeepot in loft area. Will order flowers or wine on request.

ACCOMMODATIONS
Units 3 guest rooms. **All Rooms** Sitting area. **Some Rooms** Claw-foot tub, privacy
porch, table, ceiling fan, armoire. **Bed & Bath** Queens (2), double (1). All private baths (1
detached). **Favorites** Room With A View, w/ screened private porch, feather tick on bed,
great view of the city. **Comfort & Decor** This home is full of 19th-century features,
including beveled glass, pocket doors, original wood trim, and original white pine floor
planks. In public spaces, furnishings are a comfortable mix of Eastlake pieces and newer
stuffed armchairs. The Rose Room features an antique fainting couch.

RATES, RESERVATIONS, & RESTRICTIONS
Deposit $25 **Discounts** 10% Sun.–Thurs. **Credit Cards** No; cash or check only
Check-In/Out By individual arrangement **Smoking** No **Pets** No **Kids** Over age 12 or
inquire **No-Nos** N/A **Minimum Stay** None **Open** All year **Hosts** Melanie J. Berg, 312
West Columbia St., Chippewa Falls 54729 **Phone** (715) 720-1600 or toll-free (888) 324-
1893 **Email** melanie@mcgilvraysbb.com **Web** www.mcgilvraysbb.com

OTTER CREEK INN, Eau Claire

OVERALL ★★★★½ | QUALITY ★★★★½ | VALUE ★★★ | PRICE RANGE $125–$185
WEEKENDS, $95–$145 WEEKDAYS

It's possible that Sally Hansen is the most creative and most energetic
innkeeper in the upper Midwest. From the penny fireplace to wallpaper

treatments, pretty good oil paintings, and nearly every visual vignette in the inn, Sally's designs fill the rooms. They're huge rooms to fill; the Palm Room is 610 square feet. The pool and deck are an elegant feature with a California-home quality. If you book the Jasmine Room, come in June and prepare to swoon.

SETTING & FACILITIES
Location On US 12, 2 mi. from I-94 **Near** Local parks, trails. **Building** 1920 English Tudor lodge **Grounds** I wooded acre w/ flower beds **Public Space** Entry, library, common room, breakfast nook, in-ground pool, deck, gazebo **Food & Drink** Cold beverages any time. Full breakfast includes menu choices of fruit plate, entree, cereals, bacon, limited substitutions. Guests departing early can have beverages & blueberry muffins delivered to room. **Recreation** Birding, antiquing, biking, live theater, fishing, canoeing. **Amenities & Services** Breakfast delivered to room (almost all guests eat in rooms), AC, logo bath amenities.

ACCOMMODATIONS
Units 6 guest rooms. **All Rooms** Color TV/VCR, 2 easy chairs, table & 2 chairs, coffeemaker, whirlpool tub. **Some Rooms** Canopy bed, mini-fridge, gas fireplace. **Bed & Bath** King (1), queen (5). All private baths. **Favorites** Jasmine Room w/ ornate Victorian bedroom suite, half-tester made from pieces of an old piano, sunken Jacuzzi, and glorious lilac bush outside the window—the most fragrant room in the house. **Comfort & Decor** Walk into the great room and all eyes are immediately drawn to the massive, penny-encrusted, covered-brick fireplace—the outcome of 27 years of saved pennies. A rectangular grand piano graces one corner. Decor is modified English Tudor with some country Victorian—a bit busy in some areas, but it works. All bed treatments are beautiful, from the "porcelain wrap" in the Rose Room to the Magnolia, where the bed is simply tucked into the eaves.

RATES, RESERVATIONS, & RESTRICTIONS
Deposit Credit card guarantee or full payment **Discounts** Corp. or single-occupancy **Credit Cards** MC, V, AE, D, DC, Carte Blanche **Check-In/Out** 4–6 p.m./11 a.m. **Smoking** Outside **Pets** No **Kids** Older kids welcome, but only 2 guests per room, including children **No-Nos** "We just ask people to use common sense. If you burn a candle, we ask that it be in a safe container." **Minimum Stay** None **Open** All year, except Christmas Eve, Christmas Day, Thanksgiving Day, New Year's Eve, Easter Sat. & Sun. **Hosts** Shelley & Randy Hansen, 2536 Hwy. 12, P.O. Box 3183, Eau Claire 54702 **Phone** (715) 832-2945 **Fax** (715) 832-4607 **Email** info@ottercreekinn.net **Web** www.ottercreekinn.net

BAKER BREWSTER INN, *Hudson*

OVERALL ★★★★½ | QUALITY ★★★★½ | VALUE ★★★★ | PRICE RANGE $129–$159

It's the little touches that make a bed-and-breakfast special—a shaker of talcum at the whirlpool; hand-blown glass "flower pockets," designed by a local artists, in dining room windows. Before the Kleinknechts opened their inn, they asked five family members to each decorate one guest room, and the divergent personalities show. The Kleinknechts met when both were flight attendants and their good energy pervades the inn. Staying at Baker Brewster is a seamless experience.

SETTING & FACILITIES

Location Off I-94 in the St. Croix River Valley, near Hudson town center **Near** St. Croix River, marina, beach & lakefront park, St. Croix Meadows greyhound park, Willow River State Park, Phipps Center for the Arts, Mall of America, Octagon House Museum. **Building** 1882 Queen Anne Victorian **Grounds** Double lot, flower gardens **Public Space** DR, front parlor w/ turret room, LR **Food & Drink** Beverages available any time. Full breakfast often includes signature dish, "eggs Baker"—light, cheesy soufflé w/ asparagus & ham on bottom, almond scone, French toast dessert, & coconut-milky fruit cup. **Recreation** Biking, snowboarding, snow-tubing, swimming, golf, greyhound racing, volleyball, fishing, fine arts, historic touring. **Amenities & Services** AC, bath amenities, fresh flowers in room, candlelit breakfast. Breakfast in bed on request.

ACCOMMODATIONS

Units 5 guest rooms **All Rooms** Sitting area, iron & ironing board. **Some Rooms** Clawfoot whirlpool, double whirlpool, marble fireplace, stained-glass windows, bay windows. **Bed & Bath** Queens (3), doubles (2). All private baths. **Favorites** Opal Rae, with exposed brick, Victorian furnishings and decorated with women's vintage clothing. **Comfort & Decor** These old homes teach us much about design and function. Baker Brewster's living room, for instance, features a stained-glass piano window—under which, in homes of the elite, the family's upright piano was positioned. A cherry fireplace with beveled glass and topper dominates the room; the inn's only TV also is here. Other highlights include oak trim with bull's-eye molding, two-sided pocket doors, wainscoting, and a carved oak fireplace.

RATES, RESERVATIONS, & RESTRICTIONS

Deposit 1 night's stay **Discounts** N/A
Credit Cards: V, M, AE, D **Check-In/Out** 4 p.m./11 a.m. **Smoking** On porch **Pets** Inquire; 2 resident dogs stay in innkeepers' quarters **Kids** Inquire **No-Nos** N/A **Minimum Stay** None **Open** All year **Hosts** Dawn & Keith Kleinknecht, 904 Vine St., Hudson 54016 **Phone** (715) 381-2895 or toll-free (877) 381-2895 **Email** rooms@bakerbrewster.com **Web** www.bakerbrewster.com

GRAPEVINE INN, Hudson

OVERALL ★★★★ | QUALITY ★★★★ | VALUE ★★★★ | PRICE RANGE $119–$149

If you're impressed with the diamond-pattern windows in the foyer, then you have a good eye for history: They were designed by window tycoon Hans J. Andersen, who built Grapevine Inn as his family home and created his signature diamond panes for this house. The library was the original dining room; here Andersen created his company's first board of directors—his wife and children. The home has since been updated, staying true to the transition features.

SETTING & FACILITIES

Location Off I-94 in the St. Croix River Valley, near Hudson town center **Near** St. Croix River, beach & lakefront park, Mall of America, Phipps Center for the Arts, Willow River State Park, Octagon House Museum, St. Croix Meadows greyhound park, marina. **Building** 1901 Queen Anne/Colonial Revival Transition house **Grounds** 1.5 lots w/ flower gardens, in-ground pool **Public Space** Foyer, parlor, DR w/ small gift shop area, library **Food & Drink** Snacks, beverages any time. Wake-up tray delivered upstairs. 3-course breakfast served on china & silver, can include signature individual hash brown quiche w/ Wisconsin cheeses. **Recreation** Antiquing, canoeing, downhill & cross country skiing, boating, fishing, golf, historic touring, fine arts. **Amenities & Services** AC. Breakfast in bed in master BR.

ACCOMMODATIONS

Units 3 guest rooms. **All Rooms** Fireplace, robes, radio, cassettes. **Some Rooms** Ceiling fans, claw-foot tub, double whirlpool. **Bed & Bath** Queens (3), all private baths. **Favorites** Master bedroom (Chardonnay) w/ small claw-foot tub, Eastlake table & chairs overlooking gardens, and 1880 bedroom set w/ 7-foot headboard; the only room w/ choice of breakfast in bed. **Comfort & Decor** With the mix of Craftsman touches (most notably the staircase) and English country, Grapevine Inn carries a "formal cottage" flavor. Inlaid floors, original wood trim, and, in one bedroom, original thumbprint chair rail, remind guests of the home's history. Bedrooms are named for wines (Bordeaux, Champagne, Chardonnay); grape arbors outside complete the theme.

RATES, RESERVATIONS, & RESTRICTIONS

Deposit 1 night's stay **Discounts** Cop., weekday, extended-stay **Credit Cards** V, MC, D **Check-In/Out** 4–6 p.m. or by prior arrangement/11 a.m. **Smoking** Outside **Pets** No— 2 resident cats & a dog; 1 cat is permitted in inn **Kids** Inquire **No-Nos** N/A **Minimum Stay** On holiday, summer, & fall weekends, "we try for 2 nights," but they can be Sat. & Sun. **Open** All year **Hosts** Barbara Dahl, 702 Vine St., Hudson 54016 **Phone** (715) 386-1989 **Email** info@grapevineinn.com **Web** www.grapevineinn.com

PHIPPS INN, Hudson

OVERALL ★★★★½ | QUALITY ★★★★½ | VALUE ★★★★ | PRICE RANGE
$129–$169 Sun.–Thurs., $169–$209 weekends & holidays

The elegance of this inn really sets it apart, from the Cable Crownstay baby grand in the music room to the beveled-glass panels in the parlor's fireplace. The dining room features a coffered ceiling, stained-glass windows, and built-in butler. Third-floor rooms were fashioned out of the former ballroom—one with willow furniture, giving it a "rustic" feel, one paneled in redwood with an antique walnut half-tester bed, and one with a floral and lace motif. We won't say which one the ghost likes best.

SETTING & FACILITIES

Location Off I-94 in the St. Croix River Valley, near Hudson town center **Near** Willow River State Park, Mall of America, beach & lakefront park, Phipps Center for the Arts, St. Croix Meadows greyhound park, marina, Octagon House Museum (across the street). **Building** 1884 Queen Anne Victorian mansion, white exterior, on National Register of Historic Places **Grounds** Large city lot w/ shrubs, flower beds **Public Space** Large porch, formal parlor w/ turret room, music room, billiards room, DR, side veranda, 2nd-floor sitting room **Food & Drink** Complimentary evening wine. 3-course breakfast includes homemade pastries and entree. **Recreation** Canoeing, greyhound racing, historic touring, antiquing, swimming, boating. **Amenities & Services** AC. Breakfast in bed on request. Bicycles available, pick-up service from local marinas, special packages & flowers available.

ACCOMMODATIONS

Units 6 guest rooms. **All Rooms** Double whirlpool tub, sitting area, fireplace, robes. **Some Rooms** Claw-foot tub, screened balcony porch, river view, hair dryer. **Bed & Bath** Queens (6). All private baths. **Favorites** Queen Anne Suite w/ sun room for double whirlpool w/ vaulted ceilings & stained-glass window, also double shower, vintage tile in bath & claw-foot tub. **Comfort & Decor** Phipps Inn has all the features of a true mansion: half a dozen patterns of inlaid parquet floors, ornate posts and spindles on the staircase, carved oak and maple trim, even rare pocket stained-glass windows on the side veranda. Four of the six rooms have feather mattresses; guests with allergies should notify innkeepers in advance and they'll make adjustments.

RATES, RESERVATIONS, & RESTRICTIONS

Deposit Credit card number or 1 night's stay **Discounts** N/A **Credit Cards** MC, V **Check-In/Out** 4:30–6 p.m./11 a.m. **Smoking** No **Pets** No **Kids** Over age 12; inquire for younger children **No-Nos** N/A **Minimum Stay** None **Open** All year **Hosts** Mary Ellen & Rich Cox, 1005 3rd St., Hudson 54016 **Phone** (715) 386-0800 or toll-free (888) 865-9388 **Fax** (715) 386-9002 **Email** info@phippsinn.com **Web** www.phippsinn.com

IRON RIVER TROUT HAUS, Iron River

OVERALL ★★★½ | QUALITY ★★★½ | VALUE ★★★★★ | PRICE RANGE $60–$75

Don't be put off by the low-elegance rating; Trout Haus is modest but great fun. You can't escape the trout—they even populate the placemats and dishes. The Johnsons have spun their trout pond in several entrepreneurial directions: lessons, selling smoked trout, trout farm where nonguests pay for their catch according to size—including cleaning, ice, and bagging—and they own a coffee house in town. Guests can catch their own trout for breakfast the second night, but if you don't fish, come for the deer, bald eagles, black bear, and grouse who frolic on the property. The wildflowers are a spectacle in June.

SETTING & FACILITIES

Location 2 blocks from downtown Iron River **Near** Iron River, Tri-County Corridor Trail, Brule River, White River. **Building** 1892 farm house **Grounds** 40 acres of river, trout ponds, & woodland **Public Space** DR/kitchen, sun porch, 2-level LR, porch **Food & Drink** Full breakfast, includes Belgian waffles, fresh-baked blueberry muffins, fresh sausage patties. Guests can catch own trout for breakfast w/ 2-night stay. **Recreation** Snowmobiling, mountain-biking, cross-country skiing, water sports, golf, fishing, birding, wildlife viewing. **Amenities & Services** Fly-fishing lessons available. Big-screen TV/VCR in LR; light sensors in upstairs hall.

ACCOMMODATIONS

Units 4 guest rooms. **All Rooms** Sitting area, clock, bedside reading lights. **Some Rooms** Skylight. **Bed & Bath** Queen (1), doubles (2), 2 twins (1). 2 private baths (1 detached), 1 shared. **Favorites** Trout Room w/ queen bed, private attached bath, & trout everywhere—afghan, mugs, wall hangings, even bed sheets. **Comfort & Decor** This bed-and-breakfast is ultra-casual, a working farm home, with casual furnishings. Guest rooms are themed for natural or historic aspects of the area (birds, logging, railroad), and throughout the house are artifacts and art from the innkeeper's trips around the world. The home's best feature is the large picture window in the dining area, providing a stunning view of the trout ponds and forest.

RATES, RESERVATIONS, & RESTRICTIONS

Deposit 1 night's stay, nonrefundable but transferable, or guests can take a rain check up to 1 year **Discounts** AAA **Credit Cards** MC, V **Check-In/Out** 2 p.m./11 a.m. **Smoking** Outside **Pets** No (resident Australian cattle dog) **Kids** Inquire for children under 10 years old **No-Nos** N/A **Minimum Stay** 2 nights on peak weekends **Open** All year **Hosts** Ron & Cindy Johnson, P.O. Box 662, 205 West Drummond Rd., Iron River 54847 **Phone** (715) 372-4219 or toll-free (888) 262-1453 **Email** info@trouthaus.com **Web** www.trouthaus.com

ARBOR INN, Prescott

OVERALL ★★★★½ | QUALITY ★★★★½ | VALUE ★★★★ | PRICE RANGE $145–$179

Everything about the Arbor Inn—the earth-color ambience, the innkeepers' collectibles, the antique furnishings—says "autumn." The trees along the riverbanks are spectacular in fall. Linda Kangas is a sometime antiques dealer and can direct guests to specialists for their collections. Guests who prefer sunnier seasons can choose the English Garden Room, decorated in a flower & picket fence motif, with a garden arbor quilt pattern.

SETTING & FACILITIES

Location Where the Mississippi & St. Croix Rivers meet, just off Hwy. 10 **Near** Hastings

(MN), river overlooks, bike trails. **Building** 1902 Mission-style home w/ fieldstone foundation, wood porch columns **Grounds** City lot, flower beds, beautiful lilac hedge **Public Space** Side & front porches, LR, DR **Food & Drink** Wake-up tray w/ beverage, homemade baked goods, delivered to room 1 hour before breakfast. Full breakfast served at flexible times. **Recreation** Boating, downhill & cross-country skiing, antiquing, birding, biking. **Amenities & Services** Breakfast served in bed, DR or on front or side porch—guest's choice. Robes in rooms, AC, logo soaps, intercom, movie library. Bicycles available.

ACCOMMODATIONS

Units 4 guest rooms **All Rooms** Refrigerator stocked with fruits & sodas, cable TV/VCR, CD player, table & sitting area. **Some Rooms** Extra-deep double whirlpool, gas fireplace, private deck w/ river view, double shower, private hot tub. **Bed & Bath** Kings (2), queens (2). All private baths. **Favorites** Silhouette Room, with king bed, private porch & hot tub. **Comfort & Decor** The innkeepers have chosen the perfect furnishings for this Mission home, including the upright piano. All beds feature quilts hand-sewn by Linda Kangas's sister and her quilting group. Warm wood trim, three-season porches, and a wood-burning fireplace in the common area make this a great winter getaway spot.

RATES, RESERVATIONS, & RESTRICTIONS

Deposit Entire stay must be prepaid, but 6-month rain check is given w/ 3 days' notice **Discounts** Inquire; midweek rates **Credit Cards** AE, MC, V, D **Check-In/Out** 4–6 p.m./11 a.m. **Smoking** Outside **Pets** No **Kids** Inquire **No-Nos** N/A **Minimum Stay** None **Open** All year **Hosts** Marv & Linda Kangas, 434 North Court St., Prescott 54021 **Phone** (715) 262-4522 or toll-free (888) 262-1090 **Fax** (715) 262-5644 **Email** arborinn@mn.mediaone.net **Web** www.thearborinn.com

Northeast Wisconsin

We're still in the Northwoods in Zone 24, and with similar cultural extremes as in the first zone.

To the north, **Eagle River** and **Iron County** usher travelers onto Michigan's Upper Peninsula. Historically, Iron County is an outpost from the late-1800s iron mining era that today attracts visitors for its ideal snowmobiling and to view the beautiful waterfalls on the **Montreal River.** Nearer the top of the state, Eagle River offer the quintessential great outdoors vacation; more than 1,300 lakes and half a million acres of forest wait in this county for fishers and hikers; in winter, the town hosts the **World's Championship Snowmobile Derby.** The nearby town of **St. Germain** is home to the **Snowmobile Racing Hall of Fame.** Bed-and-breakfasts in this region reflect that strong attraction to nature; those we visited in **Minocqua** and Eagle River were lakeside lodges.

As we drove south into **Oconto,** only halfway into our Wisconsin journey, we already could tell that the towns were getting larger, the forests smaller. Oconto itself isn't a destination, but the Governor Scofield Mansion bed-and-breakfasts is a dressy-casual overnight stop en route to the north country, and its owners should be credited for bringing fine dining to the area.

Turn east at **Green Bay** and you're on the **Door County** peninsula, Wisconsin's vacation playland. With 10 lighthouses, more than 80 galleries, a state park, and 250 miles of beaches, no one will be bored here. We stayed in the super-elegant Scofield House in **Sturgeon Bay,** about halfway up the peninsula; more than 30 eighteenth-century shipwrecks have been found in Sturgeon Bay's harbors alone, making it one of the Midwest's best snorkeling and diving destinations. We shopped up and down the peninsula, at upscale boutiques in **Fish Creek** and **Ephraim,** and at orchards and antiques malls all along the coast. Most bed-and-breakfasts in the vicinity are a mix of restored mansions, cottages, and inns, though a few are new constructions, such as the fun Juniper Inn in Fish Creek.

INN AT PINEWOOD, Eagle River

OVERALL ★★★★ | QUALITY ★★★★ | VALUE ★★★★ | PRICE RANGE $98–$145

City families can find plenty of new experiences at this inn—listening to loons crying in early morning; watching eagles swoop onto the lake to catch a fish; hiking into Nicolet Forest to see Majestic McArthur, a 423-year-old white pine tree measuring 17.5 feet in circumference. This is in real back country, where black squirrels, deer, and an occasional bear scamper past the dining room window. The three-bedroom home, renting for $270/night or $1,450/week (not including meals), has all the features of the inn's guest rooms plus a six-person hot tub. It's often reserved for marriage retreats, reunions, or business conferences.

SETTING & FACILITIES

Location On Carpenter Lake, 0.5 mi. off Rt. 70 **Near** Nicolet National Forest, Eagle Chain (28 lakes). **Building** 1934 log home w/ additions, former boys' academy **Grounds** 5 acres w/ woods, lakefront, sandy beach, walking trails, snowmobile trail **Public Space** "Cabin area" common room, DR, library, TV room, expansive commons area, loft sitting area, deck overlooking lake **Food & Drink** Beverages any time. Full gourmet breakfast w/ homemade muffins, egg dish, pancakes or waffles. **Recreation** Fishing, ice fishing, swimming, biking, golf, snowshoeing, snowmobiling, birding, wildlife viewing, downhill & cross-country skiing. **Amenities & Services** Book exchange program ("take it home, send us one"), logo soaps, rentals of boats, snowmobiles, canoes, kayaks.

ACCOMMODATIONS

Units 5 guest rooms, 3 suites. (Also rents 3-BR home on property.) **All Rooms** Balconies, clocks. **Some Rooms** Ceiling fan, fireplace, double whirlpool, separate water closet, 2nd bath for overflow room. **Bed & Bath** Kings (8). King & 2 twins (1). **Favorites** Honeymoon Suite w/ fireplace, view of Carpenter Lake. **Comfort & Decor** Guests love the large common room with the bowling/shuffle ball machine and the old study carrels—remnants from the boys' academy located here in the 1970s. Televisions are found in the TV room and library, and kids love sleeping in the suite's "on-stage" twin beds.

RATES, RESERVATIONS, & RESTRICTIONS

Deposit 1 night's stay **Discounts** N/A **Credit Cards** V, MC **Check-In/Out** 3 p.m./11 a.m. **Smoking** No **Pets** No **Kids** Over age 5 **No-Nos** N/A **Minimum Stay** 2 nights on weekends, can be Sat.–Sun. **Open** All year **Hosts** Bill & Jane Weber, 1820 Silver Forest Lane, Eagle River 54521 **Phone** (715) 477-2377 **Email** pinewood@nnex.net **Web** www.inn-at-pinewood.com

JUNIPER INN, Fish Creek

OVERALL ★★★★ | QUALITY ★★★★ | VALUE ★★★★ | PRICE RANGE $105–$180 IN SEASON

Located more than a mile off the commercial corridor, Juniper Inn enjoys rare isolation on the tourist-dense Door County peninsula. The cedar forest behind the inn frames a protected wetland so, Sneen says, "this view will always be here." The inn is an easy bicycle ride to the beaches at Peninsula State Park and upscale shopping in Ephraim; orchards and antiques malls dot the coast. This fresh, slightly Gothic bed-and-breakfast is a relaxing alternative to the legions of historic inns.

SETTING & FACILITIES

Location 2 mi. north of Fish Creek, just past Peninsula State Park off Hwy. 42 **Near** Resort towns of Fish Creek and Ephraim, wetlands, Lake Michigan, fruit wineries. **Building** 1995 contemporary home w/ light woods, vaulted ceilings, windowed cupola atrium **Grounds** 3.2 acres of woods on a side road **Public Space** Porch, foyer, DR/great room, screened porch **Food & Drink** Beverages any time, complimentary cream sherry in room. "Healthy breakfast" includes homemade granola, Scandinavian fruit soup, fresh-baked muffins. **Recreation** Antiquing, swimming, sailing, biking, touring, summer stock theater. **Amenities & Services** AC. Phone available, data ports in rooms.

ACCOMMODATIONS

Units 4 guest rooms. **All Rooms** TV/VCR. **Some Rooms** Whirlpool, stereo, private deck, view of cedar forest & juniper meadow, fireplace, cathedral ceiling. **Bed & Bath** Queens (4). All private baths. **Favorites** Evergreen Room w/ cathedral ceiling, spacious bay, deck, gas fireplace, double whirlpool, valley view. **Comfort & Decor** Mark Sneen built the kind of home he wanted to live in, with clean lines, few adornments, panoramic views, and a soaring atrium. "I didn't open a bed-and-breakfast to have a place where I could show off my antiques," he says. All guest rooms are on the second floor in a four-square format, and open onto a balcony overlooking the common room, an open area with maple trim and wood burning fireplace.

RATES, RESERVATIONS, & RESTRICTIONS

Deposit 1 night's stay **Discounts** N/A **Credit Cards** V, MC, prefer personal checks or travelers' checks **Check-In/Out** 2:30 p.m./10:30 a.m. **Smoking** No **Pets** No **Children:** No **No-Nos** N/A **Minimum Stay** 2 nights weekends, 3 nights holiday weekends **Open** All year **Hosts** Mark Sneen, N9432 Maple Grove Rd., Fish Creek 54212 **Phone** (920) 839-2629 or toll-free (800) 218-6960 **Fax** (920) 839-2095 **Email** juniperinn@itol.com **Web** www.juniperinn.com

FISH CREEK, Fish Creek

OVERALL ★★★★ | QUALITY ★★★★ | VALUE ★★★ | PRICE RANGE $115–$155

It's amazing to ponder this huge building inching across the ice nearly a century ago, completely furnished and sporting the same transoms, door hinges, and other features we see today. Winter guests of Whistling Swan join those of two other nearby historic properties for progressive dinners, five times each season. In addition to the gift shop, four seasonal shops operate on the lower level.

SETTING & FACILITIES

Location In Fish Creek town center **Near** Peninsula State Park, marina, Sunset Park. **Building** 1887 inn, originally built in Marinette, moved across frozen Green Bay in 1907; on National Register of Historic Places **Grounds** N/A **Public Space** Lobby, gift shop **Food & Drink** Tea & cookies at 3 p.m. Breakfast is cont'l-plus, w/ fruits, granolas, breads; in winter, guests receive breakfast voucher from nearby restaurants. Early coffee available. Bottled water in rooms. **Recreation** Swimming, boating, historic touring, antiquing, summer stock theater. **Amenities & Services** AC, logo soaps.

ACCOMMODATIONS

Units 5 guest rooms, 2 suites. **All Rooms** Cable TV, phone, sitting area w/ table. **Some Rooms** Claw-foot tub, VCR. **Bed & Bath** Queens (3), doubles (4). All baths are private. **Favorites** Suite #5, corner suite with four-poster queen bed, full sleeper sofa, French doors, VCR, 2 TVs. **Comfort & Decor** The lobby serves as a common area, with arched windows, vintage baby grand piano, game table, and gas log fireplace. Rooms are individually decorated with antiques; many of the beds are original to the inn before it was moved across the ice.

RATES, RESERVATIONS, & RESTRICTIONS

Deposit 1 night's stay **Discounts** Extended-stay **Credit Cards** V, MC, D, AE **Check-In/Out** 3–9 p.m./11 a.m. **Smoking** No **Pets** No **Kids** Yes **No-Nos** N/A **Minimum Stay** 2 nights weekends & during Christmas week; 3 nights Memorial Day, July 4, Labor Day, Columbus Day **Open** All year **Hosts** Laurie & Jim Roberts, P.O. Box 193, 4192 Main St., Fish Creek 54212 **Phone** (920) 868-3442 **Fax** (920) 868-1703 **Email** jroberts@whistling swan.com **Web** www.whistlingswan.com

ASTOR HOUSE, Green Bay

OVERALL ★★★★ | QUALITY ★★★★ | VALUE ★★★★ | PRICE RANGE $115–$156

Romantic getaways in the city and business travel are the two biggest reasons why people visit Astor House. All of his rooms suit both clientele. The neighborhood was once the town of Astor, formed by John Jacob Astor; the inn was built by one of his contemporaries. The home was renovated in 1994 but kept original features such as oak trim, pocket doors, maple floors, and beveled-glass windows in the entry.

SETTING & FACILITIES

Location On Green Bay's east side, 0.5 block from intersection of Hwys. 54 & 57 **Near** Fox River & Green Bay; downtown. **Building** 1888 Late Picturesque w/ Stick-style influence, lavender/cream exterior color scheme, on National Register of Historic Homes

Grounds City lot; flower beds **Public Space** DR, entry, wraparound porch **Food & Drink** Cont'l-plus breakfast, served on porch, in DR by candlelight, or in guest room. Complimentary wine in room. **Recreation** Boating, swimming, pro football, historic touring, museums, fine & performing arts, zoo. **Amenities & Services** AC. Morning newspaper, early coffee.

ACCOMMODATIONS

Units 5 guest rooms. **All Rooms** TV, VCR, fridge, phone, direct phone line, data port, CD players/tape decks, sitting area. **Some Rooms** Table & chairs, private balcony, whirlpool (4), fireplace (3 rooms have whirlpool plus fireplace). **Bed & Bath** King (1), queens (4). All private baths. **Favorites** Laredo Room, for the cedar Mission bench, peeled log bed, Native American artifacts, Navajo rug. **Comfort & Decor** Choosing a favorite here is not easy; other rooms feature a mahogany rocker, antique maple fireplace surround, and view of downtown Green Bay (London Room); delicate ivy-laced headboard and white-washed wicker furnishings (Marseilles Garden); private third-floor balcony overlooking flower gardens (Vienna Balconies), and black tile fireplace and original Eastern artwork (Hong Kong Retreat).

RATES, RESERVATIONS, & RESTRICTIONS

Deposit $50 per room **Discounts** Single travelers, Sun.–Thurs., $30–$60 discount, depending on room (not available holidays); also AAA, extended-stay **Credit Cards** V, MC, AE, D **Check-In/Out** 4–6 p.m./11 a.m. **Smoking** No **Pets** No **Kids** Inquire **No-Nos** N/A **Minimum Stay** 2 nights Packer weekends, select holidays **Open** All year **Hosts** Greg & Barbara J. Robinson, 637 South Monroe Ave., Green Bay 54301 **Phone** (920) 432-3585 or toll-free (888) 303-6370 **Email** Astor@execpc.com **Web** www.astor-house.com

LINDSAY HOUSE BED & BREAKFAST, *Manawa*

OVERALL ★★★★½ | QUALITY ★★★★½ | VALUE ★★★★★ | PRICE RANGE $75–$80

More than a third of Lindsay House's guests are vegetarians, so get ready to chow down some delicious carbs—especially the cinnamon rolls. If you come in berry season, you're sure to have berries grown in the backyard. Whether you garden or not, check out the eight (count 'em, eight) perennial gardens. The Secret Garden Room provides a sweeping view of them. Inside, our favorite feature was, collectively, the beds; all have high, carved headboards.

SETTING & FACILITIES
Location On Hwy. 22/110, in town **Near** Town center, antiques malls, parks, Little Wolf River (behind property). **Building** 1892 Queen Anne Victorian, white exterior w/ wrap-around porch **Grounds** 1 acre w/ gazebo, sculpted perennial gardens, rose garden, black-berry patch **Public Space** Music Room w/ grand piano, DR, LR **Food & Drink** Wine & dessert on arrival, candlelight gourmet breakfast. Specialties are amaretto soufflé and over-sized cinnamon rolls. **Recreation** Antiquing, boating, canoeing, cross-country skiing, birding, croquet, golf. **Amenities & Services** AC. Robes for detached baths, TV/VCR on request.

ACCOMMODATIONS
Units 4 guest rooms. **All Rooms** Sitting area, cable & phone access. **Some Rooms** N/A. **Bed & Bath** Queens (3), double (1). All private baths; 2 detached. **Favorites** Rose Room, has the largest bath and bright, sunny feel. **Comfort & Decor** The wood in Lindsay House is extraordinary. The floors are yellow pine, laid in an unusual pattern. Special fur-nishings in public areas include "curly Eastlake" parlor furniture—including a rocker—an 1820s fainting couch and chair, and an 1820s rifle storage bench.

RATES, RESERVATIONS, & RESTRICTIONS
Deposit Reservation guaranteed w/ credit card or 50% payment **Discounts** Special packages, including golf, movies, fresh flowers, homemade chocolates, and "the ultimate romance." **Credit Cards** MC, V **Check-In/Out** 4 p.m./11 a.m. **Smoking** No **Pets** No; resident dog comes into the house **Kids** Yes **No-Nos** N/A **Minimum Stay** 2 nights on weekends, can include Sun. night **Open** All year **Hosts** Judith & Patrick Burkhart, P.O. Box 304, 539 Depot St., Manawa 54949 **Phone** (920) 596-3643 **Fax** (920) 596-3886 **Email** lh-bandb@netnet.net **Web** www.Lindsayhouse.com

LAUERMAN GUEST HOUSE INN, Marinette

OVERALL ★★★½ | QUALITY ★★★½ | VALUE ★★★★★ | PRICE RANGE $55–$75

Joseph A. Lauerman made his fortune in early-20th-century retail and a knitting mill that supplied garments to Lord & Taylor and other depart-ment stores nationwide. Lauerman's original table, still gracing the private dining room along with the Arts & Crafts built-ins, was their meeting place: "Gimbels and Macys broke bread at this table," says innkeeper Steve Homa. More than 10,000 hours of labor went into the home's restoration, but something is missing from this grand dame—she seems depressed, a bit tomb-like, and smells badly of cigarette smoke. We want to love this lavish estate; with sprucing up, perhaps we can.

SETTING & FACILITIES

Location In central Marinette, 1.5 blocks from Hwy. 41 **Near** Downtown, Univ. of Wisconsin at Marinette, Menominee River, marina, Michigan's Upper Peninsula. **Building** 1910 Colonial Revival, Prairie design interior, on National Register of Historic Places **Grounds** Large city lot, shrubs, black walnut trees—playground to a family of chickadees **Public Space** Porch w/ 8 2-story pillars, DR, lobby/TV room, private DR **Food & Drink** Sodas any time, full breakfast. **Recreation** Golf, boating, canoeing, fishing, antiquing, theater. **Amenities & Services** AC. Morning newspaper, transport from Twin County Airport; can host meetings, weddings, parties.

ACCOMMODATIONS

Units 5 guest rooms. **All Rooms** Cable TV, phone. **Some Rooms** Bay seat w/ river view, sitting area, mirrored bathroom, whirlpool tub. **Bed & Bath** Queens (2), doubles (3). All private baths. **Favorites** Cecilia's Room, w/ large blue ceramic-tiled fireplace, bird's-eye maple woodwork, and original wall safe where jewelry was stored. **Comfort & Decor** This home's elegance needs a bit of coaxing to show itself. The lobby's stunning oak trim, ornate woodwork, 12-foot ceilings, and the original, wonderfully worn carpet, evoke a past era of grandeur. A player grand piano sits in the TV room. In the master suite hand silk-screened wallpaper and a hand-blown Italian chandelier complement rich mahogany woodwork; French doors lead to a balcony overlooking the Menominee River.

RATES, RESERVATIONS, & RESTRICTIONS

Deposit Credit card **Discounts** Corp., gov't rates **Credit Cards** V, MC, AE, D **Check-In/Out** 2 p.m./11 a.m. **Smoking** Yes **Pets** No—resident cat stays outdoors Children: Inquire **No-Nos** N/A **Minimum Stay** None **Open** All year **Hosts** Steve & Sherry Homa, 1975 Riverside Ave., Marinette 54143 **Phone** (715) 732-7800 **Web** www.wbba.org/inns/BB61.htm

M & M VICTORIAN INN, Marinette

OVERALL ★★★½ | QUALITY ★★★½ | VALUE ★★★ | PRICE RANGE $80–$150 WEEK-ENDS, $75–$125 SUN.–THURS.

The ornate carvings in the woodwork throughout this house remind us that its builder was a lumber tycoon. The elegance of the curving wood staircase, maple cherry plank flooring and elaborate wood trim, carries into the guest rooms. Dinner is served in the restaurant five nights a week; because the inn has a liquor license, guests are not permitted to drink their own liquor in public spaces. Private parties can be accommodated.

SETTING & FACILITIES

Location Central Marinette, several blocks from Hwys. 64 & 41 **Near** Menominee River, Michigan's Upper Peninsula, marina, Univ. of Wisconsin at Marinette. **Building** Approx. 1900, Queen Anne Victorian, white exterior **Grounds** City lot; flower beds **Public Space** Foyer, porch, den, French restaurant, breakfast room **Food & Drink** Full breakfast with entree such as pancakes made from organic mixes. **Recreation** Boating, canoeing, golf, fishing, antiquing, theater. **Amenities & Services** AC. Some antique furnishings are for sale.

ACCOMMODATIONS

Units 5 guest rooms. **All Rooms** Cable TV, phone. **Some Rooms** Double whirlpool tubs, pullout couch, private balcony, fireplace. **Bed & Bath** Queens (4), double (1). All private baths. **Favorites** Wedgewood Suite w/fireplace, porch, canopy bed, and double whirlpool. **Comfort & Decor** This is a beautifully kept inn originally built by a lumber baron. Features include rich, ornate oak trim, striped inlay floors in the foyer, pocket doors, and many stained-glass windows. Most light fixtures are original.

RATES, RESERVATIONS, & RESTRICTIONS

Deposit 50% of stay **Discounts** Corp. during the week **Credit Cards** V, MC, AE, D, DC **Check-In/Out** 3 p.m./11 a.m. **Smoking** No **Pets** No **Kids** Over age 10 **No-Nos** N/A **Minimum Stay** None **Open** All year **Hosts** William Mallory & Jean Moore, 1393 Main St., Marinette 54143 **Phone** (715) 732-9531 **Fax** (715) 732-0426 **Email** innkeeper@cybrzn.com **Web** www.cybrzn.com/victorianinn

TAMARACK B&B LODGE, Minocqua

OVERALL ★★★★ | QUALITY ★★★★ | VALUE ★★★★ | PRICE RANGE $100–$150

Welcome to the middle of nowhere! The roads leading back to Tamarack are narrow, winding, and remote. Innkeepers Karen Brown and Pam Graham are sisters who grew up on the West Coast; today they run the inn they built from 150-year-old logs and raise exotic chickens for eggs.

SETTING & FACILITIES

Location 12 mi. west of Minocqua, off Hwy. 70 on the south end of Squirrel Lake **Near** Lake, woodlands, Minocqua Winter Park, Indian Culture Museum. **Building** 1996 log home w/ all-glass prow front & 100-ft. wraparound deck **Grounds** 40 acres of cedar wetlands **Public Space** Great room, deck **Food & Drink** Afternoon homemade snack. Full homemade breakfast ("nothing is store-bought.") w/ egg or pancake dish, meat, sorbet. **Recreation** Canoeing, boating, birding, biking, hunting, horseback riding, snowmobiling, swimming, golf. **Amenities & Services** AC. Robes in rooms. Canoes, paddleboat, mountain bikes, & kayak are available for guest use.

ACCOMMODATIONS

Units 2 suites, 1 guest room. **All Rooms** Ceiling fans. **Some Rooms** Whirlpool tub, direct access to deck. **Bed & Bath** King (1), queens (2). All private baths (2 detached). **Favorites** Master suite, with double sink, deck overlooking wildflower garden, & sliding door opening on deck. **Comfort & Decor** Tamarack B&B is a Northwoods lodge with a woman's touch. Public areas are bright, though surrounded by forest, because of the sunny window wall overlooking the lake and skylights in the kitchen/dining area. Furnishings are casual, woody, but finely crafted.

RATES, RESERVATIONS, & RESTRICTIONS

Deposit 50% of 1st night **Discounts** Extended stay. Rates drop to $75–$100 "after the leaves fall but before the first snowfall"; also in spring, after the snow melts but before the trees bud **Credit Cards** No; cash or check only **Check-In/Out** 3 p.m./11 a.m. **Smoking** No **Pets** No; resident dog & 2 cats permitted in house but not in guest rooms **Kids** No **No-Nos** No cooking; guests can use microwave in kitchen **Minimum Stay** 2 nights on weekends **Open** All year **Hosts** Karen Brown & Pam Graham, 7950 Bo-Di-Lac Dr., Minocqua 54548 **Phone** (715) 356-7124 **Fax** (715) 358-5824 **Email** tamarack@ newnorth.net **Web** www.tamarackbandb.com

GOVERNOR SCOFIELD MANSION BED AND BREAKFAST, Oconto

OVERALL ★★★★½ | QUALITY ★★★★½ | VALUE ★★★ | PRICE RANGE $95–$125

When we visited, the innkeepers had recently opened and were still ironing out the kinks. Mario Tellez is a gracious host who brews a great cup of coffee, installed strong bedside reading lights, and serves his dry reds in the finest wineglasses—a solid start. We were surprised to find the closet in our guest room full of someone's clothes, and we tripped several times because we kept forgetting our bath sat on a small mezzanine. We'd like to see that clearly marked for guests' safety.

SETTING & FACILITIES
Location In central Oconto, on the west shores of Green Bay **Near** Green Bay, antiques malls. **Building** 1870 Italianate, white exterior, on National Register of Historic Places **Grounds** Double city lot; flower gardens **Public Space** Foyer, library, parlor, 2 DR, bar, restaurant **Food & Drink** Cont'l breakfast; cont'l-plus on weekends. Water in rooms. **Recreation** Fishing, boating, canoeing, antiquing, historic touring. **Amenities & Services** AC. Massages available.

ACCOMMODATIONS
Units 4 guest rooms. **All Rooms** Clock, sitting area. **Some Rooms** Telescope for viewing night skies. **Bed & Bath** Queens (4). All private baths. **Favorites** Scofield Suite, with French provincial furnishings and large sitting area. **Comfort & Decor** Much of the first floor of this inn is taken up by its new restaurant. The surrounds are on the formal side, yet they inspire a casual, comfortable feeling. In the parlor, the original Italian marble fireplace and original Scofield pier mirror still stand. Tables in the dining room's bayed dormer, flanked by fluted columns, look out onto the lavender-lined path.

RATES, RESERVATIONS, & RESTRICTIONS
Deposit 50% or 1 night's stay **Discounts** Wisconsin Bed & Breakfast Assoc. members **Credit Cards** V, MC, AE, D **Check-In/Out** 3–9 p.m./11 a.m. **Smoking** Outside **Pets** No **Kids** Over age 12 w/ parents **No-Nos** Don't encourage guests to bring their own liquor into the inn. Guests only are permitted in guest rooms. **Minimum Stay** None **Open** All year **Hosts** Mario & Jill Tellez, 610 Main St., Oconto 54153 **Phone** (920) 834-3846 or tollfree (877) 357-6337 **Email** govman@netnet.net **Web** www.governorsmansionbb.com

DREAMS OF YESTERYEAR BED AND BREAKFAST,
Stevens Point

OVERALL ★★★★ | QUALITY ★★★★ | VALUE ★★★★ | PRICE RANGE $62–$149

Dreams of Yesteryear is a great place for snooping, and Bonnie Maher loves to show off her stuff. Highlights include her ruby glass collection, including one piece from the 1904 World's Fair, and a Civil War–era "curtain" made of glass and leather beads. In the Gareld guest room, we also noticed a rare Arts & Crafts/Detroit E-Z recliner. This is one of those inns where you feel at home immediately.

SETTING & FACILITIES
Location Off Hwy. 10, 2 blocks from the Wisconsin River **Near** Univ. of Wisconsin–Stevens Point campus, the Green Circle 24-mile parkway, galleries, museums. **Building** 1901 Queen Anne Victorian, gray exterior, on National Register of Historic Places **Grounds** Large city lot, "formal" English garden & informal garden of perennials, herbs **Public Space** DR, side screened porch, sitting parlor, front parlor, foyer, small balcony **Food & Drink** Complimentary cookies, teas, wine in afternoon; water any time. Full breakfast may include Wisconsin burrito & blueberry pancakes. **Recreation** Antiquing, fine arts, cross-country skiing, golf, biking, tennis. **Amenities & Services** AC. Robes for rooms w/out private baths, logo soaps.

ACCOMMODATIONS
Units 2 suites, 4 guest rooms. **All Rooms** Sitting area, data ports. **Some Rooms** Whirlpool tub, cable TV, pull-chain toilet, leaded glass windows, claw-foot tub. **Bed & Bath** King/2 twins (1), queens (3), doubles (2). 4 private baths, 1 shared. **Favorites** The Ballroom Suite, w/ queen Victorian iron & brass angel bed under a chandelier & cathedral ceiling, capped window, whirlpool. **Comfort & Decor** Dreams of Yesterday has received awards from the State Historical Society for its careful renovation. Leaded glass windows in unusual patterns dominate the first floor, along with golden oak woodwork, oak & beveled-glass fireplaces, and the innkeeper's collectibles. Dining room furniture is original to the house.

RATES, RESERVATIONS, & RESTRICTIONS
Deposit 1 night's stay **Discounts** State gov't rate; extended stay **Credit Cards** V, MC, AE, D **Check-In/Out** 3 p.m./11 a.m. **Smoking** Outside **Pets** No; resident Maltese (non-shedding) lives indoors **Kids** Over age 12; younger by prior arrangement **No-Nos** N/A **Minimum Stay** None **Open** All year **Hosts** Bonnie & Bill Maher, 1100 Brawley St., Stevens Point 54481 **Phone** (715) 341-4525 **Fax** (715) 341-4248 **Email** bonnie@dreamsofyesteryear.com **Web** www.dreamsofyesteryear.com

REYNOLDS HOUSE BED & BREAKFAST, Sturgeon Bay

OVERALL ★★★★½ | QUALITY ★★★★½ | VALUE ★★★★ | PRICE RANGE $98–$155
WEEKENDS IN SEASON; WEEKDAYS & OFF-SEASON TO $70–$115

Readers of Midwest Living magazine voted this inn the best B&B in the Midwest. We enjoyed the personal touches, such as the rooms named after apples (Macintosh, Granny Smith, Cortland, Winesap), a nod to the original owner, a prominent Door County apple grower. Milwaukee transplants Jan and Stan Sekula pay attention to details, from the herb egg crêpes with champagne sauce to the manicured gardens. Be sure to notice the 1900 Murphy bed in the attic hallway.

SETTING & FACILITIES

Location In central Sturgeon Bay on the Door County peninsula **Near** Marina, orchards, antiques malls, downtown. **Building** 1900 Queen Anne Victorian w/ stone porch, gray exterior **Grounds** City lot; flower gardens **Public Space** Upstairs library loft, wraparound porch, foyer, formal parlor, casual parlor, DR, solarium **Food & Drink** Snacks, coffee, soda, water all day. Full gourmet breakfast includes homemade Danish pastries, meat, entree; innkeeper creates all of her own recipes—"I won't get my food from somewhere else." **Recreation** Antiquing, boating, biking, historic touring, cross-country skiing. **Amenities & Services** AC. Robes in suite. Birthday cakes provided, in-room champagne & chocolates for anniversaries. Innkeepers sit down w/ all first-time guests to tell them of Door County must-sees. Shared phone on 2nd floor.

Units; 1 suite, 3 guest rooms. **All Rooms** Ceiling fans, cable TV, sitting area. **Some Rooms** Whirlpool tub, fireplace, sleigh bed, cherry spindle bed, claw-foot tub, greenhouse window. **Bed & Bath** Queens (3), double (1). All private baths. **Favorites** Winesap Suite, entire 3rd floor, w/ cozy sitting room & Victorian oak furnishings. **Comfort & Decor** The public spaces all are inviting: the casual parlor with pillared oak fireplace and TV, the formal parlor with oak paneling and trim, the dining room with glass-front built-ins and oak paneling, and this writer's favorite—the super-sunny, turret-shaped solarium with stone walls. We always like to see pocket doors and beveled-glass windows; we're even happier when the rooms aren't overdone with fussy floral patterns everywhere.

RATES, RESERVATIONS, & RESTRICTIONS

Deposit 50% or 1 night's stay **Discounts** Winter specials **Credit Cards** V, MC **Check-In/Out** 4–7 p.m./11 a.m. **Smoking** No **Pets** No **Kids** Over age 12 **No-Nos** N/A **Minimum Stay** 2 nights on weekends **Open** All year **Hosts** Jan & Stan Sekula, 111 South 7th Ave., Sturgeon Bay 54235 **Phone** (920) 746-9771 or toll-free (877) 269-7401 **Fax** (920) 746-9441 **Email** jsekula@reynoldshousebandb.com **Web** www.reynoldshousebandb.com

SCOFIELD HOUSE BED & BREAKFAST, Sturgeon Bay

OVERALL ★★★★★ | QUALITY ★★★★½ | VALUE ★★★ | PRICE RANGE $98–$202

By any standard, Scofield House is the most luxurious bed-and-breakfast in Door County, and one of the most elegant in the state. Local artifacts, such as fireplace and jury-box railing from the local courthouse, blend effortlessly with the Pietreks' collectibles. Carolyn collects bride dolls, antique to contemporary, including one wearing a replica of Queen Victoria's wedding dress (the original white wedding gown), as well as bells and Capodimonti pieces. Mike collects framed letters, autographs, and photos of important people, including a letter from Mother Teresa. In the upstairs hall, he displays his collection of autographs and photos of (drum roll) the original 13 members of the Baseball Hall of Fame. Honus Wagner is there—"Men like this collection," Mike says. No kidding.

SETTING & FACILITIES

Location In central Sturgeon Bay, on Door County peninsula **Near** Downtown, marina, antiques malls, orchards. **Building** 1902 High Victorian, w/ deep green & earth tone exterior colors **Grounds** City lot; flower beds **Public Space** Porch, foyer, DR, parlor, music room **Food & Drink** Snacks, hot beverages any time; dessert buffet at night, early coffee 6:30 a.m. Breakfast is extravagant; we tasted orange frappe, hazelnut muffins, bacon double-cheese breakfast pie, turkey sausage/zucchini/cheese frittata, apple walnut crêpes, apple-glazed sausages, and red & blueberry shortcakes—all in the same meal! **Recreation** Boating, canoeing, kayaking, cross-country skiing, antiquing, historic touring. **Amenities & Services** AC. Logo bath amenities; small gift left in every room.

ACCOMMODATIONS

Units 2 suites, 4 guest rooms. **All Rooms** TV/VCR, sitting area. **Some Rooms** Private balcony, double whirlpool (5), double shower. In Room at the Top, wet bar, fridge, stereo w/ CD player. **Bed & Bath** Queens (5), double (1). All private baths. **Favorites** Water Lily Room—not the largest, but the most creative. We still can't figure out where the innkeepers found so many water lily items—including a novel leap frog checkerboard and water lily fountain. **Comfort & Decor** Every inch in this inn reflects someone's careful decision. The maple and oak trim is of virgin forest wood; the windows in the music room's curved wall are made of curved glass, original to the home. The original parquet floors are in five patterns with five types of wood, and the dining room features stained glass and glass-front cupboards.

RATES, RESERVATIONS, & RESTRICTIONS
Deposit 50% of total stay **Discounts** Special packages **Credit Cards** V, MC **Check-In/Out** 3–7 p.m./11 a.m. **Smoking** Outside **Pets** No **Kids** No **No-Nos** N/A **Minimum Stay** 2 nights; 3 nights holiday & fall color weekends **Open** All year **Hosts** Carolyn & Mike Pietrek, 908 Michigan St., Sturgeon Bay 54235 **Phone** (920) 743-7727 or toll-free (888) 463-0204 **Email** scofldhs@doorpi.net **Web** www.scofieldhouse.com

WHITE LACE INN, Sturgeon Bay

OVERALL ★★★★½ | QUALITY ★★★★ | VALUE ★★★ | PRICE RANGE $129–$239
MAY 24–OCT. 20 (UPPER-END PRICES ARE FOR WEEKENDS); LESS IN THE OFF-SEASON

They bought the first White Lace home in 1982, settling in Sturgeon Bay because of its strong arts awareness and access to Door County's natural beauty. Today, the Statzes' dream mansion has grown to a complex of four gingerbread-trimmed homes, including one that was physically moved to the property. Features such as pocket doors, beveled-glass windows, ornate oak trim, and original light fixtures have been carefully preserved, and others—an Italian tile bath floor here, French doors and hand-painted walls there—are added luxuries.

SETTING & FACILITIES
Location Residential neighborhood in Sturgeon Bay **Near** Downtown Sturgeon Bay, marina, antiques malls, orchards, state park. **Building** Four Victorian homes of various color schemes & personalities **Grounds** Central courtyard of lush, landscaped flower gardens, fountains, small pond, gazebo & brick paths connecting the 4 homes **Public Space** Porches & common room in each home; main house has foyer, DR, LR, breakfast room **Food & Drink** Full breakfast including cheesy egg bake or stuffed French toast and home-baked muffins. Complimentary cookies and beverage served in the evening. **Recreation** Boating, kayaking, canoeing, birding, antiquing, historic touring, golf. **Amenities & Services** AC. Breakfast served in room. Phones in common rooms.

ACCOMMODATIONS
Units 5 suites, 13 guest rooms. **All Rooms** Sitting area. **Some Rooms** TV/VCR, 32" TV/VCR w/ surround sound, single or double whirlpool, wood-burning fireplace, 1 or 2 gas fireplaces, CD stereo, private balcony. **Bed & Bath** Kings (4), queens (12), double (1). All private baths. **Favorites** Spring Floral Room, with full private balcony overlooking the gardens and gazebo, hand-carved plantation canopy bed, sofa, 2 chairs, windows in 3 walls, & beautiful sea foam-painted walls. **Comfort & Decor** Individually themed rooms are

conducive to nearly every guest mood, from the casually elegant Door County Orchard, with its 1840s four-poster canopy bed and tower bath, to the more refined Winter Cheer with a pencil-post king bed, entertainment center, and floral-against-winter-white Ralph Lauren upholstery. Even the wall coverings, ranging from Laura Ashley wallpaper to French toile to cottage wainscoting, create an opulent setting.

RATES, RESERVATIONS, & RESTRICTIONS
Deposit 1 night's stay **Discounts** Weeknights $20 less than full rates **Credit Cards** V, MC, AE, D **Check-In/Out** 3 p.m./11 a.m. **Smoking** Outside **Pets** No **Kids** "We welcome older children" **No-Nos** N/A **Minimum Stay** 2 nights most weekends; 3 nights select weekends **Open** All year **Hosts** Dennis & Bonnie Statz, 16 North 5th Ave., Sturgeon Bay 54235 **Phone** (920) 743-1105 or toll-free (877) 948-5223 (wht-lace) **Email** romance@whitelaceinn.com **Web** www.whitelaceinn.com

ROSENBERRY INN, Wausau

OVERALL ★★★★½ | QUALITY ★★★★½ | VALUE ★★★★★ | PRICE RANGE
$70–$100; WHOLE-FLOOR SUITES IN A SECOND HOME $150–$160 WEEKENDS

In a neighborhood listed on the National Register of Historic Places and where Frank Lloyd Wright designed two of the homes, Rosenberry Inn holds its own. Possibly designed by renowned architect George W. Maher (who designed at least four other houses in the district), the home is true to his motif-rhythm theory, combining natural and geometric elements to unify the design. The tone changes in the farm house suites across the street, featuring wainscot walls, original tin cove ceilings, wide plank floors, and, in the upstairs suite, walls covered by the home's original outdoor siding.

SETTING & FACILITIES
Location Central Wausau in the Andrew Warren Historic District **Near** Downtown Wausau, Leigh Yawkey Woodson Art Museum, Marathon County Historical Museum, restored Grand Theater, Rib Mountain State Park, Nine Mile Recreation Area. **Buildings** 1908 Prairie School brick & stucco home; also 1868 farm house across the street w/ gingerbread trim **Grounds** City lots, flower gardens **Public Space** In Rosenberry, foyer, DR, front porch, common room. Farm house has common porch **Food & Drink** Full breakfast, including 2 juices, home-baked muffins, & entree such as strata or Swedish pancakes w/ ham. **Recreation** Historic touring, museums, live theater, birding, downhill & cross-country skiing. **Amenities & Services** AC. Membership exchange privileges at nearby YMCA, YWCA.

ACCOMMODATIONS
Units Rosenberry Inn—1 suite, 5 guest rooms. Farmhouse—2 whole-floor suites. **All Rooms** Kitchenette w/ small fridge, coffeemaker, sink; TV, tape player, ceiling fan. **Some Rooms** Fireplace, tin ceiling, original claw-foot tub & sink. **Bed & Bath** King (1), queens (4), double (1). All private baths. **Favorites** Samuel Landfair Room, suite w/ exposed

brick, carved oak bed, & servants' window, where household staff once stood to watch for their masters' carriage arriving. **Comfort & Decor** Prairie School fans can bask in Rosenberry Inn's extra-deep front porch, original stained-glass lampposts flanking the front steps, wide halls, carved oak stairway, and original leaded glass windows. In the farmhouse across the street, check out the swing in the William suite: it's crafted from an old Jenny Lind bed.

RATES, RESERVATIONS, & RESTRICTIONS

Deposit Credit card number or 50% of stay **Discounts** $15 single-traveler discount on Rosenberry rooms & suite; state govt. rate **Credit Cards** V, MC **Check-In/Out** 3–10 p.m./11 a.m. **Smoking** No **Pets** No **Kids** Inquire **No-Nos** N/A **Minimum Stay** 2 nights on several select weekends **Open** All year **Hosts** Barry & Linda Brehmer, 511 Franklin St., Wausau 54403 **Phone** (715) 842-5733 or toll-free (800) 336-3799 **Fax** (715) 843-5659 **Email** innkeeper@rosenberryinn.com **Web** www.rosenberryinn.com

Southwest Wisconsin

Say cheese, because this zone is where Wisconsin's image was shaped—though we have been told that tourism has bumped dairy-producing as the state's number-one industry. Amish and Swiss communities dot this sector, and, perhaps because the region is so largely agricultural, we again found terrific bed-and-breakfasts at low cost.

The towns are small and historic. **Prairie du Chien,** on the banks of the **Mississippi River,** appeared in economic distress, but we found a fish house where we tasted our first "catfish jerky" ("approved by the sturgeon general"), and the bridge across the Mississippi took us to **Marquette, Iowa,** and a neighborhood of antiques shops. North of Prairie du Chien sits the curious riverfront town of **Alma,** consisting of two streets stretching for seven miles along the Mississippi. Stairway "avenues" take visitors up the bluffs on foot; in the fall, the annual migration of tundra swans to nearby **Rieck's Lake Park** is a major regional event.

The famous **Wisconsin Dells** are on the west side of the zone, 13 miles north of **Baraboo,** home of the **Circus World Museum.** We avoided the tourists and headed south. Our first stop was the artisan enclave of **Mineral Point,** where we toured Red Shutters bed-and-breakfasts and wished we could have browsed a few galleries. Here and in nearby towns—**Albany, Hazel Green, Monroe**—the bed-and-breakfasts were restored old homes and economically priced.

Then we hit **Madison**—the state capital, home to **University of Wisconsin,** and a metropolis compared to other towns in the zone—and bed-and-breakfast prices soared. To be fair, it's still possible to get a room under $100 at some inns here—weekdays—and the ones we saw were definitely elegant. Mansion Hill Inn is one of the most lavish bed-and-breakfasts we've seen anywhere, but we weren't shocked at the $340 weekend price for a suite; for this level of luxury, we think that's fair. Pinch yourself or you won't believe the place is real. If you can manage to leave your fancy digs, head for the water: Madison sits on an isthmus between two lakes and has been named one of the country's top canoe towns by *Paddler* magazine.

ALBANY HOUSE, Albany

OVERALL ★★★★½ | QUALITY ★★★★½ | VALUE ★★★★★ | PRICE RANGE $65–$95; 3RD-FLOOR SUITE $160

Any visitor will feel comfortable in this old house full of overstuffed furniture and flowers energizing every room. Porch sitting beneath the "vine ceiling" is the most popular sport—made easier by the abundance of books—and there's no need to stop reading when your stay ends; guests are encouraged to take home the book they've started and send back a new one. Even the gift certificates are value-added at Albany House: They actually look like gifts, hand-printed on hand-made paper. In cold weather, curling up in front of the wood-burning fireplace, surrounded by graceful green-hued vases, is a fine substitute for the hammock.

SETTING & FACILITIES
Location On the Sugar River, 30 min. south of Madison **Near** Sugar River Trail, cheese factories, wineries, Amish & Swiss communities, antiques malls. **Building** 1908 Arts & Crafts style, of local stone & concrete blocks **Grounds** 2 acres of lawns, perennial & rose gardens, sitting areas **Public Space** Foyer, LR, DR, large porch **Food & Drink** Snack on arrival, early coffee. Full 3-course breakfast includes 2 home-baked breads or muffins and entree, usually an egg dish. **Recreation** Croquet, horseshoes, antiquing, historic touring, biking, snowmobiling, cross-country skiing, fishing, canoeing, tubing.
Amenities & Services. AC. Robes for room w/ detached bath. Straw hats for guests to borrow if they'll be in the sun. Complimentary wine & cheese for whole-house rentals.

ACCOMMODATIONS
Units 4 guest rooms, 1 suite. **All Rooms** Sitting area. **Some Rooms** Ceiling fan, claw-foot tub, fireplace, TV, whirlpool. **Bed & Bath** King (1), queens (3), queen & 2 doubles (1). All private baths (1 detached). **Favorites** Master bedroom—sunny, yellow wall coverings w/ whirlpool & wood-burning fireplace. **Comfort & Decor** Innkeepers at this bed-and-breakfast successfully blend Arts & Crafts with contemporary pieces to create warm, inviting spaces. Note the Stickley rocker in the living room. Two-sided pocket doors and original quarter-sawed oak trim with tiny egg-and-dart edging, along with the original French-tiled foyer, form a rich backdrop for the collection of green Midwestern pottery. McCoy collectors, eat your hearts out.

RATES, RESERVATIONS, & RESTRICTIONS
Deposit Credit card or 1 night's stay **Discounts** None **Credit Cards** V, MC **Check-In/Out** 3–7 p.m./11 a.m. **Smoking** Outside, away from the house only (not on porch)

Pets No **Kids** Over age 10; no age restriction on whole-house rental **No-Nos** N/A **Minimum Stay** 2 nights on select weekends **Open** All year **Hosts** Margie & Ken Stoup, 405 South Mill St., Albany 53502 **Phone** (608) 862-3636 or toll-free (866) 977-7000 **Fax** (608) 862-1837 **Email** innkeeper@albanyhouse.net **Web** www.albanyhouse.net

AGES PAST COUNTRY HOUSE BED & BREAKFAST, Cashton

OVERALL ★★★★ | QUALITY ★★★★ | VALUE | PRICE RANGE $85–$125

The creaky maple floors just enhance the setting for some of Ages Past's most popular theme weekends, such as murder mysteries and wine tastings. Only long-term planners, though, can get into the inn's biggest event, sold out at least a year ahead: Titanic Night, staged every Saturday in April, when the only menu selection is the last first-class dinner served on the Titanic. Upstairs, youngsters of any age should peek into Rae Leigh's Room, filled with more than three dozen antique teddy bears.

SETTING & FACILITIES
Location Off Hwy. 33 near downtown Cashton **Near** Wild Cat Mountain State Park, antiques malls, golf courses, Amish country. **Building** 1898 Country Victorian, white exterior, former Catholic rectory **Grounds** Large lot w/ pergola, fountains, flower beds **Public Space** DR, LR, library, porch. On-site restaurant open to public for lunch & dinner **Food & Drink** Fresh ice water in rooms. Early coffee delivered to rooms 7–7:30 a.m.; full breakfast includes entree such as quiche or pecan-coconut French toast. **Recreation** Horseback riding, downhill & cross-country skiing, biking, golf, antiquing. **Amenities & Services** AC. Robes, slippers, fresh flowers in guest rooms.

ACCOMMODATIONS
Units 4 guest rooms. **All Rooms** Cable TV in cabinets, honor bar, writing desk, Belgian

chandelier, sitting area. **Some Rooms** Half-canopy bed, garden view. **Bed & Bath** King (1), queens (3). All private baths w/ claw-foot tubs & showers. **Favorites** Sarah's Room, w/ king bed, plenty of sun & decorated in soft yellows & greens. **Comfort & Decor** The furnishings are a mix of French country and Victorian. Rooms are not large, but they're comfortable, featuring fine antiques such as the 17th-century bed in Beky's Room and the carved bed in Nicholle's Room. Built-ins, transoms, oak trim, and leaded glass are found throughout; the most striking feature is the stained-glass skylight in the upstairs hallway.

RATES, RESERVATIONS, & RESTRICTIONS

Deposit Credit card number or $50 **Discounts** Whole-house **Credit Cards** V, D, MC, AE **Check-In/Out** 3–9 p.m./11 a.m. **Smoking** No **Pets** No **Kids** Over age 12 **No-Nos** N/A **Minimum Stay** None **Open** All year **Hosts** Carl & Barbara Bargabos, 1223 Front St., Cashton 54619 **Phone** (608) 654-55950 or toll-free (888) 322-5494 **Fax** (608) 654-5709 **Email** innkeeper@agespast.net **Web** www.agespast.net

WISCONSIN HOUSE STAGE COACH INN, *Hazel Green*

OVERALL ★★★★ | QUALITY ★★★★ | VALUE ★★★★ | PRICE RANGE $65–$125

This inn's history is half the fun of the place. Ulysses S. Grant, a friend of one-time owner Jefferson Crawford, visited here often; one bright corner room—possibly the room in which the president slept—is named after him. The town, settled in 1824 by lead miners and originally called Hardscrabble, is tiny; 30 years later, after the railroad had replaced the stagecoach, the inn had become Crawford's family residence. Today, an on-site restaurant serves seven-course, prix-fixe candlelight dinners Saturday nights, with a twist: the first party to make a reservation selects the menu.

SETTING & FACILITIES

Location 1 block east of WI 11 & 80 **Near** Galena (IL) & Dubuque (IA); antiques malls. **Building** 1846 stagecoach inn **Grounds** Double town lot w/ lavish flower gardens, gazebo, outdoor seating areas **Public Space** Porches up & down, LR, pub area, DR, library **Food & Drink** Snacks, candies, beverages available any time. Full breakfast is buffet w/ 5 dishes if 10 or more guests staying; if less, sit-down breakfast includes hot entree & meat. **Recreation** Antiquing, historic touring. **Amenities & Services** AC, robes for shared bath. Access to phone.

ACCOMMODATIONS

Units 2 suites, 6 guest rooms. **All Rooms** Sitting area. **Some Rooms** Garden or street view, canopy bed, desk & chair. **Bed & Bath** Kings (2), queens (4), double (2). 2-bit Suite, the entire 3rd floor, also has full bed & 2 daybeds in sitting room (sleeps up to 6). 6 private baths, 1 shared. **Favorites** Percival Suite, including Miss Helen's Room w/ walnut & rattan day beds, garden & street views. **Comfort & Decor** One feels transported in this inn— in this entire community—back to the town's early mining days. Resembling a Wild West movie set, the inn has kept the original floors and pocket doors; guest rooms are decorated in honor of the inn's history. The Chicago Room features accessories reminiscent of that stagecoach destination, and the Indian Room showcases Native American artifacts.

RATES, RESERVATIONS, & RESTRICTIONS

Deposit Credit card number **Discounts** 10% off for weeknight or multiple-night bookings **Credit Cards** V, MC, AE, D **Check-In/Out** 3–6 p.m./10 a.m. **Smoking** On porches **Pets** No **Kids** "Well-behaved children welcome." No charge for infants **No-Nos** Because inn has a liquor license, guests cannot drink their own liquor in common areas **Minimum Stay** None **Open** All year **Hosts** Ken & Pat Disch, 2105 East Main St., Hazel Green 53811 **Phone** (608) 854-2233 **Email** wishouse@mhtc.net **Web** www.wisconsin house.com

ARBOR HOUSE, AN ENVIRONMENTAL INN, Madison

OVERALL ★★★★½ | QUALITY ★★★★½ | VALUE ★★★ | PRICE RANGE $110–$220 WEEKENDS, $95–$175 WEEKDAYS

Clean visual lines and soothing music greet guests to this environmental inn, with progressive features such as hydronic heating, lpassive cooling system without air conditioning, recycled tile and Douglas fir flooring, sustainably harvested woods, and plant-derived paints and stains. Arbor House is disabled accessible, a model for urban ecology. Guest rooms in the annex are named for prominent Madison conservationists, including John Muir. One environmentally correct bonus: To encourage guests to use public transportation, Arbor House pays their bus far during their stay.

SETTING & FACILITIES

Location In the city, across from the Univ. of Wisconsin Arboretum **Near** Lake Wingra, Edgewood College, Camp Randall Stadium, State Capitol, Univ. of Wisconsin, arboretum. **Building** 1853 former tavern & stagecoach stop, one of Madison's oldest homes, on National Register of Historic Places. **Grounds** Historic home & contemporary annex w/ courtyard & gardens between, connected by an arbor **Public Space** Patios, great room in annex, "Resource Porch," 6-person sauna & sitting room, common room in historic home **Food & Drink** Welcome beverage; hot tea or herbal iced tea any time, evening sweet treat. Full breakfast weekends includes entree (one of 21 alternating dishes), weekdays home-baked goods, cereals, fruits. **Recreation** Canoeing, kayaking, birding, biking, historic touring, swimming, sailing, cross-country skiing, zoo, golf, museums, art galleries, theater. **Amenities & Services** AC. Mountain bikes available, complimentary canoeing & kayaking passes, binoculars for birding, conference facilities, sauna, environmental resource center, Aveda hair care products, & "organic robes" (made w/out bleaches, chemicals, dyes) in rooms. PC, fax available.

ACCOMMODATIONS

Units 1 suite, 7 guest rooms. **All Rooms** Sitting area. **Some Rooms** Whirlpool, chapel ceiling, arboretum view, private patio, balcony, fireplace, wet bar, CD stereo system, skylights. **Bed & Bath** King (1), queens (7). All private baths. **Favorites** Studio, a prairie-influenced suite w/ king bed, skylights, stove fireplace, whirlpool, & exposed brick wall.

Comfort & Decor Historic features meet modern conveniences in this unique, environmentally tuned inn. Each room is distinctive, with its own features—a natural stone fireplace, velvet reading chairs, hexagonal fish tank, and vaulted ceilings among them. Beds range from pine sleigh style to four-poster to more contemporary; overall, the style is closest to French country.

RATES, RESERVATIONS, & RESTRICTIONS

Deposit Required, arrangements discussed at time of booking **Discounts** Group (Nov.–April), corp., winter specials **Credit Cards** V, MC, AE **Check-In/Out** 3 p.m./11 a.m. **Smoking** On designated smokers' porch only; not on balconies **Pets** No **Kids** Yes **No-Nos** "We try to keep a scent-free inn. We have an air purifier for people who wear heavy perfume." **Minimum Stay** 2 nights weekends & during special events & football games **Open** All year **Hosts** John & Cathie Imes, 3402 Monroe St., Madison 53711 **Phone** (608) 238-2981 **Fax** (608) 238-1175 **Web** www.arbor-house.com

MANSION HILL INN, Madison

OVERALL ★★★★★ | QUALITY ★★★★★ | VALUE ★★★★★ | PRICE RANGE
$170–$340 WEEKENDS, $160–$320 MIDWEEK.

Mansion Hill Inn is pure European opulence, perhaps the most luxurious bed-and-breakfast in the Midwest, and one of the priciest—but not at all overpriced. One wants to gasp at the elaborate, gold-trimmed cornices, insets, gables, and bays. Each room creates its own ambience, from the tented sultan's bed, ottomans, and pale turquoise tile bath of the extravagantly swathed Turkish Nook to the black-and-cinnabar palette and lustrous ebony tub of the Oriental Suite. This isn't just an inn, it's a fantasy.

SETTING & FACILITIES

Location Downtown Madison between Lake Mendota & State Capitol **Near** Univ. of Wisconsin, state offices, Mansion Hill historic district, Period Garden Park, galleries, museums. **Building** 1858 Romanesque Revival mansion, on National Register of Historic Places **Grounds** City lot, flower gardens **Public Space** Entry, foyer, parlor, DR **Food & Drink** Afternoon refreshments including complimentary wine; silver-service cont'l-plus breakfast served in guest rooms. **Recreation** Theater, fine arts, historic touring, canoeing, boating, arboretum. **Amenities & Services** AC. 24-hour valet service, access to health spa & private dining club, shoe shine service, evening turn-down w/ pillow candies, wine cellar, robes, logo bath amenities, daily newspaper.

ACCOMMODATIONS

Units 11 guest rooms. **All Rooms** Sitting area, cable TV/VCR, stereo, mini-bar. **Some Rooms** Fireplace, standard or double whirlpool, private balcony, private garden entrance, veranda, skylights, floor-to-ceiling windows. **Bed & Bath** King (1), queens (10). All private baths. **Favorites** Craftsman Suite, furnished in the style of Craftsman Magazine (including

2 signed Stickley pieces), w/ French doors opening onto a private patio, double whirlpool, fireplace, & arched-ceiling bath w/ quarry tile & parquet floor. **Comfort & Decor** Marble floors, ornate cornices and medallions gracing 14-foot ceilings, a four-story staircase spiraling to the belvedere high above, and a standard of service to match the resplendence have earned Mansion Hill Inn a rare four-diamond rating. Finely carved marble mantels, damask and Chinese silk wall coverings, and round-arched windows fill the rooms with light and elegance. **Discounts** Single occupancy $20–$30 discount, depending on room

RATES, RESERVATIONS, & RESTRICTIONS

Deposit Credit card number or 1 night's stay **Check-In/Out** 4 p.m./noon **Smoking** No **Pets** No **Kids** Over age 12 **No-Nos** N/A **Minimum Stay** Inquire **Open** All year **Hosts** Anke Cramblit, 424 North Pinckney St., Madison 53703 **Phone** (608) 255-3999 or toll-free (800) 798-9070 **Fax** (608) 255-2217 **Web** www.mansionhillinn.com

RED SHUTTERS BED & BREAKFAST, Mineral Point

OVERALL ★★★★ | QUALITY ★★★★½ | VALUE ★★★★★ | PRICE RANGE $75–$95

Perched high above one of best little shopping towns in the state, Red Shutters offers a pleasant refuge. The library's brick fireplace anchors the public areas, and the original art lends a contemporary air to this space's more than 150 years. The inn's slightly New Age quality is perfectly suited to Mineral Point, a town where art galleries and studios of every medium reign.

SETTING & FACILITIES

Location 2 blocks from historic downtown, off Hwys. 151 & 39 **Near** Taliesin, Gov. Dodge State Park, Pendarvis living museum, Merry Christmas Mine Prairie (43-acre former mine site w/ walking trails), American Player Theater, galleries. **Building** 1848 Federal home w/ Italianate trim & signature red shutters **Grounds** Oversized city lot, perennial gardens **Public Space** Deck porch, LR/library, DR, stone patio **Food & Drink** Appetizers, "if guests arrive early enough." Full "elegant" breakfast weekends; weekdays choice of full or cont'l. **Recreation** Kayaking, canoeing, birding, live theater, antiquing, biking, cross-country skiing, swimming, historic touring. **Amenities & Services** AC. Robes in rooms (sarongs in summer).

ACCOMMODATIONS

Units 2. **All Rooms** Sitting area. **Some Rooms** N/A. **Bed & Bath** Queen (1), double (1). Shared bath. **Favorites** Margaret Sophia, decorated w/ intricate table covering of trapunto embroidery & crocheted edge, done by innkeeper's great-aunt. **Comfort & Decor** Ethnic textiles, vintage fashions, and very good family artwork adorn the walls in the common rooms. They join an eclectic mix of antiques and contemporary furnishings, Indonesian batiks, and artifacts from world travels. Together they create a funky but classy ambience.

RATES, RESERVATIONS, & RESTRICTIONS

Deposit 1 night's stay **Discounts** Inquire **Credit Cards** No; cash or check only **Check-In/Out** 5–7 p.m./11 a.m. or by prior arrangement **Smoking** No **Pets** No **Kids** No **No-**

Nos N/A **Minimum Stay** None **Open** All year **Hosts** Christine Tharnstrom, 221 Clowney St., Mineral Point 53565 **Phone** (608) 987-2268 **Email** info@redshutters.com **Web** www.redshutters.com

VICTORIAN GARDEN BED & BREAKFAST, Monroe

OVERALL ★★★★ | QUALITY ★★★★ | VALUE ★★★★★ | PRICE RANGE $80–$90

Victorian Garden B&B is a comfortable haven any time of year, but if you don't go in July when the perennials are at their peak, you're missing a lavish show. Two porches and backyard seating make it easy to linger. If you must go indoors, visit the extensive doll collection in the back parlor and be sure to peek in the "teddy bear room" upstairs. The stained-glass window at the landing is original. Walk downtown and buy some cheese; Monroe is known as the Swiss Cheese Capital of the United States.

SETTING & FACILITIES
Location Residential neighborhood near Monroe's town square, off US 69 **Near** Sugar River Bicycle Trail, Ice Age Hiking Trail, New Glarus Woods, Cadiz Spring State Park, Cheese Country Recreational Trail, downtown Monroe, antiques malls. **Building** 1880 Victorian, blue-gray exterior, w/ L[GOTHIC]-shaped front porch **Grounds** Large city lot w/ lush landscaped flower gardens, shade gardens, fountain **Public Space** Foyer, formal parlor, TV parlor, sitting room, library, DR, 2 porches **Food & Drink** Full breakfast w/ hot entree (egg dish and/or meats), home-baked breads/muffins, cheesecake. **Recreation** Biking, cross-country skiing, birding, canoeing, antiquing. **Amenities & Services** AC. Logo soaps.

ACCOMMODATIONS
Units 3 guest rooms. **All Rooms** Sitting area. **Some Rooms** Double shower, claw-foot tub. **Bed & Bath** Queens (2), double (1). All private baths. **Favorites** White Lace & Roses room, w/ largest bath, double shower, claw-foot tub, & view of gardens. The palette is black & white, but the room is cheery nonetheless. **Comfort & Decor** When a home is described as "picture-pretty," someone's talking about the Victorian Garden. White wicker furniture is the perfect choice for porch furniture; indoors, original beechwood trim makes a tidy backdrop for the parlor's original Tiffany ceiling light. Quilts upstairs were designed and sewn by the innkeeper's daughter.

RATES, RESERVATIONS, & RESTRICTIONS
Deposit 1 night's stay or credit card number **Discounts** Single traveler, $10 off **Credit Cards** V, MC **Check-In/Out** 4 p.m./11 a.m. **Smoking** No **Pets** No **Kids** Welcome by prior arrangement **No-Nos** N/A **Minimum Stay** None **Open** All year **Hosts** Ron & Judy Marsh, 1720 16th St., Monroe 53566 **Phone** (608) 328-1720 or toll-free (888) 814-7909

NEUMANN HOUSE BED & BREAKFAST, Prairie du Chien

OVERALL ★★★½ | QUALITY ★★★ | VALUE ★★★ | PRICE RANGE $90–$100

Innkeeping is a second career for Neumann, a transplanted Chicagoan, home economist by training and, at the time of our visit, a city council representative. We enjoyed our visit with her, but we found the cats to be a problem. For guests without allergies, Neumann House is a modest but historic structure. Originally home to a series of prosperous mercantile families, the inn served as a Jesuit boarding school for young men during the post–World War II era, becoming an inn in 1988.

SETTING & FACILITIES
Location Downtown Prairie du Chien, walking distance of the Mississippi River **Near** Wyalusing State Park, Isle of Capri Riverboat Casino, Effigy Mounds National Monument, Marquette antiques district. **Building** 1857 brick Italianate vernacular **Grounds** Small yard, flower beds **Public Space** LR, TV room, DR, deck, front porch **Food & Drink** Full breakfast includes entree & breakfast meats. Signature dish is cheese, ham & vegetable soufflé w/ waffle & fruit compote. **Recreation** Biking, birding, fishing, cross-country skiing, golf, canoeing, swimming, boating, antiquing, historical touring. **Amenities & Services** Individually controlled AC, guest fridge.

ACCOMMODATIONS
Units 3 units, plus sun porch, rented only w/ Pink Room. **All Rooms** Ceiling fans, cable TV, sitting area. **Some Rooms** Claw-foot tub. **Bed & Bath** King (1), queen (1), 2 twins (1). Sun porch has double. Roll-aways available (2). All private baths (1 detached); sun porch shares w/ Pink Room. **Favorites** Pink Room because it's the only way to rent the sun porch—really our favorite, w/ 8 windows, red oak wainscoting, antique iron bed, & easy chair. **Comfort & Decor** This Civil War home has 12-foot ceilings, a large brick fireplace and cove ceilings in the living room, and faux grain in the entryway. It's a comfy old house, unless you're allergic to the innkeeper's eight cats (seven live outside). The dander level was so high we had to leave after 30 minutes; we were wheezing painfully.

RATES, RESERVATIONS, & RESTRICTIONS
Deposit $50 **Discounts** Wisconsin Public Television members & multiple-night guests, 10% off **Credit Cards** N/A **Check-In/Out** 5–7 p.m./11 a.m. **Smoking** Outdoors **Pets** No; innkeepers have 8 cats; 7 live outdoors **Kids** Yes **Minimum Stay** 2 nights on holidays & select special-event weekends **Open** All year **Hosts** Luanne Neumann, 121 North Michigan St., Prairie du Chien 53821 **Phone** (608) 326-8104 **Email** lneumann@mhtc.net

STRAWBERRY LACE INN, *Sparta*

OVERALL ★★★★½ | QUALITY ★★★★½ | VALUE ★★★★★ | PRICE RANGE $89–$145

At this elegant inn, every touch is designed for guests' pampering. Beds are filled with mountains of pillows, and the high ceilings (12 feet downstairs, 11 feet upstairs) lend added grandeur. Only if you stay a dozen weekends will you have a repeat breakfast; innkeepers keep track of which meals are served to return guests, so you will taste all 23 entrees before you eat the same thing twice. Note the ceiling medallion and corner carvings in the sitting room—the design is replicated on the carpet.

SETTING & FACILITIES

Location Off I-90, 20 mi. east of La Crosse **Near** Elroy-Sparta State Bike Trail, La Crosse River State Bike Trail. **Building** 1875 Italianate Victorian, white exterior, w/ prominent tower & widow's walk **Grounds** Spacious lawns, flower beds **Public Space** Foyer, parlor, sitting room, 4-season side porch, DR, sun room off DR **Food & Drink** Sodas & snacks available any time. 4-course breakfast served on crystal & linen, featuring 23 alternating entrees: "We serve no pancakes, waffles, or French toast." **Recreation** Biking, golf, boating, canoeing, swimming, antiquing, downhill & cross-country skiing. **Amenities & Services** Robes in rooms, AC.

ACCOMMODATIONS

Units 5 guest rooms. **All Rooms** Ceiling fan, sitting area. **Some Rooms** Fireplace, wet bar, microwave, fridge, double whirlpool, cable TV. **Bed & Bath** Kings (3), queens (2). All private baths. **Favorites** Tower Room, a hand-painted haven w/ picket fence headboard, 4 arched windows, best views. **Comfort & Decor** Careful restoration of this historic home kept the dining room chandelier's original flues and shades, the walnut floating staircase, inlaid floors, cove ceilings, and pocket doors with rollers in the floor. Even the guest bath is elegant, with ornate parquet floors.

RATES, RESERVATIONS, & RESTRICTIONS
Deposit Credit card number **Discounts** None **Credit Cards** V, MC **Check-In/Out** 3 p.m./11 a.m. **Smoking** No **Pets** No **Kids** No **No-Nos** "If guests bring wine, we suggest they take it to the porch" **Minimum Stay** 2 nights on special weekends **Open** All year **Hosts** Elsie & Jack Ballinger, 603 North Water St., Sparta 54656 **Phone** (608) 269-7878 **Email** Strawberry@centurytel.net **Web** www.spartan.org/sbl

Southeast Wisconsin

Wisconsin's most populous zone starts in marshlands and ends in urban sprawl.

The 32,000-acre **Horicon Marsh,** straddling the boundary between Zones 24 and 25, is mostly owned and managed by the federal government as a **National Wildlife Refuge;** the remainder is owned by the state. Birders migrate along with geese, ducks, swans, cranes, and herons to watch the waterfowl descend on the march in spring and fall. Just east of the marsh is **Waupaca** on the **Crystal River,** a Class III trout stream. Also nearby is the renowned **Chain O' Lakes,** a string of 22 connected lakes known for their water sports. In this area, most bed-and-breakfasts are larger, restored pre–Civil War farm houses, with rooms available in the $75–$90 range.

Driving southeast into the **Kettle Moraine**—a forest filled with unusual land formations, created by glacial movement and melting—we reach **Plymouth,** another dairy center with several cheese factories still thriving. One of the town's biggest attractions is the 17-mile **Old Plank Road Trail,** stretching past town east to **Sheboygan,** paralleling Highway 23 and accommodating walkers, bikers, Nordic skiers, inline skaters, and horseback riders.

The closer we come to Lake Michigan, the more we see historic areas characterized by Queen Anne Victorians built by shipping and industrial tycoons. There are exceptions; Hillwind Farm is a farm house, and Sheboygan's Brownstone Inn is a brownstone mansion with Arts & Crafts influence. But the Victorian flavor is strong, and it grew as we made our way south into lake resort towns such as **Delavan, Lake Mills, Oconomowoc,** and **Green Lake.** These towns are on the outskirts of **Milwaukee,** home of breweries, the Brewers, and **Harley-Davidson.** Summer here is great fun, with more than a dozen ethnic festivals, the world's biggest outdoor music extravaganza, and a busy, accessible lakefront. **The Milwaukee Art**

Museum has a new wing, the **Milwaukee River** walkway is a promenade, and the Brewers have a new ballpark.

This is a high-energy city with character, and the bed-and-breakfast landscape reflects that quality. There's no shortage of National Register Queen Annes, most built by nineteenth-century beer and steel magnates. We found a few more modest homes as well, both in the suburbs and in the city, that compete with their flashier colleagues by pampering guests.

ADDISON HOUSE, Allenton

OVERALL ★★★½ | QUALITY ★★★½ | VALUE ★★★★ | PRICE RANGE $65–$85

Don't look for fancy digs here, just a cordial welcome and rich history. The inn is built on a Native American powwow site and later served as a trading post, an 1860s saloon, and a bordello between World War I and the Korean War. Interesting furnishings include the oak sleigh bed where Ms. Fish's mother was born, but all of the themed rooms are worth a look. Fish added the tin ceiling in the living room. Her organic garden defines the breakfast menu; eggs are from her free-range chicken.

SETTING & FACILITIES
Location In unincorporated village of Addison Center, off US 41 **Near** Horicon Marsh Wildlife Area, Holy Hill, Kettle Moraine, cheese factory. **Building** 1750s cabin w/ 1880 additions **Grounds** 3 acres of flower & vegetable gardens, meadows, trails, outdoor benches & tables **Public Space** LR, DR, 2nd-floor deck **Food & Drink** Water in room, water cooler in kitchen. 5-course country breakfast w/ tons of food. **Recreation** Birding, canoeing, swimming, kayaking, antiquing, cross-country skiing, historic touring. **Amenities & Services** AC.

ACCOMMODATIONS
Units 3 guest rooms. **All Rooms** Clock radio, phone jacks. **Some Rooms** TV. **Bed & Bath** King (1), double (1), 2 twins (1). All private baths. **Favorites** Bordello Room w/ king bed & largest bath, decorated w/ tasteful nudes. **Comfort & Decor** Furnished in overstuffed couches and comfortable chairs, this inn is decorated with the innkeeper's collections: majolica plates in one room, teapots in the kitchen, cobalt blue bottles found in beer caves on the property. The nude painting dominating the Bordello Room was painted by innkeeper Suzanne Fish; the frame is a wallpaper border.

RATES, RESERVATIONS, & RESTRICTIONS
Deposit $25 **Discounts** None **Credit Cards** No Please clarify] **Check-In/Out** Flexible, by prior arrangement **Smoking** On porch **Pets** Inquire (several resident dogs & cats are permitted in B&B but not in guest rooms) **Kids** "There are ponds and caves on the property, dangerous for kids." **No-Nos** Food in guest rooms **Minimum Stay** None **Open** All year **Hosts** Suzanne Fish, 6373 Hwy. 175, Allenton 53002 **Phone** (262) 629-9993 **Email** addisonhouse@hnet.net **Web** www.hnet.net/~addisonhouse

ALLYN MANSION INN, *Delavan*

OVERALL ★★★★★ | QUALITY ★★★★★ | VALUE ★★★★ | PRICE RANGE
$125–$185 ($100 FOR SHARED BATH)

Shuttered windows lend added richness to the harmony of textures and shapes in this 9,500-square-foot mansion. Nine marble fireplaces were a stylish status statement by the architect, and furnishings throughout the house do it justice. The queen mahogany four-poster bed in the Bishop's Room, the ten-foot-tall walnut half-tester in the Eastlake Room, and the rosewood Prudent Mallard bed in Mary E.'s room typify the quality of antiques selected for guest rooms.

SETTING & FACILITIES
Location Central Delavan off I-43 **Near** Lake Geneva, Big Foot Beach State Park, Alpine Ski Resort, Illinois border, downtown Delavan, antiques malls. **Building** 1884 Queen Anne–Eastlake in Cream-City brick, Grand Prize winner of the National Trust's Great American Home Awards (1992), on National Register of Historic Places **Grounds** Large city lot, flower beds **Public Space** Foyer, 3 parlors, library, DR, front & back porches, patio **Food & Drink** Coffee 7 a.m., wine & cheese 6 p.m. Full breakfast served on antique china & silver, usually includes "Wisconsin quiche" made of 4 cheeses, home-baked cracked-wheat bread, homemade cinnamon rolls, jams. **Recreation** Boating, swimming, biking, downhill & cross-country skiing, antiquing. **Amenities & Services** AC. Robes in rooms.

ACCOMMODATIONS
Units 8 guest rooms. **All Rooms** Sitting area. **Some Rooms** Plantation bed from 1820s or 1830s, fireplace, desk & chair, stained-glass window, marble sink. **Bed & Bath** Queens (6—some slightly over or under standard size), doubles (2). 6 private bath, 1 shared. **Favorites** Nanny's Room w/ a magnificently carved Renaissance Revival walnut bed

(slightly under queen size), stained-glass transom windows, gas fireplace. **Comfort & Decor** Billed as "the most complete Eastlake interior in the state," Allyn Mansion surrounds guests with sumptuous French walnut and oak woodwork, original "gasaliers," 13 gables, an imposing wooden tower, and more bays than this visitor could count. Ceilings on the first floor are 13 feet high; upstairs, 12-feet-wide hallways enhance the feeling of Victorian opulence. First-floor ceilings were frescoed at one time; the dining room survived.

RATES, RESERVATIONS, & RESTRICTIONS

Deposit 1 night's stay **Discounts** Single travelers, 20% off Mon.–Thurs.; "frequent sleepers" (those who've stayed at least 10 nights) get 10% discount **Credit Cards** MC, V **Check-In/Out** 3–10 p.m./11 a.m. **Smoking** Outside, away from patio in summer. "Heavy smokers who smell like ashtrays are requested to disrobe and be hosed down before entering the mansion!" (from brochure) **Pets** No **Kids** Over age 12 ("After 34 years each in the classroom, our penance is paid!") **No-Nos** N/A **Minimum Stay** 2 nights weekends May–Oct. "If guests reserve a Saturday night, they must also take a second night." **Open** All year **Hosts** Joe Johnson & Ron Markwell, 511 East Walworth Ave., Delavan 53115 **Phone** (262) 728-9090 **Fax** (262) 728-0201 **Email** info@allynmansion.com **Web** www.allynmansion.com

MCCONNELL INN BED & BREAKFAST, Green Lake

OVERALL ★★★★ | QUALITY ★★★★ | VALUE ★★★★ | PRICE RANGE $85–$100; SUITE $165

Green Lake is the oldest resort community west of Niagara Falls, and if you close your eyes, you can see the parasols and bloomer-style swimsuits on the beach. McConnell Inn fits right in, with original, golden-toned woodworking that will never be replicated: When the craftsman who created the wood and leaded windows passed away, his plans and tools were destroyed per the rules of his guild. In the attic, signatures of the house painters can still be seen on a support beam.

SETTING & FACILITIES

Location On Business 23 on Green Lake **Near** Resort community, beach, parks, boat landings. **Building** 1900 Victorian, white exterior **Grounds** Small yard, flower gardens **Public Space** Foyer, DR, 2 parlors, porch **Food & Drink** Afternoon snacks, water, candies in rooms. Full breakfast includes hot entree; house favorites are apple cheese pancakes & stuffed French toast. **Recreation** Boating, swimming, canoeing, kayaking, golf, antiquing, cross-country skiing. **Amenities & Services** AC. Bath amenities; massage weekend package, bread baking classes offered; guest fridge.

ACCOMMODATIONS

Units 1 suite, 4 guest rooms. **All Rooms** Ceiling fans, sitting area. **Some Rooms** Clawfoot tub, double whirlpool, fireplace, canopy or four-poster bed, wet bar, cable TV/VCR. **Bed & Bath** Kings (2), queens (3). All private baths. **Favorites** Master suite, entire 3rd floor w/ exposed brick, 14-foot vaulted ceilings, wet bar, sitting room. **Comfort & Decor**

Elegance begins in the foyer of this grand resort home, with inlaid parquet floors, leaded glass, and an Italianate marble coal-burning fireplace beckoning guests to continue browsing. The wood trim is quarter-sawed oak. The only difficulty here is deciding where to pause—on a porch rocker, in the book-lined turret parlor, or in the dining room, where the wall covering is an ornate, tooled leather wainscot.

RATES, RESERVATIONS, & RESTRICTIONS
Deposit N/A **Discounts** Winter discounts on 3 of the rooms **Credit Cards** MC, V, D **Check-In/Out** 2 p.m./11 a.m. **Smoking** No **Pets** No **Kids** Over age 15 (Note: A city ordinance prohibits more than 2 guests per room) **No-Nos** N/A **Minimum Stay** 2 nights weekends May–Oct.; 3 nights holidays; all weekends 2 nights in master suite. **Open** All year; closed Thanksgiving & Christmas **Hosts** Scott & Mary-Jo Johnson, 497 South Lawson (Bus. 23), Green Lake 54941 **Phone** (920) 294-6430 or toll-free (888) 238-8625 **Email** info@mcconnellinn.com **Web** www.mcconnellinn.com

STOPPENBACH HOUSE BED & BREAKFAST, Jefferson

OVERALL ★★★½ | QUALITY ★★★½ | VALUE ★★★★ | PRICE RANGE $80–$110

Large, imposing portraits of Charles and Catherine Stoppenbach grace the dining room wall. He was quite the entrepreneur, founding a saw mill, lumber yard, bank, wool mill, and his legend—Stoppenbach Meats, the largest producer of pepperoni in America today. His home is a visual intrigue and will become a showplace as restoration continues. At the moment, you have to look for the elegance—but it's there, waiting to shine.

SETTING & FACILITIES
Location Blocks from juncture of US 18 & WI 26 **Near** Glacial Drumlin bike trail, Fireside Dinner Theater, Cambridge Pottery. **Building** 1868 Italianate, white exterior **Grounds** Double lot w/ flower beds, shrubs, gazebo **Public Space** LR, DR front porch, screened side porch **Food & Drink** Welcome snack; water, soda, coffee any time. Full breakfast includes hot entree. **Recreation** Biking, birding, cross-country skiing, antiquing, live theater. **Amenities & Services** Biodegradable soaps. Breakfast delivered to room on request. Fax, copier, & computer available after business hours.

ACCOMMODATIONS
Units 5 guest rooms. **All Rooms** TV/VCR, sitting area. **Some Rooms** Garden view, double whirlpool, trundle bed, desk. **Bed & Bath** Kings (2), queens (2), double (1). All private baths, 1 detached. **Favorites** Cathedral Room, sunny corner room w/ view of 2 church steeples lit at night, double whirlpool, king bed. **Comfort & Decor** The original tin roof, maple floors, crown moldings, and 12-foot ceilings (11 feet upstairs) give a sense of history to this house. The original marble fireplace graces the living room. The disabled-friendly Cathedral Room features the original 1920s white bath with vintage floor and wall tile.

RATES, RESERVATIONS, & RESTRICTIONS
Deposit 50% of stay **Discounts** Corp. 40%; full-house **Credit Cards** MC, V, AE **Check-

In/Out 3–7 p.m./11 a.m. **Smoking** Outside or on smoking porch **Pets** Yes, if kept in guest room or w/ its owner (resident cat comes into B&B) **Kids** Yes, but discourage younger children on weekends; Inquire **No-Nos** N/A **Minimum Stay** None **Open** All year **Hosts** Karen Drews, 244 East Racine, Jefferson 53549 **Phone** (920) 674-9747 **Email** stpnbchs@jefnet.com

FARGO MANSION INN, Lake Mills

OVERALL ★★★★½ | QUALITY ★★★★½ | VALUE ★★★★ | PRICE RANGE $89–$170

Now this is history: Fargo Mansion was the original home of Enoch J. Fargo of the Wells Fargo Stagecoach Company. Lake Mills has always been a resort town—trains came regularly from Chicago to deposit the Midwest's most affluent vacationers lakeside—and Fargo clearly had visions of impressing his visitors. The house is full of ornate carved moldings with intricate beadwork, carved leaves, decorative friezes, and space for as many functions and private conversations as visiting tycoons and their families could need. This home is an original, in a town straight off a Normal Rockwell canvas.

SETTING & FACILITIES
Location In central Lake Mills, 20 mi. SE of Madison, just off I-94 **Near** Mud Lake bike trail, Glacial Drumlin State Bike Trail, Rock Lake, 16 county parks, Aztalan State Park burial mounds. **Building** 1881 Queen Anne w/ wraparound porch, prominent turret, on National Register of Historic Places **Grounds** Oversized city lot, flower beds **Public Space** Porch, foyer, 2 DRs, library, LR, 2nd-floor turret sitting room **Food & Drink** Complimentary wine, sodas, water. Full breakfast includes hot entree. **Recreation** Historic touring, biking, swimming, canoeing, kayaking, boating, antiquing, cross-country skiing. **Amenities & Services** AC.

ACCOMMODATIONS
Units 5 guest rooms. **All Rooms** Sitting area. **Some Rooms** Whirlpool, fireplace, private porch, skylights, window seat. **Bed & Bath** Queens (3), doubles (2). All private baths. **Favorites** Master bedroom, w/ fireplace, double whirlpool, private porch, largest sitting area. **Comfort & Decor** It's always a more personal bed-and-breakfast experience when the hosts are collectors, and what these guys collect can keep guests browsing for an entire afternoon. The Santas in the foyer are a beautiful spectacle, but don't overlook the antique toys and glassware. The bird's-eye birch moldings set off the treasures beautifully. A favorite spot is the tile-floored solarium area off the guest dining room, softened by quarter-sawed oak paneling.

RATES, RESERVATIONS, & RESTRICTIONS
Deposit N/A **Discounts** Jan.–April, 25% off Sun.–Thurs. Corp. discounts Sun.–Thurs. year-round **Credit Cards** MC, V **Check-In/Out** 3 p.m./11 a.m., flexible by prior arrangement **Smoking** Outside **Pets** No **Kids** Welcome but not always recommended; inquire

No-Nos N/A **Minimum Stay** None **Open** All year **Hosts** Barry Luce & Tom Boycks, 211 North Main St., Lake Mills 53551 **Phone** (920) 648-3654 **Email** frontdsk@fargo-mansion.com **Web** www.fargomansion.com

BRUMDER MANSION B&B, Milwaukee

OVERALL ★★★★½ | QUALITY ★★★★½ | VALUE ★★★★★ | PRICE RANGE $69–$175; TO $215 IN SEASON

If you've never seen a priceless work of art before, step into the dining room and gaze on the six-foot-tall fireplace designed and crafted by Niedeken, a friend of Frank Lloyd Wright who also designed the stained-glass windows, beveled glass, and woodwork throughout the mansion. The fireplace is of stained glass tile, topped with a carved oak mantel. Another must-see in this former parsonage, women's boarding house, and coffee house: the lower-level Catacombs, once a billiards room, now a 90-seat theater (actress Amy Madigan once appeared here).

SETTING & FACILITIES
Location Less than 1 mile from downtown Milwaukee and I-94 **Near** Pabst Mansion, County Stadium, Milwaukee Public Museum, art museums, Lake Michigan. **Building** 1910 English Arts & Crafts, brick **Grounds** City lot, flower beds **Public Space** Foyer, library, parlor, DR, porch, lower-level theater **Food & Drink** Cookies, wine served in afternoon. Breakfast is gourmet by candlelight, includes signature baked grapefruit w/ coconut topping. **Recreation** Fine arts, live theater, boating, swimming, cross-country skiing, birding, antiquing, historic touring. **Amenities & Services** AC. Massage therapist on staff, portable TV/VCR available.

ACCOMMODATIONS
Units 2 suites, 3 rooms. **All Rooms** Clock, sitting area. **Some Rooms** Double whirlpool, TV/VCR, fireplaces. **Bed & Bath** Kings (1), queens (4). All private baths, 1 detached. **Favorites** Gold Suite w/ original tile, tub & sink; oak columned fireplace; double whirlpool. **Comfort & Decor** Here's a cool collection: antique pantaloons. Innkeeper Carol Brumder displays them throughout the home, along with museum-quality antique ball gowns, hats, camisoles, and other remnants of long-departed lives—"eye candy," she calls them. Special features include carefully preserved oak paneling and fireplaces, a Tiffany light fixture, an intimate tea nook, and faux-painted ceilings and walls in guest rooms.

RATES, RESERVATIONS, & RESTRICTIONS
Deposit 1 night's stay or 50% of final **Discounts** Corp., extended-stay, seasonal specials—inquire **Credit Cards** V, MC, AE, D **Check-In/Out** 3 p.m./11 a.m. **Smoking** No **Pets** No (resident dog stays in innkeepers' quarters) **Kids** Older children welcome—inquire **No-Nos** Coolers of food **Minimum Stay** N/A **Open** All year **Hosts** Carol & Bob Hirschi, 3046 West Wisconsin Ave., Milwaukee 53208 **Phone** (414) 342-9767 **Fax** (424) 342-4772 **Email** brumder@execpc.com **Web** www.brumdermansion.com

INN AT PINE TERRACE, Oconomowoc

OVERALL ★★★★★ | QUALITY ★★★★★ | VALUE ★★★★★ | PRICE RANGE $80–$190

The lake country estate of an Anheuser in-law was named Mon Bijou (My Jewel) by its first owners and hosted the likes of Mark Twain, several U.S. presidents, and many members of the Miller, Anheuser, Busch, and Pabst families over the years. "Just" a summer home (with 19 rooms and 16-foot ceilings), the Inn at Pine Terrace is modeled after a French nobleman's castle outside Vienna. The interior has been carefully renovated to preserve the hand-carved wood trim, inlaid floors, and original features such as the magnificent French mirror, mantel, and bookcases in the parlor.

SETTING & FACILITIES

Location Off WI 16 & 67, 20 mi. west of Milwaukee **Near** Downtown Oconomowoc, Fowler Lake, Lac La Belle. **Building** 1879 Victorian of Cream City brick, on National Register of Historic Places **Grounds** A full city block of lawns, flower gardens, lap pool **Public Space** Entry, reception hall, sun porch, parlor, DR **Food & Drink** Sodas available any time, wine & hors d'oeuvres each evening. Breakfast is cont'l deluxe. **Recreation** Boating, swimming, cross-country skiing, birding, snowmobiling, ice skating, sleigh rides, biking, horseback riding, kayaking, canoeing, antiquing, fishing, golf. **Amenities & Services** AC. Fresh flowers & robes in rooms, massage therapist available, meeting facilities. Shuttle service downtown. Fax & copy available.

ACCOMMODATIONS

Units 16 guest rooms. **All Rooms** Sitting area, desk or table, phones, data ports, voicemail, cable TV. **Some Rooms** Recessed bay bath, double whirlpool, claw-foot tub, marble shower, double sink. **Bed & Bath** King (1), queens (9), double (1), 2 twins (2). All private baths. **Favorites** Peter Schuttler Room w/ alcove overlooking Fowler Lake. Bath sits at top of mansion's turret w/ sunken double whirlpool under chandelier & marble shower. **Comfort & Decor** In a town known as the "Newport of the Midwest," this mansion is right at home. Massive front doors with original stained and etched glass, the original eight-foot lighted newel post, custom-made headboards and armoires, and even the ornate door hinges reflect the exclusive lifestyle that once prevailed here. Wall treatments are Bradbury & Bradbury.

RATES, RESERVATIONS, & RESTRICTIONS

Deposit 1 night's stay weekends **Discounts** Winter specials to encourage 2-night stays, some partnered w/ area businesses **Credit Cards** V, MC, AE, D, DC **Check-In/Out** 3 p.m./10:30 a.m. **Smoking** In sun parlor, in select guest rooms, outside **Pets** No **Kids** Yes **No-Nos** N/A **Minimum Stay** 2 nights holiday weekends **Open** All year **Hosts** Rich Borg, 351 Lisbon Rd., Oconomowoc 53066 **Phone** (262) 567-7463 **Fax** (262) 567-7532 **Email** innkeeper@innatpineterrace.com **Web** www.innatpineterrace.com

HILLWIND FARM BED & BREAKFAST INN, Plymouth

OVERALL ★★★½ | QUALITY ★★★★ | VALUE ★★★ | PRICE RANGE $120–$168
WEEKENDS

Original wood trim is the hallmark of this farm house, along with stained-glass windows in the dining room. The inn's strongest point is its location, just a short drive outside Plymouth but at the end of a remote-feeling country road. Views from guest rooms are of farmland and woodlands—a good base for "peepers" who come to tour fall colors along the 25-mile Kettle Moraine Scenic Drive.

SETTING & FACILITIES
Location Off Rt. 67 outside Plymouth **Near** Kettle Moraine State Forest, Elkhart Lake, Crystal Lake, Sheboygan Broughton Marsh, Kohler Design Center. **Building** 1841 brick & wood Victorian farm house w/ turn-of-century addition **Grounds** 5-1/2 acres w/field, barns **Public Space** Small DR, porch **Food & Drink** Sodas & home-baked cookies available in afternoon, wine served evenings. Full breakfast includes flavored pancakes or egg dish, breakfast meats on the side or by request. **Recreation** Snowshoeing, biking, horseback riding, boating, swimming, canoeing, kayaking, snowmobiling, fishing, ice fishing, ice skating, cross-country skiing, birding **Amenities & Services** Robes in rooms, movie library, snowshoes available to guests, bath amenities, small gift shop area.

ACCOMMODATIONS
Units 1 suite, 3 guest rooms. **All Rooms** Cable TV/VCR, coffeemaker, CD player, sitting area. **Some Rooms** Fireplace, private porch area, whirlpool tub, fireplace, bay window, private entrance. **Bed & Bath** Queens (4). All private baths. **Favorites** Suite, w/ private entrance, bay, more privacy, & space. **Comfort & Decor** This inn is decorated in a flowers-and-lace-everywhere style. Rooms are spacious, but the dining room—the only public space indoors—is tiny and crowded with tables and chairs. It features stained-glass windows and impressive oak fireplace with beveled-glass mirror—a lovely room, but cramped.

RATES, RESERVATIONS, & RESTRICTIONS
Deposit 1 night's stay or 50% **Discounts** Inquire; inn offers a complicated system of multiple-night, Thurs.-or-Sun. added, and weekday/weeknight discounts **Credit Cards** V, MC, D, AE **Check-In/Out** 4–8 p.m./noon **Smoking** Outside **Pets** No **Kids** Inquire **No-Nos** Candles in rooms **Minimum Stay** Guests staying Sat. night must stay 2 nights, "but call" **Open** All year **Hosts** Kim & Art Jasso, N4922 Hillwind Rd., Plymouth 53073 **Phone** (920) 892-2199 or toll-free (877) 892-2199 **Email** info@hillwindfarm.com **Web** www.hillwindfarm.com

YANKEE HILL INN, Plymouth

OVERALL ★★★★ | QUALITY ★★★★ | VALUE ★★★★ | PRICE RANGE $80–$110

Henry and Gilbert Huson built these gracious homes next door to each other, and their admiration for quality craftsmanship is evident. Along the walkway, look for the original carriage loading block. Guests in late spring should consider staying in Mary's Room, where the scent from the lilacs outside the shuttered windows provides true aromatherapy.

SETTING & FACILITIES
Location In central Plymouth, blocks from WI 67 **Near** Kettle Moraine State Forest, Elkhart Lake, Crystal Lake, Sheboygan Broughton Marsh, Kohler Design Center, downtown Plymouth. **Building** 2 homes—1870 Gothic Italianate on National Register of Historic Places, & 1891 Queen Anne Victorian **Grounds** City lots, flower beds **Public Space** Henry's House: parlor, DR, gift shop, patio, porch. Gilbert's House: Screened porch, foyer, TV parlor **Food & Drink** Water, sodas available any time. Full breakfast includes hot entree, breakfast meat, home-baked goods. Cont'l breakfast available for guests who must leave before 7 a.m. **Recreation** Birding, historic touring, antiquing, canoeing, swimming, boating, kayaking, fishing, ice fishing, cross-country skiing. **Amenities & Services** AC. Logo bath amenities.

ACCOMMODATIONS
Units 12 guest rooms. **All Rooms** Sitting area. **Some Rooms** Private porch, canopy bed, ceiling fan, whirlpool tub, robes for rooms w/ detached baths. **Bed & Bath** Queens (9), doubles (3). All private baths, 2 detached. **Favorites** Henry's Room, w/ parquet wood floor, Eastlake bedroom suite of walnut, bay, whirlpool. **Comfort & Decor** Both homes are tastefully appointed with fine antiques, including an 1880 square grand piano in the Henry's House parlor. Butternut trim is a highlight of Gilbert's House; the favorite space there is Clara's Room with ornate walnut inlay bed, four windows, and a rose palette.

RATES, RESERVATIONS, & RESTRICTIONS
Deposit 1 night's stay **Discounts** Corp. **Credit Cards** MC, V, D **Check-In/Out** 3 p.m./11 a.m. **Smoking** None in Henry's House; on enclosed porch in Gilbert's House **Pets** No **Kids** Older children—inquire **No-Nos** N/A **Minimum Stay** On select summer weekends **Open** All year **Hosts** Jim & Peg Stahlman, 405 Collins St., Plymouth 53073 **Phone** (920) 892-2222 **Email** yankee@excel.net **Web** www.yankeehillinn.com

BREESE WAYE BED & BREAKFAST, Portage

OVERALL ★★★★½ | QUALITY ★★★★½ | VALUE ★★★★★ | PRICE RANGE $70–$80

It's easy to imagine Llywelyn Breese, Wisconsin's first secretary of state, entertaining fellow politicians and industrial giants in this gracious home. Breakfast is served by candlelight with crisp linens and silver under the romantic dining room chandelier. The elegance continues upstairs with ten-foot ceilings throughout and a Victorian sleeping porch for relaxing or intimate escapes.

SETTING & FACILITIES
Location Off Hwy. 33 in central Portage **Near** Cascade Mountain Ski Area, Devil's Lake State Park, Lake Wisconsin, Wisconsin Dells, downtown Portage, Wisconsin River, River Walk. **Building** 1880 Italianate, white w/ berry trim **Grounds** Oversized city lot w/ gazebo, flower gardens **Public Space** Front parlor, 2nd parlor, library, DR, loft sitting area, sleeping porch **Food & Drink** Early coffee, soft drinks, & snacks available all day, wine & cheese every evening. Full breakfast includes hot entrees such as soufflé w/ asparagus and hash brown casserole w/ bacon. **Recreation** Fishing, downhill & cross-country skiing, golf, antiquing, snowboarding, swimming, boating, canoeing, kayaking, historic touring. Amenities & Services. AC, robes in rooms, bikes available to guests.

ACCOMMODATIONS
Units 4 guest rooms. **All Rooms** Sitting area, clock radio, ceiling fans. **Some Rooms** Desk & chair, TV. **Bed & Bath** Queens (3), double (1). All private baths, 1 detached. **Favorites** John Muir Room w/ bay, period floral wallpaper, & parquet floor of 4 different woods. **Comfort & Decor** The warmth of this inn starts in the foyer, with original tile fireplace and decorative bull's-eye woodwork. Another working fireplace warms the back parlor. In the dining room, one is tempted to curl up with a book on the velvet-cushioned window seat, set against original oak paneling. Note the pocket door's faux finish.

RATES, RESERVATIONS, & RESTRICTIONS
Deposit $40 **Discounts** Corp., midweek, 3+ days, 7+ days **Credit Cards** No **Check-In/Out** 3 p.m./11 a.m. **Smoking** No **Pets** No; resident cat & dog stay in innkeeper's quarters **Kids** Inquire **No-Nos** N/A **Minimum Stay** None **Open** All year **Hosts** Ray & Karen Partridge, 816 MacFarlane Rd., Portage 53901 **Phone** (608) 742-5281 **Email** partridges@breesewaye.com **Web** www.breesewaye.com

JAMIESON HOUSE INN, Poynette

OVERALL ★★★★½ | QUALITY ★★★★½ | VALUE ★★★★ | PRICE RANGE $85–$165

Innkeeper Heidi Hutchison has a goal: to create a refuge for travelers where they can comfortably collect their thoughts and enjoy good food and hospitality. We think she succeeds beautifully in Jamieson House. From the massive wood table of the formal dining room to the sunny ambience of the conservatory, the inn bestows an almost spa-like atmosphere. It's very European. Weekend guests may want to dine in Emily's Restaurant, a lower-level eatery with beer & wine license, serving dinner to the public Friday and Saturday evenings.

SETTING & FACILITIES
Location Off Main St. near the town center **Near** Lake Wisconsin, McKenzie Environmental Center, Rowan Creek, Cascade and Devils Head Parks. **Building** 1878 Italianate, 1883 Victorian guest house & old schoolhouse in same complex **Grounds** 2 acres of lawns, flower gardens **Public Space** All in main building: Patios, entry, sun room, sitting

room, DR, TV parlor, conservatory **Food & Drink** Full breakfast w/ hot entree, generous portions. **Recreation** Swimming, boating, fishing, canoeing, horseback riding, biking, downhill & cross-country skiing, birding, golf, antiquing. **Amenities & Services** AC. Robes in rooms, breakfast delivered to rooms on request.

ACCOMMODATIONS

Units 3 suites, 9 guest rooms. **All Rooms** Coffeemaker, sitting area, couch. **Some Rooms** Double sink, daybed, private entrance, gas fireplace, sitting room, heart-shaped whirlpool, sleeper couch. **Bed & Bath** Kings (5), queens (7). All private baths. **Favorites** Strand, suite w/ strong British influence, bed of imported oak. **Comfort & Decor** Among the fascinating features of this inn are faux-grain painted woodwork in the main house, tall shuttered windows, Gothic Victorian dining room chairs of heavy walnut, and rare arched pocket doors. In the old schoolhouse, the two suites take on a different feel with French Country furnishings.

RATES, RESERVATIONS, & RESTRICTIONS

Deposit 50% of stay **Discounts** Corp. midweek **Credit Cards** V, MC, D, AE **Check-In/Out** 3 p.m./11 a.m. **Smoking** No **Pets** Inquire **Kids** By prior arrangement **No-Nos** N/A **Minimum Stay** None **Open** All year **Hosts** Heidi Hutchison, 407 North Franklin St., Poynette 53955 **Phone** (608) 635-2277 or (608) 635-4100 **Fax** (608) 635-2292 **Email** jamhouse@execpc.com **Web** www.jamiesonhouse.com

ELLISON'S GRAY LION INN, Princeton

OVERALL ★★★½ | QUALITY ★★★½ | VALUE ★★★★ | PRICE RANGE $80

Built as a wedding gift, this small home is a handy base for touring eastern Wisconsin parks and antiques centers. The cigarette smell is unfortunate, and doors of this bed-and-breakfast often are left unlocked. If those aren't problems, the economical price and friendly innkeepers will make this a good choice.

SETTING & FACILITIES

Location Central Princeton, 10 mi. west of Green Lake **Near** Downtown shops, antiques malls, bike trails, Amish country, Fox River, Green Lake. **Building** Small 1897 Queen Anne **Grounds** City lot, flower beds **Public Space** Entry, parlor, LR, DR, loft sitting area **Food & Drink** Water, soft drinks available. Full breakfast includes egg dish, breakfast meat, homemade bread. **Recreation** Antiquing, Amish interests, biking, golf. **Amenities & Services** AC. Hair dryer available.

ACCOMMODATIONS

Units 4 guest rooms. **All Rooms** Sitting area. **Some Rooms** N/A. **Bed & Bath** Queens (2), double (1), double & twin (1). All private baths. **Favorites** Pink Room, very feminine. **Comfort & Decor** All rooms feature an Amish quilt bed covering. In the common rooms, seating is contemporary stuffed couch and chairs. A strong cigarette smell permeates the house.

RATES, RESERVATIONS, & RESTRICTIONS
Deposit I night's stay; for multiple nights, 50% **Discounts** None **Credit Cards** No
Check-In/Out 3 p.m./11 a.m. or by prior arrangement **Smoking** No **Pets** No **Kids**
Inquire **No-Nos** N/A **Minimum Stay** 5 nights during Oshkosh air show in late July; 2
nights select summer weekends **Open** All year **Hosts** Maureen & Michelle Ellison, 115
Harvard St., Princeton 54968 **Phone** (920) 295-4101 **Email** ellison@powercom.net

BROWNSTONE INN, *Sheboygan*

OVERALL ★★★★★ | QUALITY ★★★★★ | VALUE ★★★★ | PRICE RANGE
$175–$250 WEEKENDS, $100–$225 WEEKDAYS

It was our great fortune to tour Brownstone Inn with the innkeeper's
mother, who had played in the mansion—her grandmother's home—as a
little girl. She knew all the stories about what happened in the elegant
rooms; she remembered writing on the blackboard in the registration room,
the old children's playroom. She had attended grand affairs in the third-
floor ballroom, still a striking space with its original dressing rooms, chandeliers, window seats, and stage. She knew the tycoons who had shot pool
or whispered deals with her grandfather, a coal and shipping magnate, in
the basement game room, negotiating at the billiards chairs or in front of
the old stone fireplace.

SETTING & FACILITIES
Location Residential Sheboygan, off WI 23 **Near** Lake Michigan, downtown Sheboygan,
marina, boardwalk, Whistling Straits, Blackwolf Run, Kohler Design Center, Kohler Art
Center. **Building** 1907 brownstone mansion **Grounds** City lot, flower beds **Public
Space** Foyer, LR, breakfast room, loft sitting area, upstairs hall sitting area, 3rd-floor ball-

room, LL billiards room, enclosed patio **Food & Drink** Complimentary sodas, wine, beer. European cont'l breakfast. **Recreation** Historic touring, boating, swimming, biking, fishing, golf, museums, cross-country skiing. **Amenities & Services** AC. Fitness room, winery room, billiards & poker tables, robes in rooms, logo bath amenities.

ACCOMMODATIONS

Units 4 guest rooms, 2 suites. Servants Suite can rent as 2 guest rooms w/ shared bath. **All Rooms** Cable TV, desk, sitting area. **Some Rooms** Balcony, double sinks, sitting room, fireplace, private entrance, claw-foot tub. **Bed & Bath** Kings (2), queens (4), double (1). 5 private baths, 1 shared. **Favorites** Sir Henry's Room, named for the former beloved caretaker & chauffeur, features built-ins w/ curved glass, crotch mahogany & hand-tooled leather trim, marble & wood fireplace, whirlpool. **Comfort & Decor** This is an awesome home with Arts & Crafts touches throughout, from the built-in benches flanking fireplaces to the style of the stained-glass windows. The brownstones were brought from Canada, precut and numbered for easier assembly. In the living room, look closely at the carved plaster ceiling; it matches the oak carvings of the fireplace. Guest rooms are sumptuously furnished; we love the sunset porch outside Gertrude & Carita's Suite, and the deep raspberry carpet in Mattie & Peter's Room.

RATES, RESERVATIONS, & RESTRICTIONS

Deposit 1 night's stay **Discounts** Seasonal specials **Credit Cards** V, MC **Check-In/Out** 4 p.m./11 a.m. **Smoking** No **Pets** No **Kids** Inappropriate **No-Nos** N/A **Minimum Stay** N/A **Open** All year **Host** Frank A. Ribich Jr., 1227 North 7th St., Sheboygan 53081 **Phone** (920) 451-0644 or toll-free (877) 279-6786 **Fax** (920) 457-3426 **Email** brwnstninn@ aol.com **Web** www.brownstoneinn.com

Additional Bed-and-Breakfasts and Small Inns

While our 300 profiles give you a fine range of bed-and-breakfasts and small inns, some may be fully booked when you want to visit, or you may want to stay in areas where we have not included a property. So we have included an annotated listing of 300 additional bed-and-breakfasts and small inns, spread geographically throughout the Great Lakes region. All properties meet our basic criteria for this guide: They have about 3–25 guestrooms, a distinct personality and individually decorated guestrooms, are open regularly, and include breakfast in the price (with a few exceptions). Prices are a range from low to high season. Most are highly recommended, but we have not visited all of these properties so we cannot recommend them across the board. We suggest you get a brochure, look on the Internet, or call and ask about some of the categories that are on the profile format to find out more. While some of these supplementals are famed and excellent, others may not be up to the level of the profiled properties.

Illinois

ZONE 1: Northern Illinois

Algonquin
Victorian Rose Garden Bed & Breakfast
 $70–$139
 (888) 854-9667 or (847) 854-9667
 roses@mc.net
 www.sleepandeat.com

Batavia
Villa Batavia $85–$150
 (630) 406-8182

Chicago
City Scene Bed & Breakfast $95–$195
 (773) 549-1743; cityscene@aol.com
 www.cityscenebb.com
Gold Coast Guest House $119–$195
 (312) 337-0361
 sally@bbchicago.com
 www.bbchicago.com

Illinois (continued)

ZONE 1: Northern Illinois (continued)

Chicago (continued)
House of Two Urns $79–$160
   (800) 835-9303 or (312) 810-2466
   twourns@earthlink.net
   www.twourns.com

Elizabeth
Forget-Me-Not Bed & Breakfast
      $76–$105
   (815) 858-3744; info@galena-illinois.net
   www.galena-illinois.net

Galena
Captain Gear Guest House $155–$195
   (800) 794-5656 or (815) 777-0222
   gearhouse@galenalink.com
   www.captaingearguesthouse.com
Park Avenue Guest House $95–$135
   (800) 359-0743 or (815) 777-1075
   parkave@galenalink.com
   www.galena.com/parkave
Wild Turkey Bed & Breakfast $80–$95
   (815) 858-3649

Highland Park
Ravinia Guest House $125–$135
   (847) 433-3140; dukequeen@aol.com
   www.bestinns.net

Lanark
Standish House $60–$70
   (800) 468-2307 or (815) 493-2307

Mendota
Lord Stocking's Bed & Breakfast
      $50–$100
   (815) 539-7905; lstocking@hotmail.com

Oak Park
B. R. Guest House $65–$90
   (708) 383-9977
   brguest@brguesthouse.com
   www.brguesthouse.com

Port Byron
Olde Brick House $43–$55
   (309) 523-3236; oldebrick@webtv.net

Savanna
Nest at Palisades $99–$148
   (815) 273-7824; thenest@essex1.com
   www.essex1.com/people/thenest

Woodstock
Bundling Board Inn $75–$100
   (815) 338-7054; aart@mc.net

ZONE 2: Central Illinois

Aledo
Great Escape $55–$65; (309) 582-5359

Bloomington
Burr House $55–$95
   (800) 449-4182 or (309) 828-7686
   www.bedandbreakfast.com/bbc/
      p218244.asp

Champaign
Hodgepodge Lodge $65–$85
   (217) 352-7029
   hodgepodgelodge@earthlink.net
   www.home.earthlink.net/~hodge
      podgelodge

Champaign
Norma's Hideaway $50–$60
   (217) 359-5876

Galesburg
Great House Bed & Breakfast $89
   (309) 342-8683
Seacord House Bed & Breakfast $40–$48
   (309) 342-4107; parentlj@galesburg.net

Kewanee
Aunt Daisy's Bed & Breakfast $85–$95
   (888) 422-4148 or (309) 853-3300
   auntdaisy@juno.com; www.auntdaisy.net

Illinois (continued)

ZONE 2: Central Illinois *(continued)*

Knoxville
Knox Station Bed & Rails $60–$75
  (877) 570-5042 or (309) 289-4047
  knoxsta@galesburg.net
  www.rrhistorical.com/knox

Monticello
Linda's Country Loft $45–$70
  (217) 762-7316

Nauvoo
Ancient Pines Bed & Breakfast $55
  (217) 453-2767

Oglesby
Brightwood Inn $85–$200
  (888) 667-0600 or (815) 667-4600
  brtwood@starved-rock-inn.com
  www.starved-rock-inn.com

Onarga
Dairy on the Prairie $50–$60
  (815) 683-2774

Peoria
Old Church House Inn Bed & Breakfast
  $69–$109
  (309) 579-2300
  churchhouse@prodigy.net

Ruth's Bed & Breakfast $40–$45
  (888) 825-5265 or (309) 243-5977
  ruthsbnb@aol.com
  www.bbonline.com/il/ruthsbnb

Sheffield
Chestnut Street Inn $85–$165
  (800) 537-1304 or (815) 454-2419
  gail@chestnut-inn.com
  www.chestnut-inn.com

Springfield
Henry Mischler House $75–$125
  (217) 525-2660; mischler@famvid.com
  www.mischlerhouse.com
Inn on Edwards $65–$75
  (217) 528-0240; innl@juno.com

Toulon
Rockwells Victorian Bed & Breakfast
  $45–$60; (309) 286-5201

Villa Grove
Four Oaks Inn $55–$65; (217) 832-9313

Watseka
Razzano House $60–$95
  (815) 432-4240

ZONE 3: Southwest Illinois

Anna
Goddard Place $40–$75
  (618) 833-6256

Belleville
Swans Court Bed & Breakfast $45–$90
  (800) 840-1058 or (618) 233-0779
  mdixon@isbe.accessus.net
  www.bbonline.com/il/swanscourt

Cobden
Shawnee Hill Bed & Breakfast $55–$78
  (618) 893-2211; shawnhil@intrnet.net

Collinsville
Maggie's Bed & Breakfast $45–$85
  (618) 344-8283
  maggies-b-n-b@charter-il.co
  www.bnbinns.com/maggiesinn

East St. Louis
Parker Garden Bed & Breakfast $175–$200
  (888) 298-3834 or (618) 271-2005
  www.bbonline.com/il/parkergarden

Illinois (continued)

ZONE 3: Southwest Illinois (continued)

Jerseyville

Homeridge Bed & Breakfast $75–$95
   (618) 498-3442
   howardlandon@gtec.com
   www.homeridge.com

Jonesboro

Hidden Lake Bed and Breakfast $80–$135
   (618) 833-5252; hiddenlk@aol.com
Trail of Tears Lodge & Resort $50–$200
   (618) 833-8697; ttlsr@midwest.net
   www.trailoftears.com

Nebo

Harpole's Heartland Lodge $75-175
   (217) 734-2525
   info@heartlandlodge.com
   www.heartlandlodge.com

Sesser

Gretchen's Country Home $50–$59
   (877) 495-2372 or (618) 625-6067

rcook@midwest.net
www.site.org/sitc/gch.html
Hill House $50-60
   (618) 625-6064
   nussbaum@midwest.net
   www.bbonline.com/il/hillhouse

Vandalia

Beau-Meade House $80–$90
   (618) 283-1826

Waterloo

Painted Lady Bed & Breakfast $65–$75
   (618) 939-5545
   ronhrblk@wholenet.net
Sen. Rickert Residence Bed & Breakfast
      $75; (618) 939-8242
   eweil@wholenet.net
   www.bestinns.net/usa/il/senator
      rickert.html

ZONE 4: Southeast Illinois

Arcola

Flower Patch $53–$75
   (217) 268-4876; harsh8@aol.com
   www.illinoisads.com/flowerpatch.html

Brownstown

Brazle Haus Bed & Breakfast $45–$50
   (618) 347-2207; brazlehaus@juno.com

Elizabethtown

River Rose Inn $59–$96
   (618) 287-8811
   riverose@shawneelink.com
   www.shawneelink.com/~riverose

Fairfield

Glass Door Inn $52–$72
   (618) 847-4512; gdinn@midwest.net
   www.glassdoorinn.com

Hindsboro

Breakfast in the Country $50
   (217) 346-2739

Metropolis

Isle of View $43–$125
   (800) 566-7491 or (618) 524-5838
   kimoff@hcis.net
   www.bbonline.com/il/isleofview

Mt. Carmel

Living Legacy Homestead Bed & Breakfast
      $25–$70
   (877) liv-farm or (618) 298-2476
   www.bbonline.com/il/legacy/rooms.htm

Indiana

ZONE 5: Northwest Indiana

Kokomo
Bavarian Inn $65–$85
  (765) 453-4715
  www.bavarianinn.thehideaway.com

LaPorte
Hidden Pond Bed & Breakfast $79–$139
  (219) 879-8200; edberent@adsnet.com
  www.bbonline.com/hiddenpond/

Monticello
1887 Black Dog Inn $79–$119
  (219) 583-8297
Quiet Water Bed & Breakfast $50–$80
  (219) 583-6023; quietwtrbb@aol.com
  http://members.aol.com/quietbnb/
    index/html
Victoria Bed & Breakfast $50–$75
  (219) 583-3440
  victorbb@pwrfc.com

Rensselaer
White House on Park Avenue $52–$95
  (888) 310-4455 or (219) 866-4455

South Bend
Queen Anne Bed & Breakfast Inn
    $70–$110
  (800) 582-2379 or (219) 234-5959
  queenann@michiana.org
  http://business.michiana.org/queenann/

Valparaiso
Inn at Aberdeen $94–$157
  (219) 465-3753
  inn@innataberdeen.com
  www.innataberdeen.com
Songbird Prairie B&B $95–$135
  (219) 759-4274; efnbarb@aol.com
  www.songbirdprairie.com

ZONE 6: Northeast Indiana

Bristol
Rust Hollar Bed & Breakfast $69–$89
  (800) 313-7800 or (219) 825-1111
  tim@rusthollar.com
  www.rusthollar.com

Goshen
Indian Creek Bed & Breakfast $69–$79
  (219) 875-6606
  indiancreekbandb@msn.com
  www.bestinns.net/usa/in/indiancreek.html

Kendallville
McCray Rose Inn $59–$69
  (219) 347-3647

Middlebury
Bee Hive Bed & Breakfast $55–$75
  (219) 825-5023
Tayler House $68
  (219) 825-7296
  ctayler@mapletronics.com

ZONE 7: Central Indiana

Bloomingdale
Branaghan's Pointe $85–$110
  (765) 597-2210

Brookville
Mill Street Inn $75–$125
  (765) 647-2974
  themillstreetinn@excite.com

  www.bbonline.com/in/millstreet/
    index.html

Connersville
Maple Leaf Inn Bed & Breakfast $55–$65
  (765) 825-7099
  dorrper@si-net.com

Indiana (continued)

ZONE 7: Central Indiana *(continued)*

Crawfordsville
Sugar Creek's Queen Anne B&B $75
 (800) 392-6293 or (765) 362-4095
Maples Bed & Breakfast $70–$105
 (765) 866-8095

Greensburg
Nana's House Bed & Breakfast $75–$95
 (812) 663-6607

Indianapolis
Boone Docks on the River B&B $60–$75
 (317) 257-3671
Friendliness with a Flair $55
 (317) 356-3149
Speedway Bed & Breakfast $65–$125
 (800) 975-3412 or (317) 487-6531

speedwaybb@msn.com
www.bbonline.com/in/speedway

Nashville
Allison House Inn $95
 (812) 988-0814; tammy@kiva.net

Osgood
Victorian Garden Bed & Breakfast
  $45–$85;
 (812) 689-4469
 www.bbonline.com/in/victorian

Unionville
Possum Trot Bed & Breakfast $60–$75
 (812) 988-2694

ZONE 8: Southern Indiana

Aurora
Gothic Arches Bed & Breakfast $69–$89
 (888) 747-2204 or (812) 926-2204
 mlbaltz@seidata.com
 http://seindiana.com/arches

Austin
Carousel Inn Bed & Breakfast $59–$95
 (877) 323-3334 or (812) 794-2990
 carouselinn@voyager.net
 www.carouselinnb-b.com

Bethlehem
Inn at Bethlehem $75–$150
 (812) 293-3975

Cannelton
Castlebury Inn $50–$65
 (812) 547-4714
 www.castleburyinn.com

Grandview
River Belle Bed & Breakfast $65–$75
 (800) 877-5165 or (812) 649-2500

Jeffersonville
1877 House Country Inn B&B $75–$125
 (888) 284-1877; (812) 285-1877
 house1877@peoplepc.com
 www.bbonline.com/in/1877house

Madison
Alvanna Inn $60–$85
 (812) 273-6557
 david.rader@pfizer.com
Lanham House $105–$125
 (812) 273-3198
 lanhamhse@aol.com
 www.lanhamhouse.com
Windy Hill B&B $60–$95
 (812) 265-5284
 windyhillbb@earthlink.net

New Harmony
Cholpe Guest House $125
 (812) 851-3288; cholpe@aol.com
 www.hometown.aol.com/cholpe

Indiana (continued)

ZONE 8: Southern Indiana (continued)

Paoli
Big Locust Farm Bed & Breakfast
    $55–$85; (812) 723-4856
    glendalindley@cs.com
    www.ourworld.cs.com/joellindley22

Rising Sun
Mulberry Inn & Gardens B&B $89–$125
    (800) 235-3097 or (812) 438-2206
    jwillis@one.net
    www.bbonline.com/in/mulberry

Salem
Lanning House $45–$65
    (812) 883-3484

Taswell
White Oaks Cabins Bed & Breakfast
    $65–$115; (812) 338-3120
    www.patokalake.com

Vevay
Rosemont Inn $85–$95
    (812) 427-3050
    www.rosemont-inn.com

Michigan

ZONE 9: Northern Michigan and the Upper Peninsula

AuTrain
Pinewood Lodge B&B $105–$135
    (906) 892-8300; pinewood@mail.tds.net

Bay View
Gingerbread House $100–$150
    (231) 347-3538; mghouse@freeway.net

Big Bay
Big Bay Point Lighthouse Bed & Breakfast
    $99–$183; (906) 345-9957
    keepers@bigbaylighthouse.com
    www.bigbaylighthouse.com

Charlevoix
Aaron's Windy Hill Guest Lodge
    $75–$145; (231) 547-2804
    windyhill2@bignetnorth.net
    www.members.aol.com/aaronshill/
        index.html

Charlevoix
Charlevoix Country Inn $90–$145
    (231) 547-5134; cci@freeway.net
    www.charlevoixcountryinn.com

Cheboygan
Gables Bed and Breakfast $75–$110
    (231) 627-5079; gables@northlink.net
    www.mich-web.com/gablesbb

Gladstone
Kipling House $75–$150
    (877) 905-7666 or (906) 428-1120
    info@kiplinghouse.com
    www.kiplinghouse.com

Ironwood
Meadowbrook Country Inn $74
    (906) 932-4780 ; casaari@portup.com

Kearsarge
Belknap's Garnet House $60–$90
    dbelknap@up.net
    www.laketolake.com/garnet-house

Mackinac Island
Haan's 1830 Inn $95–$175
    (906) 847-6244 or (847) 526-2662
        (winter)
    www.mackinac.com/haans

Michigan (continued)

ZONE 9: Northern Michigan and the Upper Peninsula *(continued)*

Mackinaw City
Deer Head Lodge $80–$200
  bdean@deerhead.com
  www.deerhead.com

Marquette
Blueberry Ridge Bed & Breakfast
$55–$95; (906) 249-9246
  hgreen617@aol.com
  www.members.aol.com/blueberr18

Newberry
MacLeod House $69–$95
  (906) 293-3841

fcicala@up.net
www.macleodhouse.com

Ontonagon
Northern Light Inn $75–$145
  (800) 238-0018 or (906) 884-4290
  www.laketolake.com/northernlight

Petoskey
510 Elizabeth $80–$95
  (231) 348-3830
  510elizabeth@voyager.net

ZONE 10: Western Michigan

Arcadia
Arcadia House $85–$90
  (231) 889-4394
  arcadiahouse@jackpine.com
  www.thearcadiahouse.com

Bellaire
Grand Victorian B&B Inn $115–$135
  (800) 336-3860 or (231) 533-6111
  innkeepers@grandvictorian.com
  www.laketolake.com/grand

Beulah
Elliott House $79–$99
  (231) 882-7075
  delliott@bignetnorth.net

Bitely
Cottage of Content $60–$100
  (231-745-3634; cofcbnb@carrinter.net
  www.laketolake.com/cottageofcontent

Fennville
Hidden Pond B&B $78–$120
  (616) 561-2491

Frankfort
Windchime Inn $75–$80
  (866) 352-9450 or (231) 352-9450
  fitchdg@traverse.net

Fruitport
Village Park B&B $69–$109
  (800) 469-1118 or (231) 865-6289
  www.bbonline.com/mi/villagepark

Grand Haven
Seascape B&B $85–$185
  (616) 842-8409
  www.bbonline.com/mi/seascape

Holland
Thistle Inn $90–$110
  (626) 399-0409
  patteske@triton.net
  www.bbonline.com/mi/thistleinn

Leland
Snowbird Inn B&B $125–$150
  (231) 256-9773
  www.snowbirdinn.com

Ludington
The Inn at Ludington $87–$110
  (800) 845-9170 or (231) 845-7055
  www.inn-ludington.com

Onekama
Canfield House $95–$145
  (231) 889-5756
  jane-paul@thecanfieldhouse.com
  www.thecanfieldhouse.com

Michigan *(continued)*

ZONE 10: Western Michigan *(continued)*

Pentwater
Historic Nickerson Inn $85–$250
(800) 742-1288 or (231) 869-6731
info@nickersoninn.com
www.nickersoninn.com

Saugatuck
Newnham Suncatcher Inn $65–$125
(616) 857-4249
www.bbonline.com/mi/suncatche

ZONE 11: Central Michigan

Ann Arbor
Urban Retreat Bed & Breakfast
$60–$75; (734) 971-8110
www.theurbanretreat.com

Battle Creek
Greencrest Manor $95–$235
(616) 962-8633
www.greencrestmanor.com

Coleman
Buttonville Inn $75–$105
(989) 465-9364
info@buttonvilleinn.com
www.buttonvilleinn.com

Grand Rapids
Madison Street Inn $85–$100
(800) 618-5615 or (616) 459-5954

Hastings
Adrounie House B&B $65–$125
(800) 927-8505 or (616) 945-0678

Ithaca
Bon Accord Farm B&B $58–$78
(989) 875-3136
bonaccordfarm@nethawk.com

Kalamazoo
Hall House B&B $79–$145
(616) 343-2500
thefoxes@hallhouse.com
www.hallhouse.com

Lansing
Ask Me House B&B $55–$65
(800) 275-6341 or (517) 484-3127
mekiener@aol.com
www.askmehouse.com

Lowell
McGee Homestead $49–$69
(616) 897-8142; mcgeebb@iserv.net
www.iserv.net/~mcgeebb

Perry
Cobb House $70–$95
(517) 625-7443
twillson@voyager.net

ZONE 12: Eastern Michigan

Auburn Hills
Cobblestone Manor Luxury Historic Inn
$139–$219
(248) 370-8000
stay@cobblestonemanor.com
www.cobblestonemanor.com

Bay City
Clements Inn $70–$175
(800) 442-4605 or (517) 894-4600
cleminn@earthlink.net
www.laketolake.com/clements-inn

Michigan (continued)

ZONE 12: Eastern Michigan *(continued)*

Bay City *(continued)*
Clements Inn $70–$175
  (800) 442-4605 or (517) 894-4600
  cleminn@earthlink.net
  www.laketolake.com/clements-inn

Chesaning
Stone House Bed & Breakfast
    $100–$175
  (989) 845-4440
  stonehousebnb@centurytel.net
  www.stonehousebnb.com

Dearborn
Dearborn Bed & Breakfast $105–$-175
  (888) 959-0900 or (313) 563-2200
  nancyswork@aol.com
  www.dearbornbb.com

Harbor Beach
State Street Inn $65–$75
  (866) 424-7961 or (989) 479-3388

info@thestatestreetinn.com
www.thestatestreetinn.com

Lexington
Governor's Inn $75–$95
  (888) 909-5770 or (810) 359-5770
  kutchey-lage@juno.com
  www.governorsinnbnb.com

Marine City
Heather House $85–$160
  (810) 765-3175
  www.bluewatertoday.com/heatherhouse

Port Huron
Hill Estate Bed and Breakfast $99–$145
  (877) 982-8189 or (810) 982-8187
  www.laketolake.com/hillestate

Saginaw
Cousins B&B $125–$150
  (989) 790-1728
  jhess@sbbsnet.net

ZONE 13: Southern Michigan

Brooklyn
Dewey Lake Manor $72–$130
  (800) 815-5253 or (517) 467-7122
  deweylk@frontiernet.net
  www.bbonline.com/mi/deweylake

Coldwater
Hideout Bed and Breakfast $70–$120
  (866) 872-9559 or (517) 278-4210
  hideoutbb@yahoo.com
  www.skybusiness.com/hideout-bed-
    breakfast

Lakeside
Pebble House Inn $115–$190
  (616) 469-1416
  innkeeper@thepebblehouse.com
  www.thepebblehouse.com

Marshall
Joy House B&B $90–$110
  (616) 789-1323
  edmick@ameritech.net
  http://kephart.com/joyhouse
National House Inn $105–$145
  (616) 781-7374
  www.nationalhouseinn.com

Monroe
Lotus Bed and Breakfast $105–$125
  (734) 735-1077
  rosalindreiser@aol.com

New Buffalo
Tall Oaks Inn $65–$230
  (800) 936-0034 or (616) 469-0097
  www.harborcountry.com/guide/talloak

Michigan (continued)

ZONE 13: Southern Michigan (continued)

Pittsford
Rocking Horse Inn $50–$80
  (517) 523-3826
  www.bbonline.com/mi/rockinghorse

Minnesota

ZONE 14: Northwest Minnesota

Ashby
Harvest Inn B&B $125–$145
  (218) 747-2334

Bemidji
Lakewatch Bed & Breakfast $55–$85
  (218) 751-8413; lakewatch@bji.net
  www.bjo.net/pages/lakewatch

Fergus Falls
Bergerud "B's" (Bed, Breakfast, & Bakery)
    $45-75
  (800) 557-4720 or (218) 736-4720

Frazee
Acorn Lake Bed and Breakfast $55–$65
  (888) 571-9904 or (218) 334-5545
  vpeterso@mail.nymills.mn.us
  www.detroitlakes.com/acornlake

Hackensack
Linens 'n' Loons $75–$85
  (800) 536-8309 or (218) 547-1101

Longville
Camp O' My Dreams B&B $65–$70
  (218) 363-2507
  wgriffin@djam.com
  www.camp-o-mydreams.com

Pelican Rapids
Prairie View Estate $60–$80
  (800) 298-8058 or (218) 863-4321
  prairie@prtel.com

Underwood
Aloft in the Pines $60–$80
  (888) 457-6301 or (218) 495-2862
  mjp294@prtel.com
  www.bbonline.com/mn/aloft

Warroad
Hospital Bay B&B $40–$60
  (800) 568-6028 or (218) 386-2627

ZONE 15: Northeast Minnesota

Brainerd
Pinecrest Cottage $65–$75
  (218) 746-3936
  asebasky@brainerd.net
  www.pinecrestcottage.com

Brainerd
Whitely Creek Homestead $70–$95
  (877) 985-3275 or (218) 829-0654
  whitelycrk@aol.com

Minnesota (continued)

ZONE 15: Northeast Minnesota *(continued)*

Duluth

Firelight Inn on Oregon Creek
$129–$229
(888) 724-0273 or (218) 724-0272
firelightinn@duluth.com
www.duluth.com/firelightinn
The Mansion $105–$245
(218) 724-0739
www.mansion.duluth.com
Mathew S. Burrows 1890 Inn $95–$165
(800) 789-1890 or (218) 724-4991
www.visitduluth.com/1890inn
Olcott House B&B $90–$149
(800) 715-1339 or (218) 728-1339
www.visitduluth.com/olcotthouse

Duquette

Home in the Pines Bed & Breakfast Inn
$60–$75; (218) 496-5825
julie@lcp2.net

Ely

Blue Heron B&B $75–$100
(218) 365-4720

jo@blueheronbnb.com
www.blueheronbnb.com

Grand Marais

Clearwater Lodge $65–$125
(800) 527-0554 or (218) 388-2254
clearwater@canoe-bwca.com
www.canoe-bwca.com
Pincushion Mountain Bed & Breakfast
$79–$105
(800) 542-1226 or (218) 387-1276
pincushion@boreal.org
www.pincushionbb.com
Superior Overlook Bed & Breakfast
$95–$130
(800) 858-7622 or (218) 387-1571
sobb@boreal.org
www.boreal.org/a-superior-overlook

Side Lake

McNair's Bed & Breakfast $100–$150
(218) 254-5878

ZONE 16: Southwest Minnesota

Cold Spring

Pillow, Pillar & Pine Guest House
$65–$130; (320) 685-3828

Glencoe

Glencoe Castle Bed & Breakfast
$65–$175
(800) 517-3334 or (320) 864-3043
schoenr@hutchtel.net
www.glencoecastle.com

Lake Benton

Benton House $65–$105
(507) 368-9484
bentonhs@itctel.com
http://web.itctel.com/~bentonhs

Lester Prairie

Prairie Farm Bed & Breakfast $55–$65
(888) 470-1846 or (320) 395-2055
prairiefarmbandb@aol.com

Sherburn

Four Columns Inn $65–$75
(507) 764-8861
www.bbonline.com/mn/fourcolumns

Starbuck

311 Ivy Inn $55–$65
(320) 239-4868
bnb311in@runestone.net
www.bbonline.com/mn/ivyinn

Minnesota (continued)

ZONE 16: Southwest Minnesota (continued)

Tracy
Valentine Inn B&B $85–$105
   (507) 629-3827

Willmar
Buchanan House Bed & Breakfast
   $64–$99
      (800) 874-5534 or (320) 235-7308
      www.thebuchananhousebandb.com

ZONE 17: Southeast Minnesota

Afton
Afton's Mulberry Pond on River Road
   $99; (651) 436-8086

Anoka
Ticknor Hill Bed & Breakfast $110–$150
   (800) 484-3954 ext. 6391 or (612) 421-
   9687; www.ticknorhill.com

Brooklyn Park
Meadows Bed & Breakfast $60–$85
   (612) 315-2685
   lynn@metromeadows.com

Chaska
Bluff Creek Bed & Breakfast $85–$185
   (612) 445-2735; jmeggen@aol.com

Excelsior
James H. Clark House Bed and Breakfast
   $95–$145; (612) 474-0196
   www.bbonline.com/mn/jamesclark

Falcon Heights
Rose B&B $100; (612) 642-9417

Harmony
Selvig House Bed & Breakfast $75–$80
   (888) 887-2922 or (507) 886-2200
   selvigbb@means.net
   www.selvighouse.com

Lake City
Red Gables Inn Bed and Breakfast
   $75–$95; (888) 345-2605 or (651)
   345-2605; www.redgablesinn.com

Lanesboro
Cady Hayes House $75–$115
   (507) 467-2621
   cadyhayesbb@juno.com

Marine-on-St. Croix
Asa Parker House $99–$169
   (888) 857-9969 or (651) 433-5248
   asaparkr@pressenter.com
   www.asaparkerbb.com

Minneapolis
Le Blanc House $80–$110
   (612) 379-2570

North Branch
Soleil Levant Bed & Breakfast Inn
   $50–$100; (651) 674-7361

St. Paul
Chatsworth Bed & Breakfast $70–$135
   (651) 227-4288; chats@isd.net
www.chatsworth-bb.com
Covington Inn and No Wake Café (a boat
   B&B) $135–$235; (651) 292-1411
   www.covingtoninn.com

Stillwater
Aurora Staples Inn $105–$175
   (651) 351-1187
   info@aurorastaplesinn.com
   www.aurorastaplesinn.com
Laurel Street Inn Bed & Breakfast
   $99–$189
   (888) 351-0031 or (651) 351-0031
   welcome@laurelstreetinn.com
   www.laurelstreetinn.com

Ohio

ZONE 18: Northwest Ohio

Bucyrus
HideAway Bed & Breakfast $97–$225
  (800) 570-8233 or (419) 562-3013
  www.hideawayinn.com

Catawba Island
Five Bells Inn $89–$139
  (888) 734-1555 or (419) 734-1555
  jjarc@5bellsinn.com
  www.5bellsinn.com

Findlay
Lambs Ear Bed & Breakfast $50–$70
  (419) 424-5810
Rose Gate Cottage Bed & Breakfast
  $65–$75
  (877) 614-4577 or (419) 424-1940
  rosegate@rosegateinn.com
  www.rosegateinn.com

Galion
Rose of Sherron Bed & Breakfast
  $65–$125
  (800) 368-8426 or (419) 468-3973
  rosebnb@bright.net
Presidential Inn Bed & Breakfast $65–$97
  (419) 468-3533; www.bedandbreakfast
    .com/bbc/p613360.asp

Napoleon
Augusta Rose Bed & Breakfast $65
  (877) 590-1960 or (419) 592-5852
  augrose@bright.net

Port Clinton
Marshall Inn $100–$200
  (877) 376-5531 or (419) 734-2707
  www.marshallinn.com

Put-in-Bay/South Bass Island
Vineyard Bed & Breakfast $90–$115
  (419) 285-6181

Shelby
Gamble Street Inn $50–$65
  (419) 347-3360

Toledo
Cummings House Bed & Breakfast
  $60–$90
  (419) 244-3219

West Liberty
Timberframe Bed & Breakfast $65–$85
  (800) 232-2319 or (937) 465-7565
  tmbframe@logan.net

ZONE 19: Northeast Ohio

Ashland
Winfield Bed & Breakfast $75–$125
  (800) 269-7166 or (419) 281-5587
  www.bbonline.com/oh/winfield

Cadiz
Family Tree Inn Bed & Breakfast
  $65–$75; (877) 644-4409 or (740)
  942-3641; dlgfamilytreebb@eohio.net

Chesterland
Marigold Bed & Breakfast $75–$125
  (440) 729-4000

Dover
Mowreys' Welcome Home Bed and
  Breakfast $70; (330) 343-4690
  paulola@tusco.net

East Liverpool
Sturgis House $75–$95
  (330) 382-0194

Geneva
The Grapevine at Duckhill $75–$95
  (440) 466-7300; info@debonne.com
  www.debonne.com/b&b.htm

Ohio (continued)

ZONE 19: Northeast Ohio (continued)

Hanoverton
Crystal Springs Bed and Breakfast $50
  (330) 223-2198; www.ohiobba.com

Hiram
Hiram Inn $99–$159
  (888) hiramin or (330) 569-6000
  hiraminn@hiram.edu
  www.hiraminn.com
Lily Ponds Bed & Breakfast $65–$95
  (800) 325-5087 or (330) 569-3222
  marilane@lilypondsbb.com

Medina
Reutter's Roost Bed & Breakfast
    $65–$85; (330) 483-4145
  halaluja@apk.net
  www.reuttersroost.com

Millersburg
Bigham House $79–$107
  (800) 689-6950 or (330) 674-beds
  www.bighamhouse.com

Minerva
Huston House $45–$55
  (330) 862-3141

New Concord
Bogart's Bed & Breakfast $75–$85
  (740) 826-7439

Poland
Inn at the Green $60
  (330) 757-4688

Ravenna
Rocking Horse Inn $55–$65
  (800) 457-0439 or (330) 297-5720

Youngstown
Julia's Bed & Breakfast $99–$250
  (888) 758-5427 or (330) 534-1342

ZONE 20: Central Ohio

Circleville
Braeburn Farm Bed & Breakfast $85
  (740) 474-7086

Columbus
Shamrock Bed & Breakfast $60
  (614) 337-9849

Granville
Follett-Wright House Bed & Breakfast
  $60
  (740) 587-0941
  www.bbonline.com/oh/follett-wright
WillowBrooke Bed & Breakfast
  $85–$125
  (800) 772-6372 or (740) 924-6161

Lancaster
Canalview Bed & Breakfast $40–$50
  (800) 683-1999 or (740) 862-4022

London
Winchester House Bed & Breakfast
  $65–$80
  (740) 852-0499
  winhouse@qn.net
  http://qn.net/~winhouse

Sunbury
Sondra's Bed & Breakfast $35–$65
  (740) 965-4519

Westerville
Cornelia's Corner Bed & Breakfast
  $75–$89
  (800) 745-2678 or (614) 882-2678

Ohio *(continued)*

ZONE 21: Southwest Ohio

Circleville
Braeburn Farm Bed & Breakfast $85
  (740) 474-7086

Columbus
Shamrock Bed & Breakfast $60
  (614) 337-9849

Granville
Follett-Wright House Bed & Breakfast
  $60; (740) 587-0941
  www.bbonline.com/oh/follett-wright
WillowBrooke Bed & Breakfast
  $85–$125; (800) 772-6372 or (740)
  924-6161

Lancaster
Canalview Bed & Breakfast $40–$50
  (800) 683-1999 or (740) 862-4022

London
Winchester House Bed & Breakfast
  $65–$80; (740) 852-0499
  winhouse@qn.net
  http://qn.net/~winhouse

Sunbury
Sondra's Bed & Breakfast $35–$65
  (740) 965-4519

Westerville
Cornelia's Corner Bed & Breakfast
  $75–$89; (800) 745-2678 or (614)
  882-2678

ZONE 22: Southeast Ohio

Batavia
Inn at Paxton Farm $65–$125
  (513) 625-2022
  mainoffice@paxtonfarm.com
  www.paxtonfarm.com

Centerville
Yesterday Bed & Breakfast $75–$85
  (800) 225-0485 or (937) 433-0785
  yesterdaybandb@webtv.net

Cincinnati
Symphony Hotel $69–$130
  (888) 281-8032 or (513) 721-3353
  www.symphonyhotel.com

Dayton
Candlewick Bed and Breakfast $60-65
  (937) 233-9297
  gethompson@compuserve.com
  www.bedandbreakfast.com/bbc/
    p208355.asp

Eaton
Decoy Bed and Breakfast $65–$75
  (937) 456-6154

Kings Mills
Kings Manor Inn $80–$90
  (513) 459-9959

Miamisburg
English Manor Bed and Breakfast
  $65–$95; (800) 676-9456 or (937) 866-
  2288; www.bedandbreakfast.com/bbc/
    p208340.asp

Oxford
Duck Pond Bed and Breakfast $65–$80
  (513) 523-8914
  marge.pendleton@juno.com
  www.duckpondbb.com

Ohio (continued)

ZONE 22 Southeast Ohio *(continued)*

Barnesville
Georgian Pillars Bed & Breakfast
  $75–$80
  (888) 425-3741 or (740) 425-3741
  www.georgianpillars.8m.com

Caldwell
Inn at Belle Valley $35–$55
  (740) 732-7333

Creola
Country Pleasures $85–$95
  (888) 596-3132 or (740) 596-3132

countrypleasures@hockinghills.com
www.hockinghills.com/cp

Marietta
Buckley House Bed & Breakfast
  $55–$65
  (800) 341-6163 or (740) 373-3080

New Marshfield
Bittersweet Farm Bed and Breakfast $89
  (740) 664-6011
  bittersweet@dragonbbs.com
  www.bittersweetfarmbb.com

Wisconsin

ZONE 23: Northwest Wisconsin

Alma
Tritsch House Bed & Breakfast
  $65–$115l; (608) 685-4090
  almab-b@mwt.net
  www.bbinternet.com/alma

Amery
Twin Lake Dairy Bed & Breakfast
  $89–$129; (888) 268-3775 or (715)
  268-4988; tldbb@yahoo.com

Bayfield
Cooper Hill House Bed & Breakfast
  $86–$99; (715) 779-5060
  larrymac@ncis.net
Island View Place Bed & Breakfast
  $75–$100; (800) 484-8189, Code #
  6555 or (715) 779-5307
  lorrie@ncis.net; www.island-view.com
Pilot House Inn $99–$195
  (715) 779-3561' gunderson@pilothouse
  inn.com; www.pilothouseinn.com

Chetek
Sweet Dreams Bed & Breakfast
  $50–$60
  (800) 890-0116 or (715) 924-4590

Cornucopia
The Fo'c'sle Bed & Breakfast $85
  (715) 742-3337
  info@siskiwitbay.com
  www.siskiwitbay.com
Lazy Susan's Bed & Brunch $115–$205
  (715) 742-3443
  lzysusan@cheqnet.com
  www.cheqnet.net/~lzysusan

Eau Claire
Apple Tree Inn $90–$150
  (800) 347-9598 or (715) 836-9599
  larry@appletreeinnbb.com
  www.appletreeinnbb.com
Atrium Bed & Breakfast $75–$159
  (888) 773-0094 or (715) 833-9045
  info@atriumbb.com
  www.atriumbb.com

Hayward
Mustard Seed $75–$105
  (715) 634-2908

Wisconsin (continued)

ZONE 23: Northwest Wisconsin *(continued)*

Herbster
Bark Point Inn bed & Breakfast $79–$99
   (888) 774-3415 or (715) 774-3309
   www.vnorthland.com/hotel/barkpoint/b
   arkbpoint.htm

Holcombe
Happy Horse Bed & Breakfast $65
   (715) 239-0707
   information@happyhorsebb.com
   www.happyhorsebb.com

Hudson
Jefferson-Day House $99–$189
   (715) 386-7111
   websiteinfo@jeffersondayhouse.com
   www.jeffersondayhouse.com

La Pointe
White Seagull Bed & Breakfast
   $129–$250

   (800) 977-2624 or (715) 747-5595
   www.islandrental.com/mibb.htm

Maiden Rock
Harrisburg Inn $90–$135
   (715) 448-4500
   ccbern@cannon.net
   www.harrisburginn.com

Menomonie
Hansen Heritage House $109–$179
   (715) 235-0119
   wbba@hansenheritagehouse.com
   www.hansenheritagehouse.com
Oaklawn Bed & Breakfast $79
   (715) 235-$6155
   info@oaklawnbnb.com
   www.oaklawnbnb.com

ZONE 24 Northeast Wisconsin

Appleton
Appleton's B&B, the Solie Home
   $65–$125; (920) 733-0863

Arbor Vitae
Northwoods Nod-a-Way $60–$85
   (888) nod-a-way or (715) 356-7700

Baileys Harbor
Blacksmith Inn $165–$195
   (800) 769-8619 or (920) 839-9222
   relax@theblacksmithinn.com
   www.theblacksmithinn.com
New Yardley Inn $105–$175
   (888) 4-yardley or (920) 839-9487
   yardley@dcwis.com
   www.newyardleyinn.com

Crandon
Courthouse Square Bed & Breakfast
   $60–$70; (888) 235-1665 or (715)
   478-2549; chousebb@newnorth.net
   www.courthousesquarebb.com

Ephraim
French Country Inn of Ephraim
   $65–$97; (920) 854-4001
   frenchcountryinn@dcwis.com
Prairie Garden Bed & Breakfast of Door
   County $85; (920) 854-2555
   b-bprairiegarden@dcwis.com

Fish Creek
White Gull Inn $112–$275
   (920) 868-3517; www.whitegullinn.com

Florence
Lakeside Bed & Breakfast $70–$100
   (715) 528-3259
   www.wbba.org/inns/BB58.htm

Gills Rock
Harbor House Inn $65–$175
   (920) 854-5196
   www.door-county-inn.com

Wisconsin (continued)

ZONE 24 Northeast Wisconsin *(continued)*

Hurley
Anton-Walsh House $55–$95
   (715) 561-2065; info@anton-walsh.com
   www.anton-walsh.com

Lac du Flambeau
Ty-Bach $65–$80
   (715) 588-7851; tybach1@newnorth.net

Sturgeon Bay
Colonial Gardens Bed & Breakfast
   $100–$175; (920) 746-9192

colonialgardens@dcwis.com
www.colgardensbb.com
Inn the Pines Bed & Breakfast
   $110–$150
   (920) 743-9319
   innthepinesbb@dcwis.com
   www.innthepinesbb.com

ZONE 25: Southwest Wisconsin

Blue River
Cream Pitcher $65–$75
   (608) 536-3607

Cashton
Dickson Manor $79–$135
   (608) 654-7448
   dicksonmanor@centurytel.net
   www.dicksonmanor.com

Cassville
River View Bed & Breakfast $70
   (888) 297-5749 or (608) 725-5895
   rivervu@pcii.net
   www.riverviewbb.com

Ferryville
Mississippi Humble Bush $65–$85
   (608) 734-3022

elisa@mwt.net
www.wbba.org/inns/BB69.htm

Lancaster
Maple Harris Guest House $49–$69
   (888) 216-0888 or (608) 723-4717
   maplehgh@pcii.net
   www.mapleharris.com

Mineral Point
Brewery Creek $95–$169
   (608) 987-3298
   brewpub@mhtc.net
   www.brewerycreek.com
William A. Jones House Bed & Breakfast
   $60–$95
   (800) 723-6018 or (608) 987-4651
   daviddel@mhtc.net
   www.jonesmansion.com

ZONE 26: Southeast Wisconsin

Belleville
Cameo Rose Victorian Country Inn
   $99–$149; (608) 424-6340
   romance@cameorose.com
   www.cameorose.com

Cambridge
Cambridge House Bed & Breakfast
   $105–$125

(888) 859-8075 or (608) 423-7008'
cambridgehousebandb@juno.com
www.cambridgehouse-inn.com
Lake Ripley Bed & Breakfast $100
   (877) 423-4855
   timelo@charter.net
   www.wbba.org/inns/BB270.htm

Wisconsin (continued)

ZONE 26: Southeast Wisconsin *(continued)*

Cross Plains
BBB Farm Bed & Breakfast $80–$95
   (608) 798-1123 or (608) 798-1129
   bbbfarm@midplains.net
   www.wbba.org/inns/BB227.htm

Eagle
Eagle Centre House $95–$155
   (262) 363-4700; info@eagle-house.com
   www.eagle-house.com

East Troy
Pickwick Inn $100–$125
   (262) 642-5529
   www.bbinternet.com/pickwick

Lomira
White Shutters $60–$80
   (920) 269-4056
   whiteshutters@iosys.net

Madison
Canterbury Inn $130–$375
   (608) 258-8899
   inn@madisoncanterbury.com
   www.madisoncanterbury.com

Livingston Inn $150–$290
   (608) 257-1200
   reservations@thelivingston.com
   www.thelivingston.com

Mayville
J & R's Sherm Inn $55–$70
   (920) 387-4642

Milwaukee
Crane House Bed & Breakfast $70–$91
   (414) 483-1512
   info@cranehouse.com
   www.cranehouse.com

Racine
Mansards On-the-Lake $55–$85
   (262) 632-1135

Sheboygan Falls
Rochester Inn $100–$170
   (920) 467-3123
   rochesterinn@excel.net

Subject Index